Personal Injury Major Claims Handling:
Cost Effective Case Management

Personal Injury Major Claims Handling: Cost Effective Case Management

Iain Goldrein QC
Recorder

Margaret de Haas QC
Recorder

John Frenkel FCA
Senior Partner, Frenkel Topping Chartered Accountants

Butterworths
London, Edinburgh and Dublin
2000

United Kingdom	Butterworths, a Division of Reed Elsevier (UK) Ltd, Halsbury House, 35 Chancery Lane, LONDON WC2A 1EL and 4 Hill Street, EDINBURGH EH2 3JZ
Australia	Butterworths, a Division of Reed International Books Australia Pty Ltd, CHATSWOOD, New South Wales
Canada	Butterworths Canada Ltd, MARKHAM, Ontario
Hong Kong	Butterworths Asia (Hong Kong), HONG KONG
India	Butterworths India, NEW DELHI
Ireland	Butterworth (Ireland) Ltd, DUBLIN
Malaysia	Malayan Law Journal Sdn Bhd, KUALA LUMPUR
New Zealand	Butterworths of New Zealand Ltd, WELLINGTON
Singapore	Butterworths Asia, SINGAPORE
South Africa	Butterworths Publishers (Pty) Ltd, DURBAN
USA	Lexis Law Publishing, CHARLOTTESVILLE, Virginia

A CIP Catalogue record for this book is available from the British Library.

ISBN 0 406 98862 5

Typeset by Connell Publishing Services, Thame OX9 2HX
Printed and bound in Great Britain by Antony Rowe Ltd, Chippenham, Wiltshire

Visit us at our website: http://www.butterworths.co.uk

Preface

Clinical negligence and catastrophic claims handling can so readily result in mountains of paper, delay and unnecessary expense.

The aim of this book is to accommodate 'Woolf' thus to achieve a more effective result, more speedily and with less paper.

In seeking to achieve these aims, the book is something in the nature of a multi-disciplinary partnership. Thus, in addition to 'legal' texts on risk management and preparation for trial, there are chapters on funding, project management, case management (from both claimant and defendant perspectives), structured settlements and special needs trusts, the operation of the Court of Protection, medical aspects of traumatic brain damage and spinal cord injury, brain damage at birth claims (including obstetric and neurological aspects), rehabilitation, nursing care and occupational therapy.

This work has required considerable patience from the contributors dovetailing both with each other and of course with the publishers. We are particularly grateful to them, and of course to Butterworths for acting as co-ordinator.

Iain Goldrein QC
Margaret de Haas QC
John Frenkel
13th July 2000

Contents

Contributors

Mr Roger Clements FRCS FRCOG
Consultant Obstetrician and Gynaecologist and Editor of 'Clinical Risk'

Richard Cropper

James Dadge BA (Hons) Dip Law
Frenkel Topping Chartered Accountants

Richard Follis
Solicitor, Irwin Mitchell, Birmingham

John Frenkel BA Econ (Hons) FCA
Senior Partner, Frenkel Topping Chartered Accountants and Founding Director,
Frenkel Topping Structured Settlements Ltd

Mr Brian Gardner BM BCH MA (Oxon) FRCP (UK) FRCS
Consultant Surgeon in Spinal Injuries

Iain Goldrein QC MA (Cantab) ACI Arb
Recorder, Visiting Professor (The Sir Jack Jacob Chair) in Litigation,
Nottingham Law School

Margaret de Haas QC LLB FRCA
Recorder

Caroline Harmer
Legal Training

Professor Bryan Jennett CBE MD FRCS

Professor Malcolm Levene MD FRCP FRCPCH FMedSc
Professor of Paediatrics and Child Health, University of Leeds,
Honorary Consultant Neonatalogist, United Leeds Teaching Hospitals Trust

Denzil Lush
Master of the Court of Protection

William W McKinlay BA MSc PhD CPsychol
Clinical Psychologist, Case Management Services, Balerno, Edinburgh

Robert Parr BA (Hons)

Keith Popperwell
Solicitor, Silverbeck Rymer, Chelmsford

M Rooney DipCOT
Head Occupational Therapist, Queen Elizabeth National Spinal
Injuries Unit, Southern General Hospital, Glasgow

J James Rowley MA (Cantab) DipLaw
of Lincoln's Inn, Barrister, practising at 28 St John Street Chambers, Manchester

John Sheath
Partner, Brackers

Paul Stanley FCII
Claims Audit and Training Manager

Rosemary Statham DipCOT
Head of Therapy Practice, Home Assessment and Advisory
Services

Neil Sugarman LLB (Hons)
Managing Partner, Graham Leigh Pfeffer & Co (Member of the Law Society
Personal Injury Panel)

Trevor Ward
Solicitor, Linder Myers, Manchester

A J Watkiss BSc
Psychologist, Case Management Services, Balerno, Edinburgh

Table of Statutes

Table of Statutory Instruments

Table of Cases

Case references which appear in Modules 1-12, at the end of Chapter 2, are to page, all other references are to para.

Part I

Litigation Technique

Chapter 1

Introduction to Personal Injury Actions and Major Claims Handling

Iain Goldrein QC
Margaret de Haas QC

INTRODUCTION

The Foundation of the Compensation Environment
1.1   The UK scheme of compensation under the law of tort, for personal injury victims, has to be understood in the context of the following:

- Unlimited third party liability cover.
- Protection for the victims of uninsured drivers.
- Indemnity costs provisions, which are not affected by conditional fee agreements.
- The rules for the assessment of damages were developed in order to enable judges to guide juries in assessing damages in relatively straightforward cases.

The Development of Skills
1.2   It used to be that litigation technique was the better honed with those litigators working for insurance companies. This pattern altered substantially in the 1980s, with the evolution of vast rafts of ongoing professional training for solicitors, coupled with the emergence of organisations such as the Association of Personal Injury Lawyers and Action for Victims of Medical Accidents. It is this advance in the skills of litigators acting for claimants which has helped to push the frontiers of damages so very hard and fast.

The Role of the Insurer in the New Landscape
1.3   Largely from the pressure of competition in the motor market, there has been intense consolidation of the UK insurance market, with mergers of companies leading to a few very large consortia. They, in turn, have cut back very substantially on panel solicitors. This affords the following opportunities:

(a) the pooling of experience in the long term vis-à-vis victims of brain damage and spinal cord injury;
(b) the proactive development of rehabilitation;
(c) the development of epidemiological data as to life expectation.

Life Expectation – Its Significance

1.4–1.10   The 'multiplier' so often turns on life expectation. Appendix 1 sets out an argument as to the assessment of life expectation through a legal rather than a medical prism. We are, however, on the threshold of sequencing the full human genome. We should, in due course, be able to derive assistance for the assessment of individual life expectation from the genetic make-up. Should therefore a claimant be invited to undergo a DNA test as a condition of pursuing his claim for damages in respect of catastrophic injury? Further, could an insurer protect his costs position by a Part 36 offer to settle by recourse to a structured settlement if a claimant refuses to undergo such DNA testing?

DAMAGES ASSESSMENT IN THE UNITED KINGDOM

Compensation for Personal Injuries in England and Wales

1.11   Compensation is by reference to:

- Non-financial losses.
- Past and future financial losses.

Damages are divided into 'general' and 'special' loss. 'Specials' constitute any pre-trial loss, and 'generals' are any other loss, including damages for pain, suffering and loss of amenity.

Non-financial Losses

1.12   This covers damages for pain, suffering and loss of amenity. The guiding principle is what is 'fair' or 'proper'.[1] The criteria of what is fair and proper are now set out in the Guidelines of the Judicial Studies Board, to be read in the context of the Court of Appeal guideline cases.[2]

1   See page 187 Lord Scarman, *Lim Poh Choo v Camden Health Authority* [1980] AC 174.
2   *Heil v Rankin and Another* (2000) 23 March.

Financial Loss

1.13   Vis-à-vis financial losses, Lord Blackburn said in *Livingstone v Rawyards Coal Co*,[1] the court should award:

> ' ... that, where any injury is to be compensated by damages, in settling the sum of money to be given ... you should nearly as possible get that sum of money which will put the party who has been injured, or who has suffered, in the same position as he would have been in if he had not sustained the wrong for which he is now getting his compensation or reparation.'

1   (1880) 5 App Cas 25 at 39.

1.14   This is the principle of restituo in integrum, achieved by way of a 'lump sum', a once and for all payment in the form of a single sum. This principle was endorsed by Lord Scarman in *Pickett v British Rail Engineering Ltd*[1] where he said:

> 'But, when a judge is assessing damages for pecuniary loss, the principle of full compensation can properly be applied. Indeed anything else would be inconsistent with the general rule.'

1   [1980] AC 136.

How Does a Defendant Attack a Claim Advanced by a Claimant?

1.15   In *Wells v Wells:*[1]

'In my view the Court of Appeal was right to scrutinise the individual claims which went to make up the multiplicand. Since the effect of reducing the rate of discount will be to increase the multiplier in any case, it is all the more important to keep firm control of the multiplicand'.

1   [1998] 3 WLR 329, Lord Lloyd said at 345 E-F.

1.16   Thus, when insurers attack a claim advanced by claimants, the debate covers various subjects.

Whether There is in Fact a 'Need'
1.17   This is a factor to which the attention of the medical experts on each side should be focused. For example, a defendant may argue that an item claimed will have no realistic therapeutic benefit. If the item claimed is desirable but not 'necessary' then the argument can be advanced that the claim can properly be compensated for out of the damages for loss of amenity.[1]

1   For example, a swimming pool, which was rejected by the court in *Cassel v Hammersmith and Fulham Health Authority* [1992] PIQR Q168, and a 'Philadelphia regime' was held not to be recoverable in *Dulehan v Carson* [Kemp A4-006].

Failure to Mitigate
1.18   The legal principle was expressed in *Wells v Wells* by Lord Lloyd:[1]

'The stage at which the duty to minimise loss is to be applied is at the earlier stage when the court has to identify the amount of the annual sum to be compensated for and the period over which it is to be compensated.'

1   [1998] 3 WLR 329 at 357-58. See also page 362G-H per Lord Clyde and page 370 A-C per Lord Hutton.

1.19   Thus, if 'need' is established, then the argument develops: that the facilities, care regime and/or equipment claimed can be secured equally effectively, but more cheaply elsewhere. Thus, the cost of a night-time carer was not allowed in *Leon Seng Tan v Brunage*[1] where the same result could be achieved by mechanical means.

1   Kemp A2 at 103.

Exaggeration of 'Need'
1.20   That the extent of care put forward as necessary is in fact unreasonable in extent. For example, in the moderate brain damage case of *Bristow v Judd*[1] Beldham LJ said:

'Although there had been a suggestion that, if left to fend for himself the appellant would need either a living-in housekeeper or someone coming in every day, the learned judge did not accept that full-time residential care would prove to be necessary and in my judgment, properly referred to a tendency as in many such cases for those close family members who devotedly care for an injured person in such circumstances to be overprotective. He did not see why the appellant could not, if necessary, spend more time unsupervised than he was doing, provided that regular checks were made on him and regular help was available.'

1   [1993] PIQR Q117 page Q123.

1.21   In this context it is prudent to remember that the basis for rewarding members of the family for the care they have voluntarily provided flows from the judgment of O'Connor LJ in *Housecroft v Burnett* where he said inter alia:

' ... That part of the reasonable and proper cost of providing for the [plaintiff's] needs is to enable her to make a present, or series of presents, to her mother'.[1]

1   [1986] 1 All ER 332 at 342-43.

1.22   Thus, awards for voluntary care are always discounted by up to 33% to take account of the fact that the care is not provided on a commercial basis, and that the carer does not pay tax and national insurance in respect of monies received for such care. If the carer has given up employment to provide the care, then an award can be made to cover those loss of earnings, as long as the award does not exceed what commercial care would have cost.[1] Reported cases where there has been a discount include *Nash v Southmead Health Authority*[2] and *Fairhurst v St Helens and Knowsley Health Authority* – where the discount was reduced to 25% because of the particular demands on the carer.

1   See page 343 per O'Connor LJ.
2   [1993] PIQR Q156.
3   [1995] PIQR Q1.

That the Factual Basis for the Claim was Wrong
1.23   More hours for care were being claimed than could be proved. This often happens in the context of babies brain damaged at birth – for the first year they will require very extensive care, brain damaged or not. Thus, the courts are scrupulous to avoid 'overlap'. This can happen equally if there are many members of a family who are co-operating in care, which almost invites duplication and 'overlap' of hours.

Exaggeration of 'Loss of Earnings'
1.24   If there is a claim for loss of earnings until a retirement age of 65, it can be productive for the insurer to explore with an employment consultant, the extent to which people employed in the same field as the claimant worked to the age of 65 and at what age in that field workers tended to retire.

The Judge/Jury Interface

1.25–1.26   Historically, the assessment of these figures was undertaken by a jury. Increasingly, judges increasingly performed the function of the jury. All personal injury awards are now exclusively made by the judiciary. There is no jury involvement whatsoever. The judges measure damages by reference to the same legal matrix and even given the ambit of legitimate judicial discretion, there is overall consistency in the results achieved.

THE MACHINERY FOR THE ASSESSMENT OF DAMAGES IN THE UNITED KINGDOM

The Multiplier/Multiplicand Technique

1.27 The machinery goes back certainly to the enactment of the Fatal Accidents Act 1846 and adopts the multiplier/multiplicand technique:

(a) What is the annual loss – the multiplicand?
(b) For how many years has the claimant to live – from which is assessed the multiplier.

1.28 Lord Oliver of Aylmerton expressed the position in *Hodgson v Trapp*:[1]

'Essentially what the court has to do is to calculate as best it can the sum of money which will on the one hand be adequate, by its capital and income, to provide annually for the injured person a sum equal to his estimated annual loss over the whole of the period during which that loss is likely to continue, but which, on the other hand, will not, at the end of that period, leave him in a better financial position than he would have from the accident. Hence the conventional approach is to assess the amount notionally required to be laid out in the purchase of an annuity which will provide the annual amount needed for the whole period of loss.'

1   [1989] AC 807 at 826D.

1.29 The sum paid over to the claimant or his family is arrived at on the assumption that it will be prudently invested and drawn on from time to time at the appropriate rate, so that the capital sum together with the interest that it earns will last, more-or-less, for the whole period over which it is expected that the claimant will suffer his loss and then be exhausted.

1   See *Taylor v O'Connor* [1971] AC 115.

Refinement of that Machinery

1.30 A greater scientific approach to the calculation of damages came from the mid-1960s, in three lines of cases from the Court of Appeal.

1.31 First, it was held that juries should no longer be used in the assessment of damages save in exceptional cases.[1] This heavy presumption against jury trial has been made even stronger by s 69(3) Supreme Court Act 1981.

1   *Ward v James* [1966] 1 QB 273.

1.32 Second, *Jefford v Gee*[1] ruled that given a change in the law relating to interest on damages, judges must assess separately the heads of financial loss. Until this decision, the scope for refinement of the principles by which damages were assessed was limited by the fact that judges did not have separately to value each head of claim but rather made a global award.

1   [1970] 2 QB 130.

1.33   Third, *George v Pinnock*[1] is authority for the principle that the parties were entitled to know how the judge arrived at the final figure: Sachs LJ referred to:

> ' ... considerable body of judicial opinion which held that the [plaintiff] and defendant alike are entitled to know what is the sum assessed for each relevant head of damage and thus to be able on appeal to challenge any error in the assessments. In my judgment, this court should be slow to emasculate that right of litigants.'

1   [1973] 1 WLR 118 at 126.

1.34   This is the basic machinery which is still being used to calculate claims for damages in the field of personal injury and wrongful death. However, the lump sum technique ignores the contingency that there may be a lack of capacity to manage properly the capital sum so as to ensure an adequate income stream over the necessary period of years This contingency should not arise if, through a mental condition, the intervention of the Court of Protection is necessary. If such contingency does arise the injured person will become a charge on the state. Such contingency can arise if the claimant is profligate or invests unwisely.

Actuarial Assessment

1.35   The machinery has further been refined through the admissibility in court of actuarial tables to assess multipliers.

1.36   This admissibility has been secured by the Damages Act 1996. The tables have been prepared by a Committee chaired by Sir Michael Ogden. The tables are now very sophisticated in the information they contain and give guidance not just on mortality, but on other contingencies such as employment and illness.

1.37   The tables suggest a 'discount for contingencies' very much smaller than judges previously made, often as little as 5 or 10%.

1.38   *Wells v Wells*[1] is authority for the principle that the victim is entitled to the greater security and certainty achieved by investment in Index Linked Government Securities. That net rate of return was assessed by Lord Lloyd in *Wells* as 3%. The headnote in the case reads inter alia:

> ' ... that 3 per cent should also be the guideline rate for general use until the Lord Chancellor specified a new rate under section 1 of the Damages Act 1996.'

1   [1998] 3 WLR 329.

1.39   In *Worral v PowerGen plc*[1] a precedent has been established for the use of multipliers calculated with allowance for projected rates of mortality. In practice, this means applying the multiplier given in Tables 11 to 20 of the 3rd edition Ogden Tables instead of those in Tables 1-10. The difference, particularly in respect of loss of life, can be quite significant.

1   [1999] PIQR P103.

1.40 Until the Lord Chancellor set a new discount rate under s 1(1) of the Damages Act 1996 it was not open to the court to reduce the 3% net guideline discount rate laid down by the House of Lords. Further, the reduction in the rate of return of index-linked governmental securities alone was not a sufficient change of economic circumstances to justify a change in the rate in the particular case.[1]

1 *Warren v Northern General Hospital NHS Trust* [2000] I WLR 1404 CA.

1.41 The Lord Chancellor has issued a consultation paper[1] with regard to the discount rate and how it can be consistently reviewed. The paper includes some suggestions about a possible alternative to lump sum settlements following the lead given by Lord Steyn in *Wells*.[2]

1 Damages, The Discount Rate and Alternatives to Lump Sum Settlements (CP:3/00).
2 [1998] 3 WLR 329.

What Happens in Reality?

1.42 Victims appear never to invest in ILGS. Thus, the percentage rate of return under Government Securities is an abstract yardstick to achieve the calculation of a multiplier. Were there to be investment in ILGS there would be the following disadvantages:

(a) the return is exclusively income, in contrast to the annuity under a structured settlement which is a mixture of capital and income;

(b) income from an ILGS investment is liable to tax whereas there is no taxation of the income stream from an annuity created under a structured settlement;

(c) to pay for recurring capital expenses, there will be a need to sell ILGS investments. But if one is forced to sell before redemption (in order to meet a particular need arising in a particular year) then one is subject to short-term fluctuations. For example, if one has an ILGS which is redeemable in the year 1999, and another in 2004, then one would have to sell in 1999 in order to defray capital expenditure arising before 2004. This issue was considered by the House of Lords in *Wells* as a matter yet to be resolved. Lord Lloyd said:[1]

'Secondly, it is said that there are gaps in the maturity dates. Thus there is no stock maturing in 2002, 2005, 2007, 2008 or 2010. Nor is there any stock maturing later than 2030. As for the gaps, they may be filled by new issues. According to the Debt Management Report for 1998-1999 issued by HM Treasury, the authorities are committed to a minimum annual level of £2.5 billion index-linked stock in 1998-1999 and for the foreseeable future thereafter; and the aim is to maintain liquidity 'in most maturity areas across the curve:' But even if gaps remain, there is no problem. The [plaintiff] will be assumed to purchase enough stock maturing in 2001 to cover his needs for that year as well as 2002. And so on.

'As for the period after 2030, again there is no reason to suppose that there will not be further issues. But even if there are not, the [plaintiff] knows that he will have an inflation-proof lump sum at that date which will reflect his needs for the rest of his life more accurately than any other available investment. Mr Owen put it well during argument: the court now has as its disposal a tool for calculating damages which enables it to assume a stable currency until at least 2030.'

1   [1998] 3 WLR 329.

Limitations of that 'Machinery'

1.43   This machinery was conceived in an age when:

(a) life expectancy was low;
(b) work was precarious and dangerous;
(c) there was no complexity to a claim for loss of earnings;
(d) medical opinion was as inscrutable as it was authoritative;
(e) judgment of the court was as inscrutable as it was authoritative;
(f) the measure of damages was never very large;
(g) there was little public interest and no public questioning of the system of justice.

Flaws and Solutions

1.44–1.49   Lord Steyn explained in *Wells v Wells*:[1]

(a) *the structural flaw:*
'Leaving to one side the policy arguments for and against the 100 per cent principle, there is a major structural flaw in the present system. It is the inflexibility of the lump sum system which requires an assessment of damages once and for all of future pecuniary losses. In the case of the great majority of relatively minor injuries the [plaintiff] will have recovered before his damages are assessed and the lump sum system works satisfactorily. But the lump sum system causes acute problems in cases of serious injuries with consequences enduring after the assessment of damages. In such cases the judge must often resort to guesswork about the future. Inevitably, judges will strain to ensure that a seriously injured [plaintiff] is properly cared for whatever the future may have in store for him. It is a wasteful system since the courts are sometimes compelled to award large sums that turn out not to be needed.' Page 351F.

(b) *limited statutory intervention:*
'It is true, of course, that there is statutory provision for periodic payments: see section 2 of the Damages Act 1996. But the court only has this power if both parties agree. Such agreement is never, or virtually never, forthcoming. The present power to order periodic payments is a dead letter. The solution is relatively straightforward.' Page 351G.

(c) *proposals for reform*
'The court ought to be given the power of its own motion to make an award for periodic payments rather than a lump sum in appropriate cases. Such a power is perfectly consistent with the principle of full compensation for pecuniary loss. Except perhaps for the distaste of personal injury lawyers for change to a familiar system, I can think of

no substantial argument to the contrary. But the judges cannot make the change. Only Parliament can solve the problem.' Page 351H.

1   [1998] 3 WLR 329.

WHAT ARE THE AVAILABLE HEADS OF CLAIM WHICH GO TO CONSTITUTE THE MULTIPLICAND?

The Heads of Claim

1.50   The classic case where heads of claim are fully explored is that of catastrophic brain damage or spinal cord injury. The heads of claim have become largely regularised and embrace:

1.51   *Damages for Pain, Suffering and Loss of Amenity*
These damages include:

(a) awareness of accelerated death;
(b) sexual dysfunction;
(c) loss of joy in work;
(d) loss of holiday;
(e) more work for same pay;
(f) impairment of house-keeping abilities;
(e) psychological problems including post-traumatic stress disorder.

1.52   *Past loss of earnings*
This includes the value of fringe benefits net of tax and national insurance.[1]

1   The Law Commission Report No 225 identified that the most frequent problem encountered by those who had suffered injury was their not being able to pay their ordinary living expenses. In the more serious cases, a substantial number of respondents expressed difficulty with paying for extra travel and heating.

1.53   *Past Out-of-pocket Expenses*
This includes medical treatment, value of care volunteered by third parties, cost of care commercially provided, occupational therapy aids and equipment, costs incurred vis-à-vis alterations to housing, cost of speech and/or physiotherapy, value of lost DIY services including gardening, extra cost of mobility/transport, extra wear and tear on clothing, extra domestic help, cost of travel of friends and family for visits to assist recuperation. Deductions from these damages are:

(a) state benefits;
(b) cost of maintenance in a hospital, nursing home or other institution;
(c) monies repayable to a local authority if that has provided care/housing.[1]

It is to be anticipated that there will be increasing recoupment on the part of health care or social services providers and an increased involvement from the private health care sector. The Law Commission, in its paper No 144 'The Cost of Care' recommended reform to ensure that the National Health Service could recover the cost incurred in providing treatment and care after an accident.

1   *Avon County Council v Hooper* [1997] 1 WLR 1605 CA.

1.54   *Future Loss of Earnings*
Net of tax and national insurance (consider psychometric testing).

1.55   *Pension loss*

1.56   *Cost of Future Housing/Adaptation*

1.57   *Cost of Future Care*
In this regard there is an interesting passage at page 65 in the report of the Law Commission: 'Personal Injury Compensation: How Much is Enough' No 225:

> 'Although the need for care was substantial among the sample, few received nursing care in the home, either free or purchased. The great burden of care was provided, and continues to be provided unpaid by spouses, parents, other relatives, friends and neighbours.
>
> 'Respondents were likely to require a high degree of future care, which would be provided by family and friends, and qualitative interviews provided evidence of the stress that this imposes on carers in pressure, and damage to their own work prospects.'

1.58   *Computer Aids and Equipment*

1.59   *Handicap in the Labour Market*

1.60–1.69   *Court of Protection Fees/Cost of Financial Advice*

PROVISIONAL DAMAGES

1.70   The court has power to award provisional damages in actions:

> '... for damages for personal injuries in which there is proved or admitted to be a chance that at some definite or indefinite time in the future the injured person will, as the result of the act or omission which gave rise to the cause of action, develop some serious disease or suffer some serious deterioration in his physical or mental condition.'

Pleading
1.71   This claim must be expressly pleaded and only one further 'bite' at the damages 'cherry' is permitted.

Measuring the 'Chance'
1.72   These statutory provisions are concerned only with measurable rather than fanciful chances and 'serious deterioration' refers to a clear and severable event rather than an ordinary continuing deterioration.[1]

1   *Willson v Ministry of Defence* [1991] 1 All ER 638.

What if the Claimant Dies?
1.73   Section 3 of the Damages Act 1996 provides that where a claimant dies of his injuries after receiving a provisional award, his dependants will not be precluded from claiming for loss of dependency, since that part of the provisional damages or further damages awarded before the claimant's death 'as was intended

to compensate him for pecuniary loss in a period which, in the event, falls after his death shall be taken into account in assessing the amount of any loss of support' suffered by dependants.

Obstacles to a Claim for Provisional Damages
1.74–1.79 In 1994 the Law Commission identified as one of the factors militating against a claim for provisional damages, a reluctance of respondents to go through the claim process again. Query whether this argument has such validity after the Woolf reforms.

EVOLVING TECHNIQUES OF FILE MANAGEMENT

Introduction

1.80 Until recent times, adventure and innovation were not words which were instinctively associated with common law practice. Indeed, until the 1970s, personal injury claims rarely exceeded £20,000. All that has now changed, as reflected in the following:

(a) in 1984, personal injury claims were poised to break the £½ million barrier;
(b) in 1987 they broke the £1 million barrier;
(c) in 1999 they broke the £8 million barrier.

The Trigger for Greater Awards
1.81 The initiative for change is triggered in part by medical techniques securing the continuity of a long life in those who not long ago would have died from a catastrophic injury. This interfaced with a political climate which encouraged wealth creation and creativity thus stimulating the forensic imagination of claimant litigators.

The Evolution of Contemporary File Management
1.82 File management has grown empirically to meet this demand. This highlights a feature of the English legal landscape, the division between solicitors and barristers:

(a) solicitors manage the file, which includes the instruction of experts;
(b) barristers anticipate the court room when advising and are the trial lawyers.

Lord Woolf and File Management
1.83 It is file management in particular which is the focus of the reforms of Lord Woolf. Hitherto in the field of catastrophic injury, file management has often been haphazard. There has certainly been no standard protocol. This erratic approach to file management has meant that steps have often been taken without reference to thinking through what was demanded by strict compliance with the rules of court setting out as they do, a litigation highway from inception of proceedings through to the courtroom. Lord Woolf identified in his 1996 Report that the rules of court were largely ignored.

Delay and Expense
1.84 Because there has been no standardised approach to file management, opportunities for waste, delay and expense have been generated. For example:

(a) issues of liability have been explored concurrently with quantum, irrespective of the fact:
  (i) that monies expended on the quantum investigation will be wasted if the case fails on the issue of liability, and
  (ii) hopes of compensation have been raised, only to be dashed.
(b) experts in the field of employment, nursing, housing, occupational therapy, speech therapy, physiotherapy and communication aids have frequently been retained (but not necessarily at the same time) to report but without a timetable to trial or an agenda as to the focus of the report. Should a 'nursing' report purport to be final in 2000 if trial cannot be timetabled until 2002. This necessitates further reports which demonstrate that much of the earlier reports will prove to be unnecessary.
(c) experts in the field of electronic communication aids are often instructed to report, without an educational psychologist advising as to whether in fact the victim would be intellectually able to use the equipment (given a case of intellectual impairment).

1.85 One of the problems which has arisen from this piecemeal approach to file management has been the potential for both enormous delay and the exaggeration of claims.

The Effect of Delay
1.86 In the Law Commission Report No 225, there is the following passage at page 71 in relation to delay:

> 'Qualitative interviews revealed the effect on respondents of the protracted period during which claims are investigated, negotiated and finally settled. Three main concerns emerged about the time taken to agree settlements: the stress of waiting for compensation, the financial implications of long settlement times, and in some cases, delays in being able to adapt housing to meet mobility needs. Almost without exception, respondents felt that the amount of time spent in litigation was excessive. Stress and feelings of anger and frustration about the time taken were common.'

1.87 This 1994 Report continued on page 72:

> 'The delay involved in settling claims also adds extra financial burdens on those who are not legally-aided and increases the possibility that accident victims may consider abandoning their claims ...

> 'In some instances the time taken to arrive at a settlement was said to have hindered the recuperative, or grieving process.

> 'The financial implications of the time taken to settle were often considerable, particularly where people sustained major injuries, required full-time care, or were reliant on state benefits for support. Some respondents were only able to survive financially by going into debt, using credit cards up to the limit, taking out bank loans or borrowing from others.'

The Exaggeration of Claims
1.88 The exaggeration of claims had become such that by way of example settlements could be achieved at, say £1½m when the schedule of loss was perhaps

over £3½m and the counter-schedule pitched at less than £750,000. Much of the claim in such circumstances was 'expert driven', necessarily generating the assumption that:

(a) many experts were not looking at the case with a sufficient degree of objectivity; and
(b) the file was not sufficiently subjected to the forensic discipline of the litigator.

1.89 The potential for the exaggeration of claims should now be lanced by the provisions of Part 44 of the Civil Procedure Rules 1998.

'44.3(4) In deciding what order (if any) to make about costs, the court must have regard to all the circumstances, including –
(a) the conduct of all the parties ...'

How do Lord Woolf's Reforms Change the Legal Landscape?
1.90–1.99 Lord Woolf's reforms, the Civil Procedure Rules ('CPR'), change the landscape. They do so particularly through a few, highly effective techniques:

• Openness: this is achieved through the pre-action protocols. There is no chesting of cards, no trial by ambush, no 'playing games'.
• The regulation of expert evidence by Part 35. The drive to achieve a more effective regime of expert evidence is in part facilitated by the opportunity jointly to instruct an expert.
• The 'Part 36' offer to settle: this involves a clear risk analysis of the case, given file management which must anticipate a rigorous court-imposed timetable if the action comes into the court system.
• The focus on issues: the new code ordains issue driven litigation, the word 'issue' being a constant throughout the rules, with an emphasis on narrowing their ambit (the incentive being by reference to the provision as to costs).
• The new rule militating against the exaggeration of claims.
• The issue of 'conduct' in the context of the indemnity costs rule. In particular, a failure to act reasonably pre-action, can generate an adverse costs award post-action. 'Conduct' also entails the parties co-operating:

'the "Overriding Objective" means that cases must be handled in a manner proportionate to the importance and amount at issue, and expeditiously. It also means that the parties must be much more ready to co-operate. Litigation is to be less adversarial.[1]

It is this 'overriding duty' to co-operate which opens the door to rehabilitation and the structured settlement.

1 See Part 1, CPR.

THE INTERFACE BETWEEN LORD WOOLF'S REFORMS, REHABILITATION AND STRUCTURED SETTLEMENTS

Obstacles to Rehabilitation
1.100 Insurers have always had the opportunity to volunteer a rehabilitation package financed by an interim payment. Certain factors, however, militated

against it, such as mutual suspicion between the parties, the infancy of rehabilitation as a conventional technique and the lack of perceived measurable saving.

What has Changed?
1.101   With increasingly sophisticated systems of rehabilitation coupled with soaring damages awards, the pressure for rehabilitation could be interpreted as acute. Ideally, there are no losers, for the claimant rehabilitated may recover less by way of damages, but that is because he is less damaged.

Tailoring a Package
1.102   Once both parties co-operate to explore rehabilitation, the opportunity beckons to plot the victim's lifetime needs and then to tailor a financial package to meet those needs. Thus co-operation, rehabilitation and structuring of a settlement can be interpreted as coalescing into effective claims management.

Protection Against the Unscrupulous
1.103   Insurers are naturally concerned lest claimant litigators use rehabilitation as a means of substantially increasing the damages, irrespective of the result of the rehabilitation programme. Insurers can protect themselves if, when co-operating in the funding and provision of such rehabilitation, they provide for a re-assessment of the viability of the programme at a defined date.

Taking Advantage of Pro-activity

1.104   This in turn warrants a perhaps more pro-active and imaginative stance by the insurance industry than perhaps has been the position hitherto. For example:

(a) through claims for future care, the insurance industry pays millions per year for individual nursing provision. They have all the burdens of paying for a made-to-measure product, without any of the benefits of being a mass provider. Can they not enter into a relationship with a nationwide care provider, from which provision care is drawn down case-by-case?

(b) similarly, the insurance industry must be one of the largest (indirect) purchasers of wheelchairs and occupational therapy equipment in the country but they enjoy none of the advantages of bulk purchase.

(c) cannot insurers increasingly promote rehabilitation centres, hospices and hospitals?

Purpose of Rehabilitation – a Summary
1.105   The purpose of a rehabilitation programme is four-fold:

(a) to enhance the quality of life enjoyed by the disabled claimant, or at least to improve his morale;

(b) to reduce the period of uncertainty and anxiety suffered by the claimant and his family while awaiting trial or settlement of his action;

(c) to reduce the areas of uncertainty when attempting a final valuation of the claimant's claim;

(d) to reduce the size of the losses suffered by the claimant and the consequent magnitude of the claim.

1.106–1.109   In summary, the benefits gained by the claimant on the one hand is being able to lead a fuller and more rewarding life with suitable care and accommodation and worthwhile employment. Against that there is balanced a commensurate saving to the insurers in the overall cost of the claim, even after taking into account the costs of rehabilitation.

STRUCTURED SETTLEMENTS

Background in the United Kingdom

1.110   Structured settlements evolved from three interlinked areas of concern:

(a)   the need and desirability in cases of grave injury for rehabilitation;
(b)   the inefficiency (the 'structural flaw') of the large lump sum award;
(c)   conflicts of expert opinion in the assessment of life expectancy.

Introduction

1.111   Structured settlements are evolving in part as a result of dissatisfaction with lump sums, which fail to replace like-with-like, substitute capital sums for continuing future losses and may be insufficient to meet the claimant's long-term needs, being based on considerable guesswork.

1.112   A structured settlement is an alternative method of receiving an award of damages. Rather than accept a large lump sum, the defendant will agree to provide periodical payments direct to the claimant, usually together with a smaller lump sum for contingencies. Thus, a structured settlement converts a taxable income stream into a non-taxable income stream.

1.113   The Inland Revenue has allowed those claimants to receive periodical payments under a structured settlement free of any taxation.

The Machinery of a Structure

1.115   The liability insurer will meet his liability to make periodical payments to the claimant by purchasing an annuity from a life office. As a result of s 142 of the Finance Act 1995, life offices from which the defendant's insurer purchases the annuity can now pay the annuity direct to the claimant gross of tax (existing 'structures' are assignable to the claimant). The liability insurer drops out of the picture and the claimant gets the protection of the Policyholders Protection Act 1975.

1.116   Further, the Damages Act 1996 (which came into force on 24 September 1996) has extended the indemnity provided by the Policyholders Protection Act 1975 from 90% to 100% in the case of structured settlement annuities.[1] Thus the claimant need no longer fear the possibility that the life office might become insolvent during the life of the structured settlement.

1   See s 4.

1.117   In all structures entered into subsequent to 1 May 1995, there is a direct relationship between the life office and the claimant. Thus an annuity is paid gross to the claimant directly from the life office rather than through the general insurer. The changes wrought by s 142 the Finance Act 1995 also permit the 'old' type of structured settlement entered into before that Act to be renegotiated between the claimant and the defendant's insurer. They provide for the benefit of the agreement between the life insurer and the defendant's insurer to be assigned to the claimant, so that the claimant can receive the payments of the annuity directly from the life insurer. By this means both the claimant and the defendant's insurers benefit from the new statutory regime.

1.118   The liability insurer must purchase the annuity from an independent life office. It will not be permissible for the liability insurance department of a composite company to purchase the annuity from the life department of the same company. One cannot make a contract with oneself.

1.119   The following is an actual example of a claim by a man in his late 50s, given an award of £380,000. Note: the figure was unusually high.

Option	Cost of Structure	Assuming a Level Annual Sum	Assuming an Annual Sum Indexed to the RPI	Cash lump For Contingencies
Option 1	£380,000	£57,010	£52,218	None
Option 2	£300,000	£45,008	£41,225	£80,000
Option 3	£280,000	£42,007	£38,477	£100,000

1.120   The claimant in this example is in his late 50s. Thus:

(a)   the notional yield on the level structured settlement represents a return of about 15%. Taking into account basic rate tax this is the equivalent of a return of about 19%;

(b)   the notional yield on the RPI structured settlement represents a return of about 13.7%. Taking into account basic rate tax this is the equivalent of a return of about 17.8% return;

(c)   a conventional portfolio would have to take excessive risks to match this rate of return;

(d)   To achieve the same rate of return, the claimant would have to take out capital immediately to meet cash requirements.

'Bottom up' Structure
1.121   When there is a substantial dispute over life expectation, the following factors should be considered:

(a)   is the medical analysis of the life expectation properly founded? See Appendix 1 at page 26.

(b)   what view do a variety of life offices take? A life office may be expected to weigh in the balance a commercial view flowing from their experience;

(c)   if needs are calculated 'bottom up' rather than by adopting the totality approach, a 'structure' may prove to be a satisfactory compromise.

Categories of Case

1.122 Provided that the compensation is payable in respect of 'personal injury', which includes disease and any impairment of a person's physical or mental condition (Finance Act 1996, Sch 26) then any person who is liable to pay the compensation can enter into a structured settlement. Thus the following can enter into structured settlements:

- The Criminal Injuries Compensation Authority.
- Health Trusts and the medical defence organisations.
- The Motor Insurers' Bureau (with the exception of 'hit and run' cases).

Fatal Accident Claims

1.123 Structured compensation can also be used in claims under the Fatal Accidents Act. If the dependant is a minor or a patient then the approval of the court is required for a proposed structured settlement.

Mutual Insurers

1.124 Mutual insurance companies can now use structures on the same basis as other insurers. Mutuals not liable for corporation tax on trading profits. They could not therefore recover the tax which, under the pre Finance Act 1995 regime, a life office would deduct prior to paying instalments pursuant to an annuity contract. Clearly, it made no financial sense for a mutual to offer a structured settlement if it could not recover the tax. Now that the Finance Act enables the life office to make gross payments direct to the claimant, 'Mutuals' are on the same footing as other insurers.

Note Advantages

Life-time Guarantee

1.125 The payments will continue for the whole of the claimant's life, no matter how long that may be. If a claimant does not purchase an annuity, he carries his own mortality risk. In other words, not only does he risk dying but he risks dying after the money has run out.

The Fund is Never Exhausted

1.126 The bulk of the award is 'ringfenced' in the form of 100% guaranteed, tax free, inflation proofed monthly instalments.

Income Guaranteed to be Tax Free

1.127 The annual sums payable under the structured settlement annuity are free of any taxation. The Inland Revenue now treats the annuities as tax-free income. This should be seen in the following context:

(a) tax rates are prone to change in accordance with government policy;
(b) income and capital growth produced by investments or sums deposited at the bank will attract taxation.[1]

1 If instead of a structured settlement, there were a lump sum award - then unless the tax liability generated was exceptionally high, the court would not take into account the incidence of future taxation when assessing future loss: *Hodgson v Trapp* [1989] AC 807. However, such incidence was taken into account in *Biesheuvel v Birrell* [1999] PIQR Q40 where the incidence of such taxation was particularly exceptional, involving as it did the law of the Netherlands.

No Worry about Changes in Investment Returns
1.128   The income under the structured settlement is fully guaranteed by law. There are no investment risks. In contrast:

(a) interest rates provided by bank and building society accounts are subject to fluctuations;
(b) investment in stocks and shares can potentially provide significant gains and significant losses. For example, there has been a very lengthy sustained bull market and there is an increasing perception of a bear market as a real contingency.[1]

1   The annuity payments can be index linked so that they carry an in-built hedge against inflation.

The Statutory Guarantee
1.129   The payments are 100% protected under the Policyholder's Protection Act. Should the life office providing the structured settlement payments encounter financial difficulties, then the law ensures that all payments are met in full.

The Minimum Payment Provisions
1.130   In the particular example in para 1.119 the first five years' payments are guaranteed to continue in any event. Should the claimant die within the five year minimum payments period, then the payments under the structured settlement will continue, net of tax, in accordance with the provisions under the claimant's will. The estate also has the option of receiving a lump sum instead of the balance of the guaranteed payments.

Tailoring Compensation to Individual Requirements
1.131   The UK law of tort compensation treats property damage and personal injury on the same footing. Thus if a chattel worth £1m is destroyed, restituo in integrum results in a payment of £1m. But such an approach to compensation in a personal injury context coverts a victim of serious injury overnight from a consumer into a virtual financial institution. The argument can be advanced that it is wholly unrealistic to make any comparison between an individual earning a weekly wage and an individual who suddenly receives a huge lump sum. The income stream under a structure far more closely resembles a lifetime loss. Structuring diversifies the range of remedies available to victims of personal injury. The victim's future needs may be better met by regular payments which are more likely to be spent on the purposes for which damages are awarded. The return on a structure approximates very much more closely to the income stream which a family would normally receive.

No Dissipation Risk
1.132   A lump sum award affords to a claimant of full mental capacity the opportunity to dissipate the fund with the result of the taxpayer subsequently bearing the burden of the claimant's care and attendance. Thus, the state has a significant interest in preventing recipients of damages from becoming unnecessarily dependant on welfare benefits. It is unlikely that the state will ever have to step in to provide for the claimant where a settlement is structured. The public has, in fact, paid once to compensate the victim in the form of insurance premiums. If the victim later has to fall back on welfare benefits, the public is in effect being forced to pay twice over.

Certainty
1.133   The victim has the immediate certainty of regular income. The certainty of a future income stream may be seen to be better than the prospect presented by the receipt of a lump sum which then has to be invested and managed on behalf of the victim. There is the assurance of regular payments for life and of payments to dependants if the payments are guaranteed for a period longer than the claimant's life, together with the assurance that the payments will not decline in value if they are index-linked.

Reduces the Need for Financial Advice
1.134   The claimant is relieved of the burden of managing a large sum of money. Any risk of financial prejudice to a claimant by not being able to manage his financial affairs is reduced and because the fund is structured, there are savings in the cost of administering the fund. The proper planning of a structured settlement should ensure that the claimant's financial needs are catered for as they arise, thereby obviating the necessity for continuing and costly investment advice.

Tailoring the Package
1.135   The settlement can be tailored individually to the claimant's needs. Provided the cash flow is based on projected future cash requirements, the annuity package can be set up to provide, at the appropriate time, for education, changing nursing needs, asset accumulation, housing, marriage and children, and limited work or business prospects, if any. The damages will not be spent before these needs arise. By focusing on the claimant's needs, unlike the conventionally assessed lump sum, the adversarial nature of the proceedings is reduced.

Tax Break
1.136   There is the tax break, coupled with the fact that the claimant is protected against future increases in personal tax rates. Given the tax break with a structure, the actual rate of return on the structured settlement below is the equivalent of in excess of 4.6% gross, 2.8% net. This is a higher rate of return than ILGS. For example:

> Assuming an investment of £250,000 into a structure, an annuity of about £7,000 may be generated which is a return of about 2.8% net, 4.6% gross. This £7,000 is in part a repayment of capital, and if that capital has been otherwise invested, it would have generated taxable income, potentially exposed to taxation at top slice 40%.

1.137   These features make structured settlements particularly appropriate in cases where there are serious injuries and the conventional award would be large, and particularly where the claimant is a child and a long period of future care is envisaged. Note: care should be taken when making/accepting a Part 36 offer to settle. Unless an agreement pursuant to a Part 36 offer includes terms whereby the damages are to consist wholly or partly of periodical payments, then there is an argument that the tax breaks afforded to structured settlements will not apply.

Example Demonstrating the Security Element
1.138   Take a child of 11 years who is catastrophically brain damaged. There is a very large multiplier and the damages are invested in three tranches:

(a) family house;
(b) investment of a substantial sum into a structure;
(c) the balance in equities.

1.139 The structure would be the bedrock of the investment, given a situation where the primary requirement is for security. Another approach may be to invest in a 'structure' that proportion of the damages which the Court of Protection would have invested in gilts (for example, 30%) with the balance invested in equities.

Disadvantages of Structured Settlements

The Need for Consent
1.140 The changes in the law (notably the Finance Acts 1995 and 1996) do not enable one party to insist on or the court to order a structured settlement save with the consent of the parties.

Inflexibility
1.141 They do not avoid the need for forecasting. They may place an undesirable emphasis on forward planning which is avoided where lump sums are used.

The Prophecy Problem
1.142 Whereas with a lump sum the claimant has to deal with anticipated future needs by managing the lump sum and making payments to meet the needs as required, a structured settlement requires experts and advisers to prepare a complex advance budget for life. Payments from annuities may come on stream at the wrong time or not be needed at all. Prognoses may yet prove to be incorrect, affecting decisions previously made about lifestyle. (The problem is ameliorated to a degree by building a contingency fund into the structure).

Lack of Control Over the Funds
1.143 The settlement is made and managed by outside professionals.

Irrevocability
1.144 The claimant cannot unravel a structure once it has become established. This may result in hardship to a claimant if some unforeseen eventuality should occur.

The Windfall to the Life Office
1.145 In the event of the death of the claimant earlier than estimated, the estate would be deprived of a lump sum. The annuity ceases on death (unless a provision is built into the structure for a minimum period during which payment would be made irrespective of whether the claimant dies in the meantime). The counter-point to this, of course, is that the claimant no longer carries his own mortality risk.

Irreconcilable with Provisional Damages
1.146 A structured settlement precludes a claim for provisional damages (unless the provisional damages claim is resolved contractually). This is because a provisional damages award necessarily involves a judgment and any judgment extinguishes the antecedent debt which is a vital factor in preserving the tax free status of a structured settlement. Given the relatively few provisional damages cases, this may not be too much of a problem.

No Guarantee that the Income Stream Will be Sufficient
1.147   Structured settlements do not completely remove the risk that the monies provided under them may not be adequate to meet the claimant's needs. The claimant, unless subject to supervision by the Court of Protection, will still be able to squander any monies received even if they are intended for specific purposes. Another aspect of the risk is that although structures are linked to the RPI via the index-linked security, this cannot guarantee that costs of future care will always be met. Historically, the cost of care has risen faster than the RPI, albeit that our damages system does not compensate claimants for this fact.

Personal Freedom
1.148   A severely injured claimant may wish to take a large lump sum in order to move to another country for family reasons or to take advantage of educational or business opportunities there.

Should the Courts have Power to Impose a Structured Settlement?

1.149   The question whether or not courts should have the power to impose a structured settlement is a question about the method or form of payment.

Summary of the Argument for
1.150   It has been argued that if the courts were able to impose a structured settlement against the wishes of a claimant, this would breach the established principle that claimants should be able to spend their damages awards as they wish. The corollary of this liberal principle is that claimants should be able to insist on receiving their award in the form of an immediate lump sum.

Summary of the Argument against
1.151   The Pearson Commission Report,[1] shows that the freedom of choice which is offered by the lump sum is something which claimants would not have enjoyed if they had not been injured and it is not therefore an essential part of a system based on restituo in integrum.

1   Vol 1, page 123 at para 565.

1.152   The Law Commission Report, No 225, of 1994 inter alia says:[1]

'The court has a duty to award compensation which will put the [plaintiff] back into the position she or he would have been in had the accident not occurred. It is arguable that the replacement of a lost stream of income by periodic payments and the provision of funds to meet medical and other needs created by the injury as those needs arise achieves this more effectively than the provision of a lump sum'.

1   Page 221 at pages 38-39.

1.153   There is an inconsistency in a claimant arguing that a particular need exists, such as the need for an adapted house and then using the money for something completely different.

1.154   Compare this to the view expressed in the Law of Contract:[1]

'Where a [plaintiff] is prima facie entitled to the cost of curing a defect in the defendant's performance, damages will not be assessed on that basis if there is no undertaking or proposal to undertake the cure, or at least circumstances which indicate sufficient firmness of intention to spend the damages on the cure.[2]

'The attraction of structures is that they go further than lump sums to facilitate the meeting of specific needs as they arise and, in doing so, replicate, so far as is possible, the compensatory basis on which awards are made.'

1   Guenter H Treitel, *Law of Contract* (Sweet & Maxwell).
2   Law Commission Report No 224.

Practical Problems Arising from the Power to Impose

1.155–1.159   The Law Commission Report, No 225, of 1994 inter alia says:[1]

'The small number of interviews conducted with recipients of structured settlements reveal considerable satisfaction with this form of damages payment. The chief advantages were seen as providing security for the future and the removal of responsibility for planning and managing investment of capital. However, despite the perceived advantages of the form of payment, recipients of structured settlements nonetheless expressed concerns about the adequacy of the settlements to cover future needs. In common with those who receive lump sum payments, initial satisfaction with the amount of money received at the time of the settlement can often turn to dismay later when, with the benefit of hindsight, compensated accident victims recognise the real costs of physical impairment, the true extent of their losses, and the imprecision of assessments of future needs and expenses at the time of the settlement.'[2]

1   Page 221.
2   In the UK structured settlements are invoked exclusively for personal injury claims. They do not cover for example, pollution clean-up.

THE NEED FOR INDEPENDENT FINANCIAL ADVICE

Obstacles to Structured Compensation

1.160   From a claimant's perspective there have been two pragmatic objections:

(a)   the first is the natural desire of a claimant (or his family) to recover as large a lump sum as possible in a single award;
(b)   there has been the widely held belief that low annuity rates generate a poor return for a structured settlement.

1.161   At page 264 of the Law Commission Report, No 225 1994:

'What is clear, is that given the need for the value of damages to be preserved for as long as possible, even those who receive relatively modest settlements would benefit from genuinely independent and expert advice about how to deal with their damages. Although accident victims are not profligate, they may regret the choices that they make, both about savings and expenditure. Good quality advice at an early stage would not reduce control over damages that appears to be so valued by accident victims, but it would ensure that decisions about the use of damages were well-informed.'

1.162   In summary, there is a need in the UK market for greater independent advice vis-à-vis the benefits flowing from a structured settlement, irrespective of low interest rates.

Fees
1.163–1.174   Transparency in relation to the following is probably welcomed:

(a) who gives the financial advice and the extent of its independence;
(b) how much that advice cost, and who pays for it?

SUMMARY OF THE UK POSITION

Annuity Plus Contingency Fund
1.175   A structured settlement normally consists of a conventional lump sum payment to the claimant together with an annuity or series of annuities paid to the claimant.

The Need for Consent
1.166   The structured settlement will provide for a contingency fund to give flexibility. Flexibility is required to cover:

(a) foreseeable capital needs;
(b) the gap between RPI and other inflationary increases, for example, in wages;
(c) the unexpected.

Tax-free Income Stream
1.167   The word 'settlement' connotes the need for the consent of the parties. Subject to the parties' consent, the court can, by order, provide for a structured settlement.[1] The court cannot so order in the absence of consent.[2]

1   Damages Act 1996.
2   *Burke v Tower Hamlet Health Authority* [1989] CLY 1201.

Lifetime Guarantee
1.168   The Inland Revenue treat the annuities as being non-taxable. A structured settlement may represent a substantial tax saving on the annual return to the claimant. The Law Commission Consultation Paper No 125 on structured settlements points out that the tax saving of a structure to a standard rate paying claimant amounts to a little over 8%.

Index-linked
1.169   The annuity payments can be index-linked so that they carry an in-built hedge against inflation.

Lifetime Guarantee
1.170   The majority of structured settlements are guaranteed for the life of the claimant and are indexed to cater for inflation. Thus the compensation will not

run out, no matter for how long the claimant lives. This is of particular importance in those cases where the expectation of life is uncertain.

Court Approval
1.171   If the claimant is a person under disability (child or mental patient) the proposed structured settlement will require the approval of the court. Note:

(a) the Practice Direction, which governs structured settlements, and
(b) section 96 of the Mental Health Act 1983 which provides that control over legal proceedings on behalf of a patient is given to the nominated judge (which includes the Master of the Court of Protection). He can make such orders or give such directions or authorities as he thinks fit.

The Need for Precise Wording of the Order
1.172   It is essential to ensure that the payments are not taxable on receipt by the claimant, that the agreement must be worded in such a way as to make it clear that the periodic payments, however, structured, must comply with the relevant Finance Acts.

Flexibility of Income Stream
1.173–1.174   In summary, in addition to the continency fund, the stream or streams of tax free payments may be:

(a) annual;
(b) periodic but not annual;
(c) deferred;
(d) guaranteed for a minimum period;
(e) linked to the RPI or otherwise incremental;
(f) available for life.

LOOKING FORWARD

Ongoing Victim Support
1.175   Law Commission Report, No 225, 1994:

'Qualitative interviews revealed a conspicuous lack of advice or counselling for victims of accidental injury. This is true for psychological and emotional difficulties, and for employment difficulties, as well as for the management of damages already discussed. Although accident victims have considerable contact with experts during settlement negotiations, attention at this stage naturally concentrates on those matters relevant to the claim. After years of focus on the circumstances of the accident, on the effects of injuries, on the reduced capacity to work, and the inability to perform hundreds of small daily tasks, there is a need for attention to be constructively diverted towards the future. There is a need for psychological support; there is a need to address the problem of the debilitating effects of pain; and there is a their normal work. In short, there is a need to help accident victims to adjust to their circumstances and to envisage a useful and productive future for themselves, albeit different from their pre-accident expectations.'

Clinical Disputes Forum
1.176 This forum, recently established in the United Kingdom, is looking at ways of achieving periodical payments to replace structured settlements. A question arises as to who provides the guarantee. The advantage to health trusts is that they are afforded grater cash flow. The forum is also researching the viability of the reviewability of structures, to achieve the ideal of the flexible structured settlement.

Appendix 1

LIFE EXPECTATION AND MULTIPLIERS

1.180 Introduction

- *The life expectancy/multiplier interface*: Assessment of life expectancy is central to assessment of the multiplier.
- *The significance of the multiplier in catastrophic injury claims*: Given multiplicands as high as £100,000 a year on the multiplier, generates in itself a figure for damages larger than perhaps 95% of all personal injury claims.
- *Life expectancy and structures*: If the claimant wants or needs a structured settlement, the insurer and claimant are so often apparently boxing from the wrong corners: The lower the life expectancy contended for, the cheaper an annuity, thus making a 'structure' more attractive as a solution to the insurer.

1.181 Issue

    (a) What happens if there is a sharp difference of medical opinion over life expectancy?
    (b) How is it to be resolved?
    (c) What are the arguments to put before the court?

1.182 The Legal Matrix

- *The 'person under disability' factor*: Almost invariably, a catastrophic injury results in the claimant being a person under disability warranting the approval of the court before any settlement.
- *The risk confronting the court*: The risk the court has inter alia to consider is that if there is a 'conventional award' the money will run out before death. The court therefore has to be satisfied that the issue of life expectancy has been thoroughly analysed.
- *The relevance of 'law' to assessments of life expectancy*: The backdrop against which life expectancy has to be assessed is one of law, not medicine. There is a presumption that life expectancy is normal unless proved to the contrary: *Rowley v London and North Western Railway Co* (1873) LR 8 Exch 221, see commentary in *McGregor on Damages* (15th edn at p 993).
- *The conventional techniques*: When seeking to argue that life expectation is reduced, the conventional approach is to argue by reference to literature, relating to classes of individual (for example, Bavarian veterans of 1914-1918 war or a paper as to a class of mentally handicapped children analysed in the New England Journal of Medicine (1990) 323:584–589 by Eyman et al).

- *The inadequacy of conventional techniques*: It is submitted that individual cases do not fit neatly into the pigeon holes ordained by these surveys. Is not a more legally accurate approach to consider the risk factors of premature death by reference to this individual claimant? The grounds for that argument flow from cases such as *Paris v Stepney BC* [1951] AC 367 at 389 which is authority for the principle that a duty of care is owed by the tort-feasor to the claimant *qua* individual and not *qua* class. And if the duty is owed to the individual, so the damages are by reference to the individual and not to a class: *Moschi v Lep Air Services Ltd* [1973] AC 331 at 445.
- *Risk factors, to be defined by lawyers, for the opinion of doctors*: Thus as a matter of law, it is submitted that any assessment of life expectation has to be by reference to risk factors identified medically as relevant to this claimant, and not by reference to a class.

1.183 The Medical Matrix

Risk factors identified as potentially affecting the life expectation of an individual include:

    (a) Quality of care (relevant also to the avoiding of potentially fatal accidents and also to mental stimulation).
    (b) Respiratory problems and chest infection (which can result from paralysis of the intercostal muscles).
    (c) Whole body sensation.
    (d) Whether there has been a splenectomy, epilepsy, urinary tract problems (including ascending cystic degeneration of urinary bladder), blood clots, spinal cord cyst, cardio-vascular abnormalities, kidney infection, pressure sores (which can lead to chronic sepsis), choking/coughing (levels of consciousness and the protective reflexes of the pharynx).
    (e) Autonomic disreflexia (which can manifest with headaches, sweating and high blood pressure).
    (f) Ascending syringomyelia.
    (g) Osteoporosis and long bone fracture.
    (h) Past medical history (including smoking, alcohol abuse level).
    (i) Significant family history.
    (j) Intellectual function.
    (k) Communication skills (particularly in an emergency).
    (l) Extent of any progressive degenerative disorders.
    (m) Suicide.

These factors help therefore to constitute an agenda for the medical experts to help them assess the life expectancy of this individual claimant. The following schedule explains how, by using these factors, the medical opinion can be made to hang on a framework.

1.184 Conclusion

The following is submitted:

- Issues of life expectancy involve matters of law; they are not exclusively the preserve of the medical profession. The medical experts advise by reference to a legal matrix, for otherwise the jurisdiction of the court is ousted.

- When advising, the medical experts must advise by reference to this individual claimant and not by reference to a class.
- If there is an impasse between the medical experts, given the legal matrix, then the ways through are:

  (*a*) structured settlement (conventional or 'bottom up' – but if bottom up, note the potential need for a high level of care to preserve life), or

  (*b*) hearing of a preliminary issue in respect of life expectation and multiplier: *Thermawear and Linton* (1995) Times, 20 October, CA, and/or

  (*c*) without prejudice meeting of medical experts to an agenda agreed by the legal teams on both sides.

Risk	P1 (ie First [plaintiff] medical expert)	P 2	P 3	D 1 (ie First defendant medical expert)	D 2
Introduction	'... She has recovered to the extent that despite her difficulties with communication and minor problems with swallowing, she may be considered now functionally as being simply a very high tetraplegic. The increased mortality following acute high tetraplegia is most marked in the early stages following injury, particularly in the first year. This high risk stage has been passed. 22.5.97: ... I cannot concur with Dr D1's view of Miss P having a substantially reduced life expectancy.	Life expectancy is shortened through the increased risk of particular Medical complications. The likelihood of these complications occurring in an individual is always difficult to give, and the best guide is theexperience up to this point ... ... the occurrence of a head injury does not of itself shorten life expectancy.	4.4.98: Reduction in life expectancy in severely brain damaged patient such as [plaintiff] depends on their vulnerability to a number of specific complications related to their disability.	20.7.95: The nature of her disability is such that her life expectancy has been considerably shortened ... Possible causes of early death in patients in her condition include inhalation, blood poisoning, traumatic injury and blood clots. 14.5.97: Mr T is at a disadvantage in not having examined Miss P.	3. Life expectancy in those who left mindless, as she is not, and paralysed in reflex decorticate flexion of the arms and extension of the legs, as she has been, rarely live ten years. In my own studies there was no-one as physically disabled as she has been left whose thinking brain was functioning at other than primitive levels. This is usually the case after head injury as severe as this, but occasionally, as here, there is relative preservation of the thinking part of the brain despite almost complete paralysis of the body.

Risk	P1 (ie First [plaintiff] medical expert)	P 2	P 3	D 1 (ie First defendant medical expert)	D 2
Inellectual blunting	She has recovered to the extent that despite her difficulties with communication and minor problems with swallowing, she may be considered simply a high tetraplegic. 22.5.97: I think one could reasonably take exception to (D1's) view that she be regarded as a mental retard.		8.12.93: ... She became totally independent within the college using her electric powered chair, operated by head movements – the only remaining voluntary movement available to her – she has retained a good degree of intelligence and insight, but her short-term memory is limited.	20.7.95: Intellectual faculties are reasonably well preserved. 14.5.97: Noteworthy that P 2 accepts ... 'marked cognitive impairment.'	
Limb injuries	Complete Recovery. Unlikely to Influence her life expectancy.				
Splenectomy	Theoretical risk of serious manifestations should she develop a major bacterial infection. This risk can be reduced through vaccination.		4.4.98: '... increased risk of severe infection due to her splenectomy set by Dr M as 4 times greater than that of a healthy adult after vaccine prophylaxis.'		
Sensation throughout body	Almost unimpaired.				
Breathing	No major respiratory problems, is able to breathe spontaneously.				

Risk	P1 (ie First [plaintiff] medical expert)	P 2	P 3	D 1 (ie First defendant medical expert)	D 2
Respiratory tract/chest infection	None since leaving hospital. 22.5.97: "To my knowledge she has not suffered from any major respiratory tract infection since returning home.	... clearly has an increased risk of chest infection both due to her immobility and due to her swallowing difficulties ... She has not experienced any significant chest infections over the last five years. This is despite being in schools and other settings where infections are common. Furthermore it should be noted that chest infections can be treated both using antibiotics and through chest physiotherapy. I would therefore conclude that there is no great increase in her risk of premature death due to chest infection. Any reduction in 'average' life expectancy should be measured in a few years only.	4.4.98: 'Chest infection is the commonest cause of mortality but [plaintiff's] swallowing and cough reflexes are intact and she has not had any serious chest infections at home nor during her many months in the more risky surroundings of college. Her high level of personalised care, and the fact that this is provided at home rather than in the infection-prone ... hospital further reduces the risk.'	14.5.97: 'The fact that it has not happened does not mean it will not.'	

Risk	P1 (ie First [plaintiff] medical expert)	P 2	P 3	D 1 (ie First defendant medical expert)	D 2
Epilepsy	'I do not agree with Dr D1 that she is likely to have a 3-5% risk of late onset post-traumatic epilepsy for the rest of her life. The predicted risk factors have been set out previously by Jennett and having been fit free in the eight years or so following her accident, the risk of Miss P developing late onset seizure actively is now only around 1% and would probably diminish further with time.	Life can be shortened through severe epileptic fits... She has not had any epileptic fits and her current risk of developing epilepsy is probably little above that of her contemporaries. The rise in her risk may be as little as one or two per cent. Thus there is no significant effect upon life expectancy arising from her risk of epilepsy.		20.7.95: 'So far she has not had any seizures. Nevertheless, she runs a risk of developing epilepsy as a late complication of her head injury. I would put this risk at between 3 and 5% for life.'	11.10.94: There is nothing to suggest the development of PTE and the risks of this now in that event are probably slight and in the region of 3%.
Spinal cord cyst	No				
Urinary tract problem	Not at risk. Page 3: Normal micturition.	Continent of urine, does not have an indwelling catheter, and has not had any significant urinary tract infections over the past four or five years.			

Risk	P1 (ie First [plaintiff] medical expert)	P 2	P 3	D 1 (ie First defendant medical expert)	D 2
Cardio-vascular abnormalities	No.	Theoretical risk that she might experience deep venous thrombosis and consequent pulmonary embolism. Experience from spinal cord injury would suggest that this risk is highest in the earliest months, and then reduces rapidly. She has not experienced any problems from this to this point, and there is no reason to expect any problems to develop.		14.5.97: She is and remains at high risk of deep venous thrombosis leading to pulmonary embolism.	
Dysreflexia	No.				
Pressure sores	No.	'... not experienced any pressure sores, and her care appears to be of an extremely high standard.'			

Risk	P1 (ie First [plaintiff] medical expert)	P 2	P 3	D 1 (ie First defendant medical expert)	D 2
Choking	No major problems with swallowing. She does have dysphagia but there is no evidence that she is unable to clear her own secretions nor to regurgitate food if fed carefully and therefore provided the standard of her care remains high, there is no detrimental effect on life expectancy. 22.5.97: Able to swallow secretions and no evidence that prone to inhalation or regurgitation of food if suitably cared for by experienced carers.	'... has disturbed swallowing. for example, dysphagia. She tends to choke on liquids. However she does otherwise eat a normal diet.	4.4.98: '[Plaintiff's] swallowing and cough reflexes are intact.	14.5.97: She has what is known as a pseudo-bulbar palsy that is causing impairment of both speech production and swallowing. This has implications with regard to survival that I shall refer to below.	13.12.96: Chokes a lot on food. Frequent gurgling. Coughing on excess saliva in throat.
Past medical history	None.				
Significant family history	None.				
Smoking	No.				
Alcohol abuse	No.				

Risk	P1 (ie First [plaintiff] medical expert)	P 2	P 3	D 1 (ie First defendant medical expert)	D 2
Communications skills – communicating in an emergency	Yes – Provided she has high quality constant care then this would have no detrimental effect on her life expectancy.		4.4.98: In view of her limited capacity to communicate there is another problem, that of her inability to report symptoms indicative of new life-threatening conditions such as cancer. Such conditions would therefore likely be diagnosed too late for optimum treatment, and this must be a risk for reduced life expectation.	Cannot communicate verbally.	13.12.96: Can made audible noise – can call her mother at night if requires turning.
Blood poisoning, inhalation, traumatic injury, blood clots, chest infections	Most unlikely to influence outcome particularly if preventive measures such as vaccination against pneumococcus and haemophilius influenzi as advocated by others are undertaken.			20.7.95: The nature of her disability is such that life expectancy has been considerably shortened, possibly cases of early death in particular in her condition include inhalation, chest infections, blood poisoning, traumatic injury, blood clots. Her life expectancy is about 15 years.	
Suicide	No risk.				

Risk	P1 (ie First [plaintiff] medical expert)	P 2	P 3	D 1 (ie First defendant medical expert)	D 2
Miscellaneous	Given a high quality standard of care (which would need to be virtually constant) complemented by good medical attention as and when necessary, then there is no reason why she should succumb to most of the usual medical complications related to the above factors and attendant upon tetraplegia. Claimant cannot be regarded as a mentally retarded immobile patient subject to all the detrimental risk factors relating to life expectancy as described by Dr D1. For the same reasons ... (see above) I cannot agree with D 2 in his opinion that [plaintiff] is unlikely to survive beyond her mid-thirties.	I would therefore conclude that there is no specific identifiable reason why her life expectancy should be reduced by any significant amount. There are small increases in her risk of premature death arising from her immobility, and at most I would accept a ten-year reduction in her life expectancy from her normal life expectancy.		20.7.95: The nature of her disability is such that her life expectancy has been considerably shortened. Her life expectancy is of the order of 15 years.	'It is likely to be the degree of dementia and paralysis, but principally the latter, which determine survival with brain damage. On the basis of my own studies and the available published evidence in similar states since I think she may survive another ten years and just possibly a few more years after that, but most unlikely that she will live beyond her mid-thirties.

Appendix 2

MAJOR CLAIMS HANDLING – 'WOOLF' LITIGATION TECHNIQUES FOR DEFENDANTS

1.199 Woolf: big bang in the legal profession:
  (a) The court will no longer be the repair workshop for a defective litigation product;
  (b) Litigation is to be avoided;
  (c) Words on paper define the issues;
  (d) If the words are wrong, there is no hiding place for:
      (i)   a claimant on a conditional fee agreement,
      (ii) an insurance litigator protecting his client's reserves.

1.200 To secure your business:
  (a) Tendering to an insurer/health trust which enables that customer to achieve premium fees and investment income sufficient to compete successfully in the insurance marketplace;
  (b) Enabling the insurer to achieve accurate reserving [recognising that reserving impacts on pricing and apparent profitability. Check: worst case? Reinsurance? Co-Insurance? Costs included in the reserve?]
  (c) Working to a partnership with the insurer/health trust: Access to databases/client files – ease of communication, consistency of approach, 'Woolf' orientated.
  (d) Negotiation, mediation or Litigation [consider Lord Steyn in *Wells*].

1.201 How underwriters/insurance litigators can protect themselves:
  (a) *Deny cover?* 'Incident', 'occurrence', 'claims made', – / – 'bodily injury [does this include nervous shock?]', 'death', 'disease', 'accident'.
  (b) *Contributory negligence/causation:*
  (c) *Structured settlements:*
      (i)   Assuming a return of 4% on the life office investment, then a structured settlement must be a less expensive way of resolving a claim.
      (ii) Particularly if liability is in issue, consider a 'bottom up' structure.
      (iii) Be pro-active: Offer the settlement – have recourse if necessary to the 'failure to mitigate' pleading rule.
  (d) *Life expectation:* Investigate the clinical risks which would go to reduce.
  (e) *Working life multiplier:* Explore the basis of arguments for the assumed retirement date for the accident.
  (f) *Rehabilitation:*
      (i)   Pro-active offer? Present problem of insurance money paying for

programme set by the claimant. Consider defining programme, costing it and then offering it ['failure to mitigate' if refused].

(ii) Consider effect on nursing care: *Bristow v Judd* [1993] PIQR Q 117, CA.

(iii) Note the interface between rehabilitation and residual earning capacity: should insurers offer lower premiums to those companies who offer so many places of work to the handicapped each year?

(g) *Nursing care claims:*

    (i)   At present – Bulk purchase without discount.

    (ii) Motor claims – nominated garage, and so on – is there a parallel? Note: Where the claimant has sufficient intellectual capacity to attend to and manage his own affairs, there was no need to employ a case manager: *Page v Sheerness Steel plc* [1995] PIQR Q 26.

(h) *Protocols for handling claims for loss of sole-trader/small company.* Documents which are not obvious but which may be the key are: equipment receipts, advertisements in local papers, advertising literature, names of parties approached for tenders, business plans, cash flow projections with the bank and so on.

(i) *Ill-health retirement schemes:*

    (i)   If a contributory scheme, then at present no deduction against claims for loss of earnings.

    (ii) Consider: Provision in contract of employment that payments under such schemes are to be deducted from the damages; per Lord Templeman in *'Smoker'*: 'Insurance companies and employers are at liberty to draft pension schemes in a way which will negate the effect of *Parry v Cleaver* . . .'

(j) *The profile of the claimant litigation team:* Consider in the context of the claimant:

    (i)   Legal aid merits test;

    (ii)   Conditional fee insurance – material non-disclosure;

    (iii) Legal expenses insurance.

(k) *The split-trial/payment-in interface.*

(l) *Expert witness training:* Two tips –

    (i)   Clinical negligence: What is the act or omission alleged to constitute negligence which caused the damage? What are the grounds for arguing that such act or omission was negligent, by reference to the risk benefit ratio? What are the facts which the court is invited to find to establish that opinion? What is the evidence to prove those facts?

    (ii) Quantum: What are the facts which the doctor invites the court to find to establish his opinion? Have those facts been forensically tested by medical questions and/or by reference to contemporaneous records?

(m) *Litigator training:* Witness statements – the evidence in chief – the risk arising from leading questions – cross-examination in interview/testing the evidence – certificates of truth [by telephone? By questionnaire? By post? By outside investigator? *Beachley Properties* – right first time?]

(n) *Databases:* Lexis, Newlaw Publishing, Butterworths PI On-Line, Lloyd's Law Reports Electronic, Lloyd's Law Reports [Medical], ADAM, Lawtel PI Interactive.

(o) *Schedules of loss:*

(i) Right at the beginning ask for documents which go to support the Schedule of Loss;

(ii) Check that equipment not only necessary, but capable of being used [psychologist];

(iii) Double glazing *and* extra heating?

(iv) Items which would have been purchased anyway [car, washing machine, video, TV, and so on]

1.202 Rehabilitation

(a) Establish links with rehabilitation centres around the country – working to recognised protocols vis-à-vis brain and spinal cord injury. Note: with Rehab-UK, the defendant bears the cost of rehabilitation and the assessment is made on an entirely 'without prejudice' basis.

(b) As soon as a claim is notified on the pre-action protocol:

(i) *Strategy and issues:* remembering that the priority is to find out as much as possible as soon as possible about the value of the claim – the 'reserve' issue; for example:

(ii) Do we repudiate?

(iii) Do we allege contributory negligence? The window of opportunity for a 'bottom-up' structure.

(c) Calderbank Offer/payment-in;

(d) Offer of contribution – co-insurers;

(e) Offer preliminary issue of assessment by reference to provisional damages [if the view is taken that the prospects of deterioration are very small, but a provisional damages order affords opportunity of significantly lower settlement].

(f) Early assessment for rehabilitation with the offer directly to fund, or the offer of an interim payment to fund; consider panels of experts trained to your own protocols;

(g) Ask for the opportunity to assess the experts nominated by the claimant before they are instructed; Note the ability for the defence to ask questions of the claimant experts. Alternatively, can agreement be reached that the parties respective experts visit at the same time?

(h) Can agreement be reached on a case-manager to oversee the rehabilitation plan?

(i) The pro-active counter-schedule of loss.

Appendix 3

1.203 STRUCTURED SETTLEMENTS IN THE UNITED KINGDOM – A CHRONOLOGY

1989:   The first UK structure – *Kelly v Dawes*
1992:   (a) First self-funded Health Authority structure – *O'Toole v Merseyside Health Authority*
(b) First Fatal Accident structure – *Boobyer v Highway Motor Policies*
1994:   Law Commission report
1995:   Finance Act 1996
1996:   (a) Finance Act 1996
(b) Damages Act
(c) First CICB structure (*Boulding*)
(d) First Motor Insurers' Bureau structure
(e) First Ministry of Defence structure
1998:   Judgment of House of Lords in *Wells v Wells* [1998] 3 WLR 239.
1999:   Reforms of Lord Woolf

Chapter 2

Risk Analysis

Iain Goldrein QC
Margaret de Haas QC

INTRODUCTION TO COST-EFFECTIVE FILE MANAGEMENT

Introduction

2.1 This chapter assumes that the pre-action protocols have been complied with, that the dispute has not been resolved and there is recourse to litigation. The thrust of the text is weighted towards clinical negligence litigation on the basis that this is probably personal injury ('PI') litigation in its purest form, issues of fact are rare and the expert witnesses tend to be drawn from the higher level of medical expertise.

2.2 The purpose of this chapter is to demonstrate how tort litigation can be run to a budget, cost-effectively. Its aim is to help eradicate from file management cost and delay. If litigators cannot run this litigation cost-effectively, conditional fee agreements will not be available and this will bar access to justice.

The Significance of Public Funding
2.3 The Legal Services Commission is a financier, not a legal auditor. It does not finance proceedings, rather it underwrites the risk of losing proceedings.

The Significance of Conditional Fee Agreements
2.4 For reasons explained in para 2.24, conditional fee agreements can be interpreted as justifying the removal of legal aid from areas of legal activity covered by those agreements.

Hazards of Litigation
2.5 Before considering how legal aid can be legitimately removed from the field of PI litigation, it is a useful exercise to examine the phrase 'risks of litigation.' See 2.10 onwards.

Explanation of Format of this Text
2.6 This chapter sets out a framework for litigating and fleshes out the concepts with modules which constitute practical file management tools. Those modules are:

- Module 1: Explanation of the 'legal critical path analysis' of a case.
- Module 2: Statement taking technique.

- Module 3:   Case management for personal injury claims.
- Module 4:   Organisation of trial bundles in a clinical negligence action.
- Module 5:   Limitation issues – quick access guide.
- Module 6:   Legal framework for a medical opinion in a clinical negligence action.
- Module 7:   Structure of an opening speech in court, in a clinical negligence action.
- Module 8:   Agendas for conferences. This module is tailored to clinical negligence. It can however be readily adapted to any PI claim. In smaller claims, the agenda can be used for a file review as opposed to a conference.
- Module 9:   Managing the experts to cut costs – quality control for experts.
- Module 10: Model statement of claim – clinical negligence.
- Module 11: Data about cerebral palsy claims.
- Module 12: Selection of counsel.

2.7–2.9 Access to justice is barred if the legal profession cannot cost-effectively make an accurate risk analysis. This topic is explored in more detail in Module 1.

RISKS OF LITIGATION

Rationale

2.10 This is a 'catch-all' phrase. It is used (if not invariably) in the following situations:

- To discourage a client from running an action.
- Having commenced an action, to discourage him from continuing it.
- Having continued it, to discourage him from fighting to trial (thereby to achieve a settlement).

The Hazards of Litigation?

2.11 Traditionally, there were hazards arising out of the 'chesting of cards', namely:

    (a) the court-room was the primary forum for the finding of fact;
    (b) all evidence as to fact and expert opinion was privileged until disclosure in the court-room;
    (c) thus witnesses volunteered their evidence to the other side, for the first time, in court;
    (d) facts could therefore surface which had not been anticipated and which undermined the case;
    (e) alternatively, a client's case could collapse under cross-examination by a skilled advocate on the other side.

The Consequences of 'Cards on the Table'

2.12 These traditional 'hazards of litigation' no longer apply, but the phrase is still used. Why?

2.13 What are the present hazards of litigation?

- Facts: failure to record the facts relevant to the cause of action and failure properly to communicate with the witness to foreclose the risk of the statement of truth being misleading.

- Expert evidence: failure to retain an expert of the correct calibre, properly trained in court procedure, in the relevant discipline on the relevant issue.
- Law: failure sufficiently accurately to record the legal critical path analysis of the case and to bring to the action a litigator of the relevant calibre.
- Damages: failure to have recorded in the relevant experts' reports, the relevant opinion for the issue to be proved.
- Failure to recognise the heads of past and future loss capable of being recovered.
- Failure to exercise a proper judgment in relation to the information revealed by the other side's cards which are face up on the table.
- Failure to realise that the 'go for it mentality' seduces the client with a false prospectus if confronted with a shrewdly pitched payment-in/Part 36 offer.

Hazards of Litigation and Expert Evidence

2.14 The litigator must be alert to recognise the distinction between his role as a lawyer and one who instructs experts. The published material available in the medico-legal domain is now such as potentially to seduce litigators into the belief that they can to some extent form an expert opinion vis-à-vis matters of medical practice/expertise. Here danger looms. For example, a solicitor retaining an expert will write a letter of instruction. That can have the following potential consequences:

(a) If the solicitor labours wrongly under the impression that having heard some lectures and read some material on (say) obstetrics, he is now in a position to discuss the issues authoritatively from that medical standpoint, he is at risk of causing the expert to think that the solicitor has a level of expertise in that field, which in fact he does not have. The expert, believing the letter to be accurately crafted, volunteers opinion on that basis. If the basis is wrong, monies have been wasted.

(b) The solicitor, armed with some knowledge, asks a raft of questions of the expert. The expert answers them all. In fact, none are relevant to the true medico-legal issues.

2.15 The role of any litigator is to understand the expert evidence. It is not to make oneself an expert in that field. A few lectures on medical matters and the odd textbook is no substitute for several years of tuition in medical school. Failure to understand this demarcation of roles can lead not just to wasted costs, but to total failure in the court room.

Cards on the Table and Legal Aid

2.16–2.19 Once cards are on the table, there is opened a challenge to the litigator. Why should the public purse underwrite the risk of losing?

CAN LEGAL AID BE LEGITIMATELY WITHDRAWN?

The Fail-safe Position of the Claimant

2.20 Hitherto, the Legal Services Commission has underwritten the bulk of personal injury litigation. The claimant litigator has been financially in a *'win-win'* situation:

- If the claimant has won the action, his litigator has been paid out by the health authority/insurer.
- If the claimant has lost, the litigator has been paid out by the Legal Services Commission.

2.21 All that is changing. The engine for change is 'openness'.

'Openness'

2.22 The quiet revolution in the changes to court procedure predicate 'cards on the table'. In this field the primary engines for 'openness' are the Pre-Action Protocols. After proceedings have been launched, however, the Civil Procedure Rules 1998 ('CPR') ordain 'openness' and wherever possible, 'co-operation' at every stage.

What is 'Openness'

2.23 'Openness' predicates nothing less than a revolution in our procedures. It means:

(a) The court room is not the primary fact-finding forum.
(b) The capability of making an informed risk analysis of the merits of winning/losing is accessible to the litigator who knows how to 'exploit' openness.
(c) 'Exploiting openness' means knowing the legal critical path analysis of a case, which facts and expert evidence are required to be adduced, when the relevant document should be created and at what cost. As to the legal critical path analysis, see Module 1.
(d) Knowing what facts and expert evidence to adduce and when predicates cost-effective file management.
(e) An alternative to cost effective file management is insolvency.

Why Insolvency?

2.24 Because:

(a) Once the litigator can make an informed judgment of the risks of winning or losing, the policy question arises: Why should the Legal Service Commission underwrite the risk of losing?
(b) Why cannot the Legal Service Commission withdraw its safety net and require the litigator to underwrite the risk of losing?
(c) The litigator underwrites the risk of losing in the regime of 'conditional fee agreements.'
(d) Thus the thesis is: 'conditional fee agreements' are the privatisation of the funding of litigation (just as legal aid is the nationalisation of the funding of litigation).

Summary

2.25–2.29 If the risk analysis of the claimant litigator is wrong, he goes without his fees. If his risk analysis is consistently wrong, he will fail to make an overall margin.

HOW TO MAKE A RISK ANALYSIS
Issue Driven Litigation

2.30 The CPR ordain 'issues' as the vehicle by which to achieve cost-effective case management. There can never be more than three primary issues in any piece of litigation, namely:

(a) fact;
(b) law;
(c) expert evidence.

Issues of Fact

2.31 The primary vehicle for issues of fact is the witness statement from the client, or his witnesses as to fact. By way of example, an agenda for the claimant statement as to fact in a clinical negligence action can be expressed as follows:

(a) Name and address of each GP you have had.
(b) Name and address of any hospital at which you ever have had treatment and the name of any doctor at the hospital whom you remember dealing with you.
(c) What was your condition prior to the clinical treatment you complain of?
(d) What clinical treatment do you complain of?
(e) Who administered the treatment?
(f) Where was it administered and when?
(g) What result did you expect from the treatment? Why did you expect that result?
(h) What in fact is the result from the treatment?
(i) Have you complained already to someone – if yes, to whom and with what result?
(j) Do you want to claim money compensation, or are you really looking for an apology?
(k) When did you first think that the clinical treatment had gone wrong?
(l) What made you think it had gone wrong?
(m) When did you first think of going to a solicitor and why?
(n) Has anyone said anything to you which makes you think that something has gone wrong? If yes – who, when, where, in what words?'

2.32 As to statement-taking technique, see Module 2. As to the handling of a personal injury, as opposed to a clinical negligence claim, see Module 3.

Issues of Expert Evidence

2.33 Prolix reports from experts camouflage and confuse issues. This undermines the ability to undertake an accurate risk analysis. Under conditional fee agreements, such an approach to expert evidence is a dagger pointing at the heart of the solvency of the litigation department. In respect of any liability issue, there are five primary questions for the expert. They are:

(a) What is the act or omission alleged to constitute breach of duty which caused the damage?

(b) What are the primary facts which you invite the judge to find to establish your opinion?
(c) Do you draw any inferences from the primary facts and if yes, what are they and on what basis do you draw them?
(d) What is the evidence admissible in law to support the primary facts?
(e) What are the grounds for the opinion you have expressed in answer to question (a) above.

2.34 As to the significance of the words 'act or omission' – see Module 5. As to the grounds for the opinion, the expert opinion has to be conceived by reference to a legal framework. In the field of clinical negligence, that legal framework is set out in Module 6. It sets the 'legal critical path analysis' for the following fields of medico-legal inquiry:

(a) mistreatment;
(b) failure to diagnose;
(c) informed consent.

2.35 As to the significance of the 'legal critical path analysis' see Module 1. Adopting this approach to clinical negligence assists in pre-empting a *Bolam* defence .

Issues of Law

2.36–2.39 This, it is submitted, is where the real impact of conditional fee agreements arises. How we define the legal critical path analysis of the case predicates the expert evidence which is necessary. Therefore the more analytical the legal critical path analysis, given any particular matrix of fact, so the more accurately can the risk analysis be for the conditional fee agreement. That definition can be crystallized at the first case management conference. And the opportunities for refinement arise, not just by reference to the presenting facts of a case, but perhaps also by reference to the impact of the Human Rights Act 1998.

THE TOOL-KIT FOR REFINING A RISK ANALYSIS

Litigating to a Merits Threshold

2.40 Has there been adequate disclosure? In clinical negligence, have all the case notes been disclosed? Go searching.[1]

1 *Smith v Leicestershire Health Authority* (1996) 36 BNLR 23, [1998] Lloyd's Rep Med.

2.41 Issues as to fact. What do the witnesses say? How reliable are they? How will they come over in court?

2.42 The 'litigation technique' has to be 'tight', hence the significance of 'check-lists' as the case unfolds. In the field of clinical negligence see Module 8 - Case Management Check Lists. These check lists can also be adapted for the ordinary PI claim.

2.43 Issues of expert evidence? See Module 9 – Managing the Experts to Cut Cost.

Litigating to a Budget/tender

2.44 Cost out the 'legal critical path analysis.' This should be assessed in the context of what the judge will want by way of opening at trial, see Module 7. The courtroom predicates file management: If the judge will not need it, why create the paper for it? It must be emphasised that the more accurately the legal critical path analysis is defined, the more cost-effectively can the litigation be conducted.

2.45 What evidence as to fact do we really need? Can a matrix of fact be established which shifts the burden of proof (res ipsa)?

2.46 What expert evidence do we really need, in what field and how much paper? See 'Managing the Experts' Module 9.

2.47 Cutting down the core bundles for the court, see Module 4. It is submitted that no clinical negligence action on liability need be run with a core bundle exceeding 150 pages, including pleadings, witness statements and experts' reports.

2.48 There is nothing in our experience that has trained us to work to a budget; we have consistently worked on the basis of demand-led finding on an hourly rate; consider the implications for:

(a) creating paper;
(b) instructing counsel;
(c) retaining experts.

Reducing the Price of Conditional Fee Insurance

2.49 If file management is not efficient, the premium for conditional fee insurance will be high, irrespective of whether or not it is recovered from the defence. Does this not bar access to justice? The corollary is that efficient and cost effective file management facilitates access to justice.

Using IT to Cut Cost

2.50 Uses for IT are:

(a) anatomy databases;
(b) video/tele-conferencing;
(c) computers and drafting;
(d) electronic mail;
(e) legal databases – New Law Publishing/Lexis/Lawtel and so on;
(f) medical directory on CD Rom.

Using Technique to Achieve a Clearer Focus

2.51 Statement of Case:

(a) the fundamental rule: focus and succinctness. The primary function is to set out facts material to the cause of action;
(b) purpose of statements of case: to limit the issues;

    (c) the importance of succinctness: the more succinct the statement of case the less room for misunderstanding/error/loose thinking;

    (d) the tighter the statement of case the clearer the issues – and the clearer any need to tighten up an issue by recourse to a request for further information;

    (e) requests for further information should be kept focused, and to a minium of length. The aim is to clarify, not to confuse.

2.52 For a model statement of case in a clinical negligence action see Module 10.

Limiting the Issues
2.53 See Rose LJ in *Freudiana Holdings Ltd'*:[1]

> 'Whether there should be a wasted costs hearing was clearly a matter for the judge's discretion. In his Lordship's judgment, unless the proceedings could take place in summary form on or very soon after judgment they were unlikely to be appropriate.
> '... Wasted costs orders were an imperfect means of seeking to control excess by the legal profession. They provided the courts with a tool which in some cases was equal to the task but which in many cases was inadequate.
>
> 'However the real remedy lay in the hands of the legal profession itself. The proper conduct of litigation did not require every point to be taken, it required all those involved to concentrate on the vital issues in the case.
>
> 'The legal profession must relearn, or reapply, the skill which was the historic hallmark of the profession but which appeared to be fast vanishing: to present to the court the few crucial determinative points and to discard as immaterial dross the minor points and excessive detail.'

1   (1995) Times 4 December.

When to Ask for Further Information?
2.54 Further information is required when an identified issue is not clear. Clarity is the underpinning of risk analysis.

2.55 The paradigm example is where there is information available to the other side (oral or in writing) which may be expected to support your case or damage the other side's case. For example, in the clinical negligence field, to identify medical carers involved in the care who have not been identified by the defence, or to bridge apparent gaps in the medical case notes.

Documents Destroyed or Missing
2.56 A useful authority is *Malhotra v Dhawan*[1] which explains the status of the of presumption 'omnia praesumuntur contra spoliatorem':

> Morritt LJ: 'First, if it is found that the destruction of the evidence was carried out deliberately so as to hinder the proof of the plaintiff's claim, then such finding will obviously reflect on the credibility of the destroyer. In such circumstances it would enable the court to disregard the evidence of the destroyer in the application of the principle. But that is not this case.

'Second, if the court has difficulty in deciding which party's evidence to accept, then it would be legitimate to resolve that doubt by the application of the presumption. But, thirdly, if the judge forms a clear view, having borne in mind all the difficulties which may arise from the unavailability of material documents, as to which side is telling the truth, I do not accept that the application of the presumption can require the judge to accept evidence he does not believe or to reject evidence he finds to be truthful.'

1 [1997] 8 Med LR 319, CA.

Managing the Experts to Cut Cost

2.57 For how to assess the quality of expert evidence, see Module 9.

2.58 In the field of clinical negligence, the case of *Newell v Goldenberg*[1] is a good example of how legal analysis can be invoked to cut cost. Mantell J said:

'The *Bolam* principle provides a defence to those who lag behind the times. It cannot serve those who know better. In my judgment, therefore, in failing to warn of the risk that Mr Newell might resume fertility the defendant fell below the standard required and was in breach of duty.'

Looking at this analytically, what is the judge saying? Surely it is this: tort law is based on the foreseeability of risk. A '*Bolam*' defence in this context would operate to show that a doctor did not foresee this risk. But if he does foresee a risk, he cannot hide behind '*Bolam*' on the hypothesis that he need not see it.

1 [1995] 6 Med LR 371 at 374.

Shifting Burden of Proof

2.59 There are two consequences to achieving a matrix of fact to shift the burden of proof:

(a) it strengthens the case, thus increasing the prospects of success vis-à-vis a conditional fee agreement;
(b) it may limit the amount of expert evidence required to be retained (and paid for).

2.60 In the field of clinical negligence, the leading authority is *Ratcliffe v Plymouth and Torbay Health Authority*;[1] it sets out definitively, the authorities relating to the shifting burden of proof in professional negligence actions.

1 [1998] 1 Lloyd's Rep Med 162.

USE OF COUNSEL

The Role of Counsel After CPR and Funding Changes

2.61 The role of counsel is to anticipate the court room, when advising on:

(a) the legal critical path analysis and to fine tune;

(b) how the evidence as to fact, and expert evidence would appear in the courtroom;

(c) procedural and legal technique (particularly state of the art, by reference to recent cases/concepts and the Human Rights Act 1998), to maximise the prospects of success and/or to maximise/minimise the quantum.

When to Bring in Counsel

2.62 This is very simple. If it is anticipated counsel is at some stage to be retained, bring him in right at the beginning. Similarly, bring in leading counsel if the intention is to use a leader. No longer is it sufficient to bring in counsel or a leader to sort things out if the case is coming to trial. The time to 'sort things out' is right at the beginning – to get the case into the right groove for case management, to permit the accurate definition of the issues. This is a much more cost-effective use of counsel.

Which Counsel?

2.63 What is required is the skill to see through the clutter of a case rapidly to get to the core legal/evidential issues and the forensic route to win on such issues. In the environment of conditional fees the more powerful counsel's specialist skill and grasp of both 'Woolf' and legal principle, the greater the chances of resolving the dispute favourably to one's client. Further as to the use of counsel, see Module 12.

Module 1

Defining the Legal Critical Path Analysis

COST EFFECTIVE LITIGATION TECHNIQUE AND ISSUE DRIVEN LITIGATION

Is there a future without legal aid in most civil cases or is this the end of justice as we know it? Can conditional fee agreements (the 'no win, no fee' arrangement) usher in a new era of cost-effective dispute resolution where access to justice together with freedom and equality under the law are secured?

The fact that the civil legal aid scheme as it is presently structured has run its course must not blind us to its undoubted achievements. For example:

- It has enfranchised litigants without means (irrespective of race, sex, colour or creed) who otherwise would not have had their disputes resolved.
- Equally it has enfranchised lawyers to service the needs of these impecunious litigants; lawyers who would otherwise not have achieved exposure to work in the courts. Frequently they came from classes or ethnic backgrounds which traditionally had been looked down on as not constituting the natural pool of talent from whom the legal profession should be drawn.
- Finally, through the litigation it has funded there has been woven into the tapestry of English jurisprudence so much new law relating particularly (but not exclusively) to 'everyman' which otherwise would have remained undeveloped.

Legal aid (the tax payer) does not of course finance a claim for compensation; rather it underwrites for the litigator the risk of losing. In contrast, under a conditional fee agreement it is the litigator himself who underwrites the risk of losing. Such 'underwriting' necessitates a 'risk analysis.'

To make that risk analysis, the following steps must be taken before proceedings are issued:

- First, there must be defined the 'legal critical path analysis' of the case and thus the legal issues.
- Second, there must then be identified (and weighed) what evidence as to fact, and expert evidence, is available (and legally necessary) to prove the case arising from those issues.

Hitherto, the practice of law in England and Wales has not perhaps lent itself to such strict precision, rather legal practice has worked empirically case-by-case. The underlying philosophy has been that the courtroom is the primary fact finding forum (which explains why until recently, cards were 'chested') with legal argument being the province of oral inter-change between bench and bar. The law report is in this context the accidental by-product of the immediate task of resolving the instant dispute.

This approach was, perhaps surprisingly, not inconsistent with firm forensic discipline. Discipline over the dispute resolution process was achieved through the restriction of those involved in the forensic process to a very particular and restricted social caste and culture, inheritors of an oral tradition (and it was exclusively oral) which was passed down particularly through sets of chambers. This explains the apparently idiosyncratic selection process until recent times to the bar (and indeed many firms of solicitors) and correspondingly the selection process for the bench.

The oral tradition of this culture predicated restraint, focus on the practical issue on which the case turned, finding the middle ground and negotiation. The strait-jacket of conformity predicated by this culture has, however, proved inadequate to the task of addressing the dramatic changes witnessed in our society since the 1970s.

Those changes in this context embrace:

- Liberalised entry into the professions. All are now capable of being received into our legal system irrespective of race, sex, colour and creed. Further, solicitors are now enfranchised as major estates in their own right in the realm of litigation.
- A huge increase in the number of disputes coming through the courts arising from increasing awareness of individual rights coupled with the demand to exercise them; divorce, personal injury, judicial review of decisions of government departments, criminal work and so forth.
- And of course, there has been increasing funding of the dispute resolution process. Inevitably in our commercially orientated environment, it perhaps takes the self-restraint of a Trappist monk to prevent a litigator from being seduced into measuring forensic success by reference to units billed rather than disputes resolved. Imperceptibly over the years, the importance of *precision* in defining the issues has eroded.

Restrictions in funding and particularly conditional fee agreements re-instate the central importance in our legal system of such *precision* in the definition of issues. The new discipline is entrenched by the simple expedient of identifying the interests of the litigant with that of the litigator: No win, no fee. This is the new discipline which the 'Woolf' reforms and 'case management' facilitate.

'Woolf' is to be welcomed by both litigant and litigator. For the litigant, it provides in addition to more effective dispute resolution, transparency of price and procedure. For the litigator, it secures through judicial case management a litigation highway cleared, not only of obstructions created by other parties, but also geared up for the speedy resolution of the discrete issue on which the case is going to turn. The new procedural reforms can be interpreted as a recognition that restrictions on funding spell litigator insolvency if disputes are to be resolved by the traditional 'big-bang' oral trial.

An unobstructed litigation highway which is orientated to the early resolution of disputes is a crucial prerequisite to litigating to a margin when working in a fixed fee regime, or under a conditional fee agreement.

The ultimate and classic example of cost-effective litigation technique is the pre-legal aid case of 'the snail in the beer bottle;' *Donoghue v Stevenson*. Most lawyers know that the case was tried on a preliminary issue of law (a simple, cost-effective technique to avoid the 'big-bang' trial). But how many know that the order for costs was 'in causa pauperis?' In a case where commercial interests were at stake, the claimant who had no money succeeded against the manufacture who did. Success was not secured by computer software programmed to identify every potentially discoverable document, nor with myriads of sheets of paper being spewed out of heavy duty photocopiers with a vast expensive infrastructure of machinery and staff. It was secured by the development of pure legal principle. This owed everything to the cerebral as opposed to infrastructure and expense. In summary, shrewd technique and creativity in legal approach were the cost-effective tools used to attain a result of overwhelming juridical importance.

Such cost-effectiveness and such shrewdness in technique and creativity of thought will prove to be keys to the capping of the price of the premium to the conditional fee insurance policy (which pays the defendant's costs if the claimant loses). Capping the cost can secure access to justice. If the price of the premium cannot be capped, it is the legal profession who are barring access to justice.

Once the importance of case management is recognised and the defining of the 'legal critical path analysis' as the essential tool to achieve a cost-effective result, the following perceptions evolve:

- With 'Woolf' requiring full investigation of a case before the litigation starts, the case management hearing is not an adventure into the unknown. It can develop into a forum for the definition of principle, that is, the legal issue on which the case is to turn and to which the evidence is to be called. The importance of the traditional advocate/judge relationship must surely be central to this process, as Lord Goff explained in his lecture on the English Common Law, on the occasion of the 90th birthday of Lord Wilberforce.
- Increasingly one can envisage this hearing attracting the interest of the law reporter, particularly in the light of the judgment of Lord Woolf as to the status of 'Chambers' hearings in the case of *Hodgson v Imperial Tobacco*.
- Once precise legal principle is distilled expressly as a tool for the cost-effective resolution of the dispute, the principle can, where appropriate, be refined by application of the European Convention of Human Rights. Indeed the case of *Palmer v Tees Health Authority* [1999] Lloyd's Rep Med 351 demonstrates that before one can consider Human Rights Convention law, there must be a very precise definition of the principles of common law.
- The more precise the definition of the issue, the less the opportunity for the expert evidence to be ill-focused (the quality of expert evidence is directly relevant to the risk analysis), the more focused will be the witness evidence as to fact and the narrower the ambit of the new documentary 'disclosure.'

The precise definition of the 'legal critical path analysis' of a case has huge implications for the development and refinement of legal principle. We must now revisit all our legal preconceptions and consider whether a dispute in which we are instructed can be resolved more cost-effectively if looked at from a new legal angle.

Assuming this is how the future of litigation practice will evolve, it is not difficult to foresee the growing emergence from the courts of a definable code of law consciously created to address the challenge of the future, a 'Lex Britannica', particularly for our law of obligations. Such an approach to legal practice would achieve several results, for example:

- The more precise the early definition of the legal issue on which the case is to turn, the lower the cost of resolving the dispute. This would have the effect not only of helping to facilitate 'equality of arms' under Article 6 of the Convention, but also of facilitating access to justice. Alternative dispute resolution process ('ADR') did not emerge as a concept in a vacuum, but rather as a reaction to the perceived barring of access to justice through a court dispute resolution process which was too expensive. ADR reminds litigators that they are in the business of Dispute Resolvers ('DRs').
- Further, the clearer the definition of legal principle, the easier to achieve the result of equality before and under the law. Clear and precise legal principle should be blind to race, sex, wealth, colour or creed.
- In summary, through the machinery of funding and procedural change, legal principle can be refined to achieve the following: that recourse to a lawyer generates not only a result which can be afforded, but a resolution of a dispute which does not have the appearance of being arbitrary, is transparent and in clear accordance with defined principles of law. There is an elegant symmetry to the proposition that the more refined the legal principle, the less expensive the dispute resolution process and the greater the opportunity for true equality before and under the law.

This is the significance of the concept of 'the legal critical path analysis of a case.'

In this context, the following passage in Lord Woolf's Foreword to 'Human Rights Law and Practice' [Butterworths, 1999] edited by Lester and Pannick can be interpreted as falling into sharp relief:

> 'The Human Rights Act 1998 gives individuals a raft of rights across the whole spectrum of social activity. Infringement of those rights will give the individual an entitlement to compensation where our administrative law previously provided none. It is possible to view what will be happening as the creation for this country of a new code of torts: 'Human Rights Torts' which will operate both in the fields of public and private law. These torts will redefine the relationship between the individual and the State but will go beyond this by operating 'horizontally' to influence the rights of individuals as well. The interests of minorities will be protected in a way which, up to now, has not been possible.'

The challenge to the legal profession of fashioning a new code of Human Rights Torts is awesome: the duties of a mother in relation to the fetus she is carrying? The right of the elderly to live when confronted with the commercial burden of their maintenance? The right of the individual to particular (and costly) medical treatment in the context of a health trust's resources? The rights of the individual as against the community in a society which the courts will be constantly defining under the European Convention.

The catalogue is limitless, as is the eligibility to litigate of every member of society. Unlike in previous times when only the very wealthy or the very poor (under a legal aid certificate) could afford to litigate, the new funding and procedural machinery enfranchises us all.

Of course many pre-eminent in the law caution moderation in this climate of change. This is to be expected, even welcomed. No profession more than the legal venerates the past and those rights to which legal history has been the midwife. As David Dudley Field explained so elegantly over 100 years ago in 1889:

> 'Whenever any considerable amelioration has been obtained, either in the form or in the substance of the law, in procedure or in doctrine, it has come from a minority of lawyers supported by the voice of laymen. I do not complain of this. It is in the nature of the profession. The lawyer becomes wedded to old things by the course of his daily avocations. He reposes trust upon the past. He is concerned with what is, not with what should be. The rights he defends are old rights, grounded, it may be, in the ages that have gone before him. Nor is this conservative tendency altogether to be regretted. Rooted in the past, and covered with the branches of many generations, the legal profession may be said to stand like the oak as a barrier and shelter in many an angry storm, though it may at the same time dwarf the growth. With its innumerable traditions and its sentiments of honour, it is one of the strong counteracting forces of civilisation, and we should hold fast to it, with all its good and in spite of its evil, though we may have occasions to combat and overcome its resistance as often as new wants and altered circumstances make them necessary.'

The acclaim with which 'Woolf' was received 'by the voice of laymen' demonstrates that indeed we have reached the era where there are, in the words of Dudley Field, 'new wants and altered circumstances.'

Module 2

Statement Taking Technique

PREPARATION

The statement should *not* be taken from the client as soon as he comes into the office. Rather an agenda for the statement should be given to him with a request along the following lines:

> 'Please look at this carefully. It will be the agenda when we next meet. If you have any documents which are relevant, please bring them along. If you want to make notes, or draft a statement yourself, do feel free. I cannot over-emphasise however, how essential it is for you to be accurate. Please also remember: When I have finished taking your statement, you will have to sign it as being "true." And that means nothing less than truth and accuracy - the sanction for not telling the truth can be committal to prison. Also, if you do not tell me the full truth, I cannot make a proper analysis of the merits of your case.'

No Leading Questions

A leading question is one which suggests the answer to the witness. It is potentially fatal to a case if a person taking a statement, however innocently or unwittingly, asks leading questions of the witness. The statement of truth is the warranty of the witness to the litigator, that the contents of the statement are sufficiently firm as to justify the litigator in sharing the risk in the case, just as an underwriter does with an insurance policy, after a proposal has been signed as 'uberrimaa fides.' If a statement has been taken, partly by recourse to leading questions, the statement is not that of the witness; although the witness will not realise, it is the statement of the litigator! If on the apparent strength of that witness statement the litigator runs the action (and the truth only emerges in the witness box) then the litigator not only loses the case, but also (if the action is funded by a conditional fee agreement) his costs.

Communication Skills

Litigators must learn more sophisticated techniques of communication. There is a huge raft of learning in the field of psychology and communication. What does the client really want (remedy?), what does he wish to achieve, what is his budget? How much involvement does he want (note Lord Woolf's aim that the client attend the Case Management Conference?) Is the true question: 'what is the client's real agenda?' (it may be that a commercial client gives instructions for a worldwide Mareva in support of a debt claim, when his real agenda is to exert commercial pressure on the defendant in a very different environment). In summary, find out what the client really wants and let him be a partner in the overall project management of the dispute; managing the client's expectations in partnership with him is the fulfilment of client care.

Module 3

Case Management Guide for Personal Injury Claims

OVERRIDING PURPOSE OF THIS GUIDE

Compliance with this Guide is intended to achieve the following result: the making of an accurate risk analysis for the pre-trial offer to settle, and sufficient front-end loading to comply with strict court-case-management if the action litigates. The goal of case management and clear presentation will be facilitated if those responsible for the creation of the documents orientate themselves from the beginning to what the court will require in this class of litigation, in the event of the dispute requiring resolution by the court.

Contents and Format of Statements of Case for the Claimant and Defendant

Parties: Identify the full name of the parties.

Facts: Set out succinctly those facts (and only those facts) which explain:

  (a) how the accident happened setting out any geographical location and cross-referring if practicable to plans and photographs.
  (b) the grounds for asserting that the defendant is liable.

Liability: In relation to each defendant, set out the grounds for asserting liability.

Non-pecuniary damage: If the claim is for more than one category of non-financial loss, each category should be identified (for example, orthopaedics, urology, handicap in the labour market, loss of congenial employment and so on) and if practicable the pain, suffering and loss of amenity described under such category. The age of the claimant must be expressly given.

Causation: In relation to any category of loss (financial or otherwise), set out the grounds for alleging causation (if causation is to be proved in part or entirely by way of expert evidence).

Schedule of Loss: Complete, if possible, with an ongoing daily rate.

Appendices: Provide in schedules, each to start on a fresh side of A4:

  (a) experts relied on and their respective fields of expertise;
  (b) plans and photographs;

(c) chronology, to include:

> date of accident;
> when claimant's solicitor first instructed;
> date of first compliance with Pre-Action Protocol;
> date of issue of proceedings.

NOTES FOR GUIDANCE
Preamble

- Practice Direction (Civil Litigation: Case Management) [1995] 1 WLR 262 emphasised the need to identify the issues on which the case is to turn, and warned as to the costs/wasted costs implications of failure to comply with that Direction. This ethos is entrenched and refined by the Civil Procedure Rules.
- Too much time and expense can be wasted with reports from experts which are either not focused on the relevant issues, or cover those issues too diffusely. If expert evidence is to be relied on, state the issue(s) to which it relates and the field(s) of expertise.
- It is envisaged that henceforth only experts with sufficient forensic training/ experience will be retained. It is further envisaged that given such expertise, the template for the claim can be sent to the experts to complete the parts to which their respective expertise is directed. Those experts should be capable of completing the relevant parts of the claim themselves. This in turn provides them with a verbatim agenda for their reports.
- Given the proper completion of the claim, the parties are ready for the cross-offer to settle prior to the launch of proceedings. In the event of proceedings being launched, the parties are then ready for a speedy and uninterrupted passage down the litigation highway. Front-end loading facilitates both early settlement, and in the event of litigation, a swift resolution to the dispute.
- If it be asserted that the burden of proof shifts, which facts are relied on for that assertion?
- If jurisdiction is or may be an issue, set out the grounds for the court having jurisdiction.

Parties

These include any litigation friend.

Facts

The facts relating to how the accident happened should be restricted only to those relevant to the issues of duty, breach, causation and/or damage. This Guide requires succinctness and focus as opposed to a rambling recitation of irrelevant material. Note, the only facts which are relevant are those which the court is to be invited to find to establish the claim.

Liability

The grounds should identify:

(a) any statutory duty (particularising the statute and the provision allegedly breached);
(b) in the event of negligence being alleged:

(i) what is the act or omission asserted to constitute negligence/breach of duty which caused the damage?
(ii) the grounds for the assertion should identify the precautions which should have been taken, why such precautions are contended for and how they would have caused the accident to be avoided.

These matters should be capable of transcription directly from the relevant report from the liability expert (if any) assuming he is properly instructed and his report to be properly drafted.

Causation

If this is to be proved wholly or in part by expert evidence, the grounds to argue causation should be particularised (again, taking this directly if possible from the relevant reports).

Schedule of Loss

Time and expense should not be wasted in the service of inadequate schedules of loss. Further, schedules of loss should not go outside the ambit of any supporting expert evidence. Note in particular:

- Any past or future loss of earnings has to be proved primarily by reference to medical evidence. It is for a medical expert to advise as to whether the injury caused by the accident restricted work, and if yes, what work and for how long; similarly claims for future loss of earnings and handicap in the labour market. Often too much emphasis is placed on reports from 'employment consultants' without there being sufficient medical foundation to such claims.
- Any claim for nursing, occupational therapy and so on, should again be supported primarily by relevant medical evidence. It is for the medical experts to prove the reasonable *need* for nursing. So often, too much reliance is placed on 'nursing experts.' Their role is primarily to advise on the regime of care [and its cost] generated by the need for care. Note, Lord Lloyd said in *Wells* [1998] 3 WLR 329: at 345E-F:

'In my view the Court of Appeal was right to scrutinise the individual items which went to make up the multiplicand. Since the effect of reducing the rate of discount will be to increase the multiplier in every case, it is all the more important to keep firm control of the multiplicand. [Plaintiffs] are entitled to a reasonable standard of care to meet their requirement, but that is all.'

Law

Any propositions of law on which the claimant relies should be set out succinctly in a Schedule to follow the claim. The schedule should set out:

(a) the issue to which the proposition of law relates;

(b) the proposition of law;

(c) the relevant cases (identifying the passage relied on) and/or statutory provisions.

Limitation

If the act or omission complained of took place outside the primary limitation period, state on what grounds it is claimed that the action is not statute barred?

Defence

The defence should follow the agenda struck by the claim, paragraph by paragraph. All issues of fact, expert evidence and law should be recited in a separate schedule, identifying:

(a) the issue raised;

(b) the law contended for.

Any challenge in the defence to statements of fact or expert evidence should be made in the relevant paragraph of the body of the defence.

Module 4

Organisation of Documents for Trial

STRATEGY FOR EACH BUNDLE

- On the spine and the face of each bundle:

    (a) *'Legend'* to explain contents;
    (b) number;
    (c) colour code (for example, *'Red'* for clinical notes.)

- Absolutely accurate, clear and consistent pagination and indexation.
- Name and firm of solicitor preparing it (preferably towards the bottom of the spine).
- Ensure that it is not so full as to result in either of the following:

    (a) inability properly to turn the pages;
    (b) distortion of the rings/lever which secures the documents (aim for no more than two-thirds full).

In this way, the court can in relation to each issue, contrast the respective fields of expert evidence by having both files open alongside each other.

Documents Which Should be in Entirely Separate Bundles

- Pleadings: Suggest blue ring binder. (Note: Pagination and indexation).
- Claimant and defence expert evidence: note:

    (a) the claimant expert evidence relating to separate issues (such as liability, causation, damage and so on) should be compiled together in the file – each issue separated from the next with a coloured card divider;
    (b) in a separate file, but in the same way – the defence expert evidence.

- All the medical case notes:

    (a) coloured dividers to segregate each category of note;
    (b) page numbering and indexation (which should have been agreed long before with the other side) to be absolutely accurate and consistent.

Note:

    (a) the notes may take many lever arch files. They are NOT to be given 'centre stage' in the court room. It is very rare for there to be more than 25 actual sheets of notes to be relevant in any case, and their identity will be dealt with below.;

(b) with these notes particularly, it is ABSOLUTELY ESSENTIAL not to overload the lever arch files.

- Medical literature – note:

(a) this is the literature on which experts seek to rely to buttress their opinion;

(b) the literature should be page-numbered and indexed;

(c) each article/treatise should be separated from the next by a coloured card divider;

(d) the passages in the literature central to the case of each party should be highlighted in fluorescent pen (say 'red' for claimant and 'blue' for defendant);

(e) core medical case notes and related documents:
(i) these will almost always fit into a ring binder (rather than a lever arch file);
(ii) they should be accompanied by any drawings (colour are particularly desirable) provided by experts on either side which clarify the medical opinions;
(iii) any handwritten documents should face immediately opposite, a typed up copy (the typing must be absolutely accurate). Thus handwriting can be rendered immediately susceptible to understanding without interrupting the judge's increasing grip on the detail of the case.

(f) schedules relating to damages:
(i) in a form whereby the court has a column to add its own comments;
(ii) in a separate ring binder.

Note: it is essential to screen out from this binder all the separate supporting documentation. That can be decanted into lever arch files, which are available to the court if needed but which should not block the arteries of forensic concentration and discussion.

(g) core correspondence:
(i) but only if absolutely essential to the issues;
(ii) edited to an absolute minimum.

Note: trial and document preparation goes back to the initial letter of instruction to the expert.

Module 5

Limitation – Quick Access Guide

ACTUAL KNOWLEDGE

- The test is subjective, that is, the actual knowledge of this claimant.

- The knowledge has to be of

  'the act or omission alleged to constitute negligence and which is causative of the damage'.

It is not enough that the claimant knows that the damage was attributable to an act or omission of the defendant. The act or omission of which the claimant must have knowledge must be that which is causally relevant for the purposes of an allegation of negligence: *Hallam-Eames v Merrett Syndicates Ltd* [1995] 7 Med LR 122.

- Evans LJ in *Forbes v Wandsworth Health Authority* [1996] 3 WLR 1108 at 1123H - 1124A:

  'It is impossible to identify an omission except by reference to an act which could have been done ... the plaintiff's injury cannot be said to be attributable to any omission by the defendant unless the defendant could have acted to prevent it ...'

- Litigation technique: the 'act or omission' must be defined with great precision; see *Porter v Northamptonshire Health Authority* (26 November 1998, unreported), QBD, Klevan J. This requires much forensic skill; the case may (will?) turn on this issue. Tip: the more narrowly and specifically this can be defined, the greater the prospect of proving 'date of knowledge' only on receipt of the expert's report.
- Burden of proof: is on the claimant.
- Authorities: primary cases on the interpretation of section 14 are: *Spargo v North Essex District Health Authority* [1997] 8 Med LR 125 and *Kyriacou v Camden and Islington Health Authority* (1997) unreported per Sedley J [Lexis Transcript] and *Smith v Leicestershire Health Authority* [1998] Lloyd's Rep Med 77.

CONSTRUCTIVE KNOWLEDGE

- Objective test: the rationale is explained by Evans LJ in *Forbes v Wandsworth Health Authority* [ibid] per Evans LJ at page 1125G:

- What is to be disregarded when applying the objective test: the claimant's individual characteristics which might distinguish him from the reasonable man are to be disregarded: *Smith v Leicestershire Health Authority* [1998] Lloyd's Rep Med 77 [a case of tetraplegia].

- What is to be taken into account when applying the objective test? The following characteristics can properly be taken into account:

    (a) 'he has been at all material times in a wheelchair,
    (b) 'without means of his own, and
    (c) 'virtually unable to communicate.'

- The grounds for that submission are the dicta on page 88 of *Smith* [ibid]. That submission is also supported by the dicta of Evans LJ in *Forbes v Wandsworth Health Authority* [ibid] at page 1126A-C; and also in *Forbes* [ibid] Stuart-Smith LJ adopted the same approach at page 1117B-C.
- Burden of proving the date when the claimant had constructive knowledge: On the defendant, see *Forbes* [ibid] at page 1122F-G per Evans LJ.
- Knowledge of a parent? Not knowledge of the child: *Parry v Clwyd Health Authority* [1997] PIQR P1 at page 13 per Coleman J.

Module 6

The Legal Framework for a Medical Opinion in a Clinical Negligence Action

The following constitutes the agenda for the experts on the issues of liability and causation:

Mistreatment

- Set out clearly when and why our client came to be in the care of the allegedly negligent staff – with an account of the disease/condition if any from which he was suffering, and for which he required their attention.
- Identify and itemise clearly the medical care which was in fact administered to our client, and the dates/times when it was so administered.
- As a matter of 'mechanics' – what do you say went wrong: the 'occurrence'
- As to the risk of that damage resulting?
    - (i) what was the likelihood of it occurring; and
    - (ii) how serious was the damage which would result if that risk materialised?
- What measures were in fact available to reduce that risk of damage whereby it would not have materialised?
- Should such measures in fact have been adopted taking into account:
    - (i) the risk to the patient of adopting such measurers;
    - (ii) the benefit to the patient from adopting such measures.

Note: if your view is that measures should have been taken, then could you set out with precision (because this will form part of the pleading):

- (i) what measures?
- (ii) by whom?
- (iii) when?
- (iv) on what grounds do you so advise?

Failure to Diagnose

As to the diagnosis actually made:
- (i) was it incorrect?
- (ii) if yes, what were the factors (assuming this is clear from the medical case notes) for the making of that actual diagnosis?

The symptoms complained of:

- (i)   what were they?

(ii)   should they have prompted further questioning to elicit information about other symptoms of which the patient did not complain, or other history?

(iii)   if further information should have been elicited, what information and on what grounds is that contended for?

(iv)   given the information which either was or should have been available to the diagnostician, what potential diagnoses beckoned?

(v)   in relation to each particular diagnosis which did so beckon, what was the risk of harm to the claimant if that diagnosis was not made – against the precautions/steps to be taken to make such diagnosis.

(vi)   what in fact was the correct diagnosis, and why?

(vii)   what steps were capable of being taken to make that correct diagnosis?

(viii) should such steps have been taken to make that correct diagnosis and if yes, when; and what are the grounds for your view [taking into account the risk/benefit ratio]?

If a 'wait/see' approach is adopted:

(i)   why was it adopted?

(ii)   what was the risk to the patient of so waiting?

(iii)   what was the benefit to the patient in so waiting?

Balancing risk against benefit, was the balance properly struck? If no, on what grounds (as precisely as you can) do you so advise?

(If Relevant) Informed Consent

- Was our client warned as to the risks inherent in this operation?
- If yes:

(i)   in what terms?

(ii)   were those terms sufficient?

(iii)   if yes – on what grounds do you so advise?

- If no – or if inadequately informed – on what grounds do you say he should have been better informed – and in what terms should he have been so informed?
- Was our client told of non-surgical alternatives to the treatment proposed? If not, should he have been informed? In this respect, is there a body of responsible medical opinion which would have acted as the medical men in question?

Check: there will be no claim, unless it can be proved that had the claimant been properly informed, he would not have undergone the treatment.

Resulting Damage/Causation

If you are of the view that the treatment/diagnosis was negligent, please go on to cover the following:

- State in relation to each failure of medical care, what injury/damage was sustained by our client as a result, and:

(i)   the pain and suffering and loss of amenity following that failure;
(ii) what pain, suffering and loss of amenity our client would have endured had the medical men not fallen below the standard of care;
(iii) what is the condition and prognosis resulting from the failure of medical care?

- If it is not possible to advise as to whether or not such failure actually caused the pain/damage, can you advise as to whether or not it materially increased the risk of such pain/damage? If yes:

  (i)   on what grounds do you so advise?
  (ii) by what proportion was there such contribution?

- What is the condition of the claimant today, in respect of which he claims damages?
- What did the client have a right to expect by way of outcome, if correctly treated (for example, restoration to ordinary physical fitness and capability, and to his pre-treatment employment?)
- Can failure of the medical men (if any) be rectified? If yes, when, how and to what extent will such medical intervention help the client? Would private treatment (as opposed to treatment under the NHS) be beneficial? If yes, why and at what cost?

Module 7

Structure of the Opening Speech in a Clinical Negligence Action

The following is a suggested structure. Note: it cannot be rigid, it will accommodate most claims and it must be tailored to the individual action. It is prompted by the chapter in Powers and Harris (3rd edn) by Latham J and Badenoch QC and the citations derive from their text:

Claimant's Present Condition

'Describe the condition of the claimant today, in respect of which he claims damages.'

Identify the Individuals Allegedly to Blame

'Explain who is said to have been to blame for the suffering complained about, and what their status and duties were at the material time, briefly setting out the basis for vicarious liability, if any.'

What was the Problem which Warranted Treatment?

'Set out how, when and why the [Plaintiff] came to be in the care of the allegedly negligent staff – with an account of the disease/condition if any from which he was suffering, and for which he required their attention.'

What Should Have Happened, Given Correct Treatment

'Propound, with clear reasoning, what the [Plaintiff] had a right to expect by way of outcome, if correctly treated (for example, restoration to ordinary physical fitness and capability, and to his pre-treatment employment).

Pleadings

'Now advert to the pleadings. These may be, as in the modern way, very full and detailed. It is to be hoped that the judge will indicate that he has read and digested them.'

What Should Have Happened?

'Explain step by step the care/treatment which the [Plaintiff] needed, and why, and which it is alleged should properly have been given to him if the duty of care had been discharged ...'

Treatment in Fact Given

'Detail the care/treatment in fact given to the [Plaintiff], which is said to have been negligent, doing this where possible by way of juxtaposition so that the alleged shortcomings are individually and tellingly highlighted, in chronological sequence.'

Experts

'Now advert to the expert's reports, and discover whether the judge has (a) read them, and (b) understood them.'

Clarify the Issues Between the Experts

'Subject to the judge's indication, and/or counsel's perception of the need, now present a concise summary of the arguments between the opposing experts as they emerge from the reports, and give an explanation of the crux of the dispute or disputes which require to be judicially resolved. This is obviously the opportunity which must be taken by the [plaintiff's] counsel to highlight and fix in the judge's mind the merits and persuasive force of the [plaintiff's] case, as they are perceived to be, and to attack, undermine and diminish the defence case so far as possible. Remember that with the burden of proof on the [plaintiff] the opportunity provided by the right to open the case should be exploited as efficiently and effectively as possible.'

Do Not Exaggerate

'Beware at all times during the opening of hyperbole or exaggeration, and of emotive or excessively colourful language. The media, especially the tabloid press, have the habit of latching on to counsel's more vivid excursions and turning them into headlines ('Mother left dying in pool of blood', or 'Patient fled in terror from the dentist's chair'). Unless what you describe is strictly accurate, and also a necessary part of the case, any excesses may return to haunt you. Even if they do not, they may cause considerable unnecessary pain to the professionals thus publicly pilloried, and/or give the impression (rightly or wrongly) to the judge that counsel is improperly playing to the gallery. This could prove extremely damaging to the [plaintiff's] case.'

Quantum

'Obviously, where quantum is in issue it is necessary to deal as clearly and shortly as is reasonably possible with the matters which remain to be tried. It will have been everyone's proper concern to reduce to the irreducible minimum the areas of dispute, and wherever possible to confine the triable issue to the matters of principle rather than mathematical disputation.'

To achieve a successful opening, the documents have to be satisfactorily organised.

Module 8

Agenda for First Conference with Experts

Preamble

The material which counsel needs for this conference is no more than what is set out below.

- First, the medical case notes disclosed by the other side and any information disclosed pursuant to the pre-action protocol.
- Second, if (but only if) the case turns also on oral recollection, is a *statement* from the relevant lay witness (for example, the client) required on the issue on which the case turns.
- Third, skeletal reports from the key expert or experts retained by the solicitor.

Note:
- Anything more is surplus to what is strictly necessity.
- Any more information has to be paid for under a regime of conditional fee agreements or fundholding.
- Counsel should be instructed before the conference to draft a skeletal claim. That claim should be circulated to the experts prior to the conference.
- Only those experts essential for the conference should be asked to attend. The solicitor may be paying these disbursements out of his own pocket.

What Does 'Skeletal' Mean?

It means nothing more than:

- First, those facts central to the case (and not one fact more).
- Second, a firm opinion that:

    (i) there is no case;
    (ii) there is a case;
    (iii) the expert cannot decide and is equivocal. This also has to be spelled out just as firmly as a positive or negative opinion.

Any one of these three options must be accompanied by a succinct expression of opinion, and no more.

- Third, in relation to any fact upon which the medical opinion turns, the source of that fact:

(i) if it derives from the client or other lay witness, identify precisely the page on which it is to be found, and schedule a photocopy of that page to the report or if oral, when the fact was elicited, where and when with identification of any contemporaneous note.

(ii) if it derives from medical case notes, precisely the case notes relied on, with copies of ONLY the relevant pages scheduled to the report.

Why only 'Skeletal?'

The rationale is:

- First, this conference with counsel draws a legal comb through the matrix of medical opinion of fact. Almost invariably this conference bears witness to a significant revision of any medical opinion, even if only in the form of finer turning.
- Second, every minute spent by solicitors and counsel reading passages in reports is time which is wasted if the reading of such passages is not immediately necessary. For this conference, counsel does not 'need:'

  (i)   extensive summaries of the medical notes as a preamble to the report;
  (ii) lengthy discussion as to fact;
  (iii) convoluted expressions of medical theories which gradually distil themselves to a conclusion.

Note, the word *'need'* (mentioned above) is to be contrasted with words and phrases such as 'desirable' or 'in the interests of completeness'.

- Third, this conference with counsel is the cornerstone to the litigation. It predicates all future file management. Thus until this conference, the file should be kept as slender as is feasibly possible.

The Agenda

The 'Agenda' is set out immediately below. A copy should be given to each expert attending the conference, at the time of his instruction to attend:

- First, preliminary check. Is the expertise of those experts in attendance at the conference precisely what is required?
- Second, counsel must critically assess the expert's view:

  (i)   if his report is positive, to explore in detail precisely why – to test that view by way of enquiry as to what a medical expert on the other side would be expected to argue;
  (ii) if the report is negative, counsel has the opportunity to test the grounds for the opinion;
  (iii) do the experts come over as poor witnesses (however good their medical skills?)
  (iv) most importantly, counsel rigorously to explore with the experts, the grounds for their view. The conference should be the opportunity for a firm cross-examination (as if in court, and acting for the other side). Counsel should have the experts argue the other side's case, to establish the potential strength of the defence and the potential flaws in the claim.

- Third, counsel should ensure that the experts understand the strategy:

    (i) to ensure that the other side see the strength of the expert evidence, via the content of the pleadings;
    (ii) to foreclose the opportunity to defend by plugging up potential gaps in the case.

- Fourth, as to the issues:

    (i) counsel to identify the real medico-legal issues;
    (ii) to identify whether on any issue, a further expert is required and if yes, why;
    (iii) note, if there is more than one expert already retained, it is essential as far as possible for the experts to cross-reference and appreciate the view–point of the other and how the other arrives at it.

- Fifth, medical literature. Check with the experts what literature is available to support their views. As E Anthony Machin QC explains in 'Medical Negligence' (2nd edn) Butterworths:

    'The value of carefully researched studies by acknowledged medical experts, some of whom may hold academic posts which permit greater opportunity for reflection than that afforded to the busy consultant practitioner, cannot be over-emphasised. If a medical expert witness puts forward a thesis which cannot be supported from the corpus of extant studies it runs the risk of being belittled as idiosyncratic. Thus, the medical experts forming part of a team should be asked at an early stage to research the literature in support of views advanced by them which are likely to prove controversial. This procedure should be repeated at a later stage, when reports from the defendant's experts have become available.'

    'Medical literature, such as standard textbooks and articles in learned journals, is not of itself evidence but may be used by experts in support of their views, or in cross-examination of opposing experts to destroy their opinions. The relevance of such material is discussed in *H v Schering Chemicals Ltd* [1983] 1 All ER 849, [1983] 1 WLR 143.'

Lay Evidence

At this conference, assuming the proposed claimant is present, the experts should interview the claimant to elicit such facts as are material to their opinion. As to which facts are relevant for the drafting of the claim, see Page 10.

Life Expectation – If Relevant

This is an opportunity to consider the life expectation of the claimant [see Chapter 1 Appendix 1 for a legal thesis on this issue]. Are his statements signed for Civil Evidence Act purposes? Should there be evidence on commission?

A New Approach

Use of the portable note-book computer:

- Counsel should at the conference type the allegations of negligence in the presence of the experts.
- Counsel should confirm point by point their agreement.
- When the pleading is complete, counsel should print it out (portable printer, or disc transfer to computer at solicitor's office and so on). A copy should be given to each expert.
- Each expert should then draft his report exclusively by reference to the issue(s) for which he is retained. He should keep the opinion to a minimum of length. All that is required is a medical opinion which underpins the allegations of negligence already pleaded with the experts' assistance.

Note:

- With the 'cards on the table' technique, it is absolutely essential to seek to ensure that the lay evidence, the pleading and the expert evidence dovetail. This is secured by a contemporaneous finalised drafting of the pleading.
- A carefully pleaded claim also opens the door to the other side properly to plead a defence.
- The most careful consideration should be devoted to ensuring that only such allegations are made as are relevant and can properly be supported by the evidence.

WHAT DO YOU DO WHEN THE DEFENCE IS SERVED?

The Significance of Close of Pleadings

The close of pleadings marks the time to draw back and take stock.

Take stock of what?

- The issues are identified from the pleadings once they are closed.
- The issues as distilled from the pleadings should be typed up, one by one, and set out on the front of the file for future reference.
- What is in issue constitutes the agenda for the lay witness statements and experts' reports.
- Thus the answer to the question – 'what should be decanted into the lay evidence?' – The answer is, All the evidence which is required to prove the issues of fact thrown up by the pleadings and no more.

Lay Witness Statements

The lay witness statements should follow the agenda for trial:

- The agenda for trial is the claim: *Southport Corp v Esso Petroleum Co Ltd* [1954] 2 QB 182.
- The Schedule of Loss is as much part of the Pleading as the *Particulars of Negligence*.

Check-list for Drawing up Lay Witness Statements

- Title as in action.
- Dated?

- Signed by the intended witness including a statement by him that the contents are true to the best of his knowledge and belief.
- Clear identification of any documents referred to in the body of the statement.
- Language of the witness – not the language of affidavits.
- Chronological order.
- Divided into paragraphs each numbered.
- Dates and sums/figures should be expressed in numbers and not in words.
- Paginated.
- The statement should contain no hearsay, unless:

  (i)   what is quoted is an admission of the defendant by itself, its servants or agents acting in the course of their employment; or
  (ii) what is quoted is relevant – not for the truth of what was said but the fact that the words spoken were said (that would be relevant if, for example, an issue in the case was whether anything at all was spoken).

- Does it cover all issues of fact thrown up by the pleadings to which the deponent can give evidence?

AGENDA – FILE REVIEW AFTER EXCHANGE OF LAY EVIDENCE

Introduction

By this stage:

- The defence will have been served.
- By reference to the directions at the case management conference there will have been:

  (i)   disclosure; and
  (ii) the exchange of the lay witness statements.

- The new material forthcoming will probably justify a further conference with counsel, the relevant experts and the client. Note:

  (i)   prior to the conference, the experts have to report on the pleaded defence and the lay evidence from the other side;
  (ii) in relation to the other side's witness statements, the opinion should follow the paragraph numbering of each witness statement, for ease of reference;
  (iii) any such opinion should be expressed with clinical succinctness.

The Conference with Experts and Counsel

It should be sent to the experts prior to the conference.

What Happens After This Conference?

The experts finalise their reports for disclosure. To recapitulate, those reports will (depending on the facts of the case) be divided into the following parts (paginated and with a brief index):

- First, primary opinion on the issue for which the expert was retained.
- Second, expert's opinion in relation to:

  (i) defence;
  (ii) any request for further information from the other side.

- Third, his opinion on those parts of the lay evidence he is able to comment on, statement by statement and paragraph by paragraph.
- A 'fourth' part to be prepared after exchange of expert evidence is desirable. This 'fourth' part will be his opinion in respect of the report of his opposite number for the other side.

After exchange of expert evidence, there is final opportunity to review the case as a whole. This is the pre-trial conference.

CHECK LIST FOR THE CONFERENCE WITH EXPERTS AND COUNSEL AFTER EXCHANGE OF THE LAY EVIDENCE

The issues:

- Are all the issues covered by those sufficiently skilled in relation to those issues? The primary issues being liability, causation and damage?
- Has the defence raised any positive allegations and/or blamed any other party? If yes:

  (i)   what is the riposte to the counter-positive allegation?
  (ii) have all the potential parties to the action been properly identified?
  (iii) should another party be brought in as a defendant?

Lay Evidence

- Do the lay witness statements from the other side throw up a matrix of fact different from that advanced by 'our' side? If yes:

  (i) where are the differences?
  (ii) can they be reconciled? If yes, how? If not, why not?

- If the other side's factual evidence is believed by the court, what difference does that make to 'our' expert opinion.
- Does our lay evidence constitute a proper basis for the expert opinion 'we' are calling? Is there any material in any of the statements which could prejudice 'us.' If yes, is that material relevant to any of the issues in the pleadings?
- The experts should (if they have not already) identify precisely on which parts of which witness statements they seek to rely in support of the opinions they have already volunteered. Similarly, the experts should identify what material is missing from the lay evidence which should be included and without which their expert opinion is not properly founded.
- Have all discrepancies and inconsistencies between the lay evidence for the claimant and the medical case notes been identified? Can such discrepancies be reconciled?

Expert Evidence

- Are there any inconsistencies in 'our' medical evidence? If yes, what? Why are they there? Can they be ironed out? If not, does this disclose a weak link in the armour?
- Does 'our' expert evidence dovetail with the witness statements and the pleaded case? Check this point by point in the pleading in relation to each 'issue' in the list.
- Have the experts expressed their views in the way they intended? Does 'our' pleading express the expert opinions in a way which they are content to support in the witness box?
- Have the experts restricted their opinions to advising within their own fields of specialisation? (This is the opportunity to identify whether other fields of expertise should be brought into the expert team).
- Have the experts identified the medical literature on which they wish to rely, explaining its relevance and cross referencing the relevant passages with their reports .
- Check that the experts have appreciated where the boundaries of the relevant standard of care lie (for example, to take an extreme example, alleged general practitioner mismanagement in 1989 should not be judged by reference to the standards of a consultant in the relevant speciality in the context of the standard applying in 1999).
- Draft with the assistance of the experts any amendments to the statement of claim which may be warranted in the light of the other side's defence.
- Draft with the experts the answers to any request for further information which may have been served with the defence.
- Enquire of the experts whether there is any information which the other side may have which would not be revealed on ordinary documentary disclosure (for example, if there is a hiatus in the medical case notes such as a gap in the chronology of events)
- Enquire of the experts what facts in the case, presently thrown into issue by the pleadings, cannot be disputed by the other side. In relation to those facts, again assisted by the experts, draft the Notice to Admit Facts.
- Check that the experts' reports for disclosure to the other side tie in with the pagination of the case notes.
- Check that the chronology (which should be scheduled to the statement of claim when drafted by counsel) is accurate. Any references by any expert to any date should be cross-referenced with the date in the chronology as scheduled to the pleading.
- Are all the medical terms contained in the reports readily explicable? Schedule to the statement of claim a glossary of the medical terms used in the case (to perform the role of 'mini-medical dictionary').

Note: this conference must take place to allow sufficient time for the experts to revise their reports before any deadline for exchange.

Efficient File Management

Remember that at this stage 'our' expert evidence has not yet been disclosed. Thus:

- With the experts around the table, draw up a statement of fact. This statement will contain all the factual information on which the expert opinion as to liability and causation is based.

- This agreed statement of fact can then be incorporated by reference into the report of each expert.

Rationale

- All parties and the judge read time and again, the factual background as expressed by all the individual experts in the opening pages of their reports. Sometimes, these opening pages run into several.
- This approach to file management has grown up with the Legal Services Commission paying the bill, if the claim failed.
- But with the individual solicitor now underwriting the risk analysis, this new approach will achieve a very substantial saving in costs and disbursements, if the claim fails (and will pre-empt an attack on the file management, if the claim succeeds but the Health Authority calls for a detailed assessment of costs).
- Note, in the not unrelated field of trial bundles, Mr Justice Latham and James Badenoch QC penned the following in the 2nd edition of 'Powers and Harris' Cinical Negligence' at page 823:

> 'Cases difficult enough in themselves are made longer and more complicated when the participants must battle as much with the paperwork as with the opposition. The price paid in needless loss of time, patience and concentration can be a heavy one. Judges are becoming more ready than before to question the entitlement of lawyers to costs which appear to have been wasted as a result of an undisciplined and unco-operative approach to the preparation of bundles. Lawyers may indeed find that they face orders to pay costs considered to have been wasted in this way. This is one area in our process in which co-operation between the parties – and not confrontation – is essential.'

AGENDA – FILE REVIEW AFTER EXCHANGE OF EXPERT EVIDENCE: THE PRE-TRIAL CONFERENCE

Introduction

This conference takes place after disclosure of lay and expert evidence. By now all the material should be collated. The pleadings, further information, lay evidence and expert evidence as exchanged and any further discovery.

Who Should Attend?

The experts should be in attendance, with the client (assuming the client will be testifying). That will not be the case, for example, in the usual cerebral palsy claim, in which case the parents should be present.

Purpose of Conference

At this conference, the experts and counsel will probably for the first time, see the following from both sides:

(a) all the lay evidence;
(b) all the medical evidence;

(c) the entirety of the schedule and counter-schedule in respect of special loss.

Check List for this Conference

And make sure that all witnesses (lay and expert) are prepared for the courtroom.

CHECK LIST FOR CONFERENCE AFTER EXCHANGE OF LAY AND EXPERT EVIDENCE: THE PRE-TRIAL CONFERENCE

- Issues: if he has not already done so, counsel should provide a list of issues in the case distilled from the pleadings. That list should be circulated to the experts before the conference.
- Lay witness evidence:

  (a) is there anything in the expert evidence now disclosed by the other side which lends support to 'our' lay evidence rather than the other side's on each point in dispute?
  (b) alternatively is there anything in the other side's expert evidence which lends support to their factual case rather than 'our' side on each point in dispute?
  (c) which lay witnesses are to attend court in respect of issues on liability and causation?
  (d) which lay witnesses are to attend court in respect of issues on quantum?
  (e) if necessary, initiate the service of appropriate Civil Evidence Act notices;
  (f) finally, check that each of the issues as to fact in the list are covered by the witness statements.
- Expert evidence: The check list for the conference is:

  (a) have all the case notes been disclosed?
  (b) is the chronology scheduled to the statement of claim accurate?
  (c) have all discrepancies and inconsistencies between the lay evidence on each side been identified? Can such discrepancies be reconciled?
  (d) does 'our' expert evidence cover all the issues relating to negligence and causation? If not, which issue is not covered? Can these experts plug the gap? If not, what expert is required and precisely what is the remit for this new expert? What instructions should be sent to him?
  (e) in relation to issues of opinion between the respective experts on both sides, where precisely are the areas of agreement and disagreement.
  (f) in relation to the areas of disagreement, why is there this difference of opinion? Does this demonstrate a '*Bolam*' defence? Check carefully what medical case notes each side has seen. Is it that each side is relying on different medical texts? If yes, is there a '*Bolam*' defence or is it that some materials are relevant to the issue and some are not? Can 'our' experts stand up in the witness box and justify the proposition (if acting for the claimant) that there is no responsible body of medical opinion which would disagree with them, or (if acting for the defendant) that they are a responsible body of medical opinion taking a valid stand albeit different from that advanced by the other side. Note: Check the '*Bolam*' criteria

with reference to the risk/benefit ratio: *Bolitho v City and Hackney Health Authority* [1997] 3 WLR 1151.

(g) after going through the expert evidence in relation to liability and causation, check that every other field of expertise marries up with the pleading and the schedule of loss. Check that every head of claim in the schedule of loss is covered by the medical evidence (or if acting for the defence, go through each head of claim exploring to what extent it is not backed up by expert evidence).

(h) have the entries in the medical case notes been reviewed? Is there material in the case notes which was considered to be relevant which now appears irrelevant?

This is also the opportunity to enquire the extent to which each of the experts has court experience. Check:

- Which courts?
- In relation to what type of case?
- Whether they have experience of being cross-examined.

Go on to explain to the experts (if necessary) the court process and confirm that they will be present throughout those parts of the trial relevant to the issues on which they will be testifying. In particular, it is desirable (some would argue, essential) for defence witnesses on liability and causation to see the claimant witnesses in the witness box before they themselves give evidence.

Note: This conference should be timed to allow sufficient opportunity for any amendments to the pleadings and additions to the expert evidence.

Module 9

Managing the Experts to Cut Cost and Quality Control Protocol for Experts

On What Issue is the Expert Asked to Express an Opinion?

Note: the legal matrix determines the management of the file. Do you understand the legal framework of the case?

Letter of Instruction

- Significance of Woolf ordaining openness of letter of instruction: It is central to the case.
- The significance of the letter of instruction is that it reveals the thought processes of the litigator running the file.
- Ensure that the letter of instruction does not seek to distort your opinion - that letter may come out in evidence. As to your opinion:

  (i) you will be cross examined on your opinion;
  (ii) what are the grounds for your opinion?
  (iii) how carefully have you thought through the reasoning process which generates your opinion – the critical path analysis?
  (iv) is there another field of expertise which should be invoked to target the issue? If yes, what field, and on what basis do you so advise? For example, if a complaint cannot be substantiated on clinical grounds, then is there another explanation to link that complaint with the accident (for example, psychiatry)? If no, does the fact of that complaint have a bearing on the credibility of the claimant vis-à-vis other complaints.
  (v) note Parkinson's law as expressed through the Woolf prism: A medical report is as long as there is money to spend on it.

- Causation: note the issues on causation. A simple example from the field of personal injury asks:

  (i) what pain, suffering and loss of amenity was caused by the accident? (disability);
  (ii) in relation to that disability what are the consequences for employment? Is the capacity to work impaired? If yes, for what type of work, for how long and what are the grounds for so contending? Will employment capacity be impaired in the future? If yes, when and in respect of what sort of work? On what grounds do you advise?
  (iii) does disability necessitate care/attendance? If yes, now and/or in the

future (if in the future, when?), for how many hours each day, by what status of carer? What are the grounds for your view?

(iv) would a supervening disability have arisen in any event not related to the accident? If yes, what disability and when? What are the grounds for your view?

- Aetiology and causation:

   (i)   what tests could be done?
   (ii) who does them?
   (iii) when could they be done?
   (iv) how would results of tests be relevant?

- Literature:

   (i)   to what issue does the literature refer?
   (ii)   how well researched is the literature?
   (iii) what is the status/authority of those who are responsible for the literature relied on?
   (iv)   is there any qualification to the authority of the paper?
   (v)   to what part of the literature in particular should the court's attention be focused?
   (vi)   is there any counter argument to the point made in the literature? If yes, has it been taken into account when arriving at the expert opinion?
   (vii) vis-à-vis any literature produced by the other side which we have not relied on, can we show that it is not relevant to the issue? Or that it is not from a reliable or authentic source? That it is founded on propositions of fact which can be properly challenged?

- Critique of expert opinion of the other party

   (a) Is there any part of the side's expert evidence with which you disagree? Go through it phrase by phrase, sentence by sentence, paragraph by paragraph.
   (b) Are there matters excluded which should have been included because relevant? If yes, what are those matters and what are the grounds for your view?
   (c) Are there matters covered which should have been excluded for non-relevance? If yes, what those matters and what are the grounds for your view?

- Conference with counsel. Treat this as the 'dry run.' Consider analogies:

   (i) working on a cadaver in the anatomy lab;
   (ii) the flight simulator.

- Note (1): There should be no drawing back from appreciating the following: a conference with experts should if necessary be a vigorous and robust examination of the issues, arguments and counter-arguments. Each expert must understand how his 'module' fits in with the overall structure of the case.

- Note (2): Skeleton argument:

  (a) It is critical to make sure that the skeleton argument for the court is drafted in sufficient time for experts to see it and appreciate where they fit into the legal matrix.
  (b) It is also essential for experts to appreciate that the respective skeleton arguments for each party (they should see both) are the four corners of the positive cases to be advanced by each side in relation to the definable issues.

- Courtroom technique. When drafting a report, the expert must imagine himself in the courtroom, undergoing a Viva. He must look at himself with his intellect, knowledge and judgment exposed to scrutiny while in the witness box. Characteristics to foster are:

  (i) gravitas;
  (ii) detachedness;
  (iii) objectivity;
  (iv) measured tone.

- Note: Appearance in the courtroom and the impression created in the eyes of the judge turn so very largely on the quality and focus of research conducted by that expert on the issues before committing themselves to paper and reporting in the witness box.

Techniques of Advocacy

(a) If the issue is not clear and focused in your mind, the other side has the opportunity to discredit you in public and on the shorthand transcript.
(b) The more reports from an individual expert, the greater the opportunity for confusion.Why are there so many reports from individual experts?
(c) Burden and standard of proof; for example, prognosis is not an absolute, but on the balance of probabilities.
(d) Vis-à-vis the opinion reached, what are the sources of information? Are they reliable? Can they be substantiated by other data? If yes, has that data been accessed? For example, medical records, social background, work records, DSS records?
(e) One inappropriate word can enable counsel to focus cross-examination, reveal a lack of judgment on the issue and unravel the expert's credibility.
(f) Do you know the seriousness of alleging fraud? An allegation of malingering is an allegation of fraud? What do you mean by 'functional overlay?' –weasel words have to be clarified.
(g) Note points which can be made by counsel in an appropriate case:

  'These reports are worthless and misleading'
  'He set out in his report to argue the other side's case.'
  'He has recorded in his report, an opinion which he was not able to support in evidence in the witness box;'
  'He has expressed fanciful suggestions. His second report is argumentative, inaccurate and back-pedals.'
  'The report set out to mislead'
  'There are features in the report which caused acute embarrassment in

the witness box.'
'References which were grossly misleading.'
'If that is what he meant he totally failed to say so.'
'Faced with the back-pedalling of the two medical experts from the more extreme opinion in their reports.'
'I do not think that the report he wrote was wholly frank and explicit on causation.'

Characteristics to Avoid

(a) The appearance of flippance and levity (in particular, do not try to be funny).
(b) Expressing an opinion without sufficient reflection on how that opinion will be tested.
(c) Expressing a view either glibly or with the appearance of being glib.
(d) Language: avoid jargon, vernacular, convolution, lengthy sentences.
(e) Avoid an appearance of 'mateyness' with the legal team. It contra-indicates detachment and objectivity.
(f) Spelling or grammatical errors. The more serious the case the more slipshod the appearance of thought invested in the opinion. Note the limitation of the spell-checker.
(g) Avoid the throw-away remark. If a point has to be made, make it clearly and explain why it is made.
(h) Do NOT amend a report, but keep the original date. This results both in the report telling a lie about itself and is fraught with hazard.

Risks of Litigation Through the Medico-legal Reporting Prism

(a) Not being given the legal issue(s) on which to report.
(b) Not understanding the matrix of the legal principles involved, and the legal procedures by which the court service runs.
(c) Failing to identify the medical issues.
(d) Not having the relevant medical experience.
(e) Not having the relevant forensic experience.
(f) Not being prepared to make the effort to come to conferences when required.
(g) Not being prepared to accommodate court appointments.
(h) Being partisan before one takes on the case in the first place.
(i) Being a crusader.
(j) Treating medico-legal reporting as 'pin money' rather than as central to access to justice.

SOURCE MATERIAL

Issues

The central importance of 'issues' in our system of dispute resolution was explained by Lord Salmon in a paper he delivered in 1964 entitled: 'Some Thoughts on the Traditions of the English Bar.'

He inter alia said:

'You must familiarise yourself with all the facts and documents of any case in which you are engaged and the law applicable to it. You must consider all the many points that could be made. But remember this, in few cases, however complex, is there usually more than one point that matters. Very seldom are there more than two and never, well hardly ever, more than three. Discover the points that really matter. Stick to them and discard the rest. Nothing is more irritating to a tribunal than the advocate who takes every point possible and impossible. To do so is a very poor form of advocacy because the good points are apt to be swept away with the bad ones. Stick to what matters.'

This was a paper delivered to young barristers. But it has very real practical implications for litigators today, as explained by Rose LJ in *Freudiana Holdings Ltd* (1995) Times, 4 December:

'Whether there should be a wasted costs hearing was clearly a matter for the judge's discretion. In his Lordship's judgment, unless the proceedings could take place in summary form on or very soon after judgment they were unlikely to be appropriate.

'...

'... Wasted costs orders were an imperfect means of seeking to control excess by the legal profession. They provided the courts with a tool which in some cases was equal to the task but which in many cases was inadequate.

'However the real remedy lay in the hands of the legal profession itself. The proper conduct of litigation did not require every point to be taken, it required all those involved to concentrate on the vital issues in the case.

'The legal profession must relearn, or reapply, the skill which was the historic hallmark of the profession but which appeared to be fast vanishing: to present to the court the few crucial determinative points and to discard as immaterial dross the minor points and excessive detail.'

The Quality Control Protocols for Expert Evidence

National Justice Cia Naviera SA v Prudential Assurance Co Ltd, The Ikarian Reefer [1993] 2 Lloyd's Rep 68. Mr Justice Cresswell inter alia said:

'1. Expert evidence presented to the court should be, and should be seen to be, the independent product of the expert uninfluenced as to form or content by the exigencies of litigation ...

'2. Independent assistance should be provided to the court by way of objective unbiased opinion regarding matters within the expertise of the expert witness ... An expert witness in the High Court should never assume the role of advocate.

'3. Facts or assumptions upon which the opinion was based should be stated together with material facts which could detract from the concluded opinion.

'4. An expert witness should make it clear when a question or issue fell outside his expertise.

'5. If the opinion was not properly researched because it was considered insufficient data was available then that had to be stated with an indication that the opinion was provisional ... If the witness could not assert that the report contained the truth, the whole truth and nothing but the truth then that qualification should be stated in the report.

'6. If after exchange of reports, an expert witness changed his mind on a material matter then the change of view should be communicated to the other side through legal representatives without delay and, when appropriate, to the court.

'7. Photographs, plans, survey reports and other documents referred to in the expert evidence had to be provided to the other side at the same time as the exchange of reports.'

- *Loveday v Renton* [1990] 1 Med LR 117 at 125:

'In reaching my decision a number of processes have to be undertaken. The mere expression of opinion or belief by a witness, however eminent, that the vaccine can or cannot cause brain damage, does not suffice. The court has to evaluate the witness and soundness of his opinion. Most importantly this involves an examination of the reasons given for his opinions and the extent to which they are supported by the evidence. The judge also has to decide what weight to attach to a witness's opinion by examining the internal consistency and logic of his evidence; the care with which he has considered the subject and presented his evidence; his precision and accuracy of thought as demonstrated by his answers; how he responds to searching and informed cross-examination and in particular the extent to which a witness faces up to and accepts the logic of a proposition put in cross-examination or is prepared to concede points that are seen to be correct; the extent to which a witness has conceived an opinion and is reluctant to re-examine it in the light of later evidence, or demonstrates a flexibility of mind which may involve changing or modifying opinions previously held; whether or not a witness is biased or lacks independence. Criticisms have been made by Counsel of some of the witnesses called on either side and they shall have to consider these in due course. ...'

'There is one further aspect of a witness's evidence that is often important; that is his demeanour in the witness box. As in most cases where the court is evaluating expert evidence, I have placed less weight on this factor in reaching my assessment. But it is not wholly unimportant; and in particular in those instances where criticisms have been made of a witness, on the grounds of bias or lack of independence, which in my view are not justified, the witness's demeanour has been a factor that I have taken into account ...'

Module 10

Model Statement of Claim

2001 D No.

IN THE HIGH COURT OF JUSTICE
QUEEN'S BENCH DIVISION

Claim issued the ... day of ... 2001

BETWEEN:

JOHN DOE Claimant

and

BARCHESTER HEALTH AUTHORITY Defendant

STATEMENT OF CASE

1. *Introduction*: The Defendant was at all material times pursuant to the National Health Service Act 1977, managed and administered the ... Hospital ... and provided medical specialist and other services including ... services at and for the purposes of the hospital.

2. *Chronology*: The chronology of events is set out as a schedule to this pleading *[Serve with the Summons for Directions a chronology of material events in the form of a schedule.]*

3. *Matters to be set out in brief, as agenda for opening speech to the Court*: Set out briefly:

(a) *P's Condition:* The condition of the Claimant now, in respect of which he or she claims;
(b) *The condition requiring treatment*: How, when and why the Claimant came to be in the care of the allegedly negligent staff – with an account of the disease/condition if any from which he or she was suffering, and for which medical attention was required.
(c) *What happened (the 'occurrence')*: Set out as an exercise in succinctness:

(i) What factually was the medical care provided?
(ii) How did that medical care (as a matter of 'mechanics') cause the damage?
(iii) With what result to the Claimant .

(d) *Which individuals to blame:* Who is said to have been to blame for the occurrence, and what their statutory duties were at the material time, briefly setting out the basis for vicarious liability.

(e) What should have happened: Explain what treatment should have been administered, when and by whom?

4. The said occurrence was caused by the negligence of the Defendant by itself, its servants or agents:

PARTICULARS

A. The risk of the said occurrence was reasonably foreseeable. The grounds for that averment are:

(i)
(ii)
(iii)

B. Precautions capable of being taken which would have averted such occurrence were:

(i)
(ii)
(iii)
(iv)

C. Such precautions ought to have been taken in that: [Here adopt the 'risk benefit' ratio per Bolitho]

(i)
(ii) .
(iii)

4. Because of the medical care provided, the Claimant has sustained pain, suffering and loss of amenity and has suffered loss and damage:

PARTICULARS OF PAIN AND SUFFERING AND LOSS OF AMENITY

Note: This covers causation.

PARTICULARS OF LOSS AND DAMAGE

Please see Schedule of Loss served herewith.

And the Claimant claims damages and interest thereon pursuant to section 35A of the Supreme Court Act 1981.

Etc.

GOLDHAAS QC

Module 11

Data About Cerebral Palsy Claims

There are two categories of actionable claims for cerebral palsy. In both cases the brain damage arises from a lack of oxygen.

Athetoid

This is damage to the basal ganglia occurring in the 30 minutes before birth, often through a sudden asphyxia. This can happen because of:

(a) placental abruption;
(b) cord prolapse;
(c) uterine rupture.

It frequently occurs in the second stage of labour (after full dilatation). This has midwifery implications. The duty on a midwife is to monitor the fetal heart rate after every contraction in the second stage of labour. Thus the relevant expert may be a midwife rather than an obstetrician.

Diffuse Brain Damage

This arises after prolonged partial asphyxia and is often indicated by a deteriorating CTG trace. The argument frequently is 'failure to monitor' which can involve the following experts:

(a) midwife;
(b) obstetrician.

The CTG trace will usually be characterised by increasing loss of beat to beat variation, and Type 2 late decelerations.

Causation

The problem areas are:

(a) It is not sufficient to show a general increment from the delay – that is, that delay materially increased the risk or that delay could cause injury – a claimant had to prove that some measurable damage was actually caused by the delay: *Tahir v Haringey Health Authority* [1998] Lloyd's Rep Med 104.
(b) 90% of cerebral palsy victims suffer damage through no actionable fault.
(c) Basic data – Apgar Scores: Hooper J said the following in *Hill v West Lancashire Health Authority* [1996] Lexis:

'I have already described the circumstances in which, according to Sister Dobson, the Apgar scores came to be recorded. In addition to the difficulties of remembering some 30-45 minutes later what the baby looked like, it appears that: '... precise quantification of the Apgar score varies among observers, sometimes considerably' (Neurology of the New Born, Volpe, 3 Ed., 1995, page 348). According to Mr Booth, the score 'is a very crude indicator, even Dr Apgar came to recognise that' (23.06., 43E). A similar view was expressed by Mr Gibb (22.06., 72G)'

(d) Relevant experts are:
    (i) To prove the causative link between the hypoxia and the brain damage: Paediatric neurologist or neonatologist;
    (ii) To prove the extent and timing of the asphyxia, sometimes helped by an obstetrician with a particular skill at interpreting the implications of the CTG trace.

MODEL STATEMENT OF CASE FOR THE CLAIMANT IN A
– CEREBRAL PALSY CLAIM –

Case No.

IN THE HIGH COURT OF JUSTICE
QUEEN'S BENCH DIVISION
BARCHESTER DISTRICT REGISTRY

BETWEEN:

JOHN DOE Claimant
[Suing by his Father and Litigation Friend,
Richard Doe]

and

BARCHESTER HEALTH AUTHORITY Defendant

CLAIMANT'S STATEMENT OF CASE

1. Introduction:

(a) The claimant is a minor born on the 24th Day of February 1991 and sues
     by his father and litigation friend, Richard Doe.
(b) The defendant authority at all times pursuant to the National Health
     Services Act 1977, managed and administered the Barchester General
     Hospital, and provided medical specialist and other services including
     obstetric and midwifery services required at and for the purposes of the
     hospital.

2. *Factual matrix*: The claimant suffered catastrophic brain damage peri-natally:

(a) 22nd February 1991: Admitted for induction at about 1400 hours.
(b) 23rd February 1991:
     (i)   Membranes ruptured at about 0500.
     (ii) Vaginal examination recorded on the partogram at 2115 hours.
     (iii) Partogram records the cervix as being 5 cms dilated at 2345.
(c) 24th February 1991:
     (i)   Syntocinon infusion set up at about 0145;
     (ii) Pelvic examination at 0345, with cervix recorded as being 8 cms
           dilated;
     (iii) Fetal heart rate recorded on the partogram as falling to 110/bpm at
           about 0630;
     (iv) Full dilatation of the cervix recorded as having occurred at 0645;
     (v)   Head recorded as visible at 0700;
     (vi) Delivery recorded at 0815.

3. The said brain damage was caused by the negligence of the defendant by itself,
its servants or agents:

PARTICULARS OF NEGLIGENCE

(a) The act or omission alleged to constitute negligence is the failure to deliver by 07.45. The matters hereinafter appearing are without prejudice to that averment.

(b) In the second stage of labour failed adequately or at all to heed the CTG monitoring: The Claimant will aver:

(i)   The midwife/midwives should have called a doctor by reference to the CTG trace which was showing increasing fetal distress from 0645 onwards;

(ii) In fact no doctor was informed and further, there was no medical aid throughout the second stage of labour up to and including delivery;

(iii) Permitted the second stage of labour to continue without medical aid in the face of a CTG which showed increasing fetal distress;

(iv) Failed to deliver by 0730 at the latest.

(c) Failed adequately or at all to appreciate that in the face of increasing fetal distress as obviously disclosed on the CTG trace:

(i)   There was no benefit to the litigation friend or fetus in continuing the labour beyond about 0700;

(ii) The fact that the Next Friend was a primagravida generated a risk of a prolongation of the second stage of labour;

(iii) Delay in delivery generated the increasing risk of fetal hypoxia leading to catastrophic brain damage;

(iv) From 0700 the risk of fetal hypoxia was increasingly obvious and overwhelmingly so by about 0720;

(d) Without prejudice to the foregoing: Weighing risks against benefits, the need to deliver by 0730 was obvious and overwhelming.

PARTICULARS OF CAUSATION

(a) Severe acute intra partum hypoxia;

(b) Prior to the litigation friend going into labour, the claimant was a healthy fetus who had thrived satisfactorily in utero;

(c) The degree of hypoxic stress leading to irreparable brain damage occurred right at the end of the second stage of labour.

(d) Had the claimant been delivered at any time up to 0745 he would have been preserved intact.

PARTICULARS OF PAIN, SUFFERING AND LOSS OF AMENITY

Hypotensive-ischaemic encephalopathy due to pre-natal hypoxia with refractory fits and persisting neurological abnormalities. His condition is now dystonic quadriplegic cerebral palsy.

PARTICULARS OF LOSS AND DAMAGE

The claimant will require intense nursing care for life. He has no earning capacity. The claimant is applying for a split trial.

And the Claimant claims damages and interest under section 35A of the Supreme Court Act 1981.

HAASGOLD QC

APPENDIX 1 TO MODULE 11

Dicta of Hooper J in *Hill v West Lancashire Health Authority* vis-à-vis Hypoxic Ischaemic Encepalopathy:

'HIE

I turn now to the conclusions which the expert paediatricians said could be drawn from the observed condition of the [Plaintiff] very shortly after birth, during his short stay in the SCBU and his longer stay in Myrtle Street. HIE can be described 'as a state where the new born child is encephalopathic, that is to say the child is demonstrating symptoms and signs of perturbation of brain function due to hypoxia ischaemia', ischaemia meaning 'insufficient blood flow for the metabolic requirements of the organ in question' (26.06., 33). It appears not to cause any damage but merely mark it (Chiswick, 31.10.). It was agreed that the [Plaintiff] developed HIE.

It was agreed that HIE is a predictor of a later diagnosis of cerebral palsy indeed Professor Chiswick said in evidence that that was 'its real value'. It was also agreed that it provided a diagnostic tool for what had happened earlier. However, Professor Chiswick said that there could be a 'silent vascular event' of the kind described by him or a hypoxic insult just before birth without any HIE. Babies are born with severe brain damage who do not develop HIE. There was disagreement as to the severity of the HIE. The [Plaintiff's] expert, Mr.Smith, says that the HIE was of at least moderate severity, having regard to the clinical features and the length of time during which those features were manifest (26.06., 42B) and that supported his opinion of severe fetal distress in the period leading up to the birth. The Defendant's expert, Professor Chiswick, says that the HIE was mild and that supported his opinion that there had been no such distress. Professor Chiswick did however rely, at least in part, upon assumptions as to the condition of the [Plaintiff] before and at birth which assumptions do not all coincide with my findings.

Mr Smith, who has a particular interest in neonatology, concluded his report in the following way (paras 27-28):

'I am of the opinion that Michael's disabilities have come about as a result of severe perinatal asphyxia. This has led to the passage of meconium into the liquor resulting in an aspiration of meconium causing meconium aspiration lung disease in the neonatal period. Perinatal asphyxia led to the development of an hypoxic ischaemic encephalopathy in the neonatal period which was of at least moderate severity.

1. There is no evidence in the history of the pregnancy of any pre-existing abnormality and on examination of the child there are no dysmorphic features. The initial head circumference in the neonatal period showed a good head circumference growth velocity to 38 weeks in gestation and the subsequent slowing of head circumference growth velocity suggests a cerebral insult occurring in late pregnancy. The original ultrasound scan in the neonatal period was not indicative of a primary cerebral abnormality.

2. There was evidence of asphyxia in the intrapartum period with initially clear liquor followed by passage of meconium into the liquor.

3. There was evidence of asphyxia at the birth with the child in need of resuscitation by positive pressure ventilation.

4. The baby developed hypoxic ischaemic encephalopathy of moderate severity. Symptoms of this encephalopathy emerged during the period of care at the Ormskirk Hospital and persisted at least until the 8th of May and possibly longer.

5. The later evolution of hemiplegia with global learning difficulties and microcephaly are in keeping with brain damage caused by prolonged partial asphyxia occurring in late gestation.'

In evidence he examined in detail the various contemporaneous records which supported his conclusion that HIE developed. He said:

> 'the type of abnormality which the baby shows or which the child shows now, is the sort of consequence which I believe to be that which follows prolonged partial asphyxia, rather than an abrupt reduction in the baby's ability to exchange gas.' (26.06., 51F and see also 52B)

When asked when the hypoxic events took place, he said that apart from relating it to the passage of meconium, he was unable to make any further comment because he was not qualified, as an obstetric expert would be, to interpret the fetal heart monitor traces (26.06., 51A). When asked over what period could those events have occurred he said: 'Of greater duration than perhaps 30 minutes and possibly much longer' (26.06., 52A). He went on to say that, whereas 'we have a reasonably clear idea on the abrupt asphyxia, ... we are much less clear about prolonged partial asphyxia', which he said could be episodic or continuous (26.06., 52). He said that on the information available to him he could not say whether the brain damage occurred in the last hour or in the preceding twelve hours, other than that it occurred in association with the passage of meconium (26.06., 19). In the light of my findings, much more information may now be taken into account in considering his evidence.

Professor Chiswick wrote in his report:

'49. Michael did have a mild encephalopathy, and the cause of this is unclear. It may have been caused by a degree of unrecognised intrauterine hypoxia [that is, hypoxic-ischaemic encephalopathy, HIE] but I cannot say this is probable. It is more likely that postnatal hypoxia and hypotension caused by 'persistent pulmonary hypertension' contributed to the encephalopathy. His head retraction was not necessarily part of the encephalopathy as it is commonly observed in face presentation when the head takes up the extended position it was accustomed to in the womb. Furthermore, the hypocalcaemia and hypomagnesaemia may have contributed to the baby's irritability.

50. It is most improbable that the encephalopathy was caused by brain damaging intrauterine hypoxia. There is ample evidence in the scientific literature to show that children who have cerebral palsy as a result of intrauterine hypoxia operating

shortly before birth have a moderate or severe encephalopathy with seizures as a feature. The risk of cerebral palsy in babies who have had a mild encephalopathy due to intrauterine hypoxia is virtually zero. Therefore I feel that factors other than intrauterine hypoxia shortly before birth were responsible for Michael's disabilities.'

The principle difference between the two experts related to the level of HIE. Although Professor Chiswick labelled the HIE as mild in his report and in evidence, he described it in evidence as 'a very atypical HIE'. When asked whether he could describe it as mild, moderate or severe he said: 'It is extraordinarily difficult, I would plump for mild'. What made it atypical for Professor Chiswick was that the [Plaintiff] was observed at 14.15 on April 23 to be 'stiff'. Normally he said the characteristic pattern is severe or moderate HIE is: 'floppy, lethargic, convulsions, stiffness'. The second feature which made it atypical was its duration. He agreed that a duration of 2-14 days put the HIE into the moderate category and he accepted that the duration of the [Plaintiff's] HIE was at least 14 days. He said that if HIE occurs as a result of intra-partum asphyxia and it is mild, it will normally be 'well over within three days'. Whereas the features of stiffness at the outset and the duration took the HIE into the moderate/severe category, the feature which justified the classification of the HIE as mild was the fact that no convulsions were recorded. According to Professor Chiswick if there had been severe fetal distress he would have expected convulsions within 24 hours and certainly within 72 hours. It will be remembered that stiffness, according to him, follows convulsions rather than precedes them.

The issue about convulsions became more complicated because on April 25 and thereafter until 11 May, phenobarbitone was administered to the [Plaintiff], phenobarbitone being the most commonly prescribed anti-convulsant drug (26.06. 38A). According to the records phenobarbitone was commenced on April 25 'with little effect as yet'. During his cross-examination, the records were put to Professor Chiswick showing the level of phenobarbitone. He would not accept that the levels shown could have prevented convulsions in the [Plaintiff]. He accepted that phenobarbitone could suppress fits and that the [Plaintiff] could have had unobserved convulsions but he would find that surprising.

Mr Smith gave a great deal of evidence about the published classification into mild, moderate and severe. He said how difficult it often was to make the classification because one is dealing with 'different points on a spectrum of severity' rather than stages through which a baby passes or a clinical series of events (26.06., 41 and 27.06., 33C). He said:

'I think the distinction between stage 1 and stage 2, or mild and moderate is generally agreed, and it is a brief encephalopathy. It is over quite quickly, and it is characterised by hyper alertness, hyper irritability, very brisk reflexes and pupillary dilatation, and no seizures.' (26.06., 42A)

He explained that it was often difficult particularly as long ago as 1982 to determine whether seizures were taking place (27.06., 31), particularly if the baby was being treated with anti-convulsant drugs which can effect the clinical assessment of tone and reactions (27.06., 33D). He said, further, that the absence of seizures was a feature of severe HIE (27.06., 32G). He said that what confused him about the matter:

'is how anybody can describe this child as having a mild encephalopathy when he has got features going for two weeks. It is completely out of order that that suggestion had been made.'

I have not found it easy to resolve these differences. On balance, given the confusion about convulsions and given Professor Chiswick's acceptance that early stiffness and duration would (but for the absence of seizures) take the [Plaintiff] out of the mild category, I prefer the evidence of Mr Smith. It seems to me, as Mr Smith says, that duration would be of great importance.

I find, therefore, that the HIE was of moderate severity with the consequences that flow from that.'

[This judgment was the subject of an appeal which was compromised.]

Module 12

Practice Note on Use of Counsel

(a) *Reason to instruct*: To define in the appropriate case the legal critical path analysis and to design the file management of the case up to, and if necessary beyond, the pre-action offer to settle. Counsel of the right calibre is an essential tool to achieve cost-effective litigation particularly in heavy actions.

(b) *Counsel's product*: He should aim to achieve a cost-effective result by reference to the analysis of precise legal principle, and the weighing of the strength of the factual and expert evidence necessary to establish the legal right. That 'legal right' must also be analysed in the context of the European Convention on Human Rights/the Human Rights Act 1998.

(c) *Check-list for selection of Counsel*:

- (i) Years call?
- (ii) Member of the Professional Negligence Bar Association and/or Personal Injury Bar Association?
- (iii) Specialist? [if yes, how does he show demonstrate such specialisation?]. 'Woolf' requires a particularly accurate legal analysis early on in the file management; Counsel with genuine legal scholarship are fully enfranchised in the new landscape - the skills required are by reference to legal principle; we are increasingly practising in a field of issue driven litigation, where the issues are defined by principle. This is in contrast to what for many had become general and approved practice: the jobbing journeyman using the court-room as a repair workshop for a defective litigation product.
- (iv) Thorough knowledge (and understanding) of the new procedural code?
- (v) Support/backup in Chambers? E-mail?
- (vi) Readiness and ability to undertake work on the basis of a conditional fee or to work within a budget?
- (vii) Ability to understand, and assist in costing out, the legal critical path analysis and the stages up to, and beyond, the pre-action offer to settle?
- (viii) Access to legal computer databases (for example, Butterworths PI on-line Lexis, CHH New Law, Lawtel and so on); law reports on disc etc?
- (ix) Training/learning in the jurisprudence of expert evidence/focus/succinctness.

Chapter 3

Funding –
The Claimant's Perspective

Trevor Ward

COST EFFECTIVE FUNDING – WHAT DOES IT MEAN?

3.1   The cost effectiveness of litigation has in recent times become almost a term of art. What does 'cost' really mean and what is 'effective', as far as a claimant is concerned? A claimant's solicitor is invariably instructed by a client whose prospective opponent is more than likely to be substantially solvent and able to meet their own 'costs'. For a claimant solicitor costs means funding and that funding must be:

- Available.
- Within the claimant's solicitor's control.
- Necessary.
- Secure.

3.2   Equally, 'the effectiveness' of conducting claimant personal injury claims means efficiency to the extent that the funding arrangements are:

- Necessary and not just minimalist.
- Spent in pursuance of the claimant's legal claim (in identifying those issues which have to be proven and not on ancillary irrelevant matters).
- Understood by the client.
- Sufficient to create a profit for the solicitor.
- Affordable by the client in the context of the claim.
- Recoverable from the opponents in the context of current principles of inter partes recovery.

These points must be considered, not just at the outset of instructions being received from a claimant, but throughout the course of litigation or its preparation by way of regular review, assessment and forecast.

Options

3.3   The changing face of options for funding claimant personal injury claims have never been so challenging. It has, perhaps, also never been so important to get right, particularly with the introduction of:

(a) the Solicitors' Practice (cost information and client care) Amendment Rules 1999;

    (b) the Access to Justice Act 1998;
    (c) Civil Procedure Rules (Woolf) Reforms;
    (d) the Legal Aid Funding Code;
    (e) the formalisation of previous speculative investigations and contingent claims;
    (f) the exclusivity of legal aid clinical negligence claims; and
    (g) the growth in the availability of 'before the event' and 'after the event' insurance products.

3.4   Each claimant's potential claim, whether it be in respect of a claim for damages for personal injury, a claim for damages for clinical negligence or a claim for damages for personal injury arising out of a multiparty claim will differ for:

- The particular (financial) circumstances of that client.
- The value of the claim.
- The anticipated costs and disbursements involved in pursuance of it.
- The merits on liability and causation.

3.5   While the traditional funding arrangements of the legal aid trade union funding and indeed a private paying client may be mastered by most claimant's solicitors, the following options also have to be considered:

- The specific terms and conditions of the various insurance products.
- The type of conditional fee policy.
- Premium payments.
- Reporting structures.
- Disbursement funding.
- Interest terms.
- Indemnity limit.

3.6   While the new regime does facilitate wider options for the clients and hence potentially wider access to justice, the issue arises as to how the busy litigator can assimilate the relevant data, while keeping up to date with recent law and his client base.

A Consistent Theme

3.7   Whatever the funding option chosen in connection with the cost effective conduct of a claimant's personal injury claim, a consistent theme is relevant. It is:

- Early risk analysis of prospects, merits, cost and disbursements.
- Client's formal agreement.
- A regular review of costs spent and costs forecast.
- A constant and regular cost/benefit analysis. The 'costs/benefit matrix'.

3.8–3.10   The above represents no more than best practice and indeed should have been practice adopted by the claimant's personal injury solicitors in the past. However, the likely withdrawal of 'demand led' legal aid, the introduction of what may be described as non-profitable prescribed rate funding and the restrictions on costs recovery or cash limiting will render previous best practice fundamental to the claimant's solicitors' solvency. The word 'solvency' is to be taken in its widest sense, in that failure to adopt this best practice will not only render the conduct of the litigation on behalf of your client ineffective and potentially unrewarding, but also the practitioner is likely to face an increasing number of negligence suits, increasing difficulty in obtaining reward and an increasing number of complaints to the Office for the Supervision of Solicitors.

TRADITIONAL FUNDING

The Private Payer

Personal Injury Claims

3.11   Any person, regardless of wealth, is a candidate for injury. It is conceivable therefore that even in relation to major personal injury claims instructions may come from a claimant who is prepared to provide funding a privately paying basis pursuant to the normal terms and conditions, both to fund disbursements and to provide money on account as against profit costs where appropriate. Pre-issue, this may be realistic. Post-issue, it is probable that most private clients would wish to consider one of the alternative options in the new regime, purely to protect their own position in relation to adverse costs consequences, whether they be interlocutory adverse cost consequences or final costs consequences. With a privately paying claimant who provides money 'on account', it is important to ensure that one has a regular system of interim billing, as well as cost benefit analysis, cost assessments and forecasts and that, where appropriate, there is adjusted the level of on account funding. Regular checks on the outstanding work in progress value, particularly after a spate of heavy concentrated work is essential. In the future tax will be due on this work in progress.

Clinical Negligence Claims

3.12   Considerations similar to the standard personal injury claim apply. There is a move towards agreeing with privately paying clients a 'fixed fee' for preliminary assessment tied in with a preliminary limited exposure to expert disbursements. This may or may not involve counsel. Again, while this may be conceivable for pre-issue circumstances, post-issue, (especially after there would have been compliance with the current pre-action protocol in clinical negligence cases) would probably render the claimant at great risk and therefore again the new regime may be more appropriate, subject to the affordability of the premiums and their recoverability.

Multiparty Actions

3.13   The position of a private funder in claimant orientated multiparty actions is difficult. Invariably the private funder will not be involved in financing the generic work. The funder may represent a relatively small minority of a total group participating in the action, the remaining majority having the benefit of other more secure funding arrangements, typically Legal Aid. The recent collapse of the 'tobacco litigation' which was being conducted without the benefit of legal aid serves to show the real risks solicitors run in such claims. The private funder of course will have a proportionate share of generic costs as well as individual preparation costs. It is extremely difficult for a private funder to foresee the changing landscape in connection with the levels of proportionate generic cost responsibility. The private funder will not necessarily know how many of the group remain, how many of the group settle, which members of the group have which type of funding and realistically if their adviser is not involved in the generic work, they will not have a great deal of information concerning the fluctuating risk assessments, save by periodical and usually incomplete bulletins. Again, pre-issue this may be conceivable but post-issue, with the imposition of likely cost-sharing orders, private funders are likely to seek alternative methods of cost-effective funding where the risk is shared or accepted by the lawyer. This is perhaps even more so in the post-Woolf climate of realistic considerations of proportionality and costs decisions on success of issues, rather than overall success.

Trade Union Funding

3.14 It is not within the ambit of this chapter particularly to detail considerations of criteria in respect of trade union personal injury claims. It is an option that all claimants' solicitors should consider at the time of initial instructions from their client in respect of any personal injury claim. The client, if he has the benefit of union membership, either for himself or for members of his family who may have been injured, should be referred to his union representative. Invariably, that particular union will have arrangements with a particular firm or panel of solicitors' firms. The retaining arrangements between that specific union and the firm of solicitors will govern the nature and method in which that particular claimant's litigation is investigated and pursued. The general theme (see above) applies in any event and particularly so in terms of cost-benefit analysis where there is a general conception that Union funding litigation is not as guaranteed as it was some years ago. The prospect post-Woolf of successful cases not automatically resulting in full recovery of incurred costs, and there being prospects of interlocutory cost penalties, are likely further to harden Union positions in respect of ensuring cost-effective management of cases and the use by unions of a restricted number of firms who are willing to enter into true contingency (result) arrangements.

Legal Aid/Public Funding

3.15 The Lord Chancellor on 27 October 1998 with reference to the general availability of Legal Aid said:

> 'I am determined in reforming Legal Aid to ensure that Tax payers' money should only be expended on any case that has a strong prospect of success and clear benefit to the individual concerned. That if the individual is able to fund this case out of own resources he or she should do so and accept the risk of litigation'.

Personal Injury Claims
3.16 The Lord Chancellor's statement in para 5.16 has been repeated in various sections of the Access to Justice Act 1999 and the Legal Aid Board's funding code, the latter replacing the legal aid merits test in connection with a person's eligibility for legal aid. The current code excludes personal injury from the ambit of Legal Aid in total, unless it can be brought back 'into scope' by arguing some 'connection' to the area within scope, for example a breach of contract causing injury. There is also a possible window for those cases of public interest, (and potentially those claimants under a disability and industrial disease claims) but whether the merits test in itself will be altered in those cases remains to be seen. The funding code definitions in relation to 'litigation support' and 'support

funding' belie the words used. Careful consideration of the criteria in respect of the use of those support funding aspects of Legal Aid funding illustrate how rare in the real sense that support will be. Both require a substantial upfront cost by the solicitor concerned and in respect of litigation funding the existence of insured funded Conditional Fee Agreement.

3.17 The funding code works to exclude certain categories of cases of which, in principle, personal injury is one. As indicated previously certain circumstances, for example, cases of public interest may bring the case back into scope. In any event it would appear that the merits test under the funding code, if applicable to certain limited personal injury cases, must still be an initial hurdle to be considered and overcome. It remains inevitable that the Legal Services Commission will continue to restrict those solicitors able to do the work by their franchise 'quality assured' method. It is assumed that the funding code 'prospects of success' criteria will be followed in relation to those cases where legal aid for personal injury matters is continued. The essential criteria therefore in considering legal aid funding for future PI cases, where allowed are:

Prospects of success. If no estimate can be made, funding will be refused although an application could be made for support for an investigation. The categories would be:

(a)   very good   (80% or more)
(b)   good   (60-80%)
(c)   moderate   (50-60%)
(d)   less than even.

Prospects of success mean the estimated prospect of the claim succeeding if the case went to first instance trial, as opposed to the prospect of the claim settling which would usually be much higher.

3.18 In considering the table in para 3.18, the likely benefit to be gained for the client would have to be estimated in money terms wherever this is quantifiable. In addition, to continue with the main theme costs must be estimated to apply the 'cost benefit matrix'. If the prospects of success are less than even, funding is likely to be refused, except in cases of overwhelming importance to the client or public interest, where the criteria for funding from the central budget for very expensive cases may be achieved. In respect of each of these on an application for legal aid consideration will have to be given to the alternatives to the litigation process and the availability of alternative funding mechanisms.

3.19 The cost benefit analysis is to be reviewed at each stage of the public funding certificated work and for the purposes of amendment is:

(a)   less than even   refused
(b)   moderate   damages four times the estimate of costs
(c)   good   damages three times the estimate of costs
(d)   very good   very good prospects of success would have
                          to carry at least equal if not twice as much
                          damage recovery as per the cost estimate.

Clinical Negligence

Exclusivity

3.21 The availability of legal aid funding to investigate and pursue clinical negligence claims is now the subject of exclusivity to those who have a public funding franchise in clinical negligence. Among other criteria, one criterion for successful application for a clinical negligence franchise is to have a supervising member of the department on the accredited Law Society Clinical Negligence Panel or the AVMA (Action for Victims of Medical Accidents) Referral Panel.

Limited Merits Funding

3.22 Those who satisfy the criteria are able to accept initial instructions. The onus is on those solicitors to carry out initial case screening with a view to legal merits determination. This is to confirm that the injury to the client, as sustained, could have been caused by negligence and to bear in mind with regard to initial costs/benefit analysis that claims with an estimated value of £5,000 or below would be unlikely to pass the initial screening stage, unless liability was accepted (except in cases where the estimated costs of the case are exceeded by the likely damages, to an extent that a fee paying client of moderate means would consider it reasonable to pursue the litigation).

Limitations

3.23 If a legal aid certificate is granted, it is limited in terms of scope to a preliminary investigation with a cost limitation (this is no longer a condition, but a specific costs ceiling). If a preliminary investigation is not required, that is, if liability and causation are admitted, then a full pre-issue certificate may be obtained with an increased cost limitation of £5,000. Ordinarily however, following a preliminary investigation consideration of the cost benefit analysis in respect of pre-issue certificates is highlighted in the following table:

Prospects of Success (P)	Damages Compared to Costs (A:C)
Less than 50%	Whatever the ratio the application is likely to be refused
50% - 60%	Estimated damages must be at least 1½ times costs
More than 60%	Estimated damages must be at least equal to costs

The Cost Limitation

3.24 It is clear that with consistent theme planning, the budget in terms of the cost requirements of the case at every stage, is as important in connection with legal aid assessment for amendment as it is in any other case.

Cost Benefit Matrix

3.25 Considerations in relation to the value of costs and/or benefits remain paramount in relation to amendments when sought. Amendments to cover trial have to be assessed with reference to the following table:

Prospects of success (P)	Damages compared to costs (A:C)
Less than 50%	Whatever the ratio the application is likely to be refused
50% - 60%	Estimated damages must be at least 2 times costs
60% - 80%	Estimated damages must be at least 1½ times costs
More than 80%	Estimated damages must be at least equal to costs

The reality of applying this table is to state that legal aid is unlikely to fund a case to trial which has a value of less than £50,000.

Multiparty Actions ('MPA')

The New MPA Unit
3.26   The Legal Aid Board (now the Legal Services Commission) defines a group action as one in which a number of people have an action involving the same legal or factual issues arising from the same cause or event.

3.27   The Board's multiparty action arrangements came into effect on 1 February 1999. If contracts were entered into before that day, these new arrangements do not apply. The arrangements are pursuant to Part XVI of the Civil Legal Aid (General) Regulations 1989. The Legal Aid Board have set up a multiparty action unit.[1] In brief terms under the new MPA arrangements, the Legal Aid Board will determine whether to offer a contract in connection with a multiparty action, and if so advertise for tender in respect of the contract. Tender documents will then be submitted to the particular firms of solicitors showing an interest. If a claimant's solicitor is instructed in connection with a potential involvement in a multiparty action it is important at the outset for that solicitor to determine whether the multiparty action arrangements include 'an all work contract' that is, a contract covering all representations in the action, both generic and individual or whether the same is limited to 'generic work' and separate limited legal aid certificates in connection with individual work, are issued.

1   29-37 Red Lion Street, London WC1R 4PP.

Panel of Franchised Firms
3.28   The Legal Aid Board has established a panel (20 at the time of printing) of franchised firms which are approved for the purposes of tendering under the new arrangements. If considering an application to the panel, there has to be:

• Established proven recent experience in multiparty action work and complex high value litigation.
• Sufficient resources for complex multiparty litigation.
• Evidence of the firm's financial and corporate stability.
• A franchise holder in a relevant category.

3.29   If instructed by an individual claimant who has the benefit of a legal aid certificate in respect of the nature of the multiparty action work, then one can similarly tender for the contract, although invariably such a tender itself will involve an application to the panel.

3.30 These arrangements are new and the first tenders in respect of various multiparty actions were offered in June 1999. It is not within the ambit of this chapter to consider in detail the exact criteria for panel application, nor indeed possible to consider the exact criteria in connection with individual tender applications, but some important features are:

- Detailed planned work schedules are required, dependent on the contract basis of the tender that is, all work or generic work.
- The Legal Aid Board will wish to fix a maximum acceptable hourly rate for solicitors and other fee earners and barristers. This is not subject to considerations of enhancement (see para 3.33).
- The likely costs of experts must be included as part of the work schedule.
- Payments on account will be received.
- There is likely to be a restriction to either making a claim pursuant to contract on the Legal Aid Board or on success inter partes but not a mix of both.
- Satisfying the whole of the entitlement to costs on an inter partes basis.

3.31 An application will be considered by a multiparty committee at various stages (rounds) each of these dealing with the following:

- Status and financial issues satisfaction.
- Quality criteria.
- Fee earning team information.
- Case plan.
- Pricing and pricing comparison.
- Other issues, for example, number of clients, legal aid/private.
- Extent of work already undertaken.

3.32 In reality, in considering group funding the Legal Aid Board is applying conditional fee principles where they expect contracted solicitors to share the risk of running group actions with the Board. They will be paid less for cases that fail and receive significantly more for those which succeed, subject to the usual inter partes costs arguments.

3.33 Anecdotally, it appears that the first tenders for generic work under the MPA New Regime offer an hourly rate of payment equivalent to the prescribed rates (see para 3.36). It remains to be seen whether in those circumstances, it would be profitable for any practice to take on board more multiparty action work.

Legal Aid/Public Funding

3.34 Some important matters for a claimant's solicitor to bear in mind in respect of Legal Aid remain as Legal Aid Act 1988 cases granted prior to 1 April 2000 which remain to be governed by the old regime and old considerations.

Prescribed Rates
3.35 The Legal Aid in Civil Proceedings (Remuneration) Regulations 1994 provide a prescribed rate of recovery in respect of legal aid costs incurred by the assisted person's solicitor, those rates relate to attendance, preparation, travel, waiting, telephone calls and letters. The Regulations do not distinguish rates by reference to a level of experience of the fee earner conducting the matter. The prescribed rates in principle do not include any 'uplift' for care and conduct.

However, experience suggests that although these two factors are meant to be excluded for the purposes of prescribed rates taxations (now to be detailed assessments), district judges/masters may be prepared to take them into account in allowing claims or indeed disallowing the level of claims. Taking those particular risk factors into account, it is unlikely that high quality personal injury work conducted by senior fee earners will be profitable if reliant on prescribed rates only. Seeking enhancement by reference to the qualitative way in which the work is carried out is paramount to the solicitor's profitability.

Enhancement

3.36 It is possible to get enhancement of the prescribed rates. This is dependent on the stage at which the investigation has reached at the time the claim is made against the Legal Aid Board and of course generally the complexity of the issues.

3.37 Pursuant to Regulation 5(1) of the Legal Aid in Civil Proceedings (Remuneration) Regulations 1994 provide:

'the relevant authority may allow fees at more than prescribed rates ... taking into account all the relevant circumstances ...

(a) the work was done with exceptional competence, skill or expertise;
(b) the work was done with exceptional dispatch;
(c) the case involved exceptional circumstances or complexity.

If one is able to establish that the work falls into one of the above categories, then pursuant to Regulation 5(3) in determining a percentage by which the fee should be enhanced above the prescribed rate ... a relevant authority shall have regard to:

(a) the degree of responsibility accepted by the solicitor;
(b) the care, speed and economy with which the case was prepared;
(c) the novelty, weight, complexity of the case.

Regulation 5(4) ... provides that a percentage of the above prescribed rate by which fees may be enhanced shall not exceed 100% (200% in the High Court).'

3.38 One of the main problems with interpretation of enhancement is the fact that the regulations were made in 1994 and therefore were probably drafted some time in 1992 or 1993 and continue to fail to take into account the changes in professional practice to the extent that the enhancement regulations preceded the development of specialist panels in personal injury and clinical negligence and multiparty work and the development of exclusivity in those areas. There is an absence of any specific guidelines from the Community Legal Service in connection with enhancement and reference is often made to reported cases in respect of child care enhancement considerations which appear inappropriate.

Examples of Prescribed Rates/Arguments
• Specialist panel membership.
• Specialist skill and knowledge by specialist practitioner.
• Access to up to date law, data and cases (to reduce reliance on outside parties, for example, counsel).

- The use of specially employed assistance, for example, nurses, in-house doctors, in-house surveyors, in-house accountants.
- Reduced experts' fees achieved by solicitor concentration on issues, core documents and relevant chronologies/factual matrix.
- The avoidance of use of counsel.
- The avoidance of duplication achieved by minimal delegation.
- The use of full pre-action protocols.
- The 'exceptionability' of the case.
- The value.
- The claimant – personality.
- The urgency, for example, limitation issues.
- The number of defendants.
- Unsocial hours working.
- A recognition of qualitative and quantitative input on the case.

3.39   Very little guidance has been given to the Legal Aid Board/Legal Services Commission in assessing enhancement of described rates. Although completely contrary to Regulation 5(1) and its strict interpretation, experience shows that those assessing costs at the Legal Services Commission are still referring to the Order 62 RSC 'seven pillars of wisdom'.

Prior Authority

3.40   Prior Authority-Regulations 60 to 61 of the Civil Legal Aid (General) Regulations 1989 can be utilised in order to specify the maximum fee payable for experts' reports, opinions and expert evidence. The obtaining of such authority is that no question as to the proprietary of any step or act in relation to which prior authority has been obtained shall be raised on any detailed assessment of costs, unless the solicitor knew or ought to reasonably have known that the purpose which the authority was given had failed or become irrelevant or unnecessary before the costs were actually incurred. The same principle applies in respect of instructing, with authority of Queen's Counsel, with the exception that no payment in respect of Queen's Counsel's costs will be allowed on any detailed assessment unless it would also be allowed on an inter partes detailed assessment.

3.41   The Civil Legal Aid (General) (Amendment) Regulations 1999, SI 1999/113 clarify the position on counsel's fees where there is a cost limitation. The statutory instrument provides that counsel's fees are protected except where counsel has been sent a copy of the certificate and any amendment containing the limitations and conditions.

3.42   Claimant's solicitors should consider the use of prior authority applications, particularly pursuant to the CPR where there is likely to be limitation on the recoverable inter partes element of experts and counsel's fees.

Legal Aid Contributions

3.43   Distinction must be noted in respect of those clients who are eligible for legal aid without contribution and those who are eligible for legal aid with contribution. Clearly the claimant's solicitors will have to advise clients as to their obligations in respect of maintaining contributions if they are to avoid discharge or revocation of their legal aid certificate and claimant's solicitors will have to be aware in relation to constant prospect of re-assessment, if there is a change in financial circumstances.

Claimant's Liability for Costs

3.44 Legal aid still, of course, carries a potential strategic advantage over opponents in respect of assisted person's liability for costs, but the assisted person should still be advised in relation to their potential liability for costs. The Civil Legal Aid (General) Regulations 1989, regs 1 to 4 and regs 1 to 9 set out that where proceedings have been concluded, in which an assisted person is liable or would have been liable for costs if he had not been an assisted person, no costs attributable to the period in which this certificate was in force, shall be recoverable from him until the court has determined the amount of his liability in accordance with s 17(1) of the Legal Aid Act 1988. Under regs 1 to 9 it is important to note that the court may direct either that payment under the order for costs shall be limited to such amount payable in instalments or otherwise as the court thinks reasonable, having regard to all the circumstances (including if contributory legal aid was in existence the level and amount of such contributions in total) – or where the court thinks it reasonable that no payment shall be made immediately or that the assisted person shall have no liability for payment, that payment under the order for costs be suspended either until such a date the court may determine it, or indefinitely. It is important that claimants' legal advisers make this specifically clear. It is not necessarily the case that an assisted person is free of risk and certainly not so in relation to the interlocutory cost regime under the CPR.

Payments on Account

3.45 Legal aid remains advantageous, not only tactically, but also in relation to the funding of payments on account pursuant to Regulation 100 of the Civil Legal Aid (General) Regulations 1989 that is to say 75% of profit costs every six months. With the emergence of strict cost limitations however, one will have to be careful in relation to the prospect of carrying out work beyond the cost restriction and therefore limiting the actual percentage of work in progress to be payable by the Legal Aid Board at the regular interval.

Disbursements

3.46 Pursuant to Regulation 101(1) claimant solicitors are able to obtain disbursements on account. One has to certify that disbursements claimed have already been incurred or will be incurred within the next three months following the request and that the person signing of course has a valid practising certificate. It is important to ensure that one makes applications for disbursements, either in anticipation or on immediate receipt of the voucher.

Legal Expense Insurance Funding ('Before the Event' Insurance)

3.47 This type of funding has been available for some time, although again it is the subject of significant growth. It remains the claimant's solicitors' obligation to advise the new client as to the potential availability of appropriate legal expense insurance cover, depending on the nature of the claim. Legal expense insurance cover will usually be embodied as part of an existing policy in relation to household contents, motor vehicle or other ancillary product or insurance, for example, charge and credit cards. The legal expense insurance industry have recently included claims for clinical negligence. They invariably expressly exclude involvement in multiparty actions. Most Legal Expense Insurance Companies offer indemnity by reference to a panel solicitor regime. The Insurance Companies (Legal Expense Insurance) Regulations 1990 refer to this. It is not within the ambit of this chapter to detail those arguments, save that it is necessary for claimants' solicitors to have a thorough understanding of the terms of each individual policy in terms of:

    (a) the limit of indemnity;
    (b) whether the indemnity covers claimant and opponent's costs;
    (c) reporting restrictions;
    (d) disbursement level restrictions;
    (e) hourly rate restrictions;
    (f) the impact on the indemnity principle on recovery.

THE 'NEW' REGIME

Conditional Fee Agreements

3.48 It is important to distinguish between a contingency fee and a conditional fee (a share of the spoils as opposed to a conditional fee, that is, a share of the value of costs from the spoils).

3.49 Conditional fees are undoubtedly in real terms a form of contingency, but made lawful by the provisions of the Courts and Legal Services Act 1990.[1] The key essential elements of a conditional fee agreement are:

• No fee to the client if you lose.
• Maximum of 100% uplift on the hourly rate if you win by way of success fee.
• The availability of conditional fee insurance to provide indemnity for the other side's costs and potentially client's own disbursements, both pre and post issue.

    1 Conditional Fee Agreements Order 1995, SI 1995/1674, Conditional Fee Agreements Regulations 1995, SI 1995/ 1675, both came into force 5 July 1995 and Conditional Fee Agreement Order 1998 SI 1998/1860, 30 July 1998.

3.50 Pursuant to Access to Justice Act the success fee and the premium to purchase indemnity insurance cover are (subject to challenge as to the reasonableness) in principle recoverable from the losing opponent. There is an obligation to notify the opponent as to the existence of a conditional fee agreement and a success fee, although there is at present confusion as to whether such notification is only to run with proceedings issued rather than at pre-action stage. There is apparently no obligation to give details in respect of the calculated success fee, but the timing of entry into insurance product purchase, the potential aspect of solicitors providing advice in relation to the best insurance product or the most suitable insurance product and the risk assessment at the stage of entering into a conditional fee agreement are all matters which will be subject to scrutiny by the court and potentially by the defendants. From a claimant's perspective the attractions of a conditional fee agreement are clear. The risk of litigation disappears for the client provided they co-operate with the terms of the conditional fee agreement entered into.

3.51 As mentioned before, even with the wealthy client conditional fee agreements are attractive to all potential litigants, where litigation is contemplated.

3.52 Any agreement in connection with conditional fees must state whether or not there is a cap on the amount payable by reference to the amount of any damages recovered.

3.53 The Law Society have now recommended that there should be no cap on the success fee, the recoverability of the success fee extinguishing the need such a cap.

3.54 Experts' fees and other disbursements should not be commissioned on a 'conditional' basis. To do so would undermine the independence of the expert and his duty to the court and is not necessary if proper and concise advice and instruction is given to clients in relation to disbursement funding options. There is, however, a distinction to be drawn between a disbursement being conditional fee on outcome and the timing of its payment. It is not in my view unreasonable to enter into arrangements where payment is timed to coincide with the determination of a case. This becomes a 'cash-flow' matter.

3.55 Barristers may conduct cases on a conditional fee basis. Their agreement will be with the instructing solicitor. The Bar Council has issued model terms of engagement for barristers, but the Law Society has not as yet been able to endorse the Bar's terms of engagement. This will inevitably be a matter of negotiation between solicitor and barrister and again the options should be made clear to the client. The Association for Personal Injury Lawyers and the Personal Injury Bar Association have developed model terms for their members and the agreement has been endorsed by the Law Society as representing fair terms for employing counsel.

3.56 The importance of the solicitors' obligations should not be confused with the belief that clients have to be given the best advice as they would be in respect of financial services provision, although the conditional fee agreement model agreement is somewhat contradictory in relation to the advice that solicitors have to give concerning insurance products and any interest they have in it. The definition of solicitors' interest in the insurance products is yet to be determined and may in fact cause some confusion.

3.57 While it is important for claimant solicitors to have an understanding of the various funding options, a particular claimant solicitor may decide to limit the options for his firm's clients. As long as that solicitor makes it plain, as part of his Rule 15 obligations, that there may be more beneficial policies on the market, which other claimant solicitors' practices may be willing to offer, then it is a matter of client's choice to make alternative enquiries. The solicitor is doing no more than stating that his particular practice will be prepared to fund that particular claimant's claim on that particular basis.

3.58 The Consumers Association Policy Report 1998 recommended that the Law Society should do more to make solicitors aware of the requirement to advise about insurance, particularly the newer products and the implications in terms of professional conduct in negligence claims if they breached requirements. The new practice rule (Rule 15) should include more details on cost information and makes solicitors' obligations clearer.

After the Event Insurance

3.59   At the same as the development of Conditional Fee Agreements, the 'after the event' insurance market (the event being the accident or incident) has also increased to the extent that a new body to represent after the event litigation insurance companies has been formed, known as the Official Forum of After the Event Insurers. It remains to be seen as to whether that forum seeks regularity powers.

3.60   The main theme of after the event insurance is a policy taken out when embarking on litigation to indemnify against the risk of losing. The interesting feature is that in most 'after the event insurance' policies indemnity is in respect of both sets of legal costs, that is, the claimant's and the opponent's. Therefore, they are not appropriate to be used in conjunction with conditional fees.

3.61   It is extremely important to consider as part of the analysis for a claimant's solicitor advising a client whether in comparing after the event insurance with conditional fee agreements, the aggregate of a conditional fee agreement success fee and conditional fee insurance premium exceeds the premium for the after the event insurance policy which has no success fee attached. The theme, of course, is that no solicitor and own client costs are covered by the policy until there is a claim on the policy and invariably a distinction is to be drawn between conditional fee agreements and after the event insurance policies in that the client is expected to pay the solicitor as the case progresses for his own solicitor-client costs.

3.62   New products are being developed to pay claimant's solicitors 'on account' of their work in progress, presumably with interest on such sums to be paid by the claimant out of the damages at the conclusion of the matter.

3.63   The Access to Justice Act allows success fees to be recoverable and the distinction between the conditional fee agreement and 'after the event' insurance will then disappear. It remains to be seen whether the after the event insurance market will develop its product along different lines, thereafter.

3.64   Again, it is not within the ambit of this chapter to consider the specific terms applicable to each individual policy and claimant's advisers will have to become familiar with each and every one of those policies and keep up to date with their regular developments.

3.65   Comparing conditional fee agreements and after the event insurance there are certain factors that will need to be considered which are:

- Does the conditional fee agreement provide/does the insurance provider cover insurance in respect of the relevant area of work, that is, personal injury, clinical negligence and/or multiparty actions.
- Is the policy offer mutually exclusive (for example, the Law Society's personal injury model conditional fee agreement and the insurance cover with the current provider provides that the premium level offered is dependent on all Accident

Line members insuring personal injury cases through that supplier)?
- Is there a restriction on the time when a policy can be entered into, for example, at the outset, pre issue or at any time? Is there a term preventing 'cherry picking'?
- Is there an associated disbursement funding scheme? (See para 3.74).
- Are counsel's fees included or excluded as disbursements covered by the policy?
- Are disbursements included or excluded and if so from what date?
- Does the policy cover opponent's costs or own solicitors' costs and disbursements and if so from what date?
- Is there an administration/consideration fee?
- What is the premium level and how is it revisable and if so when?
- What is the minimum/maximum level of costs/insurance cover applicable?
- How strict and to what extent are the reporting terms of the contract an administrative burden for solicitor and client?
- How reputable and liquid is the insurer?
- Are there any discounts for specialisation?
- Is there a success fee and is there a cap on the success fee?
- Is there a conditional precedent in relation to membership of a scheme or panel?

3.66 New insurance products are appearing on the market all the time. Some products offer 'stop loss' cover or own costs cover limited to a certain percentage of the work in progress. There is usually exclusivity associated with these insurance products so that all the firm's clients on conditional fee agreements are insured with that insurance provider.

Contingent Arrangements

3.67 A contingency fee involves a share in the damages. Unless the subject of a conditional fee agreement, a contingency fee is generally unenforceable in this country in litigation because it is a champertous arrangement. It is in theory possible to enter into a contingent fee agreement for personal injury and medical negligence claims where litigation is not contemplated. This may not be relevant in major claims although pursuant to the pre-action protocol and CPR that may change. Contingent arrangements have a specific definition.[1] It includes work done before proceedings are begun provided they're done 'with a view to the proceedings being commenced and that they are in fact commenced'. If one knows that a particular course of action will achieve settlement without the institution of proceedings then contingent fee agreements are in principle not barred. This may be important with pre-action protocols.

1 *Simpkin Marshall Ltd* [1958] 3 All ER 611.

3.68 Under s 57(2) of the Solicitors Act 1974 there is no breach of the Solicitors' Practice Rule to act on a contingency basis otherwise than in contentious proceedings. The section specifically authorises percentages and commissions for non-contentious fees. If a claimant's adviser is considering entering into contingent fee arrangement, Article 3 of the Solicitors Remuneration (Non-Contentious Business) Order 1994 must be considered. It provides for remuneration of such work to be on a fair and reasonable basis. This only applies, however, if there is a reference to some sort of taxation system on a contentious business footing, whereas if the matter is dealt with purely on a non-contentious business agreement basis within the definition of non-contentious business, then one is not bound by the fair and reasonable aspect of Article 3 or indeed the Solicitors' Remuneration Order at all.

3.69 It is important from a claimant's advisers' point of view that there needs to be a formal agreement in connection with the client and the contingency. In the absence of agreement a client has to be given notice of his rights to obtain a remuneration certificate unless the agreement excludes such a right. In addition, where the success fee under the Access to Justice Act becomes payable by the losing party, the idea of contingent fees per se may well be less relevant.

CICA/MIB (Untraced Driver)

3.70 The one area where, for the purposes of personal injury instructions, the relevance of a strict contingent fee may remain is of course in relation to claims to the Criminal Injuries Compensation Authority and claims to the Motor Insurance Bureau in respect of untraced drivers. Those claims are not contentious business within the definition and in view of some of the awards, albeit tariff limited, contingent arrangements may still be the preferred option.

Thai Trading Co v Taylor[1]
3.71 The essence of this case is that there is no problem entering into an agreement with the client which effectively states 'nothing if we lose, ordinary profit costs if we win'. The corollary to this is that there is, in principle, no reason not to extend the principle to 'a normal fee arrangement if we win, but a discounted fee arrangement, if we lose'. The contingent element on the win scenario will be an important consideration for a claimant's advisers and clients, especially bearing in mind the likely level of inter partes' recovery and the impact of the indemnity principle.

1   [1998] QB 781, CA.

3.72 On the basis of the *Thai Trading* case the Law Society Council approved an amendment to the practice rules in July 1998 and it came into immediate effect on 7 January 1999. The new practice rule 8 now states:

> 'The solicitor who is retained or employed to prosecute ... any action or other contentious proceeding shall not enter into any arrangement to receive a contingency fee in respect of that proceeding save one permitted under statute or by the common law.'

3.73 Recent cases include:

- *Hughes v Kingston upon Hull City Council* [1999] QB 1193; [1999] 2 All ER 49, and in particular the decision of the Court of Appeal in the case of *Gerrity v Awwad*.
- *Gerrity v Awwad* [2000] 1 All ER at p 608, which has created confusion in relation to the overall enforceability of *Thai Trading* style litigation funding arrangements. The Court of Appeal considered itself bound by the House of Lords decision in *Swayne v The Law Society*.
- *Swayne v The Law Society* [1993] 1 AC at p 598, which had not been considered in *Thai Trading* and held that the practice rules had the effect of statute and that the common law argument was also rejected. While the Conditional Fee Agreement Regulations 2000 which came into force on 1 April 2000 allow those conditional fee arrangements to be enforceable uncertainty remains in relation to true contingent agreements and those *Thai Trading* style agreements signed between January 1999 and April 2000.

Disbursement Funding

3.74 Stand alone disbursement funding schemes or tied-schemes with existing conditional fee agreement or after the event insurance policies providers are available. Hitherto, arrangements in respect of disbursements in non-legally aided cases were a matter of agreement between the claimant's solicitor and the claimant and were usually funded by way of payments on account from the client. The essence of the new disbursement funding options is that effective loan organisations enter into agreements with the claimant's solicitors who effectively broker, in the main, a separate consumer credit related agreement with, and on behalf of, their clients to fund disbursements as and when they occur periodically throughout the course of an investigation. These disbursements may include the initial premium for the insurance policy and the normal disbursements that may be incurred. Interest accrues at a relatively low rate on expended disbursements and payment options are given to effect payment immediately on conclusion or at an earlier date to minimise continuing interest. Payments may be made over an extended period of time. It is, however, hoped that the bulk of principle amounts on the disbursements will be recoverable inter partes or covered under the terms of policies of insurance taken out at the time of the conditional fee agreement or which have a retrospective element built into them.

3.75 It is important that claimants' solicitors become familiar with the various options, terms, charges and interests and any tied-in insurance arrangements.

The Potential Pitfalls

3.76 Like all new products there is potential for problems. Some of these can be foreseen and indeed have been foreseen, but others cannot. For a claimant solicitor it is important to be aware of these particular problems and their resolution. Some important aspects to consider are:

- *Work in progress*. The Finance Act 1998 contains legislation to withdraw the option for professional firms of computing tax on any other basis other than on a full earnings basis and to require all firms to use such approach for accounting standards. The Inland Revenue have indicated a willingness to offer distinction in respect of the valuation of work in progress if the fees which are payable are dependent on a contingency or a condition which has not yet been satisfied. If there are any major claims that have been considered by you, you may need to consider the value of those claims with your accountants and the Inland Revenue and have a system that readily identifies those cases.
- *Success fee and premium recovery*. It has been mentioned in paras 3.49-3.52 that the recoverability of success fees and insurance premiums will affect the distinction between conditional fee agreements, after the event insurance agreements and potentially contingency arrangements. Those considerations may be replaced with the prospect in due course of having to disclose the basis of the agreement with the client to the opponents, the potential impact on settlement offers in respect of costs and the prospect of satellite cost litigation.
- *Conflict of interest*. Practice Rule 1 states that a solicitor must not do anything that compromises or impairs his ability to act in the best interest of his client. The duty clearly means that the solicitor must not enter into any

arrangement which is unsuitable or because of some financial incentive to the solicitor. Is not a success fee a financial incentive to the solicitor? It can be argued that where the solicitor has a direct involvement by reference to his fee recovery with the client that his obligations under Practice Rule 1 are put under considerable strain when settlement negotiations, payments in or Part 36 offers are made.

- *Opponent's success fee and premium.* There is nothing to stop opponents conducting their own work on a conditional fee or other basis and seeking to recover the success fee and any incurred premium from the clients. Thus, the clients must be aware of this and have sufficient insurance cover to cover these costs.
- *Satellite cost litigation.* The potential for satellite cost litigation and the need to disclose information to allow a proper assessment of the rate of success fees and the calculations of the premiums may create a future problem for solicitor/client confidentiality which may be the subject of satellite litigation itself.
- *The new Rule 15.* Within the new standard it is necessary to include in terms of cost effectiveness a record in writing of all information required to be given by the code including decisions relating to costs and arrangements for updating cost information. Such information must not be inaccurate or misleading, it must be given clearly and in a way and at a level which is appropriate to the particular client. Any terms must be explained to the client.
- *The indemnity principle.* The general principle is that you cannot recover more from your opponent than you would have been able to recover legitimately from your client. Recent cases have discussed this and found that there would be a breach of the indemnity principle if a solicitors' profit costs as set out in the bill exceeded the amount, item by item, which he could have charged his client. Failure to abide by the indemnity principle may now be a disciplinary matter as it is important not to breach this indemnity principle and to make provision in one's cost information to the client the various factors may affect the increase in the rate, for example, the complexity of the matter and the need for annual review so as to avoid the problem of being fixed by a straightforward rate incapable of periodic assessment or variation due to complexity.
- *The dissatisfied client.* Clear and if necessary concise, but nevertheless complete information about costs and the agreement in relation to costs may avoid many potential pitfalls. It is very difficult to appreciate fully whether they have understood what has been explained to them. Anecdotally most clients probably don't understand what has so far been explained to them and hence there are not many disputes in relation to solicitor and own client taxations, success fee percentages, contingent fee percentages or hourly rate as the system becomes more sophisticated and indeed challenges from the opponents go on the increase, clients are likely to get more informed and involved.
- *The dissatisfied insurer.* In most of the arrangements on a conditional fee, after the event or before the event insurance, there are strict terms in relation to reporting and service standards. Practitioners must be aware of these and have systems to comply with them in order not to face arguments concerning coverage.
- *The insolvent client.* Beware of the position under the CPR in relation to interlocutory cost orders. The firm's liability on disbursement funding

arrangements and the prospects of recovering basic costs if clients determine for whatever reason to terminate the CFA or other insurance arrangement. Are credit checks needed on clients regardless of the method of funding agreed? The SIF would suggest that our clients are vetted!

THE CPR AND THE NEW REGIME

3.77 It is interesting to note that the new procedural code containing the overriding objective[1] makes reference to funding in that the overriding objectives includes:

(a) saving expense;
(b) dealing with cases proportionately;
(c) taking into account the financial position of each party; and
(d) ensuring (within this) that the parties are on an equal footing.

1 CPR 1.1.

3.78 It is beyond doubt that litigants and their advisers are going to have to be much more costs aware than ever before. The impact of fixed cost recovery in fast-track cases cannot be underestimated. The court will be concerned to limit the costs of an action, even in multi-track cases to the extent that it will be necessary on allocation and on listing and on every interlocutory application for estimates of costs already incurred and to be incurred per party to be provided. It will almost become a separate professional task to engineer these estimates and to provide prudent budgets for any future fees. These cost reviews clearly have to be carried out perhaps more accurately and more regularly than before. Is it cost effective for the claimant's solicitor to do this or to employ a cost specialist in-house to do it? Computer technology will clearly be of assistance in terms of accurate time recording for past purposes, but not necessarily so for future planned expenditure per file.

3.79 Part 35 should also not be underestimated and the court's duty to restrict expert evidence, to restrict recoverable fees in respect of any expert evidence that is relied on (on an inter partes basis) and to impose the instruction of joint experts. While previous litigation has been subject to scales and discretion it was never previously subject to the principle of proportionality. This will of course go hand in hand with cost/benefit analysis.

3.80 The prospect of immediate interlocutory cost orders will focus practitioner's minds. The courts need to consider directly the proportionality and the reasonableness of the costs incurred and will consider those which are unreasonable an amount and unreasonably incurred and take into account the conduct of the parties, both before and during the proceedings.

3.81 It is arguable that costs law will become so complex that there will need to be specialist costs advisers in claimant's solicitors' practices. Training programs are in fact being developed by cost organisations and also solicitors' practices will need to consider refining their current processes and approaches.

CONCLUSION

3.82   The cost effective case management of personal injury claims involves the claimant practitioner understanding the full implications, not just for the client, but for his practice in relation to the options for funding that are available. It will be the solicitors' role in understanding those costs options and deciding with the client the best option at the outset that will facilitate the easier path on costs as the matter progresses. It will be essential to have a relatively well organised planned budget in respect of litigation which will be subject of regular and precise and accurate review, the principles which are understood and explained in clear terms both by solicitor and client. The recovery of costs incurred will be no more straightforward in the future and indeed is likely to be more complicated.

3.83   Costs must not be ancillary matter to the litigation, but must be an intricate part of the litigation. Solicitors are in business and they are in business to make profit. Starting the case on behalf of the claimant with a full understanding and knowledge of the principles in respect of costs remain an essential tool for cost effective case management.

Chapter 4

Project Management in Personal Injury Cases: The Claimant's Perspective

Caroline Harmer

4.1 Project management in the context of litigation has only recently been addressed as a topic in itself. It is clear, however, that litigation is a project that must be managed as much as, say, a construction project.

4.2 It is important to make the point at the outset that most fee earners and firms will have some project management tools in place. Some of this will have been arrived at by years of experience, of trial and error. More recently, at least some project management – particularly case management has been put in place by the advent of computerised case management systems.

WHY THE NEED FOR PROJECT MANAGEMENT?

4.3 There are many reasons why project management is needed. The following are a selection:

- Because litigation can take on a life of its own and run the fee earner rather than the opposite.
- Because the danger is that litigation is run reactively rather than pro-actively, time slips away and resources are insufficient. Things are done only when they must be done rather than when they can be done and at the last minute. For example, in the run up to a trial there may not be enough time to prepare fully without disrupting the other cases being run by the fee earner, and sometimes without disrupting the rest of the solicitor's office.
- Because the danger is that the costs mount up and become disproportionate. The legal expenses insurance indemnity may be exceeded with the result that the client runs the risk of having to pay part of any adverse costs order. The costs estimate given to the court and the other side may be exceeded and neither the other side nor the court are prepared to accept the excess.
- Because all the risk analysis in the world on the topic of whether or not the case will be successful on liability and quantum is a complete waste of time if, through lack of management of the project, the case fails in some other way.
- Because losing the case on a technicality such as being stayed because no judgment or defence has been entered or filed (see CPR Rule 15.11)[1] is something that could be avoided with proper case and project management.
- Because losing an expert or counsel at the last minute is not going to help win the case.

- Because the client may lose confidence in the firm or the system and give up the case or change their legal advisers.
- Because the litigation department may not keep functioning if cases take longer than they need to reach a conclusion. This is a greater danger than losing cases. Most claimant firms do not lose a large number of cases but cases may take too long, bearing in mind high case loads. Most claimant lawyers will now not be paid until the end of case and it is evident that the longer the case takes, the longer the firm will have to fund the costs and probably the disbursements.
- Because funding may be removed at a critical moment, for example, the after-the-event adverse costs insurer may decide to withdraw cover, as in the past the Legal Aid Board might have done.
- Because if the case takes too long, everyone may lose heart. The client may lose commitment to the case and key fee earners may leave the case or the firm.

1 See para 4.130.

What is Project Management?

4.4 The temptation in litigation has always been to blame others when things go wrong or do not go as well as they were expected to.

4.5 Who or what has been seen as the main culprit? Here are some popular excuses:

The Other Side
They are responsible for delays, they do not respond to the protocol letter of claim in time, their behaviour necessitates applications to the court, they refuse to settle, insist on documentation, write too many letters and the like.

The Client
He does not tell the whole story; gives too few instructions or will never stop pestering; exaggerates his injury; is sure that his friend down the road got at least double the damages on offer or is desperate to accept the miserly offer made by the insurers because it is money available now.

The System
How a case is funded and the constraints that it places; the rules and how they are applied by district judges who demonstrate a lack of consistency and may have had little experience of personal injury litigation while in practice.

The Judge
Litigation is a lottery and the judge was having an off day

The Experts
Experts take a long time to produce reports; it is never known what they are going to say; they are unable to comply with the court timetable; even if they do produce a favourable report they only have to get to a meeting with the other side's expert to water it down or worse still go into the witness box and revise their opinion.

4.6 The tendency to lay the blame on others should be resisted. All of the above are views often expressed but with proper project management most of what is described may be avoided. On further investigation, lack of management of the case may be seen to be the cause rather than outside factors. Even if some of the above comments are justified, the case should be managed to avoid the problem or, at worst, mitigate its effect. The following practices should be considered:

- The other side – planning the litigation timetable so that it keeps to time will place pressure on the other side to do likewise
- The client – planning communication with the client and keeping him informed of the timetable, costs and progress should improve the relationship
- The system – experienced practitioners know the system and its inherent drawbacks; these should be anticipated and how to avoid them should be planned, for example, in how allocation questionnaires are completed,
- The judge – limiting issues, choosing appropriate counsel, preparing trial bundles to enlighten the judge, together with others tactics should be employed.
- The experts – involving experts in the progress and the timetable of the case is essential. Properly defining the issues to be addressed and ensuring that the expert understands their role will help avoid some of the difficulties.

4.7 It is possible to take control of the project and manage it to eliminate as many of the risks above as possible. Litigation should be viewed as a project which is of fundamental importance to the client and also to the well-being of the firm and practice.

4.8 Lawyers running cases may approach the case in different ways:

Procedure Driven
They react to the rules, they are slaves to the rules and may reach an outcome which is not consistent with the client's needs or objectives and consumes more of the funding resources than is necessary.

Case/Merits Driven
They are focused on the legal technicalities of the claim, in the justice or rightness of the case, in providing a quality service and may again go beyond or in opposition to the client's needs and pocket.

Driven by the Requirements of the Firm
Cases are seen in the context of hours worked, of fees earned.

Client Driven
The client's needs and problems are uppermost, the wish to serve the client is paramount, sympathy for the client rules decision making.

4.9 The skill of the project manager will be to harness the strengths of the various members of the project team while avoiding the difficulties inherent in any one of the above approaches to litigation. Project management is about managing the project and managing people, that is, the team.

4.10 In short, good project management includes:

- managing and meeting the client needs;
- funding and cost budgeting;

- rules and timetable compliance;
- providing and managing the necessary resources including people;
- managing the internal and external team (for example, experts).

4.11 It might be argued that this is inappropriate for personal injury litigation.

4.12 However, even in the more routine matters, for example, rear end shunt whiplash cases, some project management is evident even if undefined. In today's litigation landscape of limited funding and restricted between-the-parties costs, it is necessary if the cases are not to take too long and be unprofitable.

4.13 Although success fees will, in future, be paid by the losing party, there will have to be a large number of successes in small value cases to pay for any failure.

4.14 Success will not just be winning the case – it will be winning it with maximum costs and success fee recovery in the minimum time possible.

4.15 Project management is particularly relevant in the higher value and more complex cases. The team is larger; there will be a number of experts in different disciplines; there will probably be a number of tasks to be outsourced; the length of time taken to deal with the case will mean the missing key dates is a greater problem; the case may slow down or stop sometimes for unavoidable reasons such as the need to wait for a final prognosis.

The Project's Objectives

4.16 The first question to ask is what is the objective of this project? Clearly winning damages for the client would seem to be the main objective. However, doing so with limited exposure to adverse costs or solicitor and own client costs must be another. Achieving the result, win or lose, in the shortest possible time that is consistent to achieving a fair result for the client. Ending the project with a contented client and fulfilled fee earners is also important.

4.17 How it is to be achieved is inexorably bound up with who has the chequebook . This might be:

- the client (unlikely in serious injury cases);
- the Legal Services Commission (even more unlikely in today's legal aid desert);
- the before-the-event legal expenses insurer;
- your firm which insures the case through conditional fees;
- an after-the-event funder of your costs as well as insurer of adverse costs.

4.18 The old Legal Aid Board recognised the necessity for some sort of project management requiring a case plan for the more complex cases.

4.19 Alan Pannett writing in the *New Law Journal* deals with some of the objectives, procedures and questions to be considered in managing the litigation department, as follows:

- identifying issues early and reviewing them;
- encouraging ADR;
- avoiding court;

- using information technology, for example, to assess value of claim. Using e-mail to communicate with counsel, experts, client and so on;
- proceeding as fast as justice will allow;
- are clients aware and understand the dispute resolution process?
- educate them and manage their expectations;
- educate them and manage them in relation to fast track cases, and costs penalties;
- how to review and share knowledge, external and internal;
- selecting the right people to do the work to analyse the case, do the case plan and budget, and manage both. Will a team or an individual do it all? Assess competencies of the team.

PLANNING THE PROJECT

The Work Schedule and Litigation Timetable

4.20 It will be necessary to plan the main steps in the litigation: protocol letters, experts reports, Part 36 offers, issue, filing of defence and particularly the trial date. Identify which steps can be controlled or influenced in some way and which are subject to external control. Anticipate as far as possible the work that will be necessary and when it will have to be done.

Table 1: Litigation timetable for multi-track road accident case (straight-forward injury)

	1	2	3	4	5	6	7	8	9	10	11	12
Police accident report				x								
Interview witnesses				x								
Protocol letter				x								
Protocol response (liability admitted)					x							
Medical expert						x						
Part 36 offer + medical report schedule of damages						x						
Written questions to expert							x					
Answers to questions								x				
Negotiations								x	x			
Issue proceedings											x	

4.21 It will be seen that Table 1 is concerned with the various steps that must be taken and work that must be done. This of course will vary with the type of case – road accident or product liability for example.

4.22 Once the steps to be taken have been identified, they can be converted into the number of hours of work to be done at any particular stage and broken down into a monthly or quarterly schedule of costs and disbursements. Alternatively it is possible to consider costs and disbursements over a longer period, or up to certain stages – always remembering that costs estimates have to be given at certain known stages, for example, allocation and listing questionnaires. In addition, if there is to be any application to the court, it should be anticipated that an up-to-date costs estimate may be required. This should be easily extracted from the information available as described above.

4.23 In negotiations with the other side, the level of the claimant's costs will become a very important issue in a conditional fee case because the success fee to be paid by the defendant's insurers will be a percentage uplift on the claimant's recoverable between-the-parties costs.

4.24 In looking at the litigation timetable, it will be necessary to consider whether any one step depends on another and a way of predicting what will happen if one key step is delayed, for example, the relationship between the response of the defendant under the protocol and the end of the limitation period. If the litigation timetable/work schedule is prepared on a spreadsheet basis, then the projected effect of a step being delayed, or another step being introduced (for example, an unexpected application from the other side) can be easily understood. For example, if the other side has asked for extra time to exchange witness statements or experts reports, the timetable and work schedule should be considered and the effect this will have. The CPR allow agreement to such changes but only in so far as this does not affect the return of the listing questionnaire or the trial date. Agreement, while it might look attractive as it takes the pressure off in the short term, may build up an impossible work load for the fee earner at a later stage.

4.25 When planning the timetable as part of the project and then planning how to manage the timetable, it is important to include not only the fee earner but also counsel, experts, the client, the court, bringing in witnesses to sign their statements and any out sourced work, schedules of damages, employment consultant's figures, perusal of medical records and so on.

Resources Needed

4.26 Claimants have a choice as to when to commence litigation except that, of course, they must comply with the limitation period.

4.27 However, once litigation has commenced there are work and time constraints that may not be avoided if the case is to be pursued to a successful conclusion. The litigation timetable begins earlier than formerly, because the protocol imports pre-action requirements and a timetable into the case management process.

4.28 In relation to other parts of the case, most notably the preparation before the protocol procedure, there will be more choice as to when and what is to be done and who should do it.

4.29 The project manager should therefore plan what resources are needed and how they are to be provided.

The Skills Needed

4.30 The question concerning skills include:

- Are they to be found in house or will they be bought in, for example, reviewing medical records, calculating future loss damages?
- When will they be needed, for how long and at what cost?
- Does the case require specialist knowledge, legal or otherwise, and is it available within the firm?

Technology and Equipment

4.31   Take into account:

* Is there anything further needed?
* How extensive will the documentation be, for example, in a toxic tort case there may be numerous reports?
* Are the present methods of storing and retrieving information sufficient?
* If there will be a large team of in-house fee earners, external fee earners and experts, how will the team communicate with each other?

Funding

4.32   The factors are:

* How much is needed and when?
* If the disbursements are being paid by the firm, at what stage will this be a drain on the firm's resources?
* Is there any plan for recovery of some of this from the other side before settlement or judgment, for example, through interim payments and if so when?

Length of Time

4.33–4.39   To plan the length of time the case will last, consider:

* how long will the various resources be needed?
* how long will this substantial case tie up a fee earner's time and what happens to that fee earner when the case is finished?
* if funded through conditional fees how many years will it take to come to trial on a worst case scenario and year on year, how much of the firm's or the litigation department's budget will be tied up in this no win no fee case leading to potential losses, or payment only after a long period of time, for example, five years?

WHAT CAN BE DONE TO MANAGE THE PROJECT?

Short and Long-term Targets

4.40   Having planned the work to be done and when it is intended that it should be done or when it must be done, set short and long-term targets.

4.41   This plan is subject at varying times to more or less fixed dates, for example, the limitation period, time for giving notices, time for returning defence/allocation or listing questionnaire to the court, fixed trial dates.

4.42   There may be critical moments when too many things have to be done at once, as a result of which the fee earners' time is overloaded. This could be made worse because the case has been planned in isolation from others and suddenly, for example, several allocation questionnaires have to be filled in at once or trials are running back to back. It will never be possible to prevent this happening, but what planning and project management should do is to enable this to be forecast in advance so that remedial steps can be taken and so that resources can be reallocated or increased.

Case Allocation

4.43 One of the ways of managing this problem, as far as the fee earner is concerned, is to have a flexible case allocation system. Too often case loads are seen in terms of numbers and are not subject to review. The fee earner who has 150 straightforward road traffic cases may be completely overwhelmed if some of them become complex unexpectedly. There must be a system for dealing with this.

4.44 One interesting approach, is to decide how many 'units' a fee earner can cope with each year – for example 200. Then to grade each type of case into units, for example, simple road traffic accident ('RTA') – 1 unit; claimant with brain injury 8 units; maximum severity cases – 10 units; and so on. Add units for other responsibilities – training organiser, supervisor, team leader, preparation of updating bulletin. If a case worth 1 unit suddenly becomes a much more complex case, it is easy to increase the number of units so that the fee earner is not overburdened by new cases. However, experience shows that negotiations as to how many units to allot to particular types of work can be difficult!

A CASE STUDY

4.45 Consider, however, what planning and controls the firm has in place to deal with the following scenario:

> 'The claimant was driving home from work. She was waiting at the traffic lights when a car driven by the defendant collided with her car from behind. She has come to see you today because her car is still off the road. She needs one to travel to work. She tells you she had a very stiff and rather painful neck for about a week after the accident. She went to see her GP who gave her a collar which she wore for a few days. Since that time she has had no problem with her neck.
>
> Six months later she complains of migraine on a regular basis. She now has to take days off work from time to time.
>
> Various unsuccessful treatments have been tried including physiotherapy, pain killers and wearing collars and so on. It is now nearly two years since the accident. She attends a private clinic for an epidural injection. Complications arise. The private clinic has no facilities for intensive care. Some 18 hours later she is moved to an NHS hospital for intensive care. She nearly dies. At present she is unable to work and may never do so again.'

4.46–4.49 In using this as a hypothetical project management case study consider the following:

* What training is given to fee earners so that they may understand the characteristics of different type of injury, for example, whiplash that is peculiar in that it often worsens with time?

- Is there anything that can be done to steer a middle course between settling too early and taking too long to settle?
- Which fee earner would deal with the case initially and would they be able to deal with the case as it became complex?
- As the case may be a medical negligence case in its latter stages, what will happen to its funding (is the firm one which has a medical negligence franchise?); which experts will now be used; what is now the time scale; what will be done about the two limitation periods (personal injury and medical negligence)?
- Has the firm the necessary resources to deal with this case?

THE END OF THE CASE

4.50 It is easy to leave loose ends and move to the next case. However, the end of a case needs to be managed just as much as the earlier parts. Through this much may be learnt about how this case was run, how good the risk assessment and risk management was, whether anything could have been done better, or at lower cost, for example.

4.51 The following are some of the steps that need to be taken:

- Costs must be billed, assessed and collected, or insurance policies claimed on.
- The external team must be paid if this has not already been done.
- Outcomes should be monitored so that the initial risk assessment and plan can be matched to the actual outcome and timetable. Profitability should be monitored.
- The external team should be assessed – consider a report on the expert used for example. Most firms keep lists of experts and counsel. From time to time these are updated – annually perhaps. At this stage, each fee earner is asked to assist in the updating. This causes significant work for the fee earner which is either not undertaken or if it is, distracts them from their present cases. Consider introducing a procedure whereby a simple update on the performance of the expert is part of the process of closing the file. As always a form of some sort to complete provides an obvious reminder.
- Review with the team how the case was handled, what worked in the team and what did not, what went right and what went wrong and how to put it right. Should the client be involved in this review. It is a good way of learning how clients perceive what you do, and clients may feel really valued as a result. However, in personal injury cases this should be handled sensitively.

PLAN A BUDGET

4.52 It is obvious that a costs budget is important for a number of reasons:

- For external reasons such as preparing costs estimates and ensuring maximum between the parties cost recovery.
- For internal reasons, the case is likely to be being run under a conditional fee and the firm needs to know the commitment in terms of fee earners' time that it is putting into this case in the short and long term. Are disbursements being funded by the client or the firm and will this increase borrowing requirements? At what stage, if any, may there be some help available in the form of Support

Funding from the Legal Services Commission. Is this a case that falls into one of the few categories of cases where more than support funding is available.
- To project when, if at all, will it be necessary to seek authorisation for further expenditure, for example, from client, from funder or insurer.
- To plan cash flow. When will costs or disbursements through interim payment, costs orders, interlocutory costs, success fee, repayment of insurance premium be made.

4.53 If the work schedule has been planned then it should be possible to convert this into a budget. The number of fee earning hours can be calculated. It may be sensible to do this on a partial basis first – to likely settlement, to issue, to trial. A personal injury client is unlikely to be paying any costs as most personal injury claimant lawyers will be satisfied with between the parties costs only and the success fee. Nevertheless there is still a requirement for transparency in costs and the conditional fee agreement must comply with the Regulations and also there must be compliance with Practice Rules on costs.

4.54 If the budget begins to look something like this:

	Solicitor counsel	Expert fees	Court fees
investigation	3,500	600	

two points emerge:

- the threshold for investigative help will be exceeded and therefore some assistance from the Community Legal Services Fund is available subject to the financial eligibility criteria;
- the limit of protected recoverable disbursements under certain after-the-event insurance policies will have been exceeded.

A Budget for Each Stage of the Litigation

4.55 Each stage can be costed in this way. The detail can be decided by the firm, but, for example, it could include the following stages:

- protocol procedure;
- Part 36 and negotiation;
- issue and preparation of supporting documents;
- allocation questionnaire;
- case management conference;
- witness statements;
- expert and technical evidence;
- listing questionnaire and pre-trial review;
- brief to counsel;
- trial;
- costs recovery.

The Overall Costs Budget

4.56 This gives the overall costs and will show at a glance:

- the maximum exposure for costs unrecovered if the case is lost;
- the overall level of disbursements that will need funding;
- whether any insurance indemnity has been exceeded;
- whether any help might be available through support funding;
- whether the costs are going to be disproportionate either in total or in relation to one particular area of expenditure, for example, expert's fees.
- what success fee is recoverable – an essential part of the litigation department's financial planning.

4.57 It does not, however, give the moments at which the costs and disbursements will be incurred. It is important to know, for example, when an injection of cash for disbursements will be needed and then how it is to be provided. For this the work schedule and the costs budget must be married up. The firm then has a cash flow forecast for this case and a costs estimate should be relatively easy to provide for the court.

Divergence from the Budget

4.58 The combination of work schedule, a time-based costs forecast and an overall costs budget should be put in place with suitable monitoring procedures so that any serious divergence from the budget can be spotted in time and the reason sought. The behaviour of the other side which could not be anticipated may lead to costs escalating – this needs to be carefully controlled and the reasons recorded with warning letters to the other side. In this way, maximum costs recovery through indemnity costs orders might be achieved or, at least, a satisfactory explanation provided for the fact that the firm's costs appear disproportionate to the value of the claim.

Budget Variances can be Monitored
4.59 Costs to date can be compared with the budget, the estimated total costs compared with costs to date and future estimate, cash requirements compared with cash forecast.

Cases which have Slowed Down
4.60 Whether, for example, through fee earner fatigue, lack of commitment of client or burden of other work, cases which have slowed down can be spotted because the costs forecasts will not have been met. This, on the face of it, may look as if the fee earner is doing the case more cost effectively, but in reality it may just be piling up problems for the future when too much has to be done at once or when a larger proportion of the costs become irrecoverable from the other side, for example, difficulties of tracing witnesses after too long a time, staff turnover, time involved in reading the file after too long an absence from it.

Adjusting the Budget
4.61 It goes without saying that in something as uncertain as litigation where the activities of the other side, the performance of experts, the inefficiencies of the court, the speed of the claimant's recovery or lack of it, among other things, may cause variables, it is essential that there is some easy way not

only of adjusting work schedules and cost budgets and cash flow forecasts, but also seeing what the knock-on effect of any variable is. Suitable IT packages should be able to provide a simple way of plotting the effect of any variable.

4.62   All of this should be done understanding that the test of a successful personal injury lawyer within the firm, is not now how many fee-earning hours have been achieved. It is first, whether the case has been won and then the level of between-the-parties costs recovery and the recovery of the success fee. It is also ensuring that when a case is lost, there is no further unnecessary loss through work being done that should never have been done or should not have been done at that time.

Plan the Team – Both Internal and External

4.63   It may seem grandiose to talk about teams in personal injury litigation bringing with it as it does connotations of large city commercial practices with fee earners, paralegals, and support staff all beavering away on a multi-million pound case.

4.64   It may seem irrelevant where there is a sole personal injury litigator in the firm, or only one fee earner who specialises in serious injury cases.

4.65   Nevertheless, when looking at what happens in a case, there is always a team at work no matter what the value.

4.66   The team consists of:

- the client;
- those dealing with the case in the firm;
- the risk manager;
- the partner/supervisor/team leader responsible;
- the main fee earner or earners who work permanently on this case;
- other fee earners who may be brought in on a temporary basis;
- support staff;
- the external team;
- counsel;
- experts;
- the media;
- advisers – employment consultants, accountants, (fee earners for costs purposes?)

4.67   It is unlikely that even the core members of the team will be working only on this one case. They will be working in other teams which may be differently constituted on other cases.

Communication Within the Team

4.68   Communication within the team is clearly important for these core members but it is also important for the other team members, for example, experts. It is important to know who is in control of what. Is the client in control or do they think it is to be left to the lawyer; is the lawyer driven by procedural and other matters and not in overall control; is any person charged with communicating with the team or is it left to each member?

Setting up the Team

Plan the Team
4.69   The main partner/team leader or supervisor should plan what sort of team is needed at the outset. Again this should be pro-active rather than reactive. Is it necessary to reserve any particular person or the time of any particular person in advance?

Support Staff
4.70   Support staff should not be overlooked – they do not understand the whole picture and they cannot be full members of the team. Their role in keeping an overview of what is happening and as an early warning system in relation to things or dates that may be missed is invaluable.

Allocating Work
4.71   Work needs to be allotted to the team and the team needs to be briefed. Often work is allotted on a haphazard basis, for example because it is that fee earner's turn to take on a case. Thus those with experience end up doing run of the mill rear end shunt whiplash cases, and those with less experience take on the more complex cases. The experienced fee earner then loses interest and may be lost to the firm; the less experienced may discover that they are involved in a case beyond their capabilities but only after it has begun to drift or go wrong, or worse still do not realise its complexities at all. However, if the less experienced are left always with the less complex cases they will never develop the experience needed and also may leave the firm or become bored and perhaps less attentive to the run of the mill cases.

4.72   The make up and division of responsibilities of a team should try to accommodate these problems and to accommodate the strengths and weaknesses of the individuals concerned. All too often tasks are handed out to those least able to perform them.

The Team Leader
4.73   The team leader responsible for deciding who does what and when, giving them sufficient independence while retaining a supervisory role, protecting them from conflicting priorities, maintaining their commitment and monitoring progress.

4.74   Those readers who work in what would at first seem to be a team of one or two, that is, the sole personal injury fee earner and their secretary may see this as unnecessary, but it is not. Do not forget the external team. Is the fee earner going to do the future loss calculation or is this being done by an accountant? Is there a special damages package which can be used by their secretary, and so on?

How will the Team be Kept Up to Date?

The Internal Team
4.75   Within the firm this may be done by meeting – remember to include the whole team, for example, support staff and to decide who is responsible for convening the team.

4.76 Who is to be responsible for capturing know-how?[1]

1 See paras 4.94-4.103.

The External Team
4.77 It is more than ever essential to include the external team in the communication network. For example, a real danger to the prospect of successful litigation is that an expert may not be able to comply with the directions given by the court or the obligations imposed by the rules.

4.78 To take just one part of the rules, an expert must answer written questions posed by the other side within the time (if any) imposed by the directions. If they do not answer the questions, their evidence may not be relied on without leave of the court (see CPR Part 35). It is therefore essential that when considering the directions to be made on allocation or at a case management conference, the full timetable for experts should be thought through and discussed with them. Seek to control the date by which reports must be exchanged, thus triggering written questions within 28 days and answers within 28 days of the questions.

4.79 This involves regular monitoring of the case. This benefits not only the client but also the fee earner and their team, supervisor and their firm. Who is responsible for keeping track of the critical events? Too much monitoring can take over the case, too little and it may run out of control or not run at all. Thus it is necessary to decide who needs to know what and at what stage; when it must be monitored to provide warnings and who needs to know; whether any approval is necessary to move or not to move to the next stage.

The Client is Part of the Team

4.80 What are the objectives of the team?

To win?
4.81 The objective must be to win the case, which for a claimant may be by settlement or at trial, or for the defendant winning include a range of possibilities from successfully defending the case, to reducing the amount of damages payable, or the proportion of damages payable.

Other Objectives
4.82 However, there may be other objectives and if so the team must be clear about what they are. If the client is not happy or the other members of the team become disaffected then the prime objective may be unachievable.

4.83 Thus, as well as winning the case, making sure deadlines are met and achieving the best cost recovery, other things must be considered. Some of the client's objectives may be unexplored and therefore unstated. For example, they may wish to avoid going to court; they may be hoping for a windfall to get them out of a tricky financial position; they may wish to make an example of the defendant; they may wish to stop the same thing happening again; they may hope for a quick resolution of the case.

Relationships within the Team and with the Client
4.84 This relationship may depend on the attitude, progress reporting and inter-

personal skills of the members of the team. The happy client stays with the firm and tells six people about their experience. The unhappy client may or may not stay with the firm and will tell twelve others about their negative views of the firm.

The Client as Part of the Team

What to Tell Them, When to Tell Them?
4.85 In addition to the essential matters of which a client needs to be informed,[1] other matters should be discussed at the outset.

> 1 See conditional fee agreements and costs, paras 4.87-4.88.

4.86 CPR Part 1 sets out the overriding objective which it is the duty of the court to apply. Rule 1 also emphasises that it is the duty of the client's legal representative to assist the court in furthering the overriding objective. This may lead to possible conflict with the client. Certain matters should be discussed with the client at the earliest possible opportunity.

4.87 Having explained what will be done for the client, it is now necessary to explain their obligations. The conditional fee agreement may set these out (see Law Society Model Agreement) for example, not giving unreasonable instructions, not giving misleading information, attending medical examinations.

4.88 Other matters are very important as failure to comply with the requirement of the Rules may lead to the case having to be abandoned, or insurance cover being lost. Therefore the following should be explained:

- The client will be asked to sign the statement of truth and the disclosure statement. Failure to do this may mean that the case comes to an end. If he signs and does not have an honest belief in the facts, this is contempt of court.
- It is dangerous to exaggerate the injury or the financial consequences of it. Even though the case will not be lost for this reason alone, it is possible that not all the costs will be recovered and a costs order may even be made against him.
- If an order for costs is made, it may be dealt with by the court there and then and the amount set by the court will be payable within 14 days (subject to the costs being covered by insurance).
- Delay as a tactic is now not possible without serious costs consequences (unlikely to be a tactic employed by claimants).

4.89 The litigation process should be explained at the relevant moment. The client's attitude to litigation and going to court may be discussed. Would alternative dispute resolution procedures be a more appropriate way of proceeding than litigation if the case does not settle? Before issuing proceedings, it should be explained that on issue some of the control over the case is handed to the court. The court may not be efficient, the outcome unpredictable and unpopular.

Communication

Keep in Touch with the Client
4.90 One way is to communicate reactively – letting the case run its course with the fee earner writing every time anything happens and the client ringing up

whenever they are feeling uncertain and insecure or worrying through lack of information.

4.91   Another way is to put some structure into the communication process. Discuss with the client the best way of communicating with them and them communicating with you. It may be possible to put some structure into this communication; that is, updates on a regular basis, suggesting they limit their telephone communications to certain times of day unless in an emergency. The case plan and timetable could be discussed and built on to show where there will be delays and when you will need to contact the client, for example, for signing the statement of truth.

4.92   It may be argued that this sort of structure is not really appropriate for personal injury litigation which is unlike commercial litigation where structured communication may be put in place. The two are very different, particularly in the needs and aspirations of the clients, but some of the same techniques can be used in both types of litigation. Where defendants are concerned, it is just as important to decide the structure to put in place between the lawyers and the insurers.

4.93   It is important to keep the client involved and committed – this can be done by involving them in the matter and keeping them up to date with progress reports. A personal injury claimant may be less inclined to lose heart or change objectives than a business client may. However, it is a danger nonetheless both to the client who could have achieved a successful outcome to the case if better managed and to the firm. In the post legal aid world, cases must reach a successful outcome (with or without) success fees for the litigation department to thrive.

Keeping the Team Up to Date

4.94   How is the team going to keep up-to-date? Is this the type of case where the law is rapidly changing? For example, are we dealing with someone who has been badly treated while in care, or are we wishing to sue the police for negligence? This is an area of rapid development (see, for example, *W v Essex County Council*[1]) and someone needs to keep an eye on what is happening.

  1   [2000] 2 All ER 237, HL.

4.95   Who in the firm is charged with considering and monitoring the impact of the coming into force of the Human Rights Act?

4.96   What about the recent procedural changes and changes in funding. Who is keeping up to date with this?

4.97   The new MIB Uninsured Drivers Agreement introduces a number of new notices that must be given to the MIB and has introduced new time limits.

4.98   The new conditional fee rules (Civil Procedure (Amendment No 3) Rules) and Costs Practice Direction requires notices to be given to the other side within tight time limits if there is to be recovery of the success fee and insurance premium from the losing party.

4.99   If reminders are given through a computerised case management system, how long will it take to effect a change to the system? As soon as a change is proposed, the IT manager should be consulted so that the moment the new rules or whatever are certain, the system may be adapted to cope with the change.

What About Quantum and Recent Decisions?
4.100   Part 36 CPR creates a procedure for claimants to make offers to settle backed up by costs and interest penalties;[1] defendants(or more likely insurers) are able to make pre-action offers to settle. The most recent quantum decisions are a necessity. Updating may be provided by an on-line facility such as Lawtel or PI-Online from Butterworths. Current Law is also invaluable. The firm should consider whether it is more cost effective to have a networked system that each fee earner is able to access, or one person responsible for reviewing quantum decisions and disseminating the information to the rest.

1   See para 4.55.

4.101   Knowledge within a firm is often wasted because there is no system for sharing it. Various methods of doing this are possible. Within the firm there is a wealth of information on successful or unsuccessful cases, quantum decisions, procedural decisions of a particular county court, costs decisions, and attitudes of insurers or defendants. Too often this remains the province of the particular fee earner and emerges haphazardly. This is particularly so if fee earners are working in different locations.

4.102   Last but not least, how are the hard-pressed team going to keep up with IT developments. The introduction of a computerised case management system requires considerable training.

4.103   How often have screens and keyboards lain idle on desks for too long? This is often regarded as being the fault of the luddite tendencies of the fee earners, when in fact there may be another reason. Training may misguidedly be concentrated on the case management package to the exclusion of another essential skill – the use of the keyboard. Unfamiliarity with and therefore fear of the keyboard must be overcome before a case management system can be fully used. Keyboard skills may be replaced by voice recognition systems but in the writer's experience they are still far too slow to be a viable alternative to the keyboard.

Management of the Case – Part of the Project Management

4.104   The dispute resolution process must be planned.[1] The strength and weaknesses of the case must be analysed and from this a strategy to be followed to achieve the objectives identified. Cost budgeting and cost benefit analysis will be essential as will planning the timetable.

1   See para 4.20-4.44.

Planning for the Civil Procedure Rules

4.105   There are a number of areas of difficulty within the Rules that should be avoided.

4.106 There are a number of procedures that can be used to advantage. The strategy in the case will be influenced by both.

4.107 Areas of difficulty to avoid:

• The other side may apply for summary judgment. Plan to avoid this.
• The client being unable or unwilling to sign the statement of truth, or provide a disclosure statement.
• Written questions to experts being unanswered and that expert's evidence lost (see above); experts being unable to attend on the trial date – plan to avoid this through discussion of the timetable with the expert, consideration of other methods of providing their evidence, for example, deposition, video; expert's failing to understand their duty to the court, for example, by not attending meetings when directed to do so or failing to produce required memorandum[1] with the result that the party is debarred from using that expert's evidence and at a late stage in the case will be unable to obtain any other evidence.

1   See *Stevens v Gullis* [2000] 1 All ER 527, CA.

Procedures to Use to Advantage

4.108 The following procedures can be used:

• Summary judgment may be granted on application or by the court of its own motion. Plan for this. Careful drafting of statements of case, witness statements and the allocation questionnaire may lead to summary judgment.
• Use written questions to experts to narrow the issues, for example, had the claimant worn seat belt, helmet or goggles, how much of the injury would have been reduced or eliminated?
• Completing the allocation questionnaire as fully as possible so that the version of how the case is to be managed and the reasons why are provided as early as possible for the district judge or Master.

Managing Key Dates

4.109 There are various questions to answer before deciding on the appropriate way of managing key dates:

1. What are they?
2. Are they critical? (The action is lost).
3. When should there be reminders?
4. Who monitors these reminders, the fee earner or an external monitor?

The Dates and Whether the Action is Lost?

Issuing Proceedings
4.110 The claim form must be received by the court within three years of the accrual of the cause or action which is when damage occurs or when the claimant has the requisite knowledge.[1]

1   Limitation Act 1980 s 14.

4.111   There may be shorter limitation periods, for example, for actions concerned with carriage by air or sea, or accidents abroad.

4.112   This date is critical although an application may be made to the court under s 33 of the Limitation Act to extend the limitation period. This is a discretionary remedy. It is not available at sea or in the air.

Reminders

4.113   Part of the case plan should be to consider the intended date of issue and mark it on the work schedule. Willingness to issue proceedings is an essential tool for litigators. However, some of those who run litigation are reluctant to take proceedings, preferring to run the case right up to the end of the litigation period in the hope that the case will be settled. Fear of litigation may lead to limitation dates being missed or under settlement.

4.114   The advent of the personal injury protocol means that even in multi-track cases the claimant will have a fair idea of the insurer's attitude to the case. If they are not prepared to admit liability and to start to negotiate quantum, then issuing proceedings may be the right course of action to take sooner rather than later.

4.115   This date will need to be marked on diary systems and a decision taken as to who is able to decide that the date will not be met.

4.116   It is worthwhile considering a general policy that all cases should issue within specified time. This encourages fee earners to move their cases along – this is good for the client and also means that the firm will not be funding a conditional fee case for longer than it need.

4.117   Another way of dealing with this critical date is to regard three years as the norm for issuing proceedings and institute a number of reminders at say, two years, two years and six months, two years and nine months and so on – the countdown to disaster.

4.118   In considering when reminders should be issued account should be taken of the time needed to go through the protocol procedure and prepare all documents for court including the medical report and the schedule of special damages (although these do not need to be served with the claim form in every case since the advent of the CPR).[1]

   1   See para 4.123.

4.119   A way of managing the limitation risk, where the client has not instructed until late in the day, is to have a procedure in these circumstances of writing to the insurer asking them expressly to waive the limitation period to enable investigation and compliance with the protocol procedure. If the waiver is limited in time, this of course must be built into whatever case management system is being used.

Road Traffic Cases

4.120   Notice to insurers before or within seven days of commencement of proceedings, for example, by letter.[1] Notice to MIB within fourteen days of commencement of proceedings together with claim form and particulars of claim and other information.[2]

1   Road Traffic Act 1988, s 151.
2   See MIB Uninsured Drivers Agreement that came into effect for accidents happening on or after 1 October 1999.

4.121   These notices are critical as otherwise the insurers/MIB have no obligation to satisfy the judgment sum.

4.122   The new MIB agreement contains a large number of potential strike outs.

Service of Claim Form

4.123   This should be served within four months of issue which may be, but does not have to be, accompanied by particulars of claim, medical report and schedule of special damages and future losses. If the particulars of claim and so on are not served with the claim form, they must be served within 15 days thereafter.

4.124   This is critical especially if outside the limitation period as it will only be extended for good reason.[1]

1   *Kleinwort Benson Ltd v Barbrak Ltd* [1987] AC 597, HL.

4.125   Ensure there is a reminder in time to serve or to apply to extend within its existing validity.[1]

1   *Singh v Duport Harper Foundaries Ltd* [1994] 2 All ER 889, [1994] PIQR P87, CA.

Defence

4.126   A defence is required within 14 days of service of claim form, or within 28 days of claim form if an acknowledgment of service is filed. This is clearly a critical date for defendants but it is also a critical date for claimants who are defendants to a counterclaim (Part 20 defendants).

4.127   The date is critical as the claimant may enter judgment in default if not filed.

4.128   Defendants may wish to seek an extension of time for defence, but remember that the claimant may not give an extension of more than 28 days. Any extension granted to the defendant by the claimant must be notified to the court. Any further extension will need leave of the court.

Actions Stayed by Court as a Penalty

Transitional Provisions Practice Direction
4.129   If the case did not come before the court or no step was taken in it between 26 April 1999 and 25 April 2000, the action will have been stayed unless liability was not in dispute and the action has been adjourned awaiting a final prognosis.

Failure to File a Defence – Rule 15.11

4.130 Where six months have expired since the time for filing of the defence and the claimant has not applied for judgment, the claim shall be stayed. Any party may apply for it to be lifted. The old CCR Ord 9 r 10 has gone!

Striking Out

4.131 CPR Rule 3 combined with the overriding objective, gives the court extremely wide powers.

- Rule 3.3 allows the court to make any order of its own motion.
- Rule 3.4 makes provision for the court to strike out a statement of case or part of a statement of case if it appears that it discloses no reasonable grounds for bringing or defending a claim.
- Automatic strike out is replaced by a power to strike out on a party's application or the court's own motion.
- In certain situations, for example, failure to file allocation or listing questionnaire the court will send out a notice requiring filing within a period of time or else the claim or defence will be struck out. Where this happens the sanction will have effect unless the defaulting party obtains relief (Rule 3.8 (1)).
- Where a rule, practice direction or court order requires a party to do something within a specified time and specifies the consequences of failure to comply, the time for doing the act in question may not be extended by agreement between the parties (Rule 3.8(3)).
- If a claimant fails to pay a fee, the court may order it to be paid within a certain period or else the claim shall be struck out (Rule 3.7(4)).

Recovery of Success Fee and Insurance Premium

4.132 The Civil Procedure (Amendment No 3) Rules and the Costs Practice Directions provide that notice must be given to the defendant with the claim form within seven days of entering into the conditional fee agreement or taking out after the event insurance if later. Failure to do this means that the claimant may not be able to recover either the success fee or the premium.

Written Questions to Experts

4.133 The Rules provide that if the expert does not answer written questions it will not be possible to rely on that expert. What procedures have been put in place to control this?

Case Management Systems

4.134 Whatever system is used in the firm, be it a complete case management package, or merely an electronic diary, or even a manual diary the following should be taken into account:

- How easy is it to access the information? Suppose a fee earner hoping for a restful holiday wishes to check that all files are in order, does the system easily produce an answer to a question such as – will any cases require an allocation questionnaire to be filled in during his absence?

- How easy is it for the firm to get the necessary management information especially in the new conditional fee scenario. The firm should be able to check at any time, for example, how many cases are within three months of the end of the limitation period, how many cases have had defences filed (allocation questionnaires will have to be returned and fees paid). Does the system provide a simple answer to a simple question quickly?
- Does the system maintain only one critical date at any one time? As one critical date is met, the system should automatically calculate the next so that fee earners and managers do not suffer information overload.

Chapter 5

Personal Injury Case Management: The Defendant's Perspective

Keith Popperwell

5.1 In the late 1970s and early 1980s damages in serious personal injury cases escalated to such an extent that the Association of British Insurers were motivated to fund an investigation by the Rehabilitation Studies Unit of the University of Edinburgh.

5.2 A significant number of head and spinal injury claimants were interviewed, post settlement, and asked what they found to be the least helpful aspects of the post traumatic but pre-settlement period.

5.3 Over 50% reported that it was lack of financial help and lack of assistance from Social Workers or Occupational Therapists which had caused the most difficulty.

5.4 The report of the Rehabilitation Studies Unit concluded that, 'while it is accepted that nothing can compensate for the destruction or disruption of a young life following such major trauma the results suggest that no-one's best interests are being served by the present system of ever escalating awards without the investigation of the services available, the assessment of residual functional capacity, the needs of carers, the administration of the award and the expenses incurred. It is clear that many families are unhappy about poor rehabilitation, poor communication, inadequate family support, financial hardship before the claim is settled and insensitive administration thereafter.'

5.5 A subsequent symposium at Edinburgh advised, '… patients commonly have no individual with responsibility for their rehabilitation and resettlement and gains during treatment may be dissipated. In a number of European countries the insurers support injury assessment and medical rehabilitation centres whose staff provide the necessary care co-ordination. In North America specially trained rehabilitation counsellors provide a comparable service to support the rehabilitation and return to work of personal injury claimants.'

5.6 The principal recommendation of the Edinburgh research programme was that insurers should support the introduction and evaluation of a rehabilitation co-ordinator service.

5.7 The implementation of the above recommendation has been a lengthy process but has culminated in a Rehabilitation Code of Best Practice published by the International Underwriting Association and the Association of British Insurers Rehabilitation Working Party.

5.8   There has been widespread consultation in the preparation of the report including with, among others, the Association of Personal Injury Lawyers ('APIL'), a variety of healthcare providers and case managers in private, public and non-profit making sectors and individuals involved in the rehabilitation process.

5.9–5.14   The Code of Best Practice is not intended as anything other than a guide to those involved in the process of rehabilitation. It operates within the framework of the Civil Litigation Rules.

THE CODE OF BEST PRACTICE

Introduction

5.15   It is recognised that in many cases for which damages for personal injuries are claimed, the claimant's current medical situation and/or the long-term prognosis, may be improved by the appropriate medical treatment, including surgery, being given at the earliest practicable opportunity, rather than waiting until the claim has settled (referred to in this document as 'medical treatment'). Other cases may require non-medical treatment, such as physiotherapy, counselling, occupational therapy, speech therapy and so forth ('rehabilitation').

5.16   It is also recognised that in cases of serious injury the claimant's quality of life can be immediately improved by the undertaking of some basic home adaptations and/or the provision of aid and equipment and/or appropriate medical treatment when these things are needed, rather than when the claim is finally settled ('early intervention').

5.17   It is further recognised that where these medical or other issues have been dealt with there may be employment issues which can be addressed for the benefit of the claimant to enable him to keep the job that he has, to obtain alternative suitable employment with the same employer or to re-train for new employment. Again, if these needs are addressed at the proper time the claimant's quality of life and long-term prospects may be greatly improved.

5.18   Solicitors acting for claimants understand that, taking all these matters into account, they can achieve more for the claimant by making rehabilitation available than just the payment of compensation. The insurance industry realises that great benefit may be had in considering funds available for these purposes

5.19   It is therefore beneficial to create a Code of Best Practice which will ensure that those acting for claimants and those responding to claims against the insurance industry, or acting for such persons, act in future to ensure possible improvements in the quality of life, and the present and long-term physical and mental well-being of the claimant, are being addressed as issues equally as important as the payment of just, full and proper compensation.

The Claimant's Solicitor's Duty

5.20 It shall be the duty of every claimant's solicitor to consider, in consultation with the claimant and/or his family, whether it is likely or possible that early intervention, rehabilitation or medical treatment would improve his present and/or long term physical or mental well-being.

5.21 It shall be the duty of a claimant's solicitor to consider, with the claimant and/or his family, whether there is an immediate need for aids, adaptations or other matters which would seek to alleviate problems caused by disability and then communicate with the insurer as soon as practicable to see if this Code of Practice can be put into effect.

5.22 It shall not be the responsibility of the solicitor to decide on the need for treatment or rehabilitation or to arrange such matters without appropriate medical consultation. Such medical consultation must involve the claimant and/or his family, his primary care physician and, where appropriate, any other medical practitioner currently treating the claimant.

5.23 Nothing in this Code of Practice shall in any way affect the obligations placed on a claimant's solicitor by the pre-action protocol annexed to the Civil Procedure (Amendment) Rules 1999. However, it will be appreciated that very early communication with the insurer will enable the matters dealt with here to be addressed more effectively.

The Insurer

5.24 It shall be the duty of the insurers to consider, in any appropriate case, whether it is likely that the claimant will benefit, in the immediate, medium or longer term from further medical treatment, rehabilitation or early intervention.

5.25 If the insurer decides that a particular claim might be suitable for intervention, rehabilitation or medical treatment the insurer will communicate this to the claimant's solicitor as soon as practicable.

5.26 On receipt of such communication the claimant's solicitor will immediately discuss these issues with the claimant and/or his family pursuant to his duty as set out above and, where appropriate, will seek advice from the claimant's treating physicians/surgeons.

5.27 Nothing in this or any other Code of Practice shall, in any way, modify the obligations of the insurer under the pre-action protocols to investigate claims rapidly and in any event within three months (except where time is extended by the claimant's solicitor) from the date of the formal claim letter. It is recognised that although the rehabilitation assessment can be done even where liability investigations are outstanding, it is essential that such investigations proceed with the appropriate speed.

Assessment

5.28 Unless the need for such intervention or treatment has already been identified by medical reports obtained by either side and disclosed, the need for and extent of, such intervention, rehabilitation or treatment will be carried out by means of an independent assessment.

5.29   It must be recognised that the insurer will need to receive from the claimant's solicitor sufficient information for the insurer to make a proper decision about the need for intervention, rehabilitation or treatment. To this extent the claimant's solicitor must comply with the requirements of the pre-action protocol to provide the insurer with full and adequate details of the injuries sustained by the claimant, the nature and extent of any, or any likely, continuing disability and any suggestions that may already have been made concerning rehabilitation and/or early intervention. There is no requirement under the pre-action protocol, or this Code of Practice, for the claimant's solicitor to have obtained a full medical report. It is recognised that many cases will be identified for consideration under this Code of Practice before medical evidence has actually been commissioned.

5.30   'Independent assessment' in this context means that the assessment will be carried out by either:

   (a)   the treating physicians/surgeons, or some of them;
   (b)   by an agency suitable qualified and/or experienced in such matters which is financially and managerially independent of the claimant's solicitors, firm and the insurers dealing with the claim.

5.31   It is essential that the process of assessment and recommendation be carried out by those who have an appropriate qualification (to include physiotherapists, occupational therapists, psychologists, psychotherapists and so forth). It would be inappropriate for these assessments to be done by someone who did not have a medical or other appropriate qualification. Those doing the assessments should not only have such a qualification but should have experience in treating the type of disability from which the individual claimant suffers.

The Assessment Process

5.32   Where possible the agency to be instructed to provide the assessment should be agreed between the claimant's solicitor and the insurer. The instruction letter will be sent by the claimant's solicitor to the Medical Agency, a copy of the instruction letter being sent to the insurer.

5.33   The Medical Agency will be asked to interview the claimant at home (or where the claimant is still in hospital, with a subsequent visit to the claimant's home) and will be asked to produce a report which covers the following headings:

   1.   The injuries sustained by the claimant.
   2.   His present medical condition.
   3.   The claimant's domestic circumstances, where relevant.
   4.   The injuries/disability in respect of which early intervention or early rehabilitation is suggested.
   5.   The type of intervention or treatment envisaged.
   6.   The likely cost.
   5.   The likely short/medium term benefit to the claimant.

5.34 The report will not deal with diagnostic criteria, causation issues or long-term care requirements.

The Assessment Report

5.35 The reporting agency will, on completion of the report, send a copy of the report both to the instructing solicitor and to the insurer simultaneously. Both parties will have the right to raise queries on the report, disclosing such correspondence to the other party.

5.36 It is recognised that for the independent report to be of benefit to the parties, it should be prepared and used wholly outside the litigation process. Neither side can therefore rely on its contents in any subsequent litigation. With that strict proviso, to be confirmed in writing by the individual solicitor and insurers if required, the report shall be disclosed to both parties.

5.37 The report, any correspondence relating to it and any notes created by the assessing agency will be covered by legal privilege and will not under any circumstances be disclosed in any legal proceedings. Any notes or documents created in connection with the assessment process will not be disclosed in any litigation and any person involved in the preparation of the report or involved in the assessment process shall not be a compellable witness at Court.

5.38 The insurers will pay for the report within 28 days of receipt.

5.39–5.44 The need for any further or subsequent assessment shall be agreed between the claimant's solicitor and the insurer. The provisions of this Code of Practice shall apply to such assessments.

RECOMMENDATIONS

5.45 When the assessment report is disclosed to the insurer, the insurer will be under a duty to consider the recommendations made and the extent to which funds will be made available to bring about implementation of all, or some of, the recommendations. The insurer will not be required to pay for such intervention or treatment which is unreasonable in nature, content or cost. The claimant will be under no obligation to undergo intervention, medical investigation or treatment which is unreasonable in all the circumstances of the case.

5.46 Any funds made available will be treated as an interim payment on account of damages. However, if the funds are provided to enable specific intervention, rehabilitation or treatment to occur, the insurers warrant that they will not, in any legal proceedings connected with the claim, dispute the reasonableness of that treatment nor the agreed cost, provided of course that the claimant has had the recommended treatment.

5.47 Rehabilitation in serious personal injury cases is a complex and multi-disciplinary process. The co-ordination necessary to ensure delivery of the right services is often lacking, particularly where services are being provided in the public sector. Where no one individual takes responsibility for such co-ordination, services become fragmented and early medical gains can be lost.

5.48   Case management is the process whereby services are delivered most efficiently with emphasis on communication and with the focus entirely on the client.

5.49   There is no universally accepted definition of case management, nor is there a recognised qualification in the UK. There is the British Association of Brain Injury Case Managers which sets standards in head injury management but, at the present moment, no universally accepted standard exists and the number of claimants will substantially outweigh the number of case managers for some time to come.

5.50   When considering the appointment of a case manager, qualifications have to be considered in relation to the requirements of the rehabilitative process. While medical knowledge is an advantage it is not a prerequisite and, in any event, it is highly unlikely that a medical consultant or GP would accept such instructions.

5.51   The widest pool from which suitable candidates might emerge exists in the following professions:

- Nursing – particularly critical care.
- Therapy – particularly occupational therapists.
- Neuropsychology – head injury cases.
- Social workers.

5.52   It is a prerequisite that the case manager should be easily available and contactable by the claimant. This indicates that, where possible, the case manager should be local to the claimant. Advertisement in local papers or in professional journals often produces a suitable local candidate.

5.53   In the event of failure to find a suitable candidate for case manager the role may have to be filled by the solicitors for the claimant and/or defendant. Even if a suitable candidate is found it may be necessary to discuss the duties in some detail.

5.54   The definition of the role of case manager provided by the Case Management Society of America is 'a collaborative process which assesses, plans, implements, co-ordinates, monitors and evaluates options and services to meet an individual's health needs through communication and available resources to promote quality cost-effective outcomes'.

5.55   The primary processes of case management were considered by Dixon, Goll and Stanton in 1988. They are described in paras 5.56-5.63.

Assessing
5.56   This may be shared with a number of rehabilitation facilities, health professionals, social services, disabled living advisors and financial services consultants. Early involvement is critical. The assessment should include identification of all factors related to the injury as well a psycho-social, vocational, fiscal and legal realities.

Organising
5.57   This includes all assessments, data, professional resources and specialists, as well as organising the expectations of the patients, provides family and sponsors of care.

Co-ordinating
5.58   This includes co-ordinating assessments, medical and rehabilitation specialists, the overall treatment plan and the sequence of care. It is accomplished through communication with patients, providers, families and sponsors of care.

Referring
5.59   This includes referrals for diagnostic services, speciality examinations (for example, psychiatry, orthodontics,) entitlement to benefits and re-evaluations.

Negotiating
5.60   Advocacy is a key skill for case managers because they rarely have the power to make direct decisions. Negotiating may include:

(a) rates, with medical specialists, providers, facilities or sponsors of care;
(b) alternative settings and levels of care that are environmentally appropriate and cost effective;
(c) lengths of stay; and
(d) services and equipment.

Counselling
5.61   This is a very informal process for most case managers and occurs primarily with patients or families before or between stays in rehabilitation facilities. While patients are in rehabilitation case managers frequently serve as additional support and resource to families.

Reassessing
5.62   The continuous monitoring of quality of care, appropriateness of care, outcomes achieves and effectiveness of the ongoing treatment and discharge plan never stops.

Goal Planning
5.63   In order to promote efficient rehabilitation the case manager provides a monitoring process. Measuring the effectiveness of rehabilitation is not possible without goal planning, the basic principles of which were set out as long ago as 1971.[1] The five principles are:

1. Involve the patient.
2. Set reasonable goals.
3. Describe the patient's behaviour when the goal is reached.
4. Set a dead line.
5. Spell out the method (the rehabilitation plan should be sufficiently clear and specific such that anyone reading it would know what to do).

1   Houts & Scott.

5.64   The approach must be client based. A rigid structure approach without constant consultation with the claimant and family, consideration of their wishes and needs and detailed knowledge of their circumstances are not likely to lead to a beneficial outcome.

5.65   The requirement for an assessment of the claimant's (and family's) immediate needs is dealt with in the Rehabilitation Code of Best Practice. This is the equivalent of paramedic treatment at the scene of the accident. The intention is to deal with absolute necessities and matters which can be resolved quickly. **5.66**   An example of an immediate needs assessment is set out at Appendix 1.

5.67   Financial considerations come into the picture as soon as needs are identified. The use of voluntary interim payments by the defendant's insurer is the usual method of provision but if liability is a significant issue careful consideration has to be given to other sources of funding and the provision of services from other than the private sector.

5.68   If liability is contested either in whole or in part it follows that the claimant may be unable to recover any or some part of his damages.

5.69   Any shortfall in damages means the claimant may have to dip into the fund for other heads of damage, notably future costs, in order to pay rehabilitation costs.

5.70   Social Services are provided pursuant to the National Health Service Community Care Act 1990 by:

• Local Authority Social Services Departments.
• Health Authorities.
• Housing Departments.

5.71   The trigger for support is an assessment by the local authority pursuant to:

• Section 47 of the NHS and Community Care Act.
• The Disabled Persons (Services, Consultation and Representation) Act 1986.
• The Carers (Recognition and Services) Act 1995.

5.72   The right to an assessment is absolute and once an assessment has been carried out a written copy must be provided. A complaints and review procedure is available.

5.73   Following assessment the local authority will make a decision about whether to provide services and the type of service to be provided.

5.74   Services available are, inter alia:

• home helps or carers;
• respite breaks for carers;
• laundry service;
• therapies;
• odd job scheme;
• rehabilitation;
• carer support;

- residential care;
- transport;
- housing adaptation.

5.75 The provision of services is dependant on the resources of the local authority. Each authority publishes eligibility criteria. Certain services must be provided under a legal duty, others are in the discretion of the authority.

5.76 Section 2 of the Chronically Sick and Disabled Persons Act 1970 sets out services which must be supplied as a legal duty. These include:

- home help;
- provision of radio, television or library services;
- home adaptations for greater safety, comfort or convenience;
- holidays;
- meals;
- telephone.

5.77 The local authority will formulate a case plan which will be administered by a case manager. This will specify all needs, including those which cannot be met by reason of budget restrictions.

5.78 The Community Care (Direct Payments) Act 1996 empowers local authorities to make direct cash payments to disabled persons so that they can purchase care services for themselves. In addition, cash payments are available from The Independent Living Fund and the DSS.

5.79 Residential care can be arranged by both local authorities and health authorities. Provision of residential care by a health authority is free save that DSS. benefits are treated as if the claimant were in hospital.

5.80 A claimant can choose preferred accommodation and can ask a third party (for example, the defendant's insurer) to meet any shortfall if the cost is more than the local authority would normally pay.

5.81 If a local authority provides services free of charge then a claimant has no claim for damages in respect of those services[1]

1 *Hunt v Severs* [1992] 2 AC 350.

5.82 However, a local authority can charge for services other than residential care pursuant to s 17 of the Health and Social Services and Social Security Adjudications Act 1983. Enquiry should be made as to whether there is an intention to charge and, if so, the charges should be included in the damages claim.

5.83 The authorities right to charge for non-residential services is subject to a two stage test:

1. Whether it is reasonable in all the circumstances.
2. Whether the claimant has sufficient means.

5.84 If damages were reduced by contributory negligence or on a risk of litigation basis, it might be possible to argue that the claimant had insufficient means to pay because of future commitments to, for example, care costs. In such a case it would be wise to negotiate with the local authority before settlement.

5.85 Where residential accommodation is provided by a local authority there is a duty to charge subject to means testing – Section 22 National Assistance Act 1948.

5.86 Receipt of a fund of damages can result in losing entitlement to DSS benefits or give rise to a charge from a local authority providing services or residential care as a consequence of means testing pursuant to the Social Security Contributions and Benefits Act 1992 and the Income Support (General) Regulations 1985.

5.87 Mean tested benefits include:

- Income support.
- Family premium.
- Disability premium.
- Severe disability premium.
- Disabled child premium.
- Pension premium.
- Care premium.
- Housing benefit.
- Social Fund payments.
- Free NHS prescriptions.
- Residential nursing care.
- Disability working allowance Council Tax benefit.

5.88 Payments of compensation to a claimant or someone acting on his behalf will be treated as capital for the purpose of entitlement to means tested benefits and added to any other capital which the claimant may have.

5.89 If capital payments are exceeded deductions are made on a sliding scale and once the limit is exceeded benefits are no longer payable. This can amount to a significant loss to a claimant particularly where a discount on the issue of liability means there will be a shortfall in the damages fund.

5.90 Management of a damages fund should be made with regard to the statutory framework set out below with a view to preserving means tested benefits and/or safeguarding against a claim for local authority services.

INCOME SUPPORT (GENERAL) REGULATIONS 1987

Regulation 40

> '(1) for the purposes of regulation 25 (calculation of income other than earnings) the income of a claimant which does not consist of earnings to be taken into account shall, (subject to be paragraphs (2) to (3 (b)) be his gross income and any capital treated as income under regulations 41 and 44...'

(2) There shall be disregarded from the calculation of claimant's gross income under para (1), any sum, where applicable, specified in Schedule 9.'

Schedule 9 – sums to be disregarded in the calculation of income other than earnings

Paragraph 22 – (1) any income derived from capital to which the claimant is or is treated under regulation 52 (capital jointly held) but, subject to sub-para 2, not income derived from capital disregarded under para 12 of Schedule 10.

Schedule 10 – capital to be disregarded.

Paragraph 12 – 'where the funds of a Trust are derived from a payment made in consequence of any personal injury to the Claimant, the value of the Trust Fund and the value of the right to receive any payment under that Trust.

Paragraph 16 - 'where any payment of capital falls to be made by instalments, the value of the right to receive any outstanding instalments.'

5.91   If there is no Trust, the damages fund counts as capital, even though it is in a solicitor's hands.[1]

1   See *Thomas v The Chief Adjudication Officer* – R (S.B.) 17/87.

5.92   If the claimant then transfers the damages to Trustees, the exception in regulation 51 (1) (a) operates so that he will not be treated as having deprived himself of the capital placed on trust. It is not necessary for the Trust to be set up before the compensation is received and arguable that the disregard should apply even if the compensation was used for other purposes before being placed on Trust since para 12 refers to funds 'derived from personal injury compensation'.

5.93   CIS 368/1994 decided that the disregard in paragraph 12 applied where the compensation was held and administered by a combination of the Public Trustee and the Court of Protection – the effect of the decision is that it does not matter whether the funds are administered by the Court of Protection itself or held in the name of the Receiver or Public Trustee, the rationale being that it is immaterial whether the Trust is private or statutory.

Regulation 48 – Income treated as capital

Paragraph 4
'Except any income derived from capital disregarded under paragraph 12 of Schedule 10, any income derived from capital shall be treated as capital'.

Paragraph 44 – Schedule 10 – Capital to be Disregarded

'Any sum of capital administered on behalf of a person ... by the High Court under Order 80 of the Rules of the Supreme Court, the County Court under Order 10 of the County Court Rules 1981, or the Court of Protection where such sum derives from:

(a) an award of damages for personal injury to that person, or
(b) compensation for the death of one or both parents (where the person concerned is under the age of 18)'

5.94 Therefore:

The words 'derived from capital' in para 4 of regulation 48 are wide enough to cover payments of periodical payments as in a structured settlement.

5.95 The conflict between the exclusion of income from damages contained in paragraph 12 of Schedule 10 from para 4 of regulation 48 and its inclusion in paragraph 44 of Schedule 10 is resolved by CIS 563/1991 in which the Commissioner decided that, considering regulation 48 (4) and para 22 of Schedule 9 together, the primary rule was that income derived from capital was to be treated as capital. Therefore, the disregard in para 44 should take precedence and the payments count as capital.

5.96 The Commissioner also decided in CIS 563/1991 that the effect of regulation 48 (4) is to treat a payment of income as capital for the same length of time as it would have been taken into account as income. Therefore, if periodical payments are made monthly under a structure they will count as capital for a month from the date they are due to be paid. Money spent during the month cannot form part of the claimant's actual capital at the end of the month. Any unexpended income after that month will remain capital and be treated as such for income support assessment. Care should be taken that any unexpended annuity payments should remain remains in the hands of the Receiver or Trustee.

5.97 In the case of the claimant of full capacity, payments received from the Trust will be income or capital depending on the nature of the payment but there is scope for benefit planning, for example, if the payments are used to pay for expenses not covered by income support for it, for example, ineligible housing costs or to purchase items that are ignored for income support, for example, personal possessions or holiday.

5.98 Statutory instrument 1998 No. 497 introduced para 19, Schedule 4, to the National Assistance (assessment of resources) Regulations 1992. This mirrors para 12, Schedule 20 and disregards capital derived from personal injury compensation for the purposes of assessing liability for local authority charges for services and most importantly for residential accommodation.

5.99 The efficacy of case management techniques has lead to development of resources in the following areas:

1. *Liability Insurers.* Many large insurers, particularly re-insurers are now employing specialist case managers.
2. *Case Management Associations.* Two in particular are the British Association of Brain Injury Case Managers and the Case Management Society of the United Kingdom both of which provide regulated standards and working practices for those wishing to act in the role of case manager.

3. *Case Management Companies.* UK versions of the large providers of case management and care in the United States are becoming established.
4. *Independents.* Derived from the resources set out at page (10) above they come from a variety of professional backgrounds.
5. *Local Authorities.* The requirements of the Community Care Act have created posts within the Social Services Departments.
6. *Employers.* Personnel departments of large companies are increasingly providing health care co-ordinators.
5. *Rehabilitation Facilities.* Increasingly required to provide goal planning, monitoring and outcome assessment and co-ordination in multi-disciplinary rehabilitation establishments.

5.99 A holistic approach to a claim for damages for injuries of maximum severity demands that client care should not be restricted to maximising damages. the interests of the claimant require management of all aspects of rehabilitation and care as well as financial considerations in order to ensure the best possible outcome.

Appendix I

IMMEDIATE NEEDS ASSESSMENT

Client details.
Name:
D.O.B.
Date of Accident:
Date of Assessment:
Location of Assessment: Client's home
Clinical information for this report was obtained by reviewing medical notes from:

Orthopaedic surgeon
Plastic surgeon
Orthopaedic surgeon for her hip
Orthopaedic surgeon for her back
GP
Occupational notes from Rehabilitation Dept Trust
Ophthalmic surgeon
Dr (re her arterio-sclerosis and cervical spondylosis)
Dr.(re her oesophageal problems)

The following people were interviewed to obtain further information to complete this report.

Dr C
Daughter
Hospital physiotherapist
Social Services co-ordinator
Supervisor wheel chair assessments Hospital Rehabilitation
Health care
Senior Citizens Welfare Group
Builder
Plumber
Age concern
B.T.

PURPOSE OF REPORT

5.100 To assess functional abilities/disabilities in relation to daily living, make an assessment of the provisions required by meet immediate needs. Time frame for these immediate needs to be satisfied is one month.

LOCATION OF ASSESSMENT

5.101   Interviewed/assessed in her own home which is a bungalow. Her husband lives with her but was not present for most of the interview. Her daughter was present for the entire interview and assessment, she lives locally.

MEDICAL HISTORY

5.102   Previous medical history as follows:

1999   Presbyoesophagus
2000   Left cataract extraction with Intraoccular Implant.
2001   right cataract extraction with Intraoccular Implant (lens implant).
2002   Right Charnley hip replacement/osteo-arthritis (hip replaced due to degeneration of own from arthritis).
1987   Hemi Laminectomy L4/5 (lower back surgery with removal of part of the spinal vertebrae).
1986   Hiatus hernia.
1987   Cervical spondylosis and arterio-sclerosis. (Vertebrae of neck are degeneration, vascular changes of the blood vessels).

INJURIES FROM THE ACCIDENT

Compound comminuted fracture R. distal femur.
Degloving injury R. leg.
Fracture head of R. fibula.
Multiple lacerations L. Leg.
Degloving injury L. Leg.
Degloving injury L. heel.
Compound comminuted fracture L. calcaneum.
Comminuted fracture base of 1st metatarsal L. foot.
Fracture neck of 2nd and 3rd metatarsal L. foot.
Displacement fracture R. calcaneum.

5.103   From reading the medical reports, client was trapped in the car for one hour, no loss of consciousness. Air ambulanced post accident to Hospital. Admitted under the orthopaedic team. She was treated initially with wound debridement, skeletal traction and back slab to stabilise the injuries. Monitored in the intensive care unit, returned to Theatre for further wound debridement with partial closure of wounds on left heel and shins. Also had open reduction and internal fixation of supracondylar fracture L. femur. Transferred to another hospital for management of degloving injuries which involved skin grafts to both legs.

5.104   Weight loss during hospitalisation due to difficulty in swallowing, this had been diagnosed prior to the accident. Client weighed in at 8 st 9 lbs. She is 5 ft 2 inches tall, no new weight available at time of report. Returned to hospital after grafts were successful. Mobilising with zimmer frame and wheelchair.

CURRENT MEDICAL STATUS

5.105   Client wore brace to leg initially to add weight bearing, she is now using the zimmer frame and occasionally sticks for walking. Anything more than a few feet then she is wheelchair dependent.

5.106   Client continues to be followed up by orthopaedic team and has an appointment in the new year.

5.107   Was receiving physiotherapy three times a week at hospital, this has been gradually reduced and has now stopped as of three weeks prior to the assessment. Her physiotherapist felt she no longer required physiotherapy in the clinic setting.

5.108   Grafts to her legs are intact and she has completed her follow up with hospital.

5.109   October 1999 – client sustained fracture to left wrist when she was levering herself up in bed.

5.110   Client continues to experience a fair amount (as described by her) of pain, particularly from her right knee.

5.111   She is on Paracetamol and Dihydrocodeine with some relief, she also finds twice weekly baths ease her joints. She has been having difficulty with constipation as a result of the inactivity and codeine based analgesics.

5.112   Discussed increasing fluid intake and dietary roughage. Also discussed the frequency with which the analgesia was being taken as client was delaying taking them during the day due to concerns re the amount being take.

5.113   Counselled her to try to take them regularly if she has pain, to try with one rather than two instead of waiting 8 – 0 hours between does.

5.114   Continues to have difficulty eating and appeared to look quite frail due to her weight loss. She was to have fortified drinks to augment her calorie intake as she currently only eats small amounts of soft food due to the difficulty she has with her swallowing. She was to see a Dietician the following day at hospital for assessment. Reviewed a letter she had received from the Nutrition Clinic, no record in the letter as to who had ordered the consultation. I called the following day and established who had made the request. Called her daughter, notified her and suggested she request for them to send a report of the consultation to her mother's GP.

5.115   Client mobilises around the house with the use of a zimmer frame and occasionally with walking sticks. She no longer requires the use of the brace she had been using on her immediate discharge as she is full weight bearing on both legs.

Current Drugs

Co-danthramer	25 mg every night
Didronel	400 mgs once a day

Lansoprazole	30 mg once a day
Paracetamon	500 mg as required
Frusamide	40 mg once a day
Gaviscon	10 mls. 4 times a day as required
Lofepramine	70 mg tabs 2 at night
Dihydrocodeine	30 mg tabs as required every 4 – 6 hours

SOCIAL SITUATION

5.116   Client lives with her husband in their privately owned three bedroom bungalow, they have been there over 20 years and know the neighbours and the neighbourhood well. They have one daughter who lives close to them, she is very involved in their day to day lives.

5.117   Prior to the accident the client was the organiser/manager in the day to day running of the house. Her husband is in his 89th year and would take direction from her. This is no longer the case and their daughter is managing the day-to-day running of the house ensuring bills, and so on, are paid.

5.118   Prior to the accident, both the client and her husband belonged to a sequence dance group and would choose their vacations with dancing venues in mind. The client also enjoyed gardening and derived great pleasure in her garden, she also enjoys needlework and is just starting to show interest in this again. Since the accident she realises that dancing will no longer be possible and she no longer attends the dance sessions. They have employed a gardener that comes in once a week as she is unable to manage her garden. The gardener was to be cancelled the week I was there and to return in the spring. The client does hope to be able to return to do some light gardening such as sitting in a chair and planting flowers into pots, weeding with a long handled trowel and so on.

5.119   The client expressed that she would like a vacation this year but did not think it likely. I gave her daughter information on the rail service, reductions and facilities offered to travellers who are disabled. This may enable the client to visit her grandson and vacation with her family in France this year if the train was used as the means of transportation. Client finds it both uncomfortable and painful to sit for long periods in the car.

HOME ENVIRONMENT

5.120   The client lives as previously mentioned in a three bedroomed bungalow with an 'L' shaped floor plan. The bungalow is located in a quiet close and faces south. They have lived in the bungalow since it was built 23 years ago and know all of the neighbours. The bungalow comprises of living room, large kitchen with dining table. The kitchen is spacious with counter space along the back well and part of the right wall adjoining the hall. The left wall is broken up with door leading to a pathway to the back and front of the house. Three bedrooms and bathroom with bath, toilet, hand basin and shower. Garage to the right side to the house but no direct access from the house. There are three entrances, front, left side and back via the small back bedroom. Adjoining the back exit is a 10' 6" greenhouse that is an addition after the bungalow was built. Leading from the greenhouse to the right is an uneven flagstone patio, this leads into the garden which is mainly lawn with borders of flowerbeds. The house is heated by gas with radiators located around the house. There is a cleaning lady that comes in twice a week to do the housework. This has been in place since the client had her hip replacement and is paid for privately.

5.121   The gardener who comes in on a weekly basis, as previously stated, ceased as of the third week of December and will resume in March. This has only been in effect since the accident but will now be necessary on a weekly basis as a result of the accident.

FUNCTIONAL ASSESSMENT

5.122   The client is quite a remarkable lady. She was alert, pleasant and co-operative throughout the assessment. She was tearful at times particularly when the accident was discussed as she feels she can't discuss it with her husband as he was the driver. She is saddened by the knowledge that she can no longer enjoy her dancing by her limited mobility.

5.123   She was able to show me some of the exercises that she has been taught with the physio but has been having broken sleep over the last three weeks, waking with pain in her right knee. A course of physiotherapy was completed three weeks ago.

5.124   She is able to walk around the house with the aid of her zimmer frame and occasionally sticks. For anything further than a few yards a wheelchair has to be utilised. She has not been taught stairs or step walking and has not felt confident/strong enough to try this at this time.

5.125   She has a wheelchair supplied from the hospital. This is meant to be conducive to travelling as is reported to be easily transportable in a car. However, her daughter has found it is heavy, cumbersome and almost impossible to carry in and out of the car.

5.126   She is able to eat light soft meals which are prepared for her. Limitations in her eating are due to her hiatus hernia and her oesophageal problems which date back to prior to the accident.

ASSESSMENT OF ACTIVITIES OF DAILY LIVING

Personal Care

5.127   Since the accident the client has carers who come in and assist in dressing and undressing her. She has baths twice a week with the aid of a Lagoon Bath Lift. This is a type of platform that sits across the client's existing bath; she can then be lowered into the bath by the means of hand operated controls. There is an independent operator for this as the client requires help throughout the bathing process. The client's daughter had recently purchased this. The remainder of the days she receives a strip down wash. The client has stated that the baths relieve and ease her right knee pain and stiffness. Her current care time for the week is 7¾ hours.

5.128   She has a commode in the bedroom for use during the night.

5.129   The toilet has a Mobray toilet seat elevator which is at 17" with which this client is not having any difficulty and is able to use the toilet during the day.

5.130   She is able to eat soft meals only due to her oesophageal and swallowing problems.

5.131   Carers will prepare food that is frozen but not full meal preparation. The daughter prepares food for her mother.

Mobility

5.132   The zimmer, as previously reported for mobility in the house, has occasionally used sticks as her confidence and strength improves.

5.133   Wheelchair for anything outside of the house requiring more than a few yards of walking.

5.134   Front door used for access but has 8' step up into house from level path from the driveway.

5.135   At this time neither the side or back doors have been used by the client. The side door has an 8" step down onto narrow pathway to the front and back. The back door is a wide sliding door with an 8'! step down into the stoned tiled greenhouse with narrow glass door, too narrow for the zimmer with a 3" step up onto uneven flagstone patio.

5.136   Ambulance pick up for all Doctors' appointments.

5.137   Shopping is done by her daughter and husband.

5.138   The laundry is done by the husband with direction from the daughter.

5.139   The cleaning is done by the cleaning lady as per post-hip replacement of 1998.

5.140   I have spoken with the hospital physiotherapist and she does not feel the client requires any further physiotherapy in the clinic setting. She may benefit from the community physiotherapist.

Nutrition

5.141   When weighed three months pre-accident the client was 8 st 9 lbs, she has weight loss since the accident. No recent weight on records. The client also has problems with swallowing as previously documented. Currently being followed up with the hospital dietician.

5.142   Carers supply mid-day meal and husband and daughter assist in other meals. Meals to be augmented with fortified drinks such as Ensure. None currently in the house at the time of the assessment. The daughter is to follow on this.

STATUTORY BENEFITS

5.143   The client is on income support and will not have to pay any more for any increased care needs. Social Services can reassess these needs on request from either client or carer.

Identified Areas of Concerns and Possible Recommended Solutions

(1) Problem
5.144   Client has not really discussed the accident with anyone, she does not feel comfortable talking with her husband as he was the driver. Does not discuss it with her daughter for the same reason.

Proposed Solution
5.145   Arrange counselling sessions for client, her husband and their daughter as it appears there are a number of issues relating to the accident and the impact it has had on all of their lives that should be discussed. There could be referral to community psychiatric nurse of psychologist on the NHS, this could be arranged via the G.P. If not available in that district or the waiting lists too long, private counselling session via a group such as Alembic Behavioural Healthcare Ltd.

Initial assessment with mini report   £400.00 plus VAT

Cost for 7 sessions   £300.00 + v.a.t. Please see info.

(2) Problem
5.146   Pain over injury sites of knees and legs.

Proposed Solution
5.147   Have already mentioned the bathing. The client is on Dihydrocodene and Paracetamol for analgesia. Propose client be given education regarding her pain management and the medications she is taking with time frame between meds. Can be done via the nurse at the doctor's office or district nurse.

Cost: None.

(3) Problem
5.148   Side entrance with step, narrow path to back and front gardens.

Proposed Solution
5.149   Client will not use the side entrance as the back and front will be sufficient.

Cost: None

(4) Problem
5.150   Entrance from the back of the house involves 8" down into the greenhouse with narrow doorway with a 3' step up onto uneven flagstone patio. this would be the only access to the back of the house and garden.

Proposed Solution
5.151   Dismantle the existing lean-to greenhouse situated at the back of the house, remove the existing sliding door. Replace door with UPVC double door with

safety glass, security locks. Extend slabbed area at rear and form fanned area to ramp down to paved area. Additional handles on railing for added support.

Cost: £1,560.00

(5) Problem
5.152   Long hallway from the front door round in an 'L' to bedroom, client admitted during assessment she uses the shelf over the hall radiator to steady and support herself on the way round.

Proposed Solution
5.153   Installation of handrail along length of hall into client's bedroom. Quote from the same builder as previously. Quote is for varnished hand rail.

Cost: £260.00.

(6) Problem
5.154   Accessing the bath for personal hygiene requirements and easing of pain and stiffness in injured joints.

Proposed Solution
5.155   Lagoon bath. Lift supplied by X Health Care: Tel:

Cost: £499.00

5.156   Installation of grab rail on the side nearest to the bath for stability when transferring off of the lift.

5.157   Extra time to be added to the weekly allowance from the Social Services to allow for total of 4 baths a week with the carer. Approximately additional time, 1 – 1½ hours. No extra costs as subsidised care.

(7) Problem
5.158   Great difficulty accessing the shower in the bathroom as there is a 10" step into the shower. Shower is fitted with a seat and grab rail.

Proposed Solution
5.159   Two options:

1. Bring the existing shower tray down so there is a small step of two to three inches which will not allow wheelchair access but will make it more accessible.

   Approx; £709.00.

2. Install floor level shower tray which will allow wheelchair/commode access. Will be more expensive as will involve lowering the shower floor, present drain and pipes. Will require retiling around the shower stall. This will be more expensive as changes involved will be note extensive than plan 1. Quote not available at this time as supplier of shower stallsand so on, closed until the new year. Plumber is a local man who has done work for the client and daughter in the past and is reliable.

(8) Problem
5.160   Difficulty with wheelchair supplied by the hospital, as it is cumbersome, heavy and difficult to manage in and out of daughter's hatchback car. Daughter is the main person to take her mother out as her father does not drive since the accident.

Proposed Solution
5.161   Have arranged for the client to be reassessed at the Rehab Unit in the Hospital where the wheelchair was issued. Appointment booked into the first clinic in the new year. Unit participates in the National Wheelchair programme which consists of two parts. there is a partnership programme which is where the NHS assesses the client, allocates a wheelchair or vouchers up to the value they are assessed at. The NHS then looks after the maintenance of the chair, client has it for as long as is required. When they no longer require it the chair is returned to the NHS. the other part of the programme is independent whereby the client can buy a wheelchair and is totally responsible for its management and maintenance. The client is looking at the Stowaway wheelchair, the NHS does supply this under their scheme. If the client is not deemed eligible for that particular chair then they can make up the difference for one with cash added to the vouchers. The cost of the Stowaway is £399.00 plus extra £15.00 for non-puncturable tyres.

5.162   If, after the client's assessment, she is not deemed eligible then propose that there are funds provided for her to be able to purchase the Stowaway. This will enable much easier access in and out of the car for the client. Info on chair submitted with report.

(9) Problems
5.163   Contacting others in emergency.

5.164   Currently the client is dependent on her husband should she require any help in the night. Prior to the accident she was quite mobile and would have been able to summon help in an emergency. Her husband is in his 89th year, should he become unwell or fall, the client will not be able to assist without risking her own safety.

Proposed Solution
5.165   Age Concern Aid Call Button. Emergency response button can be worn around neck or on wrist. Can be activated from garden/house. Linked to phone system when button pressed activates response in Call Centre. Can speak to call centre through base unit without having to get to the phone. Call Centre has contact of numbers of people to call and medical details of client. Product insert included in the quote. Three payment options:

1. Initial payment £99.00 ongoing subscription of £32.50 per ¼. Equivalent to £2.50 per week.
2. Initial fee £225.00 with annual fee £78.,00 equivalent to £1.50 per week.
3. Initial fee £329.00 annual fee, £52.00 equivalent to £1.00 per week.

(10) Problem
Telephone Access

5.166   Currently there are telephone wires around the house into the living room to allow client to access the phone. Wires are a danger for her tripping when she is mobilising with her sticks and frame.

Proposed Solution
5.167 BT cordless phone with intercom. Would be able to have base phone near the phone jack and then two others, one in the living room, one in her bedroom and her husband's bedroom at night, they could also then be used as an intercom.

5.168 BT Quarter 2010 can have up to three hand sets to one base.

Cost: Initial handset £59.99 – additional bases with charger £39.99.

(11) Problem
5.169 Lack of socialising

5.170 Since client's discharge in July she has not been active with her peers, due to limited mobility she is no longer able to dance so she doesn't go the dance evenings her and her husband had enjoyed. Consequently she rarely goes out and voiced that she missed meeting people.

Proposed Solution
5.171 Two Senior Citizens groups that meet in the Chapel Hall.

5.172 'Hand in Hand' meets every other Friday. This is booked via the GP as ambulance pick up is arranged. The group meets for cards, games, interest films and so on. Cost is minimal, tea and coffee served.

Time: 14.00 – 16.00 every other Friday.

Chairperson is Mrs. B. Tel:

Senior Citizens Welfare.

5.173 Meet every Thursday in the same location. Cost again is minimal, no transportation is supplied but they do have volunteer drivers. When asked, one of the organisers of the group she did not think the volunteers would be keen to manage a wheelchair. There is a mini-bus that will take people home. They also have films, games and cards. There are four subsidised outings a year to gardens etc. Propose that cost of cab is supplied in order for client to attend the weekly group.

Proposed Case Management Hours

5.174 This will be dependent on what decisions are made to proceed with the suggestions in this report.

5.175 An estimate would be another 10 to 12 hours if all the recommendations are put into place.

5.176 No further site visit will be necessary unless specifically requested.

5.177 The client's daughter has already been extremely helpful in the case and three should be no difficulty in liaising with her for any of the building work that has been proposed.

Chapter 6

Defendant Case Management – The Defendant's Perspective

Robert Parr BA
Paul Stanley FCII

INTRODUCTION

6.1 In terms of case management, this chapter addresses the issue in terms of management of the injury rather than the mechanics of how defendants administer the case. Faced with the increasing cost of settling personal injury claims, both in terms of greater volume and also the general inflation level, one of the key steps defendants can take is to better manage the injury resolution and work in partnership with the claimant and their advisors for the benefit of all parties.

REHABILITATION AND CO-OPERATION BETWEEN THE PARTIES

The Current Dialogue

6.2 Many people are talking about rehabilitation but presently there are few opportunities to make this a reality for the majority of more seriously injured claimants. Why should this be so?

6.3 Within the defendant environment discussions and working parties are ongoing between a variety of organisations to include the Association of British Insurers ('ABI'), the Forum of Insurance Lawyers ('FOIL'), Individual Insurers and so on. The ABI has set up an 'umbrella' working party to include government agencies and departments to include the DSS, DOH, The Treasury and the Lord Chancellor's Department. Business is represented by the CBI TUC, Association of Personal Injury Lawyers ('APIL') and FOIL. While this is an entirely commendable initiative, it remains to be seen what practical solutions are generated.

6.4 Various research initiatives are also underway at present, including the follow-up to the first London International Reinsurance Market Association ('LIRMA') study on bodily injury claims. LIRMA has now become IUA (International Underwriting Association) following its merger in November 1998 with the Institute of London Underwriters. IUA is now the world's largest association of international insurers and reinsurers. It has set up a joint study with the ABI to look at inter alia 'why the UK has less effective rehabilitation procedures than other countries and to recommend effective rehabilitation and co-ordination case management, which will ensure the best possible result for victims following their accidents'

6.5   The Chartered Insurance Institute Society of Fellows is also engaged in a research project to look at 'whether the UK Insurance industry can build an occupational injury benefits and rehabilitation programme'

6.6–6.9   Individual reinsurers are becoming more active in the case management field. Not only are they now talking about the necessary requirements of a proper system, a few of them are building case management approaches and products to offer to insurers. They have recognised that, in this type of case, the settlement money spent on their behalf by insurers is their money and they ought to have a more direct say in how these cases are settled. Progress is, however, tentative.

THE CLAIMS SETTLEMENT ENVIRONMENT

6.10   The reason why there is a lot of talk but limited action is the fact that the 'environment' has not yet been created to facilitate a case management approach.

6.11   The current environment is characterised by the following:

- Historic mistrust between claimant law firms and insurers.
- An adversarial legal system.
- Diffuse expertise within the claimant community dealing with serious injury claims.
- Lack of expertise within insurer's back offices.
- No pressure from reinsurers on insurers to follow case management approaches.
- Defendant and claimant lawyers having little incentive from the system to settle cases earlier.
- Fragmentation of rehabilitation services.
- Little objective data available to validate the effectiveness of rehabilitation regimes.

6.12   Within the current environment if a defendant insurer or their lawyers wish to instigate a case management approach they must obtain the agreement of the claimant's representatives.

6.13   It is not unusual to find that by the time the claim has been reported to the insurers and details of the medical condition supplied, the optimum time to commence a rehabilitation programme has passed.

6.14   One of the greatest perceived difficulties experienced by a defendant is the reluctance or refusal of the claimant's representatives to allow a case management approach. It is felt that up to 50% of approaches to claimant law firms to provide rehabilitation services are refused. Why is this?

6.15   It is assessed that many of the negative factors cited in para 6.11 are responsible. There is a general lack of trust between claimant and defendant, which arises out of the adversarial nature of the UK justice system. Until the climate improves or changes, successful programmes of rehabilitation will arise by chance rather than design.

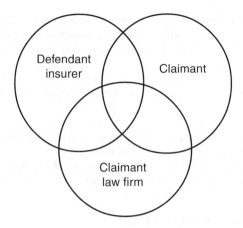

6.16–6.19 The changes in the civil justice system, the 'Woolf' reforms, will be helpful in fostering a more consensual approach to claims settlement. However, developing a climate of co-operation between claimant and defendant is in its early stages. The courts in multi-track cases may well need to intervene in a more proactive way to ensure that rehabilitation approaches have been investigated and evaluated.

WHY ARGUE IN FAVOUR OF CASE MANAGEMENT

6.20 From an enlightened defendant perspective there are benefits for everyone involved in the process of resolving a serious injury claim. The interests of all the parties overlap.

- The defendant insurer benefits from potentially lower settlement costs.
- The claimant benefits from having a better outcome in terms of optimum injury resolution, employment prospects, reduced need for care, psychological outcome.
- The claimant law firm benefits from providing a better service to the client, reducing the shelf-life of the claim, maximising profit.

6.22–6.24 There are also benefits for the community at large given that a successful rehabilitation programme funded by defendants reduces the strain on the NHS and potentially benefits the government generally through a decreased reliance on state support through the benefits system.

THE FIRST LIRMA BODILY INJURY STUDY – JUNE 1997

6.25 The conclusion of this study on behalf of the insurance and reinsurance market was that insurers should take a proactive interest in rehabilitation instead of leaving it to the NHS, social services and other agencies. They should become actively involved in the well-being of clients from as early a stage as possible.

6.26 They found that a paraplegic has a 15% chance of returning to employment in the United Kingdom, a 30% chance in the USA and a 50% chance in Scandinavia.

In other respects seriously disabled accident victims in other Western countries have a significantly greater chance of enjoying a level of independence that vastly improves their quality of life and makes them less of a burden on the state as a whole.

6.27–6.29   The study identified that skills and resources already exist to improve rehabilitation services, but are not always best deployed. A number of issues were identified:

- Could rehabilitation programmes be improved by the employment of professional care managers as exists in the USA?
- Can standards of good practice be agreed between lawyers and insurers?
- Do insurance claims staff know what services are available?

REHABILITATION – A CASE STUDY

6.30   The following actual case study was kindly provided by Sketchley Hall Rehabilitation Centre – Westminster Healthcare Group.

- Road Traffic Accident 1996.
- 35 year old male.
- Occupation: Builder
- Injuries: Fractured Right Hip, Open Fracture of Tibia and Fibula, Fractured Clavicle, Ruptured Bladder and other more minor injuries.
- Treatment: Admitted to hospital but thought to be dead on arrival. However, resuscitation proved effective. Multiple surgery required. Discharged but had serious restriction in movement.

Position Before Rehabilitation
6.31   In February 1999 medical intervention had effectively ended. At the time of the initial assessment at Sketchley Hall he was walking only with the aid of two sticks and had continuing bladder problems.

Position After Rehabilitation
6.32   A bespoke rehabilitation and pain management programme was designed.

- The individual was highly motivated to overcome the severe problems of mobility and loss of muscle in the right leg.
- Within a month the individual had made an incredible recovery leaving the rehabilitation programme walking without the aid of sticks having attained a high degree of mobility.
- The individual was ultimately able to return to his pre-accident employment in a building company.

What Conclusions Can be Drawn from this Example?

6.33   It has been said on many occasions that in the United Kingdom the accident and emergency service is world class and in this case the patient was literally brought back from the dead.

6.34   After the initial treatment and the period of hospitalisation, the individual was left with significant disability which, without the intervention of an independently funded rehabilitation regime, may well have been the extent of the recovery achieved. The fact is that in many cases the necessary rehabilitation programmes/secondary care is either not available on the National Health Service or there is a considerable wait to receive further treatment which may commence after the optimum time for maximum functional recovery.

6.35 It is significant that the individual was highly motivated to achieve the best outcome. It is recognised that factors extraneous to an accident, psychological factors, economic factors and social and cultural factors play a central role in the development of a chronic condition. Recovery from a serious injury is 50% physical 50% psychological.

6.36 In a recent study conducted by an insurer reviewing all claims with a reserve of over £50,000, 48% of all claimants had some psychological overlay to a greater or lesser extent. This is a remarkable statistic and one we believe applies to the seriously injured population as a whole.

6.37–6.39 Finally, given the right treatment regime, administered at the right time to a well-motivated individual it is not surprising that an exceptional result was achieved.

WHAT SORT OF CASE MANAGEMENT/REHABILITATION IS REQUIRED?

6.40 The most successful recovery and rehabilitation regimes take a holistic approach to the individual. The psychological as well as the physical aspects of the injury are just as important as one another and both should be treated.

6.41 Within the settlement timeframe of any large claim there are essentially three phases.

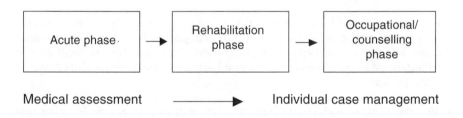

6.42 In going through the three phases the whole person needs to be addressed. Studies have shown that factors extraneous to the accident together with psychological, economic, social and cultural factors play a key role in the development of a condition which otherwise may be entirely treatable at a physical level but develops into a chronic condition.

6.43 To prevent an illness becoming chronic or to rehabilitate patients with a propensity to react negatively to the psychological factors involved then the potential needs to be recognised early, correctly diagnosed and specifically included within therapy.

6.44   Factors, which exacerbate the psychological overlay, tend to be:

- Long period of incapacitation resulting in separation from normal work routine.
- Delays in receiving state funded treatment.
- Misplaced occupational retraining measures.

6.45   The acute phase is the initial period in hospital. It is important that the patient receives the right treatment from the right specialist that the diagnosis is quick and treatment commences as soon as possible. Even at this stage of the process the injury should be addressed in an holistic way.

6.46   Defendant insurers would ideally like to be in a situation where the claim had been notified to them and their input welcomed as part of the recovery regime. Offers of assistance or private facilities could be offered if appropriate. It is helpful to an insurer to know as much about the injury as early as possible to speed up the implementation of any privately funded secondary care.

6.47   Problems occur if rehabilitation programmes are not designed to meet the needs of the individual and commenced in a timely fashion. The process needs to be completed by specialists in the appropriate discipline who have the required degree of expertise and competence. Again it is vitally necessary to address the need of the whole person in designing and delivering the physical rehabilitation package and to closely monitor progress and outcomes.

6.48   During assessment, at the rehabilitation phase, there needs to be a multi-faceted approach to include assessments of the following:

- Medical findings.
- Physical status.
- Social status.
- Economic status.
- Psychological status.

6.49   The objective is to identify any negative factors, which left untreated, may prevent optimum recovery not only recognised health and occupational factors which have already been diagnosed. This objective is facilitated by making use of the facilities available and to find the most appropriate resources for the patient.

6.50   The occupational/counselling phase must be prompt and non-bureaucratic, assisted by experts who have knowledge of the facilities and services available from both state and non-governmental institutions, together with knowledge about potential employers. This phase encompasses an assessment of the type of work likely to be suitable if returning to pre-accident employment is not possible, that is, retraining initiatives, job search and job placement.

6.51   Extensive networking is required in the occupational/counselling phase to include:

- Social services provision.
- Local and adult education establishments.

- Educational advisors.
- Occupational therapists and experts.
- Occupational medicine establishments.
- Facilities for the disabled both governmental and local charities.
- Self-help organisations.

6.52–6.59   In the occupational/counselling phase there is no reason why an employment service could not find the claimant a job with an employer. Today far too many 'experts' produce theoretical reports at enormous cost. Much of that expertise would be better utilised finding genuine opportunities. The job prospects for claimants with permanent disabilities have been enhanced significantly by the Disability Discrimination Act 1995.

THE CLAIMS SETTLEMENT ENVIRONMENT IN THE FUTURE

6.60   If the full value of case management/rehabilitation techniques in the UK is to be realised, then from a defendant perspective the following issues should be addressed:

- Development of the new Civil Justice rules – a Rehabilitation Pre-Action Protocol?
- Co-opetition – sleeping with the enemy?
- Specialisation and co-operation – insurers/reinsurers, claimant law firms.
- The end of lump sum payments.
- Creating a market for rehabilitation services.
- Research.

DEVELOPMENT OF THE NEW CIVIL JUSTICE RULES

Multi-track Rules

6.61   Part 29 of the Civil Procedure Rules deal with the multi-track. This will include a wide range of cases from the straightforward to the complex and expensive.

6.62   The major effect of the rules is to transfer management of cases from parties to the courts. What this actually means in practice will only be determined as a volume of cases go through the new procedures, however, the thrust of the changes are designed to:

- Promote co-operation between the parties.
- Identify and narrow the issues to be tried.
- Encourage Alternative Dispute Resolution ('ADR').
- Control progress of the cases through time-tabling.
- Ensure proportionality of cost and value.

6.63   When cases are allocated to the multi-track the court will:

- Give directions for the management of the case and set a timetable for the steps to be taken between the giving of directions and the trial.
- Fix a case management conference or a pre-trial review or both and give other directions relating to the management of the case as it sees fit.

6.64   The thrust of the rules encourages the parties to agree issues between themselves. The court will intervene to case manage the process only when required.

6.65   There is therefore the potential for the courts actively to encourage the parties to include issues of rehabilitation when considering how cases are to be resolved. The rules are general and allow the courts the opportunity to promote injury case management and importantly to penalise claimants and defendants who are not actively pursuing rehabilitation approaches – particularly in cases where liability is not at issue.

A REHABILITATION PROTOCOL?

6.66   Prior to proceedings, the development of pre-action protocols ensure that outside of proceedings the parties to the action progress matters in ways which are conducive to:

* The reduction of cost.
* The avoidance of delays.
* The management of cases expeditiously.
* Ensuring parties are on an equal footing.
* Ensuring proportionality.

6.67   There is as yet no rehabilitation protocol. However, claimants and defendant representatives have come together to draft a code of best practice on rehabilitation, early intervention and medical treatment which was officially launched at the International Underwriting Association in London on 22 October 1999. The code encourages all parties to consider the benefits of rehabilitation at the outset of the claims process. The extent to which the code will encourage and promote rehabilitation activity between claimants and defendants in the absence of a statutory obligation remains to be seen.

ACCREDITED CASE MANAGEMENT AND REHABILITATION SERVICES?

6.68   The defendant's responsibilities should be to ensure that only professional and, perhaps, accredited rehabilitation services are suggested. It serves defendants ill if they are proposing sub-standard products.

6.69   Proposed services should be vetted. The question of accredited case managers and rehabilitation services should be addressed. Claimants have every right to reject schemes of which they have little knowledge or no independent guarantee of professionalism. The market should not be left to its own devices.

6.70   Accreditation could be completed by a body under the auspices of the Lord Chancellor's department. There should not be a drain on the public purse for this service since companies and organisations wishing to become accredited would have to pay to join the scheme and their continued membership would be subject to annual review.

6.71–6.79   Acreditation would be a way of creating a virtual market for rehabilitation services, all collected at one location. Currently such services are fragmented and those that run them find it difficult to market their services into insurers or claimant lawyers.

'CO-OPETITION' – SLEEPING WITH THE ENEMY?

6.80   Two years ago, Adam Brandenberger, a professor of business administration at the Harvard Business School, and Barry Nalebuff, a professor at the Yale School of Management, wrote a book on the subject. It became a *Business Week* and *New York Times* best-seller.

6.81   Business is co-operation and competition. The idea, as the authors explain it on their web site, is as follows: 'Some people see business entirely as competition. They think doing business is waging war and assume they can't win unless somebody else loses. Other people see business entirely as cooperative teams and partnerships. But business is both co-operation and competition. It's Co-opetition.'

6.82   Co-opetition deals aren't just raising controversy among customers, but among regulators as well. Microsoft's $150 million investment in Apple is a case in point. The deal currently is being investigated by the Justice Department on antitrust grounds. In addition, some Apple loyalists have mixed emotions about the collaboration, worrying that ultimately it may stifle the Mac maker. On they other hand, others see the cash infusion as a needed financial shot in the arm.

6.83   What is the relevance of co-opetition to injury claims handling? Traditionally the business of settling personal injury claims is seen as adversarial – someone wins the other loses. This may be so for the law firms or the insurers but invariably even a win for the claimant turn out to be a pyrrhic victory. Inevitably they are left emotionally scarred by the experience and often have not recovered as well as they could have. While the CPR encourages co-operation or perhaps more properly co-opetition there is a need for a more enlightened approach from both claimant law firms and defendant insurers.

6.84–6.89   Any potential students of 'Co-opetition' are recommended to obtain 'Co-opetition; A Win/Win Mindset that Refines Competition and Co-operation in the Marketplace' by Adam Brandenberger.[1]

1 Published by Double Day, 1996.

SPECIALISATION AND 'CO-OPETITION' – INSURERS/ REINSURERS, CLAIMANT LAW FIRMS

6.90   Insurers have limited numbers handling large claims. Any insurer who deals with Personal Injury claims will have a limited number of personnel assigned to larger value claims handling. Many organisations have devolved this process to regional centres others have retained a head office type function. Either way the number of staff they have devoted to this work is only a very small fraction of their total claims head count.

6.91   Typically, to manage a book of 1 million motor policyholders will only require a team of four or five persons to handle claims with a value of over £50,000.

6.92   It is common that where litigation has commenced, the insurer's lawyers also handle these claims which thus creates an element of duplication. On top of that reinsurers who provide cover for larger value losses will have a team of claims experts who will regularly visit their cedents (the individual insurers who have ceded part of their risk to the reinsurer). What is built up is a duplication of effort and resources.

6.93   Most insurers do not generate a sufficient number of large value claims to generate any economies of scale. It becomes increasingly difficult to generate sufficient numbers of higher value claims to try case management approaches therefore each individual claims handler will only get involved with rehabilitation situations infrequently. Insurers therefore never build up any body of expertise.

6.94   Reinsurers are in a position to get involved in many larger value claims, which they assume responsibility for under their reinsurance treaties across a number of insurers. In the past, however, reinsurers have stood back preferring to monitor the claims handling activities of their insurer clients rather than taking over responsibility for settlement.

6.95   Certain reinsurers are taking a more active role in the run off of claims within their authority and even in some cases to take unto themselves responsibility for claims settlement.

6.96   Insurers and reinsurers could pool their large value claims to create a world-class large claims handling unit – this would provide a number of benefits:

- The creation of a claims handling unit with critical mass.
- A focal point for the development of case management and the purchase of rehabilitation services.
- The opportunity to develop world-class claims handling skills.
- The opportunity to integrate legal expertise, barristers and solicitors within the operating unit.
- Economies of scale for participating insurers/reinsurers.
- Reduction in claims costs and the cost of handling the claims.
- Collation of data across the market for the benefit of the participating companies.

6.97   There are far more claimant law firms than individual insurers or reinsurers so the concept of pooling high-value claims is probably not so viable as a strategy. However, this is not to say that the larger more imaginative law firms should not consider it. The benefits and opportunities presented through co-opetition are similar to that possible for insurers and reinsurers.

6.98   From a defendant perspective the most frustrating aspect of trying to resolve a complex high-value claim is dealing with a lawyer who is not geared up to handling this type of personal injury claim.

6.99   For commercial reasons it is quite understandable that a particular practice, which does not handle large value claims regularly, will not turn away work.

This however, creates the following difficulties:

- An over-reliance on counsel.
- A lack of awareness of case management and rehabilitation provision.
- An adversarial approach to claims settlement.
- The inclination of individual lawyers to go 'head to head' with an insurer under the mistaken impression that this is the way these types of settlement are best resolved.

6.100   What defendants would like to see is the imposition on individual lawyers of some form of accreditation to demonstrate that they have the necessary competence and expertise to handle complex/large value personal injury claims. Lawyers who wish to conduct medical negligence actions have to demonstrate their competence, before being allowed to practice in this field. Such an accreditation would potentially aid the process of a more consensual approach to the management and settlement of large bodily injury claims.

THE END OF LUMP SUM PAYMENTS?

6.101   One of the basic insurance principles is 'indemnity' which means putting the insured party back in the position they were before the loss. In the event of damage to a vehicle this can be repaired or replaced. However, in many cases of serious bodily injury this is not practically possible. Therefore an indemnity is translated into a monetary award which tries to predict the future.

6.102   Windfall payments may be inappropriate in many cases. There is sufficient research to show that a windfall payment to a person, who may not be in the most appropriate situation to handle the consequences of a large cash settlement, may provide the opposite of an indemnity. The cash may not be used for the purpose it was intended and an individual can be left in a worse financial position.

6.103   The current system is potentially disadvantageous on many levels to a catastrophically injured claimant. To the average payer of premiums it would appear eminently sensible that decisions about the future are reviewed when the future becomes the present.

6.104   Insurers and lawyers can improve the basis of compensation. Those who practice in this field could create such a system. The advantages of a system that paid on an instalment basis would be obvious.

6.105   Losses accrued to the date of trial or assessment can be readily calculated and paid as a lump sum.

6.106   Damages for pain and suffering and loss of amenity which incorporate a future element but are of a compensatory nature can be paid as a whole thus allowing the claimant some kind of windfall in an attempt to compensate for the tragedy of the accident itself.

6.107   The claimant's future needs would then be catered for on the basis of a review system. In partnership with the most relevant organisations it would not be unduly difficult to create a system professionally to assess ongoing needs for

Consumers   **Providers**

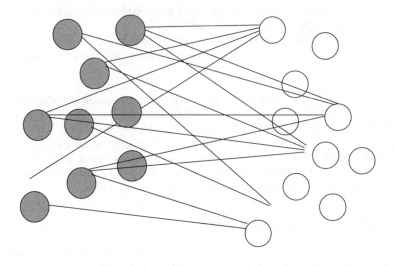

Figure 2

individuals in the unique circumstance they face. Such assessment would include rehabilitation, lost earnings, medical expenses and treatment, specialist equipment and other needs could be regularly reviewed and appropriate adjustments made to the annual funding costs. In this way both the claimant and the compensator achieve certainty.

6.108–6.109   The status quo has grown up on a haphazard basis over many years and if designing a system today to compensate the most seriously injured there would surely not be the present arrangement!

CREATING A MARKET FOR CASE MANAGEMENT/ REHABILITATION SERVICES

6.110   Currently there is a confused market for case management and rehabilitation services. The problem is one of fragmentation. There are many insurers, claims companies and reinsurers, together with captive insurers and corporate concerns who individually get involved in the settlement of large bodily injury claims. There are increasing numbers of potential products and services which are being marketed by healthcare providers and professionals, loss adjusters, reinsurers, the healthcare insurance market, and risk management companies, also consultants of various description regarding employment and so on.

6.111   The problem is that the amount of marketing effort required is huge and there is a lack of knowledge within the potential consumers of the type, availability and cost of the products and services.

6.112   Co-operation and specialisation among the potential consumers of these services would assist as would some type of accreditation of the service providers. In the short to medium term, this is not going to occur.

6.113 Customers need to be matched to suppliers. The discussions underway within the insurance industry will help the process. However, what is needed is a medium to bring together possible consumers and match them to the appropriate product.

6.114 Fortunately there is the perfect medium to facilitate the education of the consumers, identify the type of service required and match this to the appropriate service. This medium is the Internet and the schematic would look as in Figure 3.

6.115 In the USA where the pace of internet development and usage is in advance of the UK there are many internet sites, which marry up potential customers and services in an intelligent manner. The only requirement in the UK is an agency to operate and run the web site. The cost of setting it up and running could be borne by subscription from the potential providers of services.

RESEARCH

6.120 The final element in the future claims settlement environment should be research.

6.121 UK insurers, in particular, spend huge amounts of money on marketing, sponsorship and so on. However, they invest almost nothing in research and development. If these companies were operating within the manufacturing or pharmaceutical sectors a significant part of turnover would be devoted to R&D.

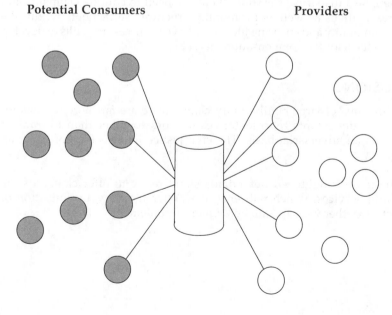

Figure 3

6.122   The fact that it does not happen from a defendant perspective does not mean that this should persist into the future.

6.123   There are some notable examples from other territories where insurers have invested in research to aid their business. One of the most successful has been a Swedish mutual insurer Folksam www.folksam.se. Folksam has a world famous auto crash test centre and has used its research to aid its own business and the community at large. Major motor manufacturers such as Toyota have used Folksam's facilities.

6.124   In the USA, companies such as Liberty Mutual who insure many workers compensation risks have their own occupational research facility in Boston where they have undertake a variety of research from driver safety to the slip resistance of floors.

6.125   Psychological factors are important. Not much is known about the resolution of large bodily injury claims. For example, it is known that after a serious injury psychological factors are as important as physical recover in the overall outcome but it is not fully understood how to minimise these effects

6.126   Given that there is a lack of information and knowledge about the services that already exist, the LIRMA study identified that it was not a case that the skills and resources do not exist. Again research and dissemination of information could play an important role in the more efficient handling of this type of claim.

6.127   Dissemination of information as an adjunct of research is an important area. For example, in the field of structured settlements there will be under 200 entered into in the UK in 1999 according to specialist accountants Frenkel Topping. In the USA about 50,000 of these agreements are entered into each year. Why should there be a disparity? Certainly there is a need to educate claimants and their representatives as well as promoting structured settlements within the insurance community and ensuring life offices have the necessary skills to develop bespoke products for the compensation market.

CONCLUSION

6.130   In the area of large bodily injury claims there are far more reasons for claimants and defendants representatives to work together than to transact settlement on an adversarial basis. The civil justice reforms support such an approach.

6.131   The more enlightened defendants stand ready to offer claimants the facilities and services, which will ensure a better recovery, optimisation of opportunity, together with an equitable financial settlement.

Chapter 7

Clinical Negligence Case Management: The Claimant's Perspective

Richard Follis

7.1 The courts are charged to take control of litigation to ensure that the excesses that have for so long given the system a bad name are not perpetuated. On the other hand, the claimant's solicitor needs to know in advance what evidence and timetable the court will allow if he is to have any hope of gathering together the resources needed to complete the project. The solution is to plan from the outset to be in the right place at the correct time armed with all the necessary information. The procedural judge can then reasonably be persuaded that the case plan proposed accords with judicial notions of good case management and hence the solicitor can be permitted to work to a scheme of his own design. The solicitor cannot wait for a judge to allow evidence at a case management hearing before obtaining it.

7.2 The likely requirements of a judicial case management timetable should be regarded from the outset. An example of such a timetable is set out at Appendix A. The challenge is in being ready to propose, justify and comply with such a scheme by the time the case is up and running. Earlier decisions to obtain evidence will be vindicated.

INTRODUCTION

7.3 Claimant-side clinical negligence litigation finally became widely recognised as a specialist field as recently as 1997 with the introduction of the Law Society's Medical Negligence Panel. Three years later, approximately 230 lawyers have gained the accreditation out of over 79,500 practising solicitors and a further 5,000 Fellows of the Institute of Legal Executives. The number of clinical negligence cases reaching trial is minute and yet the subject attracts considerable public, media and political interest. There is a suspicion among some claimant's lawyers that certain judges are hostile to clinical negligence claims. From elsewhere there are periodic calls for the introduction of a no fault scheme. What is the subject which excites such attention?

7.4 One definition of the scope of clinical negligence work is that adopted by the Legal Services Commission who regarded it as:

'... matters and all proceedings which include:
(a) a claim for damages in respect of an alleged breach of duty of care or

trespass to the person committed in the course of the provision of clinical or medical services (including dental or nursing services); or

(b) a claim for damages in respect of alleged professional negligence in the conduct of such a claim'.[1]

1 Guidance:Exercise of Devolved Powers, at p 7 Appendix 2, Internet issue 11.

7.5 Clinical negligence compensation claims form only a small sub-set of personal injury litigation. The criterion by which they are distinguished is, self evidently, concerned with the setting in which the right to damages originally arose. While this is both a common and generally a convenient means of categorising personal injury work, it is not the only basis available. Clinical negligence is a type of professional negligence litigation. More significantly, however, the outcome of the event giving rise to a claim may be more important to the injured claimant than how it arose. Hence categorisation of cases as 'head injury', 'spinal injury' or more generally 'catastrophic injury' may be far more relevant than that the injury arose in the course of health care provision as compared to elsewhere. The task involved in working up quantum for a client in persistent vegetative state is no different if the injury was caused on the road than in the recovery room of the operating theatre. While the difficulties faced in seeking to prove liability may be entirely different between the two situations, once that is accomplished, the quantum workup may be indistinguishable. The challenges of acting for a spinal cord injury victim can be as demanding as suing an NHS Trust. Indeed, the personal injury lawyer with a non-clinical negligence major claims practice is likely to spend less time on liability issues and more on catastrophic quantum work-up than the clinical negligence specialist and accordingly have more quantum experience. The labelling of work as clinical negligence ought not to serve to isolate it from other personal injury cases, which may have a great deal to teach in terms of good case management practice. Skills and techniques developed in mainstream personal injury law should be studied and emulated wherever possible.

7.6 The aim of this chapter is to examine initial case management in major clinical negligence claims only in so far as it differs from the remainder of personal injury litigation. It does not seek to reiterate the principles of case management applicable to all major claims. Good techniques in head or spinal injury practice should not be forgotten and abandoned simply because of the iatrogenic origin of the damage.

7.7 Having questioned the validity of removing the subject from mainstream personal injury practice, it is worth revisiting some of the conclusions reached by Lord Woolf who singled out clinical negligence litigation for special mention in his Access to Justice – Final Report of July 1996. He said:[1]

'Reasons for looking at medical negligence

1. Why have I singled out medical negligence for the most intensive examination during Stage 2 of my Inquiry? (I am using the term 'medical negligence' in this report to refer to any litigation involving allegations of negligence in the delivery of health care, whether by doctors, nurses or other health professionals.) It may appear a surprising choice, because medical negligence cases have no special procedures or rules of court. They are a sub-species of professional negligence actions, and they also belong to what is numerically the largest category of cases proceeding to trial, personal injury. Neither of these is singled out for special attention.

2. The answer is that early in the Inquiry it became increasingly obvious that it was in the area of medical negligence that the civil justice system was failing most conspicuously to meet the needs of litigants in a number of respects.

(a) The disproportion between costs and damages in medical negligence is particularly excessive, especially in lower value cases.

(b) The delay in resolving claims is more often unacceptable.

(c) Unmeritorious cases are often pursued, and clear-cut claims defended, for too long.

(d) The success rate is lower than in other personal injury litigation.

(e) The suspicion between the parties is more intense and the lack of co-operation frequently greater than in many other areas of litigation.

3. The cost of medical negligence litigation is now so high that smaller claims can rarely be litigated because of the disproportionate cost. It is difficult for patients to pursue a claim of any value unless they are eligible for legal aid. In the Supreme Court Taxing Office survey (see Annex 3 to this report), 92 per cent of successful parties in medical negligence cases were legally aided. An analysis by the Law Society of a survey by Action for Victims of Medical Accidents (AVMA) of 376 cases conducted by solicitors' firms on its specialist panel indicates that 90 per cent of cases which reached the stage of litigation were legally aided. If these figures are representative of medical negligence litigation generally, then in the vast majority of cases both sides are funded from the public purse. Here the cause for concern is the amount of money spent by NHS trusts and other defendants on legal costs: money which would be much better devoted to compensating victims or, better still, to improving standards of care so that future mistakes are avoided.'

1   Chapter 15 - Medical Negligence.

7.8   Historically, the rules of litigation have treated clinical negligence as a special category but only to a limited extent. The automatic directions under The Rules of the Supreme Court 1965 (Order 25 Rule 8) expressly did not apply to an action for medical negligence, so forcing an application for bespoke directions and giving the court an opportunity to take control of the action – although it rarely did so. The counterpart provisions under County Court Rules 1981 Order 17 did apply and so paradoxically an application was made to dis-apply the automatic county court timetable although again the court rarely seized the opportunity to take control of the action in any meaningful sense. For many years, the courts themselves passed by opportunities to control cases, often due to lack of resources and inclination.

7.9   It is also worth remembering that much of the success by claimants in clinical negligence litigation post-dated the landmark decision in *Naylor v Preston Area Health Authority*.[1] That decision did much to avoid trial by ambush and to place the patient on a more equal footing with the defendants by promoting mutual simultaneous exchange of expert evidence. Real gains were made towards achieving justice in consequence of *Naylor* which should not be given up lightly.[2] Even so, defendants were not, and still are not it seems, bound to own up to unanswerable breaches of duty if the claimant missed the point.

1   [1987] 2 All ER 353.

2   Some defence firms seem intent on trying to persuade case management judges at every opportunity to move back from the principle of mutual simultaneous exchange. The possibility of saving costs and speeding up resolution of disputes are held up as good reasons pursuant to the overriding objective to have sequential exchange of evidence. Extreme care should be exercised when faced with such requests.

7.10   Practice Direction 49 (1 November 1996) was a real advance and set out a detailed scheme for the conduct of clinical negligence litigation. However, it applied only in the High Court and generally only in London.[1] One of the first two pre-action protocols promulgated in early 1999 governed clinical negligence claims and yet when the Civil Procedure Rules ('CPR') were introduced on 26 April 1999 they made no special provision for the subject, apart from recognising the pre-action protocol.

1   It was adopted in some registries but by no means nationally.

7.11   At the time of writing we await the issue of the Queen's Bench Masters Practice direction[1] for clinical negligence cases which, although widely circulated in draft form, remains as yet unincorporated into the new civil justice procedural code. Thus, there is less acknowledgement of clinical negligence in the litigation rules than before 26 April 1999.

1   See Appendix A.

7.12   The CPR, which are intended to be self contained and a break with the past, are only just beginning to be interpreted and applied by the appellate courts to individual cases. Thus far, district judges who are far from consistent in their views of the rules have made the majority of decisions on interpretation. The practitioner needs to be particularly vigilant at present as new practices are developing for applying the general Civil Procedure Rules to clinical negligence litigation.

7.13   This problem may not be resolved as quickly as in other areas of litigation given the very small number of clinical negligence cases which actually reach trial. Indeed, this is a field in which methods of case preparation developed by a practitioner and repeated time after time may not be tested for their efficacy at trial for a considerable period or at all. Indeed, some practitioners regard an absence of trials as a virtue rather than a weakness.

7.14   The word 'preparation' is used deliberately, as the term 'case management' is capable of bearing several different meanings depending on who is using it. The procedural judge's view is likely to be quite different from the practitioner running high-volume low value cases on a computerised system. This in turn will involve a different view from the neuro-lawyer handling a much smaller number of high value cases. The salesman selling a software system will have yet another view of the meaning of case management. The purpose of this chapter is to examine the organisation of initial case preparation from a clinical negligence claimant solicitor's point of view. Lord Woolf's views, as expressed this time in his Interim Report on Access to Civil Justice in June 1995 were:[1]

'Without effective judicial control, however, the adversarial process is likely to encourage an adversarial culture and to degenerate into an environment in which the litigation process is too often seen as a battlefield where no rules apply. In this environment, questions of expense, delay, compromise and fairness may have only low priority. The consequence is that expense is often excessive, disproportionate and unpredictable; and delay is frequently unreasonable.'

'This situation arises precisely because the conduct, pace and extent of litigation are left almost completely to the parties. There is no effective control of their worst excesses. Indeed, the complexity of the present rules facilitates the use of adversarial tactics and is considered by many to require it. As Lord Williams, a former Chairman of the Bar Council, said in responding to the announcement of this Inquiry, the process of law has moved from being 'servant to master, due to cost, length and uncertainty.'

1   Chapter 3. The Problems and Their Causes.

7.15   Later,[1] he explained judicial case management as follows:

'The specific objectives of case management, as I see it, are:
- achieving an early settlement of the case or issues in the case where this is practical;
- the diversion of cases to alternative methods for the resolution of the dispute where this is likely to be beneficial;
- the encouragement of a spirit of co-operation between the parties and the avoidance of unnecessary combativeness which is productive of unnecessary additional expense and delay;
- the identification and reduction of issues as a basis for appropriate case preparation; and
- when settlement cannot be achieved by negotiation, progressing cases to trial as speedily and at as little cost as is appropriate.'

1   Chapter 7. The Need for Case Management by the Courts.

7.16   Claimants' solicitors have an early and valuable opportunity to influence the setting of the case management agenda in a case. In doing so we must have regard to the evils against which the Civil Procedure Rules have been drawn so that we can better pray in aid the over-riding objective in support of our strategies.

7.17–7.19   It is worth observing that since Lord Woolf expressed these views the business of clinical negligence litigation has been placed in the hands of a comparatively small number of specialist practitioners on both sides. The National Health Service Litigation Authority ('NHSLA') panel is small and rumoured to be about to contract further. High Street generalists have less to do with clinical negligence claimant work than ever before. The environment has already changed.

WHAT ARE THE ADDED DIFFICULTIES IN CLINICAL NEGLIGENCE CASES?

7.20   Having acknowledged that non-clinical negligence techniques have much to offer, the purpose of this section of the chapter is to identify and consider the differences. Generally, there are four factors.

Liability

7.21 The following render the prediction of the ultimate liability prospects difficult and uncertain:

- Less than optimal standards of care may escape liability under the test in Bolam[1] (as modified by Bolitho[2]).
- Determining whether a breach of duty occurred is dependent on expert evidence.
- Alleged breaches of duty occur against a background of pre-existing illness, disease or other processes which inherently carry varying risks of poor outcome. The existence of causation of harm frequently becomes an issue as compared to a road or factory accident which injures a previously healthy individual.
- Determining causation generally also requires expert evidence.
- The claimant is frequently unaware of the facts on which the resolution of the liability issue will turn.
- The claimant and solicitor may be unaware of the significance of facts which they can ascertain.

1 *Bolam v Friern Hospital Management Committee* [1957] 2 All ER 118.
2 *Bolitho v City and Hackney Health Authority* [1998] AC 232.

Limitation

7.22 The likely resolution of a limitation issue is particularly difficult to predict in clinical negligence actions.[1] The question of date of knowledge is frequently problematic. It arises more often than in other trauma cases. The lengthy work-up time of a clinical negligence claim compounds the problem of late instructions. A significant number of patients affected by poor outcome fail to come forward until a considerable time has elapsed since the untoward outcome. They may have:

(a) preferred to wait to see if a recovery would ensue rather than seek legal advice;
(b) been reluctant to bring a claim against the medical profession;
(c) failed to appreciate the implication of a pattern of injury into which they had no insight;
(d) failed to recognise the outcome as untoward.

1 Qualitatively, it can seem that clinical negligence claimants receive tougher treatment in the Court of Appeal where limitation is being considered than in other personal injury cases.

Proof

7.23 Proving the essential elements of liability is rendered more difficult as:

- The legal test of breach of duty in Bolam assumes the existence of ascertainable bodies of professional opinion.
- Expert evidence is frequently of a highly technical nature and difficult to verify.
- Expert evidence on breach of duty and causation issues is expensive to obtain.
- Leading experts in some fields are so inundated with medico-legal work that they have waiting lists of 12 months or more.

Quantum

7.24–7.26 The main problems are that:

- Clinical negligence can result in novel patterns of injury which, through lack of prior experience of such patterns, are difficult to quantify.
- The case law on quantum of general damages for pain suffering and loss of amenity is much more limited in clinical negligence than other traumatically caused injuries.
- Iatrogenically caused injuries are often superimposed on existing disabilities or injuries complicating the process of valuation.

THE CONTINUED IMPETUS FOR CHANGE – A YEAR 2000 PERSPECTIVE

7.27 As recently as May 1997 Iain Goldrein QC and Margaret De Haas QC identified:

> 'the contemporary problem of the creation of enormous quantities of paper, most of which is subsequently screened out with Counsel's Advice on Evidence after setting down for trial and more particularly, with the Skeleton Argument. Such screening out connotes waste'.[1]

1 Medical Negligence: Cost Effective Case Management' (1997) Butterworths, p xi

7.28 The solution proposed was a radical departure from traditional case analysis. It consisted of identifying the requirements of the trial judge and then working backwards along the litigation highway to deduce what should happen when the client came through the door of the solicitor's office for the first time.

7.29 The major catalysts for adopting such a new approach to case preparation were:

- The increasing emphasis on issue-based litigation.
- The threats posed by funding changes including the withdrawal of legal aid.

7.30 Since then change has continued apace. The most significant further developments in clinical negligence have been:

- The introduction of objective cost/benefit criteria for the grant and extension of legal aid and new litigation funding.
- The introduction of the clinical negligence pre-action protocol.
- The making of early Part 36 offers to settle payments into court by defendants.
- The advent of the claimant's ability to make a Part 36 offer.
- The creation of an obligation on the defence fully to plead their case.
- The court's increased powers of judicial case management and, particularly, control of expert evidence, sometimes against the views of specialist practitioners.

- The state's imposition of a monopoly prescribing which solicitors are permitted to take on publicly funded clinical negligence claims.
- The introduction of the CPR without a specialist practice direction to replace PD 49.
- The reduction in the number of defence firms.

7.31 These changes are in the process of altering the dynamics of clinical negligence litigation. Various reforms have succeeded in changing the status quo. However, the system has yet to settle into its new state. In terms of the exercise of judicial case management powers, individual judges' decisions in the same court centre can be hard to reconcile let alone variations in regional practice. Similarly, although the NHSLA can be felt influencing the tactics of the greatly reduced panel of defence firms, differences between individual defence practitioners within firms remain large. Funding and panel changes have occurred quite outside the CPR. The target identified by Lord Woolf is moving so much that it is difficult to assess how much benefit the rule changes are bringing.

7.32 Prior to the CPR reforms, claimant practitioners could litigate towards trial in the knowledge that a settlement might incidentally result along the way. Indeed, some of the most successful and respected litigation firms worked on the basis that pressing to trial as quickly as possible was the most effective way of forcing the defence to capitulate. All too often some defendants made little or no apparent effort to work up a case until the claimant demonstrated that he had both the ability and inclination to litigate it to a conclusion. Others would seek as much information as possible from a claimant and then appear to fail to do anything at all with it. It was not unknown to arrive at court against a defendant with liability admitted and no money in court! More proactive defendants would complain that cases could not settle because claimants failed to quantify them soon enough or at all.

7.33 Wherever the truth of the debate once lay, the litigation landscape has changed dramatically. Claimants whose cases are of doubtful merit will lose their legal aid certificate much sooner than before, assuming that they manage to obtain one in the first place. New public funding cost benefit requirements supplement a strengthened merits test. These are applied by Legal Aid Area Committees/ panels selected so that specialists decide cases within their own sphere of expertise. Specialist solicitors who in turn instruct only specialist counsel increasingly conduct claimant clinical negligence litigation. Their combined skills of expert selection are more discerning while the pool of knowledgeable experts has grown due to more training. As before, most cases still settle before trial. The difference is that fewer cases are being ignored by some defence lawyers and their clients in the hope that many will simply go away of their own accord. Defendants are becoming interventionist. Early payments-in are being made in major cases long before either side has been able to precisely value the claim. More is becoming known at a much earlier stage about the case on both sides through the pre-action protocol and the requirement for a fully pleaded defence.

7.34 Finally, to win at court is no longer a guarantee of sufficient costs recovery to retrospectively validate the approach to litigation taken to achieve the result. The emphasis on issues, the ability to make Part 36 offers in relation to individual issues, percentage costs orders and the threat of proportionality can hang over what would, until recently, have been deemed a clear victory at trial. In the absence of individual experience and appellate guidance as to the application of the new costs rules practitioners can be forgiven for being uncertain and concerned as to whether their litigation tactics will result in full costs recovery.

7.35 Against this background, case management techniques have to be re-examined if practitioners are to remain as effective as possible. As well as the experience and willingness to litigate to trial lawyers must have a preparedness to make and respond to Part 36 offers in a way that was unknown a few years ago. A pragmatic approach is needed to survive in the modern litigation landscape. Working backwards from the skeleton argument may not offer much protection against an early global sum offer to settle.

7.36–7.39 At the same time, the issue of early case selection has become more important. Traditionally, many clients chose solicitors on the basis of little more than convenience of location. The public traditionally assumed that solicitors who agreed to take on cases possessed the necessary competence to handle them effectively. The reality was too often rather different. Now, with exclusivity under community legal service franchising, increasing numbers of new claimant enquiries are going to a small panel of specialists. The available time of the experienced panel cannot stretch to investigating every possible potential claim. If deserving cases are to be progressed, systems for filtering out the remainder need to be strengthened as levels of enquiries rise. At the same time, such specialists should be able to demonstrate to case management judges that the litigation they run is already well managed. The aim must be to persuade procedural judges that cases run by specialists are best guided with a gentle touch rather than wholesale judicial intervention. In this way, cases will be run by lawyers whose experience comes from handling them regularly and who are alive to the nuances which can make all the difference in achieving a result for their client. With respect to the case management judge, the clinical negligence specialist knows more about what is needed to prepare for trial successfully than a district judge whose time is spent mainly dealing with family and other civil work.

RESOURCES

7.40 Some years ago the author had occasion to talk in detail with a man whose lawyers had just successfully concluded a claim for damages for cerebral palsy for his child. The case, arising from birth trauma, had run for several years and had been particularly demanding of the family in terms of the strain of litigation. By the end of the case the father, a successful intelligent businessman, had a first-hand insight into the workings of the legal system. He was pleased with the result, which was in its day substantial. He had been on the receiving end of 'client care' for an extended period and had closely followed the uncertainties of the litigation process. He was asked what he made of the legal system that he and his family had been through. He was well placed to comment on our compensation system. His reply was unexpected and worth recalling. He said simply that the experience had taught him that lawyers take on too many cases to deal with them as well as they otherwise might.

7.41   Case management needs to start before the client presents to the solicitor. Effective case handling requires a much broader approach than planning a piece of litigation already in hand.

Experience

7.42   The infrastructure to promote effective case management must be in place before the case presents to the lawyer. The majority of clients assume the existence of appropriate resources. In the author's experience few clients question the resources available when they ask if a particular lawyer or firm will act for them. In many respects that is a pity. Clients are entitled to expect that a properly resourced and experienced lawyer will handle their case. The ability to 'fly by the seat of ones pants' was once regarded by some lawyers as praiseworthy. In the narrow specialty of clinical negligence where the opponent will be from one of a handful of specialist defence firms, it is a recipe for disaster. It is assumed throughout therefore that the conducting lawyer has sufficient relevant experience to deal with the case proficiently. If not, he should not take it on. It is instructive to take over files from non-specialist lawyers and read the correspondence they have had with experienced defence firms. Presumably, working on the assumption that 'if you do not ask you will not get', preliminary experts' opinions on liability issues have been seen to disclose unilaterally without specific instructions for no other reason than that the defence lawyer asked for it with an air of authority!

Staff

7.43   A competent clinical negligence lawyer can run cases effectively with no more than good secretarial support and there are a number of such individuals who do so achieving good results. However, there is no doubt that cost effectiveness is more readily achieved through team working. The difficult aspects of clinical negligence work can be as demanding as any other specialist area of law. In addition, they can have an emotional dimension which some legal subjects do not carry. Conversely, some aspects of the work are utterly routine and tedious and should be delegated to junior support staff. Success in practice depends on getting the balance of delegation right.

7.44   A senior lawyer will benefit from the support of a more junior colleague working alongside on the same case. The junior will certainly gain in experience and confidence more quickly than if the traditional system of being thrown in the deep end and left to sink or swim is employed. It is also self evidently preferable from the client's point of view although this has not stoppedthe short-sighted adopting the diving pool method of training in many law firms. There is another time honoured abuse of training which is to say, 'Here is a large file you have never seen before. Please go away and come back having prepared the list of documents for service.' This is equally unlikely to advance the case in an effective manner or the reliance either senior or junior can learn to place on each other. The commitment to training by the senior must be real and not mere lip service. It must involve close co-operation. The results if this is properly done are highly rewarding to all concerned.

7.45   Good secretarial support is also essential. Economies in this area are likely to prove false. Beyond the basics of organisation and accuracy, clients are likely to have a good deal of telephone contact with secretarial support staff who require patience and understanding in equal good measures. Clients have few tangible indicators of the skill of a lawyer. Inaccuracy in paperwork will ring alarm bells straight away.

7.46   Medical support staff are becoming increasingly common in specialised teams such that many have come to regard such colleagues as indispensable. Usually nurses, although sometimes doctors or scientists, cannot simply remove delegable work from the lawyers but can provide a completely fresh insight into the case work in hand. While medical record sorting, examination and reporting can be done by freelance nurses this is no substitute for the ability to discuss the minutiae of nursing or midwifery practice with a colleague in house. Further, many cases benefit from a medical support worker who may draw out facts from the client's recollection not touched on by the lawyer. For example, a former midwife may not only be better able to explain the mechanics of a difficult delivery to a client than the lawyer can, but also is better placed (without leading) to jog a client's memory as to the precise sequence of events in the delivery room. In addition, medical support staff can provide general background briefing material on particular aspects of anatomy, physiology and medical and surgical practice supported by extracts from the literature. Two heads are also frequently better than one when it comes to deciphering and making sense of obscure/badly written medical notes.

Materials – Library

7.47   A basic set of books on anatomy, physiology and the more common diseases and conditions is essential. This is usefully supplemented by undergraduate and/ or postgraduate texts on the various medical and surgical specialties. Medical books, presumably due to economies of scale in publication, are generally cheaper than the specialised legal texts and represent good value to the specialist lawyer.

7.48   On the basics of anatomy and body system function, the colour works available to large scale are at least to me, far easier to follow than traditional fine line drawings. With a modest number of texts on site it ought to be possible, before first interview, to quickly review:

(a)   the relevant anatomy and/physiology;
(b)   a description of the condition for which health care provision was required;
(c)   an outline of the normal range of health care interventions in such circumstances;
(d)   the known inherent risks of such interventions.

7.49   This assists meaningful instruction taking enormously. If the statement taker does not know that a particular physical examination should to be conducted with the arms raised, it is unlikely that the client's statement will say that the arms were never raised throughout the clinical consultation.

7.50   On the legal side, clinical negligence law is remarkably straightforward with only a handful of key decided cases. The law of limitation is rather more complex and often requires more frequent recourse to various law reports. Beyond that, a number of specialist publications contain a steady stream of reported clinical negligence cases many of which seem to be examples of the application of settled principles, rather than ground breaking in their own right. However, what such specialist reports do provide are detailed and technical analyses of the resolution of disputes of fact in the light of expert opinion. As such, they are highly instructive if one has a case concerned with similar issues both as to the relevant issues to be addressed and the persuasiveness or otherwise of the conflicting expert opinions brought before the court. Of course the next case concerned with the same aspect of health care provision to come before a court will be decided on the basis of the later evidence adduced. The previous decision as to the facts does not stand as precedent, a fact about which the inexperienced expert may sometimes need reminding. A number of senior orthopaedic surgeons seemed to think for a long while that *Hotson*[1] decided that delay in diagnosis of femoral neck fracture was never causative of avascular necrosis.

1   *Hotson v East Berkshire Health Authority* [1987] 2 All ER 909.

7.51   The advent of searchable CD-ROM's and on-line databases greatly aids the task of searching not so much for law as for examples of similar facts and injuries.

7.52   Next, as time passes, the practitioner will accumulate an archive of past cases, each containing expert opinion, and literature extracts on the issues in that case. A number of common issues arise regularly and a system to facilitate recalling earlier case details, expert opinion and literature should be devised. Such a system should be used by and contributed to by the whole of the team. This will help deliver to the client a service based not on one lawyer's experience, however extensive, but the combined benefit of the whole team.

Systems

7.53   Litigation depends on accurately recording future dates and deadlines and allocating time to prepare to be ready to act before such dates arrive. The traditional tools were the desk diary and bring forward system, which are increasingly under pressure from the microchip. In the realm of bulk fast track litigation, the computer has become essential if any reasonable margins are to be achieved. Huge caseloads of low value claims can only be effectively managed with IT assistance. Clinical negligence litigation, while certainly capable of benefiting from direct IT support can still, for the present, be managed without computer case management software. This will probably change on two separate counts. First, as the civil justice reforms become established they may well be used more extensively to control lawyers' costs. Second, if public funding is withdrawn from clinical negligence in favour of conditional fee arrangements margins will be under threat as never before. Now is certainly a good time to be evaluating and implementing computer support in advance of such threats materialising. Beware, however, the system which requires the chosen method of working to be turned on its head simply to fit in with the software. Systems should help lawyers and not vice versa. The implementation of a computer case management system involves inordinate effort and is very time-consuming. Be clear how the chosen system will improve the practice of the law not only through reporting options but also on a case-by-case basis. Experience of case preparation with computers shows that the promised gains are rarely as great as expected while the investment in lawyer time and cost is frequently beyond all prior expectations.

7.54–7.59 Having now in place the resources with which to manage cases it is essential to directly address the issue of case selection. Cases which should never have been started are the most difficult of all to manage. The solution is to invest time in making sure that few such cases get into the case load.

INITIAL SCREENING

7.60 The scope of an action for damages for clinical negligence is poorly understood by the wider public. An office conducting such work will attract many enquiries which are beyond the reach of legal remedy. Such would-be clients may harbour dissatisfaction about:

> (a) appallingly poor health care which produced no appreciable harm (the near miss scenario);
> (b) failures of communication which did not cause compensatable damage;
> (c) lack of bedside manners ('he was so rude');
> (d) their own inability to deal with the healthcare system;
> (e) current medical problems; or
> (f) advice received from previous lawyers.

7.61 In addition, occasionally there will be an enquiry from an individual who has been in a state of constant dispute with several parts of the NHS and legal system for several years. They will be looking for their umpteenth lawyer to resolve what all others have so far spectacularly failed to do, despite having used their very best endeavours.

7.62 In practical terms, it may be impossible through legal means to help many people who fall into one or more of these categories. Experienced clinical negligence lawyers are in short supply. Those who are in practice must put in place reliable preliminary screening procedures to avoid devoting costly and scant resources to problems outside their special area of expertise.

7.63 However, in attempting to do so difficulties can arise due a number of factors:

- The would-be client may be too upset, nervous, confused or embarrassed to be able to give a coherent account of the problem.
- A healthcare provider may have been economical with the truth.
- Some clients will have received poor advice from previous lawyers and/or experts.
- The client may excite in the lawyer, consciously or otherwise, some prejudice or stereo-typing by the manner in which they present with their account.
- The nature of the problem may be so complex or imperfectly understood (whether by teller or listener) as to defy ready comprehension.

7.64 The challenge is to avoid declining help to those genuinely in need of legal advice without wasting large blocks of time and other resources on problems which lie outside the narrow band in which the law will intervene. Given the near state monopoly imposed by legal aid exclusivity arrangements, lawyers on the specialist panels owe at least a moral duty to the public to allocate their resources fairly. The creation of panels of preferred solicitors by insurers for before, as well as after, the event products leads to a similar conclusion. However, few law firms have the capacity, whether of staff, finance or management, to keep taking on all cases that present. The need for self-restraint by lawyers in not taking on too much work has never been as important as now. Ironically, the ethical problems which have beset health care providers on account of rationing may have arrived in the clinical negligence legal services market where the solicitor is in the front line. In a free market, case selection so stringent as to amount to cherry-picking may be acceptable. In an effective monopoly without a cab rank system the onus should be on the lawyer to justify turning a case away.

7.65   Enquiries may come from a would-be client direct in writing, by telephone, from a speculative personal visit to reception without an appointment or, these days, from the internet. Yet other enquiries may come via another professional or from a referrer or agent. Whichever the case, the final decision whether to offer legal advice on the problem should be made by legal staff rather than by any other person however well qualified in their field. Medical workers, whether doctors or nurses, offer invaluable support to lawyers. The ultimate decision, however, should be left to legal personnel. If fact gathering is devolved to support staff they must be properly trained, both to gather all relevant information and to recognise when they are out of their depth.

7.66   Unless the enquiry has come through an agency with appropriate experience to gather all appropriate facts and conduct its own screening, such as an experienced CHC officer or AVMA, the true nature of the enquiry is frequently best highlighted by a direct telephone conversation with the person seeking advice. Those whose problems can best be resolved through some other agency, for example, the CAB, CHC, AVMA, GP, complaints procedure, or elected political representative should be appropriately referred immediately. Only those cases which require legal redress should be further considered. That should be done, unless wholly exceptional circumstances exist, by a meeting with the potential client.

7.67   Generally this meeting should be as soon as reasonably possible. In certain circumstances it may be appropriate to delay an appointment because:

• The patient is acutely ill and still in hospital.
• The patient has just died and the relatives are in a state of shock.

7.68   Even in these situations there may be an urgent need to bring legal advice to bear. In the former situation it may be appropriate to proof a lucid, though dying individual. In the latter case, if there is to be, or should be, an inquest it is important to move quickly and offer advice on dealing with the coroner and consider whether a further post mortem should be carried out. Too many cases miss having an inquest because relevant facts were not known to the coroner immediately after the death.

7.69   The lawyer needs to balance the conflicting risks of causing unnecessary additional anxiety to the gravely ill or recently bereaved against the limited circumstances in which speed is important to capture some evidence or seize some opportunity which may not endure. The prospect of a lawyer sitting at a hospital bedside taking instructions in muted tones from a gravely ill patient while clinicians and other patients drift in and out of hearing requires clear justification.

7.70 The lawyer should take care, even once a potential case has passed through preliminary screening, not to agree to act until first meeting the potential client. The most cursory examination of papers in the would-be client's possession and/ or detailed face-to-face discussion with them at interview may reveal insuperable problems with the case or reasons why the lawyer should not act. Many practitioners have rued the day they agreed by telephone to take a transfer of an existing legal aid certificate without first seeing the client and at least some of the papers. Conversely, many experienced specialists will have achieved notable successes on cases regarded by previous lawyers as being without merit. Careful selection is the key once more on transfers as well as new enquiries. Lawyers should:

- Avoid getting embroiled in a mire of unattainable expectation.
- Not turn away deserving cases which at face value appear flawed due to previous poor work up.
- Not take on cases for which the law is never likely to provide a remedy.
- Quickly identify those cases which require legal advice.
- Avoid delay which may compound the difficulties already suffered by the client.

7.71 Case selection is so important that it should be done at as high a level as possible. Just as a decision to turn away a case should not be made by inexperienced staff, so initial interviews should preferably be conducted by experienced specialist lawyers. It may be useful for a senior practitioner to meet the would be client with a more junior member of the team. Too much delegation at this stage will bring problems later. Conversely early parallel involvement by a junior lawyer will bring benefits in the form of confidence both for the client and lawyers.

7.72–7.79 Case selection is an acquired skill and benefits from involvement of senior fee earners. More junior fee earners need exposure to the process to develop their own skills.

THE FIRST INTERVIEW

7.80 The first interview is the most important single meeting in the life of a case.

7.81 Many lawyers and their staff routinely refer to a first interview as a 'new client' meeting or similar and for convenience this chapter will also do so. Strictly though, the meeting is with a potential new client and the decision to agree to accept instructions and act should not generally be made until some time after the start of the first interview. For their part, an increasing number of clients wish to meet their prospective lawyer and discuss finance before giving their instructions to act. Obviously in the case of young children the interview will be with parents or sometimes one parent. If the latter, why isn't the other there if available - are they at one about the possibility of legal action? Such problems do not become apparent by telephone.

7.82   Initial screening will already have taken place and from the preliminary enquiry and questions asked on that screening, a good deal should already be known about the nature of the health care delivery problem which has given rise to the request for legal help. In addition the new client will have been asked to send in any documents he holds in advance of the meeting, including items such as complaint correspondence, any patient held records and any other records if already obtained by the client. This permits pre-interview reading and consideration of the anatomical and physiological background to the health care delivery issue. The first technical challenge for the lawyer is generally obtaining a sufficient understanding of the factual matrix to enable a view to be taken of the possibilities which arise. However, before that the new client needs to be given an opportunity to express, in his own terms, the basis of his concerns and aspirations for a resolution. Early closed questioning to clarify details of what is already known of the problem can set the interview off to a bad start. Much better to rely on an open style along the lines of, 'How can I help' or, 'Tell me what has happened' with appropriate eye contact and other empathetic body language. The frequent response, 'Where shall I start?' is best met with, 'at the beginning' followed by as long a period of listening on the part of the lawyer as is required to understand not only the client's story but their state of mind and motivation. Occasional light touches can help steer the story away from side alleys although it is noteworthy if the client regards side issues as significant. As the story is winding down and if it has not already emerged, the gentle 'and how are you now?' will often elicit new information. A supplemental, 'and what do the doctors say will happen to you after this' can also be revealing.

7.83   Some lawyers prefer to make brief notes as aide memoirs as the story is told rather than make a full note and thereby risk the client feeling they are not getting personal contact. These can then be used to ask specific detailed questions, to ensure the facts have been explored as fully as possible. Having bottomed the story as known to the client the question, 'before I start talking about the law what would you personally like to see done about all this?' may add insight into the client's instinctive wishes.

7.84   Beware the over-protective relative or accompanying companion who insists, frequently from the outset, on giving their views of the facts and proper remedy by helping with every answer, often to the complete exclusion of the client. In a few cases the client has such significant communication problems that help from a companion is required. Generally though, the effort taken to obtain the history direct from the client is energy well spent. The lawyer should be looking to form preliminary though detailed impressions as to the client's:

(a) pre-injury condition and level of function;
(b) insight into what has happened to them;
(c) condition and prognosis;
(d) own wishes and expectations;
(e) ability to give evidence effectively.

7.85   It is essential that the lawyer should understand the client's wishes and expectations before agreeing to act. It is worth fathoming any already held expectations before moving on to advise as to which of the following options are open to the client:

(a) return to same personnel at healthcare provider to discuss concerns;
(b) see another clinician – perhaps either the GP or second opinion;
(c) if problem is seemingly down to breakdown of trust with own GP – procedure to change GP;
(d) enlist assistance from Community Health Council;
(e) invoke NHS complaints mechanisms;
(f) refer to General Medical Council or similar[1] for possible action;
(g) seek to publicise the problem through the media;
(h) alternative dispute resolution;
(i) choosing to do nothing or;
(j) claim for compensation.

1 For example, GDC, UKCC.

7.86 On one view, the clients who come to see you are a self-selected group who, by their presence, evince a preparedness to contemplate litigation. Many come wanting to hear only the legal option explained. Nevertheless, do not let the opportunity pass without considering all available options. Having done so, the litigation option can be considered in detail. One by-product of this discussion will be to inform the client in a way which should help shape their expectations of the process under consideration so as to bring such expectations into line with cold legal reality.

7.87 When considering litigation it seems to me essential to explain:

• That the possibility of compensation depends on invoking a fault based system.
• That litigation has a very narrow goal – the recovery of money.
• That the process must halt if sufficient money is offered to satisfy the monetary claim.
• The burden of proof.
• The standard of proof.
• The means of proof.
• The Bolam test as modified by Bolitho.
• The need to establish causation.
• That damages are compensatory.
• The broad bracket within which damages might lie, if the case could be won.
• Limitation.
• Case duration and, last but by no means least.
• Funding.

7.88 There was a time when eligibility for legal aid might have been the first and sometimes only question to be addressed when considering taking on a new case. Equally the 'strength' of a case of wholly uncertain merits might be gauged by putting in an application for legal aid and awaiting the response. Those days are long gone and rightly so – sealed finally with the advent of the Legal Aid Board three-stage approach to investigative work before a certificate will be amended to permit proceedings to issue.[1] Today, and more importantly looking to the future, the availability of public funding is but one consideration to be factored into the advice to be given to a client as to whether they should further consider litigation. The topic of funding has been dealt with in detail in Chapter 4 and this chapter will not go over the same ground. Suffice to say that identifying funding options which the client can afford has become firmly part of the lawyers remit. Which brings back the question of whether to offer to take the case on after meeting with the potential client.

1   This has now been further modified still by Legal Services Commission Funding Code requirements.

7.89   The decision whether to offer to act will generally be made during this first interview. A much better assessment will by then be possible of the prospects of the case as well as the presence (or absence) of complicating factors which might mitigate against being reasonably able to expect to satisfy the client's informed expectations.

7.90   This should be coupled with an explanation of the relevant funding options. Consider in advance how far to take matters if your firm's risk assessment procedures require you to refer an intention to offer a pre-conditional fee work-up to another for approval. In turn, the client will decide either then or later to instruct you or not. A great deal of time has already been expended up to this point. If the client decides not to instruct you then it is wasted. However, that cost is significantly less than it would be in the long run if less thorough screening procedures were employed.

7.91   If a significant part of the conduct of the matter is to be delegated to a more junior lawyer he should be present throughout the interview. It may be helpful to call in a medical support colleague for part of the meeting but beware of overwhelming the client by weight of numbers of participants from the firm.

7.92   The process is likely to take two hours or so, sometimes up to three in cases involving injuries of utmost severity or twins. Ensure sufficient time is available in the diary to avoid spoiling the careful build up by having to rush at the end. Assuming that both the lawyer and the client wish to proceed, there remains only the inevitable paperwork. Skimping at this stage is also a false economy in the long run. Wherever possible this should not be postponed to another day. The case will not be as fresh in the mind as it is now either later the same day or, more likely, in a few days time. Prepare:

• The client's first proof of evidence, paying particular regard to getting on paper their detailed account of the events said to give rise to a breach of duty. The account will never be as detailed or fresh if retold days or weeks later, particularly after it has all been explained once before. Sending the client away to 'write it all out' is no substitute for the technical skills lawyers develop as statement takers. Dictating the initial statement in the client's presence remains the best check that the client's view of the case has been properly understood. In some cases a client's recollection may later change after seeing medical records. In most cases though it is important to establish at the outset how much, if anything, the client can remember. As public funding and insurance product merits testing procedures become more refined, a good initial statement is often essential to secure finance. If it is thought that the effort at this stage is wasted and unpaid try running an appeal against refusal of funding and see how long that takes. Although this is intended as a preliminary statement, there may be cases in which the client will be assisted by later showing that their original recollection was consistent with later evidence or that they recalled certain matters before disclosure of records and receipt of expert opinion. Although it will probably not be disclosed in this form remember that it might be and so exclude material which is irrelevant to the case. Use file notes for extraneous reminders – not the client's proof. Finally, bear in mind that the statement may have to be used in evidence if something subsequently happens to the client which prevents them from giving evidence.

- A case plan setting out briefly in summary a view of the next six to nine months work.
- A list of the records which must be obtained to complete the detailed investigation. Identify where relevant imaging investigations are likely to be held.
- The first summary of the case setting out briefly.
  - The facts.
  - The suspected breach of duty.
  - The anticipated consequences thereof.
  - The heads of damage which will be claimed.
- The funding application documentation (if required).
- Diary entries for the limitation expiry date provisionally identified from the client's instructions.

7.93–7.99   Part of this documentation may conveniently and properly be delegated to a junior colleague provided they are clear on the conclusions and plan reached. As soon as possible afterwards provide the client with:

- All requisite client care information.
- A copy of the proof for signature and return.
- A copy of the case plan either as already signed at first interview or for signature and return.
- Instructions on preserving/sending to you relevant documents such as diaries, correspondence and so on.
- Instructions on obtaining/keeping records of special damages.

DETAILED INVESTIGATION

7.100   The file is open and the client has signed the client care documentation. What next?

The Medical Records

7.101   Those certainly required for the purpose of the detailed investigation have already been identified. The Law Society protocol form should be used for all hospital NHS records. Stock letters will be required for GPs as well as private health care records. Remember that in private medicine the consultant will hold clinical notes while the hospital will keep the remainder of the records. Specify whether imaging investigations are or are not required. These may include CT, MRI and ultrasound as well as traditional x-rays. Hospitals frequently keep written reports on imaging investigations 'filed' in the x-ray packet. If in doubt, ask for a list of the imaging investigations held by the record keeper. Then select which films are required. If the case is about the standard of fixation of a femur do not inadvertently end up paying for pre-operative chest x-rays. Increasingly GP notes, or part of the record, are held on computer. Specify that any such computer held data is also required. Avoid double sided photocopies. Standardise everything to single side copying.

7.102   The potential for delay to creep in at this stage is great. Record collection is a tedious job and the temptation to put a couple of kilogrammes of copy notes aside until another day can be overwhelming. Ideally, there will be in-house medically trained staff to review, sort, paginate and analyse incoming notes. If not there a number of nurses who offer this service on a case-by-case basis. Whatever system adopted, the temptation can be to wait until all notes are in before beginning an examination of the material. The review of the material will thus take place after receipt of the last and slowest notes to arrive.

7.103   Better to carry out a preliminary review of each set on arrival.

• Have both clinical and nursing records been sent?
• Does the bundle contain correspondence and test results?
• Have imaging investigations and their associated reports been provided?
• Particularly in the case of GP notes, how far back does the material extend?
• Does the GP correspondence reveal treatment for the index condition at another unit not originally identified as relevant?
• Are cardiotocographs (where relevant) included? Are they all there?
• If CTGs are relevant are the copies well reproduced on continuous paper rather than cut A4?

7.104   Obvious deficiencies can be noted and appropriate steps taken for them to be remedied sooner rather than later. Thus when the eventual detailed review of the material begins the investigation will not have to halt while major omissions are made good.

7.105   If there are legibility problems with CTGs, specify that a further copy is required which should be professionally made at a specialist facility. The cost is justified having regard to how long an obstetric expert may spend trying to interpret a poor copy.

7.106   It is also good practice to check that the principal dates given by the client in instructions are accurate, so as to confirm that the correctness of the limitation expiry date originally identified. Some clients may be inaccurate by a year or more.

7.107   Once apparently complete, the various sets of records should be arranged in a logical order and paginated. From these prepare:

(a) a chronology of the principal events cross referenced to the pagination in the bundle;
(b) a short précis of past medical history;
(c) a detailed check-list identifying any remaining inadequacies in the completeness of disclosure from which further requests for disclosure can be made and against which receipt of outstanding material noted.

7.108   If the relevant anatomy, physiology, condition or treatment were not capable of being identified from the client's original instructions this is the first chance to carry out some medical research in the appropriate literature to gain an understanding of the clinical background to the events complained of.

7.109 In most cases it will then be necessary to go through the relevant part of the records with the client to see whether the client's recollection of events coincides with the records or can at least be reconciled with them. The result of that process can usefully be recorded in a short free-standing statement dictated as the client goes through the records. This is also an opportunity to begin to attribute names to the various personnel who played a part in the client's original account of events.

Witness Statements

7.110 At this stage importance should be attached to obtaining statements which have a bearing on liability (as opposed to quantum) issues. A good initial proof taken at first instructions, with a supplemental taken on going through the records, is frequently useful to forward to the expert.

7.111 The client's recollection is irrelevant in some cases and vital in others. The significance of such evidence may not be appreciated until after receipt of expert evidence. Be alive, however, to try to identify cases where factual witness evidence may be important. For example, if relatives visited the bedside and saw the patient's condition decline over a period when it is alleged medical staff did not, the relatives must be proofed at an early stage as to what they saw. Cases involving alleged failure by a GP to suspect and refer for meningitis may also turn on precisely what symptoms those people who saw the patient around the time of the medical consultations can recall. If the father was present throughout the delivery his recollection may be better than the mother's depending on the pain relief she was taking. Equally, after a Caesarean section the father may have seen the state of the neonate long before mother was well enough to visit the special care baby unit.

7.112 It is impossible to generalise as to which categories of case will turn on lay evidence. That said, look closely at omission cases, where failure to act is alleged. Here, lay observers may add to the sum total of knowledge available to an expert to draw informed conclusions. Look closely also at cases where there is a mismatch between the course of events described in the records and that described by the client or other witnesses. If it appears that lay evidence may add to the facts disclosed by the records or challenge them, ensure that you proof available witnesses before instructing the expert. It is no good complaining later to the funder who is looking at a negative medical report that it is based on incomplete facts.

7.113 The importance of medical records in clinical negligence litigation cannot be over-stressed. In the majority of cases the case notes will be an accurate, although sometimes incomplete, record of events. Expert opinions will be greatly influenced by them and trial judges will start from the premise that the records are more accurate than witnesses recollections. In a minority of cases the records will be inaccurate or in error. Here the absence of available lay evidence may condemn the claim to wrongful rejection. Given the implications for the client and the effort already expended on preliminary screening such a result is a disaster.

7.114   The author once acted for a client, as second solicitor, where it was alleged that an amniocentesis needle had negligently been allowed to penetrate the foetal brain causing major damage and lifelong disability. The claim was unconscionably old when it was taken over and would have been struck out long ago had one of the clients not been under a disability. Everything was in issue. Ultimately it was demonstrated that the injury was caused by a needle penetration. The outstanding issue was whether the stab was negligent or not. This turned on whether it was the first or second attempt to obtain a sample that produced the bloody tap. The client and her partner had observed the procedure. Had they been proofed at the outset, in simple terms, as to what they saw the issue could have been resolved. However, they were not asked to commit their account of events to paper for several years, by when their recollections were much less likely to be relied on by a judge, particularly as the significance of this simple observation was not appreciated until shortly before trial.

7.115   While one cannot literally expect the unexpected, the discipline of committing witness accounts to paper at an early stage is very much part of the clinical negligence lawyer's role.

7.116   Later, after positive expert opinion on liability is in hand, can the work-up begin on the lengthy quantum statements.

7.117   There is one final point on statements. It is not always necessary, or even desirable, to prepare before exchange of witness evidence, a single all encompassing consolidated document into which the contents of all earlier statements are subsumed. There may be tactical advantages in having the client's evidence presented in a series of statements taken sequentially over a period of time. The client's original state of knowledge, or lack of it, may be well demonstrated by an evolving series of proofs. The first statement will have been taken closer to the events complained of and so the client will not lose the advantage of being able to demonstrate the contemporary nature of that early account. In addition, why waste time reformatting witness evidence if you took the trouble to record it accurately in the first place?

Complaint Generated Documentation

7.118   Documentation coming into existence as a result of a complaint or adverse incident reporting system should be sought. It should then be presented (paginated and so on) with the same care as the master bundle of records. Indeed, it can usefully be kept as an appendix to the record bundle. It may contain important insights into the factual matrix that the defendant will rely on. If the complaint went to a hearing, a note of evidence may be invaluable material to cross-examine from later.

Expert Selection

7.119   Legal aid franchise and other quality assurance systems require that a degree of control is maintained over the experts who are instructed in cases. A desire to have any reasonable chance of winning renders this mandatory and the most important single aspect of case preparation after selection. A whole chapter could be devoted to this issue alone. In brief, in selecting experts to report on breach of duty issues look for someone:

- Who has extensive clinical experience in the relevant field.
- Whose relevant experience had been acquired by the time the events complained of occurred.
- Who was practising at an institution and in a post comparable to that occupied by the alleged tortfeasor.
- Who is still in clinical practice if possible.[1]
- Who has been exposed to the discipline of academic teaching alongside clinical practice.
- Who has experience of reporting as an expert in clinical negligence litigation.
- Who does not always report for one side or the other (not a 'hired gun').
- Who has actually given evidence as an expert witness in a personal injury or clinical negligence trial before.
- Who is recommended by an experienced solicitor or barrister contact or AVMA as a reliable and knowledgeable expert.
- Whose ability to report, deal with subsequent enquiries, conferences and meetings and present a list of available dates for trial fits within the overall time constraints of the matter in hand.
- Whose fee structure is acceptable to your properly advised client.

1 This may not be possible in very old cases, for example, on behalf of persons under a disability – such as 25-year old obstetric claims.

7.120 The requirements for causation experts are similar except that as scientific and technical knowledge acquired after the events complained of is also relevant the second and third of these requirements do not apply.

7.121 Bear in mind that experts can go off. Yesterday's favourite of the circuit can become short of supporters after a bad performance in the witness box. Recheck the standing of your experts from time to time.

Which Speciality Should be First?

7.122 There is no easy answer to this question.

- Sometimes a single expert can deal with all breach of duty and causation issues.[1]
- More frequently one expert will have to deal with breach and another with causation.[2]
- Some cases will cover more than one specialty in relation to breach of duty.[3]
- Others will require more than one causation expert.[4]

1 Orthopaedic surgeon sets long bone with inadequate reduction. Single expert can report on breach and consequences.
2 For example, GP misses malignant abdominal mass, oncologist needed to report on whether earlier diagnosis would have altered outcome in addition to GP to report on breach of duty.
3 For example, both health visitor and GP fail to refer infant for abnormal increase in head circumference hence late diagnosis of hydrocephalus made. GP and HV experts needed to report on breach of duty plus Neurosurgeon as to consequences of late surgical intervention.
4 What do the appearances of the cerebral scanning reveal as to the nature and aetiology of the alleged neo-natal brain injury? Neuro-radiologist required in addition to paediatric neurologist to explain significance of neo-natal clinical presentation, both in relation to causation.

7.123   The permutations are numerous. If there is a requirement for multiple experts on liability consider:

- Will a negative view from, for example, the sole breach of duty expert render irrelevant opinions from several causation experts?
- Does one of the experts provide specialist analysis of data which might assist others? For example the conclusions of a histopathologist on certain samples or a neuro-radiologist on imaging investigations may add to the sum of the knowledge of the case in a way which assists experts from other clinical specialties to reach conclusions with more certainty.
- The relative and overall waiting times for reports from the different specialties involved. If the obstetrician will take 15 months to report and the paediatric neurologist 18 months there is little justification in deferring instructing one until after the first has reported.
- On the other hand, if a GP expert can report in a few weeks on breach of duty it may be worth deferring sending instructions to the vascular surgeon or cardiologist on causation until after the GP has reported.
- Experience from similar cases and/or information from the literature may lead the lawyer to be relatively confident about one aspect of the case but have doubts about another. Consider starting with the weakest perceived link in the chain first.

The Initial Approach to Experts

7.124   It has long been regarded as poor practice in clinical negligence cases and a source of irritation to experts to despatch a set of papers cold to an expert without first ascertaining if they wish to accept instructions. There are several reasons, apart from etiquette, for this which should be obvious but as experts still complain that it happens they can be listed as follows. The expert:

- May not wish or have time to accept the instructions.
- May already have been approached by the other side.
- May perceive an actual or potential conflict of interest raised by the case.
- May not be able to act within the time constraints of the case.
- May regard the matter as falling outside of his sphere of expertise.

7.125   Good practice requires that an initial detailed letter of enquiry is first directed to the expert so that the expert can decide whether they can assist and if so on what basis. The letter of enquiry should accordingly identify:

- The parties.
- The institution or place at which the negligence is alleged to have occurred and the identity of the key personnel.
- In summary form, the facts on which expert opinion is sought.
- The issues on which the opinion is required.
- Any special time constraints inherent in the claim.

7.126   The lawyer will also wish to ask for the expert's:

- Confirmation that the matter falls within their expertise.
- Details of turn around time for reporting.
- Confirmation of ability to meet any unusual or onerous timetable.

- Basis of charging and other terms of business.
- View as to whether it will be desirable to examine the client for the purpose of preparing the report.

7.127 Only after receipt of confirmation of these matters should detailed instructions and supporting documentation be despatched.

The Instructions to Experts

7.128 The expert should be provided with:

- A detailed letter of instruction clearly identifying:
  - the facts on which the alleged cause of action is thought to arise.
  - the issues to be reported on (standard of care, causation and so on).
  - the relevant legal tests (unless the expert is personally known to the instructing solicitor to be aware of such matters) such as standard of proof, Bolam test, but for test, relevance of material contribution and so on.
  - whether the expert's opinion should be presented as advice or a report for disclosure.
  - a reminder to refer to and provide copies of literature to support conclusions reached.
  - a request for the report to contain or be accompanied by a short CV.
  - confirmation that terms of business previously supplied are accepted.
  - details of the time constraints currently applicable to the case (which may have changed since the original letter of enquiry).
- Bundle of paginated ordered records.
- Relevant imaging investigations.
- Statements of fact from client and any lay witnesses.
- A précis of past medical history and chronology of events prepared following receipt of the records.
- Confirmation as to how an appointment with the client should be arranged if it is required (that is, direct, via a named relative, through the solicitor's office and so on).
- It may also be helpful for the time being at least, to provide the expert with a note, by way of an aide memoire, as to the requirements of Part 35 CPR.

7.129–7.139 It is more difficult to determine whether to provide from the outset an expert with a report from another expert already obtained in the same case. Where the opinion of the first is on an aspect of the case separate and distinct from the issues to be considered by the second then my preference is to provide from the outset the latter expert with the report of the former. However, where the same or overlapping ground is covered then it may be preferable to allow the second expert to form his own view independent of the first before learning of the former's conclusions.

REVIEWING THE EXPERTS' OPINION

7.140 In an ideal world every expert's advice or report would:

- Accurately and correctly identify the factual matrix/matrices on which the opinion is based.
- Draw alternative conclusions where multiple possible factual matrices exist.

- Address each of the issues raised in the instructions.
- Draw attention to other matters within the expert's field not specifically raised by the instructions but relevant to the case.
- Demonstrate internal logic and consistency.
- Express conclusions with clarity.
- Convey the relative certainty with which conclusions are drawn.
- Support by reference to supplied literature extracts conclusions reached.
- Demonstrate that such conclusions were reached in the light of an awareness of the relevant legal framework (proof on balance of probabilities, test of breach of duty and so on).
- Stay within the expert's own sphere of expertise.
- Refrain from expressing value judgments on the client.
- Comply with the requirements of Part 35 CPR.

All too often the reality falls short of this.

7.141   The lawyer's role is to critically review the expert's advice/report. The above forms a convenient checklist against which to do so. Having done that the client should then be seen and the report gone through line-by-line.

7.142   Generally, it is better to see the client with the report rather than sending a copy by post. At interview the client should be given a copy of the document to follow as the lawyer reads it through. In this way the lawyer can explain the meaning and significance of terms of art and science so as to convey the full meaning and implications of the report. It is not sufficient to turn immediately to the conclusions without first exploring the route by which the expert arrives at them. The client is often best placed to detect factual errors in the report. These and other disagreements should be recorded in a supplemental proof dictated there and then or immediately afterwards from notes made at the meeting. A dispassionate examination of several pages of history and background can be very difficult for a client who feels aggrieved from the outset by advance sight of the final adverse conclusion. Of course there may be situations in which this process cannot be followed but these should be the exception rather than the rule. An important opportunity is lost if the report passes to the client by post without further ado.

7.143   In other fields of personal injury practice, particularly fast track, there may be strong economic arguments as to why medical reports should be sent to the client for comment and approval. In clinical negligence liability may depend on a report often written in language which may be obscure or technical. It is a false economy not to address this major piece of evidence face-to-face with the client.

7.144   Having reviewed the opinions of the expert the report can then be looked at to see how it relates and compares to any other expert opinions obtained in the case.

7.145   The outcome of these processes will normally indicate whether the obtaining of an alternative opinion is justified. While private fee paying clients are sometimes shown more latitude than others in this respect, shopping around for more favourable second opinions should be done on the basis of demonstrable shortcomings in the first advice report rather than bare disagreement to and objection with the former's unfavourable conclusions.

7.146 The analysis of the expert's opinion will often dictate what should happen next namely whether the case should:

(a) be considered further by the reporting expert either on paper or in conference;
(b) be abandoned without further work-up;
(c) be the subject of a second opinion and/or;
(d) be the subject of further fact gathering and/or;
(e) be the subject of further expert opinion from a different specialty and/or;
(f) proceed immediately to letter of claim or, if there are limitation problems, issue of proceedings and/or;
(g) go to counsel.

7.147 Individual solicitors should be aware of their own limitations and experience which will assist in determining whether and if so when to instruct counsel. If counsel (and particularly leading counsel) is going to be brought in at some stage then it is better to do so before issue of proceedings than afterwards. On the other hand the days have gone when it was considered mandatory for counsel to be instructed in every clinical negligence claim whether to plead or advise on evidence. Good case management demands that the instruction of counsel is a considered step rather than a reflex action.

7.148 Certainly an increasing number of experienced solicitors are pleading their own cases and holding conferences with experts to test and examine the nature and quality of their evidence and the merits of a case.

7.149 Following receipt of supportive expert opinion decisions need to be made which will bear on case management as it is practised by procedural judges.

CASE MANAGEMENT – PRE-ACTION PROTOCOL

7.150 The pre-action protocol for the resolution of clinical disputes ('PAP-CN'), prepared by the Clinical Disputes Forum, is presently one of only two pre-action protocols approved by the Head of Civil Justice and thereby recognised under the Civil Procedure Rules. Others are in the course of preparation.

7.151 Compliance with the protocol is required by PD – protocols with sanctions available against a defaulting party. Although there are many similarities between the personal injury and clinical negligence protocols there are more important differences. PAP-CN requires:

- A letter of claim to be sent to the healthcare provider/potential defendant 'as soon as practicable' after 'the patient/adviser decides there are grounds for a claim' following 'receipt and analysis of the records, and the receipt of any further advice (including from experts if necessary.)'

7.152 Thus, the letter of claim is required not when all possible investigations and a quantum work-up have been completed but as soon as practicable following the decision that there is a claim. The PAP-CN expressly envisages that the decision that there are grounds to claim may be based on records without any expert opinion. Of course, if the obtaining of quantum evidence has been delayed pending receipt of favourable liability opinions, then the period when the defence are considering the letter of claim is an ideal opportunity to put in hand outstanding work on quantum

7.153   PAP-CN provides the following further guidance:

- '... a template for the recommended contents of a letter of claim:
- The letter should contain a clear summary of the facts on which the claim is based, including the alleged adverse outcome, and the main allegations of negligence. It should also describe the patient's injuries, and present condition and prognosis. The financial loss incurred by the plaintiff should be outlined with an indication of the heads of damage to be claimed and the scale of the loss, unless this is impracticable.
- In more complex cases a chronology of the relevant events should be provided, particularly if the patient has been treated by a number of different healthcare providers.
- The letter of claim should refer to any relevant documents, including health records, and if possible enclose copies of any of those which will not already be in the potential defendant's possession, for example, any relevant general practitioner records if the plaintiff's claim is against a hospital.
- Sufficient information must be given to enable the healthcare provider defendant to commence investigations and to put an initial valuation on the claim.
- Letters of claim are not intended to have the same formal status as a pleading, nor should any sanctions necessarily apply if the letter of claim and any subsequent statement of claim in the proceedings differ.
- Proceedings should not be issued until after three months from the letter of claim, unless there is a limitation problem and/or the patient's position needs to be protected by early issue.
- The patient or their adviser may want to make an offer to settle the claim at this early stage by putting forward an amount of compensation which would be satisfactory (possibly including any costs incurred to date). If an offer to settle is made, generally this should be supported by a medical report which deals with the injuries, condition and prognosis, and by a schedule of loss and supporting documentation. The level of detail necessary will depend on the value of the claim. Medical reports may not be necessary where there is no significant continuing injury, and a detailed schedule may not be necessary in a low value case.' The Civil Procedure Rules which followed the PAP-CN now set out the requirements for making offers to settle.

7.154   The PAP-CN goes on to provide guidance on the response:

- 'a template for the suggested contents of the letter of response.
- The healthcare provider should acknowledge the letter of claim within 14 days of receipt and should identify who will be dealing with the matter.
- The healthcare provider should, within three months of the letter of claim, provide a reasoned answer:
  - (a) if the claim is admitted the healthcare provider should say so in clear terms;

(b)   if only part of the claim is admitted the healthcare provider should make clear which issues of breach of duty and/or causation are admitted and which are denied and why;

(c)   if it is intended that any admissions will be binding;

(d)   if the claim is denied, this should include specific comments on the allegations of negligence, and if a synopsis or chronology of relevant events has been provided and is disputed, the healthcare provider's version of those events;

(e)   where additional documents are relied on, e.g. an internal protocol, copies should be provided.

- If the patient has made an offer to settle, the healthcare provider should respond to that offer in the response letter, preferably with reasons. The provider may make its own offer to settle at this stage, either as a counter-offer to the patient's, or of its own accord, but should accompany any offer by any supporting medical evidence, and/or by any other evidence in relation to the value of the claim which is in the healthcare provider's possession.
- If the parties reach agreement on liability, but time is needed to resolve the value of the claim, they should aim to agree a reasonable period.'

7.155   In most cases it ought to be possible for an experienced solicitor to prepare the letter of claim. This will elicit the defence response to the allegations being made on which in turn the views of the experts can be sought as well as the client before proceeding further. Assuming acceptable admissions are not received, a further review of the merits of the case must then be undertaken. If the case survives this re-evaluation despite the defence's response then the time has come for proceedings to be commenced and pleaded by the solicitor or papers prepared for consideration by counsel. Review at this stage has the advantage over previous practice where generally little or nothing was known about the defence position until at best, receipt of a defence and, at worst, exchange of expert evidence.

7.156   As part of the planning process, in anticipation of commencement of proceedings, work should begin on quantum with:

- The gathering of documentary evidence bearing on quantum.
- The preparation of outline or preliminary quantum proofs of evidence to assist when instructing quantum experts.
- Approaches to the medical experts who will need to report on condition and prognosis and future needs.
- Approached to the other (non-medical) quantum experts who will need to be instructed to fully value the claim.

One cannot wait to see what the case management judge will allow by way of expert evidence. Besides, his decision is as to what evidence may be called. The decision now bears on what evidence should be gathered.

7.157   The protocol has important guidance on expert evidence at s 4. It differs greatly from the requirement of the PI protocol which demands that:

- 'Before any party instructs an expert he should give the other party a list of the name(s) of one or more experts in the relevant speciality whom he considers are suitable to instruct.'

7.158   Thus, in PI the parties are required to co-operate before an expert is instructed. In clinical negligence on the other hand the protocol acknowledges that:

- 'In clinical negligence disputes expert opinions may be needed:
  (a) on breach of duty and causation;
  (b) on the patient's condition and prognosis;
  (c) to assist in valuing aspects of the claim.'

7.159   The parties are then given far greater freedom as to choice of their own experts:[1]

- 'The civil justice reforms and the new Civil Procedure Rules will encourage economy in the use of experts and a less adversarial expert culture. It is recognised that in clinical negligence disputes, the parties and their advisers will require flexibility in their approach to expert evidence. Decisions on whether experts might be instructed jointly, and on whether reports might be disclosed sequentially or by exchange, should rest with the parties and their advisers. Sharing expert evidence may be appropriate on issues relating to the value of the claim. However, this protocol does not attempt to be prescriptive on issues in relation to expert evidence.'

1   This approach was supported in *S v Birmingham Health Authority*, LTL 23 November 1999.

Planning

7.160   Traditionally, much personal injury litigation proceeded in a tennis-like manner. Each side would play one shot and then await the response of the other. Reaction was the order of the day. Progress was thus at the pace of the slowest participant. Further steps to prepare would be delayed until after the opponent responded to the last initiative. Case work-up consisted of a series of consecutive rather than concurrent moves. Years would be spent obtaining a series of quantum reports only to discover that the defendants were not amenable to settling after all but that liability was in issue. The result was that overall the case proceeded at snails pace. Proceedings would be issued at the last possible moment before limitation expired. Several years might elapse after issue of proceedings before the end appeared in sight.

7.161   The delay was often fuelled by inexperience, excessive case numbers and the desire of some defendants to ultimately steer the case towards a strike-out for want of prosecution.

7.162   One response to this was to become proactive and conduct all aspects of case preparation simultaneously. Quantum would be worked up from the outset in parallel to the liability investigation. Soon the claimant would be ready to issue a fully valued claim if the defendants did not settle on demand.

7.163   There are real problems associated with applying this model to clinical negligence litigation as compared to personal injury.

- It is harder to form a view on prospects at the outset.
- Many more clinical negligence cases investigated will have to be abandoned due to a failure to establish liability. Costs expended in the meantime on quantum issues will be wasted.
- The work-up costs of liability are much higher than in routine PI due to the reliance on and cost of expert opinion.
- Expert evidence on causation is frequently required to establish what part of the current disability is due to the breach of duty as against an underlying disease or illness. Non-medical quantum experts may not know how much disability can be attributed to the breaches of duty alleged until liability has been worked up.

7.164 These considerations mitigate against an immediate full case work up. The consequence of this is that project management like decisions have to be taken as to when to devote time and money to the various facets of a case.

7.165 The following questions need to be addressed to construct a considered plan to bring the case to a conclusion.

1. What funding is available for the case and what conditions apply to it?

2. What are the prospects of obtaining early admissions as to breach of duty and/or causation?
   2.1. Does anything arising from the complaint process help predict the attitude of the proposed defendant?
   2.2. Is this an unanswerable barn door type of case (retained swab, misfiled result and so on)?
   2.3. Can a letter of claim be drawn before expert opinion is obtained?
   2.4. May the resolution of the case turn on the outcome of a well defined factual issue?

3. To prove breach of duty and causation what evidence is required:
   3.1. From lay witnesses and;
   3.2. From experts?
   3.3. Are any of the experts that will have to be consulted prone to excessive waiting time for reports?

4. When will it be possible to form a reliable view on condition and prognosis having regard to:
   4.1. The extent of the claimant's recovery from the injuries;
   4.2 The need for further treatment; and
   4.3. The claimant's age?

5. To prove the extent of injury, loss and damage what evidence is required:
   5.1. From a causation expert (see 3 above) before a view can be taken as to how much of the claimant's condition is due to negligence and how much attributable to the underlying condition to which the clinical intervention was or should have been directed;
   5.2. From lay witnesses;
   5.3. From medical experts on condition and prognosis;
   5.4. From quantum specialists (therapists, care, employment and so on) and;

5.7. What will the cost of the quantum investigation amount to?

6. Should liability be dealt with as a preliminary issue?
 6.1. Is the claimant's age or health such as to require early resolution of liability?
 6.2. How long ago did the events complained of occur?
 6.3. Is there a risk that a fair trial will not be possible if resolution of the liability issue is delayed while quantum is worked up?
 6.4. Conversely, did the events occur so long ago that an early liability trial will bring little or no advantage in terms of witness recollections?
 6.7. Is the cost of the quantum work-up so great that it cannot be justified/ afforded until after there is a result on liability?
 6.6. Will the ultimate outcome of the case significantly benefit from obtaining a substantial interim payment to obtain accommodation and/or implement a care regime etc which can only be provided after a decision on liability?

7.166–7.169   The answers to these questions will suggest:

- the likely timescales required to work-up the whole case as compared to liability;
- when proceedings should be issued;
- whether a preliminary trial of liability or some other severable issue is desirable.

CONCLUSION

7.170   The claimant clinical negligence practitioner should focus on four questions:

 1. Should the case be taken on in the first place?
 2. Does expert opinion prove the complaint?
 3. Can the defence be persuaded to settle?
 4. If no settlement, how soon can a trial be held?

7.171   This chapter has concentrated on the detailed practicalities of dealing with the first and second of these issues. The clinical negligence pre-action protocol then begins to provide a mechanism for resolving the third question. If the case does not settle after letter of claim but still stands up to scrutiny despite the defence response then the lawyer must devise the route most economical of time and money to reach a final resolution – which usually means trial.

7.172   Formal ADR remains a largely theoretical possibility as a means of resolving clinical negligence claims for damages. A stated commitment to ADR by the NHSLA is frequently not matched by any enthusiasm on the part of defence lawyers. Informal ADR by negotiation between legal teams and experts discussions plays a vital part in the process but if that fails then trial is currently the likely forum to resolve the dispute.

7.173   Once the response to the letter of claim has been analysed, and yet it appears that the case should still proceed, then litigation should be run so that procedural steps all lead to the earliest possible trial date. The identity of the pool of experts needed will be known by this stage and their availability for trial can be ascertained before the first case management hearing. A draft set of directions should be forwarded to the defence for agreement at the earliest opportunity before the CMH and they should be encouraged to agree a trial window before the hearing. If agree, this can be built into an agreed set of directions. All of this material should be before the judge as he looks at the allocation questionnaires. Early disclosure of witness statements and documents should not present any difficulty since the majority of the work has already been done.

7.174   At first CMH the procedural judge should have, in addition to the allocation questionnaires:

- A case summary prepared by claimant indicating the extent of the issues.
- A set of proposed directions which the claimant has attempted to agree with the defence.
- A proposed agreed trial window failing which details of claimant's side trial availability.

7.175   The claimant in that position will have a much better prospect of persuading the procedural judge that the case is being handled well and efficiently and so obtain an order which the claimant can readily work with towards trial. Waiting for allocation orders before undertaking this work is fraught with danger as judges in some courts are prone to make initial directions on paper the effect of which may be to delay rather than speed up the overall conduct of the claim. Better to obtain a comprehensive order at an early stage against which future timetabling of preparation can be managed. Besides, there is still no better way of securing a trial fixture in some centres than if the case management judge picks up his telephone during the CMH and arranges it direct with listing.

7.176   There follows as appendices to this chapter a specimen set of directions and an example of a timetable of a piece of litigation run under the last days of the old rules which may be of interest to readers. Care is required to ensure that under the new regime of the CPR round of allocation questionnaires, (potentially) multiple preliminary hearings followed by listing questionnaires do not become procedural delays particularly as some parts of the court service are suffering problems with levels of resource to process paperwork, let alone follow up cases.

7.177   Present the claimant's case in well developed form to the procedural judge from the outset, alongside a planned route to early resolution and it is more like to have the ear of the court.

Appendix 1

MODEL CASE STUDY – CLINICAL NEGLIGENCE CASE

The Background

7.180 S was born in November 1958. She obtained 11 O levels before leaving school aged 17 during her A level studies, having met her future husband, to begin work in a bank. She was married two years later to R, who was four years her senior. Daughters were born in 1983 and 1989 after which the couple decided to try for a son. The resulting pregnancy was of twins and a son and daughter were born in 1993. The family was complete and S decided to have a sterilisation.

7.181 In the meantime S had continued to work for the same employer taking only six and eight weeks maternity leave respectively when her first two children were born. Following the birth of the twins S returned to work once again despite having a family larger by one than originally expected. This time she took up a once-only career break scheme offered by her employers which enabled her to work part-time hours for two years after which she was bound to return to full-time working. She had shown aptitude for a role in sales and had reasonable expectations of a promotion ultimately to the higher grade of personal banker after a full-time return to work.

7.182 R was employed on a rotating three-shift arrangement as a machine operator. He frequently worked overtime which was regularly available to employees as well as being expected by his employer. He had an exemplary work record having had no absence due to sickness in eight years. He had previously been a self-employed builder and plumber and in 1988 the couple purchased a plot of land in a pleasant rural location which had planning permission for two dwellings. S and R laid services on to the site and had a four bedroomed house constructed for themselves to a high specification. Planning permission for two further dwellings was obtained (four in total) and the remaining plot divided into three, each part having permission to build a house. Two of the plots were sold off for, in total, nearly twice as much as the whole site had originally cost. The result was that S and R had a country home built to their own design and only a nominal mortgage. Both commuted to work in nearby towns for which they were reliant on each having a motor vehicle.

7.183 S relied on R's widowed mother, who was 62 when the twins were born and who lived in the town where the children attended school, to help with child care both before and after nursery and school hours.

THE CAUSE OF ACTION

7.184 On 10 April 1995 S underwent a laparoscopic sterilisation by the application of a falope ring to each fallopian tube at the local hospital as an NHS patient. The surgery was performed by a registrar in obstetrics and gynaecology. The procedure was seemingly uneventful. She did not recall being given any warning of any risk of failure inherent in the procedure.

7.185 In July 1995 S began to lose blood PV. Later that month, on holiday S noticed that her jeans were becoming tight and that she disliked drinking tea, which was normally associated with her being pregnant. She began to suffer tiredness and nausea. Once home S carried out a pregnancy self test which was positive. As a result, she consulted her GP who took her straight to the local cottage hospital where an ultrasound scan confirmed a single pregnancy. The GP thought it may well have been a twin pregnancy originally and that the PV blood was a miscarriage of one twin. S felt guilty that she had pushed herself so hard at work that she might have caused the miscarriage.

7.186 S was referred to the consultant who had carried out the sterilisation and saw him in early August 1995. He appeared 'shocked' and offered a termination to take place five days later. He said the termination would be 'straightforward' and arranged counselling to take place beforehand. Alternatively he said S and her husband could buy a people carrier for a larger family. S was in tears and worried they could not afford to buy such a vehicle. S later said that she was devastated.

7.187 S began to worry about whether a termination might give rise to long-term problems. She spoke to her GP who doubted that she was a suitable candidate. S saw a midwife who raised doubts as to how she could cope with another child. Still very concerned, S consulted a local solicitor. The 'advice' given was that the solicitor had previously had a termination and that if she could have her time over again she would not have gone through with the termination. S still wanted legal advice and so consulted a medical negligence specialist, to whom she had to travel some distance. There, S was advised of the legal implications of her decision after which she decided not to terminate the pregnancy. In just four days S saw her GP, Consultant, a midwife and two solicitors before making what she viewed as her unborn child's 'life or death' decision.

7.188 S returned to work full time when her two-year career break ended but almost immediately on doing so her maternity leave began with this unplanned pregnancy.

7.189 S went into labour in February 1996 around term and was admitted to the hospital where the sterilisation had been performed. She was booked for the GP unit but on arrival was told that the GP would be unable to attend. The labour became complicated. A doctor was called and the Registrar who had performed the sterilisation attended. He performed a scan which revealed that the baby was engaged but not that the presentation was in fact face first. The delivery did not proceed as expected. The Registrar was called again this time to perform a forceps delivery. The child's heart slowed and the cord was found to be around the neck. S was aware of panic around her and of being told 'push or this baby will be a dead one' before she passed out. With an episiotomy the baby, a boy C, was delivered requiring resuscitation and having a bruised face although otherwise well. S felt traumatised and did not ask for her son for over an hour. She went on to become depressed and felt both physically and mentally exhausted.

7.190 R was given four days compassionate leave from work to assist in getting the children to and from school after which he had to take further unpaid time off work to help with domestic arrangements. His mother had to stay with the family for ten weeks to help S. A midwife on a home visit told S that she must have been pregnant when the sterilisation was performed.

7.191 Later that year the remaining development plot had to be sold to raise money to buy a people carrier vehicle after S was told by the police that it would be unlawful to carry all of the children together in a conventional car.

FURTHER STERILISATION

7.192 S sought advice about having a further sterilisation performed and after consultation with her GP was referred to the Professor at a regional centre. He saw S himself and agreed to perform a repeat procedure. He volunteered that he was legally as well as medically qualified and further volunteered to S that frankly she would not get any compensation. He repeatedly told S that she had signed an appropriate form of consent and that there had been no negligence. In a letter to the GP he wrote, 'I hope that she is now satisfied with the position she now finds herself'.

7.193 S underwent a further sterilisation procedure by way of bilateral salpingectomy under general anaesthetic in June 1996.

THE CONTINUING EFFECTS OF THE ALLEGED NEGLIGENCE

7.194 S was due to return to work from maternity leave in November 1996 but felt unable to manage both employment and her newly extended family. She had accrued over 18 years continuous service with one employer. The family's income was reduced and they ran into debt. R found it impossible to sleep between shifts with the increased occupancy in the house as S was no longer out at work and C was always there. In May 1997 he took a new job, which promised only day working. He was dismissed in June when it transpired that, despite being led to believe that the position was permanent, he had only been taken on to cover for an employee on long-term sick leave who became able to return to work. R became unemployed finding only occasional work. S considered returning to the bank, while R would remain at home with the children. However, the break in service meant she would have to work much further from home than before and her pay would reduce considerably as she would be taken on at a lower grade. R stopped at home while S took employment as a nursery nurse but her pay was low and she found it unsatisfactory looking after other people's children when she had so many of her own to look after. The family incurred expenses in seeking to relocate to another area where employment prospects would be better for R but no good employment could be found in an area where property prices were lower.

7.195 In June 1997 the family's second vehicle became unroadworthy and was sold as they could not afford to repair it.

7.196 In October 1997 they sold their house at less than the asking price to move to a smaller property in the town nearer to the children's schools and shops as transport had become a major problem with only one vehicle and a further young child to look after. There was no local shop in the village where they previously lived.

7.197   Ultimately, in January 1998 R was able to return to his former job as a machine operator on shifts. However, he was unable to return to his former pattern of regular overtime working because of the need to help S with the child care burden which had increased with C's arrival. Despite R's return to work the family income was still greatly reduced as compared to what it would have been but for the C's birth.

7.198   S became depressed. Her personality changed and she found it difficult to cope as she had before. Around the house S found herself doing housework in the night-time as she had no time when the children were awake. She was unable to devote as much time to her other children as she wished and felt that their development was being hindered by her commitment to C. In the summer of 1998, in an effort to facilitate an eventual return to work, S started a part-time course leading to a BA Ed. in child care. However, she found she had insufficient time available to devote to studies even on a flexible modular course.

LEGAL ACTION

7.199   S decided to investigate whether she had a claim for compensation arising out of the failed sterilisation of April 1995. She returned to the specialist solicitors she had consulted for the second opinion at the time of making the 'life or death' decision. While she was working she was not eligible for legal aid. After C was born she became eligible and a certificate was granted in July 1996. The progress of the claim is set out in the following chronology.

1996

15 November   Letter before action requesting copy hospital records and asking for explanation if Trust thought unfavourable outcome explicable other than by reason of negligence.

1997

13 June   Defendant's solicitors point to comments of Professor who carried out repeat sterilisation and ask for confirmation of proposed course of action.

18 June   Defence told independent opinion being obtained.

1998

18 February   Defence told that expert opinion indicated that falope ring had been inadequately applied to the left fallopian tube and that a claim would be persued. Defence asked whether they intended to defend the claim and if so what their views were on a split trial.

27 February   Defence write, 'We are clearly disappointed that this is a matter which you intend to persue. Our current instructions from both

our client and the Clinical Negligence Scheme for Trusts is to defend any proceedings issued and we have reverted for their views as to the advisability of a split trial.'

13 May   Writ served.

5 June   Statement of claim served with outline schedule of damages and short report substantiating the birth. Defence asked to agree a split trial in view of:
(a) C's age – still only two;
(b) the expense of investigating quantum which would require several experts;
(c) The desirability of resolving breach of duty sooner rather than later.
They are asked to accept outline schedule failing which application for split trial will issue immediately.

9 June   Defence request fully pleaded schedule.

11 June   Defence asked to reconsider their position over schedule in view of matters advanced in support of case for split trial.

15 June   Defence send summons for issue to stay action until fully pleaded schedule served. Issued returnable 21 July.

22 June   Defence refuse to serve defence until schedule served.

3 July   Admission made in open correspondence of breach of duty causing C's birth.

10 July   Defence told that Claimant would rely on expert evidence in relation to care, employment, property valuation, psychiatry and gynaecology. Cross summons sent for issue to enter judgment and for directions including mutual simultaneous exchange of expert evidence.

20 July   Defence insist their summons for fully pleaded schedule should stand and issue a further summons seeking strike out or stay over schedule and in relation to directions seeking sequential exchange of expert evidence. They suggest transfer down to county court as 'this is no longer a complex claim.'

21 July   Terms of order agreed after lengthy telephone discussion. Order by consent later that day.
• Judgment for damages to be assessed.
• Lists of documents 28 August.
• Witness statements exchange 28 August.
• Medical expert evidence primary mutual simultaneous exchange 31 December.
• Secondary mutual exchange 31 May 1999.
• Schedule on information currently available 28 August.
• Full schedule 31 December.

- Claimant's quantum reports 31 December.
- Defence schedule 30 April 1999.
- Defendant's quantum reports 31 May 1999.
- Authorities and literature from experts with their reports and final such material by 31 May 1999.
- Set down by 28 August 1998 Judge alone category B time estimate 3-5 days.
- Action be allocated first open date on or after 31 May 1999.

24 July Defence informed that speech and language expert also to be instructed due to concern over C's development in that area.

4 August Defence provide details of their psychiatric expert and request Claimant attends him.

25 August Action set down for trial.

27 August Extensive list of documents (12 pages) served together with statements by S and R.

28 August Further schedule of loss served.

3 September Defence asked to serve formal list after they fail to do so.

9 September Defence request a small selection of documents from claimant's list as 'very much a first trawl and that as a result we may be coming back to you with a request for further documentation in due course'. Defence ask for copy of claimant's personnel file.

18 September Copy documents from list supplied.

20 October Defence informed that bank refuse to release staff file voluntarily.

26 October Defence asked to provide dates of availability for June to October 1999 after claimant's solicitors have liased with listing office.

27 October Agreement reached on interim payment of £5,000 to come from money in court.

5 November Claimant's supplemental list of documents served.

9 November Claimant prescribed anti-depressant following suggestion made by her own psychiatric expert but currently contra-indicated.

1999

6 January Claimant discloses:
- medical evidence;

- gynaecological condition and prognosis report reporting complications of pregnancy and delivery;
- Psychiatric report;
- quantum reports;
- child rearing costing;
- employment report;
- property valuation report;
- short witness statement from R's mother;
- second supplemental list of documents.

Defendant discloses:
- medical evidence;
- gynaecological report;
- psychiatric report.

11 January	Claimant's further schedule of loss served.
15 January	Listed before s 9 Judge for mention to fix a date. Window of 25 to 29 October 1999 already agreed and trial listed accordingly for regional trial centre with time estimate 3 to 5 days.
2 February	Agreement in principle that psychiatric experts should meet.
17 March	Request for further voluntary interim payment of damages.
15 April	Claimant proposes that meeting of psychiatric experts should be delayed until after second psychiatric examination due to take place in July for purpose of updating report on condition and prognosis following course of anti-depressant medication. Further interim payment agreed. Defence request clarification as between witness statements and such limited documentation as they have seen and again ask for S's personnel file.
28 April	Agreement reached that S should visit defendant's psychiatric expert on same day as she sees her own expert (both psychiatrists are in London).
6 May	Defence disclose: • care cost report • employment report • architect's report on property valuation issues. They indicate an intention to submit supplementary reports on care and property after receiving counsel's opinion.
11 May	Claimant's third supplemental list of documents served together with additional documents requested by defence dealing with plot sales.
12 May	Defendant's counter-schedule served.

24 May	Defendants seek written authority for disclosure to them of personnel file as a pre-cursor to discovery application against bank (C's former employer).
23 July	Defendants supply copies of documents they have obtained from bank most of which were already contained in lists served on claimant's behalf.
23 August	Defendant invited to signify they are ready to effect secondary exchange of employment and psychiatric reports
20 September	Defendant unilaterally discloses revised schedule of damages supported by supplementary reports from their psychiatrist, care cost consultant and architect without previously signifying that they were ready to exchange pursuant to the order.
1 October	Claimant discloses supplemental psychiatric, valuation and employment reports. Defendant's sent draft trial bundle indices for agreement and reminded that they had still not asked for sight of the balance of the documentation listed on discovery. Defendant's put on notice that in absence of rate of return being set under Damages Act claimant would contend for award based on 2% return and further that reliance would be placed on Ogden Tables 11-20 rather than 1-10 following *Worrall v Powergen plc* [1999] Lloyd's Rep Med 177.
4 October	Defendant asks for copies of all documents disclosed in claimant's lists
8 October	Copies of documents sent to defence. Invitation issued to them to meet/discuss to attempt to compromise numerous small differences between counter-schedule and schedule. Further supplemental employment report served on defence.
11 October	Defence invited to abandon as unsustainable the allegation in the final counter-schedule that an interim payment should have been sought instead of selling the family home – given that on 27 February 1998 in correspondence liability was denied by them.
22 October	Civil trial centre telephone in the afternoon to indicate no judge available to hear fixture. Matter moved to London as Floater.
25 October	Trial at RCJ commences.
28 October	On fourth day of trial negotiations lead to settlement of claim for £180,000 after claimant concedes in cross-examination that she would like to return to work sooner than previously indicated.

Appendix 2

Draft

Clinical Negligence Practice Direction

1.1 This Practice Direction applies to all Clinical Negligence cases. A Clinical Negligence case is one which contains a claim for damages in respect of an alleged breach of duty of care committed in the course of the provision of clinical or medical services (which services include dental or nursing services).

1.2 The provisions of all other relevant Practice Directions will apply to Clinical Negligence cases save the extent that they are superseded by the matters set out below

2. All parties in Clinical Negligence cases must comply with the Clinical Negligence pre-action protocol. Failure to do so may attract sanctions in the form of costs orders and the granting of refusal to grant extensions of time.

3.1 All Claimants must serve with the particulars of claim, a medical report on the Claimant's condition and prognosis. A claimant who does not wish to do so, must apply to the court within 14 days of service of the particulars of Claim to dispense with service of a medical report and justify their reasons for so dispensing. If she cannot so justify the Claimant's statement of case may be struck out.

3.2 It is not necessary for a Claimant to serve with the particulars of Claim a Schedule of loss and damage. If a defendant wishes the Claimant to serve such a Schedule, he must apply to the Court within 14 days of service on his of the Particulars of Claim for such Schedule to be served and on the hearing of any such application, the onus will be on the Defendant to justify the need for such Schedule.

4.1 In London, all Clinical Negligence cases of a financial value over £15,000 may be commenced in the Royal Courts of Justice. The Court may then transfer cases to a county court.

4.2 Outside London, any Clinical Negligence case commenced in a county court other than a Civil Trial Centre, will be transferred at the allocation stage to the most convenient Civil Trial Centre.

5. In Clinical Negligence cases, there is a presumption that the case will be allocated to the multitrack but the court may order or the parties may by

agreement, opt for the case to proceed on the Fast Track in which case the court will give directions appropriate to a case in the Fast Track and paragraphs 7,8,9 and 10 of this Practice Direction will not apply.

6. Clinical Negligence cases will wherever practical, be assigned to designated Masters or District Judges as Procedural Judges and the Royal Courts of Justice and each Civil Trial centre will from time to time publish the names of the designated Masters or District Judges.

7. After allocation, the Court will fix a date for holding a Case Management Conference. The Court may however, instead of fixing the date of a Case Management Conference either give directions under Rule 29.2(I) (a) or fix a date for a pre-trial review under Rule 29.2 (I)(b).

8. Not later than 7 days before the date of the Case Management Conference the following steps must be taken by the parties:

8.1 The Claimant must file with the Court and serve on all Defendants, a summary of the case (limited to 250 words) and a Chronology.

8.2 Each Defendant must file with the Court and serve on all other parties a list of issues (limited to 250 words) and its comments on the Claimant's chronology.

9. At the hearing of the Case Management Conference (which must be attended by Counsel instructed to the case or by the Solicitor having conduct of the case) the following matters will be considered:

9.1 Whether all previous directions (for example, any given on allocation) have been complied with.

9.2 Whether the Defendant's list of issues can be agreed and if not what provision should be made for drawing up an agreed list of issues.

9.3 Whether provision should be made for updating the list of issues and for filing any admissions.

9.4 The scope for settling any particular issues.

9.5 Any directions for the separate trail of certain issues including whether there should be separate trails of liability arid causation and of quantum.

9.6 The scope for Alternative Dispute Resolution.

9.7 The timetable for the case including the date of trial or the trial period or the date by which a trail date must be obtained.

9.8 Disclosure.

9.9 The need for non-expert witnesses, the provision of lists of such witnesses and the service of statements of such witnesses.

9.10 The need for-expert evidence. There will be a presumption that such evidence will be given orally at trial but consideration will be given as to whether some or all experts need not give oral evidence.

9.11 Whether and if so when experts should discuss the issues in the case.

9.12 The costs incurred at the date of the Case Management Conference so as to ensure that the cost incurred are not disproportionate to the damages claimed.

9.13 The date of any further hearing of the Case Management conference or a Pre-trial Review and the date by which the parties must file a listing questionnaire. If there is to be a Pre-Trial Review, this will be held if possible by the Judge who will hear the trial.

10 At any further hearing of the Case Management Conference or at any Pre-Trial Review, the Court will enquire into compliance with its earlier directions and require justification for any non-compliance. Any failure by a party to comply with directions may result in the striking out of the Statement of Case of that party.

11 At the hearing of applications for summary judgement

11.1 The application must be supported by signed witness statements by all experts relied on by the Claimants which statements must:

(a) Exhibit all of the expert's reports and any answers he has given pursuant to Rule 37.6(3).
(b) Contain a certificate that there is prima facie evidence of substandard case.

11.2 Defendants opposing such applications must, if they wish to rely on expert evidence, serve signed witness statements by all experts to be relied on by them which statements must

(a) Exhibit all the expert's reports and any answers which he has given pursuant to Rule 37.6(3)
(b) Contain a certificate that there is no prima facie evidence of sub-standard case.

11.3 All experts' reports must comply with Paragraph 13 of this Practice Direction.

12 While the Court will consider the scope for the giving of a direction that a single joint expert give evidence as to a particular issue it will not be the usual course in Clinical Negligence Cases to insist on a single joint expert for issues of liability and causation or condition or quantum but as between Defendants shared experts on condition and prognosis and quantum will frequently be ordered.

13 Every experts' report in Clinical Negligence Cases must comply with Rule 35 and the Practice Direction relating to that Rule and the Court may refuse to read a report which does not so comply.

Appendix 3

IN THE HIGH COURT OF JUSTICE   2000 C No
QUEEN'S BENCH DIVISION
DISTRICT REGISTRY

Before   sitting in public

B E T W E E N:

ABC
(A minor by his Father and Litigation Friend DEC)
Claimant

- and –

XYZ
Defendant

CONSENT ORDER FOR
CASE MANAGEMENT DIRECTIONS

On hearing the Solicitors for the Claimant and Defendant
And by consent
It is ordered:

Allocation

1. The case be allocated to multi-track. Leave to dispense with filing allocation questionnaires.

Exchange of Witness Statements on Liability

2. The parties do mutually simultaneously exchange by way of signed and dated written statements the substance of evidence of all witnesses as to fact on issues of breach of duty and causation that they intend to rely on at trial by 4pm on **Monday 3 April 2000.** For the avoidance of doubt the witness statements to be disclosed include the statements of any medical, nursing and ancillary staff dealing with matters of primary facts or recollection as well as including any expert opinion of that witness that it is proposed to rely on. Such statements to be agreed if possible. Where a party fails to comply with this direction he shall not be entitled to adduce evidence to which this direction relates without the permission of the Court.

Expert Evidence – Liability and Life Expectancy

Primary and Secondary Exchange
3. The parties do mutually simultaneously exchange the substance in writing:

(i)   Of all medical and other experts evidence (if any) that they propose to rely on at trial as to the issues of breach of duty, causation and life expectancy by 4pm on **Monday 31 July 2000** (Primary exchange).
(ii) Of all further expert evidence (if any) as to the said issues prepared by the experts whose evidence has been disclosed pursuant to sub-clause (I) hereof that they propose to rely on at trial by 4pm on **Monday 25 September 2000** (Secondary exchange).

All such evidence as is mentioned in sub-clauses (i) and (ii) above be agreed if possible. Permission to call expert witnesses at trial to give opinion evidence limited to those witnesses the substance of whose evidence has so been disclosed pursuant to this clause and to the specialties of:
    Neuro-radiology
    Obstetrics
    Paediatric neurology.

Expert Authorities

4. If any expert witness proposes to rely on any textbook, article or other published item in any expert or other learned journal, or unpublished scientific, technical or other research data, a first list and photocopies be served on the other party at the time of primary exchange and any supplemental list and photocopies at the time of secondary exchange.

Expert Meetings

5(a) By 4pm on Monday 23 October 2000 the solicitors for the parties shall communicate with each other and use their best endeavours:
    (i)   to define the main issues to be tried and
    (ii) to eliminate or reduce the issues to which expert evidence is directed and
    (iii) to prepare agreed agendas to experts for the purpose of clause 5(b) below.
5(b) By Monday 27 November 2000 there be a meeting without prejudice of the opposing experts in like disciplines, or alternatively telephone communication between them, for the purpose of identifying those parts of their evidence which are in issue. Such experts to prepare a joint statement by Monday 11 December 2000 indicating those parts of their evidence on which they are, and those on which they are not, in agreement.

Claimant's Schedule

6. The claimant do file and serve a fully pleaded Schedule of damages by 4pm on Monday 25 September 2000. Such Schedule to include the substance in writing of all lay and expert evidence the claimant intends to rely on at trial in relation to quantum.

Defendant's Counter-Schedule

6. The defendant do file and serve a fully pleaded Counter-Schedule of damages by 4pm on Monday 18 December 2000. Such Counter-Schedule to include the

substance in writing of all lay and expert evidence the defendant intends to rely on at trial in response to the claimant's Schedule of Damages. The Counter-Schedule shall state which heads of damage are agreed and (if not agreed) the reasons why not and all counter-proposals.

The parties shall be limited to one expert witness each on quantum issues in each of the following areas of expertise:

Care
Employment
Educational Psychology
Orthopaedic
Occupational therapy
Technological aids (computers etc)
Architect
Speech & language
Physiotherapy

Updated Expert Evidence on Condition and Prognosis

7. The parties do simultaneously exchange the substance of all further witness statements and expert evidence (if any) as to condition and prognosis, calculated up to the trial date, no later than 3 calendar months before the dates fixed for the trial.

Further Schedules of Damage and Expert Evidence – Quantum

8(a) The claimant do file and serve an updated, fully pleaded Schedule of Damages by not less than 3 months before the date fixed for trial.
8(b) The defendant do file and serve an updated Counter-Schedule of Damages not less than 1 month before the date fixed for trial.

Listing availability

9. The solicitors for the parties shall communicate with each other and use their best endeavours to agree dates of availability for a trial window in the period of to inclusive. The parties are to provide the Listing Office Multi track section with the agreed dates of availability, or in default, if agreement cannot be reached, their own dates of availability, for the said period by 4.00pm on.

Pre-trial Review

10. There be a pre-trial review of this action before a Section 9 Judge with a time estimate of one hour being not later than one month before the date fixed for trial.

Trial

11.   Venue: Birmingham
        Mode: Judge alone
        Listing category: A
        Time estimate: 10 days

Costs

11.   The costs of and consequent on today's hearing be costs in the cause.

Chapter 8

Clinical Negligence Claims

John Sheath

INTRODUCTION

Woolf on 'Clinical Negligence'

'The ailments from which the Civil Justice system suffered are peculiarly relevant to my audience tonight. They are that it has become excessively adversarial, slow and expensive. It is especially true of litigation over alleged medical negligence in the delivery of healthcare, whether by doctors, nurses or other health carers. If litigation is in general slow and expensive, then medical negligence is even slower and even more expensive than other litigation. Further, there is greater mistrust in this area than any other.'

Lord Woolf – UKCC Lecture 24 April 1997

8.1   Lord Woolf's comments epitomise the delay and cost traditionally associated with major claims pre Civil Procedure Rules ('CPR').

Mistrust and Public Perception

8.2   There can be no doubt that the previous mistrust and suspicion between the parties and their advisers involved in major claims has, in the past, undermined and devalued the whole process in the public eye. What the public are not told behind the headline '£3.5m for birth blunder' are the legal issues regarding what acceptable standards were current at the time of the incident or the effect on the hospital or staff of such an incident. How often does the media announce a multi-million settlement with the broadcaster adding the negative postscript 'the hospital denied liability' without any further explanation. The value of the claim is newsworthy, the details of the defence are not.

Cover-up Defendants and Exaggerating Claimants

8.3   The adversarial approach presumed that the hospital claims officers would be as obstructive as possible, stonewalling requests for documents and covering up the errors of the doctors. Their lawyers would then use technical litigation skills to undermine claims such as limitation or, worse still, prolonging the litigation in the hope that the ordeal of a contested trial would dissuade the long-suffering victim. On the other hand, the defence litigator assumed that all claimants exaggerate their damages and that with the benefit of what was so readily interpreted as the 'legal aid meal ticket', spurious experts supported unmeritorious claims at the taxpayers' expense.

8.4   Woolf concluded, 'it was in the area of medical negligence that the civil justice system was failing most conspicuously to meet the needs of litigants ...'

The Changing Landscape

8.5   How times have changed! The 'Med Neg' term of endearment is no longer in vogue. Clinical negligence more accurately reflects the broader scope of accountability for the healthcare professionals. Alongside the development of patients' rights under the Patients Charter and Complaints Procedure and the advent of better representation and advocacy on patients' behalf, clinical mishaps have been catapulted to the forefront of media attention. Matters such as enforced Caesareans, human embryo consent, DNR (do not resuscitate) policies and NHS resources now make headlines. However, with the advent of Woolf there has been a sea change in culture as illustrated in the objectives set out in para 1.2 of the Clinical Disputes Forum ('CDF') Pre-Action Protocol:

> 'It is clearly in the interests of patients, health care professionals and providers that patients' concerns, complaints and claims arising from their treatment are resolved as quickly, efficiently and professionally as possible. The climate of mistrust and lack of openness can seriously damage the patient/clinician relationship, unnecessarily prolong disputes (especially litigation) and reduce the resources available for treating patients. It may also cause additional work for, and lower the morale of, health care professionals.'

8.6   It is in this new co-operative environment that the effective handling of major claims falls to be considered. Major claims signify those attracting quantum in excess of £1 million, ranging from cerebral palsy baby cases to adult brain damage and permanent paralysis claims, where the lives of infants and adults have been irreparably damaged in consequence of medical malpractice.

The Legitimate Clinical Defence

8.7   No lawyer involved in this speciality can remain unaffected by the extent of human misery and tragedy that can result from a single incident. However, from the outset, the claim must be critically assessed and analysed in the legal context of new *Bolam/Bolitho* and in the clinical context of modern day practice. There is a legitimate defence to many of the claims that are pursued pre- and post-action for alleged clinical negligence. Forty-three year old *Bolam* is now subject to judicial critical analysis and there is the rare *Bolitho* overruling of expert evidence on grounds of 'illogicality and irrationality'. There is the prospect of *Bolam* being further challenged or eroded by the Human Rights Act 1998 depending on interpretation of Article 2 of the Convention

8.8   However, the current position is that there is a legitimate defence to a claim where the doctor or nurse practitioner has followed a practice accepted by his peers. A responsible body of opinion would endorse such a defence in accordance with the current acceptable standards, notwithstanding the disappointing outcome for the patient. Injury is not tantamount to liability. This is recognised in the objectives of the NHS Litigation Authority's ('NHSLA') framework document 'to minimise the overall cost of clinical negligence to the NHS, and thus maximise the resources available for patient care by defending unjustified actions robustly, settling justified actions sufficiently and creating incentives to reduce the number of negligent incidents'.

8.9–8.11 It will be interesting to observe the impact on clinical standards of the Clinical Negligence Scheme for Trusts ('CNST') in encouraging and imposing better and improved guidelines for care and treatment. There is also the growing influence of the National Institute for Clinical Effectiveness ('NICE') and the introduction of Clinical Governance combining to improve standards and ensuring there is an increasing accountability for health care professionals. Protocols, guidelines and up-dated regulatory professional codes are already having a significant impact on the defensibility of claims. The *Bolam* 'responsible body of medical opinion' will have to take all these matters into account now when experts provide a Woolf report to the court. Legitimate defences exist to claims for professional negligence in any field and medicine is no exception no matter how unpopular. In practice, a great number of defensible clinical negligence claims are settled for a multitude of reasons, evidential, technical, litigation risk, economics and political expediency but that should not detract from the fact that as a matter of current law and clinical practice there still exists the legitimate defence.

TRADITIONAL MAJOR 'MEDICAL NEGLIGENCE' CLAIMS HANDLING

8.12 In a forward-looking book of this nature, war stories and dwelling on past ineffective case management seems an inappropriate exercise to perform. However, it is a valuable lesson to reflect on past cases to see how modern case management would have affected the outcome. The reflective process in litigation is greatly undervalued and ignored because of case workloads and time pressures but much is to be gained from reviewing 'what happened', concluding 'so what' do we draw from this experience and planning 'now what' do we do next time. Three examples of cases which lasted more than a decade from incident to resolution are set out below along with a reflective view showing how the matter would have been processed more efficiently today.

CASE STUDY 1

Facts

Child DC suffered athetoid cerebral palsy, all limbs affected following birth on 13 December 1985.

Issues

1. Failing to heed:

    (i) CTG trace
    (ii) obstetric history
    (iii) signs of fetal distress

2. Failing to perform:

> (i) fetal blood sample
> (ii) caesarean section
> (iii) adequate assessment before forceps.

3. Doctor of insufficient experience.

4. Forceps rotational technique incompetent.

Defence was a blanket denial of all allegations.

Chronology

13.12.85	Delivery of child DC
07.04.87	Letter requesting records
26.01.88	Originating summons for pre-action discovery
23.11.88	Writ served
01.04.91	Statement of claim
31.05.91	Defence
31.12.92	Request for further and better particulars of defence
27.01.93	Summons for directions
28.01.93	Plaintiff's notice of intention to proceed
22.03.93	Hearing for directions
05.05.94	Application for further and better particulars of defence
24.05.94	Admission of liability by defendant
04.01.95	Request for interim payment
06.02.95	Consent order for directions, quantum only
23.03.95	£8,500 voluntary interim
24.01.96	Application for schedule of loss to be served
01.03.96	Order requiring service of Schedule of Loss
21.03.96	Schedule served with supporting reports and documents
27.03.96	Quantum experts instructed by defence
16.05.96	Counter-schedule served
24.06.96	Payment into court £950,000
15.07.96	Settlement negotiation
16.07.96	Consent order £1.1 million deferred for structure
02.05.97	Structure approved

Reflective Review

- No letter of claim or before action.
- Originating summons issued before medical records disclosed.
- Liability admitted eight years after event, three years after statement of claim and defence served.
- Interim payment limited because of eligibility for legal aid.
- No experts meeting.
- Settled day before trial following discussion between counsel.
- Ten months before structure approved following consent order.

Likely Outcome Today

An admission would have been made pre-action and a substantial Part 36 offer/payment within 6 months of issue of proceedings which would have resolved the litigation. A far stricter timetable would have been directed regarding the structure.

CASE STUDY 2

Facts

Baby DB suffered severe quadriplegic cerebral palsy of the mixed spastic dyskinetic type following birth on 10 February 1985.

Issues

Failure to maintain oxygen equipment in the delivery room, failure to intubate and/or provide a paediatrician to supervise resuscitation caused a delay of 12 minutes, failure to provide staff with sufficient skill or a safe system of delivery. Defence denied all allegations, alleging injuries caused by cord around neck and delay contributed by mother's non co-operation.

Issue between experts as to whether delay in delivery or intrapartum factors caused hypoxia and brain damage.

Chronology of Events

10.02.85	Date of delivery
30.09.87	Writ endorsed with statement of claim
23.11.87	Request for further and better particulars of claim
15.02.88	Defence
12.05.88	Further and better particulars of claim
15.07.88	Claimant amends statement of claim
18.04.91	Claimant's solicitors served notice of intention to proceed
22.04.91	Notice of change of solicitor
29.05.91	Application for directions (claimant)
02.07.91	Application by defence for split trial
02.08.91	Order directing split trial
13.02.95	Notice of change of solicitor
13.10.95	Order by consent for leave to set matter down on issue of liability
29.10.96	Order for directions regarding expert evidence
13.11.96	Interim payment voluntary £10,000
06.12.96	Liability and causation conceded following discussion between experts to the extent of 75%. Judgment entered for claimant for damages to be assessed
15.03.97	Order for judgment
16.01.98	Defence pay into court £890,000
05.02.98	Notice of acceptance of payment
10.02.98	Infant settlement approval by consent. Structure not agreed.

Reflective Review

• Two changes of solicitor

- Writ issued within 2½ years after events but inordinate delay by claimant's advisors, 1988 to 1991, 1991 to 1995
- Defence initiative to request split trial
- Discussion between experts did not take place until 1996, resulting in agreed apportionment
- No structure agreed.

Likely Outcome Today

A meeting between experts would have occurred pre or shortly after issue and a Part 36 offer made on liability. Ironically earlier settlement may have led to a higher award in this case because the child responded well to therapy but would certainly have avoided 13 years of legal costs.

CASE STUDY 3

Facts

Claim by 37 year old male arising from undiagnosed fracture of cervical spine at C7 level following traumatic accident at work on 6 January 1990. Diagnosis delayed by two weeks by which time the claimant suffered permanent paralysis.

Issues

Failure to diagnose unstable broken neck within reasonable period in the event until 14 days. Relied on incomplete radiological evaluation of cervical spine, failed until 20 February 1990 to take any image of lower neck, caused or permitted claimant to be treated as if neck were stable, failure adequately or expeditiously to diagnose or treat fracture C7/T1. Failure to take specific care when turning or moving or intubating plaintiff.

Defence denied negligence on basis the injury had been caused in the initial accident by employer first defendant's negligence or breach of statutory duty. Substantive causation issue.

Chronology

08.02.91	Writ of summons
11.07.91	Statement of claim against employer, first defendant
08.07.91	Schedule of special damages
22.07.91	Defence of first defendant
22.01.92	Further and better particulars (of the first defendant)
24.11.92	Order for interim payment of £40,000 by first defendant
23.01.93	Reply to defence (of first defendant)
09.09.93	Order giving leave to the plaintiff to join the second defendant Health Authority and to amend writ and statement of claim.
09.09.93	Order for interim payment of £120,000 against first defendant
27.09.93	Amended writ and statement of claim
25.10.93	Amended defence of the first defendant
13.11.93	Defence of second defendant
12.04.94	Order for split trial and order for directions (liability and causation)

29.11.96	Consent order requiring first defendant to make a further interim payment of £89,000
21.04.97	Calderbank offer. Second defendant offering 30%, first defendant reduction 7½% contributory negligence.
01.05.97	Order by consent agreeing Calderbank, further interim £100,000 (Trial date 12.05.97 vacated).
10.06.97	Summons for directions.
22.12.97	Order varying date by which schedule of special damages and counter schedule must be served.
13.02.98	Consent order varying time limits of the order of 22 December 1997
23.07.98	Consent order re service of expert evidence on quantum
03.06.98	Consent order. Further interim payment of £100,000
06.10.98	Summons requiring service of first and second defendants' schedule of special damage
22.10.98	Summons for leave to serve re-amended statement of claim
05.11.98	Order giving leave to re-amend statement of claim
05.11.98	Re-amended statement of claim served
05.11.98	Amended schedule of damages served
12.11.98	Counter-schedule of damages served
12.11.98	Payment into court of £1.8 million (first defendant 70%, second defendant 30%)
07.12.98	Order approved, £1.8 million (trial vacated)

Reflective Review

- Decision to join second defendant 2½ years after issue of writ of summons.
- Numerous piecemeal applications for small interim payments rather than a global sum pending trial.
- No meeting between experts.
- Following exchange of expert evidence on liability the defence made a Calderbank offer resulting in agreed apportionment of liability and admission.
- The claimant's advisers were slow to deliver schedule of special damages and an amended schedule was served one month from trial date.
- A payment into court by the defendants close on trial eventually resulted in settlement.

Likely Outcome Today

A split trial would have been directed within six months of service of statement of claim. A 'without prejudice' meeting between experts would have resulted in earlier apportionment and settlement. The claimant would not have been allowed to supplement special damages so close to trial. The defence would have made Part 36 offer or payment much earlier thereby reducing legal costs for both parties. In this instance the claimant's solicitors legal costs claimed in excess of £250,000 would have been reduced to £50,000.

CURRENT MAJOR 'CLINICAL NEGLIGENCE' CLAIMS HANDLING

The Impact of Practice Direction ('PD49')

8.13 Before Woolf, major claims management had already been radically changed by PD49 which had identified medical negligence cases as requiring 'special treatment' and a need for a more efficient system. Following the publication of the Access to Justice Report in July 1996 in the High Court, new rules were imposed for all medical negligence cases where pleadings closed after 1 November 1996 and were subsequently amended on 1 January 1998. Practice Direction 49 was a first step towards the establishment of a High Court medical negligence list. Its aim was to:

• Impose time limits on parties.
• Achieve greater openness to identify the real points of issue between the parties as early as possible.
• Give information to the courts so that effective case management can occur.
• Make the parties consider alternative methods of resolution.
• Ensure that the lawyer dealing with the case attends the summons.

8.14 A major advance for defendants in managing claims was that PD49 specified that the claimant should serve a letter before action at least three months before proceedings are issued, setting out the fullest information available. It provided that a Summons for Directions must be issued within 28 days after close of pleadings, when the claimant is obliged to serve a summary description of the case limited to 250 words, a chronology of events and a list of initial witnesses. The defendant should respond within 14 days, producing a list of outstanding issues limited to 250 words and a response to the claimant's chronology and list of initial witnesses. The object was that the parties should not be able to agree a timetable without the court's approval and each party should produce a list of potential witnesses and experts, including number and discipline. They should ensure that a lawyer who has the conduct of the matter, or one who is fully briefed, attends the hearing when the court considers fixing either a further hearing for directions or a trial date. All the above provisions are now taken for granted but the impact on the management of major claims should not be understated. PD49 was a long overdue revolution in the management of major claims pre-Woolf. That situation existed between 1 November 1996 and 26 April 1999.

CDF Protocol

8.15 The Clinical Disputes Forum ('CDF') Protocol has been effective since January 1999, and the Woolf multi-track case management system more recently. The current defence of major claims is greatly influenced according to when a claim is first notified to the hospital, but long before the arrival of Woolf, claims managers had recognised the need for pro-active steps being taken prior to formal notification of a claim.

Early Warning Devices

8.16 The defence strategy is to speed up the process before the claimant has begun his action. This is achieved by identifying potential claims, obtaining statements, instructing in-house and external experts to reach a decision on liability and causation well in advance of any notification of a claim. The consequence for hospitals has been to install early warning devices. These devices facilitate immediate communication to the claims department on the occurrence of one or more of the following events:

(a) within a short time, preferably four weeks, of any untoward incident occurring;

(b) on the receipt of a complaint which contains a potentially litigious element;

(c) on receipt of an application for records either under the Access to Health Records Act 1990 (now superseded by the Data Protection Act 1998);

(d) on receipt of a request for pre-action discovery (old rules), pre-action standard disclosure (new rules) whether or not in the approved Law Society form.

Claims Handling and Risk Management

8.17   The current aim for the defence is not just to beat the claimant to the finishing post but to beat the claimant to the starting post in reaching a decision on liability. The traditional approach of waiting for a letter before action or issue of court process is no longer acceptable. This is particularly so in cases involving minors where notification of a claim may not be received for 20 years and for the children or patients without capacity well beyond the limitation date. Good clinical risk management strategy enables Trusts to identify potential claimants within four weeks of birth or in adult cases within four weeks of the incident. There can be no doubt that risk management in all fields, but particularly obstetrics, anaesthesia and orthopaedics is now an essential tool in setting up untoward incident reporting systems of events and near misses on which the foundations of effective claims management can be built. The disadvantage might be that time and costs are incurred in investigating claims which ultimately are not pursued but the positive side is that whether or not a claim is pursued the lessons learnt from that exercise can be passed on to the regular unit audits to improve standards and reduce risks.

Identifying the Claim

8.18   The identification of potential claims depends on the local claims officer's skill and the standard of communication within the Trust, between clinicians and management and between complaints and medical records officers and claims managers. The initial intended purpose of incident reporting was an audit function identifying risks specific to the hospital or the unit but its adopted function enables potential claims to be identified at an early stage ensuring essential evidence is preserved and vital witnesses interviewed and statements obtained shortly after the events.

Early Steps

8.19   A defendant lawyer is frequently frustrated by not being able to locate key witnesses or having to rely on unexplained notes of witnesses who have moved out of area, or abroad. Written records rarely afford a complete defence to the claim without some explanation behind the contemporaneous note. Effective claims management of major clinical negligence claims start here. The preserving and obtaining of evidence in form of records, CTG traces, X-rays and scans is essential if there is to be any prospect of a successful defence.

Identifying Potential Claims

8.20   It is an internal matter for the Trust to decide which events should be reported and investigated but modern defence strategy necessitates all potential claims being reported and investigated pro-actively. Many hospitals now have an in-house panel, comprising the consultant in charge, clinical director and hospital claims manager to review all incident reports on a regular basis and liaison between complaints and claims departments is imperative.

Beating the Front Loaded Claim

8.21   From the defence lawyer's perspective, instructions cannot be received soon enough. Although the Woolf rules incorporating the CDF Protocol recommendation of sending a letter of claim three months prior to issue of proceedings is an improvement, in reality the parties are still not on an equal footing. The claimant's case is front loaded, having collated over a long period all their factual and expert evidence, often obtained counsel's advice, assessed quantum and included a Part 36 pre-action offer. The defence have only three months to carry out a similar exercise. For this reason, waiting until the letter of claim has arrived is too late in major medical negligence claims. The sooner a potential claim can be identified the better. The more efficient Trusts tend to seek legal advice at a much earlier pro-active stage. Having gathered basic preliminary evidence themselves and taken the in-house view of consultants they can seek legal advice on the issues of liability and causation enabling independent expert opinion to be obtained pre-action and hopefully before receipt of the letter of claim.

Early Analysis

8.22   Having received instructions from the client together with all relevant papers, including statements from the treating consultant, junior doctors, nurses and midwives and a full set of medical records and any correspondence from the patient or their representatives, the skill of the defence lawyer is to prepare an early analysis of the case.

8.23   The key to analysing issues is not to lose 'the wood for the trees'. In a celebrated paper by Lord Salmon in 1994, entitled 'Some Thoughts on the Traditions of the English Bar' he commented that 'very seldom are there more than two and never, well hardly ever, more than three points that matter in a case'. Whether you are handling a major or a small claim, early identification and analysis of those two or three material issues is imperative.

Identifying Issues – The Chronology

8.24   To identify the issue, it is essential to have a proper and detailed chronology, not just a superficial list of events but an informed list highlighting significant medical findings or omissions which are likely to be relevant to material issues. One of the practical problems for defendants is if the claimant has moved from the area, changed hospital, where there are third-party hospital or GP records which are essential to fill in the gaps. This generates a delaying factor which can only be overcome by the claimant or his solicitors' co-operation in consenting to release of records. Once the overall picture on the jigsaw is in place, it is much easier to identify the likely points of dispute. There are familiar patterns of negligence in all cases. In the excellent publication on *Safe Practice in Obstetrics and Gynaecology*[1] Roger Clements identified in relation to obstetrics the cascade of errors, delay and communication as the regular pattern leading to claims. Most cases can be categorised under those headings whatever the discipline involved.

1 Clements R, *Safe Practice in Obstetrics and Gynaecology* (1995) Churchill Livingstone.

Case Analysis and Case Theory

8.25 The defence identification of issues should not be dependent on the allegations made by the claimant if they are known. In particular, there are often matters apparent from clinicians' statements that are not obvious on the face of the medical records, which are the only documents on which claimants, their experts and advisors initially rely. It is not uncommon for the claimants to raise additional or fresh issues once the records have been disclosed and the letter of claim procedure does not prevent issues being raised subsequently. Often claimant experts raise fresh issues following an exchange of factual evidence. For defence purposes, identification of issues and the formulation of a case theory is the foundation on which the future management of the case is based. Case analysis is now a fundamental part of any professional practice training. The traditional litigators' method of compiling detail on detail from the client, feeding evidence piecemeal to counsel and experts and only eventually painting the whole picture for the client to see close on trial, led to the notorious 'on the steps settlement' of so many cases which could and should have been resolved sooner. The Woolf reforms with the new pre-action openness and 'cards on the table approach' has helped, but the key is the effectiveness of the client's early warning device systems which should enable an early analysis to be reached and case theory formulated on the issues of liability, causation and quantum.

8.26 Modern litigation practice is driven by the client's needs, not the lawyers' timetable. In clinical negligence the client must be encouraged to devise early identification of claims and in-house risk management systems to collate the evidence as soon as possible.

NHSLA Protocol

8.27 The NHSLA recognise the importance of this pro-active approach in their Existing Liability Scheme ('ELS') claims management protocol which requires a detailed analysis from the defence lawyers within 15 working days of receipt of instruction. To effectively do this the bulk of the work in obtaining evidence and in-house and external independent expert reports must have already been completed prior to instruction of solicitors.

8.28 The CNST Reporting Guidelines January 2000 for hospital claims officers now require a Preliminary Analysis within 40 days of receipt of a request for medical records.

8.29 The issue of liability for negligence having been identified and investigated, the equally important substantive issue in all major claims which must be fully investigated is causation.

CP and Spinal Claims Causation

8.30   In cerebral palsy cases, having established with the experts an agreed time by which earlier intervention should have taken place, causation experts namely neonatologists, paediatric neurologists and neuro-radiologists should be instructed to advise on the balance of probabilities of the effect of the period of hypoxia. Similarly, in serious spinal injuries advice from orthopaedic spinal specialists, neurosurgeons and neuro-radiologists is essential to ascertain precisely when the patient's condition became irreversible and whether earlier diagnosis or referral would have altered the outcome.

The Early Admission

8.31   Having obtained advice on liability and causation, the defence strategy is to make an early admission of liability and/or causation to prevent unnecessary costs being incurred by the claimant. It is important that the wording of that admission accords with expert opinion and the wishes of the client and the NHSLA. Early admissions have the effect of 'taking the sting' out of the litigation, relieving already distressed parents or carers of the burden of worrying whether they will have to prove fault. It also enables sensible voluntary interim payments to be made in deserving cases to facilitate the NHSLA objective of getting 'the right money to the right people at the right time'.

Defensible Claims – Cards on the Table and Pre-action Expert Meetings

8.32   In cases where the expert evidence confirms defensibility on liability or causation that view will, of course, be expressed in any letter of response to a letter of claim but there is no reason why pro-actively, even before the letter of claim is formulated, the claimant's solicitors should not be advised of the likely grounds for defence and invited to attend a 'without prejudice' pre-action meeting between experts. At the very least, this will reduce the issues or clarify the differences between the parties experts at this early stage. Local experience has shown that even post-action claimants' solicitors and the courts are currently reluctant to allow or direct experts to meet, without prior exchange of all factual and expert evidence. Is it not in both clients' interests that experts meet pre-issue before they become too entrenched? Experts often find themselves committed to an opinion previously expressed in writing, from which it is difficult to withdraw whereas following a 'without prejudice' oral discussion the issues may be crystallized and a greater understanding arises of 'where the opposing experts are coming from' before any views are committed to print. The lawyer's fear is that experts will 'carve up' the case pre-issue of proceedings rendering the entire legal process obsolete.

Defensible Claims and Post-action Expert Meetings

8.33   Post-action, in all major claims where there are live issues of liability and causation, courts now direct (regardless of the parties' wishes) discussions between experts, either face-to-face or by telephone conference or video link. It is essential an agenda is agreed before the meeting. Following such a meeting, an agreed note is produced which should enable lawyers on both sides to review their client's position on liability and either to seek client's approval of an admission or to draft further directions for the court's approval at a case management hearing. The status of the agreed note is the subject of debate at present, as is the format and role for lawyers, if any, at these meetings. We must await the outcome of the Experts Working Party for further guidance.

Split Trials

8.34 Most major claims are now subject to a direction for split trial. There are rare occasions where defence lawyers believe that credibility issues on quantum might affect the outcome on liability but for the most part the court will seek to limit, not broaden the issues and have separate and discrete issues tried first. One of the major problems for the defence in trying to resolve major claims quickly, where they receive unfavourable expert advice on liability and causation, is the lack of available information on quantum. Post-Woolf 'proforma' (rather than detailed) schedules of damages often accompany the statement of case and the accompanying medical reports set out the past chronology in some detail but regrettably scant evidence as to current condition and future prognosis.

Quantum Only and Joint Experts

8.35 Where there has been an early decision on liability for negligence and causation, effective case management on quantum depends on the claimant or his advisor's co-operation. If issues of liability are not live, there seems no reason why instruction of single experts on condition and prognosis should not be agreed. There is a difficulty for an expert who is requested to deal with causation as well as condition and prognosis, particularly where there are two schools of thought which might place him in the difficult position in reaching a definitive conclusion. Provided however, the issues of liability and causation have been resolved or dealt with by other independent experts, the modern common sense approach is joint instruction of a single expert. Apart from the obvious saving in costs and less inconvenience to the patient, the new Woolf obligations under CPR Part 35 should ensure an independent and objective report on which realistic quantum calculations can be achieved. In cerebral palsy cases, a great deal of money can be saved by joint instruction in relation to the therapists namely, physio, occupational, speech and language but there remains a need for independent paediatric neurologists' reports because of the difficult issue of life expectancy which has such a vital influence on calculation of the multiplier. Set out below are two recent case studies which show how the court process is stayed pending development of the child.

CASE STUDY 4

Facts

Baby MK born on 22 November 1995 with shoulder dystocia, difficulty in resuscitation, now microcephaly, quadriplegic cerebral palsy and significant learning difficulties.

Issues

Failure to monitor, failure by midwife to refer to medical staff, failure to follow protocol, delay in delivery, failure to resuscitate and intubate.

Defence admitted liability for breach of duty but initially disputed causation. Issue remaining relates to quantum. See Chronology below.

Chronology

22.11.95	Date of birth
21.06.96	Pre action disclosure of records.
28.10.96	Originating summons for discovery of disciplinary papers.
19.12.97	Defendant admission of liability for breach of duty.
05.06.98	Writ of summons and statement of claim.
09.07.98	Defence (as to causation and quantum).
06.08.98	Cranial MRI performed. Report disclosed to both parties.
21.08.98	Defence conceded causation of damage.
04.09.98	Consent order (judgment entered for plaintiff for damages to be assessed). Defendant makes interim payment of £150,000.
17.09.98	Summons for directions adjourned to be restored onapplication by either party on or before 22 May 2002 (claimant will be 6½) for directions on assessment of damages.

Reflective Review

- No letter of claim in this pre-Woolf action but pro-active steps taken by defence immediately on request for documents.
- Two years from birth before admission of liability (could have been three months if earlier authority to obtain expert evidence).
- Causation not conceded until 21 August 98 once expert advice had been obtained on cranial MRI.
- If MRI had been performed earlier, admission could have been made sooner (dependent on parents' consent because required general anaesthetic).
- Quantum, not resolved, matters deferred until plaintiff 6½ years old.
- Would be possible to make Part 36 offer or payment now but life expectancy uncertain.

CASE STUDY 5

Facts

WB born on 7 July 1995, delay of 23 to 28 minutes in delivery, profound asphyxiation leading to severe cerebral palsy.

Issues

Failure to monitor, failed to interpret CTG trace correctly, failure to call medical staff, failure to follow protocol, caused delay. Pre-action admission by defence. See chronology.

Chronology

07.07.95	Date of birth.
06.02.97	Letter before action.
20.03.98	Defence admission of liability for negligence and causation.
03.09.98	Voluntary interim payment, £20,000.

22.12.98	Writ of summons.
14.01.99	Order for directions, judgment entered.
15.02.99	Further interim payment, £30,000. Summons for directions adjourned 26 May 1999.
26.05.99	Hearing for directions. Contested. Defence requested disclosure of claimant's evidence on quantum, claimant solicitors refused until child aged seven years old. Order adjourning matter until 21 December 2001 but thereafter fast tracked to assessment hearing.

Reflective Review

- Benefit of an early admission of liability is seen.
- Could have been obtained even earlier within 3-6 months of birth avoiding claimant's costs of preliminary experts' opinion and letter before action.
- Dilemma for defendants in not able to obtain order for disclosure of quantum evidence but need to make realistic assessment of Part 36 offer and payment.
- Debatable whether claimant would be penalised in costs even if the Part 36 offer/payment proves to be sufficient.
- No letter of claim in this pre-Woolf case but even if there had been 3 months before issue, would have been insufficient time to obtain the range of specialist expert advice required on liability and causation.
- Need for pro-active steps by defence on request for records.

Defence dilemma

8.36 The defence objective is to resolve the claim as soon as possible by negotiating or making a substantial payment, by way of Part 36. The claimant's problem is that they may not be able to properly advise on the adequacy of the offer or payment until their experts confirm they are able to predict life expectancy.

8.37 In the meantime, defence solicitors and experts are expected to make realistic assessments of claims at a very early stage with a view to early settlement. It will be interesting to see how the courts deal with this dilemma, namely whether the claimant or his advisors will be penalised in costs if the defence make a sufficient Part 36 offer or payment some years before the claimant's experts are willing to confirm life expectancy. From a defence point of view client protocols require a realistic assessment at the inception of the case and to prepare a 'counter schedule' years before the claimant's schedule of damages will become available.

Early Realistic Assessments of CP Claims

8.38 It is essential to identify the type of cerebral palsy concerned. Cerebral palsy is a non-progressive but dynamic disorder of motor function, secondary to damage of the motor pathways in the developing brain. As most of this development takes place between conception and the birth and the first two years of life it is possible to identify the type of cerebral palsy concerned as follows:

(a) Spastic cerebral palsy results from damage to the pyramidal pathways and signs including fisting, abnormal limb posture, increased limb tone and increased deep tendon reflexes.

(b) Dyskinetic cerebral palsy results in damage to the basal ganglia and extra pyramidal pathways and signs including fluctuating tone, abnormal posturing and involuntary movements and rigidity.

(c) Ataxic hypotonic cerebral palsy which is due to a lesion of the cerebellum or its connecting pathways and is evidenced by low tone, poor balance, inco-ordination of movement and in the very young child often by delay in motor milestones. Quadriplegia implies involvement of all four limbs and any type of cerebral palsy could be represented.

The Evidence Required

8.39 It is essential therefore to have up-to-date medical notes on assessments by paediatricians of the claimant child, which should be available in the acute hospital notes or in some cases in the Community Trust notes if that Trust has the management of the paediatric service. It is therefore vital to have available copies of the most recent notes from your clients or failing that obtain consent to release from the claimant's solicitors, on the understanding you will provide them with full disclosure of their client's notes in return for the consent being supplied promptly. MRI scans are a particularly helpful indicator and an up-to-date paediatric assessment of motor skills and intellectual ability also form key evidence of likely life expectancy.

The Research Data

8.40 The research data[1] regarding life expectancy in children with cerebral palsy, reflecting the UK population, has indicated that children with cerebral palsy and two severe disabilities in the areas of ambulation and manual dexterity have an 80.5% chance of surviving to 27 years from birth. If children have three disabilities in the areas of ambulation, manual dexterity and learning ability then they have a 44.7% chance of surviving to 27 years from birth. There are, of course, other factors involved and the higher standard of care, education, stimulation, monitoring and family support which were lacking in the past do tend to optimise the Pharaoh figures for the prospects of survival. Other research,[2] in particular Strauss (1997/98) has indicated the most useful prognostic factors for survival are mobility and feeding skills. Evidence from defence experts on risks from respiratory infection and other consequences of immobility (osteoporosis, fractures, urinary tract infections and joint contractures) accidents and mental stress will be needed. The general quality of care also influences the risk from these factors, which is why as much information regarding the current care regime as can be gathered from the recent notes is essential in making a realistic assessment.

1 Hutton, JC, Cooke, T and Pharaoh POD, Life Expectancy in Children with Cerebral Palsy [1994] 309 BMJ at 431-35.
2 Strass, DJ et al [1997] 131(5) P.

The Realistic Assessment

8.41 All the above enables the defence to take an early view on life expectancy on a 'rough and ready' basis. The risk for the defendant is that the child does not follow the predicted pattern or that modern, more proactive therapies will have a significant impact on the child's development but advice can only be provided in the light of current medical knowledge. Having assessed the likely life expectancy it is possible to calculate the multiplier in relation to the Ogden tables and the various heads of claim, pain, suffering, loss of amenity and past losses, future care, earnings, therapies, equipment, technology, accommodation, health, transport, education and miscellaneous in order to reach a global figure for reserves and negotiating purposes. Similarly, with spinal injuries it is possible, with the benefit of expert assistance, for an early expert view on life expectancy to be obtained to enable arithmetical calculation of future loss to be made on the basis of the multiplier tables and an offer of settlement or Part 36 payment to be effected either pre-action or early post-action.

Structure or Capital Sum

8.42   Needless to say, that in all major claims for clinical negligence having assessed quantum, consideration should now be given to a structured settlement and to try and ascertain the claimant's solicitors views on this at an early stage. From a defence point of view, depending on the extent of quantum, there is a requirement to inform the NHS Executive as well as the NHSLA. A value for money report ('VFM') is required from the Health Authority or Trust to the NHSLA if a structure is to be proposed.

Joint Care and Rehabilitation Assessments

8.43–8.49   Whether or not quantum is agreed, considerable savings can be made in relation to the care and rehabilitation element of the future loss by the instruction of a single expert jointly agreed by both parties. A working party is currently considering standardisation of past care rates with reference to the appropriate rate/index and drawing up a standard model for reasonable and necessary care for a 'normal' child. In essence, each case must be decided on its own particular facts and there are variations of carers rates according to geographical region. As to future care, it should be possible to agree thresholds for the rates of a residential carer/night carer and this is a key area where the instruction of a single expert should also prove cost effective. This should avoid the current comparison of the minutiae in care experts' detailed schedules. At the very least, a joint report should enable a realistic assessment to be made of the patient's future needs so that reasonable interim provision can be agreed, securing proper care for the patient pending resolution of the claim.

FUTURE MAJOR 'CLINICAL NEGLIGENCE' CLAIMS HANDLING

Advanced Front Loading

8.50   Front loading is the order of the day, not just for claimants but for defendants and their advisers. With improved incident reporting and communication between clinicians and managers it is hoped that the early warning devices for identifying potential claims will prompt the obtaining of factual evidence and in-house and external expert reports close on the incident. In the event of a major claim being anticipated, whether obstetric, anaesthetic or orthopaedic, one recent proposal is for the formation of a central or regional panel of experts to give a preliminary view, (similar to the former Cases Committee of the Medical Defence Organisations whose function has not been replaced since the introduction of Crown Indemnity). The problem for such a panel might be that their opinion will be regarded as defendant biased but there seems no reason why in the halcyon days of 'Ikarian Reefer/Woolf' experts, such a panel should not produce an objective balanced view on liability and causation to disclose early admissions or alternatively legitimate grounds for defence. There might also be a possible disadvantage in such a scheme as independent experts subsequently instructed by the parties might be disinclined to oppose the panel's view for fear of disagreeing with a responsible body of opinion.

Trial by Experts – Redundant Lawyers

8.50   The future for experts must be viewed in the context of Woolf reforms under Part 35, the new Practice Direction for experts, the Clinical Disputes Forum Working Party on Experts and Louis Blom Cooper's guidance on the code for experts. Taken to its ultimate conclusion, courts and lawyers will have a very restricted role limited to arranging expert meetings, preparing agendas, informing clients of the outcome and drawing up consent orders for the court's approval. With the advent of the wide powers for the court now to appoint its own experts, for all experts to seek court directions without lawyers and for without prejudice meetings to be arranged by the court not the parties, it is likely the small percentage of cases that currently reach trial will be reduced or resolved by other means. This will leave the question of quantum and it can only be a matter of time before such calculations will be available to judges relying on computer software, based on current actuarial valuation, rather than lawyers' lengthy schedules and counter-schedules and counsel's submissions.

Human Rights Act 1998

8.51   This is likely to have a significant impact on the management of claims both in relation to civil litigation procedure and in the wider context of confidentiality of personal records (the right to privacy) and the provision and availability of medical treatment (the right to life) and consent issues. There is plenty of scope for Euro-lawyers to challenge 43-year old UK *Bolam* principles.

Alternative Dispute Resolution ('ADR')

8.52   Apart from resolution by the new Woolf experts, the future of ADR and mediation in clinical negligence should not be understated. The early mediation pilot schemes have not met with great enthusiasm from lawyers on both sides. However, it is now a requirement for lawyers to justify to the court why they have not attempted mediation at the allocation stage. It would not be surprising if, in the near future, mediation became a mandatory preliminary direction as in the commercial court. At the very least, the courts might impose costs sanctions on all parties who do not attempt resolution by ADR. On the horizon, we have a renewed policy drive by the NHSLA to support ADR and mediation whenever appropriate. Not surprisingly the mediation advocates are critical of the small number of cases referred in practice. The patient and hospital's desire to have cases resolved with minimum involvement of legal costs from lawyers and with a solution being agreed between the parties rather than imposed by the court, must be an attractive proposition for both parties. The advantages of earlier resolution, absence of counsel and experts, addressing non-monetary issues and letting the parties, not the lawyers, set the agenda are certainly appealing factors for clients. Mediation can never provide a binding legal precedent but is an important option to litigation which can be invoked at any stage of a major clinical negligence claim, pre- or post-action, particularly where the patient or relatives resources to fund litigation are limited and the risk of success is uncertain.

Epitaph by Woolf

8.53 'The openness on the part of both parties which the protocols will encourage will in turn provide the information which is necessary for disputes to be resolved whenever possible by recourse to the now justifiably fashionable ADR ... there is everything to be gained by the hospital using its resources to make available mediators and neutral claim evaluators at their own expense'.[1] There has been much discussion about ADR in clinical negligence but regrettably little evidence to show its implementation. The future of ADR in clinical negligence will depend on the extent to which the NHS might be prepared to resource Woolf's proposal.

1 Lord Woolf 24 June 1997, UKCC Annual Lecture.

Part 2

Medical Issues

Chapter 9

Acquired Brain Damage

Bryan Jennett CBE MD FRCS

9.1 Acute brain damage can rapidly produce a life threatening situation, yet it can be difficult in the early stages to predict what the outcome may be. This outcome may be death in the first few hours or after days of intensive treatment, or it may be complete recovery. Many survivors, however, suffer a wide range of disabilities, from impaired motor and sensory skills, intellectual performance and memory, as well as changed personality and behaviour and loss of mental well-being.

9.2 Claims for victims of brain damage usually relate to acute insults to the brain, which may be traumatic or non-traumatic. Most non-traumatic insults produce brain damage by hypoxia – reduction of the oxygen supply to all or part of the brain. However, the initial mechanical damage sustained by the brain in a head injury is often followed by processes that result in secondary hypoxic brain damage. There are therefore many similarities in the disabilities resulting from traumatic and non-traumatic brain damage, although the initial mechanisms of causation are different. In parts of this account it will therefore be necessary to deal separately with head injury and non-traumatic brain damage.

VULNERABILITY OF THE BRAIN

9.3 There are physical and chemical features of the brain that make it peculiarly susceptible to both mechanical and hypoxic insults. The jelly-like consistency of the brain makes it liable to bruising, tearing or distortion when the moving head rapidly decelerates by hitting an immovable object. The surface of the cerebral cortex impacts against the rough internal surface of the skull, causing bruising (contusions). These are usually most marked on the poles of the temporal and frontal lobes, no matter which part of the head was hit. But sometimes the contusions are limited to the opposite pole from the point of impact (frontal damage from an occipital impact). This is termed contra-coup injury. It is therefore difficult to relate brain damage reliably to the site of impact. Such contusional brain damage can occur without a skull fracture, but it is often more severe under a fracture of the skull vault or base, when it may amount to laceration of the brain surface.

9.4 Quite a different type of impact damage accounts for most patients who are in deep coma from the outset, and some of whom recover only to severe disability or the vegetative state. It depends on the vulnerability of the fine nerve fibres that make up the white matter of the cerebral hemispheres and brain stem, which are stretched or ruptured by shearing stresses when the head abruptly decelerates on hitting an immovable object. The resulting lesion is known as diffuse axonal injury ('DAI'). In such cases there is often no severe contusion of the cortex, no skull fracture and no raised intracranial pressure. Indeed, the brain may look almost uninjured on gross examination at post mortem. The true extent of the damage is evident only on microscopic examination by a neuropathologist, dissecting the brain after it has been fixed in formalin for two to three weeks. This is therefore not a diagnosis that could be made by a coroner's pathologist who limits his observations to immediate slicing of the unfixed brain. Damage of this kind usually results from a severe impact such as occurs in road accidents or falls from a height. However, it has been found also after assault, probably because the victim has fallen his length and hit unyielding ground.

9.5 The other mechanical feature of the brain is that it is contained in an unyielding bony cavity. Consequently, if there is an increase in the volume of the intracranial contents by the accumulation of extruded blood in multiple contusions or in a discrete clot (haematoma), or by swelling of the brain from bruising, vascular engorgement or oedema, the intracranial pressure must rise. This will impede the flow of blood into the brain and will eventually cause hypoxia. This secondary hypoxic brain damage may be accentuated in parts of the brain where blood vessels have been occluded by distorting shifts of parts of the brain that occur in response to accumulating haematoma or areas of swollen brain. Hypoxic brain damage is a common finding in the brain after fatal head injury and is presumed to be a feature also in patients who survive with brain damage.

9.6 Hypoxic brain damage after head injury may be aggravated by, or even mainly due to, systemic hypoxia or hypotension due to associated extracranial injuries or complications. Blood loss from haemorrhage, inadequate respiration due to chest injury, or a poorly maintained airway (for example, by the unconscious patient swallowing the tongue or inhaling vomit) may lead to reduced cerebral oxygenation and may even lead to cardiorespiratory arrest.

9.7–9.9 The chemical or metabolic feature that distinguishes the brain from other organs is its dependence on a continuous supply of oxygenated blood. The brain consumes oxygen at a high rate both when awake and asleep and it has neither oxygen stores nor any shut-down mechanisms for dealing with shortage of oxygen, such as many other organs have. Moreoever, a critical shortage of oxygen for only two to three minutes not only stops the machine but wrecks the machinery, causing irreversible structural brain damage. There is, however, some degree of selective vulnerability, the cerebral cortex being more sensitive to oxygen starvation than the more primitive brain stem.

SEQUENCE OF EVENTS AFTER HEAD INJURY

9.10 The significance of contusional impact damage from head injury is not that brain function is greatly affected by it, for such patients often recover completely. The danger is that secondary brain damage may occur due to complications. The torn blood vessels on the surface of the brain may result in an acute subdural haematoma, while those deep in the brain may cause an intracerebral haematoma. Often there is a combination of the two, resulting in a "burst" lobe, usually in the frontal or temporal regions. A haematoma causes life-threatening brain compression by virtue of raised intracranial pressure and distortion of brain structures, eventually reducing the blood supply to vital parts of the brain. Urgent evacuation of the clot may save life and the patient may then recover well or be left permanently disabled.

9.11 Even without the formation of a discrete haematoma, cerebral contusions can result in brain swelling from vessel engorgement and oedema. The resulting raised intracranial pressure can be as life-threatening as a haematoma, but is less easy to treat because surgical removal is not an option. Medical management in intensive care may bring the intracranial pressure under control but this is not always successful.

9.12 Even without significant initial brain damage, complications can have serious implications after certain types of head injury. If a skull fracture tears the middle meningeal artery in its groove in the temporal bone, bleeding may result in an extradural haematoma that threatens life by brain compression. Such a fracture quite often results from a blow that has caused brief unconsciousness or none at all.

9.13–9.19 The same goes for a penetrating skull fracture from a sharp object, screwdriver or an airgun pellet, or for a more extensive scalp laceration with an underlying compound depressed fracture. The brain damage is usually very limited, causing only brief or no unconsciousness. However, unless adequate surgical cleaning and antibiotics are available there is threat of intracranial infection leading to meningitis or brain abscess. A blunt injury may be an open injury if a skull base fracture tears the dura over the air sinuses of the frontal region or the middle ear cavity. The result is leakage of cerebrospinal fluid (rhinorrhoea or otorrhoea) which, if it persists, carries the risk of meningitis which may develop only after months or years.

NON-TRAUMATIC BRAIN INSULTS

9.20 The most common is an incident leading to cardiac arrest, followed by resuscitation that is in time to restart the heart but too late to save the cerebral cortex, although the more resistant brain stem survives. Such cardiac arrest may be the result of a heart attack, of primary respiratory obstruction leading to hypoxia, which affects both the brain and the heart. Such respiratory obstruction may be due to choking on food or vomit, to a severe asthmatic attack or bronchospasm as a reaction to some drug, to near drowning or strangulation. These respiratory events may themselves be enough to cause brain damage without cardiac arrest occurring. Another situation is during the course of general anaesthesia when there may be difficulty in endotracheal intubation, laryngeal or bronchospasm in response to drugs, or there may be inadequate oxygen supply in the inhaled gases due to technical problems with the anaesthetic machine. In these cases cardiac arrest usually occurs due to systemic hypoxia, but the hypoxia may be enough to damage the brain without cardiac arrest. Sometimes brain damage occurs from severe arterial hypotension without cardiac arrest.

9.21   Other non-traumatic insults include severe hypoglycaemia, usually in diabetics, in whom a suicide attempt may be suspected. Insulin may be injected by mistake, or in too high a dose, as part of certain diagnostic tests. Depriving the brain of the nutrient glucose has the same effect as reducing the oxygen supply, producing similar damage.

9.22   Other non-traumatic intracranial conditions may cause severe brain damage, such as spontaneous haemorrhage, severe meningitis, brain abscess or brain tumour. These may cause brain damage abruptly as with haemorrhage or as a result of slow progression that cannot be controlled, as with infection or tumours. The mechanism of damage with these conditions is similar to an accumulating haematoma after head injury, with raised intracranial pressure, brain distortion and impaired blood flow.

9.23–9.29   A striking difference between the two types of insult is that after most non-traumatic events the brain damage is maximal at the outset. Although the crisis might have been avoided there is little that can be done once the brain is damaged. By contrast, after head injury there are a number of sequences that can lead to secondary brain damage so that there is a range of potentially avoidable factors that can lead to damage or even death after an initial injury that was not serious. This can lead to disputes about liability for severe brain damage when the impact injury was not severe. Attempts are sometimes then made to blame inadequate care at some stage for the ultimate outcome. This may be relevant when compensation for medical negligence is at issue. But it is seldom successful in other cases because it is usually maintained that there has been no break in the chain of causation.

ASSESSING BRAIN DAMAGE AFTER RECENT HEAD INJURY

9.30   The most consistent evidence of diffuse brain damage when the head as a whole has been decelerated, leading to contusional damage or DAI, is impaired consciousness. This may range from a few minutes of confusion to many days of coma. The extent and duration of this impairment of consciousness is the best guide to the severity of diffuse brain damage and it is assessed using the Glasgow Coma Scale (Table 1). This scale records three aspects of behaviour – eye opening, motor response in the best limb and verbal response. By ascribing a score to each response it is possible to add these to describe the patient's conscious state on a scale of 3-15. It is now convention to describe patients admitted with a Glasgow Coma Score ('GCS') of 13-15 as having a mild injury, GCS 9-12 moderate and 8 or less severe. Only a minority of injuries are severe but, as already explained, complications often result in less severe injuries having an unfavourable outcome. Because less severe injuries are so much more common they make a major contribution to poor outcomes. Thus, about 40% of patients who develop an acute intracranial haematoma needing surgery were initially moderately or mildly injured, and that accounts for over 40% of patients whose outcome is severe disability. Apart from assessing initial severity of injury a practical use of the GCS is in regular monitoring of the recently head-injured patient, in order to recognise any deterioration in conscious level. This is the earliest and most consistent sign of complications, in particular of intracranial haematoma, and immediate action is then required to avoid further deterioration.

TABLE1

Glasgow Coma Scale

Eye opening	E
spontaneous	4
to speech	3
to pain	2
nil	1

Best motor response	M
obeys	6
localises	5
withdraws	4
abnormal flexion	3
extensor response	2
nil	1

Verbal response	V
oriented	5
confused conversation	4
inappropriate words	3
incomprehensible sounds	2
nil	1

E + M + V = 3-15, the coma score

Duration of Coma and PTA

9.31 While the GCS on admission after injury allows an initial assessment of the severity of impact injury, the duration of coma adds further information. Some patients with a low coma score on admission rapidly improve, sometimes because of resuscitation restoring normal breathing and blood pressure, sometimes because the effects of alcohol wear off or simply by reason of spontaneous improvement. It can then be concluded that the initial injury was not very severe. If coma persists for many hours or days then clearly the injury has been more severe.

9.32 For purposes of rehabilitation and when making a legal report, a doctor may first see a patient months after injury, when the original medical records may be unavailable or prove incomplete. It is then very useful to assess the severity of the brain damage by the duration of the post-traumatic amnesia ('PTA'). After diffuse brain injury associated with any impairment of consciousness, patients suffer a period of loss of memory for ongoing events. Even when the injury is followed by only a period of confusion without actual unconsciousness it will be some time before the patient remembers "coming to" and has continuous ongoing memory. This is always much longer than the period of actual reports by bystanders. Thus, onlookers or family may report that the patient started speaking or recognising them at a certain stage, yet for some time after that the patient has no continuous memory. Only an approximate estimate of PTA is needed to categorise severity (Table 2).

Table 2

Severity grading by PTA

Less than 5 minutes	–	very mild
5-60 minutes	–	mild
1-24 hours	–	moderate
1-7 days	–	severe
1-4 weeks	–	very severe
>4 weeks	–	extremely severe

9.33   Some patients who are initially unconscious, perhaps only for a few minutes, regain the ability to talk and sometimes even to be completely oriented, before lapsing again into coma from complications. They are said to have had a 'lucid interval'. It is known that 30-40% of head injuries who die in hospital have talked. In these 'talk and die' cases there are often so-called 'avoidable adverse factors' in their management that could have contributed to death (or to severe disability in survivors). Such factors are delay in recognising deterioration or in taking appropriate action when it occurred, or failing to prevent or expeditiously to deal with systemic complications such as airway obstruction, low blood pressure or blood loss – usually due to associated extracranial injuries. When patients who had a lucid interval lapse into coma, their PTA may be continuous from the time of injury, but it will still be valid to record that their initial injury was not very severe.

Skull Fracture

9.34   It is damage to the brain that matters after head injury. While a fracture is evidence of the head having been subjected to a certain amount of violence, it is only certain types of fracture that are important because of the risk of secondary brain damage. A closed fracture of the vault increases the risk of an intracranial haematoma. Fractures that result in an open injury with risk of infection are also important – compound depressed fracture of the vault, or skull base fracture with dural tearing.

9.35–9.39   While a fracture may indicate that violence to the head has occurred, or that there is a risk of certain complications, the absence of a fracture does not indicate lack of violence. Indeed the most severe type of DAI is frequently found in the absence of skull fracture.

ASSESSING BRAIN DAMAGE SOON AFTER NON-TRAUMATIC INSULT

9.40   The Glasgow Coma Scale is again the best indication of the severity of the brain damage. If, in addition, the pupils are fixed and dilated this is a sign of serious brain stem damage and if it persists survival is unlikely. In contrast to head injury, when the concussive damage in severe cases leads to eyes-closed coma for 2-3 weeks, after severe non-traumatic coma the eyes may open after 24 hours or so. This may signal the beginning of recovery but in some cases it indicates the onset of the vegetative state (see para 9.53).

9.41 Investigations by CT scan are of little value, as they may show only evidence of brain oedema and cannot indicate the extent of the diffuse hypoxic damage at this stage. As for treatment, the only question at issue is how quickly resuscitation was established – to establish an airway by intubation, to restore blood pressure or inhaled oxygen supply, or in the case of cardiac arrest to restart the heart by external massage or defibrillation.

MANAGEMENT ISSUES FOR HEAD INJURIES

9.42 For the Accident and Emergency Department the main issue is how to deal with the large number of mild injuries, with a view to identifying the few with risk factors for complications. These questions are who should have investigations, who should be admitted for observation and who should then be considered for consultation with or transfer to regional neurosurgeons. It is now widely recognised that in the past too many mildly injured patients were admitted for observation and it is now held safe to send home patients without a fracture who are fully conscious even if they have been briefly unconscious or amnesic. The proviso is that there is a responsible adult at home to whom instructions can be given about contacting the hospital if symptoms suggestive of complications should develop. For the more severe cases the decision to transfer is the important one as is the safety of transfer. There is evidence that unless precautions are taken and trained escorts are provided, there is a risk of complications developing during such transfer and these may aggravate the brain damage.[1]

1   Gentleman D, Jennett B 'Audit of Transfer of Unconscious Head Injured Patients to a Neurosurgical Unit' [1990] 335 Lancet pp 330-34.

9.43 In patients with major associated extracranial injuries another problem is deciding priorities. If there is shock or haemorrhage from extracranial injury these must be treated, otherwise secondary brain damage may occur. On the other hand it is a mistake to embark on definitive reconstructive surgery for some extracranial injuries, with the attendant risks of anaesthesia and added shock, as well as making observation for complications of head injury difficult.

Skull X-ray and CT Scan

9.44 There is some controversy about the value of skull X-ray in the management of head injuries, since the availability of imaging techniques that directly show brain damage and accumulating intracranial haematoma. Experience shows that only about half the patients after a recent head injury have a plain X-ray and that only 1-2% have a fracture. There is no indication for skull X-ray in the Accident and Emergency Department for a seriously injured patient who is obviously going to be admitted and will have a CT scan then. A problem is when the concern is whether or not a fully conscious patient should be admitted or not, and whether a CT scan can help this decision.

9.45 CT scan is now available in many Accident and Emergency Departments but only a minority of cases justify its use. It can show contusions but is often normal when there is serious brain damage. Moreover, a CT scan done very soon after injury may be normal or show only limited contusions in a patient who subsequently develops a significant intracranial haematoma. It is therefore important to be willing to repeat the CT scan if there is clinical signs of deterioration. The microscopical lesions of DAI will not show on CT scan although accompanying macroscopic lesions in certain areas may suggest that such damage has occurred. MRI gives better definition and may show abnormalities when the CT is normal but its limited availability makes it a tool of use only in specialist centres or for research purposes. A problem may arise when CT scans are done in general hospitals without neurospecialists to interpret the pictures, leading to false alarms or false reassurance. In some places telephone transmission of the CT images to the regional neuro centre deals with this problem.

Guidelines

9.46 In an attempt to clarify these difficult issues guidelines for the initial management of head injuries have been issued.[1] These deal with indications for skull X-ray, for admission to a general hospital, for CT scan in a general hospital and for transfer to a neurosurgical unit. For the management of head injuries in childhood some recommendations were made some years ago by paediatricians.[2] However, the recently published guidelines are taken to apply also to children. Because of geographical considerations and variations in the availability of certain facilities from place to place, it is recommended that the Accident and Emergency Departments and the regional neurosurgical unit should draw up their own local guidelines, derived from these national recommendations.

1   Working Party of the Society of British Neurological Surgeons. Guidelines for the Initial Management of Head Injuries [1998] 12 British Journal of Neurosurgery pp 349-52.
2   Working Party of the British Paediatric Association and British Association of Paediatric Surgeons. Guidelines on the Management of Head Injuries in Childhood. London, British Paediatric Association 1991.

9.47 These guidelines are concerned mainly with the initial management of head injuries, most of which are mild. They emphasise the interaction between Accident and Emergency Departments and Neurosurgical Units. For the minority of severely injured patients other considerations apply. Recommendations for the care of patients with continuing impairment of consciousness, especially during transfers between or within hospitals have been made by anaesthetists.[1] The continuing treatment in intensive care of patients remaining in coma for days remains controversial and there is considerable variation in the methods used.[2] However, an American consortium did agree guidelines in 1996[3] and a year later a European group produced another document.[4] These could be described as permissive rather than the more prescriptive tone of the recent UK recommendations for initial management. In any event it is important to recognise that guidelines are only that. They are not rules or standards. The complexity of head injury makes it essential that the locally involved clinician has the freedom to make what decisions seem best in any particular case at any particular time. He should of course be prepared to justify decisions that a given guideline was not appropriate in his circumstances.

1 Working Party of the Neuroanaesthesia Society and Association of Anaesthetists. Recommendations for the transfer of patients with acute head injuries to neurosurgical units. London, Neuroanaesthesia Society and the Association of Anaesthetists, of Great Britain and Ireland, 1996.
2 Jeevaratnan DR, Menon DK, 'Survey of Intensive Care of Severely Head Injured Patients in the United Kingdom' [1996] 315 Br Med J pp 944-47.
3 Bullock MR, Chestnut RM, Clifton G et al., 'Guidelines for the Management of Severe Head Injury' [1996] 13 Journal of Neurotrauma pp 639-734.
4 Naas AIR, Dearden M, Teasdale GM et al (on behalf of the European Brain Injury Consortium) 'EBIC Guidelines for Management of Severe Head Injury in Adults [1997] 139 Acta Neurochirur (Wein) pp 286-94.

Questions About Early Care of a Head Injury

9.48 In concluding this account of the acute stage after head injury, certain questions might be asked in order to verify that management has been appropriate.

(1) Before the patient reached hospital were there delays or difficulties that might have aggravated the brain damage?
(2) Was management of the patient's airway and associated extracranial injuries appropriate and adequate at the roadside, at the first hospital and during the subsequent transfer?
(3) Was the nature and severity of head injury properly assessed – GCS applied and recorded – open skull fractures recognised and extracranial injuries diagnosed?
(4) Was continuous observation of the head injured patient adequate and was appropriate action taken expeditiously when there were signs of complications?
(5) If the patient was either not admitted, or was sent home after a day or so of observation, was the patient's state adequately assessed before discharge? Was a responsible relative or friend given a head injury information sheet or card indicating symptoms that might indicate complications, with clear instructions to telephone the hospital or bring the patient back?

LONG-TERM OUTCOME

9.49 There is extensive literature on the outcome after severe head injury but virtually none on that after non-traumatic insults, which are less common. What follows is largely an account of the sequelae of severe head injury, with brief notes about other types of brain damage where relevant.

9.50 Most clinicians classify outcome after acute brain damage using the Glasgow Outcome Scale.[1] In addition to dead and vegetative there are three categories of outcome for conscious survivors, which focus on the patient's social capacity rather than on details of the neurological deficit .[2] In each of these categories the mental impairments are more important than the physical in more than half the cases.

(1) Severe disability is summarised in the term 'conscious but dependent', and the degree of dependency varies greatly. Some require 24 hour nursing care,

while others are mobile and capable of self care but, by reason of cognitive and behavioural disorders, are not safe to leave without supervision for a 24 hour period, in many cases for more than a hour or so.

(2) The moderately disabled are independent, able to use public transport, to shop and to live on their own. Some are capable of work, usually in a reduced capacity but in some occupations and with a sympathetic employer normal work may be resumed.

(3) Good recovery indicates the capacity to return to work and to resume normal social life. It does not, however, imply that there are no sequelae and indeed a quarter of those so categorised have not fully integrated into their former life and in particular may not have resumed previous employment.

1 Jennett B, Bond M, 'Assessment of Outcome after Severe Brain Damage.' [1975] 1 Lancet pp 480-84.
2 Wilson JTL, Pettigrew LEL, Teasdale GM 'Structured Interviews for the Glasgow Outcome Scale and the Extended Glasgow Outcome Scale: Guidelines for Their Use [1998] 15 Journal of Neurotrauma pp 573-85.

9.51–9.52   In a series of 600 survivors of severe head injury in the UK the outcome six months later was 2% in the vegetative state, 28% severely disabled, 28% moderately disabled and 42% good recovery. These broad categories of outcome are of most use for clinicians assessing the efficacy of various treatment regimes in the acute stage after brain damage and in planning rehabilitation. For personal injury claims a more detailed assessment is required which relates specific deficits to the circumstances of an individual patient. The exception to this is the vegetative state, the rarest outcome category. Not only is this a clearly defined clinical entity, but it has special legal significance by reason of the size of claims for damages that it attracts, and because its medical management in the UK is subject to legal constraints.

THE VEGETATIVE STATE

9.53   This term was introduced in 1972 by Jennett and Plum[1] to describe the clinical condition resulting from loss of function in the cerebral cortex with the brain stem continuing to function. About half the cases result from a head injury when severe DAI results in isolating the cerebral cortex, which may also be affected by secondary hypoxic damage. In non-traumatic cases the cerebral cortex is extensively damaged. In both types of case the thalamus is severely affected on both sides, further impairing cortical function. Vegetative patients have long periods with the eyes open (thus they are not in coma), and they can breathe on their own (as distinct from brain dead patients who are ventilator-dependent). The eyes may move in a roving fashion and in some patients may occasionally briefly appear to focus or follow and the spastic limbs move reflexly when touched or pinched. Facial grimacing or groaning noises are frequently observed. But no words are uttered, no commands are obeyed and there is no evidence of a working mind. Research investigations indicate that the metabolism of the cerebral cortex is reduced to levels found in deep barbiturate narcosis. The patient is awake but not aware, and it is widely accepted that in this unconscious state the patient is unable to feel pain or suffer mental distress. Some vegetative patients can swallow small amounts but in practice adequate hydration and nutrition depends on tube feeding. Sometimes this is through the nose but usually by a percutaneous gastrostomy ('PEG') – a tube introduced surgically into the stomach through the skin of the abdomen.

1   Jennett B, Plum F, 'Persistent Vegetative State after Brain Damage [1972] 1 Lancet pp 734-47.

Diagnosis

9.54   Diagnosis depends on a careful observation over a period of time, because no radiological or laboratory tests can make the diagnosis.[1] It is not uncommon for families and sometimes professional carers unfamiliar with this condition to interpret reflex activity as meaningful responsiveness. It can require patient and careful assessment by experts over a period of time to make the diagnosis and it is not uncommon for non-expert doctors to fail to detect limited levels of responsiveness .[2] These require that the patient be diagnosed as in a minimally conscious state. While this may represent the first stage of recovery to a better state many patients remain permanently minimally conscious. It is particularly important to exclude the locked-in syndrome, resulting from brain stem damage. Such a patient is fully aware but totally paralysed, although able to communicate by code, using the sole remaining motor power by blinking the eyelids or moving the eyes.

1   Wade DT, Johnston C, 'The permanent vegetative state: practical Guidance on Diagnosis and Management' [1999] 319 BMJ at 841-43.
2   Andrews K et al, 'Misdiagnosis of the Vegetative State: a Retrospective Study in a Rehabilitation Unit [1996] 313 BMJ pp 13-9.

Prognosis

9.55   The 1972 paper described the persistent vegetative state ('PVS'), and specifically stated that this did not imply permanent. The Multi-Society Task Force in 1994[1] set out statistics for recovery from PVS, based on patients declared in this state one month after an acute insult. Recently there have been recommendations in several countries to discontinue the use of persistent and to use only the vegetative state, until the criteria for permanence had been satisfied, when it is appropriate to refer to the permanent vegetative state. It is not yet widely recognised, however, that the P in PVS has changed its meaning and the use of this abbreviation may therefore be misleading.

1   Multi-Society Task Force on the Persistent Vegetative State 'Medical Aspects of the Persistent Vegetative State [1994] 330 N Engl J Med pp 1499-1501 and 1572-79.

9.56   The American Task Force reviewed 754 cases published in the world literature and showed that about half of those vegetative one month after a head injury regained consciousness, with a reducing proportion doing so of those still vegetative after three or six months. Only 14% of non-traumatic cases vegetative one month after the insult regained consciousness. Many patients who recover consciousness, particularly after several months in a vegetative state, remain very severely disabled and dependent, often failing to speak and still requiring tube feeding.[1] The Task Force recommended that permanence could reasonably be assumed after three months in non-traumatic cases but not until one year after head injury, while recognising that very occasional cases with slight degrees of recovery had been reported later than this. In the UK the more conservative period of six months for non-traumatic cases has been recommended by the Royal College of Physicians .[2]

1   Andrews K 'Recovery of Patients after Four Months or More in the Persistent Vegetative State' [1993] 306 Br Med J pp 1597-1600.
2   Royal College of Physicians Working Group, 'The Permanent Vegetative State [1996] 30 Journal of the Royal College of Physicians London pp 119-21.

Life Expectancy

9.57   There are many fewer data about this than there are for recovery. The Task Force acknowledged that several survivals of more than 20 years had been reported, some for 30 or 40 years. Its conclusion that average expectancy was 2-5 years and that survival beyond 10 years was based on patients vegetative only one month after an acute insult. Only a quarter of these are alive and in a vegetative state after one year, the rest having died or made some recovery. For those who have already survived a year in the vegetative state the chances of more prolonged survival are therefore considerably greater. A more recent report records 10 years as the median survival for those in a vegetative state aged 19-21 years.[1] Another report indicates 14-15 years survival at age 15 years and 11 years at age 40.[2]

1   Ashwal S, Eyman RK, Call TL 'Life Expectancy of Children in a Persistent Vegetative State' [1994] 10 Paediatric Neurology pp 27-33.
2   Strauss DJ, Shavelle RM, Anderson TW, 'Long-term Survival of Children and Adolescents after Traumatic Brain Injury' [1998] 79 Arch Phys Med Rehabil pp 1095-1100.

9.58   A Channel 4 telephone support line following a documentary on the vegetative state in 1994 logged 458 calls from people with relatives or friends in a vegetative state. Of these, 78 had been vegetative for 10 years or more.[1] Clearly it can no longer be maintained that survival for more than 10 years is unusual. However, claims that because vegetative patients have no progressive disease they have a normal life expectation are quite unrealistic. These patients are vulnerable to chest and urinary tract infections, the usual causes of death. Moreover they are unable to report the symptoms of disease that may be curable or controllable, such as cancer or heart disease. Another factor is whether a policy has been adopted not to treat infective complications with the antibiotics, which is commonly the case. By the time legal claims are being settled the patient has often already been vegetative for several years and it may be clear whether or not they are subject to repeated infective episodes. Clearly younger people are likely to live longer. For the patient already five years in the vegetative state it is reasonable to assume a further ten years as the probable expectation of life.

1   Jennett B, 'A quarter century of the Vegetative State: an Internatinal Perspective' [1997] 12 J Head Trauma Rehabil pp 1-12.

Management of the Permanent Vegetative State

9.59   The question of where it is most appropriate to care for the permanently vegetative patient is sometimes an issue of legal importance. Most such patients are in long-term care, either in rehabilitation units, in units that care for dependent patients of various kinds or in nursing homes. Perfectly adequate care can be provided in such settings and this is where the very long-term survivors have lived. Some relatives, usually parents of teenagers or young adults, request that provision be made for care at home. This usually requires alterations to the house or the acquisition of a larger house, to allow for hospital-type bathing and showering facilities and to accommodate live-in carers. While such arrangements are feasible to make they involve expenditure of four to five times that charged by a nursing home. It is difficult to sustain a case that there is any benefit to the patient in being cared for at home, and the purpose of the enterprise is mainly to satisfy the wishes of the parents.

9.60 There is a widespread consensus in many countries that survival for years in a permanent vegetative state is of no benefit to the patient and that it is therefore appropriate to withdraw life-sustaining treatment once permanence is declared.[1] Many institutions and courts in the USA and the UK have agreed that artificial nutrition and hydration is medical treatment that can be withdrawn by a doctor if judged to be of no continuing benefit to the patient. Once this is done a peaceful death occurs in 8-12 days, the cause of death being regarded as the original brain damage. In the USA many such cases went to state courts in the 1980s and one to the US Supreme Court. It is now considered inappropriate in the US to bring such cases to court unless there is a dispute that cannot be otherwise resolved.

1 Jennett B, 'A Quarter Century of the Vegetative State: An International Perspective' [1997] 12 J Head Trauma Rehabil pp 1-12.

9.61 In the UK the case of *Bland*[1] established that withdrawal of tube feeding from a permanently vegetative patient is lawful and this was confirmed in the unanimous decision in the House of Lords. It was, however, stated that each further case of this kind should require a declaration by the High Court (Family Division). In the subsequent six years 18 cases came to court, in all of whom a declaration was made.[2] In these cases the Official Solicitor acts as *guardian ad litem* for the patient and the rules for applying to the court have been set out by him in a Practice Note.[3] He requires that the patient has been in a vegetative state for 12 months after a head injury or 6 months after other insults. A second expert opinion is required from the applicant (next of kin or health authority). The diagnosis should be in accord with accepted guidelines, and those of the Royal College of Physicians are mentioned. However, the court has been willing to grant a declaration in cases in which certain eye signs listed by the Royal College of Physicians were not satisfied because the experts in court considered them to be irrelevant to the central issue of whether the patient had any awareness.[4] There is concern that only in England is a court required to sanction treatment withdrawal, and it is hoped that some alternative formality may eventually be allowed.

1 *Airedale National Health Service Trust v Bland* [1993] AC 789; [1993] 1 All ER 821.
2 Hinchliffe M, 'Vegetative State Patients' [1996] NLJ Practitioner pp 1579-80 and 1585.
3 Official Solicitor to the Supreme Court Practice Note, 'Vegetative State' [1996] 2 FLR 375.
4 *Re D (1997)* 38 BMLR 1, [1998] 1 FLR 411.

SPECIFIC DEFICITS IN CONSCIOUS SURVIVORS

9.62 As indicated above, these comprise both neurophysical and mental, the combination resulting in the overall impairment of function with resulting disability and social handicap.

Neurophysical deficits

Cerebral Hemispheres

9.63   About half the survivors six months after severe head injury have some evidence of damage to the cerebral hemispheres – the cortex or its connections. This is more common in patients who have had evacuation of an acute intracranial haematoma but secondary ischaemic brain damage is probably also an important cause of such focal deficits. Hemiplegia or hemiparesis (paralysis or weakness of the arm and leg on the side opposite to the brain damage) is the most common deficit. As after a stroke, the arm and hand are worse affected than the legs and most patients are able to walk again - sometimes with persisting spasticity and a limp. If the dominant hemisphere is affected (left side in right handed and some left handed people) then language function may be affected. Dysphasia may affect both speaking and understanding spoken and written communications. Again, considerable recovery in the first year is usual, but when dysphasia persists it can be very disabling. If the visual tracts in the cerebral hemisphere are damaged the patient may be left with a homonymous hemianopia – loss of the visual fields on the opposite side. This affects both eyes and if it is complete is a bar to holding a driving licence.

Brainstem and Cerebellum

9.64   Damage to these structures is much less common but a few patients suffer ataxia (unsteadiness of gait) and sometimes difficulty in articulation of speech (as distinct from problems with language).

Cranial nerve Deficits

9.65   About a third of survivors at six months have one or more of these, and in half such cases these are the only persisting neurological signs.

Anosmia

9.66   Loss of the sense of smell results from damage to the skull base in the frontal region, and is common in patients with CSF rhinorrhoea. If surgery has been necessary for this there is more likely to be anosmia. Recovery after three months is unusual. The patient with anosmia loses an important pleasure of life – the smell and taste of food, and the scent of flowers. For cooks, food handlers and tasters, this can affect their employment. There is also the loss of the ability to detect dangerous smells (for example, escaping gas or burning).

Visual Pathways

9.67   Damage to the optic nerve in or behind the orbit can result in blindness in one eye, or loss of part of the visual field on that side. Recovery is rare after three to four weeks. Hemianopia due to cortical damage has already been noted.

Oculomotor Nerves

9.68   Damage to these nerves either in the orbit or further back results in squints and double vision (diplopia). When the deficit persists for longer than six months corrective ophthalmic surgery may be required.

Seventh and Eighth Nerves

9.69   Facial palsy is common after skull base fractures and often recovers over the first six to eight weeks. These fractures often damage the vestibular apparatus in the inner ear, resulting in vertigo and nystagmus. Specialised tests can often indicate such damage when ordinary clinical examination reveals no abnormality. Hearing loss is common after basal fractures, but when due to blood in the middle ear is usually temporary. Damage to the ossicles can cause persisting deafness which may be improved by surgical correction.

Traumatic Epilepsy

9.70 This delayed complication is of significance because of its effect on the eligibility to hold a driving licence. After severe head injury epilepsy is of most significance in patients who have otherwise made a good recovery. However, even in patients already disabled epilepsy may further limit their activities, and it makes a small contribution to reducing expectation of life. Some 5% of patients admitted after recent head injury have one or more seizures in the first week (early epilepsy) but it is late epilepsy that matters for the patient's future. Only about 5% of admitted patients develop late epilepsy, but the risk is much higher after certain types of injury and early complications.[1] After evacuation of an intradural intracranial haematoma the risk is 45%, but for an unoperated (CT diagnosed) intracerebral haematoma it is only half this. Extradural haematoma with associated intradural damage on CT carries a risk of 20%, without such damage only 2%. Compound depressed skull vault fracture has an overall risk of 17%, but this varies from less than 3% to over 50% according to combinations of four risk factors (PTA more than 24 hours, dural tearing, focal signs and early epilepsy). Early epilepsy carries a 25% risk of late epilepsy developing regardless of the type of injury, but it is of most significance when there are no other risk factors. A severe injury without any of these risk factors or marked contusional damage on CT has a risk of less than 2%.

1   Jennett B, 'Epilepsy after Non-missile Head Injuries (2nd edn, 1975) London, Heinemann. Jennett B 'Epilepsy after head injury and intracranial surgery' *Epilepsy*, Hopkins A, Shorvon S, Cascino G (eds) (2nd edn, 1995) London, Chapman and Hall.

9.71 More than half the patients who develop late traumatic epilepsy have their first seizure within the first year but in a quarter it is four years or more before this occurs. There are data indicating the residual risk after various seizure-free intervals after injury.[1] Over 70% of sufferers have seizures involving unconsciousness, but some have complex attacks involving altered feelings and behaviour without unconsciousness and these may not initially be recognised as epileptic. EEG examination is of limited value in diagnosing traumatic epilepsy, as there are often abnormalities related to the original brain damage without their being epilepsy, while the record is often normal in patients with undoubted epilepsy. In many patients the seizures are infrequent and well controlled by drugs, but in others they are frequent. The tendency for recurrence persists, even when seizures are infrequent. Prophylactic anticonvulsant drugs are of no value in preventing the development of traumatic epilepsy patients at high risk.

1   Taylor JF (ed) *Medical Aspects of Fitness to Drive: a Guide for Medical Practitioners* (5th edn, 1995) London, The Medical Commission on Accident prevention.

9.72 The Driver and Vehicle Licensing Authority has established guidelines for revoking private or vocational licences after head injury. These regulations are understandably more rigorous for those wishing to resume vocational driving (for example, buses or heavy goods vehicles). After an early post-traumatic seizure a period off driving is recommended because of the risk of recurrence. In other cases who have not yet had a seizure driving may be disallowed for a period because there are risk factors.

Mental Sequelae

9.73 These constitute the most common and most disabling sequelae of severe head injury. While only patients with more than four weeks PTA end up with severe disability and a quarter of patients with a month's PTA make a good recovery, almost all patients with more than three weeks PTA have some impairment of mental performance on formal tests of cognitive function. Mental sequelae are best considered under two headings. These are defects of cognitive function that can readily be tested by formal psychological methods (extension of IQ testing). More common than these are changes in personality and behaviour, which can occur even in some patients who do well on cognitive tests.

Cognitive (Intellectual) Deficits[1]
9.74 Traditional IQ tests depend heavily on verbal ability and these disadvantage both those with limited pre-traumatic educational attainment and those with damage to the dominant hemisphere resulting in dysphasia. They also tend to reflect the crystallised intellectual ability, reflecting a lifetime of intellectual habits, motivations and cultural expectations. Pre-traumatic ability can, to some extent, be judged by school performance and occupational status. Fluid intelligence is more relevant to present performance, as reflected in the ability to solve new problems, undertake visuo-spatial and motor tasks without verbal content. Such performance tests can go on improving over the first year after injury whereas verbal tests seldom improve after the first three to six months. Yet another aspect of performance is slowness of information processing, impaired attention and vigilance, poor attention span, distractibility and reduced speed of reaction time. Recently tests have been devised to test these aspects of mental function. These features may in part account for the frequent finding that patients perform better in the formal situation of the psychologist's test room than they do at home, where there may be no motivation to perform well and distractions abound. In that situation there is need for a carer to prompt the patient, to remind him what to do next and to ensure that a task begun is finished. Another frequent problem is poor short-term memory. This makes it difficult for patients to organise and get through even the routines of daily life and it also impairs their ability to learn new tasks. The value of psychometric testing is that it enables the patient's strengths and weaknesses to be identified, which can be helpful in planning rehabilitation and in suggesting strategies for minimising the effects of cognitive deficits in daily life.

1   Brooks DN, Hosie J, Bond MR et al, 'Cognitive Sequelae of Severe Head Injury in Relation to the Glasgow Outcome Scale' [1986] 49 J Neurol Neurosurg Psychiatry pp 549-53.

Personality Change[1]
9.75 This is the most consistent and often the most disabling sequel of a severe head injury. Three aspects of behaviour may be affected.

(1) Drive is usually reduced, with lack of motivation to initiate activities or to persevere with them. This may be reported as laziness or slowness. It can be an obstacle to successful rehabilitation, and even for activities of daily life it

may only be overcome by a relative or other carer acting as a daily god.

(2) Affect most often changes in the direction of depression, which is evident in half the patients several years after injury.

(3) Social restraint and judgment are qualities that normal people exhibit to varying degrees.

1   Brooks, N, 'Personality Changes after Severe Head Injury [1988] 44 Acta Neurochirurgica (Supplement) pp 59-64.

9.76   A common feature after head injury is that a previously well-behaved person becomes tactless and embarrassing in their social interactions. In addition, the patient may be short-tempered, apt to verbal aggression in response to minor rebuffs or refusals of requests. In some there is sexual disinhibition, resulting in verbal or physical approaches that are inappropriate. The whole picture of lack of social restraint is often summarised as childish behaviour. Personality change can become more evident as the months pass and physical recovery plateaus.

Patient Insight and Family Reactions

9.77   Many patients are so blunted that they have little insight into their disabilities, particularly mental impairments. The patient may therefore deny important disabilities and it is only by questioning relatives or other carers that the true picture emerges. Relatives can also provide information about the patient's pre-traumatic characteristics. Sometimes, however, relatives idealise the patient's previous psycho-social status. It is important to recognise that head injured persons do not form a true sample of the normal population Risk taking and aggressive behaviours are commonly a feature before injury, as are social deprivation and high alcohol intake. There is no consistent relationship between pre-morbid personality and the kind of change that follows trauma. Sometimes previous traits are exaggerated after injury. More often a previously quiet and courteous person becomes disinhibited, or a previously very active person becomes apathetic.

9.78   The effect of mental sequelae on caring relatives is an important aspect of disability after head injury – parents, spouses and siblings all being affected. Far from adjusting to the stresses of living with the disabled patient, many relatives report increasing burden as the years pass and the fact that disability is permanent becomes clear.[1] This burden often results in other members of the family leaving home and to divorce. While depression is not uncommon in patients with enough insight to appreciate their plight, other psychiatric reactions are rare and it is difficult to ascribe psychotic illness to previous head injury. Post-traumatic stress syndrome, based on reliving the stressful aspects of the accident is very uncommon, because there is almost always amnesia for these events. The first the seriously head injured patient knows is when he wakes in hospital days or weeks later. Some comment has already been made about recovery of certain neurophysical deficits.

1   Oddy M, Coughlan T, Tyreman A et al, 'Social Adjustment After Closed Head Injury. A Further Follow-up Seven Years After Injury [1985] 48 J Neurol Neurosurg Psychiatry pp 564-68. Brooks N, Campsie L, Symington C et al, 'The Effects of Severe Head Injury on Patients and Relatives Within Seven Years of Injury [1987] 2 J Head Trauma Rehabil pp 1-13.

Timescale of Recovery

9.79   Medical reports on overall outcome after severe head injury usually specify assessment after six months. It is acknowledged that some improvement occurs after this, but 90% of those who attain a moderate or good recovery by one year have done so by six months. Only 5% of patients show sufficient improvement after 12 months to change their category on the Glasgow Outcome Scale. Later recovery often proves to be a reflection of better social adjustment to a fixed disability than measurable gains on physical or cognitive tests. It is reasonable to regard two years as a time to assess outcome for personal injury purposes. Although minor improvement may occur later than this, it is unlikely to affect the degree of disability that has to be compensated and it is unfair to postpone the final settlement in the hope of further material improvement. Indeed studies as late as seven years after injury show no improvement after two years nor should it be assumed that the adverse situation in the home is likely to improve, as evidence is that in time it tends to get worse.

9.80   Life expectancy in conscious survivors after severe head injury with major disability is reduced only by about five years according to one study,[1] and by even less in a more recent study. Most premature deaths are due to accidental death, epilepsy and suicide. As the average age of disabled survivors is 27 years, they face some 40 years disability.

1   Roberts AH, *Severe Accidental Injury* (1979) An assessment of longterm prognosis (London, MacMillan).

Chapter 10

Dissecting the Spine: A Model Report

Brian Gardner BM BCH MA(Oxon) FRCP (UK) FRCS

INTRODUCTION

10.1 A model report in a claim relating to spinal cord injury should confine itself to answering fully all questions raised by the instructing solicitor. These instructions should be stated at the beginning of the report.

10.2 The report must comply fully with the Civil Procedure Rules 1998 ('CPR'). In particular it should be addressed to the court to which the expert owes his duty. A statement of truth must be included.

10.3 All literature and other material that is relied on should be stated clearly in the report. Where there is a range of opinion on any aspect then this should be indicated, together with the reasons for the expert reaching his own conclusions.

10.4 The expert should not offer opinions or advice in areas in which he has no knowledge. A curriculum vitae should be appended to assist the court in this regard.

10.5 The effective resolution of a personal injury claim in a spinal cord injury case is dependent on a comprehensive medical report that covers all aspects of the claimant's situation. Incomplete or otherwise inadequate reports prolong the litigation process. This not only increases costs but also, and more important, delays financial restitution to the severely disabled person at a time when he is in great economic need.

10.6 It is likely that the medical expert will increasingly be required to act as lead expert in spinal cord injury cases. Even when this is not the case the court is unlikely to approve an item claimed without implicit or explicit medical support.

10.7 The purpose of this chapter is to help the medical expert to construct a report that incorporates all aspects relevant to the spinal cord injured claimant so that the rest of the legal team of experts, including specialists in care, therapy, psychology, housing, employment and special equipment, can be pointed in the correct direction from the outset.[1] The headings in Appendix 1 of this chapter indicate those areas that should be covered in a comprehensive report.

---

1 Grundy D and Swain A (eds) 'ABC of Spinal Cord Injury' [1993] British Medical Journal.

10.8–10.11   After all experts have assessed the claimant a case conference should be held to clarify any uncertainties. The schedule of expenses should then be prepared. Claims approached in this way will result in an appropriate and cohesive case being prepared with the minimum of correspondence. The claimant will receive appropriate compensation at the earliest possible time after the prognosis has become clear. This will enable him to restart his life early. It will also reduce the financial impact on the defendant.

DEFINITIONS

10.12   A spinal cord injury is complete if there is no somatic motor or sensory function below the level of injury. If the arms are spared the claimant has paraplegia. If they are involved he has tetraplegia. The level of injury is the lowest intact spinal cord segment. If there is residual sacral sensation then the injury is incomplete. If there is useful function several segments below the injury then the claimant has either paraparesis or tetraparesis. Use of the terms quadriplegia and quadriparesis should be avoided.

CLINICAL ASSESSMENT

Liability – Negligence and Causation

10.13   Medical experts are sometimes requested to advise regarding the extent to which different negligent incidents have caused the disability, for example in multiple vehicle accidents or when there was inappropriate handling of the spinal cord injured person at the scene of the injury.

10.14   Spinal cord injured persons may have contributed to their injury, for example by not wearing a seat belt. In these cases the determination of the appropriate reduction in quantum may be assisted by medical advice based on the nature of the injuries sustained and the pattern of the accident. An understanding of the mechanism of injury of the spine and spinal cord is required.[1]

1   White AA and Panjabi MM (eds) Clinical Biomechanics of the Spine (1990) JB Lippincott Co.

10.15   When medical negligence is alleged, medical expert advice is crucial. There is considerable variation in opinion regarding the correct management of spinal cord trauma. Provided that the particular treatment selected is reasonable and is carried out competently and with an acceptable degree of care then there is no negligence.

10.16   Missed fractures are an important area of medical negligence. Common sites include the cervico-dorsal junction and spinal fractures below the major one. Simple basic principles are sometimes overlooked. Accurate radiological evaluation may not be possible immediately after the accident. If there are reasonable grounds for believing that the patient has sustained an unstable spinal injury then appropriate steps must be taken to immobilise the spine until such time as the diagnosis can be confirmed or refuted.

10.17   Causation is often a major area of dispute. Although multiple secondary factors arise in the spinal cord after trauma,[1] these rarely cause spontaneous deterioration. Negligent treatment of a patient with a complete spinal cord injury results in much less harm than when the injury is incomplete. In general, those with some voluntary movement below the level will improve to gain useful function provided that their care is good.

1   Tator H and Fehlings M 'Review of the Secondary Injury Theory of Acute Spinal Cord Trauma with Emphasis on vascular mechanisms' [1991] 75 J Neurosurgery pp 15-26.

10.18   The most comprehensive studies on neurological prognosis following spinal cord injury can be found in the various National Acute Spinal Cord Injury Studies ('NASCIS').[1] In these prospective double-blinded randomised multicentre studies the newly spinal cord injured were examined immediately they entered the emergency rooms. Another useful guide is the USA spinal cord injury database.[2]

1   Bracken MM et al 'Administration of Methylprednisolone for 24 or 48 Hours or Tirilazad Mesylate for 48 Hours in the Treatment of Acute Spinal Cord Injury' [1997] 277 JAMA pp 1597-1604.
2   Stover SS, DeLisa JA and Whiteneck GG (eds) Spinal Cord Injury Clinical Outcomes from the Model Systems (1995) Aspen p 173.

10.19   The presence shortly after trauma of widespread deep tendon reflexes below the injured level points to the spinal cord lesion being incomplete. Conversely, an early flexor plantar response is unhelpful as it may be the deep plantar response that is frequently found in the early stage after acute spinal cord injury.[1]

1   Ko H-Y, Ditunno JF et al 'The pattern of Reflex Recovery During Spinal Shock' [1999] 37 Spinal Cord pp 402-409.

10.20   Other pointers to an incomplete lesion in high thoracic and cervical spinal cord damaged persons are normal blood pressure and pulse. These cardiovascular parameters are usually reduced with complete sectioning of the descending sympathetic nervous pathways.

10.21   Complications such as pressure sores can usually be avoided with good care. Early transfer to a dedicated comprehensive spinal cord injury centre is required.[1]

1   Carvell J and Grundy D 'Patients with Spinal Injuries. Early Transfer to a Specialist Centre is Vital' [1989] 299 BMJ pp 1353-1354. Donovan WH, Carter RE, Bedbrook GM, Young JS, Griffiths ER 'Incidence of Medical Complications in Spinal Cord Injury: Patients in Specialised, Compared with Non-specialised Centres' [1984] 22 Paraplegia pp 282-92.

Quantum

10.22   To clarify the quantum issues it is advisable to divide the consequences of spinal cord injury into categories. In each, acute and chronic aspects should be considered.

10.23   Before these categories are described in detail the history of the spinal cord injured person since injury should be given. Relevant family, medication and past medical history should be stated. Smoking should be highlighted as this interacts with and augments most of the important causes of morbidity and mortality in the spinal cord injured.

Associated Injuries

10.24   Associated injuries can be very important in determining the quantum consequences of spinal cord damage. They must be described in the report. Some of the more relevant are described in paras 10.25-10.33.

Brain
10.25   The duration of unconsciousness and post-traumatic amnesia must be stated. The latter is the best guide to the severity of a brain injury though sometimes sedative drugs and artificial ventilation preclude an accurate estimation. Whenever significant brain damage has occurred a full psychological and psychometric assessment is mandatory.

10.26   Successful rehabilitation following spinal cord injury is dependent on the total involvement of the disabled person. Impairment of personality, memory, concentration and intellect can profoundly alter outcome. Good executive function is of particular importance in enabling the spinal cord injured person to lead a safe and well-integrated life. Relatively minor degrees of higher cerebral impairment can interact with the other problems associated with spinal cord injury to make employment much more difficult.

10.27   The commonest cranial nerve abnormality following head injury, and the most frequently overlooked in spinal cord injury cases, is the loss of sense of smell and the altered taste sensation that results from olfactory nerve damage.

Limb Joints, Bones and Soft Tissues
10.28   Injuries to limb bones, joints and soft tissues should be described, in particular where residual deformity or loss of movement has occurred. An orthopaedic opinion is required when the prognosis for a joint or bone abnormality is uncertain.

10.29   Spinal cord damaged persons are more dependent on their arms than prior to injury. Joint damage, and to a lesser extent long bone fractures, can severely impair transfers and wheelchair skills. Contractures are frequently very disabling.

10.30   Because arm joints, especially the shoulders, are put under stress by the routine activities of wheelchair life, problems commence in them at an earlier age. The onset of these joint problems is accelerated by joint damage sustained at the time of injury.

Peripheral Nerve Injuries, Especially Brachial Plexus
10.31   The nature, degree and prognosis of any peripheral nerve or brachial plexus injury must be stated.

10.32   Paraplegics require both arms for most activities. An affected arm cannot cope as well as an unaffected one with transfers and wheelchair control. The functional impact of a disabled arm can be reduced by trick movements that may take years to develop.

Chest and Abdominal
10.33   Chest and abdominal injuries, though life threatening at the time of the original event, are seldom important in quantum terms because they do not often

result in an increased requirement for care or equipment, and rarely alter life expectation after the acute stage.

Neurology

10.34   The level, degree of completeness and pattern of the spinal cord injury must be clearly stated in the report as they are of central importance in determining outcome and prognosis. There is no level of neurological disability, including ventilator dependency, that is incompatible with life in the community.[1]

1   Whiteneck G et al *The management of high quadriplegia* Demos.

10.35   Incomplete injuries are associated with a longer expectation of life.[1] Preserved sensation enables the paralysed person to become aware of complications as they arise below the level of injury. Complete spinal cord injured persons also learn to recognise signals coming from the paralysed and denervated parts of the body but these are less precise. It is not just pressure sores but also other complications such as intra-abdominal events and long bone fractures which are recognised in this way. When there is useful muscle as well as sensory function below the level of injury then life expectation is further improved.

1   Coll JR, Frankel HL, Charlifue SW and Whiteneck GG 'Evaluating Neurological Group Homogeneity in Assessing the Mortality Risk for People with Spinal Cord Injuries' [1998] 36 Spinal Cord pp 275-79

10.36   Every neurological level in the cervical region is of vital importance. In paras 10.37-10.45 typical features relating to the different cervical, thoracic and lumbar spinal cord injury levels are described.

10.37   Patients with complete lesions at C3 and above usually require a greater or lesser degree of ventilatory support, such as intermittent positive pressure ventilation and phrenic nerve pacing . Non-invasive ventilation by mouth carries a lower risk to life as tracheostomy related complications are avoided.

10.38   C4 level persons can almost always breathe independently but are otherwise totally dependent. Electric wheelchair mobility and control of the environment is achievable using retained head and neck control.

10.39   C5 level patients have good shoulder control as well as elbow flexion. With aids, such as feeding straps, limited function is possible. Assistance is required with every activity.

10.40   C6 level persons have good wrist dorsiflexion. Elbow extension is achieved by means of trick movements. By locking the elbow, transfers are sometimes possible. Wrist dorsiflexion is associated with passive tenodesis of the fingers and the thumb.

10.41   Upper limb reconstructive procedures can be of great benefit at this level of injury. Active elbow extension can be achieved by the Moberg posterior deltoid to triceps transfer procedure. A stronger and more active key grip can be achieved by tendon transfers around the wrist, such as insertion of the extensor carpi radialis longus into flexor digitorum profundus and the brachio-radialis into flexor pollucis longus. Upper limb electronic implants are also beneficial in selected cases. These procedures do not usually increase transfer capability but they do improve upper limb control and so lead to an improved quality of life.[1] When these upper limb reconstructive procedures are done the upper limb is temporarily immobilised in plaster.

> 1   Moberg E *The Upper Limb in Tetraplegia: A New Approach to Surgical Rehabilitation* Georg Thieme.

10.42   C7 and C8 level persons have sufficient upper limb function to achieve a degree of independence in transfers and activities of daily living, but not those functions that require precise hand control.

10.42   Upper thoracic, T2 to T6, level persons lack the abdominal and lower paraspinal muscle control that is essential to achieve good truncal balance. Backwheel balance control and transfers are impaired as a result. Spontaneous spasms are likely to cause problems in transfers. Ambulation in long leg callipers is difficult and usually requires braces that stabilise the upper body, such as the reciprocating and hip guidance orthoses.

10.43   Lower thoracic, T7 to T12, persons have greater abdominal and paraspinal muscle control and hence better truncal balance. Higher kerbs can be negotiated because better backwheel balance can be achieved.

10.44   L1 level persons frequently achieve ambulation though this is seldom of functional benefit.

10.45–10.49   Mid-lumbar level persons have good quadriceps control that usually allows functional ambulation.

LONGER-TERM NEUROLOGICAL CONSEQUENCES

10.50   The report must incorporate potential future hazards that could have a serious impact on the care and equipment needs of the spinal cord injured person in the future. Spinal cord deterioration is the most important of these risks. In recent years it has become clear that the incidence of tertiary spinal cord change is much commoner than had previously been recognised. These changes continue to develop throughout the life of the spinal cord injured person. The most important tertiary change is the spinal cord syrinx.

10.51   The previously quoted incidence of syrinx formation was between 2% and 4%. This was largely based on clinical diagnosis. It is now clear that the incidence of syrinxes is much greater than this because the majority do not have diagnostic clinical features. In a recent study carried out in Stoke Mandeville Hospital on 153 patients whose spinal cord injury was more than 20 years ago, the overall incidence of syrinx formation was 20%. The longer since the injury the more likely the spinal cord injured person was to have a syrinx.[1]

> 1   Wang D, Bodley R, Sett B, Gardner BP, Frankel HL 'A Clinical Magnetic Resonance Imaging Study of the Traumatised Spinal Cord More Than 20 Years Following Injury' [1996] 34 Paraplegia pp 65-81.

10.53 The aetiology and management of syrinxes remains controversial. Surgery may be required. Continued review is advised.[1] If a person has a spinal cord syrinx he needs to alter his lifestyle so as to avoid those abrupt stresses, strains and other events that can cause serious spinal cord deterioration. Falling out of the wheelchair, for example, can be associated with the loss of the use of a hand or an arm.

1   Nielsen OA, Biering-Sorensen F, Gardner BP et al 'Clinical Case of the Month. Post-traumatic Syringomyelia' [1999] 37 Spinal Cord pp 680-84.

10.54   A person with a spinal cord syrinx needs a greater degree of care assistance at an earlier age because of his need to avoid the risks associated with deterioration, such as falls during transfers.

Spine

10.55   The spinal column injury and its management should be described in the report. Great detail is seldom necessary because following the acute event spinal problems are not usually a major concern.

10.56   Arthritis may occur at an earlier stage in the intact spinal joints above and below the injured segment. This can give rise to increased spinal pain and stiffness in older years. This contributes to the greater dependence that occurs with ageing. Deformities such as gibbus are seldom functionally important.

10.57   Long spinal fixations can be very disabling. A young person with paraplegia and a long fixation is usually totally independent in his younger years but when older his loss of truncal mobility cannot be so readily compensated for by increased movement of the hips. This brings forward the stage at which dependence increases. Long fixations in the cervical region prevent the tetraplegic person from looking around.

10.58   Approximately 10% of spinal injured patients have fractures at multiple levels. Those below the level of the main fracture are important if they cause neurological damage or significant spinal deformity. A thoraco-lumbar fracture, for example, can damage the spinal cord conus giving rise to loss of bladder, bowel and erection reflexes.

10.59   Progressive skeletal deformity is a particular problem in children. Regular careful spinal column review is required until skeletal maturity. Whereas gibbus does not significantly increase disability, scoliosis can be a significant problem. Sitting posture, the pattern of pressure on the ischial areas and transfers are impaired. Surgical correction is often required.

Pain

10.60   It is essential that the report gives a detailed description of any pain, its characteristics, its prognosis and the manner in which it affects the spinal cord injured person.

10.61   Musculo-skeletal and neurogenic pains are common following spinal cord injury. They can be intractably disabling. Treatment is frequently difficult as well as limited within the NHS, especially the non-pharmaceutical approaches.[1] Pain clinics seldom have the resources required to provide the ongoing support that many spinal cord injured persons need.

1   Richards JS 'Chronic Pain and Spinal Cord Injury: Review and Comment' [1992] 8(2) Clin J Pain pp 119-22.

10.62   Sometimes pain makes it necessary for the spinal cord injured person to shift from one position to another or to lie down at intervals during the day. Employment can be difficult for this reason and also because both pain and its medication can affect concentration.

Bladder

Lower Urinary Tract
10.63   The report should describe past, present and future urological care. The method by which urine is drained, urological complications to date and current uro-renal status should be stated.

10.64   Bladder sensation and control are impaired in the spinal cord injured. The precise pattern of bladder management varies with the individual.[1]

1   Parsons KF and Fitzpatrick JM (eds) *Practical Urology in Spinal Cord Injury* (1991) Springer-Verlag.

10.65   All methods of bladder care are associated with events that can be distressing and inconvenient. With intermittent self catheterisation there is incontinence. Toilets are frequently inaccessible. With reflex voiding the urinary sheath occasionally comes off causing the spinal cord injured person to become soaked. Minor penile skin problems can prevent application of the sheath, forcing the person either to remain in bed or to insert an indwelling catheter.

10.66   When partial control remains there is usually urgency and frequency that impairs the spinal cord injured person's quality of life, for example by forcing him to plan his journey according to the location of accessible toilets.

10.67   Bladder management for females is particularly difficult. There are no satisfactory external urine collection appliances. The risk of incontinence and the awareness that there may be a smell of urine impairs self-confidence and femininity.

10.68   Several urological procedures exist that benefit certain groups of patients. The more commonly used include augmentation cystoplasty, distal urethral sphincterotomy, the artificial urinary sphincter and the Brindley sacral anterior root stimulator. The latter is of particular benefit in females.[1] Newer techniques of sacral root stimulation that obviate the need for sensory nerve ablation are being developed.

1   Brindley GS, Polkey CE, Rushton DN et al 'Sacral Anterior Root Stimulators for Bladder Control in Paraplegia: The First 50 Cases' [1986] 49(10) J Neurol Neurosurg Psychiatry pp 1104-10.

10.69   Many patients elect to have an indwelling suprapubic or urethral catheter. Although associated with an increased risk to life because of the inevitable infection, life-style is often improved. Indwelling bladder catheter associated problems include bladder stones, intravesical bladder changes, urethral discharge and the problems associated with catheter blockage, especially autonomic dysreflexia.

Upper Urinary Tract
10.70 Continued vigilance of the upper urinary tract is required throughout the life of the paralysed person. Asymptomatic problems such as calculi and dilatation can occur.

10.71 The pattern of review that is required varies with the individual. An annual evaluation usually suffices to ensure early diagnosis and treatment before problems arise.

10.72 Improved urological techniques, such as percutaneous and whole body lithotripsy, have reduced the morbidity of upper tract stones.

10.73 Uro-renal causes of death were the most common. They are still important but much less so than previously as a result of better urological care.

Bowels
10.74 Bowel management can be distressing, time consuming and dependent on care. The report should include a full account of its impact on the claimant, including potential future problems.

10.75 Upper gastrointestinal problems are seldom significant.

10.76 Faecal evacuation is usually a major problem. A disciplined pattern of bowel control is essential. Most spinal cord injured persons require suppositories or digital stimulation. Some require aperients.

10.77 Episodes of incontinence occur and can be very distressing. They are minimised by the avoidance of precipitating factors such as hot curries and similar foods.

10.78 Most paraplegics are able to manage their bowels by transferring onto the toilet followed by suppository insertion or digital evacuation. The rectum needs to be checked after bowel emptying to ensure that no faeces remain.

10.79 Most tetraplegics need a greater or lesser degree of assistance. Bowel evacuation while seated on a shower chair over the toilet and followed by a shower at the end of the evacuation is a popular pattern. After the shower the spinal cord injured person is dried. He then has his top half dressed while still sitting on the shower chair and his bottom half after transfer onto the bed.

10.80 Bowel problems often increase in chronic spinal cord injury.[1] Faecal evacuation takes progressively longer. Aperients become less effective. If it takes several hours to evacuate the bowels then employment is difficult to maintain. Colostomy and colonic irrigation, either antegrade or retrograde, are occasionally required.

1 Banwell JG, Creasey GH, Aggarwal AM et al 'Management of the Neurogenic Bowel in Patients with Spinal Cord Injury' [1993] 20(3) Urol Clin North Am pp 517-26.

Hygiene
10.81   Good hygiene helps to maintain the integrity of the skin. A description of the pattern of bathing is required. It should include the time taken and the level of care required.

10.82   The report should indicate if special equipment, such as shower chairs, specialised baths and driers are required,

Joints/Limb Soft Tissues

10.83   A full account must be given in the report of all problems in this area. The impact on independence and lifestyle of contractures, heterotopic ossification and joint wear can be profound.

10.84   Because of increased use, wear and tear on upper limb joints is increased. As paraplegic patients get older, episodes of upper limb joint pain and stiffness occur with increasing frequency. Extra help is needed at these times.

10.85   Heterotopic ossification can occur in the early stage following injury.[1] Hip mobility can be severely impaired. Transfers and activities of daily living become more difficult.

1   Daud O, Sett P, Burr RG et al 'The Relationship of Heterotopic Ossification to Passive Movements in Paraplegic Patients'[1993] 15(3) Disabil Rehabil pp 114-18.

10.86   The ossification process eventually becomes quiescent. Surgery is rarely required and should only be undertaken after ascertaining that there is no residual bony activity. There is a small place for radiotherapy immediately following excision.

10.87   Contractures interfere with independent living, mobility and transfers. They cause pain. In tetraplegics, contractures of the shoulders, elbows and wrists are a particular problem. In paraplegics, lower limb contractures prevent ambulation and interfere with transfers.

Spasms
10.88   The impact of spasms and spasticity on the claimant's normal daily life must be fully described in the report, together with an indication of the treatment required and any adverse effects.

10.89   Spasms and spasticity are usual accompaniments of spinal cord injury. They are sometimes helpful but more usually a hindrance. They cause embarrassment. They can be dangerous if they occur abruptly during a transfer or when driving. Spasms throw the legs out of position in bed. The sleep of both the paralysed person and the partner may be disturbed. They can assist, but more usually impair, transfers and activities of daily living.

10.90   The treatment of spasms includes the eradication of any precipitating causes, in particular those that are bladder and bowel related, good physiotherapy including standing, systemic drugs such as Baclofen and Dantrium and, in rare circumstances, operative intervention such as insertion of the intrathecal Baclofen pump.[1]

1   Sindou M, Abbott R and Keravel Y (eds) *Neurosurgery for Spasticity: a Multidisciplinary Approach* (1991) Springer-Verlag.

10.91 Systemic medication for spasticity has adverse effects. Baclofen causes drowsiness and interferes with concentration, affecting employment.

10.92 Intrathecal drug delivery can cause complications that may be serious.[1] Tubing dislodgement and kinking occurs necessitating revision. Pump replacement is sometimes necessary, in particular with the battery driven types. Regarding the latter, when a steady continuous delivery of drug is effective then the computerised pump can be replaced by a continuous infusion one that has no battery and hence should not require replacement.

1 Teddy P, Jamous A, Gardner BP et al 'Complications of Intrathecal Baclofen Delivery' [1992] 6 BJNeurosurg pp 115-18.

Respiratory

10.93 Because respiratory factors are so important in causing or contributing to morbidity and mortality following spinal cord injury, a full description of upper airway and chest problems must be given, especially those that have arisen following discharge into the community.

10.94 Respiratory functional impairment is the most important increased risk to life in tetraplegics. Carers need to be fully instructed in the relief of choking, assisted coughing, postural drainage of the chest and clearance of secretions.[1]

1 Clough P, Lindenauer D, Hayes M et al 'Guidelines for Routine Respiratory Care of Patients with Spinal Cord Injury. A Clinical Report' [1986] 66(9) Phys Ther pp 1395-402.

10.95 Permanent ventilator assisted individuals ('VAIs') can live safely in the community provided that they have sufficient care.[1] A trained carer must be in-line-of-eye of the VAI at all times and capable of suctioning, bagging, reconnecting to the ventilator and re-positioning the tracheostomy tube. Alarms to summon immediate help are required. With a portable ventilator, supplemented where appropriate by the phrenic pacemaker and other systems, free movement of the VAI out of doors including aircraft travel is possible. Tracheostomy problems can occur but the risk is minimised by good care.

1 Carter RE 'Experience with Ventilator Dependent Patients' [1993] 31 Paraplegia pp 150-53.

10.96 Mid and low cervical persons have good diaphragmatic control but no intercostal or abdominal muscle function. Their cough is weak and may need to be assisted.[1] Physiotherapy may be required during chest infections.

1 Jaeger RJ, Turba RM, Yarkony GM et al 'Cough in Spinal Cord Injured Patients: Comparison of Three Methods to Produce Cough' [1993] 74(12). Arch Phys Med Rehabil pp 1358-61.

10.97 Mid-thoracic paraplegics lack a good cough because their abdominal muscle control is absent. They may require help with chest infections in their older years.

Cardiovascular

10.98 Cardiovascular factors are an important source of morbidity and mortality in the spinal cord injured. They should be dealt with fully in the report.

10.99   Postural hypotension in the seated position is a common problem in the early stage following spinal cord injury. It is seldom disabling thereafter though tetraplegics may require occasional assistance with being tilted back when hypotension occurs.[1] A recent discovery is the linkage of postural hypotension with fatigue and 'coat-hanger' pain. The latter is felt in the neck and shoulders after the tetraplegic person has been in his wheelchair for some time.[2] Quality of life and employment prospects suffer.

1   Groomes TE and Huang CT 'Orthostatic Hypotension after Spinal Cord Injury, Treatment with Fludrocortisone and Ergotamine' [1991] 72(1) Arch Phys Med Rehabil pp 56-8.
2   Bleasdale-Barr KM and Matthias CJ 'Neck and Other Muscle Pains in Autonomic Hypotension: Their Association with Orthostatic Hypotension' [1998] 91 J Roy Soc Med pp 355-59.

10.100   The blood pressure in tetraplegics is usually reduced. This may be protective in life expectancy terms, though this is offset by other negative cardiovascular factors.

10.101   Autonomic dysreflexia is a serious potential problem in all patients with injuries at T6 and above.[1] It can be precipitated by any stimulus arising below the level of injury. The most common are those from the bladder and the bowels. Some events, such as rectal electrostimulated semen emission and vibrator induced ejaculation, are particularly potent stimuli.

1   Mathias CJ et al 'Clinical Manifestations of Malfunctioning Sympathetic Mechanisms in Tetraplegia' [1983] 7(3-4) J Auton Nerv Syst pp 303-312.

10.102   During autonomic dysreflexic episodes the arterial blood pressure can rise to dangerously high levels. Cardiac dysrhythmias can occur. Spinal cord injured persons describe that their heads are bursting open with pain. Their sweating can be so profuse that a change of clothes or bedding is necessary.

10.103   Because tetraplegics cannot deal with the factors that precipitate autonomic dysreflexia, carers need to be available to ensure that should such an attack occur then it is dealt with promptly and effectively. In intractable cases sacral root deafferentation is sometimes required.

10.104   In spite of immobility and leg dependency, deep venous thromboses and pulmonary emboli are uncommon except in the early stage following spinal cord injury. Anti-coagulation is seldom required following the acute stage.

10.105   Peripheral oedema and superficial lower limb skin changes are common. Careful attention must be paid to the feet so that cellulitis and other complications are avoided.

Skin

10.106   The history of the skin since injury, with particular reference to pressure sores, is a good guide to the quality of care that the spinal cord injured person has received. The report should deal with this aspect as well as all the facets required to minimise the risk of skin complications in the future. These include hygiene, seated posture, cushions, beds, mattresses, hoists, level and type of care, lifts in the wheelchair and turns in bed at night.

10.107 Immobility and loss of sensation contribute to the risk of pressure sores.[1] Careful discipline and good care will largely prevent their development. The insensitive skin must be inspected morning and evening.

1 Fuhrer KJ, Garber SL, Rintala DH et al 'Pressure Ulcers in Community-resident Persons with Spinal Cord Injury: Prevalence and Risk Factors' [1993] 74(11) Arch Phys Med Rehabil pp 1172-77.

10.108 The minor red marks and skin abrasions that occur during transfers are best treated by rest in bed until the skin has returned to normal. This can interfere with employment as well as quality of life. When confined to bed in this way extra care is required.

10.109 With ageing, the skin and its underlying tissues become less resilient. The risk of pressure sores increases. Spinal cord injured persons may go many years without a pressure sore and then develop a serious one.

10.110 During the acute stage following injury two-hourly turns in bed are necessary. Thereafter the gap between turns can be gradually increased. The required time-gap between turns in bed at night depends on the individual. It decreases with ageing.

10.111 Prone lying is an excellent way of maintaining the hips, minimising spasticity and preventing pressure sores.

10.112 Paraplegics are usually able to turn in bed independently in their younger years. They require increasing help as they get older. Various aids such as monkey poles are helpful. Tetraplegics usually require assistance with turns from one or more persons.

10.113 Whether one or two persons are required for turns depends on the spinal cord injured person. European regulations must be applied. These frequently mean that two people are required for activities, turns or transfers where, prior to these EEC rulings, one person sufficed.

10.114 The selection of the appropriate bed is important. The type required may change during the life-time of the person concerned. Variable height beds help carers by making transfers easier. The ability to elevate the head of the bed is useful. Rotating beds are seldom popular.

10.115 Most spinal cord injured persons prefer double beds with double mattresses that they can share with their partners. Beds that appear normal are preferred to beds which, though functional, retain a hospital-like appearance.

10.116 An appropriate mattress will increase the gap between turns and hence reduce the burden on the carers. Many different types are available. Some permit the spinal cord injured person to remain in one position for long periods. Conversely they can also make turns and transfers more difficult.

10.117 Many different types of cushions are available. The appropriate one for the individual is best selected in a posture and seating clinic because in the prevention of pressure sores it is not just the cushion and its characteristics that are important but the whole posture and seating status of the person concerned.[1] A spare cushion should always be to hand in case the main one is damaged.

> 1   Dover H, Pickard W, Swain I et al 'The Effectiveness of a Pressure Clinic in Preventing Pressure Sores' [1992] 30(4) Paraplegia pp 267-72.

10.118   The Jay Back is a useful aid to maintaining a correct posture.

10.119   The Jay Protector enables spinal cord injured persons to go up and down steps on their bottoms and to travel more safely in vehicles when other methods for buttock support are not available.

Sexual Function

10.120   The various ways in which sexual functions have been adversely affected should be described, including sexuality, fertility, intercourse and the effect of the injury on the partner and the children. The report should indicate any special aids to intercourse and fertility that are required.

10.121   Sexuality is severely impaired following spinal cord injury. A spinal cord injured man sometimes feels incomplete because not only is normal sexual intercourse impossible but in addition he cannot be a full husband, father and breadwinner, or be involved in masculine activities.[1]

> 1   Alexander CJ et al 'Sexual Activities, Desire, and Satisfaction in Males Pre- and Post-spinal Cord Injury' [1993] 22(3) Arch Sex Behav pp 217-28.

10.122   Spinal cord injured women can lose their self-respect. Wearing attractive clothes such as skirts is limited by the leg-bag and the wheelchair. Urinary incontinence is dreaded.[1]

> 1   Charlifue SW, Gerhart KA, Menter RR et al 'Sexual Issues of Women with Spinal Cord Injuries' [1992] 30(3) Paraplegia pp 192-99.

10.123   Although many approaches are available to achieve erections, including implants, intracavernosal injections, external aids and Viagra, the spontaneity, sensation and orgasm of normal intercourse are lost.[1] Viagra can be prescribed to the spinal cord injured within the NHS but the amount allowed is usually rationed.

> 1   Derry FA, Dinsmore WW, Fraser M, Gardner BP, Glass CA, Maytom MC, Smith MD 'Efficacy and Safety of Oral Sildenafil(Viagra) in Men with Erectile Dysfunction Caused by Spinal Cord Injury' [1998] 51 Neurology pp 1629-33.

10.124   Fertility in spinal cord injured men is usually severely impaired. For such a person to become a genetic father it is usually necessary for the services of a fertility centre to be used, first to prepare his semen and second to treat his female partner to increase her fertility.

10.125   Methods for obtaining semen include the penile vibrator, rectal electrostimulated semen emission, vas cannulation, micro-epididymal sperm aspiration and the hypogastric plexus stimulator. The quality of such semen is usually severely impaired.[1]

> 1   Seager SW and Halstead LS 'Fertility Options and Success after Spinal Cord Injury' [1993] 20(3) Urol Clin North Am pp 543-48.

10.126 Intra-cyto-plasmic sperm injection into oocytes ('ICSI') has a high fertilisation rate. Because the take-home-baby rate per embryo replacement cycle is only 25% several such treatment cycles are usually required. A major benefit of ICSI is that non-motile sperm can be injected. As a result frozen stored sperm can be used. This means that a single harvesting of semen from the spinal cord injured man may suffice. With other assisted reproductive techniques fresh semen is needed because only motile sperm are effective. Motility, which is severely reduced following spinal cord injury, is still further impaired by freezing.

10.127 Female intercourse is possible but passive. Orgasm does not occur except in women with lower levels of injury. Fertility is usually unimpaired.[1]

1 Berard EJ 'The Sexuality of Spinal Cord Injured Women: Physiology and Pathophysiology: A Review' [1989] 27(2) Paraplegia pp 99-112.

10.128 Both male and female spinal cord injured persons are unable to be parents in the full sense. They cannot take their children out to the park or play with them as previously.

10.129–10.139 Spinal cord injured persons who are not married at the time of injury have reduced prospects for developing firm and lasting relationships. Those already in existence are put under great stress following injury.[1]

1 Kreuter M, Sullivan M and Siosteen A 'Sexual Adjustment after Spinal Cord Injury (SCI) Focusing on Partner Experiences' [1994] 32(4) Paraplegia pp 225-35.

MOBILITY

10.140 A full description of the present and future pattern of mobility must be given. This should include a consideration of wheelchairs, vehicles, walking orthoses and aids to recreational mobility. The ability to cope with stairs must be described. The effects of ageing and upper limb problems must be outlined.

10.141 The wheelchair must be carefully selected. A spare is always required. Different wheelchairs are necessary for different purposes. For example, a sports wheelchair, a lightweight wheelchair and an electric wheelchair for outdoor use may all be required by the same person for use at different times.

10.142 The pattern of wheelchair requirement varies with the individual. It also changes with age. A young tetraplegic can cope with a lightweight wheelchair indoors on level surfaces and up shallow steps. In his older years, an electric wheelchair is required indoors instead.

10.143 The range and type of wheelchairs that are available is enormous and constantly changing. Before the appropriate wheelchair for an individual can be selected it should be both seen and evaluated by the spinal cord injured person in a practical setting.

10.144 The most sophisticated wheelchairs, such as the Permobil, allow control of the environment. These chairs can also take portable ventilators. They offer a stand-up or a reclining facility.

10.145   The wheelchair must be integrated with an appropriate vehicle for satisfactory mobility out of doors. Either the spinal cord injured person must be able to get the wheelchair in and out of the car or he must be able to get into the vehicle while still seated in the wheelchair. A portable ramp is useful when visiting friends or other places where access is difficult.

10.146   The selection of the appropriate vehicle and its controls often requires assessment in a specialised centre, such as MAVIS. The individual characteristics of the spinal cord injured person must be considered. Tall people have a restricted range of vehicle that they can use while seated in an electric wheelchair. One adjunct that assists transfers in and out of the car is the swivel seat.

10.147   Vehicle mileage is usually increased. Mobile telephones are important. If the vehicle breaks down then the paraplegic person cannot easily get to a local telephone. The vehicle must be well-maintained as the paralysed person is so dependent on it.

10.148   Spinal cord injured persons who have not passed their driving test should do so if possible. At present those at C4 cannot drive though modern controls are being developed that will permit this. Tetraplegics at the level of C5 and below are usually able to drive. Those at C5 usually require joy-stick control. Some at C6 and most at C7 and below can usually cope with vehicles with hand controls, automatic transmission, servo assisted brakes and power assisted steering.

10.149   While ambulation is seldom a functional form of mobility for paraplegics or tetraplegics, it does confer dignity and is a form of exercise. For persons with poor truncal balance, such as low tetraplegics and high thoracic paraplegics, orthoses that provide truncal support are necessary. With lower levels of thoracic and upper lumbar injury, the knee-ankle-foot orthoses suffice. Those with good quadriceps control usually cope with ankle-foot orthoses alone. While the majority of spinal cord injured persons cease to use their walking devices even when they have successfully learned to ambulate in them, few regret having mastered the technique.

10.150   Public transport, such as on trains and buses, is difficult or impossible. Air travel is usually feasible.

10.151   There are a number of recreational mobility devices, such as the three-wheeler cycle, the hand cycle and the motorised quadbike, that some individuals need. Those involved in country pursuits often need the quadbike for mobility over rough ground.

Transfers

10.152   These are the way in which a paralysed person gets from one position to another. It is important in a quantum report to deal fully with this aspect as significant care consequences flow from it. The manner in which it will change with ageing and intercurrent illness must be described. The equipment required to enable safe transfers, such as hoists, must be identified.

10.153   Nearly all paraplegics become independent in level transfers. Most achieve the more difficult ones as well, such as from the easy chair into the wheelchair and out of the bath. The most difficult transfers, such as getting from the floor into the wheelchair, and from the floor into the upright position having fallen in calipers, are achieved by only the most able.

10.154 There is great individual variation between paraplegics in their transfer capability. Factors associated with reduced ability include increasing age, poor truncal balance, spasticity, spasms, obesity and upper limb problems such as muscle strains, nerve injury and joint contractures. Those with a low arm to trunk-length ratio, for example achondroplastics, seldom achieve independent transfers. A few low level tetraplegics become totally independent in transfers, usually with the aid of a sliding board. Most require help.

10.155 The minimum pattern of help required by each individual is best determined following a course of rehabilitation in a spinal cord injury unit.[1] Spinal cord injured persons who have not been to a spinal unit are more dependent.

1   Smith M *Making the Difference* (1999) DESA Limited, Alfreton Road, Nottingham. Bromley I *Tetraplegia and Paraplegia: A Guide for Physiotherapists* 4th edn (1991) Churchill Livingstone. Sargant C and Braun MA 'Occupational Therapy Management of the Acute Spinal Cord-injured Patient' [1986] 40(5) Am J Occup Ther pp 333-37. Woods BM and Jones RD 'Environmental Control Systems in a Spinal Injuries Unit: A Review of 10 Years Experience' [1990] 12(4) Int Disabil Stud pp 137-40.

10.156–10.159 Hoists are important aids. Portable ones are versatile but ceiling mounted types take up less space. Strengthening of the ceiling is required with the latter. EC regulations must be applied when advising on numbers of carers required to assist hoisted transfers.

ACTIVITIES OF DAILY LIVING

10.160 It is important to deal fully with this aspect in the report as significant care consequences emanate from it. The simplest way of determining how a spinal cord injured person deals with his normal daily life is to ask him to describe how he manages first in a typical day and second when faced with unusual challenges. The report should point out the important aids that are required to ensure maximum independence. The ability of a spinal cord injured person decreases with ageing.

10.161 In general, young paraplegics are fully independent and tetraplegic partially independent in activities of daily living. Tetraplegics usually need help with lower-half washing, dressing and personal hygiene. Obesity, poor truncal balance, increasing age, upper limb musculo-skeletal problems, spasms, spasticity and short arms all impair ability.

10.162 Higher level tetraplegics require environmental control systems. Provided that the person can voluntarily control, in an accurate and predictable manner, a single muscle then he can control his environment, such as opening and closing curtains and using the telephone. Speech control is becoming the method of choice. The optimum application is best determined at a home visit. There should be a system in the bedroom, living room and study.

10.163 Most paraplegics and tetraplegics benefit from a remote control door-opener. If a paraplegic is sitting in an easy chair and someone calls at the house, there may be insufficient time to transfer into the wheelchair to get to the door.

10.163 Regarding showering, paraplegics are usually able to use a shower seat. Higher level paraplegics and low tetraplegics find the shower chair system more practicable.

10.164–10.167 With baths, most paraplegics can manage a normal one while they are young. This becomes more difficult with ageing. A bath-board may then help. Eventually a specialised bath is required to relieve the carer.

PSYCHOLOGY

10.168 The psychological impact of the paralysis on the spinal cord injured person should be indicated in the report, together with how much support and counselling will be required in the future. The report should indicate if a report from a psychologist or a psychiatrist is required, for example if there is a significant brain injury or a risk of suicide.

10.169 The effects of sudden paralysis, potential double incontinence, impotence, infertility, loss of relationships and all the other manifestations of spinal cord damage, affect every aspect of the person's life. The impact can be devastating. In spite of this, depression is not a major consequence of spinal cord injury and the incidence of suicide is not much greater than in the able-bodied.

10.170–10.171 Most paraplegic and tetraplegic persons who have been through a spinal cord injury unit have learned to minimise the effect of their disability. They seldom concentrate on what they cannot do. It takes careful questioning to elicit the various ways in which the quality of their lives has been irretrievably altered by their condition. It is essential that the report conveys this if the true impact of the condition is to be understood.[1]

1 Trieschmann RB 'Psychosocial Research in Spinal Cord Injury: The State of the Art' [1992] 30(1) Paraplegia pp 58-60.

FAMILY

10.172 Because the global well-being of the spinal cord injured person depends in significant part on his closest relationships, the latter must be addressed in the report.

10.173 The enormous impact of paralysis on the family including parents, siblings, spouses and children must be considered. Relationships can be destroyed. The old age of parents can be shattered by paralysis in their children. The ability of the spinal cord injured person to be a full partner or parent is severely impaired.[1]

1 Oliver M et al (eds) *Personal and Social Implications of Spinal Cord Injury: A Retrospective Study* (1987) Thames Polytechnic.

10.174 Careful questioning will elicit the precise manner in which the family has been affected. These adverse effects may rebound on the spinal cord injured person who sometimes feels guilty for the suffering caused.

10.175   The view that family members should look after their spinal cord injured relative is no longer widely accepted. It is better for normal relationships to be retained. This will increase the likelihood of the integrity of the family being preserved. In particular a partner should remain partner, parent and lover rather than become nurse and carer.

HOME

10.176   Satisfactory housing is a very important determinant of independence and quality of life following spinal cord injury. A housing expert will advise on detail but the medical specialist needs to point out in his report those housing alterations that are reasonable and necessary as a result of the injury. Any special needs of the particular claimant, such as a gym for an athlete or a study for a student, should be highlighted.[1]

1   Selwyn Goldsmith *Designing for the Disabled* (3rd edn, 1976) RIBA Publications Limited.

10.177   The accommodation that a spinal cord injured person has at the time of his injury is seldom suitable for life in a wheelchair. Re-housing is usually required. The precise requirements depend on the person concerned and the pattern of his disability.

10.178   Incomplete paraplegics who can ambulate and cope with stairs in their younger years find this increasingly difficult as they grow older. Many eventually become wheelchair dependent. Tetraplegics and complete paraplegics are safest in ground-floor wheelchair-accessible accommodation from the outset.

10.179   Among the many housing aspects that must be considered are the following:

(a)   A covered way for the vehicle and from the vehicle to the front door together with adequate space to get in and out of the vehicle under cover.
(b)   Appropriate, usually ramped, access to the house.
(c)   Doorways and corridors of sufficient width to accommodate the wheelchair base and turning circle.
(d)   Adequate storage space to avoid equipment cluttering up corridors and living areas.
(e)   A bedroom of sufficient size for easy wheelchair mobility and with storage space for catheters, urinary sheaths and other personal equipment.
(f)   An en-suite toilet and bathroom because the spinal cord injured person usually needs to get to and from the bathroom and toilet while seated in the wheelchair in a state of undress.
(g)   Appropriate hoists for intermittent use when unwell in younger years and regular use when older.
(h)   A second toilet and bathroom for use by family, guests and carers as spinal cord injured persons take a considerable time to empty their bowels.
(i)   Carer accomodation for tetraplegics throughout their lives and for paraplegics in their last years. Carer accomodation must be comfortable and attractive to help ensure satisfactory recruitment of carers.
(j)   Paraplegic and tetraplegic persons are less able to maintain their body temperature. In the case of tetraplegics, temperature control is further

compromised by altered sympathetic nervous control. Central heating is advised in all cases. Because tetraplegics can become overheated in hot weather, at least two rooms in the house should have air conditioning.

(k) Spinal cord injured persons are more vulnerable to the destructive elements in society. Household alarms are recommended.

(l) Wear and tear on carpets and skirting boards is increased by the wheelchair.

RECREATION

10.180 The report should include an indication of the recreations enjoyed before injury and those that are now possible. The equipment required to facilitate the latter should be stated if possible, though this is a specialist area. Where recreations have medical benefit this should be identified.

10.181 It should be noted that some recreational equipment might have been purchased in any event, such as a home computer system, while others, such as a page turner for high tetraplegics, would not.

10.182 Although some paraplegics and tetraplegics enjoy wheelchair sports the majority are no more sporting that the rest of the population.[1]

1 Guttmann, Sir L *Textbook of Sport for the Disabled* (1976) HM and M.

10.183–10.184 Because the range of recreational opportunities is limited and employment is often precluded it is essential that regular holidays are taken to maintain morale and family relationships. Holidays are usually more expensive as cheaper hotels are often inaccessible to wheelchairs. Accomodation in the centre of a resort reduces mobility problems but is usually more expensive. Extra help is required on holiday.

EMPLOYMENT

10.185 The pre-accident employment history should be outlined, followed by an assessment of the prospects of the spinal cord injured person returning to this or similar work in the future.

10.186 The prospects for employment following spinal cord injury are greatly reduced. Retraining centres exist. The disablement resettlement officer can also advise. Many universities have facilities where spinal cord injured persons can study.

10.187 There is a great difference between obtaining a qualification and achieving employment. The wheelchair dependent are often overlooked when there is competition. Although many paraplegics and some tetraplegics achieve employment, compared with the able-bodied it is more likely to be part than full time, intermittent than continuous and to end in early retirement.

10.188 Those who had physical outdoor manual employment prior to injury and, in particular, those with poor academic backgrounds are at a great disadvantage and usually remain unemployed.

10.189 Academically capable spinal cord injured persons and those who succeed in retraining clerically still face many problems. It takes longer to get up and get going in the morning. At work the car must be under cover and with access from it to the workplace. The latter must be wheelchair accessible. Getting from one floor to another and from one building to another may be difficult or impossible. There must be facilities to allow for episodes of incontinence. Employers have to accept that complications such as red marks and urinary tract infections will result in time off work. Drugs such as Baclofen interfere with concentration and mental agility.

10.190 Recent data on the current employment situation of the spinal cord injured population in the UK indicates that only one-third of spinal cord injured persons, mostly paraplegics, are in paid part-time or full-time employment. Poor access is a major problem.

10.191–10.194 The employment expert will advise not only regarding the ability of the individual concerned but also the relevant opportunities available where he lives.

MEDICAL CARE

10.195 Good medical care is essential for the quality and duration of life of the spinal cord injured person to be optimal. The report must indicate what future medical care will be required and the likelihood of this being met satisfactorily within the NHS.

10.196 The recent review by the Spinal Injuries Association has demonstrated once again that spinal cord injured persons who do not have a course of treatment in a spinal cord injury centre are more dependent, develop more complications and are less likely to gain employment.

10.197 The clinical needs of the spinal cord injured should be met by the spinal cord injury units and general practitioners.

Preventative Maintenance Reviews

10.198 The purpose of these reviews is to detect medical complications while they are at an early stage so that they can be treated effectively before they cause trouble.

10.199 Problems can arise in many different areas including, among others, the spinal cord, spine, urinary tract, bowels and skin. The review should be done in a spinal cord injury unit on one day in every year and cover all relevant areas. It should include medical, nursing, physiotherapy, occupational therapy and psychology input. Investigations that include the urinary tract and the spinal cord should be done. A fully effective review system should cover all areas where asymptomatic pathology could arise so that this can be dealt with before it becomes a problem.

Hospital Readmissions

10.200 Spinal cord injured persons should always be re-admitted into spinal cord injury centres whenever possible. Non-specialist centres lack the necessary knowledge and expertise in their care in, amongst others, the following ways:

(a) Spinal cord syrinxes are frequently overlooked or misdiagnosed.
(b) Spinal and other pain may be misdiagnosed as musculo-skeletal when other causes, such as spinal cord change or hypotension, are responsible.
(c) Asymptomatic serious urological problems are overlooked.
(d) Bowel evacuations are not carried out because the nurses lack the necessary skills, so family members or outside carers need to be involved.
(e) Disabling joint contractures are allowed to develop through inexpert therapy and inadequate treatment of spasticity and spasms.
(f) Respiratory problems are not predicted and pre-empted, or are treated inappropriately.
(g) Life threatening autonomic dysreflexia is induced or overlooked or misdiagnosed.
(h) Pressure sores are allowed to develop and progress in those who have been free from them for many years.
(i) Psycho-social problems that predispose to physical complications are overlooked.

10.201   Spinal cord injury units are the victims of their own success. While the incidence of new cases is broadly steady in Great Britain at around 700 per annum, the prevalence is increasing with the improving life expectancy that has resulted from good care.

10.202   Historically spinal cord injury units undertook to follow-up their patients and to readmit them for treatment whenever necessary. This is no longer possible. Savic et al[1] at Stoke Mandeville have shown that over 40% of readmissions are now into non-specialist centres.

   1   Savic G, Short D, Gardner B et al, 'Hospital Readmission in People with Chronic Spinal Cord Injury' [2000 in press] Spinal Cord.

10.203   Hospital readmission is greatest in the early years after injury and shortly before death. When these periods of maximal hospitalisation are excluded, the hospital bed-occupancy rate of stable chronic spinal cord injured persons in Great Britain is 4.9 bed-days per person at risk per annum. This compares with 1.5 days for the general population, therefore bed occupancy rate is 3.26 times higher for stable chronic spinal cord injured persons than the general population.

10.204   The average bed occupancy rate in bed-days per spinal cord injured person at risk per annum is greater than 4.9 if spinal cord injured persons in the final period prior to death are included. An accurate UK figure on this is not available, but an average of around 7 days per spinal cord injured person per annum is likely.

10.205   It has been estimated that there are between 30,000 and 40,000 spinal cord injured persons alive in Great Britain who have survived the early years following their spinal cord injury. Using the data above, this equates to a total bed-occupancy for stable chronic spinal cord injured persons of between 147,000 and 196,000 bed days per annum, or between 450 and 600 beds at an occupancy rate of approximately 90%.

10.206 In Great Britain the total spinal cord injury unit bed complement is about 500. Of these, approximately two-thirds are required for acute admissions. Therefore only about 165 are available for readmissions when 450 to 600 are required to meet the readmission need defined above. This means that if spinal cord injured persons are to have prompt readmission when the need arises then they will need to purchase at least some hospital care privately.

10.207 In general, emergency admissions for life threatening conditions take precedence over less dangerous ones, or those that are merely to improve independence or quality of life.

10.208 Examples of life-threatening conditions are severe urinary tract infections, respiratory tract infections and autonomic dysreflexia. An example of a less threatening condition is a pressure sore. An example of a condition that will improve quality of life is upper limb reconstructive surgery.

10.209–10.213 Some complications, such as most pressure sores and urinary tract infections, can be treated successfully at home. Extra care is then required.

AGEING

10.214 A clear indication of the likely effects of this must given in the report. There is no stereotypical pattern of ageing. Some people are intrinsically more able than others. Others have the effects of ageing brought forward by problems such as limb contractures and joint problems.

CARE ATTENDANT NEEDS

10.215 The medical expert should indicate in the report those areas where care is needed. The care expert will then quantify the hours required to meet these needs.

10.216 A brief description of past care should be given. This should be followed by a description of the current care being provided and any care not being given that should reasonably be provided. Finally, the manner in which care needs will evolve in the future should be stated.

10.217 In determining future care needs many factors should be considered including the effects of ageing, the superimposition of intercurrent problems such as illness and upper limb strains, child-bearing, the effect of altered environment and holidays. In giving predictions for the future the expert should indicate first the age at which increased care will be required, second the reasons for this increased need and third the rate at which the care needs will increase. The expert should advise as to the level of expertise required by the carer, in particular whether a trained nurse is required for any aspect.

10.218 Low-level paraplegics are usually independent when young, apart from needing help with domestic activities, shopping, certain obstacles out of doors, gardening, do-it-yourself work and home maintenance. They usually require stand-by assistance when ambulating in calipers or similar devices.

10.219   Mid-level paraplegics often require, in addition, assistance with getting into and out of the standing frame, out of the bath, in and out of the car and with lifting the wheelchair in and out of the car. Spasticity, spasms, intrinsic ability, obesity, truncal balance and age are important.

10.220   While a few low level tetraplegics are almost independent, the majority require substantial assistance. For example, they can use a fork or spoon for eating but not cut up meat. They can drive vehicles but not transfer in and out or lift their wheelchairs in and out.

10.221   Because tetraplegics can get autonomic dysreflexia or choke on food, someone should always at hand to deal with an emergency should the need arise. Notwithstanding this, many tetraplegics live on their own for substantial periods of time. This is a reflection of the inadequacy of resources available in the community rather than the particular needs of the tetraplegic person. In general, one person should be present at all times. A second should be present when there are activities that require two persons.

10.222   Ventilator-assisted tetraplegics should always be in line-of-eye of someone who can reconnect them to the ventilator, suck out secretions, reposition a dislodged tracheostomy tube and carry out bagging via the tracheostomy. In some cases two persons need to be present for these activities, necessitating the presence of two trained carers at all times.

10.223   As mentioned above, it is not generally appropriate for family members to be involved in the physical and personal care of their spinal cord injured relatives. Nevertheless, they frequently choose to do so and then usually provide excellent care.

10.224–10.226   Carer accomodation must be adequate if carer recruitment is to be assured.

PHYSIOTHERAPY

10.227   The report should indicate those areas where physiotherapy is required now and will be required in the future. If specialised equipment is required then this should be indicated.

10.228   The pattern and type of physiotherapy required depends on the individual. In general, carers can carry out the straight forward physiotherapy activities of joint range of motion and assisting the spinal cord injured person into the standing frame. Training, supervision and the more specialised physiotherapy tasks require a chartered physiotherapist.

Occupational Therapy

10.229   The report should indicate those areas where occupational therapy is presently required and will be required in the future. If specialised equipment is needed this should be stated.

10.230 A regular visit from an occupational therapist is helpful in bringing the spinal cord injured person up to date with modern developments in aids, equipment and recreations. Disabled clubs and societies are also a useful source of information.

10.231 Housing adjustments or home moves should be accompanied by adequate occupational therapy advice.

Chiropody

10.232 Good foot care is essential, especially in the ageing spinal cord injured person, if lower limb infections and other complications are to be avoided. The report should indicate how this need is being met, whether or not this is satisfactory and how provision should alter in the future.

Dental Treatment

10.233 Good dental care is essential for the spinal cord injured. If access to NHS dentists is difficult then private treatment should be provided.

Other Therapy not Considered Elsewhere

10.234 Spinal cord injured persons frequently have problems, such as pain, that are not relieved by conventional approaches. In exploring alternative ways of dealing with their problems other treatments are sometimes found to be helpful, for example acupuncture. The report should indicate if any of these are relevant.

Equipment

10.235 The report should indicate the equipment that is required in the present and will be required in the future as ageing and changing expectations supervene. Each of the headings above should be considered in determining the appropriate list.

10.236 There is no such thing as a standard equipment list. The latter should instead be honed to the particular requirements of the spinal cord injured person being considered.

10.237 It is important to note that the equipment should be necessary and reasonable as a result of the accident, not just desirable. Items that would have been purchased in any event should be mentioned only if their use has been increased by the injury.

10.238 Problems can arise when the spinal cord injured person has not had the opportunity of evaluating different types of equipment because of inadequate resources and time. This can in part be overcome by the spinal cord injured person visiting one or more of the established exhibitions, such as NAIDEX. Ideally, the equipment expert should accompany the spinal cord injured person on such a visit to provide advice. The medical expert can more readily support an item of equipment that the claimant has personally evaluated and found useful than one thought by an equipment expert to be helpful.

RELEVANT POTENTIAL DEVELOPMENTS DURING THE REMAINING YEARS OF LIFE

10.239 This is a difficult and important area. A 20-year old paraplegic with 45 or so more years of expected life will undoubtedly encounter many developments in treatment, equipment and technology that will be beneficial to him. Many of these will not be available from exchequer funds. During the last 15 years, for example, there have been important developments that have been available to only a limited extent within the NHS. Examples include male fertility treatment, impotence therapy, imaging techniques, drug delivery systems, alternative treatments for pain, sophisticated implanted upper limb controllers etc. The report should allude to this area, though applying a figure that is appropriate for the spinal cord injured person being considered will be difficult.

Expectation of Life

10.240 An assessment of expectation of life is an essential component of any report because it determines the appropriate multiplier for the claim. The following paragraphs will assist the expert in arriving at the correct figure.

10.241 The expectation of life of a spinal cord injured person is reduced. Although some experts state that the expectation of life of paraplegics is normal there is no evidence to support this view.[1]

> 1 De Vivo MJ and Stover SL *Long-term Survival and Causes of Death*, in Spinal Cord Injury: Clinical Outcomes from the Model Systems, Stover et al (eds) Aspen (April 1995) pps 289-310. De Vivo M, Krause SJ and Lammertse DP 'Recent Trends in Mortality and Causes of Death Among Persons with Spinal Cord Injury' [1999] 80 Arch Phys Med Rehabil pp 1411-19. Yeo et al 'Mortality Following Spinal Cord Injury' [1998] 36 Spinal Cord pp 329-36. Frankel et al 'Long-term Survival in Spinal Cord Injury: A Fifty Year Investigation' [1998] 36 Spinal Cord pp 266-74. DeVivo MJ and Ivie CS 'Life Expectancy of Ventilator Dependent Persons with Spinal Cord Injuries' [1995] 108 Chest pp 226-32

10.242 The assessment of the expectation of life of any spinal cord injured person cannot be deduced simply by referral to life expectancy tables, such as those of Frankel et al, De Vivo et al and Yeo et al. These publications are an important guide but factors relating to the individual must also be carefully considered.

10.243 Although the usual approach is to take a standard published average life expectancy figure and then to calculate where the spinal cord injured person in question lies in relation to this, there is much to be said for the alternative approach of taking the life expectancy figure appropriate to an able-bodied person and then applying a reduction that takes into account the factors that pertain to the person being considered.

10.244 In considering life expectancy the following should be taken into account:

1. Date of injury.
2. Age at injury.
3. Present age.
4. Years since injury.

5. Level and completeness of injury.
6. Statistics of life expectancy for the country concerned.
7. Factors relating to the sex, social class and environment.
8. Published literature on the subject. Most estimates of expectation of life in these publications are based not on known deaths but on predicted deaths using standard mortality ratios. For example, an SMR of two implies that the mortality rate of persons with spinal cord injuries in that strata is twice the rate of the general population of comparable age, sex and race. When the ratio is multiplied by 100 a percentage figure is obtained.
9. Family history.
10. History to date in relation to known causes of death in spinal cord injured persons, especially infection, uro-renal, cardiovascular and respiratory.
11. Medication history.
12. Reliability in attending follow-up appointments. Asymptomatic complications can be detected early and treated appropriately through such follow-up visits.
13. Pattern of care.

10.245 The importance of adequate care is well-recognised by spinal cord injury specialists as being of great importance in determining the life expectancy of a spinal cord injured person. Such care includes not only that in the community but also the possibility of admission into an appropriate hospital for suitable treatment immediately the need arises. Although there has been no quantification of the importance of good care, the recent disturbing USA findings of De Vivo et al point to it being of central importance. The latter has demonstrated that life expectancies for the spinal cord injured in the USA, which had risen steadily from 1973, have recently shown a significant fall that coincides with the health provision restructuring that severely pared the medical care available to the spinal cord injured.

10.246–10.248 With the exception of the recent USA findings described in para 10.245, the expectation of life of the spinal cord injured continues to increase with improved treatment. Newer techniques that have assisted the diagnosis and treatment of life threatening complications include magnetic resonance imaging scans for spinal syrinx detection, the Brindley stimulator, newer and more effective antibiotics, percutaneous and whole body lithotripsy devices to shatter kidney and bladder stones without recourse to major surgery, computerised and other drug delivery systems for the eradication for intractable spasticity, the artificial urinary sphincter and other urological operative advances, and improvements in intensive care and anaesthesia. Even the most vulnerable of spinal cord injured persons, the ventilator assisted, now have life expectancies that are approaching those of their ventilator independent counterparts.

LIST OF OTHER EXPERTS REQUIRED

10.249 The medical report should indicate those other experts who will be required to deal with certain aspects, such as specific medical problems, housing, employment, care, equipment and therapy.

SUMMARY

10.250   The summary at the end of the report should indicate the key areas relevant to the questions posed by the instructing solicitor.

10.251   Where there is a range of opinion on any aspect this should be summarised together with the reasons for the expert arriving at his own opinion.

Appendix 1

TABLE OF HEADINGS FOR A MODEL REPORT IN A SPINAL CORD INJURY CASE

Claimant's name
Claimant's address
Date of report
Date of birth
Date of injury
Age at injury
Current age
Weight
Height

When and where the claimant was examined
Who else was present

A. Civil Procedure Rules requirements

Statement of duty to the court
Instructions of solicitor
List of material and literature relied on
Abbreviated curriculum vitae
Statement of truth

B. Past history – especially that relevant to current state.

C. Family history – ages, causes of death, state of health, familial factors.

D. Medication history.

E. Alcohol and smoking history.

F. History of claimant from time of injury to the present.

G. Liability issues – seat belt, alcohol, medical/other negligence, causation.

H. Quantum issues.

1. Associated injuries

Brain
Limb joints/bones/soft tissues
Peripheral nerves/brachial plexus
Chest/abdominal

2. Neurology – level, completeness: syrinx
3. Spine – deformities, arthritis
4. Pain
5. Bladder – upper and lower urinary tract
6. Bowels
7. Hygiene – method of bathing, shower chair, bath
8. Joints/soft tissue – heterotopic ossification, contractures, strains
9. Spasms/spasticity – implants, treatment
10. Respiratory
11. Cardiovascular – hypotension fatigue, coat-hanger pain: autonomic dysreflexia
12. Skin – turns in bed, mattress, cushion, bed
13. Sexual function – fertility, intercourse, sexuality, relationships
10. Mobility – wheelchair, car, orthoses, recreational mobility, ramps, AA, phone
15. Transfers – hoists
16. Activities of daily living – environmental control systems
10. Psychology – counselling
18. Family
19. Home
20. Recreation – holidays
21. Employment
22. Medical Care – in-patient and out-patient
23. Ageing
24. Care Attendant Needs
25. Physiotherapy Needs
26. Occupational Therapy Needs
27. Chiropody
28. Dental treatment
29. Other therapies – hydrotherapy, acupuncture, dietitian, osteopathy and so on
30. Equipment
31. Relevant potential developments during the remaining years of life
32. Expectation of Life
33. List of other experts required
34. Summary of Conclusions reached.

Chapter 11

Rehabilitation after Brain and Spinal Cord Injury

W W McKinlay BA MSc PhD CPsychol
A J Watkiss BSc
M Rooney DipCOT

INTRODUCTION

11.1 The purpose of this chapter is to outline the process of rehabilitation after brain and spinal cord injury. Specifically, the chapter will outline:

- The challenge for rehabilitation: the problems which arise after such injuries, giving rise to the need for rehabilitation.
- The process of rehabilitation, including the components which go to make up rehabilitation.
- The effectiveness of rehabilitation.
- Access to rehabilitation.
- Community re-integration. (What happens after rehabilitation?)
- Medico-legal considerations.

11.2 The overall aim of rehabilitation is to maximise an injured individual's level of functioning. Key aims are, so far as possible, to enable the injured person to be constructively occupied and to allow him to be as independent as possible in the basic activities of daily life. The amount of care and supervision needed in the long-term, and the eventual prospects for gainful employment, are key considerations in relation to quantum of damages after injury. These key aspects of outcome are affected by the availability and effectiveness of rehabilitation.

11.3–11.4 Catastrophic injury usually means brain injury and/or spinal cord injury, although there are other cases in which severe injuries have been suffered, for example, burns or severe internal injuries. Nevertheless, this chapter will concentrate on brain injury and spinal cord injury. Brain injury is a major traumatic cause of severe injury and disability in adult life.[1] Spinal cord injury is less common, accounting for about 10% of cases of disability due to brain injury,[2] but nevertheless sometimes resulting in very extensive needs for care and special equipment, housing and so on.

1 McKinlay WW and Pentland B 'Editorial: Developing rehabilitation services for the head injured: A UK perspective' [1987] 1(1) Brain Injury pp 3-4.
2 Jennett B Foreword in Rosenthal M, Griffith E, Bond MR and Miller JD (eds) *Rehabilitation of the Head Injured Adult* (2nd edn, 1983) FA Davis Company, Philadelphia, PA.

THE CHALLENGE FOR REHABILITATION

Brain Injury

11.5   Brain injury is common. The precise frequency with which it occurs is difficult to determine with great precision because much depends on the severity of the injury. Traditional methods of recording the diagnosis of head injury paid more attention to certain aspects of the type of injury than they did to injury severity, and they were therefore not a particularly good guide to the extent of disability after brain injury. Nevertheless, a number of studies have appeared and two in particular will be highlighted.

11.6   Miller and Jones[1] reported on all the head injuries admitted to a UK brain injury unit which served a population of 1.2 million, that is, from Edinburgh and the surrounding area. They found that there were 1,919 admissions to the head injury unit in a year. They found that 133 of these cases were severely disabled or worse in terms of the Glasgow Outcome Scale[2] at one month post-injury. A conservative estimate would be that all of these, plus further cases with lesser disabilities, will have substantial ongoing long-term difficulties. A further study[3] based on a population of about 900,000 found approximately 3,000 hospital admissions per annum after head injury. Less than half of these admitted cases made a good recovery (in Glasgow Outcome Scale terms), leaving over 1,500 moderately disabled or worse, a year post-injury.

1   Miller D and Jones PA 'The work of a Regional Head Injury Service' [1985] 1 *Lancet* pp 1141-44.
2   Jennett B and Bond M 'Assessment of outcome after severe brain damage' [1975] 1 Lancet pp 480-84.
3   Thornhill S, Teasdale GM, Murray GD, McEwen J, Roy CW and Penny KL *A prospective cohort study of disability after admission with a head injury: the importance of 'mild' injuries* BMJ in press.

11.7   The severely head-injured are predominantly young (especially late teens and twenties) and male (male to female ratio 4 or 5 to 1). They also have, other things being equal, a near normal life expectancy, although certain specific features (for example, severe respiratory problems, poorly controlled epilepsy) make for exceptions.

11.8   An attempt to look at the long-term difficulties after brain injury was made by Tennant et al.[1] They carried out a follow-up of 190 patients who had been admitted to regional neurosurgical units an average of seven years previously. The average age at injury of 29 was typical for such patients. They found that some 36% of those followed up were unable to occupy their time in a meaningful way and for these individuals and their carers quality of life was severely curtailed. They note:

> 'The shortfall in ... provision (of rehabilitation-relevant services) means that in the UK patients often fall between the separate responsibilities of health, social, and employment agencies, and have no recourse to informed advice about retaining or finding new employment after head injury.'

1   Tennant A, Macdermott N and Neary D 'The long-term outcome of head injury: implications for service planning' [1995] 9(6) Brain Injury pp 595-605.

11.9 What are the particular problems, arising after brain injury, that give rise to the need for rehabilitation? One of the first things to note is that the need for rehabilitation depends, to a considerable extent, on the severity of the injury. Head injuries range from trivial blows through to severe life-threatening or even fatal injuries. The methods generally used to gauge head injury severity are level of responsiveness, assessed by the Glasgow Coma Scale ('GCS'), and duration of post-traumatic amnesia ('PTA'). The degrees of severity of injury conventionally associated with GCS and PTA levels are shown in Table 1.

Table 1: Severity of Injury as Indicated by Glasgow Coma Scale (GCS) and Duration of Post-traumatic Amnesia (PTA)

GCS Total Score	Severity	PTA Duration	Severity
3-5	Very severe	Up to 5 minutes	Very mild
6-8	Severe	5-60 minutes	Mild
9-12	Moderate	1-24 hours	Moderate
13-15	Minor	1 day-1 week	Severe
		1 week-1 month	Very severe
		Over 1 month	Extremely severe

References:
Glasgow Coma Scale: Teasdale G and Jennett B'Assessment of Coma and Impaired Consciousness [1974[ii Lancet pp 81-84.
Russell WR *The Traumatic Amnesias* (1971) Oxford University Press, Oxford.
Jennett B and Teasdale G, *Management of Head Injuries* (1981) FA Davis Co, Philadelphia.

11.10 Sometimes these two measures give somewhat different estimates. In particular it is worth noting that there is a sub-set of patients who are never in particularly deep coma and never have low GCS scores, thereby implying an injury of no great severity, but who do have long post-traumatic amnesia. Wilson et al[1] have shown that there is a group of patients with contusional injuries to the frontal and temporal lobes of the brain. These patients have long post-traumatic amnesia but may never be deeply comatose. In these patients it is the long post-traumatic amnesia which is the better predictor of outcome than the GCS score.

1 Wilson JTL, Teasdale GM, Hadley DM, Wiedmann KD and Lang, D 'Post-traumatic amnesia: still a valuable yardstick?' [1994] 57 Journal of Neurology, Neurosurgery and Psychiatry pp 198-201.

11.11 The nature of the injury also matters and, in particular, features such as subdural haematoma have been associated with a higher likelihood of adverse outcome.[1] Moreover, while most civilian head injuries are described as 'closed' head injuries where acceleration and deceleration forces do the damage, penetrating head injuries may be caused by missiles or sharp objects. In these cases GCS scores and duration of post-traumatic amnesia are less good guides to eventual outcome.

1 Gennarelli TA, Spielman GM, Langfitt TW et al 'Influence of the type of intracranial lesion on outcome from severe head injury' [1982] 56 J Neurosurg pp 26-32.

11.12   In general, the more severe the injury, the more likely it is that there will be long-term problems. Unfortunately, it tends to be the case that only those with the more severe injuries get access to rehabilitation, but it is not necessarily only the more severe who may benefit. Indeed, one could make a case for saying that those who have injuries of intermediate severity would be likely to derive more benefit from rehabilitation than the most severe cases who may have little capacity to benefit.

11.13   The specific problems which render these patients in need of rehabilitation are the deficits and other changes which follow from head injury. These may be stated relatively simply and are well established now by a large number of follow-up studies. A convenient source of further information on these is a recent text on rehabilitation edited by Rosenthal et al.[1] There may be physical changes, including neuro-muscular changes (weakness/paralysis), poor co-ordination and balance, numbness and also sensory changes. There may also be other physical injuries, not due to the head injury as such, but sustained at the same time. Other problems which may arise in the physical realm include post-traumatic epilepsy.[2] This should always be considered in the medico-legal context. The risks of epilepsy can be quite precisely determined by a suitably experienced neurologist or neurosurgeon.

1   Rosenthal M, Griffith ER, Kreutzer JS, Pentland B *Rehabilitation of the Adult and Child with Traumatic Brain Injury* (3rd edn, 1999) FA Davis Company, Philadelphia.
2   Hammond FM and McDeavitt JT 'Medical and orthopedic complications' in Rosenthal M, Griffith ER, Kreutzer JS and Pentland B (eds) *Rehabilitation of the Adult and Child with Traumatic Brain Injury* (3rd edn, 1999) FA Davis Company, Philadelphia.

11.14   There are also emotional and behavioural changes which are described in the Rosenthal book.[1] The changes in this area include:

- *Undercontrol*: a reduced capacity to control both temper and mood state. Aspects of this include short-temper, with a difficulty in shrugging off minor annoyances; in some cases a proneness to verbal and sometimes physical aggression; rapid mood swings; and inappropriate sexual and social behaviour.
- *Lack of insight*: a failure to appreciate the presence of deficits and the implications of these deficits. Some patients will mistakenly maintain that all is well with them, and it has long been accepted that great care must be taken, especially in a medico-legal context, not to do them an injustice as a result.
- *Apathy and tiredness*: initiative and motivation may be lacking, and some will suffer from extreme tiredness. Indeed tiring easily is one of the most common sequelae of severe brain injury, and tiredness will often exacerbate other problems.
- Depressed and anxious mood are common. While there is some debate as to how many such patients might usefully be diagnosed as having psychiatric disorders in terms of DSM-IV,[2] it is clear that the symptomatology often comprises elements of anxiety or depression rather than full-blown anxiety or depressive disorders. In this context, it is worth noting that it is very rare for post-traumatic stress disorder to arise after serious brain injury[3] as the injured persons do not generally recall the point of injury. This is due to retrograde amnesia (loss of memory for events leading up to injury) and post-traumatic amnesia (loss of memory for events following injury). The combined effect of these is that following most serious head injuries the last memory is some time

before injury and the next memory some time afterwards. Phobias are uncommon, even travel phobias after road traffic accidents, again because the individual does not recall the accident.

1 McKinlay WW and Watkiss AJ 'Cognitive and Behavioral Effects of Brain Injury' in Rosenthal M, Griffith ER, Kreutzer JS and Pentland B (eds) *Rehabilitation of the Adult and Child with Traumatic Brain Injury* (1999) FA Davis Company, Philadelphia.
2 Diagnostic and Statistical Manual of Mental Disorders, 4th edn 1994) (DSM-IV) American Psychiatric Association, Washington.
3 McMillan TM 'Post-traumatic stress disorder following minor and severe closed head injury: 10 single cases' [1996] 10 Brain Injury pp 749-58.

11.15 The cognitive changes which may arise were also outlined in our chapter[1] and include:

- *Memory and learning deficits.* Of the cognitive changes, one of the most common and important is the reduction in capacity to learn new information. 'Old' memories (that is, 'remote' memories, memories of early life) may be retained, but capacity to form 'new' memories, that is, to remember recent events, and to keep track of appointments, work duties and so on, is impaired.
- *Concentration/attentional deficits.* The capacity to sustain concentration, in particular 'divided attention', is particularly prone to impairment. Individuals with divided attention deficits will have difficulty keeping track of more than one task at a time. They may be engaged in one particular task and be distracted by a supervening task, and the initial task is forgotten about. This inability to keep 'balls in the air' is an obvious handicap in demanding professional or managerial employment. However, the fact must not be overlooked that even less demanding forms of employment very often require such skills.
- *Deficits in executive function.* Such difficulties are among the most difficult to describe and yet are among the most devastating deficits found after brain injury. Such problems are especially associated with damage to the frontal lobes of the brain, especially where this is bilateral. In extreme cases the affected individual may simply do little or nothing, sitting inactive and seemingly not especially distressed or bored. He may continue with any task he is given, doing it over and over until told to stop. Essentially, the control mechanisms which regulate behaviour are damaged. In mild to moderate form such problems can be both subtle and pervasive and can render the individual unable to behave flexibly, to show initiative, and to plan and organise their time, although if clearly and unambiguously directed they may still be able to carry out familiar tasks.

1 See para 11.14.

11.16 It is worth noting that cognitive problems are very common and also important practically. In particular, problems with verbal memory and with concentration have been strongly linked to failure to resume employment.[1]

1 Brooks DN, McKinlay WW, Symington C, Beattie A and Campsie L, 'Return to work within the first seven years of severe head injury' [1987] 1 Brain Injury pp 5-19. McMordie WR, Barker SL and Paolo TM 'Return to work (RTW) after head injury' [1990] 4 Brain Injury pp 57-69.

11.17 Brain injury, therefore, commonly gives rise to a broad range of problems – physical, cognitive and emotional-behavioural. In the one to two years after injury some recovery takes place, although this applies to physical and cognitive function, whereas emotional behavioural adjustment often becomes worse.[1] Substantial problems very often persist, especially in cognitive and emotional behavioural realms. The latter, especially, are a considerable burden for family members who find it particularly difficult to cope with emotional and behavioural changes[2] and family/marital breakdown are by no means uncommon.[3]

1   McKinlay WW, Brooks DN, Bond MR, Martinage DP and Marshall MM 'The short-term outcome of severe blunt head injury as reported by relatives of the injured persons' (1991) 44 Journal of Neurology, Neurosurgery and Psychiatry pp 527-33.
2   Brooks DN, Campsie L, Symington C, Beattie A and McKinlay WW, 'The five year outcome of severe blunt head injury: a relative's view' [1986] 49 *Journal of Neurology, Neurosurvery and Psychiatry* pp 764-70.
3   Wood RL and Yurdakul LK 'Change in relationship status following traumatic brain injury' [1997] 11 *Brain Injury* pp 491-502.

11.18   Given the young average age of injury and given that life expectancy is not greatly reduced in most cases, it follows that head injury gives rise to many years of 'disabled surviving'. This is something which should give considerable impetus to the need for rehabilitation in order to get the best possible outcome.

Spinal Cord Injury

11.19   Spinal cord injury ('SCI') is a complex, life-threatening condition, most commonly caused by trauma. Road traffic accidents are recorded as being responsible for 46% of cases, with domestic, industrial and sporting injuries at 48%.[1] The incidence of violence, drug and alcohol abuse related injuries continue to be on the increase.

1   Spinal Injuries Association Annual Review [1992].

11.20   Damage to the spinal cord means messages to and from the brain are interrupted, causing impaired motor and sensory function in the body. The severity of loss of function is dependent on two main factors.

The Level of the Lesion
11.21   How much of the body is paralysed depends on where on the cord damage has occurred. Essentially, the higher on the cord the damage, the more of the body is affected. The spine is divided into four sections. The cervical spinal cord in the neck feeds the neck, shoulders, arms, hands and diaphragm. Injury here results in tetraplegia – all four limbs are affected. The higher the lesion the more of the upper limbs are affected. In higher tetraplegia, the individual is ventilator dependent and requires 24-hour care in the home. With technology they are able to operate a wheelchair and environmental control units and adapted information technology.

11.22   Those with a mid-cervical lesion generally do not require ventilation but still require full care support for domestic and self-care tasks. In lower cervical lesions, the individuals can carry out some care for themselves, for example, feeding, shaving, pushing their wheelchair. Only the fit, motivated person with the lowest cervical lesions can be expected to be independent in self-care.

11.23   Injuries to the thoracic, lumbar or sacral areas result in paraplegia. Upper limb function is normal. The thoracic spinal cord supplies nerves to the chest and abdominal muscles. The lumbar cord supplies the hips and legs while the sacral spine is responsible for the bowel, bladder and sexual function. Those with paraplegia have the potential to be independent at a wheelchair level (given the appropriate environment), while those with lower lumbar injuries can ambulate and may even be independent of a wheelchair.

The Extent of the Injury
11.24   When there is no preserved motor or sensory function below the level of the lesion, the injury is complete. In an incomplete injury there is some sparing of function. This can vary tremendously from having a little sensation spared in a small area to having sufficient function to allow walking. Often those with an incomplete injury will have sufficient lower limb function to allow walking but their upper limb deficit will be more marked resulting in them requiring assistance in self-care.

11.25   It is generally thought that paralysis only affects the limbs. However, spinal cord injury results in multi-system impairment. There is loss of bladder and bowel control and sexual function. Respiratory function is affected in those with tetraplegia and higher paraplegia. The reduced sensation and circulation means spinal injured are more prone to development of pressure sores. Loss of vaso-motor control means many spinal injured cannot control the temperature of the body. Autonomic dysreflexia is a condition peculiar to spinal cord injury and is a life-threatening condition if not quickly identified and treated. Chronic pain related to the damaged cord appears to becoming an increasing problem as the proportion of incomplete injuries continues to increase.

11.26   In addition to the level and extent of injury there are other factors which will impact on rehabilitation: see Table 2.

Table 2: Factors Influencing Rehabilitation Potential after Spinal Cord Injury

Factors Increasing Potential	Factors Decreasing Potential
Age - young adult	Age - elderly
Anthropometry - long arms, short trunk, wide shoulders, narrow hips	Anthropometry - short arms, long trunk, narrow shoulders, wide hips
Motivation	Associated injury, for example, head injury
No spasm or minimal to moderate spasm	Past medical history
Good body awareness	Pain
Any sparing of motor or sensory function	Poor motivation
	Severe spasticity
	Contractures
	Poor body awareness
	Lifestyle, for example, drug/alcohol abuse

11.27–11.34   As well as adjusting to all these physical changes, the spinal injured also have to cope with loss. This may include loss of their perceived role in society and/or of their family role. The young tetraplegic may feel forced to return to the care of his parents. Loss of job, social and financial independence must also be considered. Despite all these stresses it is surprising that research has shown that the incidence of depression in the acute phase following spinal cord injury is only between 10 and 30%.[1]

   1 Davidoff G et al 'Depression among acute spinal cord injury patients: a study utilizing the Zung self-rating depression scale' [1990] 35(3) Rehabilitation Psychology pp 171-79.

THE PROCESS OF REHABILITATION

Brain Injury

Forms of Rehabilitation
11.35   There are many forms that rehabilitation may take after brain injury. Leaving aside those minor injuries where a full spontaneous recovery occurs, for those with significant brain injury the following are possible elements in a rationally planned and run rehabilitation system.

- Acute hospital care
- In-patient rehabilitation
- Employment rehabilitation programme
- Out-patient therapies.

11.36   Some patients will need to progress through these in order. Others may be able to omit a stage. However, this should happen on the basis of an appropriate clinical assessment, rather than on a haphazard basis as too often occurs.

11.37   Some patients, usually with less severe injuries, will have relatively circumscribed problems. Out-patient physiotherapy and speech therapy might be necessary in some cases. Others might need advice on overcoming memory problems, which can be provided by a suitably experienced clinical psychologist on an out-patient basis. However, there are too many cases who need more than this and do not get it. It is worth remembering Tennant's[1] finding at follow-up that about a third of those discharged from neurosurgical care ended up unoccupied. Rehabilitation staff should not be content with small gains. One member of rehabilitation staff was overheard saying, approvingly, that an 18-year old patient was 'doing really well' because he had made a cup of tea. While that was undoubtedly progress in the circumstances of the case, such progress is not enough. Rehabilitationists should not be overly pleased, and certainly should not rest content with small gains but should always consider how the person will be occupied in the longer term and how they will reach that goal.

   1 See para 11.8.

11.38   While too many are provided with only out-patient rehabilitation or no rehabilitation at all, too few receive the 'total push' of broad-based multi-disciplinary rehabilitation. Generally, it will be those with the more severe injuries who need such an approach. For them rehabilitation should be directed towards some or all of a range of aspects, including physical, cognitive, emotional-behavioural aspects and social adjustment. Where substantial input is needed to deal with a range of problems, rehabilitation programmes will ideally begin when the patient is medically stabilised. Such programmes are referred to as 'post-acute' and should encompass a variety of rehabilitation-relevant professionals including medical and psychological practitioners, physiotherapists, occupational therapists and speech and language therapists. There may also be a role in such programmes for other professionals including those involved with employment rehabilitation (for example, job coaches and trainers) as well as dieticians and others.

11.39 It is important to remember that rehabilitation involves not so much undoing what was done by the injury, but rather retraining the individual to recover certain skills or sometimes to learn certain compensatory skills or strategies. A man who becomes blind may need a white stick or guide dog, which of course he did not require before injury. Some brain injury patients protest, for example, that before injury they did not have to use diaries or other aids to memory and may have to be convinced that they will have to learn new compensatory strategies. In other words, rehabilitation is not just a matter of relearning things that which the individual knew before but is also a matter of learning new compensatory skills.

11.40 Moreover, there is a small number of very severely damaged individuals with behavioural problems who cannot learn the skills they need to function in the outside world. For this small group it is a matter of tailoring the environment to achieve the best management of their problems. In someone with a very severe behavioural disturbance it may be that by a certain regime of care, involving regular prompting and reminding that certain behaviours are unacceptable, and insulating the patient from potential 'provocation', will enable behaviour to be maintained on an even keel. Such patients may be dependent on their 'environment' and prone to deteriorate without it.

Assessment
11.41 The appropriate sequence of events for a rehabilitation programme will be as follows. First, there must be an assessment. The length of this varies – for an inpatient programme it may well be a week or longer. The assessment will involve various members of the team. The team should encompass professionals from a number of different disciplines. This is particularly important in rehabilitation, as the outcome of the various elements of the programme will depend on the outcomes of other elements. For example, someone who has problems with mobility may be able to make good progress during physiotherapy, but this may not be maintained unless, for example, they have sufficient social competence to take part in activities. This will give them some place to go and something to do in order to use their mobility.

11.42 A good point is made by Zasler[1] in describing assessment by a rehabilitation physician (or physiatrist – the North American term). He notes:

> 'One of the biggest problems in our field is the continued disparity in nomenclature used by physiatrists as well as by other medical specialists ... We need to make a concerted effort to agree on a common nomenclature ...'

1   Zasler ND 'Physiatric assessment in traumatic brain injury' in Rosenthal M, Griffith ER, Kreutzer JS and Pentland B (eds) *Rehabilitation of the Adult and Child with Traumatic Brain Injury* (3rd edn 1999) FA Davis Company, Philadelphia.

11.43   The lack of a standard nomenclature in rehabilitation and indeed the lack of widely agreed and accepted measurement instruments continues to be a problem. In fact, if anything, there are too many measurement instruments around, few attracting widespread support.

11.44   The assessment should include the following elements:

- The physiotherapist's assessment will deal with such issues as balance, mobility, fitness and endurance, posture, and so on.
- The speech and language therapist's assessment will include articulation and language ability (both understanding and expression). Increasingly, speech and language therapists also take an interest in 'pragmatics' – the non-verbal aspects of communication including turn-taking, and social appropriateness.
- The assessment by a clinical neuropsychologist is crucial. After brain injury, mental (rather than physical) limitations usually underlie the major long-term handicaps (for example, the need for supervision, inability to work). Neuropsychological assessment will involve examination of a range of mental capacities. These include premorbid and current IQ, memory, information processing ability and other skills. Emotional status (including anxiety and depressive features) should also be considered.
- The occupational therapist's assessment will involve tests and observation (for example, in a kitchen setting). This will deal with certain basic skills and the ability to perform Activities of Daily Living ('ADLs') such as washing and dressing and other self-care tasks, and household tasks including cooking safely. More advanced ADLs will also be assessed such as the ability to plan for shopping needs and handle money.
- The rehabilitation physician ('physiatrist' in North America) will carry out an assessment directed towards such issues as cranial nerve function, neuromuscular problems (tremor, spasticity and so on), epilepsy, as well as medical status more generally.
- The assessment by nurses/care workers will vary depending on the nature of the unit. In an in-patient unit, they will comment on such issues as whether the patient is settling, sleep-wake pattern, compliance with medication, and so on.
- There may be other assessments (for example, by a dietician). Moreover, a variety of medical specialists may need to be called on depending on the particular problems the patient presents. These may include an ophthalmologist, orthopaedic surgeon, neurosurgeon, neurologist or psychiatrist.

11.45   At the end of the assessment period, the team will generally meet to review the various elements of the assessment and agree a view of what would be the best way forward in rehabilitation. Apart from the most severely impaired, the patient will then have to be persuaded that there would be value in taking part in the programme. Rehabilitation is not a treatment or cure which can be administered to a passive patient. It requires the active participation of the injured person. So far as possible, family members also have to be 'on board' this process and to be supportive and co-operative.

11.46 To succeed, rehabilitation will generally require hard work for the injured person. From an emotional point of view, it may also be a difficult time for both the injured person and family members. Media coverage of injuries or assaults inadvertently encourages a false view. News items often end with the injured person 'recovering in hospital'. In reality, months of struggle are often required to achieve a degree of independence, and even at the end of the process the injured party remains 'not the man he was'.

11.47 As the long-term and limited nature of recovery becomes ever more apparent, then – sometimes for the first time – patients and family start really to appreciate that life is not going to return to what it was. The assessment and rehabilitation process is therefore potentially a difficult time for both patient and family members. Staff members have to be prepared to be the focus of families' frustration as the limited prospects for recovery become clear. Jennett's observation that a good outcome for the doctor can be a disaster for patient and family needs to be borne in mind.

Rehabilitation
11.48 The rehabilitation process itself, like the assessment, involves input from a number of different health professionals. There is something of a balancing act in the different professions collaborating and at the same time bringing their own distinctive contribution. Ideally, rehabilitation should be 'seamless' as inter-professional distinctions do not matter for the most part to the recipients of the rehabilitation. On the other hand, it is important for the various professionals to bring their own distinctive contribution - otherwise there would be no point in having all of the members of the team. Bearing in mind these comments, for convenience and clarity it may be helpful to consider the input of the various professions and this is outlined in Table 3.

Table 3: Key Members of the Brain Injury Rehabilitation Team

Physiotherapists

The problems they treat include movement and sensation. They can plan and help carry out a programme of exercise to build up fitness and improve mobility. They can also give advice on posture. A high level daily gym fitness programme is of great benefit to patients without any physical disabilities as such, as it stimulates their general blood circulation and musculature and is also good for motivation.

Speech and Language Therapists

While a minority of head injured patients suffer severe speech or language problems, those who do should see a speech therapist. He will carry out a diagnostic assessment to see if treatment or communication aids would be of help. If necessary, they will help patients with speech or language difficulties to try to re-adjust to the demands of work and so. Even where dysphasia as such is absent, there may be problems of speech 'pragmatics' – including turn-taking and other aspects of social skill – with which they can help.

Neuropsychologists/Clinical Psychologists

Careful neuropsychological assessment is crucial after brain injury, as mental (rather than physical) limitations underlie the major long-term handicaps (for example, dependence, inability to work). Neuropsychological rehabilitation may involve training in the use of memory aids and mnemonics, training in anger management methods, social skills training, training in methods of problem-solving and planning and cognitive and behavioural treatments for anxiety, depression and other reactive psychological disorders.

Occupational Therapists ('OTs')

Patients will often have forgotten how to perform 'Activities of Daily Living' (ADLs) – including self-care, household tasks, community skills (for example, from crossing a road to managing money/shopping). Occupational therapists can help with the retraining of these skills. Those who are now unable to perform the practical daily functional skills, for example, self-care, domestic activities, community skills will need the support of an OT who can teach adaptive techniques, retrain the skills, or recommend the use of adaptive equipment, or environmental changes to maximise function.

Rehabilitation Physician ('Physiatrist' in North America)

In some units, the Rehabilitation Physician will lead the team and attend to basic medical needs. In other units, a key worker system is used with a local GP tending to basic medical needs. The further medical input from such a physician may include management of common medical issues which may arise in rehabilitation settings include epilepsy, neuromuscular problems (tremor, spasticity, and so on).

Care Worker/Nurses

Their role will vary widely depending on the nature of the unit. In some units, usually the more traditional, they will carry out basic nursing duties (washing, dressing, administering medications and so on) while in others their role may be much wider. The latter may include participating in, and reinforcing, a broad range of rehabilitative measures in conjunction with the other team members (for example, regularly prompting patients to use their memory aids).

Other Contributors to the Team Effort May Include

Dietician
Orthopaedic surgeon
Neurosurgeon/Neurologist
Psychiatrist

11.49   The precise mode of operation of the rehabilitation unit will depend to some extent on the model or approach used. Some rehabilitation programmes, particularly traditional NHS ones, are physician-led. The case has been put that rehabilitation teams may be led by a rehabilitation physician.[1] The case has also been made for neuropsychologist-led teams.[2] In other instances, a 'key worker' system is used. Here, experienced staff members from a variety of professions may act as key worker, each key worker typically having responsibility for a very small number of patients. The key worker will convene and chair meetings relating to that patient's progress, and act as point of first contact for that patient and his family. The advantages suggested for such an approach include that each key worker, having only a few patients under their wing, can form a close relationship with patient and family, and can keep fully 'up to speed' with the case. This would not be possible for a busy consultant. This should, therefore, carry the advantage that family members have a single point of contact who should be well-informed about the details of the case and who, when unable to answer a question, is able to find out from the relevant health professional an answer to the query.

1 See para 11.42
2 Oddy M, 'Taking the lead at rehabilitation centres' [2000] 13 *The Psychologist* pp 21-23.

11.50 Once goals have been set, a variety of rehabilitation inputs will be provided. Ideally, the various professions will work well together, and will provide a mixture of one-to-one sessions and group sessions. The latter can be a cost-effective way of providing some of the elements of rehabilitation. Groups can also have the advantage that some patients will be more persuaded of the value of, for example, memory aids or mnemonics when they hear a fellow patient extolling their usefulness. There is much to be gained by good collaboration between professions, for example between psychologists and occupational therapists, on such aspects of rehabilitation as social skills and memory training in which each discipline has something to contribute. In working through all of these processes, it is good rehabilitation practice to have in mind clear goals. So far as possible these should be so specified that it should be possible clearly to determine whether or not they have been attained.

11.51 Given the variety of approaches to rehabilitation, the choosing of an appropriate unit for an individual is an issue which must be considered. There are a very large number of units which claim to offer rehabilitation, especially to the brain injured. These vary from well-developed units specialising in brain injury, to poorly resourced units which claim to include brain injury but are in fact non-specialist. The Appendix provides a list of some main units in the UK. There are many others and the Directory of Rehabilitation Services[1] is a useful source. However, caution should be exercised. Standards which are applied, for example, the CARF standards in the USA, are not in general use in the UK where there is a lack of agreed standards as regards what staffing and resources a brain injury rehabilitation unit should have. Units should therefore be chosen carefully. A visit should form part of the process of choosing a unit, and Johnson and Brooks[2] offer advice on making this choice.

1 Paton ML and Hellawell DJ 'Directory of Rehabilitation Services for people with traumatic brain injuries, spinal cord injuries, orthopaedic injuries, burns' (1999) Rehabilitation Studies Unit, Edinburgh.
2 Johnson C and Brooks N 'How to choose and monitor an organisation providing services for the individual with brain injury' [1996] 3(2) Personal Injury pp 99-111.

Insight

11.52 Lack of insight is the bane of rehabilitation. One of the most common reasons for lack of progress or failure in rehabilitation is that the patient will not accept that there is anything wrong with him. Equally, some patients agree there is something wrong, but expect to wake up one day fully recovered. Fleming et al[1] have provided a very useful discussion of this. It is common for individuals to be lacking in insight early in their admission. For example, a patient said he was physically 'fine' although it was plain that he was confined to a wheelchair. When tactfully asked about the chair in which he was sitting, he said that he 'didn't bother with it' and that he 'just gets up and walks about'. Of course, this was entirely untrue and he was in fact confined to the wheelchair. This is someone who is showing an entire lack of insight. At a later stage, such an individual might acknowledge that he has difficulty walking and requires to be in a wheelchair, but nevertheless may express an intention to return to some physically demanding job, such as labouring. Nevertheless, the acknowledgement of physically limitation is a step in the right direction. The final step would be to acknowledge the physical limitation, its implication (that they will not get back to labouring), and to form a realistic plan for some other alternative activity (for example, sedentary work).

1   Fleming JM, Strong J and Ashton R 'Self-awareness of deficits in adults with traumatic brain injury: how best to measure?' [1996] 10 Brain Injury pp 1-15.

11.53 Sometimes lack of insight is both severe and persistent. It is by no means unusual to encounter an individual who is both unable to return to work at his previous level, while lacking the insight to accept that he can only cope with less demanding work. Rosenthal[1] gave a good example of this problem:

'Peter sustained a severe closed head injury in an automobile accident at age 21. At the time, he was a senior in college, achieving high grades, and planned to attend law school after graduation. After 3 months of hospitalisation, he returned to college and managed to complete his BA degree in Economics. Physically, he was left with mild left-sided weakness but could ambulate independently without assistive devices and was totally independent in activities of daily living. Neuropsychologic examination revealed that his IQ returned to bright-normal range, somewhat below his estimated premorbid level of function. Memory assessment resulted in the finding of mild short-term memory defects. Reading skills were good, though slower than normal, and comprehension was at a 10th grade level. Despite advice to the contrary, he persisted in pursuing law school entrance immediately. His performance on the Law School Admission Test was marginal. Nevertheless, he did not acknowledge the possible persistence of mental deficits and proceeded to enter a law school program. Within four weeks after entry, he dropped out, claiming that his professors were unfairly grading him. He searched for another law school which would accept him but failed in this effort and became quite despondent.' (p 204).

1   Rosenthal M 'Behavioral Sequelae' in Rosenthal M, Griffith E, Bond MR and Miller JD (eds) *Rehabilitation of the Head Injured Adult* (2nd edn, 1983) FA Davis Company, Philadelphia.

11.54 Given that there is often lack of insight early after injury, it is perhaps not surprising that anxiety and depression are not particularly prominent in the early stages. Indeed, the development of anxiety and depression, rather than representing a worsening of the case, may in fact be a sign of progress, as the individual achieves a degree of insight.

Discharge Planning

11.55 It would be uncontroversial to say that good rehabilitation practice requires that a discharge plan, at least in outline, should be in place from the outset. The dictum that 'discharge should never be a surprise' is one that should be remembered. Rehabilitation unfortunately cannot turn the clock back and make the patient entirely 'better' so that he can simply be discharged without further thought. Rather, rehabilitation seeks to attain the best possible level of function. However, it is nearly always necessary to have in place, for after rehabilitation, continuing support or help and advice. With suitable further help, it will often be possible to build further on the gains made in rehabilitation. Without a proper discharge plan, the effort and money spent on rehabilitation may well be wasted.

Family liaison

11.56 Families do, of course, take an interest in all the various matters which rehabilitation seeks to address, such as achieving reduced dependence on others and more constructive occupation (in the broadest sense). Families, however, are especially aware of the more subtle changes in personality which may not be apparent to those who did not know the injured person prior to injury. Many spouses of injured individuals will say that this is not the person that they married, but that their personality has changed. Unfortunately, rehabilitation can do little to reverse changes of this sort and cannot, at least in the present and foreseeable state of knowledge, undo the more subtle changes which follow from brain injury. Rehabilitation is instead geared towards trying to achieve the best possible level of functioning, that is, the least dependence possible, so that the individual regains so far as possible the ability to live independently and to work, or at least be occupied, at some level.

Spinal Cord Injury

11.57 Spinal injury rehabilitation in many spinal injury units can be viewed as being started on admission to the acute unit. Many of the medical and physical therapies used are preventative in nature and are used to ensure the patient can optimise the rehabilitation when they are able to become actively involved in the post acute phase. Most units in the UK are using a patient focused/keyworker/ goal-planning system of rehabilitation. Patients with little or no cognitive deficit are encouraged to become responsible for directing the focus of their own rehabilitation. This 'ownership' is believed to increase the patient co-operation and therefore maximises the opportunities the rehabilitation process offers. As mentioned previously, assessment, reassessment, discharge planning and a multi-disciplinary approach to include family and patient are fundamental to the success of rehabilitation. Rehabilitation may continue post discharge as an out-patient. Also, later in life, should any post-SCI complications arise resulting in a decrease in functional status, the patient may be re-admitted to the local spinal unit for further treatment and rehabilitation or receive the 'top up' as an out-patient. This is in stark contrast to the level of rehabilitation and follow-up available to the brain injured population.

11.58 Rehabilitation includes:

- Education and training in bladder and bowel care.
- Prevention of sores.
- Physiotherapy to maintain range of motion in paralysed limbs, maximise function in muscles unaffected and to maximise skills in wheelchair skills, transfers and mobility.
- Occupational therapy to teach adaptive techniques in carrying out activities of daily living, use of adaptive technology, and recommendations for adaptations and equipment for the home and work.

11.59 All of this is augmented by:

- Clinics for fertility.
- Clinics for sexual function.
- Clinics for pain.
- Support from social work and clinical psychologists.

This is all to ensure that new spinal-injured can survive the trauma and that they can lead their life as normally as is possible.

THE EFFECTIVENESS OF REHABILITATION

Brain Injury

11.60 A key question is whether or not all the rehabilitation works. This is not an easy question to answer with great confidence. There is a large volume of research in rehabilitation. Much of it is of relatively technical interest and it is important in helping rehabilitation practitioners refine and develop methods which show promise in tackling particular problems. An example of this would be research into the treatment of memory disorders.

11.61 However, of more pressing concern to those involved in funding rehabilitation is the question of whether there is real overall benefit which makes a difference to the lives of the individuals involved. There has been some research which attempts to tackle this question, in particular the work of Nathan Cope.

11.62 Cope[1] has provided a recent review of the area from which the general picture being produced by studies suggests that there is benefit to be gained from rehabilitation. Nevertheless, this is not a view which finds favour in every quarter. One brake on the development of rehabilitation is undoubtedly a view among some medical practitioners, for example some neurosurgeons, that rehabilitation does not make much difference. Scepticism is not wholly unjustified in this area, but at the same time available evidence points in the direction of rehabilitation making a worthwhile difference. However, further research remains necessary.

1 Cope DN 'The effectiveness of traumatic brain injury rehabiliation: A review.' [1995] 9 Brain Injury pp 649-70.

11.63 How is the 'effectiveness' of rehabilitation gauged? There is no single measure. Everything depends on the goals which were set at the start of rehabilitation. These should be specific and measurable, and the staff should monitor progress closely. These will generally be formulated in terms of achieving greater independence in day-to-day function, for example, being able to self-care, go out and about safely and to engage in productive activity. However, the precise goals will be specific to the individual.

11.64 The following case example is an instance of limited goals which, nevertheless, led to a major reduction in care costs by obviating the need for a waking carer and allowing 'sleep-over' care to be substituted. This case, a 50-year old male who had severe brain injury, intimidated his carers, and would be up at night soiling, moving furniture and making a good deal of noise. The goals of rehabilitation here were to achieve control of behaviour and a settled night-time routine. This was of course a limited goal – which was achieved. He did remain dependent on a care team, but there was an annual reduction in overall care costs of over £10,000 per annum in 1995.

1   McKinlay WW and Watkiss AJ 'Long-term Management' in Rose FD and Johnson DA (eds) *Brain Injury and After: Towards Improved Outcome* (1996) John Wiley & Sons, Chichester, England.

11.65 Another instance, which arises quite commonly, is that the aim of initial rehabilitation is to get the individual 'vocational rehabilitation ready' i.e. to meet the criteria for acceptance onto a vocational rehabilitation programme. This will generally entail that the individual should have:

• Reasonably good self-care.
• Basic cognitive skills.
• Basic social skills.
• No undue anxiety.
• Reasonable insight.
• The ability to travel independently to the vocational rehabilitation programme and/or work placements.

11.66 Goals will be set, in such a case, to achieve these requirements, and naturally the precise areas where improvements are needed to attain these goals will vary from case to case.

Spinal Cord Injury

11.67 Rehabilitation post spinal cord injury is more established and developed than for brain injured. Prevention of the complications associated with the multi-system impairment is one of the prime goals of rehabilitation. During the 1914-1918 war, life expectancy post-SCI was two weeks.[1] In the 1960s the mortality rate in tetraplegia was 35%.[2] Developments in medical treatment, rehabilitation and education over the last 50 years have meant that life expectancy for the young tetraplegic can now be within five to ten years of normal and more are surviving the highest levels of cervical lesion requiring ventilatory support.

1   Stover SL and Fine PR *Spinal Cord Injury the Facts and Figures* (2nd edn, 1986) University of Alabama.
2   Grundy D and Swain A *ABC of Spinal Cord Injury* (2nd edn, 1993) *BMJ.*

11.68–11.74   With the clear benefits to life and quality of life, spinal cord injury rehabilitation has become a distinct speciality. There are now regional and national units throughout the United Kingdom providing the necessary rehabilitation and lifelong post discharge support to the victims of SCI.

ACCESS TO REHABILITATION
Brain Injury

11.75   A recent study[1] of all admissions to hospital after head injury in the Glasgow area (catchment population 900,000) found that 2,995 patients were admitted to hospital following head injury in a year. A particularly striking finding concerned those found at follow-up at one year post-injury to be 'moderately disabled' or 'severely disabled', as gauged by the Glasgow Outcome Scale. In only 25% of those who were moderately disabled was contact reported with either rehabilitation services or social work services. Moreover, only 39% of those who were severely disabled had such contact.

> 1   Thornhill S, Teasdale GM, Murray GD, McEwen J, Roy CW and Penny KL *A prospective cohort study of disability after admission with a head injury: the importance of "mild" injuries* BMJ in press.

11.76   This lack of access to rehabilitation is, in some ways, a surprising finding. Unfortunately, however, it will come as no real surprise to many who work in the field who are all too aware that services for head injury are very patchy and often very limited indeed.

11.77   Because of the small amount of brain injury rehabilitation available through the NHS, private sector rehabilitation has filled the gap. Some of these units provide the bulk of their services to the NHS. Where a client has a personal injury claim there is the possibility of privately funded rehabilitation, without the need to wait for the possibility of rehabilitation being offered via NHS funding. This is particularly relevant when it is considered that early rather than late, and some rather than no, rehabilitation is likely to produce a better outcome.

11.78   Costs of rehabilitation vary widely, with £1,600 plus per week common (at 2000 prices). Given relatively few rehabilitation places relative to the number of cases, cost can seldom be the key driver of choice of unit. Location is important. A unit local to the patient's home enables 'phased' discharge, or weekend discharges, which allow the patient to adjust from the rehabilitation setting to the community. A local unit also allows the family to visit, and might persuade those unsure of a residential setting that they are never far from home and those close to them. Consideration needs to be given to what is provided, what therapies are provided, what are the staff:patient ratios, whether there is over-reliance on groups rather than one-to-one treatments for cost reasons, and so on.

Spinal Cord Injury

11.79–11.81   With the clearly defined benefits to saving and prolonging life which aim, hopefully, to allow the individual to return to their place in society as a tax-payer, along with the fact that SCI rehabilitation has been physician led, means it is now viewed as a necessity.

COMMUNITY RE-INTEGRATION

Brain Injury

What Happens After Rehabilitation?

11.82 After discharge from rehabilitation units or general medical wards (where rehabilitation has not been received) individuals who have suffered head injuries return to pick up their lives. Very often they return to live with family members. This is often their parents, even in the cases of adult survivors who had left home before injury, or to be cared for by a spouse. The burden placed on family members as a result of caring for their injured relatives is well documented in research studies[1] and is well known to clinicians.

> 1 McKinlay WW and Watkiss AJ 'Cognitive and Behavioral Effects of Brain Injury' in Rosenthal M, Griffith ER, Kreutzer JS and Pentland B (eds) *Rehabilitation of the Adult and Child with Traumatic Brain Injury* (3rd edn 1999) FA Davis Company, Philadelphia.

11.83 The re-integration of brain injury survivors back into the community remains an outstanding problem.[1] In the long term, brain injury survivors are often out of work, socially isolated, depressed and withdrawn from society. Unfortunately, although living in the community, they are often effectively not part of it or contributing to it.

> 1 Morton MV and Wehman P 'Psychosocial and emotional sequelae of individuals with traumatic brain injury: a literature review and recommendations' [1995] 9(1) Brain Injury pp 81-92.

11.84 Individuals achieve better outcomes following brain injury when they have an effective structure to their day, and are constructively occupied. There are often activities, day centres, work schemes and college courses of which individuals could take advantage. The problem is in accessing these services and in knowing where to find them. It takes someone with knowledge of what is available to put the individual and their family members in touch with these resources. It can be very difficult indeed for the individual to negotiate their own way around services, especially considering the cognitive and other limitations which often follow injury. It can be equally difficult for family members to do this on their behalf, particularly where they are over-stretched in spending their time caring for their relative, and in managing day-to-day life. Many families will state that they do not plan more than a day ahead, but just attempt to cope with the day ahead of them.

Case Management

11.85 The reason for having a brain injury case manager is that very many brain injured individuals have difficulty in obtaining the support they need to live as stable and full a life as possible in the community. There are, however, often many potential sources of help available, including support/voluntary groups, day centres, 'special needs' courses, employment retraining services, clubs and societies. The individuals may need assistance in finding day-time occupation, whether vocationally based or in a more general sense. They may also need help to find suitable carers or home helps, who should be briefed as to the limitations the individual has, and how best to help them (for example, what to do for them and what to prompt them to do). They may need a case manager to help them identify local therapists who have experience of working with brain injured individuals. The case manager's overall remit is to identify possible local sources of help, explore just what may be available, and help the brain-injured individual to structure his time.

11.86   A brain injury case manager would be expected to:

(1) Co-ordinate the client's further placement, care, rehabilitation and training, working flexibly and proactively to prevent problems or solve problems should they arise.
(2) Liaise between hospitals, clinics, day centres, educational institutions, social workers and others involved in providing elements of placement, care, rehabilitation and training.
(3) Liaise between such agencies and the client, family members, care workers, nurses and others involved in providing care and treatment in the client's place of residence.
(4) Arrange such further assessments, placements, rehabilitation training and care as necessary. If these cannot be obtained in the public sector, to recommend suitable private sector sources.
(5) Organise the recruitment and participate in the selection of care workers or others who are to be employed in the care, training and rehabilitation of the client in the client's residence.
(6) Train, supervise, and obtain progress notes from such care workers by means of regular meetings with them.
(7) Meet regularly with any family members or close others involved with the client, in order to ensure that their expectations and needs are being met.

11.87   The overall aim of the brain injury case manager includes increasing the social involvement of the individual. Often when a case manager is introduced, the individual is not interacting in society, has no commitments and may be very withdrawn. The case manager should work towards increasing the individual's commitments to a level where they are leaving the house and beginning to take a part in the community, through to regular commitments, such as day centres or college courses, to also possibly vocational placements or structured weekly activities with the assistance of a carer/companion.

Employment Re-entry
11.88   Estimates of those who return to work after brain injury were traditionally low, below 30%, and attention has increasingly been paid to methods of achieving and sustaining employment. This topic is well reviewed by Wehman et al[1] who developed a programme in Virginia.

> 1   Wehman P, West M, Johnson A and Cifu DX 'Vocational rehabilitation for individuals with traumatic brain injury' in Rosenthal M, Griffith ER, Kreutzer JS and Pentland B (eds) *Rehabilitation of the Adult and Child with Traumatic Brain Injury* (3rd edn 1999) FA Davis Company, Philadelphia.

11.89   A key approach is that of 'supported employment'. This utilises a 'place then train' approach (rather than a more traditional 'train then place' approach) whose advantages include that training is 'on the job'. For individuals with cognitive impairment, this means they do not have to transfer skills to the workplace. Job coaches are an integral part of this approach. On-going support is also important.

11.90 One member of the Virginia group, Jeff Kreutzer,[1] has recently commented on some of the issues which arise. He notes that they used a Monthly Employment Ratio to gauge outcome. This was the proportion of available time that the person actually worked and it was used to characterise employment stability over time. He notes:

'We've known people who have held as many as 12 jobs in less than two years. On average, they are unable to hold a job for more than two or three months. Many people wouldn't consider holding so many jobs in a short time period an indication of "success". We found that the employment ratio provided a better gauge of employment stability than, for example, the more standard practice of contacting people every 6 or 12 months and simply asking them if they were working.'

1 Kreutzer JS [2000] International Neurotrauma Letter 3, pp 7-8.

11.91 It is important, therefore, to consider not only whether a return to work has been achieved, but to ascertain the stability of employment over a period.

Spinal Cord Injury

11.92 Returning to the community as an active, fully participating individual is one of the prime goals of rehabilitation. This is limited to a great extent by environmental barriers and lack of transport. Although the recent Disability Discrimination Act is making progress in developing an equally accessible society, this country still has a long way to go to equal many areas of the USA, and in particular Sweden where legislation demanding equal access has led to 80% of those with spinal cord injury living in the community, being in employment or further education.[1]

1 Slösteen A, Lundquist C, Blomstrand C et al 'The quality of life of three functional spinal cord injury subgroups in a Swedish community' [1990] 28 Paraplegia.

11.93–11.95 This is in stark contrast to a study[1] carried out in Scotland which reviewed the employment rate of those injured in 1992/93 after a six-year period. Prior to injury, only 36% were in education or employment. Of those unemployed prior to injury, none are now working. Only 26% returned to work post-injury, 33% stated they did not want to work while 13% were unable to work due to additional cognitive impairment, due to either head injury or alcohol abuse. Others felt they were caught in the 'benefit trap' and could not afford to work. The vast majority of spinal injury units have sports and recreational clubs or associations attached to them. Their aim is to introduce the spinal injured to leisure activities. This offers the opportunity to remain active, socialise and can give focus to the day. However, the ultimate goal should be for those individuals to participate in mainstream organisations, but this is unlikely to happen until society and environment allows their integration.

1 Walker, A. Presentation of Study at IMSOP, Copenhagen 1999

MEDICO-LEGAL CONSIDERATIONS

Brain Injury

Access to Rehabilitation

11.96 Given the haphazard and often limited access to rehabilitation that brain injury survivors have in the UK, the legal system has a role to play in achieving better access. From the claimant's perspective, access to rehabilitation and, if necessary, brain injury case management is desirable, as it enables greater independence to be achieved. There must also be advantages, at least in some cases, from a defender's perspective, in ensuring that rehabilitation is received. If a reduction in disability can be achieved, the long-term costs of care may be less, sometimes substantially so.

Past and Future Needs

11.97 Rehabilitation professionals are often asked to address various questions which relate to the quantum of damages. By virtue of their experience, they are well placed to consider the long-term outcome of the catastrophic injury sustained in terms of dependency for care, and in terms of employment prospects.

11.98 Reports in this area go under a rather bewildering range of titles. They include:

- Needs reports.
- Care reports.
- Rehabilitation cost reports.
- Functional reports.
- Services report.

11.99 In the end, someone has to consider the impact of the injury on everyday life and make plans for realistic future management. The main areas that should usually be covered, either by one report or a raft of reports, are:

- Need for further rehabilitation and therapies, including any need for ongoing review and advice and the resulting cost.
- Value of past care and costs of future care.
- The need for a case manager, often required in brain injury cases but not often required in spinal cord injury cases, except where the individual has undergone some compromise to cognitive functioning.
- Costs of equipment (special aids and adaptations).
- Accommodation – an architect may be needed here, but the rehabilitation professional should specify broadly what is needed (for example, wheelchair entry, low work surfaces and so on).
- Extra living expenses (extra heat/light, transport, telephone and so on).
- Loss of earnings and superannuation rights and liability to repay benefits, are not clinical matters and would usually not be covered in such reports.

11.100 The comprehensiveness, or otherwise, of reports in this area varies widely. Some reports deal only with care, others with accommodation/equipment and so on. In some cases, a whole raft of reports (sometimes overlapping) is instructed, while in others a single report may cover a broad range of past and future needs. In any event, it is important that all the key areas are covered, and do not 'fall between stools'.

11.101 Such reports, in particular consideration of the care element may form key evidence as regards the largest part of many claims arising from severe catastrophic injury.[1] There would seem to be an advantage in ensuring that these reports are prepared by experienced rehabilitation professionals with a non-litigating practice, so that they can speak with authority on the subject.

1 Braithwaite B 'Legal Considerations' in Rose FD and Johnson DA (eds) *Brain Injury and After: towards improved outcome* (1996) John Wiley & Sons, Chichester, England.

Impact of Legal Proceedings on the Injured Party
11.102 Lawyers should be aware of the impact on the injured person and their family of on-going legal proceedings. The problem which may arise has been summarised by the Australian psychologist Jennie Ponsford:[1]

'Legal proceedings usually continue over many years, often commencing at the point when the TBI[2] individual and the family were beginning to adjust to the impact of the injury and look to the future. A multitude of assessments may be conducted, requiring the injured person and/or the family to reiterate the history and consequences of the injury many times. This can be very stressful. There may be pressure to prove the degree of disability, leading at times to exaggeration of problems and discouragement of return to previous activities, such as work, in order to maximise compensation. This can be extremely counterproductive, undoing rehabilitative attainments' [pp 288-89].

1 Ponsford J with Sloan S and Snow P *Traumatic Brain Injury: Rehabilitation for Everyday Adaptive Living* (1995) Lawrence Erlbaum Associates, Hove, UK.
2 TBI: Traumatic Brain Injury.

Experts
11.103 Members of many rehabilitation professions have the potential to provide useful testimony. Many are wary of getting involved in medico-legal work, because of concerns about having to give evidence. The first author, in teaching rehabilitation professionals and encouraging them not to shy away from giving evidence has found the comments of the American psychologist Paul Deutsch[1] especially useful. He advised rehabilitation professionals giving evidence as follows:

- Maintain intellectual honesty/consistency from case to case.
- Avoid dogmatism/unsupported statements.
- Don't be afraid to say 'I don't know'.
- Stay within your area.
- Don't get flustered or angry.
- Don't get bogged down in minutiae.
- Be an educator – not an advocate.

1 Deutsch PM *Rehabilitation Testimony: Maintaining a Professional Perspective* (1985) Matthew Bender Albany, NY.

11.104–11.109 This advice, especially the last point, is very comforting to many potential expert witnesses, conveying the idea that they are outside the 'quarrel' of the adversarial encounter. That they should treat court in a similar frame of mind to addressing a seminar, giving the court the benefit of their knowledge and experience without being drawn into supporting or attacking either party's position, a stance very much in accord with the spirit of the Woolf reforms.

SUMMARY OF MAIN POINTS AND NOTES ON LEGAL CASE MANAGEMENT

11.110 The main points of the chapter are summarised here with key medico-legal points bulleted.

Brain Injury

11.111 Brain injury is common, young males are most at risk, and life expectancy is near-normal, resulting in many years of 'disabled surviving'. The more severe the injury (assessed by GCS and PTA in Table 1) the greater the disabilities. Deficits are physical, cognitive and emotional-behavioural.

- Medico-legal assessment requires a report from a neurologist or neurosurgeon, to describe the injury and initial management, and a report from a clinical neuropsychologist, to describe the cognitive and emotional-behavioural sequelae, which are the key drivers of disability.

11.112 The main aim of rehabilitation is to minimise care needs and maximise constructive occupation. Rehabilitation takes several forms but not everyone needs to progress through all forms. Assessment for rehabilitation requires the involvement of many professions. The assessment should lead to specific and measurable goals. These will vary widely, depending on the individual's deficits. The process of rehabilitation should be 'seamless', with the various professions co-operating closely. Table 3 sets out what each profession should bring.

- An overall medico-legal report on the need for, and prospects of, rehabilitation can be given by a suitably experienced rehabilitation consultant and/or clinical neuropsychologist.

11.113 Lack of insight can be a key barrier to rehabilitation.

- Medico-legally, one must be wary of taking what the injured person says at face value. They may under-state their problems and over-state their progress.

11.114 The benefits of rehabilitation vary from case to case as goals are individualised. Improvements are generally gauged in terms of gains in independence. Rehabilitation units should not accept clients they cannot help, nor give them rehabilitation for longer than necessary.

- There may be a case for assessment of outcome by a professional independent of a unit. However, it is important to use professionals who have rehabilitation experience.

11.115 Access to rehabilitation is startlingly limited in the United Kingdom, compared to many other countries.

- Lawyers can be proactive in getting clients access to rehabilitation, by securing the funds to pay for it where adequate NHS provision has not been made.

11.116   After rehabilitation, social integration and, for some, return to work are the key issues. A brain injury case manager is the key to social integration for many, while job coaching and supported employment are often needed to achieve employment.

• As with access to rehabilitation, access to brain injury case management and employment rehabilitation may also be gained by securing funds in compensation
• It is important to ascertain the stability of employment over a period, as there may be failure to sustain employment.

11.117   Costs of rehabilitation vary widely, but cheapest is not always best value.

• Location and available services are key considerations.

11.118   The assessment of rehabilitation needs as well as care needs may form part of Needs, or similar, reports.

• Suitably experienced rehabilitation professionals should be well-placed to provide such reports.

Spinal Cord Injury
11.119   This is also more common in young males. The level of the lesion in the spine and whether the lesion is complete or incomplete, are key variables in determining loss of function. (For further factors see Table 2). Rehabilitation starts at the acute unit and includes education/training, prevention of complications, physiotherapy and occupational therapy, as well as further clinics to aid adjustment.

• Medico-legal reporting should cover the nature and extent of injury and medical/surgical management and prognosis.

11.120   Rehabilitation is well-established with good access.

• Some individuals obtain privately-paid rehabilitation as a supplement. Whether this is reasonably necessary should be investigated.

11.121   On return to the community, very extensive care may be needed. This can, in some cases, be as much as 24-hour care from more than one carer at a time. There may be very extensive needs for adaptations to the home and for equipment, which may sometimes reduce the need for care. There will often be extra living expenses.

• Needs reports (which go under a variety of names) are important to deal with the wide range of costs arising.

Chapter 12

Brain Damage at Birth

Roger Clements FRCS FRCOG

12.1   Damage to the baby's brain at birth may be:

(a)   traumatic;
(b)   asphyxial.

12.2   The distinction is somewhat artificial, for trauma and asphyxia may occur together and in any event it is notoriously difficult to differentiate the impact of birth trauma from asphyxia on ultimate neurological damage.

DIRECT TRAUMA TO THE BRAIN

12.3   The birth process may involve considerable distortion of the fetal head. The accommodation, in change of shape of the baby's head, to the birth canal, is brought about by powerful uterine contractions and is called moulding. The five bones at the vault of the fetal skull (Figure 1) are joined by membranes (sutures) and, to a limited extent, the bones may move independently of each other and be made to override. The effect of moulding is to elongate the fetal head and reduce its side-to-side measurement. The effect may be considerable. If a severely moulded fetal head is measured at birth and again 24 hours later, the side-to-side measurement (biparietal diameter) may be found to have increased by up to 5 mm. Moulding of moderate extent is a physiological phenomenon, occurring in normal labour. Excess moulding, particularly without corresponding descent of the fetal head, is an ominous sign for the fetus.

12.4   The rapid development of moulding is a particularly serious finding and suggests that there is insufficient room for the baby's head safely to descend the birth canal (cephalo-pelvic disproportion). While absolute cephalo-pelvic disproportion is uncommon in United Kingdom practice, relative disproportion caused by abnormalities in the position of the fetal head is common, particularly in first pregnancies. It is a common and accepted practice to use drugs (oxytocics such as Syntocinon) to stimulate the uterus so as to overcome this disproportion. However, the abuse of Syntocinon and its use in inappropriate circumstances, particularly in multiparous pregnancy, may lead to excessive moulding and damage to the fetal head.

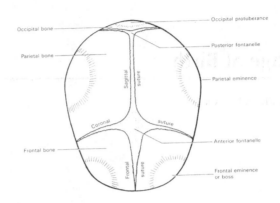

Figure 1: View of Fetal Head from Above (Head Partly Flexed)
from Myles' Textbook for Midwives (V Ruth Bennett and Linda K Brown, 12th
edition, 1993, Churchill Livingstone p 58).

12.5   Attempts have been made to quantify moulding but it is not easy. The best
known method is that recommended by Stewart[1] who suggested a system of
assessment by digital examination of the fetal head, awarding +s as shown in
Table 1.

Table 1: Assessment of Moulding

Degree of Moulding	Clinical Findings
–	Bones normally separated
+	Suture lines closed. No overlap
++	Overlap of suture lines. Reducible
+++	Overlap of suture lines. Irreducible

Two suture lines are added together to provide a moulding score. Four or five
plusses constitute marked moulding

1   Stewart KS, *Second Stage* in Progress in Obstetrics and Gynaecology (ed J Studd) (1984) Vol 4.

12.6   In Stewart's method moulding is assessed by the midwife or doctor at two
or more locations on the fetal head, at the junction between bones. Such junctions
(Figure 1) would be at the sagittal suture, between the two parietal bones, at the
coronal suture between the anterior and frontal bones or at the lamdoidal suture
between the parietal and occipital bones. The two scores are then added together
and Stewart suggests that it may not be safe to continue with attempts at vaginal
delivery with moulding scores as high as 5 or 6. In practice, such elaborate methods
of assessing moulding are seldom employed and the best that can be hoped for in
most labour wards is an assessment as slight, moderate or severe.

12.7   With more sophisticated techniques for detecting intracranial
haemorrhage, it has become clear in recent years that slight intracranial

haemorrhage is common and, without imaging, would pass unnoticed. The vast majority of babies with such small haemorrhages are born normally. The factors which increase the likelihood of haemorrhage and the likelihood of sequelae from it include:

    (a) prematurity;
    (b) prolonged labour;
    (c) operative vaginal delivery.

12.8   In particular, the length of the second stage of labour appears, at least in some reviews, to be relevant. Considerable controversy concerns the length of the second stage of labour.

12.9   The traditional demarcation between the first and second stages of labour has been full dilatation of the cervix. Without regional analgesia, the woman whose cervix is fully dilated usually has an irresistible urge to push. The onset of pushing therefore traditionally coincided with the onset of full dilatation. It is pushing which puts the baby at increased risk.

12.10   With the advent of epidural analgesic block there was no longer a correlation between full dilatation and pushing, as the epidural obtunds the pushing reflex. The mother with a dense epidural will not become aware that the cervix is fully dilated and the head distending the vagina and therefore will have no desire to push. She can of course push on command but her efforts are likely to be much less successful. Only with the return of sensation and the desire to push will spontaneous vaginal delivery usually be effected. What matters in such patients is not the length of time which passes from full dilatation of the cervix but the length of the 'active' or pushing phase of the second stage of labour.

12.11   Two factors operate during the second stage of labour to the potential detriment of the fetus:

    (a) further compression of the fetal head;
    (b) asphyxia.

As noted in para 12.1, the influence of the two cannot necessarily always be separated.

12.12–12.14   The solution to the prolonged second stage may be operative vaginal delivery. Operative vaginal delivery is one of the factors tending to increase birth trauma. There is therefore a tension between the length of the second stage of labour and intervention by operative delivery. In a difficult labour and with evidence of cephalo-pelvic disproportion, the choice, time and method for operative delivery become critical.

OPERATIVE VAGINAL DELIVERY

Which Instrument?

12.15   Two types of instrument are available to shorten the second stage of labour and to rescue the baby from asphyxial stress. There is lively debate as to whether a ventouse (vacuum extractor) is preferable to forceps for this purpose.

12.16   The choice of instrument is more likely to be determined by geography and the individual preference of the operator than by any objective criteria. The choice of the operator is, in turn, likely to be influenced strongly by training and experience. The obstetric forceps have been available for over 250 years in a variety of models. While there were early attempts at ventouse design dating back to the eighteenth century, it was not until Malmstrom's design of the ventouse in 1954 that the instrument established any kind of credibility. In the 1950s and 1960s, at least in Northern Europe, forceps remained more popular. In the developing world the ventouse achieved rapid popularity. The developed world has followed. Part of the reason for the change has been an improvement in design with the development of the 'posterior cup' for the malrotated head and the use of synthetic materials for the suction cup. Modern cups are less efficient than the old metal Malmstrom variety and will therefore tend to pull off more readily with extreme traction.

12.17   The initial popularity of the ventouse in the third world (where cephalo-pelvic disproportion is more common) was due partly to this inherent safety factor. Whereas an unskilled and brutal operator with the obstetric forceps can drag a fetal head through a contracted pelvis, even the old metal cups on the ventouse would pull off given extreme traction. Another likely reason was probably that, by common consent, basic proficiency with the ventouse can be acquired quicker than with obstetric forceps.

12.18   It follows that, with reduced junior doctors' hours and less exposure to labour ward duty, there is a reduced opportunity for proficiency in operative delivery skills and the ventouse becomes more attractive. Operative vaginal delivery cannot be taught from a book or even by watching someone else do it. It has to be done, under supervision, by the junior doctor himself. It is a one person operation, much of it is done by feel and only the operator can tell how much traction or rotation force is being exerted. Judgement comes only with practice. The generation of doctors trained before 1970 had ample opportunity to learn operative delivery skills and to become proficient with a variety of different instruments. Those opportunities are now severely curtailed and for the majority of obstetricians in training there is little opportunity to learn the more difficult and complex forceps delivery techniques.

The Ventouse

12.19   The theoretical advantages of the ventouse are that:

    (a) it takes up no room in the pelvis;
    (b) it requires less operative dexterity;
    (c) it is capable of less harm to the fetus.

The truth of the last is open to debate and it should not be assumed that the ventouse is a benign instrument. Even with the modern silc cups, harm to both baby and mother is possible and has been described. While serious intracranial injury is rare, its occurrence is amply documented, particularly in circumstances where the ventouse is used from the mid-pelvis and where there are repeated applications with prolonged traction. It is in this context that moulding takes on an added significance. Inside the skull the brain is separated both vertically and horizontally by thin membranes. Within these membranes run large vessels. If the supporting membranes (the falx cerebri and the tentorium cerebelli) are already stretched, as a consequence of moulding and head compression, further mechanical stress resulting from traction by the ventouse may be sufficient to cause significant haemorrhage. Where moulding is already well established the wisdom of traction with the ventouse must be questioned by the operator and in any event, the number of pulls limited. There have been attempts to codify such advice, one of which, from Munro Kerr's Operative Obstetrics is reproduced as Table 2.

Forceps Delivery

12.20   With one minor exception all of the forceps commonly in use in the United Kingdom were developed before the beginning of the first world war. They belong to an age when the primary objective of the obstetrician was to save the life of the mother. Thus, in the context of mechanical difficulty, it was common practice to sacrifice the baby so that the mother avoided the worst ravages of obstructed labour or, occasionally, the alternative of primitive Caesarean section which at that time carried a high maternal mortality. Forceps were designed to overcome obstruction by dragging the head through the pelvis at no matter what cost to the fetus. The obstetric forceps now have a very different purpose but it is important to bear in mind that they are designed so as to be easily applied to the head obstructed high in the pelvis and, if used for that purpose inadvertently today are just as lethal as they were at the end of the last century.

Table 2: Scheme for Selecting the Method of Delivery (After Stewart)

Amount of head palpable (fifths)	0/5		1/5		2/5		3/5		4/5
Moulding score	Regardless	0-4	5-6	0-4	5-6	0-4	5-6		Regardless
Mode of delivery	Ventouse or forceps		Trial ventouse unless fetal distress		Symphysiotomy + ventouse		Caesarean section		
Group number	1		2		3		4		

12.21   Although the Chamberlen family must be credited with the development of the obstetric forceps in the seventeenth century they did nothing to popularise them, rather keeping them as a commercial secret. It was not until the advent of William Smellie, the father of British midwifery, towards the middle of the eighteenth century that the obstetric forceps were perfected and popularised. The Chamberlens recognised the need for the instrument to be curved so as to fit the baby's head (the cephalic curve) but it was Smellie who introduced the second curve in the instrument (the pelvic curve) to fit the shape of the birth canal. One hundred years later Simpson modified the instrument slightly with the addition of a lock so that the blades could not be squeezed together. Simpson's instrument remains in use today with a dozen eponymous variations of no great importance. The Simpson forceps are shown in figure 2, illustrating the cephalic curve to accommodate the baby's head and in figure 3, illustrating the pelvic curve.

Figure 2: Simpson Forceps
from John Patrick O'Grady, *Modern Instrumental Delivery* (Williams and Wilkins at p34).

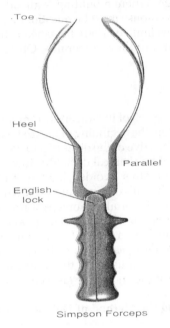

Simpson Forceps

12.22 Curved forceps can be applied to the head at any height (the only limitation being the length of the handle), provided that the head is in the correct position in relation to the mother's pelvis. The baby's head must be facing directly backwards or directly forwards to allow the blades to be correctly positioned, as

Figure 3: Lateral View of Simpson Forceps
from John Patrick O'Grady, *Modern Instrumental Delivery* (Williams and Wilkins, at p34).

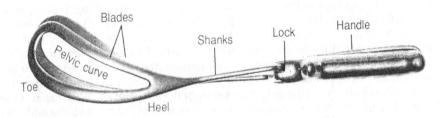

Anatomy of classic obstetric forceps. Lateral view of Simpson forceps Note pelvic curve of the fenestrated blades.

there is no possibility of rotation. But the fetal head was frequently arrested high in the pelvis in a transverse position (facing left or right) and it was to permit the application of the forceps to a head in such a position that Christian Kjelland introduced his instrument in 1910. The Kjelland's forceps (Figure 4) has a cephalic curve but no pelvic curve. Neither does it have a fixed lock. This allows the instrument to be applied accurately to the fetal head irrespective of its position in relation to the maternal pelvis and irrespective of its tilt (asynclitism) toward the front or the back. The Kjelland forceps is a most elegant and versatile instrument in the proper hands, but because it is capable of delivering a head from almost any level and almost any position, the opportunity for abuse is great.

12.23   Correct application is to the side of the fetal head (Figure 5). The blade of the forceps grips the baby's head between the ear and the eye, exerting its traction over the zygoma and mandible. When correctly applied the blades of the forceps frequently leave a mark on the baby's face which quickly fades.

12.24   Forceps may cause brain damage in three principle ways:

    (a) compression of the fetal head;
    (b) rotational injury;
    (c) asphyxia.

12.25   Compression of the fetal head can be achieved with forceps of any design. It is particularly likely to happen with the Kjelland's forceps because there is no fixed lock. If the operator squeezes the handles of the instrument together he also directly squeezes the blades. It is therefore axiomatic that in applying traction to the Kjelland's forceps the operator uses only finger traction on the shoulders of the instrument, never employing a hand to squeeze the handle.

Figure 4: Kielland Forceps
from John Patrick O'Grady, *Modern Instrumental Delivery* (Williams and Wilkins, at p43).

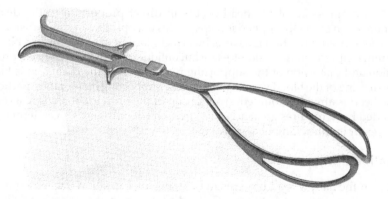

Figure 2.12.   Kielland forceps (ca. 1916). Note sliding lock and absence of a pelvic curve.

Figure 5: The Correct Application of the Obstetric Forceps
from *The Obstetrical Forceps* (L V Dill, Charles C Thomas 1953, p 38.)

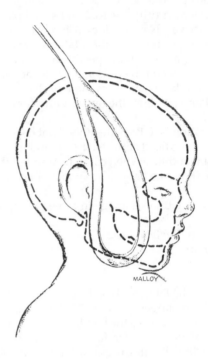

12.26   The fixed lock is not, however, a complete safeguard against crushing injury by the curved forceps. There is nothing to prevent the toes of the forceps coming together and although the operator cannot directly squeeze the blades together, traction through a limited bony pelvis will crush the baby's head within the forceps blades. The blades do not protect the fetal head against crushing in the event of strong traction.

Moulding

12.27   Compression of the head occurs in direct proportion to the degree of traction. Even correctly applied forceps blades may produce a compression injury of the fetal head if traction is severe. Incorrect placement of the forceps blades (so that the compression is not side-to-side but oblique or even front-to-back) produces tension and distortion of the supporting membranes to the brain and is likely to cause tearing of the blood vessels within those supporting membranes, particularly if the head is already moulded. Application of the obstetric forceps to a severely moulded head requires great accuracy. In such circumstances, even light traction may result in intracranial haemorrhage.

Rotational Injury

12.28   If the baby's head presents in the transverse position (facing left or right) a 90° rotation is required with the Kjelland's forceps, in order to effect delivery. If, however, the baby faces forwards (the occiput-posterior position) the operator may have to rotate the head 180°. It is this long rotation which is sometimes associated with a specific rotational injury, usually to the fetal cervical spine.

12.29   Rotional forceps delivery is more dangerous because:

    (a) accurate placement of the blades is more difficult;
    (b) the fetal head may already be moulded;
    (c) rotation may not be possible at the level of arrest and the head may have to be displaced upwards or downwards before rotation can be achieved.

12.30   In modern obstetrics rotation of the fetal head is only acceptable from a level in the pelvis which precludes significant cephalo-pelvic disproportion. If more than one fifth of the fetal head is palpable abdominally, rotational forceps delivery should not be attempted.

12.31   Sometimes it may be permissible to deliver the malrotated head in the direct occipito-posterior position. This can be achieved by the use of conventional curved forceps but should not be attempted unless the head is very low in the pelvis and already bulging the perineum. Because the diameters of the fetal head are larger in this presentation, a generous prophylactic episiotomy is essential.

ASPHYXIAL INJURY

12.32   At the end of a long labour in which the baby has been exposed to chronic partial hypoxia (see paras 12.97-12.99) a difficult rotational forceps delivery provokes collapse of the fetal circulation. Little has been written about this phenomenon but all experts with experience of cerebral palsy litigation have seen the results. The mechanism is unclear. It may be that in such circumstances compression of the fetal head is sufficient stimulus to the brain stem to provoke a vagal discharge and bradycardia which, the fetal resources having been partially exhausted already, leads to circulatory collapse. It may be that in some cases the cord becomes entangled with the toe of the forceps, either at the time of application or during rotation. In any event, the result is a collapse of the fetal circulation and a profound bradycardia. If delivery is effected quickly the fetus may well recover to normal function but if, as sometimes happens, the forceps delivery fails and there is an interval before Caesarean section can be accomplished, asphyxial injury may result.

Trial of Forceps

12.33   It is because the penalty for failure is so great that the concept of 'trial of forceps' has arisen. If the operator believes that there is a significant risk of failure then forceps delivery should not be attempted in the delivery room but should be carried out as a planned procedure in the operating theatre. In the event of failure there, the blades may be removed and immediate recourse had to Caesarean section. To undertake a proper trial of forceps it is mandatory that the operation not only finishes but starts in a properly equipped operating theatre. In this way, the operator will be less tempted in circumstances of difficulty to pull just that little bit harder to overcome the resistance, for the opportunity for abdominal delivery will be readily available. Furthermore there will be no delay between the removal of the blades and the Caesarean section. Forceps delivery in such circumstances requires mature judgment. As Ian Donald famously remarked:

> 'Trial of forceps is like lion taming; it is not the sort of exercise one would willingly undertake in expectation of failure'.[1]

1 Donald I *Technique and Pitfalls of Instrumental Delivery. Practical Obstetric Problems* (5th edn, 1979) Lloyd Luke. Chapter XIX p 648.

Breech Delivery

12.34   Because the head of the human fetus is so large in proportion to its body, vaginal breech delivery presents special mechanical difficulties. With a cephalic presentation there is plenty of time for the head to rotate, flex and mould within the maternal pelvis to negotiate a passage even in circumstances of borderline disproportion. If the passage cannot be negotiated safely there is plenty of time for the obstetrician to intervene to rescue the baby well before there is any real danger of trauma or asphyxia. This is not so with a breech presentation. Because the head must negotiate the birth canal last, and at a time when there is no longer an efficient oxygen supply, there must be no question of disproportion between the baby's head and the maternal pelvis. It is unsurprising therefore that vaginal breech delivery is more dangerous to the fetus than cephalic vaginal delivery. Exactly how much more dangerous is very difficult to assess.

12.35   Breech presentation is associated with:

  (a) prematurity;
  (b) fetal abnormality.

12.36   For these reasons the infant presenting as a breech is more likely to perform unfavourably, regardless of the mode of delivery. Nevertheless it is inescapable that even in the term infant the excess perinatal mortality of vaginal breech delivery is between two and five times higher than that associated with planned Caesarean section, even after excluding infants with lethal congenital abnormalities. The major hazards in breech delivery are:

  (a) entrapment of the fetal head;
  (b) prolapse of the umbilical cord.

Prolapse of the Cord

12.37   Because the presenting part fits less well into the maternal pelvis, there is a danger that the umbilical cord may slip past the baby and when the membranes rupture prolapse into the cervix and vagina. The consequences of prolapsed cord are considered in paras 12.66, 12.67 and 12.1000.

12.38   The varieties of breech presentation are illustrated in Figure 6. The frank (or extended) breech fits the pelvis better than the other varieties. Where the knees are flexed the umbilical cord may become entangled with the baby's feet and, particularly in a footling presentation the risk of cord prolapse is so high that most obstetricians would counsel against vaginal breech delivery.

Figure 6: Varieties of Breech Presentation
from *Dewhurst's Integrated Obstetrics and Gynaecology for Postgraduates* by Whitfield (Blackwell, 1986).

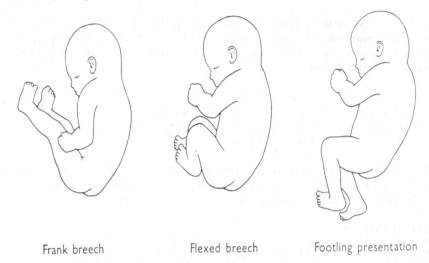

| Frank breech | Flexed breech | Footling presentation |

Reproduced with permission of Blackwell Science Ltd.

Entrapment of the Fetal Head

12.39   When the baby's body is delivered and the fetal head engages in the maternal pelvis there is little available space for the umbilical cord and it will usually be squeezed between the head and the maternal pelvic brim, reducing if not completely obstructing blood flow. From this moment the baby is effectively without oxygen and must be delivered before damage can result. Delivery too fast, particularly if the baby's head is a tight fit in the maternal pelvis may produce a 'springing' injury to the supporting membranes of the brain, causing intracranial haemorrhage. Too slow delivery, on the other hand, risks asphyxia. Provided that the baby is well grown and has not previously been exposed to asphyxia during labour, it will probably withstand up to ten minutes without injury. Once the mouth reaches the perineum the baby can of course breathe and the last part of the delivery of the head may be taken at leisure.

12.40   A number of methods are described[1] to encourage flexion of the baby's head and engagement in the pelvis. The obstetric forceps should generally be applied to the baby's head once it has fully entered the pelvis so that the operator can control the speed of delivery of the baby's head. Forceps delivery allows the operator greater control than the older jaw flexion and shoulder traction manoeuvre (Mauriceau-Smellie-Veit).

1   Donald I *Breech Presentation. Practical Obstetric Problems* (5th edn, 1979) Lloyd Luke. Chapter XIII.

12.41   If the fetal head cannot be made to enter the maternal pelvis then all is lost for the baby. Jaw and shoulder traction can be applied by the skilled operator to the fetal head above the brim and of course the obstetric forceps can be used to overcome disproportion but both are likely to result in severe fetal trauma.

12.42   Because of the impossibility of treating this dreaded complication it is essential to make sure that there is no possibility of cephalo-pelvic disproportion before vaginal breech delivery is permitted. Careful ante-natal assessment is essential and should include:

(a) assessment of fetal well-being;
(b) exclusion of other obstetric complications;
(c) estimate of fetal weight and attitude (by ultrasound);
(d) assessment of maternal pelvic size.

12.43   When the assessment has been made it is of course essential that the obstetrician shares with the parents the information obtained and obtains consent for the course of action recommended.

Breech Extraction

12.44   Planned vaginal breech delivery is assisted by the obstetrician but at no time[1] should the operator employ traction on any part of the baby's body. To do so risks extension of the arms or head and increased mechanical difficulty. The art of assisted breech delivery is all about masterly inactivity until the operator assists with the delivery of the head.

  1   Donald I *Breech Presentation. Practical Obstetric Problems* (5th edn, 1979) Lloyd Luke. Chapter XIII.

12.45   The operation of breech extraction is entirely different. Justification for breech extraction is speed, either because the fetus is distressed or the mother is bleeding. In order to hasten breech delivery, the obstetrician 'breaks up' the complete breech and if possible pulls down a leg. Alternatively in an extended (frank) breech the operator exerts traction in the fetal groin. In modern obstetrics there is practically no place for such a manoeuvre. If there are reasons to speed delivery before the baby's buttocks have been delivered the correct solution is Caesarean section. The only exceptions to this rule are the dead fetus or, occasionally, the delivery of a second twin.

Caesarean Section for the Premature Breech

12.46   There is considerable controversy at present as to whether the pre-term breech baby is better delivered vaginally or abdominally. If the decision is made to delivery the term baby by Caesarean section there is usually no difficulty at the time of operation. However, with the pre-term breech, particularly in extreme prematurity, Caesarean section may be as hazardous to the baby as vaginal breech delivery. The conventional lower segment operation often provides inadequate space (for the lower segment is poorly formed) for the baby's head to be delivered. The tiny body can be extracted easily through a small transverse incision in the lower uterine segment, however poorly formed. But once the shoulders are born the head is firmly stuck and the obstetric forceps are no use because they are too large. Traction on the baby's shoulders is likely to produce severe soft tissue damage to the trunk, traction injury to the head and asphyxia. In such circumstance the operator is forced into making a T-shaped incision. In order to avoid this dilemma Caesarean section to the severely pre-term breech should be a longitudinal incision which can be extended swiftly and sufficiently to provide space for the baby's head.

12.47–12.60 Caesarean section is sometimes undertaken when the lie of the baby is not longitudinal. It is dangerous to embark on a Caesarean section for transverse or oblique lie without first correcting the lie. This can be done either before or after the abdomen is open but it is essential as otherwise the operator, again opening the lower segment, may need to insert a hand and manipulate the baby through a small incision. The result is likely to be trauma to both mother and baby.

ASPHYXIAL BRAIN INJURY

12.61 Asphyxial injury to the fetal brain is best considered as:

(a) chronic;
(b) acute;

although both varieties may operate in any particular case.

Oxygen Supply to the Fetus

12.62 The fetus obtains oxygen and all nutrients from the maternal circulation by way of the placenta. The chorionic villi of the placenta, carrying fetal blood vessels (Figure 7) are suspended in the intervillus space, a pool of maternal blood. Gas and nutrient exchange occur across the membrane separating the fetal vessels from the maternal reservoir. The health of the placenta is essential for fetal wellbeing during pregnancy. If the placenta is defective or small the baby may be starved of nutrients and eventually of oxygen. The placenta communicates with the baby by the umbilical cord and blood flow through the cord is critical for the baby's survivial.

Chronic Asphyxia

12.63 In its most extreme form chronic asphyxia occurs during pregnancy and will be responsible for fetal damage or death before labour. Ultrasound measurements of babies starved of nutrients have characteristic appearances because of the 'head-sparing' effect. Growth of the brain is preferentially protected so that the baby loses weight, causing a reduction in the rate of growth of the abdominal circumference without a corresponding decrease in head circumference. This is asymmetric growth retardation and is characteristic of the starving baby. Eventually, when starvation and oxygen supply become extreme head growth too will be affected. Occasionally fetal death may occur in utero. More commonly the baby survives intact but is vulnerable to further asphyxial insult in labour.

Figure 7: Chorionic Villi of the Placenta Carrying Fetal Blood Vessels
Reprinted from *Myles' Textbook for Midwives*, 12th edition, edited by V Ruth Bennett
and Linda K Brown, p 44, 1993 by permission of the publisher Churchill Livingstone.

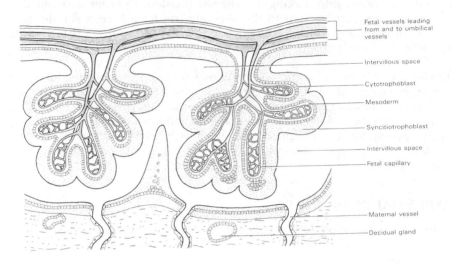

Fetal vessels leading from and to umbilical vessels

Intervillous space

Cytotrophoblast

Mesoderm

Syncitiotrophoblast

Intervillous space

Fetal capillary

Maternal vessel

Decidual gland

12.64   Uterine contractions are present throughout the second half of
pregnancy. They become painful and expulsive during labour. When the uterus
contracts the intervillus space is squeezed of blood and once the uterus relaxes
it fills again. This has a beneficial effect on the baby's oxygenation, only if the
labour is normal. Provided that there is relaxation between contractions, that
the contractions do not last too long and that the contractions do not occur
too frequently, the baby benefits from this secondary pump action of the uterus.
However, where uterine activity is excessive or where the baby's reserves are
depleted uterine activity becomes a threat to fetal oxygenation. Repeated
exposure to uterine contractions may then produce chronic intermittent
asphyxia. Evidence of that asphyxial stress may be observed as changes in the
fetal heart.

Acidemia

12.65   Uniquely, the fetus has the capacity for limited respiration in the absence
of oxygen. The energy source (carbohydrate) may, in the fetus, be partially
broken down so as to release some of its energy without oxygen. This anaerobic
respiration produces acid metabolites which accumulate in the fetal tissues.
Where oxygen is in short supply, there is usually a concomitant difficulty in
disposing of carbon dioxide. Thus, in the fetus exposed to chronic asphyxia
there is both accumulation of carbon dioxide and acid metabolites. This
metabolic acidosis is associated with a fall in pH (acidaemia) which can be
measured both before and after birth. It is also associated with a reduction in
available base (paradoxically reported as negative base excess!). Measurements
of pH and base excess give some indication of the severity and duration of the
asphyxial stress.

Acute Asphyxia

12.66 Acute asphyxia is uncommon before labour. The causes of acute asphyxia are set out in Table 3.

Table 3

CORD COMPROMISE
Prolapse
Compression
Entanglement
PLACENTAL ABRUPTION
RUPTURE OF THE UTERUS
MATERNAL HYPOTENSION
Epidural analgesic block
Supine caval occlusion
Amniotic fluid embolus
Blood loss
SHOULDER DYSTOCIA

12.67 In any of these circumstances fetal oxygen supply is suddenly compromised and again characteristic changes may be observed in the fetal heart. In some cases, the change is intermittent, as with cord entanglement. In others, such as rupture of the uterus or shoulder dystocia, the asphyxia is inexorable until the baby is rescued.

12.68 In very severe and short-lived asphyxia there may be little time for a change in pH. With slightly longer periods of acute asphyxia the pH may fall but the fall is due to the accumulation of carbon dioxide (respiratory acidosis) there will be no time for the build up of acid metabolites and the fetus may show no evidence of a metabolic acidosis at birth.

The Physical Sign of Intrapartum Asphyxia

12.69 Hypoxia is known to produce certain changes in the fetus which the obstetrician recognises as fetal distress. Fetal distress in labour is recognised by:

(a) the passage of meconium;
(b) abnormalities of the fetal heart.

12.70   The term fetal distress is much criticised by modern authors as it cannot easily be defined. It does not readily equate to hypoxia and acidosis in the fetus. Nevertheless, hypoxia and acidosis are commonly associated with the appearance of meconium in the liquor and abnormalities of the cardiotocograph trace. The term 'fetal distress' denotes only the anxiety produced in the birth attendants by the appearance of these physical signs, in case they should indicate hypoxia and acidosis. Many babies are born with both abnormalities present, but in excellent condition. Few babies are born with evidence of hypoxia and acidosis in the absence of these physical signs.

The Cardiotocograph Trace

12.71   The cardiotocograph is an electronic apparatus for monitoring fetal heart rate, and maternal uterine contractions. The contractions are monitoried by an external tocodynamometer or by an intra-uterine pressure transducer (Figure 8).

12.72   The fetal heart may be recorded by ultrasound, using an external monitoring transducer (Figure 9), or by an internal electrocardiograph record obtained by the application of a screw or clip to the baby's scalp (Figure 10).

External monitoring transducer

Figure 8: External Monitoring Transducer
from *Fetal Heart Rate Patterns and Their Clinical Interpretations* (PJ Steer, 2nd edition, Oxford Sonicaid Limited).

Figure 9: External Tocodynamometer
from *Fetal Heart Rate Patterns and Their Clinical Interpretations* (P J Steer, 2nd edition, Sonicaid Limited).

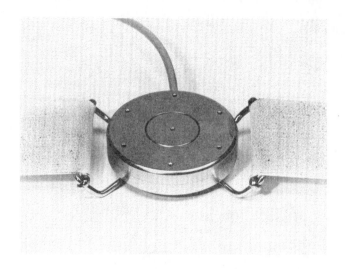

Figure 10: Screw Electrode and Clip Electrode
from *Fetal Heart Rate Patterns and Their Clinical Interpretations* (P J Steer, 2nd edition, Sonicaid Limited).

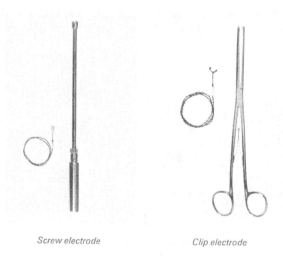

Screw electrode   Clip electrode

12.73   These two recordings are combined on a single CTG printout, the main features of which are illustrated in Figures 11 and 12.

Figure 11:   Terms Used in the Study of Continuous Records of FHR
from *Fetal Heart Rate Patterns and Their Clinical Interpretations* (P J Steer, 2nd edition, Sonicaid Limited).

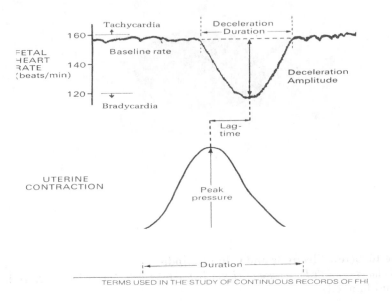

Figure 12: Fetal Heart Rate Patterns and Their Clinical Interpretations
from *Fetal Heart Rate Patterns and Their Clinical Interpretations* (P J Steer, 2nd edition, Sonicaid Limited).

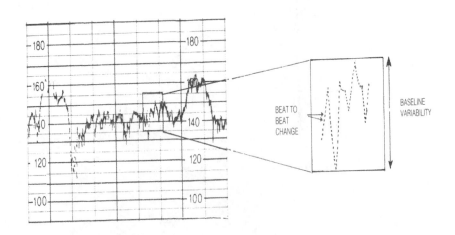

Figure 13: Signficance of FHR Traces Relative to pH
from *Fetal Heart Rate Patterns and Their Clinical Interpretations* (P J Steer, 2nd edition, Sonicaid Limited).

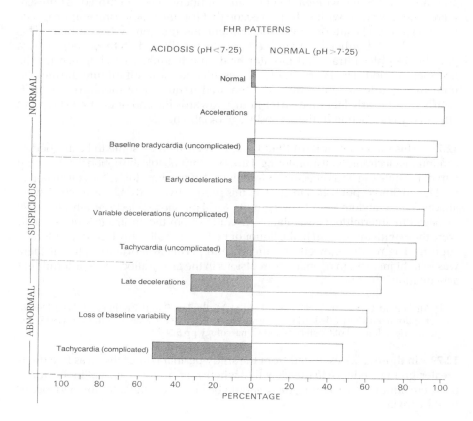

12.74 The significance of some of the heart rate patterns is illustrated in Figure 13.

12.75 In considering the analysis of the cardiotocograph trace ('CTG') it must be clearly understood that the CTG is only one of the indicators available to the obstetrician. Labour is not managed on the basis of the appearances of the CTG. Labour is managed on the overall clinical picture. The CTG is but one part of it. Other factors in the labour, such as the presence of a Caesarean section scar, maternal bleeding, slow progress, signs of disproportion, abnormal presentation of the fetus will influence management profoundly.

12.76 The attachment of a CTG machine to a labouring mother conveys no benefit. A trained observer is necessary in order to interpret the signals of the CTG and to convey that benefit.

12.77 There is a general perception that routine use of electronic monitoring increases the incidence of intervention in labour, particularly the incidence of Caesarean section. It has been remarkably difficult to show that continuous electronic fetal monitoring has a measurable beneficial influence on fetal mortality and morbidity. Some women do not want routinely to be monitored. At present there is no consensus within the profession that routine monitoring is appropriate for all labours. The alternative is intermittent auscultation by the midwife. This can be achieved either by a simple ear-trumpet (Pinard stethoscope) or by a portable Doppler ultrasound monitor held onto the maternal abdomen for the necessary period. The heart should be auscultated for a full minute during and immediately after a contraction. The required frequency of monitoring is half-hourly during early labour, quarter-hourly towards the end of the first stage and after every contraction in the second stage of labour.

12.78 This method of intermittent monitoring is held by some to be as good as continuous electronic fetal monitoring. However improbable the notion that listening part of the time can be as effective as listening all of the time, this is the conclusion of the Dublin Study,[1] published in 1985. In this prospective study 12,964 mothers were allocated on a random basis to two groups, 6,474 monitored electronically and 6,490 managed by intermittent auscultation. Excluded from the groups (6% of the total) were those with meconium in the liquor or no liquor at all at the time of membrane rupture. The results showed no difference in perinatal mortality rate but there was a slight increase in neonatal convulsions in the group allocated to intermittent asucultation.

1   McDonald D, Grant A, Sheridan-Pereira M, Boylan P and Chalmers I, 'The Dublin Randomized Controlled Trial of Intrapartum Fetal Heart Rate Monitoring' [1985] 152 American Journal of Obstetrics and Gynaecology pp 524-39.

12.79 In those cases excluded from the study perinatal mortality was five times greater, giving credence to the view that where meconium is present in the liquor or where liquor is very scanty, there should be increased vigilance for evidence of fetal hypoxia.

12.80 As a compromise, for those women who do not want or are perceived not to merit continuous monitoring, a short 'admission trace' is often taken. If this is normal and all other factors are favourable, the patient may then be allocated to intermittent monitoring rather than continuous electronic surveillance.

The Analysis of the CTG

12.81 The (lower) contraction channel (tocograph) records maternal contractions but is not quantitative. It is possible to tell by examination of the tocograph the frequency and length of contractions but not, with any accuracy, their strength.

Figure 14: The Normal CTG (cf figure 16)
Reprinted from *Myles' Textbook for Midwives*, 12th edition, edited by V Ruth Bennett and Linda K Brown, 1993 by permission of the publisher Churchill Livingstone.

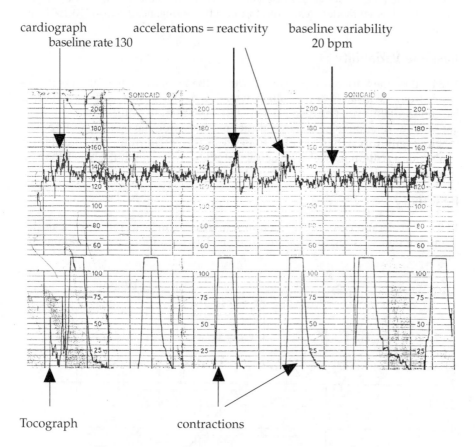

cardiograph   accelerations = reactivity   baseline variability
    baseline rate 130   20 bpm

Tocograph   contractions

(The gain control has been poorly adjusted (high) so
that the peak of the contraction goes off the scale)

12.82 Four components of the fetal heart trace (cardiograph) must be examined separately, in order to determine whether or not the trace is normal:

(a) baseline heart rate;
(b) baseline variability;
(c) reactivity;
(d) decelerations.

A normal CTG is illustrated in Figure 14.

Baseline Heart Rate

12.83 The baseline heart rate is the average heart rate, the same heart rate that would be detectable by simple auscultation for a minute. It is the mean heart rate between accelerations and decelerations. There is some dispute concerning the normal range. Traditionally it was 120 to 160 beats per minute. 110 to 120 may also be considered normal if all other features of the CTG are normal. Recently some authors have considered rates above 150 suspicious, particularly if the heart rate rises during labour. This has led modern textbooks to adjust the normal heart rate to 110-150 beats per minute.

Baseline Variability

12.84 Baseline variability or band width is the extent to which the heart rate varies from the mean over the course of a minute. The normal cardiograph has a baseline variability of between 5 and 15 beats per minute. Values greater than 15 are often normal but sometimes indicate recovery from an episode of hypoxia, labelled saltatory when greater than 25 beats per minute. An undulating (sinusoidal) pattern may also be abnormal if the wave length is greater than 30 seconds.

Reactivity

12.85 Acceleration is defined as a transient increase in heart rate of 15 beats per minute or more, lasting for 15 seconds. When two or more such accelerations are

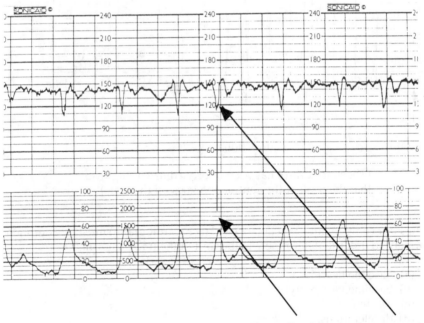

The nadir of the deceleration and the peak of the contraction coincide

Figure 15: Early Decelerations
Reprinted from *Myles' Textbook for Midwives*, 12th edition, edited by V Ruth Bennett and Linda K Brown, p 178, 1993 by permission of the publisher Churchill Livingstone.

present in a 20-minute period of recording the trace is said to be reactive. Accelerations are an indication of fetal health, the fetus responding to stimuli such as uterine contractions or its own movement.

Decelerations

12.86 A slowing from the baseline of 15 beats per minute or more, lasting for at least 15 seconds is a deceleration. Decelerations are essentially of three types and have four components:

   (a) amplitude – depth from the baseline;
   (b) duration – time from onset until return to normal baseline rate;
   (c) shape – V-shaped or U-shaped;
   (d) lag time – the time between the peak of the contraction and the nadir of the associated deceleration.

Table 4: Decelerations

Early	– synchronous with contractions – V-shaped – amplitude less than 40 beats per minute – associated with head compression – usually, but not invariably, benign
Late	– lag time of more than 15 seconds – usually U-shaped but may be asymmetric – can be of any amplitude or duration – usually, but not invariably, pathological – often represent chronic intermittent hypoxia
Variable	– no fixed relationship with contractions (variable lag time) – synchronous contractions exceeding 40 beats per minute – any amplitude or duration – may or may not indicate hypoxia – common in the second stage of labour – often seen with cord complication

12.87–12.90 The types of decelerations and their significance are explained in Table 4. Examples of early decelerations are shown in Figure 15, late decelerations in Figure 16 and variable decelerations in Figure 17.

Figure 16: Late decelerations. The same patient as figure 14. After many hour of labour there is a baseline tachycardia at 170 - 180 beats per minute, complicated by persistent late decelerations and loss of baseline variability. There is a paradoxical increase in variability associated with the peak of the hypoxia, at the bottom of each deceleration.

Baseline rate 180 bpm

Increased variability at the bottom of the deceleration

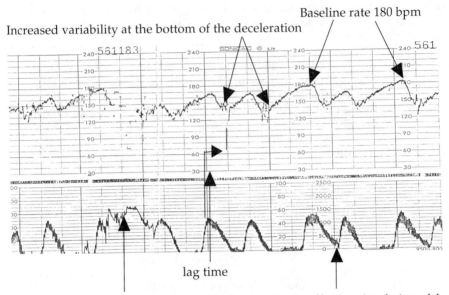

lag time

Uterine hyperstimulation, with elision of contractions

Further evidence of hyperstimulation of the uterus with coupling of contractions

Figure 17: Variable Decelerations. The vertical lines illustrate that the relationship between the nadir of the deceleration at the peak of the contraction is not constant. Even though some of the decelerations are very nearly coincident with contractions, they cannot be classified as early because they exceed a depth of 40 beats per minute.

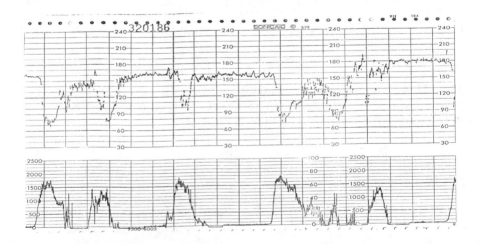

CLASSIFICATION OF THE CTG IN THE FIRST STAGE OF LABOUR

12.91 The CTGs may be broadly and simply classified into three patterns, as shown in Table 5.

Table 5

Normal
> Baseline rate between 110 and 150
> Baseline variability between 10 and 25 beats per minute
> Two accelerations in 20 minutes
> No decelerations

Suspicious
> Baseline heart rate above the normal range, between 150 and 170 or below the normal range between 100 and 110
> Amplitude of variability between 5 and 10 beats per minute for more than 40 minutes
> Increased variability above 25 beats per minute
> Variable decelerations

Pathological (Abnormal)
> Baseline heart rate below 100 or above 170
> Persistence of heart rate variability of less than 5 beats per minute for more than 40 minutes
> Severe variable decelerations or severe repetitive early decelerations
> Prolonged decelerations
> Late decelerations: the most ominous trace is a steady baseline without variability and with small decelerations after each contraction

---

Meconium Staining of the Liquor

12.92 Meconium is the substance present in the fetal bowel during intra-uterine life. Unlike faeces, meconium is sterile and contains mostly dead cells desquamated from the fetal bowel mixed in with biliary secretions, giving it its typical green appearances. The significance of meconium in amniotic fluid is hotly debated. There are two principle reasons why meconium is passed by the fetus:

(a) maturity;
(b) stress.

12.93 A fetus of less than 34 weeks gestation rarely passes meconium in response to hypoxia or any other stress whereas a third of fetuses of gestation greater than 43 weeks will pass meconium without being hypoxic, in response to the normal stress of labour. Thus meconium has only a limited association with 'fetal distress'. Attempts have been made to classify the extent to which the liquor is contaminated with meconium and one such classification is given in Table 6. Classifications are of limited value and are in any event highly subjective.

Table 6

Grade 1	– A good volume of liquor stained lightly with meconium, often brownish/yellow in colour
Grade II	– A reasonable volume of liquor with a heavy suspension of meconium, often dark green in colour
Grade III	– Thick meconium undiluted and resembling spinach puree

12.94–12.95   The context of the meconium staining is of the greatest importance. In a breech presentation, particularly when the buttocks are being squeezed by descent through the birth canal, the presence of undiluted thick 'pea-soup' meconium is common and is of little significance. In a cephalic presentation, on the other hand, with the fetal anus near the fundus of the uterus the passage of thick meconium indicates not only that much meconium has been passed but also that there is little liquor in which to dilute it. Some guidelines are suggested in Table 7.[1]

1   Steer PJ, *Intrapartum Care Including the Detection and Management of Fetal Dysfunction*, in Safe Practice in Obstetrics and Gynaecology: A Medico-Legal Handbook (ed Roger V Clements) 1994.

Table 7

Significance of Meconium in the Liquor

- If the CTG pattern is normal, the risk of a fetus being acidotic is no greater when there is meconium than when there is not. Therefore the presence of meconium is not an automatic indication for fetal blood sampling (FBS) **so long as the CTG is normal.**
- However, if meconium is present in the liquor, there is a risk of meconium aspiration at delivery even if the baby is not hypoxic and a paediatrician should therefore always attend the birth.
- If the CTG becomes abnormal, and particularly if the fetus becomes acidotic, the risk of meconium aspiration is at least doubled. Thus the CTG must be observed particularly closely in any labour with meconium staining of the liquor, and FBS or delivery considered promptly if any abnormality develops.
- If meconium is inhaled into the fetal lung it sets up a pneumonitis and may be responsible for post-natal asphyxia. The chances of aspiration are greatly increased by subsequent hypoxia for hypoxia induces deep inspiratory efforts on the part of the baby.

Figure 18: Abnormal CTG in the second stage of labour.
This trace shows a complicated tachycardia with a baseline rate of 160 to 170 beats per minute and severely reduced, sometimes absent baseline variability. There are no significant decelerations suggesting a previous (and not necessarily deteriorating) hypoxic injury. A flat baseline is very unusual in the context of the second stage when stress to the fetus is maximal.

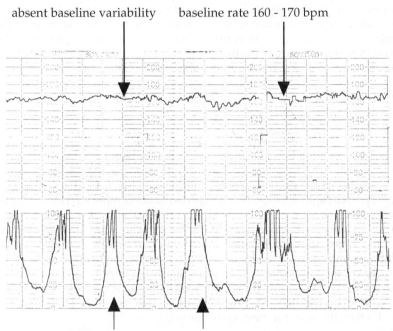

absent baseline variability   baseline rate 160 - 170 bpm

contraction showing picket-fence distortion produced
by maternal pushing

Reprinted from *Myles' Textbook for Midwives*, 12th edition, edited by V Ruth Bennett and Linda K Brown, p 58, 1993 by permission of the publisher Churchill Livingstone.

CLASSIFICATION OF THE CTG IN THE SECOND STAGE OF LABOUR

12.96 Second stage labour patterns are much more difficult to assess. Full dilatation of the cervix is of little significance to the fetus. It is maternal bearing down efforts which add increased stress in the second stage of labour. When the mother starts to push the tocograph shows characteristic distortion, a 'picket-fence' appearance with maternal bearing down efforts superimposed on the contraction pattern (Figure 18). Variable decelerations are common in the second stage of labour and, provided that they do not go on for too long, may be of no sinister significance to the baby. Bradycardia is of much more ominous significance and demands immediate delivery. Variable decelerations, on the other hand, may be tolerated for 15 to 20 minutes provided only that:

(a) there have been no previous significant abnormalities on the CTG;
(b) the baseline fetal heart rate returns to normal between the decelerations;
(c) variability is maintained.

Characteristic Heart Rate Patterns in Chronic Asphyxia

12.97   Chronic partial asphyxia during labour is associated with uterine contractions. It may occur because the fetus is especially vulnerable, the placenta inefficient or small or because the uterine contractions are abnormally strong. Oxytocic stimulation in the form of prostaglandin or Syntocinon may be responsible for excessive uterine contractions (hypertonus). In any of these circumstances asphyxial stress on the baby is usually indicated first by late decelerations. Gradually, often over the course of several hours, two other changes are added:

(a) baseline heart rate rises;
(b) baseline variability is lost.

12.98   Provided that the baseline heart rate remains within the normal range and provided that the baseline variability is retained, the fetus is unlikely to become acidaemic. If the hypoxic stress continues fetal tachycardia results and with chronic partial asphyxia the CTG usually displays a complicated tachycardia, a tachycardia associated with loss of baseline variability and with decelerations. Once that stage is reached acidaemia is likely. Fetal reserves and the capacity for anaerobic respiration are soon exhausted and delivery should be effected without delay. If labour continues and the hypoxic stress is maintained, fetal reserves will eventually be completely exhausted and neurological injury result. Eventually, the fetal circulation collapses and the complicated baseline tachycardia is no longer maintained, the heart rate falls to below the normal range (a terminal bradycardia) leading to fetal death unless immediately rescued.

12.99   Chronic partial asphyxia produces a characteristic pattern of neurological injury. However, the final phase, represented by the baseline bradycardia represents a near-total asphyxia and a baby born in such circumstances may have a pattern of neurological injury which is a mixture of that normally seen in chronic partial asphyxia with that seen following a shorter period of near-total asphxyia.

Characteristic Heart Rate Patterns in Acute Asphyxia

12.100   Two principle patterns are seen, depending on whether the asphyxia is sudden and complete or intermittent. With massive placental abruption or rupture of the uterus a previously normal fetal heart rate pattern may deteriorate to a terminal bradycardia within only a few minutes. Figure 19 shows the typical tocograph appearances of early placental abruption. The cardiograph is not reassuring but is not yet abnormal. The rate remains normal and variability is still acceptable but there are no accelerations. At this stage the fetus is probably not damaged but if the abruption extends further deterioration may be rapid. Figure 20 demonstrates rapid deterioration from a relatively normal CTG to terminal bradycardia when the uterus ruptures. It is a myth that rupture of the uterus is reliably heralded by fetal distress. Sometimes, with oxytocic stimulation producing hypertonus, the fetus may

Figure 19: The CTG in early placental abruption
Reprinted from *Myles' Textbook for Midwives*, 12th edition, edited by V Ruth Bennett and Linda K Brown, p 58, 1993 by permission of the publisher Churchill Livingstone.

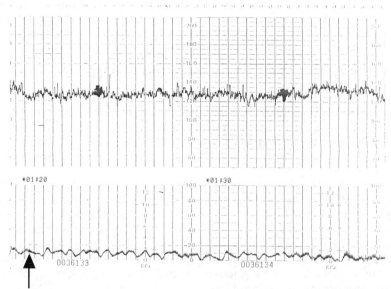

tocograph showing uterine 'irritability' with no clear pattern of contractions

Figure 20: The CTG When the Uterus Ruptures
Reproduced with permission of Carfax Publishing Co, a member of the Taylor & Francis Group (http://www.tandf.co.uk/journals/carfax/014443615.html) from Meagher, Bhatt, Macauley and Fisher 'Accidental Bolus Infusion of Oxytocin. Journal of Obstetrics and Gynaecology' (1990) 10:5:404 1990.

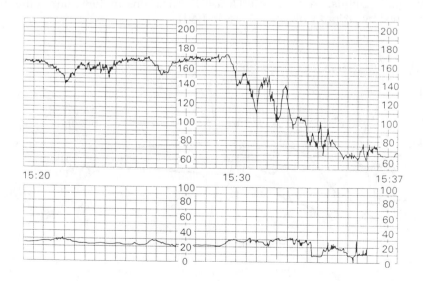

become distressed before the uterus ruptures – but not always. Rupture may occur without any previous warning of any kind.

12.101–12.109 Where the acute asphyxia is, at least initially, intermittent variable decelerations are the common finding. Thus in cord compression and even in cord prolapse, variable decelerations usually precede the terminal bradycardia.

THE PLACE OF FETAL SCALP PH MEASUREMENT

12.110 Although electronic fetal monitoring remains the most reliable method of intra-partum assessment of the fetus, abnormalities of fetal heart rate pattern, even when pronounced, are not invariably associated with poor neonatal outcome. Reliance on cardiotocographic evidence alone for the diagnosis of fetal distress may result in an unnecessary increase in operative intervention.

12.111 Fetal blood sampling, used as an adjunct to electronic fetal monitoring, has been shown to facilitate the detection of fetal distress and rationalise the management of labour. However, randomised control trial in high risk patients has not always demonstrated any difference in the Caesarean section rate or neonatal outcome, whether or not the facility of scalp pH measurement was employed. Moreover, a recent review article indicates that only 40% of major obstetric units in the United Kingdom used fetal blood sampling to supplement electronic monitoring in the late 1980s.

12.112 The technique of fetal blood sampling (Figure 21) is described in the standard textbooks and has been the subject of numerous review articles·

Figure 21: Schematic Diagram of Endoscopic Fetal Blood Sampling
Reproduced by permission of Oxford University Press from Saling E and Langner K 'Fetal Acid-Base Measurements in Labour' in *Fetal Monitoring: Physiology and Techniques of Ante-Natal and Intra-Partum Assessment*, Ed John A D Spencer (originally published by Castle House Publications in 1989, subsequently published by Oxford University Press in 1991).

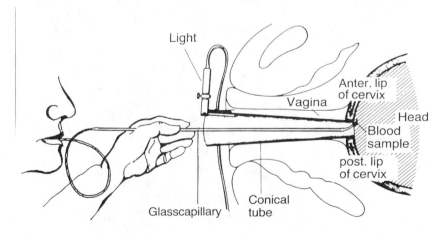

12.113 It should be clearly understood, however, that false positive and false negative results occur in up to 10% of samples and the results need to be interpreted within the clinical context.

12.114 The pH of the blood sample is currently believed to be the most reliable indicator of fetal oxygenation. The base excess, although derived from the pH, will usually indicate whether the hypoxic insult to the fetus has been a short lived event or is of a more long-standing nature. These are the most basic principles in interpreting fetal blood sampling, with which every obstetric registrar should be familiar.

12.115 There are occasions when fetal scalp samples should not be performed. Gibb and Arulkumaran explain:[1]

'Fetal scalp sampling is often not appropriate under the following circumstances:
(1) when the clinical picture demands early delivery ... 42 weeks gestation, cervix 3 cm dilated, thick meconium;
(2) when an ominous trace prompts immediate delivery;
(3) when the FHR trace is reassuring;
(4) when the changes are due to oxytocic stimulation ...
(5) when there is associated persistent failure to progress in labour
(6) during or soon after an episode of prolonged bradycardia ...
(7) if spontaneous vaginal is imminent or easy instrumental vaginal delivery is possible' (pp 131-33).

1   Gibb D and Arulkumaran S, *The Role of Scalp pH. Fetal Monitoring in Practice*, Chapter 11, (1st edn, Butterworth Heineman).

12.116 Fetal blood sampling was introduced by Saling in the 1950s and pioneered at Queen Charlotte's Hospital in the early 1960s. Although recommended as an adjunct to electronic fetal heart monitoring by the Royal College of Obstetricians and Gynaecologists, it remains available as a routine procedure in a minority of hospitals. It is not always possible to gain reproducible results with the high turnover of resident staff. Critical delay because of unnecessary fetal scalp samples (when circumstances demanded urgent delivery) is a recurrent cause of litigation. For these reasons many hospitals, including some prominent teaching establishments, have abandoned the practice. However, scientifically sound the theory of fetal scalp samples, to verify the impression of cardiotocography, CTG monitoring alone remains the staple method of most obstetric departments.

Chapter 13

Brain Damage at Birth: Causation

Malcolm Levene MD, FRCP, FRCPCH, FMedSc

BRAIN DEVELOPMENT

13.1   The first evidence of brain tissue appears approximately 18 days after conception. The rudimentary neural tissue first appears over the back of the embryo and develops into the neural tube. The first evidence of brain development occurs at approximately 21 days after conception, with rapid growth at the top end of the neural tube which becomes convoluted and by 32 days after conception the cerebral hemispheres start to divide. Brain growth is at its most rapid though pregnancy, but continues well after delivery and the brain is not anatomically fully mature until about 12 years.

13.2   Brain development starts at a somewhat later time than other organs and insults occurring shortly after conception that may disrupt development of some organs such as the heart or bowel, may not affect the brain as development of that organ has not yet commenced. The full complement of neurones is complete by 18 weeks after conception, but there then begins a process of migration of neurones and other supporting cells to their point of final destination. Neuronal migration is complete by 30 weeks after conception.

13.3   Brain development during pregnancy and the early months of neonatal life represents a very vulnerable stage due to rapidly changing structural anatomy. An insult which compromises the brain will have differing effects depending on the developmental age of the brain when the insult occurs. Thus an insult in the first month of pregnancy will cause massive disruption of the rudimentary brain structures. One that occurs at 20 weeks will also have a major effect to many as yet poorly differentiated areas. Insults at 28 weeks will impose themselves on a brain which has already largely determined its structure although functional organisation is poorly developed and an insult at term will cause yet different types of pathology which may have a more profound effect than insults occurring earlier in development.

13.4   The developing brain is considered to show 'neuronal plasticity'. This concept implies that the immature brain has the capacity to compensate for damage. Undifferentiated areas may take over function from damaged structures, with better functional outcome than anticipated from the extent of anatomical damage seen on a scan. This adds a further complexity to understanding the subsequent functional ability of the brain as the timing of the insult on one hand contributes towards its severity (the earlier the more devastating) but on the other hand a moderate insult in a relatively immature and plastic brain may be compensatable.

Brain Abnormalities and the Timing of the Insult

13.5   The abnormal brain may occur due to an abnormality in normal development, referred to as a malformation or a deformation which arises in previously normally developing brain damaged by an external insult. Sometimes distinguishing these two patterns of brain abnormality may be relatively easy. Spina bifida (an open lesion of the neural tissue over the back) is usually a malformation in development at about 28 days after conception when the neural tissue of the spine is at or near the surface. A deformation in brain development may occur as the result of an insult that occurs, lasts for a short period, and then disappears. An example of this may be a viral infection in early pregnancy such as rubella (German measles). If this occurs in the first 8 weeks of pregnancy the brain will show massive abnormalities with the result of both blindness and deafness as these organs are differentiating and developing rapidly at that stage. The same infection at 28 weeks of pregnancy may have a much less damaging effect because the particular cells susceptible to damage in the brain are well differentiated and stable.

13.6   An insult occurring late in the first half of pregnancy may cause an abnormality which is difficult to distinguish between a malformation and a deformation. The majority of malformations are due to genetic factors, although acquired abnormalities of blood flow leads to bilateral cerebral injury which may be confused with a symmetrical congenital malformation such as schizencephaly. Disruption of neuronal migration may also produce a neuronal migration disorder. The major form is referred to as lissencephaly and more subtle forms as heterotopias. The latter condition refers to abnormal migration of neurones through the brain substance so that nests of neurones are malpositioned. Studies of groups of children with cerebral palsy report that up to 25% of children have been shown to have neuronal migration disorders. Whether all these are deformations or malformations is not known.

13.7–13.8   An ischaemic or asphyxial insult to the developing brain early in the third trimester will cause a particular type of damage in the periventricular white matter (PVL, see para 13.53-13.59), but if the same insult occurs at term a completely different pattern of brain injury will develop. It is clear that defining the pattern of brain damage may allow a more careful forensic examination of the timing of the insult in pregnancy or the newborn period.

COMMON DISABILITIES AS A RESULT OF PERINATAL BRAIN INJURY

Cerebral Palsy ('CP')

Definition
13.10   Cerebral palsy is defined as a disorder of movement present by five years of age and due to a static insult in the developing brain. These terms must be qualified:

- A disorder of movement refers to a heterogenous group of conditions with abnormal neurological signs including spasticity, choreoathetosis, and ataxia (see para 13.157).
- A static insult refers to a discrete form of pathology which is present for a relatively short period of time and then resolves. Examples of this include infection, asphyxia, and haemorrhage. The timing and localisation of the insult will determine the pattern and type of cerebral palsy.
- The developing brain refers to maturation occurring up to the end of the first month of life after birth. Some authorities include the first three months of life but this is not widely accepted.

13.11 The incidence of cerebral palsy is 2½ to 3½ per thousand children in a community. Only about 10% of cases of CP are due to asphyxia in full-term babies. It is probable that an early or mid-pregnancy insult leads to CP in approximately 50% of cases.

Clinical Features
13.12 Signs of CP are often not apparent in early life and may not be detected until the child is a year of age or more. In general the more severe the cerebral palsy the earlier it is diagnosed. It is well recognised that the pattern of CP can appear to change in the early years of life. This is particularly common in children with developing choreoathetoid CP who may initially be thought to have a spastic form of motor disorder. The apparent change in neurological signs do not indicate an ongoing cerebral lesion, but that as the brain matures the abnormal neurological signs appear to change.

13.13 70% of children with CP have spasticity, the hallmark of which is increased tone (abnormal stiffness in muscle groups at rest) and abnormally increased tendon reflexes with loss or reduction in function. The distribution of the spasticity can be further defined as quadriplegic (involving all four limbs), hemiplegic (arm and leg on the same side), diplegic (lower limbs predominantly involved compared with the upper, sometimes the upper limbs are functionally normal) and monoplegia (spasticity of only one limb).

13.14 The second most common type is choreoathetoid or dystonic cerebral palsy which accounts for approximately 15% of cases. This involves uncontrolled writhing movements usually of all four limbs and commonly involving the tongue and throat muscles making speech and swallowing difficult. Intelligence may be normal in this group. The neurological lesion causing this pattern of CP involves the basal ganglia, a collection of grey matter deep within the brain.

13.15 Ataxic cerebral palsy accounts for 5% to 10% of cases and is manifest by abnormality in co-ordination resulting in an unsteady rolling gait and a tremor exaggerated by intention. The tremor is absent at rest. This form of CP is due to an abnormality in the cerebellum. Mixed patterns of cerebral palsy occur, mainly with signs of spasticity with choreoathetosis. Hypotonic cerebral palsy is very rare and there may be considerable difficulty in distinguishing this from non-cerebral neuromuscular disorders.

13.17 Cerebral palsy is associated with significant learning disabilities in about 50% of cases and with epilepsy in 25%. Blindness is particularly likely in severe spastic quadriplegia. Deafness is more common in athetoid cerebral palsy when it occurs due to hyperbilirubinaemia (kernicterus, see para 13.74-13.84).

Causes

13.18   Cerebral palsy is a very heterogenous condition and should not be considered a diagnosis, but rather a symptom or general description of a disability. The same insult operating at different times in brain development may result in different patterns of CP and many conditions can damage a particular neurological region resulting in an abnormal pattern of movement referred to as CP.

13.19   The insult that has caused CP may be classified by the timing of its occurrence. This is most commonly defined as prenatal (before the onset of labour), perinatal (onset during labour or in the first week of life) and postnatal (an insult unrelated to birth and usually occurring after the first week of life and before the end of the first month). There is sometimes confusion in allocating a cause to either the perinatal or postnatal period. If the baby develops a condition unrelated to birth and usually after discharge from hospital (for example, near-miss Sudden Infant Death Syndrome or non-accidental head injury) even if these occurred within a week of birth then it is more likely that these will be allocated to a postnatal cause.

13.20   Table 1 lists the commoner causes of CP according to whether they are prenatal, perinatal or postnatal in origin. Some of these are discussed in more detail later in this chapter.

Table 1: Commoner Causes of Cerebral Palsy

Prenatal
cerebral malformations
congenital infection
Cytomegalovirus
Toxoplasmosis
Rubella
metabolic disorders
Perinatal
complications of prematurity
Intraventricular haemorrhage
Post-haemorrhagic hydrocephalus
periventricular leukomalacia
intrapartum trauma
birth asphyxia
hypoglycaemia
Postnatal
meningitis
cardiopulmonary arrest
non-accidental injury
accidental head injury

Mental Handicap (Learning Disability)

Definition
13.21 This is the most common of the severe disabilities affecting children. Mental handicap is defined on the basis of intelligence measured by standardised IQ tests and the limits of normal are defined by how far below the normal range the child performs. Mild mental handicap are those with IQ 50-70 and those with severe handicap have an IQ of below 50.

13.22 The incidence of mild mental handicap is 30 per 1,000 school age children and of severe is 3 per 1,000.

Clinical Features
13.23 The diagnosis of mental handicap is entirely dependent on being able to assess intellectual performance and in particular, reasoning ability. It is not possible to test reasoning in normal children until at least three years of age and therefore the diagnosis of mental handicap cannot be reasonably made until at least this age. In young children, general development is closely related to physical development and in the presence of severe physical problems such as cerebral palsy the child will be developmentally delayed. This must not be mistaken for intellectual impairment and the child may actually be shown to have normal intellectual capacity (reasoning ability) as he gets older, despite very severe physical disabilities.

13.24 The assessment of IQ in severely physically disabled people may be extremely difficult and requires much skill and patience by psychologists especially trained in this area. It is a great mistake to label an individual as mentally handicapped simply because he cannot make appropriate physical or language responses. One must also consider whether the physical problem (cerebral palsy or deafness) may have prevented the child from achieving appropriate stimulation and learning opportunities. In these cases, the mental impairment may be secondary to loss of opportunity rather than primary brain involvement.

Causation
13.25 Mental handicap may either be an isolated disability or associated with other forms of disability such as CP. In general, isolated mental handicap is not likely to be due to an acquired cause in the second half of pregnancy although there may be some rare exceptions (see paras 13.158-13.160). It is a paradox that a child with high genetic potential for intelligence (for example, very bright parents) may have sustained a very significant brain insult and have an overall loss of 50 IQ points, but if his measured IQ does not fall below 70 he is not by definition mentally handicapped.

13.26 The cause of mild mental handicap is usually very difficult to identify. Intelligence is a polygenic determinant based on genetic make-up, environment in the home and opportunities at school. Families living in deprived areas with limited educational facilities may not achieve their genetic potential for intelligence and their lower IQ does not imply that there is a single 'cause' for it but is actually multifactorial.

13.27 Severe isolated mental handicap usually has a recognisable cause, but if associated with other disabilities is most likely to be similar to the causes in Table 1.

Blindness

Definition
13.28   Blindness is not an absolute term and visual impairment better describes the disability. Blindness describes the child whose visual impairment is so severe that he is unable to be educated by methods that involve sight. A child is defined as partially sighted if he requires special education but can use methods which depend on sight, such as large print books. One in 2,500 children are registered as blind or partially sighted and 50% of these have additional disabilities such as hearing impairment or learning difficulties.

Causation
13.29   The cause of visual impairment can be considered as those that have a genetic (approximately 50% of cases) or early onset and those that are acquired. In a medico-legal context retinopathy of prematurity is the most important and this is discussed in para 13.88.

Deafness

Definition
13.30   Hearing impairment refers to a severe reduction in auditory perception. Hearing loss can be divided into two major categories: sensorineural (nerve deafness) and conductive (bone) deafness. In the former group the abnormality lies in the cochlear or auditory nerve and hearing impairment is often present from birth or shortly afterwards, but in some genetic forms it develops slowly and insidiously later in life. Conductive deafness is usually acquired as the result of middle ear infections and failure of adequate drainage of secretions through the Eustachian tube. This is referred to as 'glue ear'. It is common and does not usually cause serious long-standing hearing impairment.

13.31   Approximately 4% of school children have hearing impairment, but most are mild due to conductive problems. Two per 1,000 have moderate deafness and require a hearing aid and a further one per 1,000 are severely deaf and require special education.

Causation
13.32   Sensorineural hearing loss is most commonly due to genetic causes, but there are a number of important acquired causes which have medicolegal implications (see Table 2).

Epilepsy

Definition
13.33   Epilepsy is a condition of recurrent seizures resulting from paroxysmal involuntary disturbances of brain function. The term seizure is synonymous with 'fits' and 'convulsions' and all refer to episodes of impairment or loss of consciousness, abnormal motor activity or sensory disturbances. Seizures may occur as the result of a temporary impairment of brain function such as asphyxia, head injury, or meningitis without being termed epilepsy unless these episodes continue once the acute insult has resolved.

Table 2: Causes of Sensorineural Hearing Impairment with an Approximation of Frequency to the Total Number of Cases

Genetic (50%)
     various types
 	
Intrauterine (8%)
     congenital infection eg rubella, cytomegalovirus
 	
Perinatal (12%)
     severe jaundice (kernicterus), drugs
     intracranial haemorrhage, meningitis
 	
Postnatal (30%)
     meningitis
     encephalitis
     head injury

13.34 Epilepsy is classified as generalised (involving the whole body) or partial (localised to a discrete area of the brain) and the latter can be complex (with associated impairment of consciousness). The tonic-clonic seizure (formerly known as grand mal) and simple absences (petit mal) are examples of generalised seizure disorders and the condition formerly known as temporal lobe epilepsy is now known as complex partial seizures.

13.35 Epilepsy is common and affects approximately 1% of school age children. Convulsions in the newborn period are very common and indicate an acute or chronic abnormality of brain function. Most children with neonatal convulsions do not develop epilepsy.

Causation
13.36–13.39 Epilepsy is a multifactorial condition with a significant genetic contribution. Focal acquired damage to the brain may cause a type of epilepsy involving paroxysmal abnormalities such as temporal lobe epilepsy from ischaemic injury to the temporal lobe. The brain that is damaged and scarred is also more likely to show epilepsy as a complication. Imaging of the brain and EEG studies may help to define whether there is a focal abnormality and its location. Epilepsy occurs in approximately 50% of children with CP and is a common sequelae of acquired perinatal brain injury.

RISK FACTORS FOR THE DEVELOPMENT OF BRAIN DAMAGE

13.40 Cases in which medico-legal actions are commenced usually fall into a relatively few groups where the child has been perceived as being at risk of injury. The following risk factors represent those which are most commonly recognised as the cause of the disabilities discussed in paras 13.10-13.36.

Prematurity

13.41   Prematurity is defined as birth before 37 completed weeks of pregnancy and accounts for 7% of babies born in Britain. There is a very close relationship between mortality and prematurity, but the increased risk of dying as the result of being born pre-term does not significantly increase until the prematurity is quite severe. With modern intensive care given in a regional centre, a baby born at 30 weeks and above has over a 95% chance of survival, at 27-29 weeks an 80% chance of survival and at 25-26 weeks a 60% chance of surviving to discharge. Delivery at 24-25 weeks carries a 40-50% chance of survival, but delivery at 23 weeks is associated with very few survivors and virtually none at 22 weeks.

13.42   The risk of neurodevelopmental handicap in very premature infants is some 30 times higher than that for a full-term infant. Approximately 10% of babies born at 30 weeks and below will survive with some significant disability apparent at two years of age. About half of these will have severe disability including CP, mental handicap, deafness or blindness. It is now well recognised that children who do not have these 'hard' disabilities at five years may have significant impairments recognised in their early school years, such as clumsiness, attention deficit disorder (hyperactivity), a reduced IQ score, delayed reading and other specific learning problems. The cause of these latter impairments are not clear.

13.43   Neurodevelopmental disabilities in premature babies arise from a number of different insults which occur in the perinatal period. These include intraventricular haemorrhage, post-haemorrhagic hydrocephalus and periventricular leukomalacia.

Intraventricular Haemorrhage ('IVH')
13.44   This is a common finding in premature infants and approximately one third will have bleeding into or around the lateral ventricles which is referred to as IVH. The bleeding is usually small and confined to the caudate nucleus, with some leakage into the lateral ventricles. Babies who develop IVH confined to the ventricles and who do not progress to post-haemorrhagic hydrocephalus are not at increased risk of neurodevelopmental disabilities. In approximately 10% of cases the haemorrhage involves the cerebral white matter on one side. This is referred to synonomously as a parenchymal haemorrhage, venous infarction or grade IV haemorrhage. If the infant survives, then a porencephalic cavity develops in the region of the parenchymal haemorrhage. Infants with this type of lesion are likely to have disability later on, most commonly a spastic hemiplegia on the opposite side of the body to that of the haemorrhage. Intellectually these children may not be severely impaired and may be able to attend a mainstream school.

13.45   The cause of IVH is related to rupture of fragile immature capillaries lying just below the lateral ventricles. Acute changes in cerebral blood flow are thought to be the underlying factor in bleeding and these changes are most commonly related to respiratory complications. Those babies with respiratory distress syndrome, high levels of arterial carbon dioxide (hypercapnia) and particularly those with major complications of their lungs, such as pneumothorax, are statistically most likely to develop IVH. Additional factors are coagulation disorders which predispose the baby to more extensive haemorrhage if the germinal matrix capillaries rupture.

Medico-legal Considerations

13.46   As IVH is a relatively common condition, and if confined to the ventricles is unlikely to cause significant disability, its medicolegal significance is not high. In more severe cases involving the cerebral parenchyma, disability certainly is common and the most important factors in assessing the quality of care which may have exacerbated the lesion is focused on the respiratory management. Antenatal steroids given to the mother 48 hours prior to delivery is known to reduce the risk of IVH and failure to give this drug where time exists must be considered to represent a poor standard of care.

13.47   Too high level of arterial carbon dioxide (hypercapnia) increases the risk of IVH, but modern respiratory care for premature infants recognises the concept of 'permissive hypercapnia' whereby the baby is deliberately slightly underventilated allowing the carbon dioxide level to be higher, thereby protecting the lungs. This does not represent sub-standard management.

Post-haemorrhagic Hydrocephalus

13.48   In approximately 20% of babies with IVH progressive hydrocephalus develops secondary to blood in the cerebral ventricular system. The ventricular system of the brain is a convoluted series of connected compartments through which the cerebrospinal fluid ('CSF') travels. CSF is secreted by the choroid plexus in the lateral and third ventricles, passes through the aqueduct of Sylvius to the fourth ventricle and then exits the brain to the surface of the brain or down the spinal canal to bathe the spinal cord. The CSF is eventually reabsorbed over the surface of the brain in small tufts called arachnoid granulations. If there is obstruction to this flow of fluid due to blood in the ventricular system, then progressive build up of CSF occurs and the ventricles enlarge in size. This progressive dilatation of the ventricles, particularly the lateral ventricles, is described as posthaemorrhagic hydrocephalus.

13.49   As the ventricles increase in size there may be a concomitant rise in intracranial pressure which causes cerebral compromise, particularly if this is long standing. The newborn can compensate for the accumulation of fluid by enlarging the head size because the skull bones have not fused. The sutures (gaps between the skull bones) become enlarged and the fontanelles bulge. Treatment for post-haemorrhagic hydrocephalus is intermittent removal of CSF or a ventriculoperitoneal shunt which offers a permanent alternative route to CSF drainage from the lateral ventricle to the peritoneum.

13.50   Post-haemorrhagic hydrocephalus is diagnosed by repeated ultrasound scans and should be anticipated in any baby who has had IVH. The size of the lateral ventricles should be measured regularly and once a critical dilatation has occurred treatment instigated. There is no agreed treatment paradigm for post-haemorrhagic hydrocephalus, but intermittent drainage of CSF should be undertaken to assess whether spontaneous resolution will occur and if this fails then a neurosurgeon should be involved. The intracranial pressure is probably important in determining when treatment should be instigated. Those babies with high pressure (>10 mm Hg) should be treated earlier than those with lower pressure. The only reliable way of measuring pressure is directly when fluid is removed at lumbar puncture or ventricular tap. The baby may develop symptoms related to the increased intracranial pressure including apnoea, bradycardia, irritability, lethargy and convulsions. These symptoms should always cause the clinician to consider raised intracranial pressure as the cause.

13.51   The effect of post-haemorrhagic hydrocephalus on disability is not clear. In general terms a baby who has hydrocephalus secondary to a small IVH is probably not at significantly increased risk of adverse outcome. Babies with post-haemorrhagic hydrocephalus secondary to a large parenchymal haemorrhage are much more likely to have severe disability, but this may be due to the severity of the underlying haemorrhage rather than the hydrocephalus. In addition, increasing hydrocephalus may make determination of white matter pathology such as periventricular leukomalacia (see paras 13.53-13.59) difficult to exclude and it may be the PVL that causes the bad outcome rather than the hydrocephalus.

Medico-legal Considerations
13.52   The standard of care in the management of this condition is whether the condition was anticipated by regular scanning after the IVH and whether the management of the hydrocephalus was timely in terms of rises in intracranial pressure. Without clearly agreed standards of care, establishing what was less than satisfactory care is clearly more difficult.

Periventricular Leukomalacia ('PVL')

13.53   This is the most common cause of severe disability in prematurely born infants. PVL describes a form of pathology with scarring in the periventricular white matter with resultant cerebral palsy.

Causation
13.54   PVL is a condition of the immature brain, although its cause is not clear. The periventricular white matter appears to be most vulnerable to the insult that leads to PVL between 24 and 34 weeks gestation. It may occur in the fetus or the newborn as a result of an acute compromise during this developmental stage. The traditional understanding of the cause of this condition is that the periventricular white matter is a vascular watershed (the tissue between two vascular territories) and if blood flow falls to the brain, the watershed bears the brunt of the ischaemic insult, which causes infarction in this region. Consequently, its cause has been (and to some extent still is) believed to be due to a critical underperfusion of the brain as a result of acute fall in cardiac output and/or blood pressure. It is important to emphasize that PVL is a lesion of the developing brain and can affect the fetus or newborn. It is estimated that 25% of babies with PVL have a prenatal origin for this condition. The commonest prenatal cause is probably twinning, particularly when the twins are identical and share a common placental circulation (see para 13.62). More recently other causes have been described including infection and hypocapnia.

Infection
13.55   There is a well recognised association between infection of the amniotic fluid and fetal membranes and the development of PVL. This is probably due to the initiation of an inflammatory cascade mediated by proteins called cytokines and there is now good circumstantial evidence that cytokines cause PVL. Postnatal septicaemia, particularly due to bowel bacteria that leak into the blood stream in

a condition called necrotizing enterocolitis is well recognised as a cause. It is also postulated that infection of the amniotic fluid causes release of prostaglandins which stimulates the onset of premature labour, thereby predisposing the baby to all the risks of prematurity which in turn may damage the baby's brain. The precise relationship between maternal and fetal infection, the onset of premature labour and the development of PVL, need to be further elucidated.

Hypocapnia
13.56 Hypocapnia refers to low levels of arterial carbon dioxide which have been strongly implicated in the development of PVL in premature babies by reducing blood flow to the brain. There are now a number of reports describing the association between very low arterial carbon dioxide levels (paCO2) and the development of PVL. Two studies[1] have shown that a paCO2 of<2.6 Kpa (20 mm Hg) within the first days of life is an independent risk factor for the development of severe PVL.

> 1 Graziani et al 'Mechanical Ventilation in Preterm Infants: Neurosonographic and Developmental Studies [1992] 90 Pediatrics pp 515-22: Fujimoto S et al 'Hypocarbia and Cystic Periventicular Leukomalacia in Premature Infants [1994] 71 Arch Dis Child pp 17-110.

Diagnosis and Timing of the Lesion
13.57 PVL can be recognised in its acute stages by ultrasound imaging. The scan shows a sequence of changes from its inception to healing and to some extent the onset of the lesion can be timed on the basis of these appearances. The first sign is increase in echodensity of the periventricular white matter. There is a considerable degree of subjectivity in the interpretation of degrees of echodensity, but the important features are the relative echodensity of the white matter compared with the choroid plexus (at least equivalent density is required for abnormality) and the fact that the abnormality is apparent in two planes. In severe PVL, cavitation or cyst formation occurs, at about 10-14 days after the echodensity is first seen. The ultrasound appearances change from marked echodensity through resolution of the severity of the echodense appearance to the development of discrete cysts. If cysts are present in the first week of life then the conclusion is that the lesion that caused the cysts happened prior to birth (that is, at least 10-14 days before the cysts were first recognized). Postnatal onset of PVL can be recognized by the initial appearance of normal echodensity in the periventricular white matter evolving to marked increase in echodensity and 10-14 days later cyst formation.

Prognosis
13.58 The presence of cystic PVL on ultrasound is a marker of brain damage and carries a significant risk of cerebral palsy. The presence of multiple cysts, large cysts (>5 mm in diameter) or cysts in the periventricular occipital region carry a very high risk of disability. More subtle cystic lesions, and persistent or transient echodensities are much less able to predict the risk of significant neurodevelopmental abnormality.

Medico-legal Considerations
13.59 If PVL is present on scanning a baby with cerebral palsy, it is probable that the lesion which caused the PVL occurred at 24-34 weeks of gestation irrespective of the maturity at birth. Changes on the neonatal ultrasound scan may allow an estimate of when the insult that caused PVL actually occurred. In

evaluating the quality of care, persistent very low carbon dioxide tensions ($<$2.6 Kpa), represents a potentially avoidable risk factor.

Multiple Birth

13.60 It has been known for many years that multiple birth confers a significantly increased risk of cerebral palsy in surviving twin pairs compared with singletons.

13.61 There is a five to ten-fold increased risk of cerebral palsy in a twin compared with a singleton birth and the risk is 17½ to 19-fold increased for triplets compared with singletons.[1] This increased risk is partly related to the fact that babies born as the result of multiple birth tend to be more premature than singletons. When the weights of premature multiple birth infants are compared with singletons of similar birthweight then there is virtually no difference in rates of CP. For twins weighing $>$2,500 g, the risk of CP is 3½ fold greater than that of singletons of the same birthweight.

> 1 Petterson B et al 'Twins, Triplets and Cerebral Palsy in Births in Western Australia in the 1980s [1993] 173 BMJ pp 1239: Pharoah POD, Cooke T 'Cerebral Palsy and Multiple Births [1996] 75 Arch Dis Child p 174.

13.62 The risk of cerebral palsy is also increased eight-fold if one of the twin pair is born dead compared to the risk if both twins survive. This is partly explained by monozygotic (identical) twins being more likely to share a common blood flow through the placenta with the risk of vascular accidents to one or both twins. One study has shown that PVL was 10 times more common in identical than non-identical twins[1] and that placental vascular connections and death of a co-twin were the most important independent variables associated with PVL in these babies.

> 1 Bejar R et al 'Antenatal Origin of Neurologic Damage in Newborn Infants II Multiple Gestations [1990] 162 Am J Obstet Gynaecol pp 1230.

13.63 The second-born twin is also more at risk of cerebral palsy than the first-born twin. This is due to the fact that after the birth of the first baby, there is increased risk of malposition of the second twin, birth trauma and premature separation of the placenta causing fetal asphyxia.

13.64 Recently, it has been suggested that brain injury occurs as the result of twin death very early in pregnancy.[1] It is well known that in a significant minority of twin pregnancy recognised by ultrasound scanning in the first eight weeks of gestation, one of the twin pair disappears: the so called vanishing twin syndrome. This occurs as the result of one twin dying and being absorbed. The mother is not aware of the loss of her fetus. By analogy with death of one twin at an older age it has been suggested that the death of one twin very early in pregnancy may damage the surviving twin and cause cerebral palsy. There is little hard data to support this suggestion. If an insult occurs to a developing twin in the first 8-12 weeks then brain development is at a very early stage and any damage will be massive and should be recognised on subsequent imaging. For this reason if the vanishing twin syndrome does cause cerebral palsy due to very early fetal demise it is, in the author's view, likely to be associated with obvious abnormality on imaging at birth or when the child presents with cerebral palsy.

> 1 Pharoah POD and Cooke T 'A Hypothesis for the Aetiology of Spastic Cerebral Palsy – the Vanishing Twin [1997] 39 Develop Med Child Neurol p 296.

Medico-legal Considerations

13.65 It is clear that as a group twins and triplets are at considerably increased risk of a bad perinatal outcome with cerebral palsy a particular consequence. Some of these risks are directly related to being a twin and sharing the intrauterine environment and others are related less directly to being a twin, but rather to the growth restriction that is inherent in being a twin pair, particularly in the third trimester. The obstetric management of twins needs to be particularly careful in recognising this high-risk status.

Infection

13.66 Infection can cause brain damage by at least three different mechanisms. First, infection may trigger inflammatory mediators (cytokines, see para 13.55) and cause damage to the periventricular white matter leading to periventricular leukomalacia. Second, infection in the newborn may lead to shock with a sudden fall in blood pressure, apnoea (cessation of breathing), or severe acidosis and these systemic problems may damage the brain by an ischaemic or asphyxial event. Third, infection may cause brain damage by organisms invading the brain and causing meningitis or encephalitis.

Clinical Features of Infection

13.67 Infection in the newborn period is insidious in its onset and, unlike in older children, often shows no specific signs or symptoms until quite well advanced. The early signs suggestive of infection are apnoeic episodes, bradycardia spells (intermittent slowing of the heart), pallor, unstable temperature (episodes of low body temperature is as common as elevated temperature), vomiting, lethargy and irritability. Coma, convulsions, and bulging fontanelle are late signs of infection in meningitis. It is a general rule in all of newborn medicine to consider infection as a possibility in any child who is non-specifically unwell. The child must be assessed by an experienced doctor as soon as concern is expressed and if it is considered that infection is a possibility, then an infection screen must be performed. An infection screen involves a full blood count, blood cultures, swabs from skin, throat, rectum and a specimen of urine. A lumbar puncture is mandatory in babies with features suggestive of infection and a chest X-ray is often carried out as well. Having taken these specimens a positive result for infection is unlikely to be obtained immediately unless the child has meningitis (see paras 13.68-13.73) as the bacterial organisms must be grown on culture medium in the laboratory and this may take 24-48 hours. While awaiting the results from the laboratory a decision must be made whether to treat the baby for suspected infection 'blind' without knowing what organisms are present. This requires a broad spectrum antibiotic on a 'best guess' principle. In summary, any baby with suspected infection requires an immediate infection screen including a lumbar puncture and a decision as to whether to treat with broad spectrum antibiotics. If the decision to investigate and treat is left too late then the baby may die or be seriously damaged as the result of the infection.

Meningitis

13.68 In this condition organisms invade the membranes surrounding the central nervous system, the meninges, and cause severe inflammation to the brain. Any organism can cause neonatal meningitis, but bacteria are most common followed by viruses and, rarely, fungal infections.

13.69   Meningitis, like most infections, can be contracted from the mother (perinatally) or from the environment after birth. Neonatal meningitis is most commonly due to the organism group B beta haemolytic streptococcus. This is a bacterium of relatively low virulence outside the neonatal period, and about 10% of pregnant women have genital colonisation with this organism without causing symptoms. During birth a proportion of babies themselves become colonised with the GBS bacterium and only about 1% of those colonised develop serious infection. Infection presents either as septicaemia with predominant respiratory problems which may be rapidly fatal if treatment (penicillin) is not started early or may present with meningitis. In some cases meningitis presents later and the baby may already have been discharged home when the first signs of infection emerge. Prolonged rupture of the membranes is a risk factor for early neonatal meningitis.

13.70   Herpes simplex encephalitis infection involving primarily the brain substance rather than the meninges is a very rare condition but one that often has devastating effects. Herpes simplex is usually acquired from the female genital tract, and the baby born vaginally to a women with recent new genital herpes infection is particularly at risk. The baby presents with non-specific symptoms but there is often herpetic lesions on the skin, although these may be subtle. Convulsions are a frequent symptom in these babies. The diagnosis may be made at lumbar puncture if the meninges are inflamed, but in a proportion of cases the lumbar puncture is normal and the diagnosis must be considered on clinical grounds. There is specific antiviral treatment for this condition (acyclovir) which needs to be given early and intravenously if the disease is to be limited. Unfortunately, even with early diagnosis and treatment the outcome may be poor.

13.71   Meningitis may also occur after discharge from hospital in a baby who had been completely well in the first week or more of life. The early signs of meningitis are insidious and it requires a high index of suspicion for serious infection in any young baby who presents to their GP or Health Visitor.

Medico-legal Considerations
13.72   The mortality due to meningitis is about 10-20% depending on the organism and its virulence. Approximately 40% of survivors are seriously neurologically damaged including severe cerebral palsy, intellectual impairment, deafness and blindness. Poor outcome does not necessarily indicate a low standard of care.

13.73   The principles of management of infection are early diagnosis based on a low index of clinical suspicion for non-specific signs, judicious and rapid commencement of 'best guess' antimicrobial therapy and treatment of ensuing complications such as low blood pressure, apnoea and respiratory complications. Delay in diagnosis because non-specific signs were not investigated and inappropriate choice of antibiotics do represent a less than acceptable standard of care.

Kernicterus

13.74   The jaundice pigment (bilirubin) is toxic to the developing brain and may cause irreversible brain damage which in many cases is preventable. It is thought that the insoluble component of jaundice (unconjugated bilirubin) crosses from the blood to the brain and damages the basal ganglia and the hearing component of the eight cranial nerve leading to severe long-term consequences.

13.75 Kernicterus was a term originally used to refer to yellow staining in various areas of the brain that occurred in newborn babies as the result of excessive jaundice. More recently kernicterus has also been used to refer to bilirubin encephalopathy, a pattern of abnormal neurological activity, that occurs as a result of bilirubin entering into the brain in toxic amounts. Bilirubin toxicity (kernicterus) is a preventable condition.

13.76 The fetus is able to excrete bilirubin via the placenta so that high levels of jaundice develop only after birth. Excessive breakdown of red blood cells, a condition known as haemolysis, causes severe hyperbilirubinaemia and the most common predictable cause of this is rhesus haemolytic disease. In this condition the mother is rhesus negative and the baby rhesus positive. There is commonly leakage of fetal cells into the maternal circulation which causes maternal antibodies to be produced to the rhesus positive cells. These cross to the fetus and cause break down of fetal red cells leading to anaemia and excess bilirubin production.

13.77 With each sensitisation of the mother by fetal rhesus positive red cells, her antibody level increases and the severity of fetal haemolysis gets worse. Thus the first affected pregnancy is only mildly affected but this gets worse with successive pregnancies. All pregnant women should have their blood group analysed so that if they are rhesus negative precautions can be taken. The mainstay of the prevention of rhesus haemolytic disease is anti-D prophylaxis which was developed in the 1960s. It has been shown that specific anti-rhesus antibodies can be injected into the mother after birth or termination of an affected pregnancy which will neutralise rhesus positive fetal cells entering her circulation before they can induce immunisation. The policy of giving all rhesus positive women anti-D prophylaxis has made kernicterus due to rhesus haemolytic disease a rare condition.

13.78 Unfortunately, severe jaundice can still occur due to other maternal-fetal blood group incompatibilities and although the D-antigen is the commonest one to cause rhesus incompatablity there are other less common antigen (c) which are not neutralised by anti-D. Therefore severe jaundice as a result of haemolytic disease of the newborn still occurs and may not be predictable antenatally.

13.79 Although the baby with haemolysis is particularly at risk, some premature babies can develop quite severe hyperbilirubinaemia without apparent haemolysis. All jaundiced babies should be closely monitored for the potential risk of kernicterus.

Management
13.80 In a woman at risk of haemolysis, careful management in pregnancy can reduce fetal and neonatal morbidity and mortality. All at-risk women should be screened at booking for the presence of antibodies and should have antibody measurements repeated at monthly intervals from 20 weeks of gestation. Once a woman has been found to have antibodies, her pregnancy should be managed in

a regional centre experienced in the management of rhesus problems. Women with increasing antibodies should have amniocentesis (removal of a specimen of amniotic fluid by a needle through the abdominal wall) for estimation of the severity of haemolysis. The management of the pregnant woman can be expectant if the levels are not high, the baby can be delivered prematurely if levels are increasing to a potentially dangerous level or if the baby is likely to be seriously affected but too immature to deliver then in-utero transfusions are necessary.

13.81 The aim of antenatal treatment is to deliver affected fetuses in good condition and before they become too anaemic. After birth the management of excessive haemolysis is to measure the bilirubin and haemoglobin on cord blood and then to monitor the rise of bilirubin very carefully (four-hourly) to assess the rate of increase. Several forms of treatment are available for controlling hyperbilirubinaemia. Phototherapy is a form of light treatment which breaks down the toxic bilirubin in the baby's skin. This may reduce the rate of jaundice accumulation but is not likely to avoid the need for exchange transfusion in affected infants. Exchange transfusion refers to a procedure where twice the baby's circulating blood volume (180 ml per kilo birthweight) is exchanged with rhesus negative blood. Severely affected babies may require multiple exchange transfusions before all the antibody is washed out.

13.82 The level at which high levels of bilirubin damage the brain is unknown. It is thought that premature babies are at considerably greater risk of kernicterus at lower levels of jaundice than more mature babies and consequently exchange transfusion is undertaken at lower levels of bilirubin in premature babies. It is also thought that if a baby is ill he is more sensitive to kernicterus and the level at which exchange transfusion is carried out is lower. There are a number of published charts which give guidelines for when phototherapy and exchange transfusion should be started. Each neonatal unit should have clear policies for the management of this condition.

Medico-legal Considerations
13.83 Kernicterus is usually (but not always) a preventable condition. Women at risk of haemolysis (particular those with rhesus disease) should be very carefully monitored by skilled Obstetricians. Treatment in utero may be necessary and must be finely judged. Judicious delivery is also essential with good communication between obstetricians and paediatricians.

13.84 The paediatric team should have a clearly written policy of the management of hyperbilirubinaemia with close monitoring of bilirubin levels from birth in high risk babies. The need for exchange transfusions must be anticipated and must be timely with the bilirubin and antibodies washed out before the baby's levels become significantly high.

Retinopathy of Prematurity ('ROP')

13.85 ROP (formerly known as retrolental fibroplasia) is the commonest cause of blindness in children born severely pre-term. ROP develops as the result of a variety of poorly understood factors causing the developing retina to scar and in the most severe cases become detached from the back of the eye. High levels of arterial oxygen to the developing eye is known to be a factor, but is by no means the most important underlying cause. The causation of ROP is still uncertain.

13.86 Approximately 50% of very premature infants (with birthweight <1500 g) develop some evidence of ROP, but in the majority this is mild, self-limiting, requires no treatment and does not cause any impairment of vision. The risk of visual impairment increases in the most immature babies. Approximately 1-2% of babies with ROP will lose the vision in at least one eye as the result of this condition. With appropriate treatment vision can be saved by judiciously timed intervention.

Principles of Management
13.87 There are two important factors to consider in the management of ROP:

- Diagnosis: it is only possible to diagnose this condition by examining the baby's retina on a regular basis. This must be done by an ophthalmologist experienced in the diagnosis of ROP. The babies are often ill, fragile and cannot be moved from their incubator. Examination takes time, skill and experience of working with tiny babies. In 1992 Fielder and Levene[1] described a screening regimen for all babies at risk of this condition. They recommended that all infants of <1500 g and/or <31 weeks gestation should be regularly screened for ROP. The first examination should be 6-7 weeks after birth and then every 1-2 weeks until they reached 36 weeks of postmenstrual age (gestational age + postnatal age). The aim of screening is to detect those babies with rapidly progressive or aggressive retinal disease who require treatment.
- Therapy: the second aspect is treatment of eyes with threshold ROP that may progress rapidly to severe visual impairment. Delay in treatment must be kept to a minimum in order not to miss the opportunity of best visual outcome. It has been shown that treatment with cryotherapy will prevent or reduce the poor visual outcome in this condition by 50% compared with no treatment. The aim of screening is to recognise those babies who require cryotherapy and to ensure that these babies are assessed and treated by ophthalmologists most experienced in the management of this condition.

1   Fielder AR and Levene MI 'Screening for Retinopathy of Prematurity' [1992] 67 Arch Dis Child pp 860-67.

Medico-legal Considerations
13.88 In any baby who has visual impairment due to ROP consider the following:

- Was the baby's oxygen therapy reasonably monitored in the neonatal period? This will require careful review of all the intensive care records and blood gas estimates. It is not enough to simply show that the baby had high arterial oxygen concentrations, but if they were monitored were they acted on appropriately by reducing high levels.
- Did the neonatal unit have a protocol for screening for ROP by experienced ophthalmologists as recommended in the paediatric literature in 1992?
- Having recognised severe ROP at a treatable stage, did the baby receive cryotherapy (or suitable alternative treatment) in a timely manner?

Asphyxia

Definition
13.89   There is no satisfactory clinical definition of asphyxia. The components of asphyxia are similar to the effects of suffocation, that is, a reduction in oxygenation due to respiratory embarassment with impairment of blood flow to the brain and other organs. This may occur either before, during or after birth and at any stage later in life.

Incidence
13.90   The incidence of birth asphyxia will clearly depend on its diagnostic criteria. As mentioned in para 13.124 there is no generally accepted definition so that the incidence must best be described as a range. In general, it is accepted that asphyxia occurs in 3-9 cases per 1,000 liveborn full-term babies although many will escape with no long-term disabilities. The concept of asphyxia in premature babies is more difficult as they usually display different forms of pathology such as intracranial haemorrhage or periventricular leukomalacia and the incidence of these are described earlier in this chapter.

Physiology
13.91   The physiological definition of asphyxia is one of progressive tissue hypoxia leading to a build up in lactic acid, a byproduct of anaerobic metabolism. Therefore, metabolic acidosis which may be measured in the fetus or newborn is taken as a marker of asphyxial insult.

13.92   The fetus is entirely dependent on the placental gas exchange for its respiratory needs. The fetal lungs have no respiratory function prior to delivery. Oxygen and glucose cross the placenta to the fetus and waste products from the fetus in turn cross into the maternal circulation to be excreted. The placenta perfuses the fetus via the umbilical cord. Thus, 'suffocation' or asphyxia of the fetus usually occurs as the result of a placental or cord problem. The most common chronic situation is poor placental function which may cause long-standing fetal growth restriction. The fetus grows poorly and shows signs of compromise on various assessments of fetal well-being, but is able to protect its brain during times of placental insufficiency. The brain is the last organ to slow its growth rate, so affected fetuses usually show differential growth retardation with a head circumference that is appropriate for the duration of gestation but a weight that is considerably lower than the gestational age (asymmetrical intrauterine growth restriction). Under these circumstances the brain will show no anatomical or functional deficit. In general, fetal growth restriction does not cause brain damage, but the fact that the fetus is less well metabolically protected against the rigours of labour makes brain compromise more likely during a complicated labour than a well grown baby with an equally difficult delivery.

Causes of Asphyxial Insults
13.93   An acute event affecting the feto-placental unit may cause a rapidly progressive onset of asphyxia. This most commonly occurs during labour but may occur before the woman goes into labour. Pre-labour causes of acute asphyxial insult include the following:

- Severe maternal illness. Mothers who develop medical complications in pregnancy which lead to severe hypoxia will cause their fetus to become acutely hypoxic. Severe asthma attacks, coma due to maternal subarachnoid haemorrhage and prolonged epileptic seizures have all been described as causing brain damage to the fetus.

- Maternal asphyxia. This may occur accidentally as in carbon monoxide poisoning or deliberately in attempted suicide. In both cases the mother and her fetus will become acutely and severely hypoxic with potential brain injury to both.

- Trauma to the mother as occurs in high-velocity car accidents are well recognised to lead to associated fetal injury by direct or indirect trauma. A less well recognised problem is a low-velocity car shunt (approximately 30 mph rapid deceleration force) during pregnancy. The gravid uterus will continue to move forward until its momentum is suddenly restrained by a sash seat belt. This rapid deceleration causes a shear force on the intrauterine contents with potential partial separation of the placenta possibly causing an acute non-fatal asphyxial injury to the fetus. The brain may be irreversibly damaged by this acute placental abruption. There are now more than 50 cases in the medical literature of fetal damage as a result of a pregnant woman being involved in a low-velocity car crash.

13.94 It is much more likely that a fetus is exposed to an asphyxial insult during labour than before its onset and two different patterns of asphyxial insult has been described.

Asphyxial Brain Damage
13.95 It is not known how long a baby can be deprived of oxygen to the brain yet survive to be normal. Animal experiments in fetal monkeys and sheep suggest that total brain asphyxia (no blood flow) lasting 10-15 minutes can be tolerated without brain damage and clinical experience in humans coincides with this.

13.96 Brain damage as the result of asphyxia can be classified into a number of patterns that were initially recognised at post-mortem examination and more recently by imaging. In addition experimental animal studies have attempted to produce patterns of brain damage by imitating different types of asphyxial models. Basically two models of asphyxia have been produced.

Partial Intermittent Asphyxia
13.97 During each contraction the placenta is squeezed and the maternal blood within the maternal intervillous spaces is forced out. During the relaxation phase between contractions the intervillous spaces refill with oxygenated blood and the fetus is reperfused. If the contractions are too frequent or too prolonged adequate reperfusion may not occur between them and the fetus is subjected to a process of attrition during which he becomes more severely compromised and eventually clinically asphyxiated. This is referred to as partial intermittent asphyxial insult. During this form of asphyxial insult characteristic changes are seen on the CTG trace.

13.98 Studies in mature fetal monkeys have produced partial asphyxia in a number of different ways, but in all there has been maintenance of some blood flow despite very low oxygen concentrations. In these studies brain injury affects primarily the cerebral cortex with severe brain swelling. The distribution of injury is described mainly in areas of brain between two arterial supplies; the so-called vascular watershed distribution. Deeper structures in the brain are either spared or significantly less badly affected. Human post-mortem studies have found similar types of brain damage with prolonged partial asphyxia and imaging in living children support this.

Acute Total Asphyxia

13.99   In this condition the fetus is tolerating labour normally until a major, sudden and often unexpected insult occurs. This may be a large placental abruption where up to a third or more of the placental surface detaches from the uterine wall, a cord accident or uterine rupture. Under these circumstances the fetus will rapidly decompensate and become acutely and severely hypoxic and acidotic. In clinical practice complete asphyxia rarely occurs as the primary event, and what is described as total asphyxial insult is, in fact, a form of severe and sudden partial asphyxia. Perhaps the most common event to illustrate this is cord prolapse. All the blood flow from the placenta to the fetus is through the umbilical cord and if it is merely compressed, it is rare that no blood flow at all will get to the fetus. The duration that the fetus can survive will clearly depend on the duration and severity of the cord compression and this makes calculation of the duration of 'total' asphyxia somewhat difficult.

13.100   Although cord compression occurs most commonly in the second stage of labour, intermittent cord compression may occur earlier in labour, particularly if there is relatively little amniotic fluid (oligohydramnios). Under these circumstances there may be characteristic features on the CTG trace which are described elsewhere.

13.101   An important feature of total asphyxia is the fact that the fetus will very rapidly develop critical failure to maintain adequate cardiac output so that as well as being hypoxic he becomes ischaemic (with critical impairment of blood flow). The feature on the CTG trace will be a fixed bradycardia of 80 beats per minute or less.

13.102   Animal studies show that total asphyxia by complete compression of the umbilical cord causes damage to the brain stem and the nuclei of the basal ganglia in distinction to partial asphyxia. Other studies in a monkey fetus has shown that a period of total asphyxia superimposed on an animal that has already suffered partial asphyxia develops injury in both the cortex and basal ganglia. More recently fetal sheep exposed to repeated relatively brief (10 minute) but total episodes of cerebral asphyxia were shown to develop basal ganglia type injury. Post-mortem studies have found a similar distribution of brain injury in cases of sudden circulatory arrest in newborn babies.

13.103   Although two ends of an asphyxial insult can be described as above, in clinical practice a fetus may move from intermittent asphyxial insult to one of total asphyxia in a number of ways. The fetus has many physiological mechanisms to protect vital organs during labour and can withstand either intermittent or total asphyxia for a period of time. It is not until these mechanisms are overwhelmed that the fetal brain and other organs are exposed to potential irreversible injury. The duration of these brain-sparing reserves depends on both the vigour of the fetus and the severity of the asphyxial insult. As mentioned above, the growth restricted fetus will have less in the way of physiological reserves and therefore will be less likely to cope with a period of severe intermittent partial asphyxia than a well grown baby. A baby who has sustained partial asphyxia in the earlier stages of labour will be able to survive a more acute asphyxial event later in labour.

13.104 Asphyxial insults may occur after birth. A common event is failure to make the transition between intrauterine and extrauterine life. The baby must be able to switch rapidly from an aquatic environment to one where the lungs expand, oxygenate and perfuse the newborn's body. Failure to make this adaptation may cause ongoing hypoxia and asphyxial damage. This is why expert resuscitation at delivery needs to be available for all babies wherever they are born because the need for such resuscitation cannot always be predicted. A baby who is severely asphyxiated prior to delivery may continue to remain in a severely depressed and asphyxiated state without appropriate resuscitation.

13.105 In summary, our understanding of the relationship between asphyxia and brain damage is that the fetal brain is very resistant to up to 10-15 minutes of total asphyxial insult. A total asphyxial insult lasting at least 15 minutes where there is virtually no oxygen delivered to the brain causes basal ganglia injury. A partial asphyxial insult where there is hypoxia (not anoxia) with some preserved flow to the brain seems to lead to mainly cortical injury in a watershed distribution. Total or partial asphyxia may damage both cortex and basal ganglia.

Resuscitation

13.106 It is not necessary for a paediatrician to be the first person available to resuscitate babies as all staff working on a delivery suite should have at least basic resuscitation skills. All personnel should receive formal training and regular retraining to keep their skills at an acceptable level. Basic resuscitation means being able to use a bag and mask to artificially ventilate a newborn baby who is not breathing. With this treatment alone most babies will recover. Some with more severe asphyxial injury may require additional skills from a person with advanced resuscitation training and this person is usually a paediatrician. This person should be able to pass an endotracheal tube into the baby's airway (intubate) and give artificial respiration through this as well as give external cardiac massage if this is appropriate, together with cardiostimulant drugs intravenously.

13.107 It is also necessary for each delivery unit to have a written protocol agreed with the paediatric department as to which deliveries it is necessary to call a paediatrician to attend. Table 3 lists examples of higher risk deliveries where it may be appropriate for a paediatrician to be in attendance. These indications will vary between units, depending on what is appropriate for their own organisation and availability of staff. It is essential that written protocols exist, equipment is serviced regularly and training and retaining programmes are available for all staff.

Table 3: Indications for a Paediatrician to Attend Delivery

Caesarean section under general anaesthetic
Fetal distress
Multiple births*
High or rotational forceps delivery
Breech delivery
Pre-term delivery
Antepartum haemorrhage
Prolonged rupture of the membranes
Thick meconium staining of the liquor
Polyhydramnios (excess amniotic fluid)
A known major fetal anomaly

*The number of skilled resuscitators should match the number of babies to be born.

13.108   Asphyxia may occur rarely after delivery, most commonly associated with an episode where the baby stops breathing (apnoea). This is usually due to infection or some other underlying cause, but if the baby is apnoeic and hypoxic for too long a period of time then brain damage may occur. The commonest example in the few weeks after birth is the near miss sudden infant death baby who is found pulseless and not breathing in their cot, but who can be resuscitated and their heart starts to beat again. Irreversible brain damage is unfortunately a relatively common sequelae of this situation.

Prognosis
13.109   Asphyxia is potentially the commonest cause of preventable brain damage in babies born at full-term. Various follow-up studies have attempted to predict outcome on the basis of a variety of measures in the first few days after asphyxial birth. The best predictor is the severity of hypoxic-ischaemic encephalopathy (HIE). The term HIE refers to abnormal neurological behaviour that occurs as a result of an asphyxial insult occurring within 48 hours of birth in a full-term baby and is graded into mild, moderate or severe. There are a variety of ways of defining the three grades of severity, but Table 4 summarises the salient features of all of these methods. In summary, the outcome for babies with Grade I HIE (recovery within 48-72 hours and have no convulsions) is excellent with virtually no reports of death or disability.

13.110–13.119   There have been a number of follow-up studies of babies with HIE and there is a close relationship between severity and outcome (Table 5). Death is very uncommon in babies with moderate HIE, although 20-25% of the infants will show significant neurodevelopmental disability. The prognosis for severe HIE is very poor, 60% of babies die and 70% of the survivors are severely handicapped.

Table 4: Definition of the Grading of Severity of Hypoxic-Ischaemic Encephalopathy ('HIE'). This only applies to mature neonates

Grade I (Mild)	Grade II (Moderate)	Grade III (Severe)
Irritability	Lethargy	Coma
Hyperalert	Seizures	Prolonged seizures
Mild hypotonia	Increased tone	Severe hypotonia
Weak sucking	Requirement for tube feeding	Loss of gag reflex
		Failure to maintain spontaneous respiration

Table 5: Outcome Following Severity of HIE

Severity of HIE	Estimated mortality	Estimated severe handicap
Mild	0%	0%
Moderate	0%	20-25%
Severe	60%	70%

A FORENSIC APPROACH TO 'BIRTH ASPHYXIA' AS A CAUSE OF DISABILITY

13.120 The commonest and potentially most expensive medical negligence claims are disability due to birth asphyxia. With increasing scientific knowledge of the effects of asphyxia and with more sophisticated imaging modalities it is now possible to apply a number of 'rules' to the approach to such cases. Over the course of the last ten years the author has seen many cases of disability allegedly due to birth asphyxia and has developed the following method to decide whether the putative asphyxial insult is the probable cause of the disability.

13.121 As discussed above, the effects of asphyxial insult vary considerably depending on the maturity of the brain. In very immature babies particular forms of pathology develop which are rarely seen in full-term babies and for that reason, this approach to asphyxia causing disability is only relevant to the relatively mature infant of 35 weeks gestational age and above.

13.122 There are four major questions that need to be examined and although a positive answer is not required for each, the weight that is given to each question is discussed in each section. Once information has been obtained in each of the four questions an overall assessment can be made as to the probability that 'asphyxia' caused the disability.

13.123   The four questions are:

- How many positive features of asphyxia are present?
- Have alternative causes of disability been excluded?
- Is there any supporting data?
- Is the pattern of disability appropriate for the likely cause?

Positive Features

13.124   As discussed above there is no single or generally accepted definition for what constitutes asphyxia. There are a number of recognised features of the condition which can individually be examined. The more of these features that are present the more likely that the diagnosis of asphyxia will be generally accepted.

Evidence of Fetal Distress
13.125   The fetus can only react to compromise in a limited number of ways which can be measured by the clinician (midwife or obstetrician) and the one that is used to assess fetal well-being in labour is patterns of heart rate change. This chapter will not discuss CTG monitoring or intermittent auscultation, but decelerations in the fetal heart rate may indicate fetal distress. The normal fetus may show some decelerations in the heart rate with contractions and this may represent the normal reaction to fetal stress and is not a feature of distress. The distinction between fetal heart decelerations which distinguish distress from stress is discussed elsewhere in the book.

13.126   In general, the slower the fetal heart rate (particularly if it falls to 60 beats per minute or below) and the longer the decelerations last, the more concerned the clinician will become that the fetus is distressed. Other important features of distress include the interval between the uterine contraction and the recovery and the quality of the trace (beat to beat variability) between decelerations. It is only possible to assess beat to beat variability on the CTG trace and this cannot be determined by intermittent auscultation.

Passage of Meconium
13.127   The fetus who is distressed may have vagal nerve stimulation which causes anal relaxation and passage of meconium into the amniotic fluid. Meconium staining of the liquor occurs commonly (10-20% of full-term deliveries) and it is only heavy contamination that is associated with fetal distress. Meconium staining in a breech baby is common and usually not significant. On its own meconium staining of the liquor is a very weak marker of the baby at risk of brain injury and it is reported that only 0.4% of babies with this sign were later found to have cerebral palsy.

Metabolic Acidosis
13.128   Cellular metabolism may continue despite very low levels of tissue oxygen. The cells are able to switch to a form of anaerobic metabolism which is considerably less efficient in energy production that aerobic metabolism. A result of anaerobic metabolism is the production of lactic acid which causes a metabolic acidosis. Blood acidosis is expressed as a measurement of pH. Normal pH is 7.4 and the lower the pH the more severe the acidosis although

the scale is not arithmetic but logarithmic, so that for a progressive reduction in pH there is a greater accumulation of acid at lower pH than higher. A low pH may not indicate a metabolic cause for it, and measurement of the base excess is required to estimate the degree of lactic acid production. The base excess expresses the amount of metabolic acids in the blood and by convention is shown as a negative number. (Normal base excess is +5 to -5 mmol/L). The more negative the base excess the more metabolic acid is present.

13.129 Blood pH can be measured in the fetus from a fetal scalp sample if the baby is presenting by the head. Serial estimates can be made to assess changes with time. At birth, blood can be taken from the umbilical cord for an estimate of pH at birth. A scalp or cord blood pH of <7.20 is usually taken as a sign of preceding hypoxia. The severity of the metabolic acidosis may reflect either the duration or the intensity of the asphyxial event. There is normally a difference in blood pH depending on whether it is taken from the umbilical vein or artery. Arterial values reflect blood coming from the fetus and venous pH reflects blood from the placenta. The arterial level is normally slightly lower than venous blood. In acute asphyxia the differential between arterial and venous pH values are increased, which may be used as a feature of the rapidity at which the acidosis (and by implication the hypoxia) has developed. Large differences are usually the result of cord compression. Blood may be taken from the newborn after birth, but the longer after delivery that this is measured the less reliable it becomes in reflecting what the fetal situation was. In general, neonatal blood pH one hour after delivery cannot reliably be used to estimate fetal acidosis and even when taken earlier than this one must consider the effect of drugs given with neonatal resuscitation to reverse and correct a metabolic acidosis.

13.130 Acidosis at birth is a poor predictor of irreversible brain damage and it is not until cord pH is <7.05 that there is a significantly increased risk of bad outcome, although the majority of babies with acidosis of this severity are later normal.

Depression of Apgar Scores
13.131 The Apgar score takes its name from Virginia Apgar who first described a system for describing the baby's condition at timed intervals after birth in 1953. The details of the score are shown in Table 6. The maximum score is 10 and the minimum zero. It is usual to describe the total score at one and five minutes after birth and at longer intervals if the baby remains depressed. The Apgar scores in the first five minutes after birth actually describe the baby's adaptation to birth rather than implying a low score to mean that the baby was asphyxiated, but the longer the score remains low after five minutes the more likely it is that a significant asphyxial event may have occurred within a short time before birth. The score may be affected by factors other than asphyxia, including maternal sedation with opiates administered for pain relief birth trauma and, rarely, neuromuscular disorders affecting the onset of spontaneous breathing.

Table 6: The Apgar Score

Sign	0	1	2
Heart rate	Absent	<100 bpm	>100 bpm
Respiratory effort	Absent	Weak cry	Strong cry
Muscle tone	Limp	Some flexion	Good flexion
Reflex irritability to suctioning pharynx	No response	Some motion	Cry
Colour	White	Blue	Pink

(bpm – beats per minute)

13.132   Depression of Apgar scores has a weak correlation with outcome. In full term infants the risk only becomes significant if the Apgar score remains 0-3 at 20 minutes. Depression of the score to this degree at 15 minutes is associated with a less than 10% risk of subsequent cerebral palsy in surviving infants. A score of 0-3 at 5 minutes carries an overall risk of 3% of handicap in surviving infants. Conversely, a very low score (0 at one minute and/or 0-3 at 5 minutes) is entirely compatible with normal outcome and in one study 93% of infants with such scores were normal at follow-up.

Delay in Establishing Spontaneous Respiration
13.133   Respiratory activity is a component of the Apgar score but has been suggested as a feature of asphyxia in its own right. The time to establish spontaneous respiration is used by many as an index of the severity of preceding asphyxial insult and a delay of 10 minutes or more is significant. Delay lasting as long as 20 minutes is a relatively poor predictor of outcome as in one study 71% in this group were normal or had only minimal handicap. For prognostic purposes it is not until the delay is 30 minutes or longer that outcome is generally poor.

Hypoxic-ischaemic Encephalopathy ('HIE')
13.134   This refers to a consistent pattern of abnormal neurological signs which occur over a period of time. Table 5 lists the signs according to severity of HIE. Convulsions are often a prominent feature of HIE, but convulsions occur as a result of many different neonatal brain problems. The feature of HIE is that the neurological signs increase over the first 6-12 hours of life, then remain constant for a number of days before gradually reducing in severity. Convulsions occur most commonly between 12-36 hours, and are rare within the first three hours of life. With recovery of HIE the baby may show little or no persisting neurological abnormality even if the brain has been irreversibly damaged and the child is subsequently shown to have cerebral palsy and other disabilities. The prognosis of HIE is discussed in paras 13.109-13.110.

13.135   The clinical pattern of neurological abnormality will also depend on the developmental age of the baby. Mature babies usually show the characteristic features of HIE whereas premature babies may show little or no abnormal neurological behaviour which reflects the under-developed nature of their central nervous system.

Multi-organ Involvement

13.136 Severe asphyxia is likely to cause a transient compromise in a number of potentially vulnerable organ systems, most commonly the brain, kidneys, heart and bowel. Evidence of acute and transient compromise to more than one organ system suggests that an acute asphyxial event occurred in the 48 hours prior to birth and was the common pathway by which these organs were affected. Recognition of renal involvement includes a clinical description of oliguria (reduced urine production), haematuria (persistence of blood in the urine) and biochemical abnormalities of renal function (elevation of serum creatinine or blood urea).

Summary

13.137 If a baby shows six to seven features of asphyxia, there can be little doubt that he had been asphyxiated in the hours prior to delivery. Five features are suggestive of asphyxia, but if there are only three to four features then the probability that there had been a significant asphyxial event depends on the pattern of these features and their duration and severity, as well as considering the other conditions set out below. If a baby only has one or two features it is difficult to argue that significant asphyxia had occurred. The presence of HIE is the most reliable sign of asphyxial brain compromise and if this is absent, the significance of the other features is weakened.

Timing of Asphyxial Insult

13.138 In order to consider the liability aspects of any case of asphyxial brain injury it is necessary to consider timing the injury. This can be looked at in a number of ways and a picture built up. Timing the onset of the severe asphyxial injury requires both paediatric and obstetric expertise.

Condition at Birth

13.139 If a baby is suffering from a severe asphyxial insult at delivery he will be profoundly depressed at birth with very low Apgar scores (0-3 at one minute) and require vigorous resuscitation, usually including intubation and artificial respiration. If these conditions are met then it can be assumed that birth marked the end of a severe asphyxial insult.

CTG Trace

13.140 This may give an indication of the length of the period of potential fetal distress present. As discussed above changes on the CTG trace do not necessarily correlate with brain impairment, but if the CTG only became abnormal in the last hour prior to birth and the baby was born in a very depressed state then it is probable that the severe brain damaging asphyxial insult occurred no longer than an hour prior to birth but longer than 15 minutes. It is estimated that 15 minutes is the minimum time that a healthy baby can sustain a period of severe total asphyxia without sustaining permanent brain damage. A CTG trace which shows few or no severe abnormalities shortly before birth will make it difficult to time the onset of the severe asphyxial event immediately before delivery.

Nucleated Red Blood Cells ('NRBC's)

13.141 Recently it has been suggested that measurement of the number of immature red cells in the peripheral blood indicates whether the baby has been subject to a severe hypoxic stress prior to delivery. NRBCs are immature red cells which in the peripheral circulation suggest an activated bone marrow and increased levels are seen in growth retarded fetuses, maternal diabetes mellitus, rhesus haemolytic disease and prematurity.

13.142 Phelan et al[1] have shown that asphyxiated full term newborn babies have a significantly higher NRBC count than non-asphyxiated babies of the same gestation. They were unable to show a statistically significant difference in the numbers of asphyxiated babies who had evidence of a more prolonged asphyxial insult as opposed to a terminal severe asphyxial event. They suggested that those babies with more long-standing asphyxial compromise had a longer duration of NRBCs present in their blood film. The chronically asphyxiated group still had NRBCs present >80 hours after birth compared with babies who had sustained a more acute asphyxial event.

> 1   Phelan JP et al 'Nucleated Red Blood Cells: A Market for Fetal Asphyxia? [1995] 173 Am J Obstet Gynecol pp 1380-84.

13.143 These data are of interest when attempting to time the onset of potentially brain damaging asphyxia, but there are a number of methodological problems with this study and the conclusions may not be fully sustainable.

Imaging Studies
13.144 The role of MR brain imaging in assessing the type of asphyxial brain injury is discussed in paras 13.149-13.153. Briefly, two patterns can be recognised, one arising as the result of acute total asphyxial insult and the other due to a more intermittent asphyxial process. Evaluation of the scan findings along with CTG changes and condition at birth may be very helpful in deciding what was the most probable duration of the asphyxial event.

Exclusion of Alternative Causes

13.145 A number of disorders can lead to features consistent with asphyxia and alternative conditions must always be considered. Table 7 lists some of the more common conditions that may cause brain damage and which may be confused with asphyxia. These include abnormal neurological behaviour such as meningitis, brain haemorrhage, or severe hypoglycaemia (critically low blood sugar). The baby with a congenital brain disorder may show delay in adapting to birth with low Apgar scores and depression of spontaneous respiration. Further investigations are required to exclude these conditions as far as possible. Brain imaging, blood and urine biochemical assessment and careful examination for subtle dysmorphic features should be part of the assessment of all infants in whom asphyxia is suspected.

13.146 It is possible that a baby may be predisposed to a severe asphyxial event in labour by an existing underlying brain disorder such that if not for the asphyxia, the baby would have been less severely damaged than was actually the case. The possibility that such an event makes a material contribution to bad outcome must of course be considered.

Table 7: Conditions to be Excluded when Considering the Causation of Asphyxial Brain Damage

Meningitis
Cerebral haemorrhage
Neonatal stroke
Brain malformation
Dysmorphic or chromosomal conditions
Inborn errors of metabolism
Severe hypoglycaemia

Supporting Data

13.147 In addition to the features of asphyxia there are a number of other pieces of information which may help in weighing the evidence that asphyxia was the cause of disability.

Head Growth
13.148 All babies should have an accurate measurement of head circumference made at, or shortly after, birth. This is plotted on a growth chart together with birthweight and length. Most infants will have a head circumference in proportion to their weight at birth, but following very severe brain injury at birth progressive measures of head size shows failure of brain growth. This indicates that brain growth had been normal up to birth and a severe insult close to the time of birth caused brain growth failure. This does not allow determination of the cause of the brain injury or accurate timing of the event (whether it was the week before or after birth) but may give some additional weight to an already relatively strong causation argument. Some babies who have sustained severe brain injury during birth do not show a change in their brain growth trajectories.

Imaging
13.149 Magnetic Resonance ('MR') brain imaging has given new insight into understanding the causation of brain injury. MR is a technique that involves placing the patient in the core of a strong magnetic field to generate cross-sectional images of the brain. The technique involves no radiation and is safe, but currently the acquisition of images is relatively slow and the technique is very sensitive to movement artefact. Therefore, very young children, those with intellectually impairment or abnormal movement disorders must be anaesthetized to keep them still and this has a measurable (but small) risk of severe complications. Fully informed consent from the parents, and where appropriate, the child is necessary with an explanation of risk.

13.150 Over 90% of all children with cerebral palsy will show abnormalities on MR scanning performed some years after birth and these images may allow determination of the underlying cause and to some extent its timing.[1]

1 Truwit CL, Barkovich AJ, Koch, TK, Ferriero DM 'Cerebral palsy: MR findings in 40 patients' [1992] 13 AmJNeurorad at 67-78.

13.151 Congenital malformations will be obvious on the scan and if it shows a true malformation then the question of causation is clear. Some disorders of neuronal migration (see above) may arise as the result of a hypoxic-ischaemic insult early in the second half of pregnancy and this should be considered and expert neuroradiological interpretation of the scan obtained.

13.152 PVL causes the damaged myelin in the periventricular white matter to show a particular abnormality and this can be readily recognised on MR scans taken years after the acute episode. The timing of the lesion that causes PVL is most likely to be 24-34 weeks of gestation.

13.153 Asphyxial insult in mature babies leads to one of two patterns of abnormality seen on MR which relate to acute total asphyxia or partial intermittent asphyxia as described above. Abnormal MR signal in the basal banglia with relative sparing of the cortical structures occurs in acute asphyxia. Specific cortical injury in the perirolandic area has also been associated with acute total asphyxial damage. In a more partial asphyxial insult, the injury affects mainly the cortical watershed distribution with sparing of the basal ganglia.

Pattern of Cerebral Palsy

13.154 There are only two types of cerebral palsy that are commonly associated with asphyxia as the cause. The first is described as spastic quadriplegia and is usually a devastating form of disability because it is usually associated with severe cortical damage and profound intellectual handicap, microcephaly and sometimes severe visual impairment. If asphyxia causes this pattern of disability it is usually due to a partial form of intermittent asphyxial insult (see above).

13.155 The second well recognised sequelae of asphyxial insult is a choreoathetoid form of cerebral palsy. In this condition the predominant abnormality is uncontrolled writhing movements of all four limbs, usually with involvement of muscles of mastication, swallowing and speech so that eating, drinking and verbal communication are severely affected. Surprisingly, the intelligence may be preserved but due to the severe physical disabilities, accurate measurement of intelligence is difficult. This pattern of disability is most likely to be due to an acute total episode of asphyxia.

13.156 The two other forms of spastic cerebral palsy that are commonly seen, hemiplegia and diplegia, are less likely to be due to an asphyxial event in full-term babies although in each case careful forensic assessment should be made to weigh all the evidence.

13.157 Approximately 10% of children with CP have ataxia with the major problem being co-ordination. Cognitive function may also be impaired. It is most unlikely that pure ataxic cerebral palsy arises as a result of birth asphyxia in the fullterm infant.

13.158 In general terms, if asphyxia in a mature fetus causes disability, part of the constellation of abnormalities is cerebral palsy and this may be associated with intellectual impairment, sometimes severe. It is sometimes asked whether asphyxia can cause learning problems on their own without cerebral palsy. The author's view is that this is very unlikely, but again some additional factors must be taken into consideration.

13.159 First, is there evidence on MR scanning of pathology that is associated with asphyxial insult? The combination of characteristic MR changes, with a reasonable number of positive features of asphyxia would lead me to believe that cognitive impairment without cerebral palsy may have been due to an asphyxial insult prior to birth.

13.160 This can be supported by some, albeit relatively weak, scientific data. There are very few long-term follow-up studies of babies who had suffered asphyxia as defined by HIE. One study suggests that babies who have suffered moderate HIE may show a reduction in IQ without cerebral palsy, but the impairment in intelligence in relatively mild with an average IQ of about 80 compared with a control of 110. In other words survival with a 30 point reduction in IQ may occur as the result of asphyxia in the absence of motor deficit.

Part 3
Quantum Issues

Chapter 14

Introduction and Overview of Financial Matters

John Frenkel FCA

INTRODUCTION

14.1 Although the really interesting part of litigation is dealing with all the cerebral issues like liability, causation, contributory negligence and case management, at the end of the day the focal point of litigation is to come up with an amount of money, which takes into account all the issues associated with the litigation. Thus money-men can never be too far from the process, although it is clear that there are plenty of occasions when it is apparent that, notwithstanding the vast sums of money that are at stake, there are plenty of practitioners who would rather not see them at all.

14.2 In 1983 the author was closely involved in what was then the largest award in a road traffic accident and the client, who was aged eight years old at the time of the trial, received £380,000. Although the case of *Biesheuvel v Birrell*[1] is the largest award at £8,200,000 (the case did compromise on appeal but the terms of that compromise are not in the public domain), there are a significant number of cases where damages total in excess of £3,000,000. Thus, over a 16-year period when the Retail Price Index has about doubled, the amount of damages in the largest cases has gone up by a factor of nine to ten times. New ways of calculating damages and new heads of damage constantly appear, the effect of which require a far more scientific approach to the whole question of financial matters in cases involving catastrophic injury.

1 [1999] PIQR 3 Q40.

14.3 Financial input into these types of cases is essential. The practitioner inevitably concentrates on the question of the litigation, often having little time, awareness and expertise for the clients' needs in the post-settlement period and in fact in the pre-settlement period as well. The case of *Hurlingham Estates Ltd v Wilde & Partners*[1] has imposed a much greater burden of responsibility on the solicitor, in that it is now clearly incumbent on the solicitor to be aware of all potential related matters when handling professional work for a client. The practitioner's obsession with focusing litigation on a single lump sum figure at point of settlement may not fully address the long-term needs that the client will have. Experience of these large cases is that clients have more problems post-settlement and that it does not all end when they get their damages cheque, but rather a new type of problem begins for the client and the family.

1 [1997] STC 627.

14.4 In Chapters 14 to 16 on financial matters, attention has been focused on the following key areas:

Assessing Quantum
- Assessing quantum is exclusively a pre-settlement issue.
- A detailed case study is analysed from both the claimant's and defendant's perspective.
- Detailed consideration is given to the issue of multipliers.

The Need for Independent Financial Advice
- Financial advice is certainly *not* exclusively a post-settlement issue.
- Clients in receipt of means-tested benefits must be wary of interim payments and how this might impact on these benefits. Woe betide the practitioner who is not live to these issues. A simple but highly effective trust can be the solution for such cases. The advice is needed before settlement as the entitlement to such benefits could otherwise be impaired.
- Protecting the principal family carer and the much more detailed requirement for proper portfolio planning is essential to match the vast number of financial instruments on the market with the specific needs of each client. These matters can be dealt with post-settlement;
- Financial advice will include the question of a structured settlement and at the time of writing it is 10 years since we implemented the first case of Cathy Kelly. Structures have become an integral part of the way that the catastrophic cases (and indeed cases of much lower value as well) are handled. Significant legislative changes took place in 1995 and 1996 which have made our structured settlement environment the envy of places like the USA and Canada, where structures preceded the United Kingdom, but where they still have a fair number of impediments that we do not. Structures can only be implemented *at point of settlement*, and only with the *consent* of both sides. Thus by the time the practitioner is contemplating settling the case, consideration must have been given for the structure so that the claimant (and the defendant as well) have ample opportunity to consider the various merits and issues associated with this type of settlement.

OVERVIEW OF FINANCIAL MATTERS

14.5 A vast array of information on the various financial problems that arise in dealing with personal injury litigation has been included. These are complicated matters and it is not reasonable to expect the legal practitioners to be able to answer all the financial questions that will arise. Rather, the practitioner should be live to these problems and must obtain experienced independent advice on behalf of the client as early as possible in the litigation process. In the opinions of many, the failure to advise properly on such financial matters is nothing short of negligence. The competent practitioner need do no more than recognise the problem and retain the appropriate advisers, in exactly the same way as would be expected in relation to medical expertise, for example.

* I must add that I am particularly grateful to my colleagues Richard Cropper and James Dadge from Frenkel Topping Structured Settlements who have respectively contributed to the Chapters on The Need for Independent Financial Advice and Structured Settlements while still maintaining all their client responsibilities.

Chapter 15

Quantum Issues

John Frenkel FCA

INTRODUCTION

15.1 A key feature of personal injury litigation over the last few years has been the successful way that costs associated with the action have been driven down. Forensic accountants have certainly not been immune from these changes. However, the need to keep costs to a minimum does not obviate the need to instruct accountants, but merely that their role should be confined to that which they know best, that is, the assessment and presentation of the schedule of damages with minimal commentary.

15.2 The example on which the case study is based is a matter in which the author is currently involved. The action follows negligent obstetric treatment for a young boy who is now aged seven years old. A full case summary is set out below.

15.3 The summary of losses and costs is set out in the way that it would now be reported, but in order to explain the reasoning for some of the figures adopted, a more detailed explanation by way of footnote is included at the bottom of the schedules to the summary of losses and costs. The claimant is referred to as William Darby, although of course that is not his actual name.

15.4 The NHS Trust who are the defendants in this matter have not accepted all of the schedule and an extract of the key issues that they have taken is included, together with further commentary.

15.5–15.9 Also included is a separate section on multipliers, to take account of some of the current thinking on multipliers and how they can interrelate with structured settlements.

CASE STUDY

Facts to the Case Study

- William was born on 1 May 1992 and following negligent obstetric treatment he has athetoid cerebral palsy.
- Judgment has been entered into against the Health Care NHS Trust.
- William will be subject to the Court of Protection.

- The claimant's evidence is that he has a reduced life expectancy and that he should live until he is aged 45. The defendants do not take much issue with this assessment.

Summary Calculations

15.10   The detailed calculations and supporting notes are set out at Schedules 1 to 13 and they can be summarised as follows:

William Darby – Summary of Losses and Costs
(Calculations based on a discount rate of 3%)

General damages including interest	128,798
Past losses and costs	96,548
Future losses and costs	2,864,894
Total	£3,090,240

CONCLUSIONS ON THE CASE STUDY

15.11   This is a typical case of its nature. The differences between both sets of experts are the usual items, with plenty of room to manoeuvre and negotiate being allowed by both parties. By any reckoning, this is going to settle at a substantial sum of money and discussions are already taking place about structuring the case. This will certainly assist in the risk associated with how long William will actually live. On the investment front, the structure will take out that slice of capital from generating income that would otherwise have been taxed at the highest rates and hence provide an excellent return for him. Further details about structuring are covered in Chapter 17.

MULTIPLIERS

Introduction

15.12   The high profile nature of *Wells et al* in July 1998 has meant that the issue of multipliers has been to the forefront of the mind of all practitioners, not just on the cases of utmost severity, but on all cases where an element of future loss is involved.

15.13   There is a limited amount that can be added usefully to the debate but set out below is a summary of the current situation (September 2000) and some thoughts as to where it may well finish up in the future. Some observations on the interaction between multipliers and structured settlements are set out as the two concepts do have a much closer bearing on each other than perhaps is fully appreciated.

15.14   At the time of drafting, the discount rate applicable on multipliers is 3%. Below is a summary of the current key issues affecting multipliers:

- There is now no ceiling to the multiplier that can be adopted.
- Once the life expectancy has been agreed/compromised the multiplier is taken straight from the Ogden Tables.
- Tables 11 to 20 from the Ogden Tables are now those adopted following the decision of *Worrall v Powergen plc.*[1]
- Multipliers are now effectively taken on a tariff basis.
- Multipliers for loss of earnings can be subject to judicial discounting for the vicissitudes of employment.
- The Lord Chancellor has still not exercised his power under the Damages Act 1996 to proscribe the discount rate. The word from the Lord Chancellor's Department is that this is unlikely to be done until the end of 2000 at the earliest.

1 [1999] PIQR Q103.

15.15   For illustrative purposes only, the summary of losses and costs adopting a discount rate of 2% has been recalculated. While this chapter does not deal with the detailed calculations, the big impact on the assessment of damages based on a lower discount rate is summarised.

William Darby – Summary of Losses and Costs
(Calculations based on a discount rate of 2%)

General damages including Interest	128,798
Past losses and costs	96,548
Future losses and costs	3,271,651
Total	£3,496,997

15.16   It is apparent from the above that the impact on the total award of changing the multipliers based on a discount rate of 2% would be to increase the amount claimed by 13%. The increase is not as much as it might have been as there is only a 38-year life expectancy from date of trial. Had William not had a reduced life expectancy, then the impact of the change in the multiplier would have been significantly higher. Nevertheless, the impact in cash terms is in fact in excess of £400,000. Little wonder there is such lively debate over the multiplier.

Quantum Issues – Appendix 1

William Darby

CASE DETAILS

Date of Birth	1 May 1992
Assumed Date of Trial	31 December 1999
Age at Assumed Date of Trial	7 years 8 months
Nature of Injuries	Athetoid cerebral palsy with epilepsy
Life Expectancy	To age 45
Current Care	Provided by parents
Future Care Required	24 hour care regime
Employment Status	Unemployable

Schedule 1

WILLIAM DARBY
Summary of Losses and Costs

		£	£
General Damages	Schedule		120,000
Interest at 7.33%	4		8,798
		A	128,798
Past Losses and Costs			
Care and attention	2	57,735	
Sundry costs	3		
Taxi costs		6,274	
Equipment		1,490	
Increased costs		15,846	
Holidays		3,495	
		84,840	
Interest at 31.48%	4	26,708	
State benefits		(15,000)	
		B	96,548
Future Losses and Costs			
Earnings	5	248,564	
Care and attention	6	1,273,091	
Therapies	7	136,910	
Transport	8	170,181	
Housing	9	430,219	
Aids, appliances & equip	10 (p 4 of 8)		
Initial cost		68,312	
Remainder		252,684	
Increased costs	11	160,022	
		2,739,983	
Court of Protection costs	12	38,325	
Receiver's fees	12	86,586	
		C	2,864,894
Total		A+B+C	**£3,090,240**

Schedule 2

WILLIAM DARBY
Past Care

	Hours per Week	Total Hours	Hourly Rate £	Total £
Gratuitous Care				
6 August to 31 December 1992	42	888	3.88	3,445
Year ended 31 December 1993	42	2,184	4.04	8,823
Year ended 31 December 1994	42	2,184	4.20	9,173
Year ended 31 December 1995	41/56	2,357	4.44	10,465
Year ended 31 December 1996	41/56	2,357	4.56	10,748
Year ended 31 December 1997	41/56	2,357	4.69	11,054
Year ended 31 December 1998	41/56	2,357	4.84	11,408
Year ended 31 December 1999	41/56	2,357	5.03	11,864
				76,980
Allowance for fact that care provided gratuitously, say 25%				(19,245)
				£57,735

Notes

1 25% deduction is based on Housecroft.
2 Hourly rate is labour rate only and does not include any agency profit or overhead hence the only deduction is only for tax and NI.

Source of information is the nursing report.

Schedule 3-1

WILLIAM DARBY
Sundry Past Costs

		£	£
Taxi Costs			
1992	Appointments at Hospital		228
1993	Appointments at Hospital		6
1992	GP appointments		3
1993	GP appointments		9
1994	GP appointments		9
1995	GP appointments		3
1996	GP appointments		9
1997	GP appointments		3
1994	Appointments at Hospital		63
1995	Appointments at Hospital		35
1996	Appointments at Hospital		7
1992	Appointments at Hospital		84
1993	Appointments at Hospital		84
1994	Appointments at Hospital		24
1995	Appointments at Hospital		12
			579

	£	£
Additional cost of Fiat Brava – based on AA Tables 1998		
October 1997 to December 1999 (27 months)		
Standing costs, 1,400 Road tax	150	
Insurance	342	
AA subscription	72	
Depreciation, estimate	1,250	
	1,814	
Total for 14 months		4,082
Running costs, assuming 5,000 miles a year		1,613
		£6,274

	£	£
Equipment Purchased		
Car seat		90
Push chairs/buggies		155
Toys, age 2 to date, May 1994 to December 1999, at £100 pa	566	
Videos, age 2 to date, May 1994 to December 1999, at £120 pa	679	
		£1,490

Increased Costs – May 1992 to December 1999

Nappies, one year only from age 2	364
Cost of drinks, £371 per annum	2,842
Heating, £210 per annum	1,609
Electricity, £60 per annum	460
Laundry, £100 per annum	766
Consumables (e.g. tissues), £600 per annum	4,596
Telephone, £80 per annum	613
Clothing, £200 per annum	1,532
Increased bedding costs, £200 per annum	1,532
Wear and tear, £200 per annum	1,532
	£15,846

Holidays

Age 3 to date, at £750 per annum	£3,495

Information provided by the family. Information on increased costs from reports of OT specialist and architect.

Schedule 4

WILLIAM DARBY
Interest on Damages

From	To	Days	Rate	Factor %
General Damages				
7/23/97	12/31/99	892	3.00%	7.332
Rate for application to general damages				7.33%
Special Damages				
5/6/92	1/31/93	271	10.25%	7.610
2/1/93	12/31/99	2,525	8.00%	55.342
				62.952
Half rate for application to special damages				31.48%

Schedule 5

WILLIAM DARBY
Future Earnings

	Age 16 to 18 £	Age 19 to 25 £	Age 26 to 35 £	Age 36 to 45 £	Total £
Skilled Manual					
Gross annual earnings	8,605	13,171	20,802	26,813	
Personal allowance, 1999/2000	(4,335)	(4,335)	(4,335)	(4,335)	
	4,270	8,836	16,467	22,478	
Income tax 10%	150	150	150	150	
23%	637	1,687	3,442	4,825	
National insurance 10% (excess over £66 pw)	517	974	1,737	2,257	
	1,304	2,811	5,329	7,232	
Net annual earnings	7,301	10,360	15,473	19,581	
Multiplier Schedule 13	1.46	4.50	5.01	3.30	
Total	10,659	46,620	77,520	64,617	199,416

Lost Years' Claim

Multiplicand	19,581
Multiplier from age 46 to 65 Schedule 13	5.01
Multiplier for claim, half	2.51
Total	49,148
	£248,564

Gross annual earnings from employment consultant report.

Notes

Claimant's Position
1   Loss of earnings split according to four key periods of employment and multiplier allocated accordingly.
2   Future earnings based on employment as skilled manual worker, that is, the same as his father.
3   Lost years' claim based on death at age 45 and loss to his estate for the remaining part of his working life. A deduction of 50% is made to represent expenditure he would have incurred on himself exclusively.

Defendant's Position
1   Loss of earnings split according to seven key periods of employment and multiplier allocated accordingly. Allowance argued for falling income from age 50.
2   Claimant would have been a skilled engineer or in factory employment.
3   Lost years' claim accepted as is the 50% deduction.
4   Defendant seeks 20% discount overall on the multiplier to reflect possibility of not reaching age 45, for periods of sickness and unemployment and fact may not have worked until age 65 but he may have retired younger.

Further Comments
1   There will need to be some compromise between the parties on the above points as they all represent legitimate argument.
2   For periods of sickness it is likely that the claimant would receive some amounts of sick pay. Periods of unemployment would have been made up by the receipt of unemployment benefit for at least part of the wages loss.
3   Discount to be conceded likely to be lot less than 20% as the period when being out of work is more likely when he is older and the multiplier appropriate to that period is heavily discounted.

Schedule 6-1

WILLIAM DARBY
Future Care and Attention

		Rate £	Weeks	Total £
To age 18	Resident carer	300.00	58	17,400
	Employer's NIC 10.0%			1,740
	Weekend relief	150.00	58	8,700
	Food & other expenses	40.00	52	2,080
	Recruitment advertising costs			800
	Case management			5,750
				36,470
	Multiplier Schedule 13			9.25
	Total		**A**	337,348
Age 19 onward	Two live-in carers	600.00	58	34,800
	Night care	252.00	58	14,616
				49,416
	Employer's NIC 10.0%			4,942
	Food and other expenses	50.00	52	2,600
	Recruitment advertising costs			600
	Case management			6,750
				64,308
	Multiplier Schedule 13			13.24
	Total		**B**	851,438

Enablers

	Cost £	Multiplier (Sch 13)	
To age 11	13,000	3.72	48,360
Age 12 to 18	6,500	5.53	35,945
Total		**C**	84,305

Total Future Cost	**A + B + C**	**£1,273,091**

Notes

Claimant's Position

1 The claim is based on two periods for care, that is up to age 19 and thereafter for the rest of his life. Weekend relief claimed for the period to age 19 when only one carer claimed.

2 Claimant requires two carers from age 19 when he returns home full-time from school.

3 As originally referred to in the case of Page and Sheerness Steel, the claimant is claiming the costs of an enabler to assist him with going out and generally looking after his social activity and also to assist in providing individual attention at school.

4 Case management is claimed and is now quite a common head of damage.

Defendant's Position

1 The counter-schedule is based on four periods for care, that is, three up to age 19 and thereafter for the rest of his life. Assumed family will provide the bulk of the care at a discounted rate. No weekend relief allowed. Family to do everything all the time to age 19.

2 Only one full-time carer allowed with mid-week and weekend relief also included.

3 In principle an enabler is allowed but at a lower annual cost ie £7,500 throughout as compared to £13,500 to age 11 and £6,500 from age 11 to age 19. The defendant also allows for NI on cost of employing an enabler.

4 Case management costs are allowed but at a much reduced rate to age 19 as it is argued that the family should be able to carry out the function. A higher rate is allowed from age 19.

5 The allocation of the multiplier for the respective periods is not in dispute, albeit the total multiplier as put forward by the claimant is not accepted. (See Schedule 13).

Further Comments

1 While there is some £550,000 between the parties on the question of future care it really only boils down to three main differences:

Approximate difference in £ terms

(a) Family or paid care to age 19?	£ 76,000
(b) Weekend relief or no relief to age 19?	£ 86,000
(c) One or two carers from age 19?	£ 266,000
Total	£ 428,000

2 While families do often shoulder added responsibility, hence saving third party costs, there has to be some realism as to how much stress a normal family can cope with.

3 There will need to be some compromise between the parties on the above points as they all represent legitimate argument.

Schedule 7-1

WILLIAM DARBY
Future Therapies

		Annual £	Total £
Occupational Therapy			
Initially	12 sessions at £55 a session		660
To age 19	52 sessions a year at £55 a session	2,860	
	Multiplier Schedule 13	9.25	26,455
Thereafter	4 sessions a year at £55 a session	220	
	Multiplier Schedule 13	13.24	2,913
Speech Therapy			
Initially	12 hours at £50 an hour re eating/drinking		600
	104 hours at £50 an hour re communication aid		5,200
To age 19	52 hours a year at £50 an hour	2,600	
	Multiplier Schedule 13	9.25	24,050
Thereafter	40 hours a year at £50 an hour	2,000	
	Multiplier Schedule 13	13.24	26,480
Chiropody			
	6 sessions a year at £15 a session	120	
	Multiplier Schedule 13	22.49	2,699
			89,057
Physiotherapy			
To age 7	2 sessions a week at £52.50 a session	5,460	
	Multiplier Schedule 13	0.97	5,296
To age 15	1 session a week at £52.50 a session	2,730	
	Multiplier Schedule 13	6.05	16,517

To age 19	1 session per fortnight at £52.50 a sessio	1,365	
	Multiplier Schedule 13	2.93	3,999
Additional sessions to age 19			
	6 sessions a year at £52.50 a session	315	
	Multiplier Schedule 13	9.95	3,134
Thereafter allow for 26 sessions at £52.50 a session			1,365

Swimming/Riding for the Disabled

For life	1 session a week at £15 a session	780	
	Multiplier Schedule 13	22.49	17,542
			£136,910

Information from reports of OT and physiotherapy experts.

Notes

Occupational Therapy
1 This is accepted by the defendant as claimed.

Speech Therapy
1 Agreed by the defendants as claimed to age 19.
2 After leaving school, only 4 hours per annum is allowed by the defendants and that is to train the carers.

Chiropody
1 Not allowed at all by the defendants as would ordinarily be done by the parents or carers at no additional cost. This is based on the claim being for the routine cutting of toe-nails.

Physiotherapy
1 Physiotherapy need accepted in principle but argued by the defendants that this will be provided at school so only allowed for the school holiday period.
2 Future fortnightly sessions from age 19 are agreed by the Defendants.
3 The defendant takes issue with the cost per session at £52.50 and argues for a figure of £45.00 including a travelling allowance.

Swimming/Riding for the Disabled
1 The defendant does not agree the cost per session at £15.00 but argues for a figure of £7.50.
2 At any event the defendant takes the view that these are not *additional* costs as he would have enjoyed different leisure pursuits in the normal course of events.

Schedule 8-1

WILLIAM DARBY
Transport Costs

	Initial Cost Yrs	Replacement Period £	Annual Cost £	£
Mercedes V class per OT expert	28,435			
Residual value, say	(9,478)			
	18,957	3	6,319	
Car phone	100	3	33	

Annual costs (AA 1998 tables)
(Car licence excluded)

Insurance, assuming a 3,000cc to 4,500cc vehicle and 60% no claims discount		661
AA subscription		72
Total Standing costs		7,085
Running costs, assuming a 3,000cc to 4,500cc vehicle, 5,000 miles a year		1,316
Car phone		180
Service call		5
		£8,586

But for Accident

	Initial Cost	Replacement Period	Annual Cost
Second hand car, say	3,500		
Residual value after 5 years, say	(1,250)		
	2,250	5	450

Annual costs (AA 1998 tables)

Car licence	150
Insurance, assuming a 1,100cc to 1,400cc vehicle and 60% no claims discount	342
AA subscription	72
Running costs, assuming a 1,100cc to 1,400cc vehicle, 5,000 miles	717
	£1,731

£

Future Additional Costs

			£
To age 19			8,586
Multiplier　Schedule 13			9.25
Total		A	79,421

From age 19 onwards

			£
Required vehicle			8,586
Vehicle that may have been acquired but for accident			(1,731)
			6,855
Multiplier　Schedule 13			13.24
Total		B	90,760

Total Additional Cost		A + B	**£170,181**

Notes

Claimant's Position
1　Claim based on 5,000 miles pa that claimant would have done at any event.
2　Based on keeping car for three years and then changing it to ensure reliability.
3　No credit for transport costs up to age 19 as claimant would not have been earning.
4　Credit given for car would have had at any event from age 19 but lower value car that could have been kept for five years.

Defendant's Position
1　Defendant argues that a Citroen Berlingo would be a more appropriate vehicle. They state that this could be bought under the Motability Scheme at a much reduced cost.
2　Defendant argues that credit should be given for transport at any event in the period to age 19 and seeks credit in the same sum of £1,731 as the claimant gives in the post 19 period. This figure is not disputed by the defendants.

Further Comments
1　Claimant's case for more expensive resource such as the vehicle has more chance of success if the more costly option is actually incurred using interim payments.
2　The family did not have a car on a regular basis, hence no credit for the costs of a vehicle at any event in the period up to age 19. Some credit for transport costs at any event does seem reasonable.

Schedule 9-1

WILLIAM DARBY
Housing

	£	£

Projected Costs

Capital costs

Purchase price of bungalow	110,000	
Betterment value of adaptations	50,000	
	160,000	
Value of current property	(65,000)	
Increased capital cost	95,000	

Other purchase costs

Legal fees	2,121	
Estate agent commission	1,146	
Removal costs	411	
Surveyors' fees	1,528	
	5,206	

Cost of adaptations

Extensions	51,500	
Extending garage	4,250	
Conservatory	12,500	
Drainage works	2,450	
Central heating modifications	5,100	
Electrical work	365	
Internal modifications	12,300	
Disabled person's bathroom	16,865	
Heat resistant working surface	615	
Redecoration	4,250	
External ramps etc.	3,800	
Intruder alarm system	950	
Grab rails and fire extinguishers	655	
Contingencies	1,000	
	116,600	
Hydrotherapy pool	80,000	
	196,600	
VAT on adaptations	13,857	
VAT on hydrotherapy pool	9,400	
	219,857	

Betterment value of adaptations	(30,000)	
Betterment value of hydrotherapy pool	(20,000)	
	169,857	
Architects'/surveyors' fees etc on adaptations	18,603	
Architects'/surveyors' fees etc on hydrotherapy pool	10,400	
Planning permission, building regulation fees	453	
	199,313	

Calculation of Additional Costs

Costs thrown away

Purchase costs	5,206	
Adaptation costs	199,313	
Carpets and curtains	11,100	
		215,619

Additional annual costs

Annual interest on capital cost £95,000 x 3%	2,850	
Council tax	96	
Water rates	175	
Heating	1,015	
Electricity	360	
Telephone	80	
Property maintenance	1,341	
Equipment maintenance	486	
Building insurance	227	
Contents insurance	236	
Building insurance for hydrotherapy pool	176	
Running costs for hydrotherapy pool	2,500	
	9,542	
Multiplier Schedule 13	22.49	
		214,600
Total Cost		£430,219

All details from report of housing expert.

Notes

Claimant's Position

1 Claiming abortive costs of acquisition and adaptations in full.
2 Claiming the finance costs of the increased capital tied up in the family home ie the cost of the property, plus the retained value ie the betterment following the adaptations, with due credit being given for the capital cost of the home at any event.
3 The cost of a hydrotherapy pool is claimed.
4 All the additional costs associated with a larger house are claimed for the claimant's lifetime.

Defendant's Position

1 Defendant argues that the adapted bungalow will have six bedrooms, two more than they say is required.
2 They do not accept that a conservatory is required by virtue of the claimant's disability.
3 They argue that the family could move outside of the area, albeit still reasonably close, and purchase the required bungalow at a reduced total cost.
4 They argue that the claimant does not require a hydrotherapy pool.
5 They have only allowed a relatively small amount for increased annual running costs on the basis that the new home would not cost that much extra to run.

Further Comments

1 Claimant's case for more expensive resource such as the home has more chance of success if the more costly option is actually incurred using interim payments.
2 Hydrotherapy pools are often claimed but are rarely recovered.
3 While the defendant's comments that the total cost of extra housing is particularly high does seem well founded, they have been quite unrealistic regarding the extra running costs that will clearly be incurred in running a larger home.

Schedule 11-1

WILLIAM DARBY
Future Increased Costs

	£	£
Sundry costs		
Report of OT expert		
Clothing	200	
Toys/recreational items	400	
Holidays	1,072	
Consumables (e.g. tissues)	600	
Wheelchair seating assessments	1,000	
Carpet wear and tear	200	
Increased bedding costs	200	
Equipment assessments	1,000	
Incontinence materials	1,000	
	5,672	
Multiplier Schedule 13	22.49	
Total		127,563
Other		
DIY	300	
Multiplier, age 19 on Schedule 13	13.24	
Total		3,972
Medical costs		
Periodic review by physician to age 19 – annual cost 45 minutes every 4 months at £150 per hour 0.75 x 3 x £150	338	
Multiplier Schedule 13	9.25	
Total		3,127
Periodic review by physician from age 19 – annual cost	150	
Multiplier Schedule 13	13.24	
Total		1,986
Periodic orthopaedic review – annual cost	150	
Multiplier Schedule 13	22.49	
Total		3,374
Cost of orthopaedic surgery		20,000
Total future costs		**£160,022**

Notes

Claimant's Position
1 No particular points of principle arise in this Schedule

Defendant's Position
1   The defendant takes issue with the following major points:
(a) Certain items would have been incurred at any event and only small annual increases are allowed, for example, clothing, consumables and toys.
(b) Certain items will not need to be paid for, that is, equipment assessments (provided by the occupational therapists) and incontinence materials (now provided free and will continue to be so).
(c) Wheelchair seating assessments agreed but only from age 16 for the rest of his life at £1,000 pa.
(d) Holidays agreed at £1,072 pa.
(e) Orthopaedic review agreed by defendants but only on the basis on every three years.
(f) Many other items agreed in full, for example, DIY, bedding, medical reviews.

Further Comments
1 Certain items should be capable of being agreed as it should be a question of fact as to whether or not they have to be paid for.
2 There will need to be some compromise between the parties on the above points as they all represent legitimate argument.

Schedule 12

WILLIAM DARBY
Court of Protection and Receiver's Fees

	Note	£
Future losses	1	2,739,983
General damages		128,798
		2,868,781
Annual interest on fund at 3.0%	2	86,063
Annual Court of Protection Fee		
On income in excess of £25,000		1,750
Annual visit fee		75
Annual fee		1,825
Future annual cost (x 21.0)	3	38,325
Initial costs		
Application fee		100
Medical fee		50
Legal fees		646
		£82,042
Annual Receiver's Fee	4	2,350
Cost of tax and accountancy assistance for Receiver		1,500
		3,850
Future cost (x 22.49, Schedule 13)		£86,586

Notes
1 Estimated after allowing for initial expenditure.
2 Per *Cassel v Riverside Health Authority* (CA 1993).
3 The multiplier has been reduced from 22.49 to 21.00 to reflect the fact that the capital sum, and the interest earned thereon, will diminish.
4 Estimate based on the 'going rate' of £2,000 plus VAT. Income will be in excess of £25,000 for a very high proportion of the period so only a small reduction in the multiplier and considered appropriate.

NB Court of Protection and charges are due to change again to a flat fee of £205 p a with effect from 1 September 2000.

Schedule 13

WILLIAM DARBY
Multipliers

Years from Date of Trial (31 December 1999)	Age of Claimant	Present Value of £1 at 3.0%	Arithmetic Multiplier 0.0%	Rounded Muliplier
0	7			
1	8	0.9709	0.9709	0.97
2	9	0.9426	1.9135	1.91
3	10	0.9151	2.8286	2.83
4	11	0.8884	3.7170	3.72
5	12	0.8625	4.5795	4.58
6	13	0.8374	5.4169	5.42
7	14	0.8130	6.2299	6.23
8	15	0.7893	7.0192	7.02
9	16	0.7663	7.7855	7.79
10	17	0.7440	8.5295	8.53
11	18	0.7223	9.2518	9.25
12	19	0.7013	9.9531	9.95
13	20	0.6809	10.6340	10.63
14	21	0.6611	11.2951	11.30
15	22	0.6418	11.9369	11.94
16	23	0.6231	12.5600	12.56
17	24	0.6050	13.1650	13.17
18	25	0.5874	13.7524	13.75
19	26	0.5703	14.3227	14.32
20	27	0.5537	14.8764	14.88
21	28	0.5376	15.4140	15.41
22	29	0.5219	15.9359	15.94
23	30	0.5067	16.4426	16.44
24	31	0.4919	16.9345	16.93
25	32	0.4776	17.4121	17.41
26	33	0.4637	17.8758	17.88
27	34	0.4502	18.3260	18.33
28	35	0.4371	18.7631	18.76
29	36	0.4244	19.1875	19.19
30	37	0.4120	19.5995	19.60

31	38	0.4000	19.9995	20.00
32	39	0.3883	20.3878	20.39
33	40	0.3770	20.7648	20.76
34	41	0.3660	21.1308	21.13
35	42	0.3553	21.4861	21.49
36	43	0.3450	21.8311	21.83
37	44	0.3350	22.1661	22.17
38	45	0.3252	22.4913	22.49

Chapter 16

The Need for Financial Assistance

John Frenkel FCA
Richard Cropper

INTRODUCTION

16.1 Following the House of Lords decision on the three cases of *Page*, *Wells* and *Thomas*, the whole basis as to how personal injury damages are calculated was affected. While those decisions have meant that claimants are not entitled to recover the costs of investment advice, they have certainly not rendered obsolete the actual need for independent financial advice following the receipt of a large award of damages.

16.2 The amounts awarded for future losses have always been calculated by taking into account the accelerated receipt of the money, with the claimant utilising both the original capital and income generated by it into the future. The assumption (pre-*Wells et al*) was that the claimant could, with sound financial advice and a prudent approach, achieve a return of between 4% and 5% after tax and above inflation. In *Wells et al* the claimants maintained that such a return was unachievable in the current economic climate without exposure to a degree of risk that was unacceptable.

16.3 The Lords agreed that a claimant should not be forced to take risks in order to meet their future needs. In addition, since Index-Linked Government Stocks ('ILGSs') have become available which provide a secure return that increases in line with inflation, they should be used as the benchmark. But what are ILGSs?

16.4 Index-linked government stocks are special government securities where both the rate of interest and capital repayment are linked to the rate of inflation as measured by the Retail Prices Index ('RPI'). The link is eight months in arrears for administrative and pricing reasons. They provide returns that are uncertain in money terms, but they do provide the certainty that the purchasing power will be protected if the investor holds the investment until redemption.

16.5 It follows that if claimants are to be compensated in a way that ensures they receive a lump sum that is sufficient to buy a portfolio consisting solely of ILGS, which will provide for their annual needs, increasing each year in line with the cost of living and be virtually free of risk, why do they require any financial advice?

16.6 Unfortunately, although this approach has been successful in increasing the level of damages recovered by claimants, actually it has fallen short of providing them with the certain knowledge that their damages will not run out.

16.7 First, the claimant will often not recover the total amount claimed. Indeed, given the uncertainties of the litigation process, contributory negligence and the give and take of negotiation, the final award is likely to be well short of the figure claimed in the Schedule of Damages.

16.8 Second, an award based on ILGSs takes no account of future changes in economic and social conditions. Although an allowance is made for projected inflation, there is no allowance for adverse variations in the taxation regime. The recent, large case of *Biesheuvel v Birrell* has extended the boundaries for the multiplier to be increased where the claimant is a foreign national and resident, whose own country's taxation levels are appreciably higher than our own. However, no allowance is currently made for potential future increases in the British income or capital gains tax regime that could have a detrimental effect on the net return on ILGS.

16.9 Third, the longest dated ILGSs are currently only available until 2030. It is quite conceivable that claimants receiving awards of damages today will survive beyond that date. No consideration has been given as to in what a claimant will invest if there are no further issues of long-dated ILGS.

16.10 Furthermore, although a portfolio of ILGSs will provide the claimant with a guaranteed income that will increase in line with the Retail Prices Index, it is generally recognised that their needs will not follow such an index. The main element of expenditure in catastrophic personal injury awards is future care. Care costs do not tend to increase in line with retail prices, but at a rate estimated at about 2% higher. Without the existence of additional monies, or a contingency fund to meet this shortfall, a portfolio of ILGSs will only prove to guarantee insufficient income.

16.11 Despite changing the discount rate inherent in the multiplier, the greatest problem associated with a lump sum compensatory system was not addressed: the issue of future life expectancy. At the time of settlement, expert medical opinion is sought with regard to how long the claimant will live, attempting to take into account developments in medical science and, of course, such opinion is based on average life expectations. Compensation is then paid to cover this period and not beyond it. If the claimant were to hold a portfolio of ILGS and utilise the income and capital over the assumed lifetime, the monies would be fully exhausted on the exact average date agreed by the medical experts. If the claimant were to live longer, then there would be no funds remaining to provide for the continuing needs. Effectively, the claimant is penalised for the misfortune of living too long.

16.12–16.14 Consequently, even though the claimant has been compensated on the basis that he will purchase a portfolio of ILGS and require no investment advice, the reality is that this approach cannot meet the needs for life with any degree of comfort or certainty. Only with effective financial planning can the damages be maximised and the risks be at best mitigated against.

NATURE OF FINANCIAL PLANNING REQUIRED

16.15   There is a need for effective financial planning at all stages of the litigation process and throughout the claimant's lifetime. For the sake of convenience the times have been summarised when financial advice should be taken into account and the nature of such advice.

Before Settlement

Structured Settlements
16.16   This is, of course, a whole subject in its own right and has been set out at Chapter 17. The key point to note is that the structure should be considered as part of the overall financial planning requirements of the claimant and to use a client's phrase, 'the structure is the bedrock of my investments'. Claimants should be introduced to the structure well before settlement so that they understand the concept and have maximum opportunity to have the whole idea explained to them.

Income Support and Local Authority Financial Assistance
16.17   The point to note is that claimants are very likely to be in receipt of a variety of state benefits some of which might cease *after* the damages have been paid over to the claimant. It is possible to retain such benefits by the simple but effective use of trusts, which we have termed Special Needs Trusts.[1] The key point is that the damages must flow into the Trust at point of settlement and there are some restrictions (albeit relatively modest) that relate to the Trust and the claimants should have the concept explained to them well before settlement.

1   See paras 16.20-16.32 for detailed consideration of such trusts.

Post-Settlement

Portfolio Planning
16.18   There is a massive array of financial products available in the marketplace, each attracting its own benefit or drawback. The needs of the claimant will be many and varied and so advice is essential to match the products available with the needs of the client. This whole process is considered in detail in paras 16.50 to 16.63.

Family Carer Protection
16.19   Complete financial advice recognises that, in the vast majority of cases, there will be a disabled family and not just a disabled individual. Protecting against both the inevitable and further disaster is an essential to a rounded solution to all the claimant's problems and considered below are the issues that arise in such situations.

STATE BENEFITS AND SPECIAL NEEDS TRUSTS

16.20   The solicitor should advise the claimant how to maximise his entitlement to Income Support and local authority assistance and due consideration must be given to the implications of receiving interim payments. An interim payment, for example, without prior planning can prejudice the claimant's entitlement to means-tested benefits and leave the claimant in a worse position than if he had never received it.

Example 1

A claimant with spinal injuries receives an interim award of £150,000 to purchase and adapt a suitable property. However, the purchase takes two months to transact and a further three months to do the adaptations. During that time the money is held on the solicitor's client account. The claimant is in receipt of Income Support. Without planning and the use of a Trust, the claimant will lose his entitlement to these benefits over the five-month period and he may well have to reapply for them once all the money held on client account has been expended on the property.

What is a Special Needs Trust?

16.21   A Special Needs Trust is a means to maintain a sui juris claimant's entitlement to means-tested benefits and local authority assistance following receipt of an award of damages for personal injury.

Why is a Special Needs Trust necessary?

16.22   The easiest way to illustrate the need for a Special Needs Trust is by way of example.

Example 2

The claimant, aged 26 at point of settlement, was rendered tetraplegic following an accident. On a full liability basis the claim was valued at around £2 million. Due to major issues with regard to liability and contributory negligence, damages in the sum of £500,000 were recovered. After interim payment and the repayment of CRU, the net award was £450,000.

Prior to settlement the claimant lived in a council house that was wholly unsuitable for his needs. It was envisaged that he would be moved into a fully adapted bungalow, furnished with the necessary equipment. The total cost of the property, adaptations and equipment was almost £250,000. This effectively left £200,000 to cater for his future care needs for the rest of his life.

His care was costing £32,000 per annum and his life expectancy was estimated at a further 30 years. Obviously, at such a rate the award of damages would have been fully exhausted within eight years or so.

The care was being provided partly by the local authority and partly by the Independent Living Fund ('ILF'). The local authority assistance within the home is discretionary and means-tested and the ILF's contribution was also discretionary. If the claimant had received the award of damages in his own name he would probably have lost his entitlement to both, until his damages fund had been spent.

A Special Needs Trust was effected by the claimant at point of settlement. Under Regulations 45 & 53 of the Income Support (General) Regulations 1987 and National Assistance (Sums for Personal Requirements) and (Assessment of Resources) Regulations 1998, personal injury damages held within a trust are disregarded for the purposes of assessing relevant capital and income. Therefore, the claimant continued to receive funding for care from the local authority in the sum of £18,000 per annum.

Further discussions were held with the ILF who agreed to continue to fund the remainder of the care as long as the claimant contributed £5,000 per annum himself. A structured settlement was implemented to provide this amount for his lifetime, tax-free and RPI-linked, at the cost of £100,000.

Consequently, the Special Needs Trust, together with the Structured Settlement, secured the claimant's continuing care needs, ensured he retained his Income Support, council tax relief and free prescriptions, while allowing for a contingency fund of £100,000 to provide for replacement of his equipment and upkeep of his property.

This could not have been achieved by any other means.

When does the Special Needs Trust Need to be Established?

16.23   In order to ensure that the claimant's entitlement to state benefits and local authority assistance is not affected by the award of damages, the Special Needs Trust needs to be established at the point of receipt of any interim payments or on final settlement of the case.

Can One Disregard the Option of a Special Needs Trust if the Claimant is not Currently in Receipt of Means-tested Benefits?

16.24   The option of a Special Needs Trust cannot be disregarded because although the claimant is not currently entitled to means-tested benefits it does not mean that he may not become entitled in the future. Indeed, given that there are current plans to make more benefits means-tested, the award of damages could preclude them from claiming benefits in the future unless the monies were put into a trust.

Example 3

The claimant suffered a severe head injury at work. Consequently he will never work again. Although he can manage to look after himself with help at the moment, he will probably require residential care in the future. Just before his case settled, the claimant's father died and it was suggested that the claimant purchase his father's house from the estate. This is the house in which the family had been raised and had much sentimental value.

If the claimant had received his damages in his own name and purchased the house he would have lost his Income Support payments, Council Tax Relief and free prescriptions. Furthermore, he could have prejudiced himself for the future. Without a Special Needs Trust, when it came to needing residential care, the local authority would require him to utilise his assets before he became entitled to state help. Therefore, he would probably need to sell his home to pay for his care. Consequently, unless his family could afford to buy the home at market value, he would have to sell it outside the family.

With the Special Needs Trust, the claimant has had the house purchased on his behalf, but the Local Authority cannot take the asset into account. Subsequently, on his death, the trust is dissolved and the house will fall to his younger brothers, as are his wishes.

What Type of Trust is a Special Needs Trust?

16.25 Although Discretionary Trusts can be used as Special Needs Trusts, the most effective type of trust involves the claimant as the sole beneficiary, because:

- It is easy to understand and administer.
- Although, the claimant is the sole beneficiary, the trustees do have the discretion as to when and whether or not to distribute capital and income;
- For an individual the position is tax neutral, as tax is payable on the individual as if the trust did not exist.
- The claimant does not forego the absolute right to the capital. In the event that the claimant's circumstances change and he is no longer entitled to means-tested benefits, then he can dissolve the trust returning the capital to their individual control, that is the trust contains a revocation clause.

16.26 However, the type of trust that is most effective for any given claimant will depend on their own specific circumstances, tax position and objectives. Careful examination needs to be undertaken to establish the implications of each option, especially following the case of *Hurlingham Estates Ltd v Wilde & Partners* that imposed responsibility on the solicitor to be aware of all client issues.

On What Can the Monies Held in the Special Needs Trust be Spent?

16.27 The trustees may pay someone for services and benefits provided for the claimant. Such payments must be for items other than those covered by the benefits.

Typical Items Purchased by Special Needs Trusts:

Care provision
Suitable property purchase and upkeep
Specialist equipment
Vehicles
Audio visual equipment
Computer equipment
Telephone bills
Holidays, and so on

16.28   By contrast the Special Needs Trust cannot be used for payments which are intended to be covered by Income Support.

The Special Needs Trust Can Provide for Items Other Than:

Housing costs (covered by Housing Benefit)
Council Tax
Food
Ordinary Clothing
Ordinary Footwear
Heating Costs
Lighting Costs

16.29   The aim of the Special Needs Trust is to secure the claimant's current position and maintain entitlement to means-tested benefits and local authority support both now and into the future. There are costs incurred in running a Special Needs Trust, potentially for a professional trustee and accountancy/tax advice, so a viability check should be undertaken by the specialist establishing the Special Needs Trust.

16.30–16.39   Regardless, you must ensure that the claimant is fully aware of the option of a Special Needs Trust. Following *Hurlingham Estates Ltd v Wilde & Partners*, you need to ensure that the claimant is aware of all of the implications following receipt of his/her personal injury award. It follows then that if a claimant loses his entitlement to future benefits because he/she was not advised of the option of a Special Needs Trust at the point of settlement, then there is a potential loss due to negligence.[1]

---

1   At the time of writing, the authors are aware of a firm of solicitors who are being sued for failing to advise a personal injury client to create a trust to protect against the loss of means-tested benefits.

Special Needs Trust Checklist

Always consider a Special Needs Trust when your client is:

- Sui juris.
- Receiving means-tested benefits.
- Receiving local authority assistance at home.
- In residential care.
- In possible need for residential or home care in the future
- In employment but this has an uncertain future and would be entitled to means-tested benefits if unemployed.

Consider wider implications of the award and the Special Needs Trust

- Income Tax implications.
- Capital Gains Tax implications.
- Inheritance Tax implications (including drafting a will).
- Specialist advice on the investment of the trust funds.

SECURING THE CURRENT POSITION – FAMILY CARER PROTECTION

What is Family Carer Protection?

16.40   Probably the greatest asset any claimant has is the help and support of his family and friends. In many cases family members will, post-settlement, continue to provide a part if not the mainstay of care. Having a family member provide part of the claimant's care does raise some financial issues that must be considered.

16.41   In many cases, the overall settlement figure may have been reduced as a family member is providing care. This reduction might not adequately take into account what may happen to that family member in the future and its effects. The claimant may have to confront one or more of the following events in the future:

- The family carer gets older and can no longer manage to undertake the tasks they are currently able to do. At that point, the claimant will need increased outside care and assistance to be able to cope, at additional expense. This is likely to be a transitional process that can be undertaken over time. But, sufficient funds must be available at this unknown point in the future to provide for this.
- The family carer is diagnosed with a dread disease, such as cancer, and/or dies. Then not only will the claimant have to cope with the loss of a loved one, but will instantly have to replace the care they provided. This has instant implications and further funds need to be available to cope at this time.
- The family carers themselves must also consider their own financial position. Many family carers will refuse to be fully recompensed for the help they provide, while at the same time they have either reduced their working hours or have stopped work to administer the care. They need to address how they will pay for their own living expenses and care in old age. If they have not worked for a substantial period then currently their state pension will even be reduced (this issue is being addressed in new provisions for carers' pensions under the government's pension review).

Example

Miss T is cared for predominantly by her mother. As her mother gets older she is unlikely to be able to cope without a professional carer's assistance. It was envisaged that at that point she would adopt a case manager role overseeing the care that was being provided. Therefore, an insurance policy was purchased that will provide additional income, free of taxation, to pay for professional care, as and when her mother was unable to cope. In addition, when her mother could no longer oversee the care regime, further annual payments would become payable and a lump sum cash payment would be made upon her death.

16.42–16.48   There are a vast array of plans and insurance products that can be used to cover the above problems. Each claimant's requirements will be different and need to be individually assessed. Such cover provides both the claimant and the family carer peace of mind that in the event of their death, the claimant will continue to receive the best of care.

PORTFOLIO PLANNING
Where do you Start?

16.49   In order to ensure that the claimant has access to all of the products available in the marketplace, he must receive independent financial advice. An adviser should be either independent or a tied agent of a particular firm. If the adviser is a tied agent the claimant will only be offered products from the range available from that specific provider, who may not be the optimum provider for the claimant's circumstances. By contrast, an independent adviser can advise on any company's products. A further important distinction is that the independent adviser owes the client a much stronger duty of care than does the tied agent who is responsible to his own company.

What Then?

16.50   The independent adviser is required to gather sufficient information that will identify the claimant's current position, personal circumstances and future needs. Although the Schedule of Special Damage is a good starting point, one cannot assume that the information contained within it reflects the claimant's precise needs post-settlement. In order to fully understand the claimant's needs, the financial adviser will need to complete a confidential client questionnaire or 'factfind'.

16.51   The factfind will provide the adviser with the following information:

- The claimant's personal circumstances.
- The claimant's state of health and future prognosis.
- The claimant's current income.
- The claimant's benefits entitlement.
- The claimant's current assets.
- The claimant's current liabilities.
- The claimant's income requirement, for care, for living costs and anticipating changes in care requirements in the future.
- The claimant's immediate and projected capital requirements, for a house, for adaptations, for specialist replacement requirements.
- The claimant's current will and estate planning.

16.52   From this information the adviser can then identify the claimant's financial objectives, identify the need for protection cover, investments and review of the claimant's projected change in personal circumstances, for example, the spouse no longer being able to look after the claimant at below market cost.

Financial Objectives – Protection Cover

16.53   Often protection cover is overlooked due to the fact that the claimant himself may be uninsurable or the cost of insurance is prohibitive due to the injuries sustained. However, in many catastrophic personal injury cases the claimant's spouse and family provide care, assistance and the income for the rest of the family. Even with effective investment advice, the award of damages will often not be able to solely provide for their replacement if they were to die. Consequently, the following need to be considered by the claimant and his family.

Life Assurance and Family Protection

16.54   Is there a concern with the amount of capital and/or income that would be available for the claimant in the event of the death of the main carer, based on current arrangements?

Claimant's Life Insurance
16.55   Family members often give up work to provide care or may be dependent on the loss of earnings element of the damages. Life assurance can protect them in the event of the untimely death of the claimant.

Carer's Life Insurance
16.56   There are also circumstances when a family member is providing care that must be replaced in the event of their death. Thus there is clearly a form of mutual inter-independence.

16.57   The need for Family Protection Cover is even more obvious when the claimant has children.

16.58   As the claimant is ultimately the beneficiary of any such insurance proceeds, it is usual to ensure that the cost of such policies are taken into account when identifying the amount of income required from the investments. This would also ensure that no additional costs fall on the family. The Court of Protection will typically approve such expenditure, provided of course it is modest.

Critical Illness

16.59   Are you concerned with arranging for a lump sum to be paid to the main carer, in the event of serious illness or disability?

Carer's Critical Illness
16.60   Critical Illness cover for the main carer can typically be added to the life assurance and would pay out in the event that the carer could not fulfil the normal care duties due to suffering from certain illnesses, for example, cancer.

Income Protection Cover

16.61   Is it your objective to arrange for an income to be paid to you, to replace your salary, in the event of long-term illness?

16.62   The need for income protection cover may be for example for the claimant's spouse. However, in cases where the claimant is still working, this type of cover should also be considered.

16.63–16.69   In addition to the above policies, the adviser should consider the need for long-term care and inheritance tax planning. However, the personal injury award will almost certainly cater for long-term care and ensuring sufficient monies are available for the life of the claimant takes priority over providing for others following death. This does not mean that inheritance tax planning should not be considered. Indeed the use of trusts can ensure that the claimant maximises allowances without incurring significant costs.

FINANCIAL OBJECTIVES – INVESTMENT ADVICE

16.70 If you were to ask anyone what their financial objectives are when it comes to investment advice, they would probably say that they want a good return without taking any risk. Unfortunately there is an inherent relationship between risk and reward that makes this objective an impossible task. The greater the level of risk one is willing to take, the greater the expected returns. However, the greater the level of expected return, the greater the risk of fluctuations in the value of the capital. Conversely, the lower the level of risk, the safer the investment and the lower the level of expected return.

16.71 What compounds the importance of risk in personal injury cases is the fact that, almost without exception, if the award were depleted due to a fall in the value of the investments the claimant is not in a position to replace the capital by other means. Therefore, advising a recipient of an award of damages is wholly different from advising a lottery winner for example, although the sums may be of similar amounts. The judgment in *Wells v Wells* clearly sets out the court's view that PI claimants are a special class of investor for whom minimum risk is the only appropriate investment strategy.

16.72 Unless the amount of risk to which the portfolio is exposed is managed adequately, the claimant will not have peace of mind. There are two main ways of managing risk. First, to invest in range of investments over a range of inherent risk levels (for example, investing in a Russian Recovery Unit Trust is of higher risk than a With Profits Bond). Second, to pool the investments with others to increase the spread the risk within the investment (for example, investing in an insurance company's fund where assets are pooled with millions of others over thousands of individual companies has far less risk than a stockbroker investing the funds alone in a small number of shares in the UK market).

Risk Levels

16.73 Risk can be classified in many different ways. For illustrative purposes, the list below separates risk out into five categories.

Risk Level 1 (Low Risk)

I am cautious and dislike the risk. I prefer security of capital and predictable investments. I accept that this may result in low rates of return being earned on my portfolio. I also accept that interest returns from deposit based investments move up and down, sometimes quite suddenly and therefore there is no security of income.

Risk Level 2 (Below Average Risk)

I am prudent in my outlook. I am attracted to the security of lower risk investments, but I am willing to accept limited exposure to equity investments (stocks and shares). I am therefore prepared to accept a limited degree of fluctuation in the value of my capital in the hope of improved medium to long-term returns.

Risk Level 3 (Average Risk)

I regard myself as a balanced investor. Part of my portfolio should contain investments, which are for security of capital and/or access to capital. For medium to long-term investments, I will accept a broadly based approach which includes a significant proportion in equity based investments (stocks and shares). I am therefore prepared to accept a degree of fluctuation in the value of my capital in return for the potential of good medium to long-term rewards.

Risk Level 4 (Above Average Risk)

I am prepared to accept a higher than average degree of risk in my portfolio, in the hope of achieving well above average long-term returns. I accept that this strategy requires a high degree of exposure to equity investments (stocks and shares), and I understand the performance of such investments may be volatile.

Risk Level 5 (High Risk)

I am willing to accept a high level of risk in relation to my portfolio. I realise that such an approach may include investments in specialist funds and products whose performance may be highly volatile. I also appreciate that certain high-risk investments may not be readily realisable, as there may not be a ready market for the sale of such investments and that access to reliable data for valuing such investments may be restricted.

16.74   Most claimants cannot afford to expose their entire fund to Risk Level 5, because although the potential for exceptional returns is high, so is the risk that the value of the investments could fall sharply. However, the claimant probably will not be in a position to opt exclusively for Risk Level 1 due to the fact that the funds will be depleted in real terms if they do not realise returns above inflation and it is highly unlikely that there will be sufficient damages available to adopt this approach exclusively.

16.75   But what types of investments fall in each of the categories? The following list is by no means exhaustive.

Risk Level Type of Policy

1   Purchase of a property for the claimant; Bank and Building Society Accounts; National Savings Certificates; Structured Settlements; Gilts.

2   With Profits Bonds; Open-Ended Investment Companies (depending on the fund chosen); Unit Trusts (depending on the fund chosen).

3   Distribution Bonds; Open-Ended Investment Companies (depending on the fund chosen); Unit Trusts (depending on the fund chosen); Managed Bonds; Discretionary Portfolio

Management (depending on the shares chosen); Investment Division of the Public Trust Office Investment Scenario.

4   Open-Ended Investment Companies (depending on the fund chosen); Unit Trusts (depending on the fund chosen); Managed Bonds; Discretionary Portfolio Management (depending on the shares chosen); Investment Division of the Public Trust Office Investment Scenario.

5   Open-Ended Investment Companies (depending on the fund chosen); Unit Trusts (depending on the fund chosen); Managed Bonds; Discretionary Portfolio Management (depending on the shares chosen); Investment Division of the Public Trust Office Investment Scenario; Specialist Funds.

Insurance Company Investments v Stockbroker Funds

16.76 It was often considered that the optimum means of investing in stocks and shares was by way of a portfolio managed by a stockbroker. Insurance company investments were often considered less viable, not due to the returns realised, but because of perceived relatively high level of charges imposed. However, this is no longer the case. Indeed, due to the fact that they offer competitive returns at lower risk and compounded by recent tax changes, insurance company investments can be a much more tax efficient and safer means of investment than direct investments in the stock market via a stockbroker.

16.77 Insurance company investment bonds are basically a pooled form of equity investment funds that are offered by life insurance companies. The fund managers at the life companies will invest in a pool of stocks and shares. Rather than directly investing in shares on an individual basis, the funds will effectively be split into units and issued in the investment bonds.

16.78 For 'with profits' bonds, their aim is to grow in value and protect the investor from the inevitable fluctuations in the stock market. In addition, the return on the stocks and shares held within the fund are converted into annual bonuses that are added on to the bond. These bonuses, once added, cannot be taken away. The result is that the bond smoothes out the peaks and troughs of the performance of the underlying stocks and shares.

16.79 Under current tax legislation there is no personal liability to either basic rate income tax, or capital gains tax. These taxes are accounted for within the life company's fund, and also cannot be reclaimed. It is possible to withdraw up to 5% of the original investment each year with no immediate personal income tax liability. This applies for the first 20 years of the investment or until the full amount originally invested has been withdrawn. With good management the tax can be deferred even longer if the investment is rebased every few years, thus increasing the amount that can be withdrawn without incurring a tax liability.

16.80 From April 1999 taxation changes announced in the 1998 Finance Act replaced the indexation allowance with taper relief, for Capital Gains Tax ('CGT') purposes. This will significantly affect the ability of a stockbroker to actively manage the investment portfolio to achieve optimum equity returns. This is due to the fact that an actively managed portfolio of individual shares will, by definition be bought and sold on a regular basis. Under the old taxation system, relief was given for the rise in the cost of living index in the form of "indexation allowances". Following the imposition of taper relief, a reduction in the level of taxation will only be available if one asset is held for more than three years. As an actively managed portfolio is required to achieve an optimum shareholding, this will result in disposals of shares over the three year period which may result in higher CGT charges than under the pre-1998 tax regime. The new rules therefore act as a severe restriction to any actively managed, directly held portfolio of shares.

16.81–16.89   Each individual's own situation will determine which is the best route for him, or indeed whether that is a mixture of both. However, expert advice is required with regard to the tax implications of receiving the award of damages.

REMUNERATION FOR ADVISERS – COMMISSION v FEES

16.90   The way in which financial advisers are remunerated is often discussed. Should they should be retained on a contingent commission basis or a time-fee basis. The simple answer to the question is that they should be paid what they are worth and what both parties agree. Therefore, what they will do for their money needs to be considered.

16.91   Those retained on a fee basis may often be cheaper initially, however, it must be remembered that they will charge each and every occasion they service the portfolio and will charge for any work subsequently undertaken. The commission payable on significant portfolios might well be higher in the first instant but such an adviser should not charge for all subsequent servicing. Some investments do cost in an annual management fee (trail commission) which will remunerate the intermediary. There are clearly different ways to remunerate the adviser, which should be agreed up front in the initial client terms of business engagement letter.

16.92   The most important factor however, is the value an experienced adviser will add to the portfolio. Their expertise and experience should provide answers to the multitude of questions the client will have. Furthermore, having a lump of personal injury damages will more often than not cause the client more worry than it takes away. The adviser's job is to provide, over a period of time, steady but strong returns that allow the claimant to plan the rest of their life, safe in the knowledge that they have sufficient funds to provide for their needs. This is no simple task and it will not happen overnight. It is the expertise, knowledge and understanding that the client is paying for.

CONCLUSIONS

16.93   Investment advice is probably the most overlooked aspect of a personal injury claim. When it is considered it is almost invariably at the very last moment and usually it is not considered at all. If the client has been told to take independent advice, some obligations have been fulfilled. However, just fulfilling obligations is not enough. Without effective advice, at worst the client is likely to find himself in severe financial crisis, and at best he is likely to have ongoing concerns about his financial future.

16.94   Advisers should not tell the client what he can or cannot spend his damages on or when to spend them. They act merely as a financial conscience, explaining the consequences of any set of actions. They advise and allow their clients to make informed decisions. History has illustrated that, in the long run, markets have always grown. However, the adviser does not have a magic wand and there will be instances when economic conditions will conspire against the portfolio, but that is when the balance and flexibility built into the portfolio will hopefully allow for the tide to turn.

16.95   Without due consideration of the low level of risk a recipient of personal injury damages can accept, the portfolio will not provide the claimant with a secure future. But at the same time it should be accepted that such a strategy may realise lower returns. However, if a strong secure base that will provide safe and steady returns is built, other parts of the portfolio can be invested for the longer term in the higher risk investments. As with so many other aspects of life, it is all about a proper, informed basis.

16.96   The decision in *Wells v Wells* highlighted clearly the problems that face the investment requirements of a PI claimant. While Risk Level 1 strategies are not very sexy, the courts now compensate claimants for this by changing the mechanism by which future losses are calculated by increasing the multipliers. There is the inherent assumption by the courts that PI investors should not have to carry anything other than the minimum level of risk. It therefore makes most sense for the client to have a mixed portfolio, one that provides the bedrock of the essential requirements, typically a suitable home and a structured settlement to provide a lifetime tax-free income. Thereafter more adventurous strategies can be bolted on to the portfolio.

16.97   Ensuring that the client receives effective financial advice at all stages of the litigation process will maximise the damages regardless of the level of the award. Remember that every client is an individual and his needs are individual. What may be best advice for one client may be wholly unsuitable for another. Ensure that each client has the opportunity to make the most of his award. In the most catastrophic cases, the client will only get one chance to get it right. The damages have to last his lifetime and that will not happen by accident.

Chapter 17

Structured Settlements

John Frenkel FCA
James Dadge

INTRODUCTION

17.1 Structured settlements are now entrenched in the personal injury litigation framework. This may seem like a bold statement to practitioners who are considering a structured settlement for the first time, or have only handled a few such settlements. However, considering that the first structured settlement in the United Kingdom was only implemented in 1989,[1] an estimated 1,000 cases have compromised by way of a structured settlement. This is a noteworthy achievement given the fact that the lump sum method of compensation has been in existence for centuries.

  1 *Kelly v Dawes* (1990) Times, 27 September.

17.2 In this chapter the aim is to provide the personal injury practitioner with a brief background of the historical development of structured settlements in the United Kingdom, to set out a practical guide to the use of structures and to illustrate their advantages to claimants, defendants and the litigation process as a whole. The practitioner will be shown that structured settlements are a dynamic tool which are useful in many different personal injury litigation circumstances, providing pre-settlement negotiation assistance, saving time and costs for the defendant seeking an early settlement and providing tax-free financial security for the lifetime of the claimant.

17.3 Structured settlements are unique products, and cannot be placed into any one category. Their subject matter overlaps the boundaries of forensic accountancy alternative dispute resolution and investment advice. They have received glowing tributes and support from claimants, defendants, lawyers, barristers, the judiciary and even from politicians.

THE HISTORICAL DEVELOPMENT OF STRUCTURED SETTLEMENTS

What is a Structured Settlement?

17.4 A structured settlement allows those receiving an award of damages following a personal injury or fatal accident to receive a proportion of their damages in the form of a series of guaranteed tax-free, index linked annual payments for life.

17.5   A structured settlement can only be implemented with the consent of both parties. There can be no formal acceptance of all the settlement monies by the claimant, as this will taint the tax-free status of the structured settlement.

The North American Experience

17.6   Settlements have been a feature of personal injury and workers compensation awards in the USA for over 25 years. While such forms of settlement are now extremely popular, they are principally driven by the general insurers and rely heavily on agreement between the parties. In only a handful of states does the judiciary have the power to formally award a structured settlement and even then only in very limited circumstances.

17.7   In Canada, structured settlements have been in existence for over 15 years and are principally claimant driven. It was only in the late 1980s that a formal statute was passed which simplified the mechanics of paying structures, providing a clear framework to be followed by those involved. The judiciary has the power to award a structured settlement but, as in the USA, only in very limited circumstances. For a judge to award periodical payments a number of criteria are applied to the circumstances of the case, for example, if the claimant is a minor, if accepting the award will mean a large liability to tax or where there is a considerable need for future care costs.

The Development of Structures in the United Kingdom

17.8   Structured settlements first arose in the UK as a result of discussions between the Inland Revenue and the Association of British Insurers ('ABI') in 1985. From these discussions a framework was devised by 1987, which allowed for structured settlements to be given tax-free status without having to specifically change current tax law. Based on the obscure 1936 tax case of *Dott v Brown*[1] it was held that the instalment payments made under a structured settlement were to be viewed as a capital debt, being discharged by instalments over the lifetime of the claimant, and not income. The validity of any structured settlement centered around a single document drawn up between the parties known as the 'model agreement'. The model agreement had to be drafted in the form as approved by the Inland Revenue and the ABI and any deviation from that form prejudiced the tax advantage of the structure.

1   [1936] 1 All ER 543, 154 LT 484, 80 Sol Jo 245, CA.

17.9   The practical framework created allowed for damages in personal injury or fatal accident cases to be paid, wholly or in part, by means of tax-free periodic payments for the life of the claimant and essentially consisted of:

(a) the defendant insurer agreeing to provide periodic payments to the claimant for his lifetime;
(b) the defendant insurer then reinsured his obligations to the claimant by purchasing an annuity from a life office;
(c) the life office made monthly payments, less tax (as they were obliged to deduct tax at source), to the defendant insurer;
(d) the defendant insurer 'grossed-up' the annuity payment and passed it on to the claimant;

(e) the defendant insurer then reclaimed the tax from the Inland Revenue at the end of the tax year.

17.10 The defendant insurer was obliged to administer the transfer of payments to the claimant. In addition, it suffered a loss of cash flow as it could only reclaim the tax deducted at source by the life office at the end of each financial year. The case of *Burke v Tower Hamlets Health Authority*,[1] in which the court of first instance held that an award for periodic payments could only be made if both parties consented, affirmed that a structured settlement could not be imposed on either party. As a result, the defendant insurer would often seek a discount on the award of damages in order to secure its agreement to implement a structured settlement. Discounts typically ranged from between 5% and 15% of the amount structured.

1   (1989) Times, 10 August, [1989] CLY 1201.

The Impetus for Change

17.11 The above position was seen as cumbersome and restricted the wider use of structured settlements. In order to address the limitations of the model agreement and formulate potential alternatives, the Law Commission published Consultation Paper No 125 in October 1992. Having received responses from parties as wide-ranging as The Public Trust Office, The British Coal Association, the British Medical Association and Lloyds of London, the Law Commission recommended sweeping changes to the structured settlement system in Paper No 224 published in September 1994.

17.12 They advocated that '[a] life office should be able to make payments free of tax direct to the claimant as the annuitant under an annuity bought for her or him from the office by the defendant (or defendant insurer) who will apply for this purpose as part of the damages, which would be payable by the defendant to the claimant'. Effectively, this would allow the claimant to own the structured settlement annuity policy purchased by the defendant insurer on his behalf and release the defendant insurer from any future administrative burden. In addition, those in receipt of payments from structured settlement annuity policies should have the protection under the Policyholders Protection Act 1975 ('PPA 1975') increased from 90% to 100%, to give complete security of payment in all eventualities.

17.13 Having considered the responses to the Discussion Paper No 125, the Law Commission remained against the introduction of the claimant, the defendant or the judiciary having the authority to impose a structured settlement on one or other of the parties involved. They concluded that at this stage it was premature to grant the power of imposition to the court, preferring instead that the 'reform of structured settlements should be confined to rationalisation and building on the voluntary system'.

THE PRESENT POSITION

17.14 The Law Commission reports were clearly taken to heart and a number of legislative changes took place.

The Finance Act 1995

17.15   The first and probably most significant legislative change came with the Finance Act 1995. Section 142 inserted the provision into s 329A of the Income and Corporation Taxes Act 1988 that where:

> ´...
>
> (a) an agreement is made settling a claim or action for damages for personal injury;
> (b) under the agreement the damages are to consist wholly or partly of periodical payments; and
> (c) under the agreement the person entitled to the payments is to receive them as the annuitant under one or more annuities purchased for him by the person against whom the claim or action is brought, or, if he is insured against the claim concerned, by his insurer ...
>
> (3) Subsection (4) below applies where:
> (a) a person receives a sum as the annuitant under an annuity purchased for him pursuant to a qualifying agreement; or
> (b) a person receives a sum on behalf of the annuitant under an annuity purchased for the annuitant pursuant to a qualifying agreement.
>
> (4) Where this subsection applies the sum shall not be regarded as the recipient's or annuitant's income for any purposes of income tax and accordingly shall be paid without any deduction under s 349(1).´

17.16   This was an important piece of legislation for all involved in structured settlements as it gave legislative ratifification to the tax-free status of structured settlement payments. The previously cumbersome system was now replaced by a more streamlined system for establishing the periodical payments under the structure, that is:

(a) the defendant insurer agrees to provide periodic payments to the claimant;

(b) the defendant insurer purchases an annuity from a life office, with the claimant as the policyholder;

(c) the life office makes monthly payments free of taxation and direct to the claimant;

(d) the defendant insurer closes its files on the case and has no further liability.

17.17   Essentially, this enabled the defendant insurer to purchase an annuity from a life office on behalf of the claimant and the life office could make these payments gross of tax and direct to the claimant. This eliminated the ongoing involvement of the defendant insurer allowing it to close its file on completion of a case. Consequently, the justification for discounts to cover the defendant insurer's administrative burden had also been removed.

17.18   Section 142, in para 17.15, refers to an agreement setting out damages which can consist 'wholly or partly' of periodical payments. Thus, to structure is not an all or nothing decision. Depending on the circumstances of the case the claimant can agree with the defendant to receive the entire award on a structured basis or, much more likely, just a proportion.

17.19 Unfortunately s 142 fell short of the provision for all circumstances in which structured settlements may arise. The section only provided for those 'entitled to the payments' to have the structured settlement annuities 'purchased' by the 'insurer'. The cases where annuity policies were not actually purchased by the defendant insurer were: they would have been provided by a self-funding arrangement (see 'self-funded structured settlements'); by the life arm of a mutual insurer (as one cannot by law purchase something from yourself); because there was no insurer involved in the action; or because the claimant was not actually entitled to the monies awarded, the legislative changes did not apply.

17.20 For example, cases involving the Criminal Injuries Compensation Board (where the applicant is not entitled to damages as such but compensation is in the form of an award from the Board), the Motor Insurers' Bureau ('MIB') (for uninsured drivers as there is no insurer), and the Medical Defence Organisations (as they indemnify and not insure) were all excluded from s 142.

17.21 The anomaly with regard to awards made in respect of criminal acts was remedied by the Criminal Injuries Compensation Act 1995. Section 8 of that Act inserted the provision into s 329B of the Income and Corporation Taxes Act 1988 which allowed awards from the CICB to be used to purchase a structured settlement.

The Finance Act 1996

17.23 Effectively, a two-tier system remained prevalent consisting of those that could and those that could not benefit from incorporating a structured settlement into their award until the Finance Act 1996 ('FA 1996'). Section 150, Schedule 26 of FA 1996 provided the required amendments to the 1995 Act thereby ensuring that:

> 'The periodical payments ... [may] consist of payments under one or more annuities purchased or provided for, or for the benefit of, [the plaintiff] by the person by whom the payments would otherwise fall to be made.'

17.24 Consequently, structured settlements could now be provided either by a self-funding arrangement or the provision of a policy by the life arm of a mutual insurer. FA 1996, by referring to 'the person by whom the payments would otherwise fall to be made', placed the onus of funding the structured settlement on those who indemnify, rather than insure, known or unknown individuals. For example, a structured settlement could now be funded by payments from the MIB in the case of an uninsured driver.

The Damages Act 1996

17.25 Finally, the most recent piece of legislation to impact upon structured settlements was the Damages Act 1996 ('DA 1996'). Indeed, no less than six of the eight sections were concerned with completing the reforms required to establish structured settlements as the safest form of 'investment' available in the UK. In line with the Law Commission's recommendations, s 4 of DA 1996 increases the 90% policy protection afforded under the terms of the PPA 1975 to 100%. Therefore, in the event that the life office from which the annuity was purchased should go into liquidation and could, therefore, no longer provide the periodic payments, then the Policyholders Protection Board guarantees to provide in full for the provisions of the policy.

17.26 The overall result of the above legislative changes was to significantly simplify the payment process and to ensure the tax-free status and security of structured settlements. They are now the most secure form of guaranteed return currently available in the investment market. The Acts have finally created a level playing-field, allowing all recipients of personal injury or fatal accident awards the opportunity to benefit from structured settlements. Indeed, all of the proposals put forward in the Law Commission's Report No 224 have now been enacted, making it their most successful recommendation paper to date.

17.27 In summary, the present framework for cases where structured settlements are implemented, consists of:

(a) the defendant insurer purchases an annuity from the life office on behalf of the claimant to provide periodic payments;

(b) the life office makes gross monthly payments, free of tax, direct to the claimant;

(c) as no tax is payable, the Inland Revenue have no involvement. However, there must still be a qualifying agreement signed by both parties to the action;

(d) the defendant insurer closes its file on implementation;

(e) the claimant receives a series of tax free, periodical payments, 100% secured by statute.

17.28 In addition, as the Acts were retrospective, structured settlement annuity policies already in place under the previous framework could be assigned from the defendant insurer to the claimant. Accordingly, following the assignment; the claimant received full cover under PPA 1975 and the defendant was discharged from their ongoing administration responsibilities.

17.29 It is essential to remember that the monies providing the periodical payments under the structured settlement must come from the defendant. If they are seen as coming from the claimant then the tax-free status of the payments will be tainted. However, there can be an interlocutory judgment, on liability or quantum, and this will not prejudice the tax-free status.[1] It is clear that the claimant must not formally accept the damages. It is acceptable for a claimant to indicate that sums standing in court are acceptable and to request that a structured settlement is investigated, but formal acceptance should be contingent on the satisfaction of a suitable investigation into the structure.

1 *Everett v Carter* [1991] 7 PMILL No 8.

THE CLAIMANT'S PERSPECTIVE

17.30 The overriding principle of damages is to put the claimant back in the position he would have been in but for the accident, as far as is possible in financial terms. This means that usually a claimant will receive a 'lump sum' which has been calculated with reference to the claimant's future recurring annual losses, taking into account his life expectation and future rates of investment returns. Once the claimant receives the award, it is invested to produce income that is withdrawn, together with capital, to provide for those annual losses.

Risk of Dissipation

17.31 The lump sum investor (that is, the claimant) is faced with many vagaries, which can affect the lump sum investment. On receiving an award of damages for personal injury, the claimant and his advisers are faced with the difficult task of providing for the claimant's future income, taking into account future rates of taxation, investment returns, inflation and the claimant's own life expectation. The further difficulty arises where the claimant's capital is more likely to be fully eroded later in life, when perhaps his care costs are greater.

Risk of Exhaustion

17.32 The adviser must, therefore, balance the need to provide income, especially in the later years, against the requirement to preserve capital. Taking all these matters into account, the claimant is either over-compensated for the loss, and will have large amounts of capital left for the benefit of his estate, or under-compensated, in that the lump sum will be fully exhausted before the claimant dies. The Law Commission's Consultation Paper No 125 makes specific reference to this point (page 16). Structured settlement payments are linked to the life of the claimant. There is, therefore, no danger of the structured element of the award being exhausted, as payments will continue for the life of the claimant.

Taxation

17.33 An award of damages is paid over to the claimant free of any taxation. However, once that award is invested it will be subject to income tax and capital gains tax. This can effectively reduce the claimant's income as required to provide for loss of earnings, annual care costs, rehabilitation costs and other annual requirements. Also, awards over £500,000, once invested, will potentially generate levels of income that would take the claimant into punitive levels of high-rate tax. Awards are made without any reference to future levels of taxation, and are only increased to take into account the possibility of paying punitive levels of high-rate tax in *exceptional circumstances*.[1]

1   *Hodgson v Trapp* [1989] AC 807, [1988] 3 All ER 870, HL; *Wells v Wells* [1999] 1 AC 345, [1998] 3 All ER 481, HL.

17.34 It is axiomatic that by receiving a proportion of his damages via tax-free periodical payments, the claimant is placed in an extremely tax efficient way of limiting the tax liabilities. Taking the example of a paraplegic who receives an award of £750,000, an investment of this size would almost certainly attract tax at the highest rate. A basic and efficient way of managing the taxation problem would be to 'invest' £250,000 under a structured settlement. The residual funds available to the claimant would be £500,000, which when invested would produce an income beneath the higher rate threshhold. This method of limiting the claimant's future liability to tax is known as 'top-slicing' and is illustrated by the following examples.

Example 1
Top-slicing: Implications of damages of £750,000 all as lump sum
Assuming an investment return of 5% on £750,000 in year one, the immediate implications to income tax are as follows:

Gross income produced	£37,500	A
Personal allowance	£4,335	
Taxable income	£33,165	
£28,000 taxed at 20% = Tax liability of £5,600		
£5,165 taxed at 40% = Tax liability of £2,066		
Total tax liability	£7,666	B
Net income =	£29,834	that is A–B

Example 2
Top-Slicing: Implications of receiving £500,000 as a lump sum, plus £250,000 placed in a structured settlement

£250,000 in structured settlement providing tax-free income of £9,000; (A)
Assuming an investment return of 5% on £500,000 in year one, the immediate implications to income tax are as follows:

Gross income produced	£25,000	B
Personal allowance	£4,335	
Taxable income	£20,665	
£20,665 taxed at 20% = Tax liability of £4,133		C

Total net income is therefore £29,867 (A+B+C) with no liability to punitive levels of high rate tax.

Rates of Return

17.35   The returns achieved on structured settlements are expressed net of tax. To determine the real rate of return the notional yield must be grossed up to include taxation at the applicable rate. Assuming a structured settlement costing £300,000 produces an immediate annual sum of £10,000 the notional net yield produced would be 3.33%. This net return would equate to a gross return of 4.33% for a basic rate taxpayer, and 5.55% for a higher rate taxpayer.

17.36   With a retail price index linked structured settlement, the rate of return would increase in line with the corresponding increase in the retail price index. Assuming inflation increases at 3% per annum, after 10 years the structured settlement payments would be at £13,048, which, based on the original cost, would equate to a net yield of 4.35%, and a gross return of 5.65% for basic rate tax and 7.25% for higher rate tax.

17.37   Furthermore, if the same scenario is adopted assuming inflation at 5%, after 10 years, the structured settlement payments would be £15,513, a net yield of 5.17%, equating to a gross yield of 6.72% for basic rate tax and 8.62% for high rate tax. Thus, while an initial yield of 3.33% may not appear to be attractive at first glance, the fact that the majority of structured settlements are linked to the retail price index must be considered, as the yield will therefore increase with inflation. While we are currently experiencing low levels of inflation, it is interesting to note that only nine years ago, in 1990, inflation was as high as 9.3%.

Life Expectation

17.38 Where the claimant and defendant are in dispute over life expectation there is a potential problem with regard to the multipliers to be applied. A structured settlement can resolve these issues over life expectancy. On investigating a structured settlement, medical reports relating to the claimant's life expectation are submitted to the structured settlement life offices for an underwriting decision. In catastrophic personal injury claims, there are often significant disparities on future life expectancy between the defendant and claimant's medical reports.

17.39 The underwriting decision obtained for the structured settlement is an independent view of the claimant's life expectation. As is pointed out in the Law Commission's Paper No 125, the Master of the Court of Protection undertook an informal survey from 1988, which revealed that in some of the personal injury cases dealt with, the medical prognosis was substantially incorrect. The mistakes covered forecasts as to expectation of life and, in general, an unrealistically pessimistic view of life expectation was taken. Damages based on such prognoses were seen to both over- and under-compensate, leading to a 'hit and miss' basis of compensation on the multiplier and multiplicand system.

17.40 Structured settlements can, at least in part, overcome this problem since the payments on life contingent structured settlements will continue for as long as the claimant is alive. Thus, if the claimant survives beyond even the most optimistic of medical prognosis, there will be no danger of the award being exhausted. Additionally, it means that the claimant can 'benefit' from the pessimistic medical reports obtained on behalf of the defendant, as the structured settlement rates are worked out on an impaired life basis. The more severe the injury and the greater the reduction in life expectation, the greater the increase on the structured settlement yield.

Peace of Mind

17.41 Receiving a large award of damages can also be a daunting prospect for many claimants. A large cash fund requiring frugal investment planning can expose claimants to risks of dissipating the award, resulting in recourse to public funds, and/or possible destitution. There have been many studies commissioned both in the UK and the United States investigating the use of awards of damages and the overwhelming evidence is that there are very great risks of dissipation of the award.

Restoration of Near Financial Normality

17.42 The Law Commission Paper No 224 refers to an empirical study in the late 1970s in the USA, which found that 25% of recipients had dissipated their awards at the end of one month, with 90% having nothing left after five years. While this evidence may not be the best comparison to large awards for catastrophic injury in the United Kingdom, Professor Hazel Genn of Queen Mary & Westfield College, London, was instructed by the Law Commission in 1993 to examine the adequacy of settlements in meeting the needs for claimants. Claimants who had received £100,000 or more were asked if they would have preferred to have received a proportion of their award in the form of periodical payments. Of those questioned, 31% expressed a preference. Structured settlements allow for the claimant to receive a series of manageable periodical payments into their bank accounts. In some instances, the structure will assist with rehabilitating the claimant. The payments can be made monthly, much like a salary, which can make financial and investment management decisions so much easier to plan.

Investment Risks

17.43 A further problem arises with the fact that the claimant requires security from the lump sum. The case of *Wells v Wells* established that recipients of awards of damages are not in the position of ordinary investors, and that they should not be expected to take unnecessary investment risks. It was, therefore, held that claimants should expect to invest in a portfolio of secure stocks, such as index linked government stocks. Structured settlements have the same level of investment security as index linked government stocks, as this was conferred to them under the Damages Act 1996. In the event of the body making the structured settlement payments encountering financial difficulties then the law ensures that the structured settlement payments are met in full.

17.44 The claimant also needs to be able to rely on the fact that sufficient income can be produced to provide lifetime income for rehabilitation, care, loss of earnings and so on. There are no other investment vehicles that provide lifetime, tax-free, guaranteed investment returns. The rate of interest offered by banks and building societies is very much set by the rates prevalent in the Bank of England's base rates. The dividend yield on equities is dependent on the economic performance of individual companies in which the share is held. Over the last 20 years the annual dividend yield has fluctuated from a high of 27.7% in 1979 to a low of 0% in 1992. In no two successive years has dividend yield been the same. This uncertain return is clearly not the type of guaranteed return that claimants require.

17.45 The coupon returned on gilts is a guaranteed return, but only if the coupon is held for the duration of the gilt, otherwise the returns on these investments are not guaranteed. It is possible to invest in certain investment products that guarantee a minimum rate of return, but often the rates offered are not competitive. There is always a direct relationship between risk and reward. The higher the reward demanded, the higher the risk that has to be taken.

Effects of Inflation

17.46 The claimant must also be advised on the erosive affect that inflation will have on the award of damages. Over the last 20 years, annual inflation has fluctuated from a high of 15.2% in 1980, to a low of 1.9% in 1993. In no two successive years has inflation been the same. One way claimants can protect themselves against the effects of inflation is to invest in a portfolio of index linked government stocks. The majority of structured settlements written in the United Kingdom have been linked to the retail price index. This ensures that the payments will rise in line with the cost of living and, thus, maintain their purchasing power against inflation.

Investment Choices

17.7   Investing an award of damages can be a daunting prospect for the claimant and his advisers. There are four essential links in the chain in a catastrophic personal injury claim, namely liability, causation, quantum and investment advice. It is often the last link in the chain that is given the least consideration. Although the legal advisers will have finished their jobs once the liability, causation and quantum have been resolved, from the claimant's point of view the most difficult and important link has yet to be addressed. How the claimant should deal with the money to produce income and capital growth, in an uncertain investment and inflation environment, where tax regimes change are always complicated and all this over an indeterminable period, that is, the claimant's lifetime (and possibly beyond as well).

17.48   In cases where the claimant is a patient under the Court of Protection, the directions of the Investment Division of the Public Trust Office will govern the investment choices.

17.49   In making comparisons with other investment vehicles one must remember that the structured settlement is currently the *only one* that offers 100% protection and 100% tax free status for life.

The Court of Protection

17.50   Approval of the Court of Protection is required in cases involving claimants who by reason of mental disability cannot handle their own affairs. This will usually mean that should a structured settlement be implemented in such a case, a report will be required detailing the structured settlement's merits in the particular case as compared to the merits of receiving the award in the conventional lump sum manner.

17.51   The report should deal with the claimant's individual circumstances and anticipated future levels of income requirements given his likely life expectation. The report should include an appraisal of the taxation advantages of the structured settlement, the advantages of any index-linking under the periodical payments against the relative disadvantages of receiving a proportion of damages in the structured fashion.

17.52   While a report has always has to be done to justify a structured settlement, to date there has been no reciprocal obligation, that is, a report satisfying why a structured settlement is not being done. Given that a structured settlement has traditionally been seen as a departure from the 'conventional' route that has made sense to date. However, given the widespread adoption of structured settlements, it is debatable whether or not financial reports should be done in both sets of circumstances; that is, to justify having a structured settlement and to justify *not* having a structured settlement. The report should then be submitted to the Court of Protection for consideration of the structured settlement, typically with counsel's opinion endorsing this method of settlement.

The Defendant's Perspective

17.53 Since the Finance Act 1996 effectively ended the practice of defendants benefiting from the right to negotiate discounts due to the continuing administrative burden, their involvement now ends with the signing of the agreement. Many insurance companies have taken the view that once the level of damages has been agreed all the benefits of structuring fall in favour of the claimant. Consequently, they consider that they should not bear any costs involved in the investigation of the structured settlement.

17.54 Indeed it has been argued that in the case of a 'top down' structured settlement, where a compromised lump sum figure has been reached with the claimant being given the option to structure any portion he sees fit, the investigation constitutes future financial advice. In *Francis v Bostock*[1] it was held that a claimant could not claim from the defendant any costs to cover future financial advice (as compared to tax advice regarding the completion of tax returns and so on, which are generally recoverable), as any advice given should add value in its own right. Therefore, as the defendant insurer's consent is still required, most consider it only equitable that while they are willing to allow the claimant the opportunity to benefit from a structured settlement, they do not see why they should pay for the claimant's privilege.

1   (1985) Times, 9 November.

17.55 Once a conventional lump sum award has been compromised between the parties, it can be more difficult for the defendant insurer to benefit from the structured settlement process. It was always considered that in order for structured settlements to evolve, both parties should benefit in some way: the 'win-win' scenario. Therefore, a different approach is necessary. As an alternative, if negotiations are considered from a 'needs-based' perspective, both sides are able to work together to meet the claimant's needs at a cost acceptable to the defendant.

17.56 By removing the contentious nature of the litigation process, the 'bottom-up' structured settlement can assist in achieving compromise in a cost effective and time efficient manner. By examining the claimant's future annual requirements, investigations can be carried out as to whether it is cost effective for the defendant to provide for those needs via a structured settlement. This is known as the 'bottom-up' approach. The defendants should have the possibility of discharging their liability much sooner than considered achievable by the lump sum method and at an acceptable total cost. Although this approach will not work in every case, settlements of this type are becoming much more common. Drawing a parallel with US cases, many US casualty insurers contend that by taking this route they can save on average between 8% and 18% per case due to the savings in time and costs.

17.57 With the consolidation of the UK life and insurance markets, many general insurers have acquired vested interests in companies providing life insurance products. There is obvious benefit in the defendant insurer providing the structured settlement annuities from their own life arm. In effect, the insurer can pay that part of an award that is structured to another part of its own group. In addition, government departments such as the Ministry of Defence and the

Department of Health have considered that investigating a 'bottom-up' structured settlement will have numerous advantages in terms of saving time and costs to the Treasury.

17.58–17.59 Changes under the Civil Procedure Reforms have meant that defendants should consider alternative means of resolving claims, with particular regard to alternative dispute resolution. The introduction of structured settlement intermediaries to investigate and discuss the possibility of settling claims using periodical payments may increase, as there may well be tactical advantages to the defendant in introducing the question of a structured settlement much earlier on in the process.

THE JUDICIARY'S VIEW

17.60–17.64 The judiciary have been very much in favour of structured settlements as is shown in the following judgments approving the settlement of cases by this means:

Per Turner J (March 1991, unreported):
One is prompted to wonder why greater use is not made of the enormously beneficial process of structured settlements in these cases, and it is manifestly not only to the claimant's collective advantage but also the defendant's as well ... which may be a suitable prelude to the fact that I have no hesitation in approving the method of disposal of this action.

Per Judge J in *Moxon v Senior* (10 July 1991, unreported)
'... it is difficult to see any reason why the parties should not at the very least always consider whether a structured settlement would not provide the most advantageous arrangement for the claimant. If, after such a settlement has been considered, it may emerge for a whole variety of reasons that it would not suit the particular claimant then that is well and good and he can make his own decision about it. But where in a case such as this the claimant is either under disability or indeed may be an infant and the settlement requires the approval of the court, I should have thought, speaking for myself, that hereafter I should be likely to require to be satisfied that a structured settlement has been fully investigated on behalf of such a claimant and if it is considered inappropriate in the particular circumstances the reasons for that conclusion explained in court to me.'

Per Sedley J in the Royal Courts of Justice (9 October 1992, unreported) said that the purpose of the structured settlement is:
'... to remove as many of the uncertainties as can be removed from the perennial problem of either over or under compensating a claimant in making projections for the future. It is a valuable tool which can relieve the courts of many of the worries that future projections of loss inevitably involve and which, with the use of actuarial methods, makes it possible to distribute the burden through annuities.

As per Holland J in *Wells v Mehes* (October 1996, unreported)
'I am entirely satisfied that a quite excellent settlement has been arrived at, and what particularly pleases me about it is the fact that it is now going to be

converted into a structured settlement so that [the claimant] will be getting these payments tax free with the benefit of index-linking for the rest of his life.

One thing I learned, both as a barrister and as a judge, was just how advantageous that is. I vividly remember meeting the mother of someone very like [the claimant] whom I had to advise some years after the settlement. I met her in the street and she told me then that the one thing that had gone absolutely right over the intervening period was the structured settlement, the regular arrival of cheques without the worry of tax, without the worry of retail price index going up. So from her, through me, you have a personal commendation of the advantages of this.'

Per Lord Steyn in *Wells v Wells* [1999] 1 AC 345, [1998] 3 All ER 481
'... there is a major structural flaw in the present [lump sum] system ... which ... causes acute problems in cases of serious injuries with consequences enduring after the assessment of damages. It is a wasteful system since the courts are sometimes compelled to award large sums that turn out not to be needed. It is true, of course, that there is a statutory provision of periodic payments. But the court only has this power if both parties agree ... The solution is relatively straightforward. The court ought to be given the power of its own motion to make an award for periodic payments rather than a lump sum in appropriate cases. Such a power is perfectly consistent with the principle of full compensation for pecuniary loss.

THE IMPACT OF THE CIVIL PROCEDURE RULES

17.65 Structured settlements and the Woolf reforms are inter-linked. The overriding objectives of the Woolf reforms are to enable the courts to deal with cases fairly, to ensure that the parties are on an equal footing, to allow cases to be dealt with expeditiously and generally to save time and costs.

17.66 There are a number of rule changes in the reforms that directly affect the role of structured settlements in personal injury litigation, principally Part 36 and the role of alternative dispute resolution.

Part 36 Offers/payments In

17.67 Either the claimant or the defendant can make Part 36 offers. The offer of settlement can be made for a specific part of the claim or for the entire settlement. It can be made prior to the commencement of proceedings, and, if made, can be taken into account by the trial judge should the case proceed to trial.

17.68 The important point to bear in mind for a Part 36 offer to be effective is that the offer to settle the claim only needs to be more 'beneficial' for the claimant than the award made by the judge. Therefore, the offer to settle need not be quantified in a lump sum basis. Either party can make the offer of settlement and it can apply to the whole or a specific part of the award, for instance future care costs.

17.69 Although at present a judge cannot impose a structured settlement, the rule changes do seem to add weight to the pro-imposition lobby via the possibility of a costs sanction to either side. If a structured settlement is raised and rejected at an early stage, then if later that party obtains a less favourable settlement the question arises as to what sanction the courts possess given the current inability to formally impose a structure on either party. A possible solution is that a costs sanction on the offending party could ensure that litigants are compelled to consider seriously a structured settlement as a means of settling personal injury claims.

17.70   An unnamed solicitor was quoted in the Financial Times on 26 April 1999 as saying:

> 'I am acting for an insurance company. I have to use any tactic I can, to pay as little as possible to the claimant. I intend to put the claimant to as much trouble as possible ... mediation is simply not appropriate where you have institutions like insurance companies.'

We can all assume that following the Woolf reforms, with its emphasis on joint instruction, mediation, saving time and costs, the above unnamed solicitor should hopefully find life rather difficult in the future.

Self-funded Structured Settlements

17.71   The single difference between a self-funded structured settlement and an annuity backed structured settlement is that no annuity policy is ever purchased by the defendant. The periodic payments are made directly from the defendant to the claimant. The defendant agrees to match the most competitive structured settlement annuity quotation available in the open market, retaining out of the damages the notional purchase price that would have otherwise funded the structured settlement.

17.72   Although this option is available to any defendant or his insurer/ indemnifier, it is usually only acceptable to the claimant when offered by a government department, such as the Department of Health, the Ministry of Defence or the Welsh Office. This is due to the fact that if no structured settlement annuity is purchased, no policy exists and, therefore, the PPA 1975 does not protect the claimant. The self-funded alternative will only be acceptable to claimants if it offers the same benefits, terms and guarantees as the annuity backed option. In the case of a government department, the NHS (Residual Liabilities) Act 1996 and the Damages Act 1996 provided a statutory guarantee that the future payments would be met in any event. Section 1 of the NHS (Residual Liabilities) Act 1996 ensures that if a health authority or trust ceases to exist the Secretary of State has statutory powers to transfer all liabilities, thereby ensuring that all payments are met. The Damages Act 1996 broadened this guarantee to encompass all government departments and public sector bodies. No such guarantee exists if an insurer/indemnifier were to self-fund the payments.

17.73   Government departments now opt to self-fund almost all of the structured settlements they establish. It is considered that, by retaining the notional purchase price of the structure and funding the periodic payments out of future budgets, significant cash flow savings are made. Indeed, the Treasury considers that it can almost always provide an annuity more cheaply than that provided by any commercial life office, based on the assumption that they do not cost in profits, income collection, advertising and they do adopt a different discount rate to the private sector.

17.74 The only provision insisted on by the National Health Service Litigation Authority ('NHSLA'), is with regard to the inclusion of minimum payment periods. They regard their liability to be to the injured party only for the duration of their lifetime. It is not considered to be the public purse's responsibility to continue making payments to an individual's estate following death. Therefore, the NHSLA tends to insist on any structured settlement payments being guaranteed for life only, with no minimum payment period. Exception is only granted in the possible event of the claimant's immediate family being rendered with no other option than to recourse to public funds in the event of the claimant's early death.

17.75 Such is the success of self-funded structured settlements within the Health Service, the NHS Executive issued guidelines (FDL (96) 34 in July 1996), which stated that:

> 'Structured settlements should always be considered for settlements of £250,000 and above, and may represent good value for money for smaller settlements as well.'

The Ministry of Defence has also issued similar guidelines.

17.76–17.79 By 'consideration' one must assess whether the implementation of a self-funded structured settlement would provide the public purse as a whole with 'value for money'. Not only must one assess the cash-flow savings made by self-funding, but also such implications as the amount of income tax foregone because of the tax-free status of that to a portion of the award. One must calculate the possibility of the alternative capital lump sum being fully exhausted, and the cost of the state providing care thereafter. These considerations are then set out in a formal report and submitted for approval. Only if the self-funded structured settlement indicates a saving to the Department of Health and Treasury will authorisation be given.

STRUCTURED SETTLEMENTS IN PRACTICE – A CASE STUDY

17.80 In this section we will consider a catastrophic case scenario.

Case Study – Background Data

Mr Smith (the claimant) was injured in a road traffic accident, sustaining severe injuries to his spinal column. As a result of the accident he was rendered paraplegic and is now wheelchair dependent. Liability is not in issue and the claimant can expect to receive 100% of his damages from the defendant, who is covered by an insurance policy issued by Northsouth Insurance.

The claimant now aged 25 was formerly employed as a motorcycle mechanic. He has not returned to work since the accident and is unlikely to return to work as a mechanic. He is, in reality, likely to have a sporadic earning capacity at best. He is married and lives in a terraced house with his wife. They hope to move to a more suitable accommodation following the receipt of the award of damages.

Due to the injuries that he has sustained his expectation of life has been reduced. Various medical reports have been produced for both the defendant and claimant. The defendant's expert is of the opinion that his life expectancy has been shortened by as much as 20 years, whereas the claimant's expert is much more optimistic, and considers that he will survive beyond the age of 70, which is a reduction of just a few years.

The issues will be dealt with from the claimant's and defendant's perspectives. It will be assumed that a claim form has been submitted to the defendants, and that the defendants have filed their defence to the claim. The case has been allocated to the multi-track. A trial date has yet to be fixed. Various medical, care, rehabilitation and housing reports have been prepared by both parties. The case is heading for trial.

A case management conference has been held between the parties, and the following points were raised as principle points of contention between the parties:

Issue	Claimant	Defendant
1. Interim payment	£200,000 has been paid, most of which has been used to purchase a suitable home	Objected to this figure as £200,000 was considered too high for the home given the claimant's injuries and circumstances
2. General damages	£90,000 claimed for pain, suffering and loss of amenity	In broad agreement
3. Past losses	£120,000 claimed for past care to date, loss of earnings to date and other sundry expenses	Opposes this figure, and is working to a much lower quantification of £80,000
4. Future loss of earnings	£14,500 per annum net claimed until age 65	Will argue that the claimant has a residual earning capacity of at least £7,500 per annum, and would have retired at age 60 in any event
5. Future costs of care	£25,000 per annum is claimed for the rest of Mr Smith's life, for respite care for his wife, and a regular care regime.	Contends that £7,500 is a valid annual figure according to the defendant's own care report, and that his wife provides the majority of his care in any event.
6. Future costs of physiotherapy and rehabilitation	£7,500 per annum claimed for life	Opposes this head of damage completely.

Issue	Claimant	Defendant
7. Future transportation costs	£15,000 required every five years to replace a suitable vehicle	Will argue that the claimant would have incurred many of these costs in any event, but is willing to concede £7,500 every five years.

For simplicity we have ignored many other heads of damage which are applicable to Mr Smith's case. Both parties have issues over other multiplicands.

Due to Mr Smith's prognosis, the defendant and claimant are in issue over his future life expectation, and consequently the multiplier for future loss of earnings and lifetime needs are in contention.

We have summarised the quantum of the claimant and defendant schedules in order to illustrate to differences between the parties.

The defendant's multipliers for future losses is 20.61 for life, and 14 for his loss of earnings to age 65, whereas the claimant is arguing for 24.66 for life, and 20.10 to age 65, based on the Ogden Tables Third Edition Table 11, discount factor 3%.

The alternative assessments of future losses can be summarised as follows:

Head of Damage	Claimant	Defendant
1. Future loss of earnings	£14,500 * 20.10 = £291,450	£7,000 * 14 = £98,000
2. Future care	£25,000 * 24.66 = £616,500	£7,500 * 20.61 = £154,515
3. Future costs of physiotherapy and rehabilitation	£7,500 * 24.66 = £184,950	Nil
4. Future transport	(£15,000/5) * 24.66 = £73,980 = £30,150	(£7,500/5) * 20.10costs
Total future claim	£1,166,880	£282,725

Taking into account sums in respect of past losses and general damages, the claimant is looking towards a conventional settlement of over £1.5 million, and the defendant is working towards limiting the claim to under £500,000. The two parties are a long way from settlement, and it would seem that there is no other option than to start preparing evidence for trial.

The difficulty arises in this instance in considering whether it is now a suitable time for the claimant to consider the merits of a structured settlement? The answer to this question is that given the likely size of the award, there will be significant advantages to both parties in exploring the suitability of a structure at this stage.

STRUCTURED SETTLEMENTS AS ALTERNATIVE DISPUTE RESOLUTION

17.81 The new Civil Procedure Rules ('CPR'), which came into effect in April 1999, were drafted with the intention of creating a culture of alternate dispute resolution, aiming to allow both parties to a claim to formulate practical solutions to legal problems. The CPR allows for alternative dispute resolution to take place at any one of the following stages:

- (a) allocation questionnaire – r 26.3;
- (b) stay to allow for settlement – r 26.4;
- (c) case management conference – r 29.3;
- (d) pre-trial review – r 29.3 (1);
- (e) listing hearing – r 29.6 (1).

17.82 Alternative dispute resolution, or third party assisted settlement as it is also sometimes known, involves examining a case from a different angle. Mr Smith and Northsouth Insurance are clearly a long way from obtaining a meaningful settlement. If either, or both, of the parties considered the merits of a structured settlement as a practical form of alternative dispute resolution, then the management of the case could be improved, with consequent potential for savings in time and costs of the action.

Consideration

17.83 It is important at this stage to define consideration. Early consideration of structured settlements is recommended by the Law Society in the 'Structured Settlement Guidelines for Solicitors',[1] which states that:

> 6.1 The possibility of structuring a settlement should be considered early in the case, indeed as soon as possible, particularly where liability and causation are not seriously in dispute.
> 6.2 The claimant's solicitor should raise the concept with the claimant and/or his family at an early stage, explaining the possibilities, advantages and disadvantages. The question is not simply whether or not to structure as there will be claims where it will be appropriate to structure part of the award.
> 6.3 An early decision to seriously consider a structure will enable the claimant's solicitors to look at the claimant's financial position (including tax status) while gathering the evidence on quantum. This information will be required if and when a structured settlement agreement is made.

1 September 1996.

17.84 Here the Law Society places the onus of considering a structure on the claimant's solicitor. However, given the advantages to both sides, there is no reason why the defendant, be it via the insurer (in our example Northsouth Insurance) or the solicitor instructed to defend the case, should not take it on himself to instruct an intermediary.

17.85 The ultimate decision rests with the instructing solicitor. From the claimant's perspective, will the possibility of not fully examining the merits of a structure returning to haunt him at a later date? Does the solicitor possess the financial experience to advise on the consequences of accepting a large lump sum in light of taxation, inflation and investment returns?

17.86 Since structured settlements are based on the circumstances of each claimant, it is not sufficient to dismiss the possibility of a structure by following, at best, a superficial consideration of apocryphal stories of the yields structures provide. Given the 100% guaranteed nature of structured settlement payments and their tax-free status, consideration from the claimant's perspective should mean undertaking a complete financial assessment of the claimant's future financial requirements and examining the best way to provide them. It is important to make the distinction between simple consideration, perhaps a file note on the client's file stating 'raised possibility of structured settlement with client, outcome was that it is not relevant in this case' and serious consideration, which would imply that a more thorough investigation is required, involving the use of experienced financial advisers.

17.87 From the defendant's perspective, the possibility of achieving a more prompt and appropriate settlement together with reducing time and costs associated with the case should encourage greater involvement of structured settlement intermediaries.

17.88 There are a number of structured settlement intermediaries available in the marketplace that are willing to examine the relative merits and disadvantages of structured settlements given the circumstances of the claimant.

Intermediaries

17.89 In considering which intermediary to consult, the instructing solicitor should have regard to the experience and fee structure of the intermediary. A number of intermediaries offer their services on a time fee basis which, like any other expert instructed in the course of an action, would only be recoverable from the defendant in the event of those costs being submitted to taxation once the matter is resolved and if they were accepted by the defendants or the district judge.

17.90 Other intermediaries work on a commission basis. They will conduct the broking exercise of the structured settlement annuity market, and examine the viability of the structure on the basis that should a structured settlement be implemented, they would then be remunerated by way of a commission derived from placing the structured settlement business with the life office. Such intermediaries usually work on a contingent basis, that is, should no structure be implemented then they will not submit a fee note. The commission generated will be comparable to the commission that an independent financial adviser would receive were the lump sum invested conventionally.

17.91 The Law Commission Paper on Structured Settlements (No 224) did not make any specific recommendation on either fee-based intermediaries or those who are remunerated by commission.

17.92 Commission-based intermediaries have been seen as being detrimental to the claimant, since the commission would reduce the sums produced under the structured settlement. However, those acting on a fee basis will submit a bill to the defendant in any event, regardless of whether a structured settlement has been implemented or not. Thus, the claimant may have to make the shortfall in costs at taxation in obtaining the advice on the non-implemented structure.

17.93 Given the fact that the defendant might not be asking to structure the case, it cannot be said with any certainty that such costs would be recoverable under the normal taxation process. This is probably so that should the claimant decide, following advice from the intermediary, not to structure as the defendant may well not have to meet such costs. Additionally, deciding whether or not to structure is akin to an investment decision, and advice on investment decisions are not recoverable by the claimant against the defendant as made fully clear in the decision by the House of Lords in the case of *Wells v Wells* and associated appeals.

17.94 The claimant's advisers should, therefore, be aware that the costs incurred by an intermediary working on a time fee basis might reduce the award of damages available.

17.95 Which intermediary to instruct depends on the circumstances of the case and the judgment of the instructing solicitor. The Law Society has expressed no preference to either the intermediaries who act on a time-fee structure or those who derive their fees from commission contingent on the implementation of the structured settlement. Ultimately, when considering which intermediary to instruct, one should bear the following in mind, as is the case in involving any professional, that is, the experience of the intermediary, their reputation and quality of service, and the fee basis.

Claimant's Perspective

17.96 Reverting to Mr Smith's case, a structured settlement should be considered for the following reasons.

17.97 First, Mr Smith is likely to receive a very substantial sum by way of damages. If the sum were accepted and invested in a conventional manner then there is no doubt that Mr Smith would incur significant liabilities to tax at the highest rate. A structured settlement should therefore be considered from the point of view of being a tax-efficient vehicle. A proportion of the damages could be utilised to limit Mr Smith's liability to significant levels of high rate tax. A conventional level of quantum does not need to be quantified for a structured settlement to be implemented.

17.98 Second, a large proportion of Mr Smith's claim is for future care and loss of earnings. These sums are future recurring items. It is often difficult to adopt an investment strategy that is guaranteed to produce a secure level of income, whilst taking into account future tax rates, investment returns and the erosive affect of inflation. All these factors have to be considered alongside Mr Smith's life expectation, which could mean an investment strategy with a 'lifetime' of over 50 years. In this instance, a structured settlement could be utilised to 'ring fence' certain aspects of his future costs, for example a proportion of his care costs.

17.99 Third, since the decision in *Wells v Wells*, it was held that claimants were not in the same position as ordinary investors, and they should therefore not be expected to take investment risks with their awards of damages as ordinary investors might with their investments. This altered the assumption that the claimant should be expected to invest their awards in a mixed basked of equities and gilts, with a net return of 4.5%. The Law Lords held that the claimants should not be expected to take unreasonable risks with their awards, and should be able to invest in more secure products such as index-linked government stocks ('ILGS'), with an assumed rate of return of 3%.

17.100 The consequence of this for claimants such as Mr Smith is that the search for an investment product with 100% guaranteed income is extremely limited. Bank and building society accounts are only secure for the first £18,000. Other investment products such as with-profit insurance bonds have the benefit of 90% of the value of the investment should anything happen to the life company that has issued the bond, and stocks and shares are only as secure as the company in which you have invested. The only other investment vehicle that can provide 100% security are government backed bonds (ie gilts) and payments under structured settlements. For this reason Mr Smith should consider investigating a structured settlement.

17.101 Part 36 of the civil justice reforms has allowed for the development of a 'claimant offer of settlement'. The overriding objective of this particular initiative is to encourage a settlement culture. If the claimant makes an offer of settlement to the defendant, and that offer is rejected, then should the case proceed to trial and the claimant matches, or beats, his earlier offer then the claimant will potentially be awarded the 'premium rate' of interest and possibly indemnity costs.

17.102 It is therefore in the interests of Mr Smith for a structured settlement intermediary to become involved at this stage.

Defendant's Perspective

17.103 Following from the case management conference, it was clear to Northsouth Insurance that their reserve would be seriously exposed if this case were to proceed to trial and the claimant won the majority of his claim. To this end, it would now be an appropriate time to broach the subject of a structured settlement.

17.104 The claimant is claiming a significantly different sum for future care than the defendant's own valuation. It may therefore be possible to provide a significant proportion of the claimant's care requirements on an annual basis via a structured settlement, thus, using the structure to bridge the gap between the different levels of quantum on a conventional basis.

17.105 Early consideration of the structure via alternative dispute resolution may also move the two parties away from talking about obtaining lump sums for their clients, and may allow for a practical approach to settlement. The claimant has made a significant claim for future care and future loss of earnings. If the defendant makes a Part 36 offer of these annual sums then he could promote a settlement of this claim.

17.106 The defendant could also use the structured settlement to solve the difference of opinion over the claimant's life expectation. All medical evidence that relates to Mr Smith's life expectancy must be submitted for an underwriting decision to the structured settlement annuity life office. The underwriters will take a completely independent view on life expectation, and will take a commercial view on Mr Smith's life. This will also solve the potential problem of either under compensation or over compensation due to Mr Smith's uncertain prognosis.

17.107 If there were exceptional circumstances in this case, for example if the claimant was resident in a country that had particularly high levels of taxation, then the claimant may wish to make an additional claim for the fact that his damages, if accepted on a conventional basis, will almost certainly attract tax at the highest rate. The introduction to the Ogden tables makes reference to this point,[1] and the defendant may wish to protect himself against this eventuality. A structured settlement is paid free of any taxation whatsoever, so the claim may be reduced in this way. Indeed we have currently been involved[2] in two cases in which an additional claim has been made due to the fact that the claimants involved are resident overseas and will be subjected to punitive levels of high rate tax following the receipt of their awards. Both cases are on appeal by the defendants as they consider the sums awarded by the court to be excessive.

1 See *Hodgson v Trapp* [1989] AC 807, HL.
2 Frenkel Topping Chartered Accountants, *Van Oudenhoven v Griffin Inns Ltd* [2000] PIQR Q276.

The Broking Exercise

17.108 When the structured settlement intermediary investigates the viability of a structure, a broking exercise is undertaken. This will involve submitting all relevant medical reports, which relate to Mr Smith's condition and prognosis to the structured settlement life offices for an underwriting decision. Each structured settlement is specific to each claimant, as it is based on their date of birth, sex and future life expectancy. If the claimant has an injury that reduces his life expectancy, as in Mr Smith's case, then the life office underwriter will consider the claimant to be older than they actually are. This is known as an 'up-rated' age, and the claimant will receive an enhanced structured settlement rate as a result of this.

17.109 No two structured settlement quotations are the same as they are based on each prospective claimant's age, sex, life expectation and prognosis. The basis on which to quote is a skilled area and will be on the advice of the structured settlement intermediary, given the circumstances of the claimant and the objective of the structured settlement.

Types of Structured Settlement

17.110 Although structured settlements are inflexible, inasmuch as once they are established they cannot be undone, there are a number of different options available:

(1) Immediate structured settlements provide payments that commence immediately. In Mr Smith's case, it could be utilised to provide for his immediate care requirements, or to provide him with income for loss of earnings.
(2) Deferred structured settlements can be used in cases where a definitive income is required at a specified point in the future. For example, if Mr Smith's

wife were certain that she wanted to cease providing care to Mr Smith in 15 years' time, then a deferred structured settlement could be considered to incorporate additional periodical payments after this time.

(3)   Step structured settlements provide capital lump sums at specified regular intervals. For example a step-structured settlement could be utilised in Mr Smith's case to provide him with the replacement costs of his vehicle every five years.

These options are all open to the defendant health authority.

Structured Settlement Features

17.111   The above three basic structured settlements can have the following features incorporated into them:

(a)   Lifetime linked structured settlements are almost invariably linked to the life of the claimant, no matter how long that may be. Thus, if Mr Smith were to surpass his life expectancy of a further 50 years, then the payments would continue.

(b)   Term certain ensure structured settlements can be specified to continue for a certain period, for example, to provide the cash for a dependant child's education.

(c)   Minimum payment periods mean that once a structured settlement is entered into all the capital is forgone. For example, in a case where the claimant has dependants, then a minimum payment period can be incorporated to ensure that payments will continue for a specified period in any event. Our advice to Mr Smith would be to ensure that he has a structured settlement with a 20-year minimum payment period. Should anything happen to him in the first 20 years, then the beneficiaries under his will would have a choice. They could either agree to continue receiving payments under the structure, (subject to a deduction of tax) until the remainder of the minimum payment period, or they could elect for a commutation of the remaining payments into a lump sum. Where a minimum payment period is commuted, the body making the structured settlement payments will take into account the number of years of payments remaining, and various factors relating to the terms of the structured settlement. It should be noted that for inheritance tax purposes, a commutation value would be required in any event.

(d)   Level structured settlements are where payments will continue at the same specified level for the duration of the structured settlement.

(e)   Fixed escalation structured settlements mean that the payments under the structure can increase at a specified percentage on an annual basis, for example they could increase at 2%, 3%, or 5%.

(f)   Retail price index linked use the RPI to measure the annual increase in a basket of consumer goods which is generally seen as the measure of inflation. Structured settlements can be linked to increase in line with RPI. On the anniversary of the structured settlement, the increase will be made according to the appropriate increase in RPI. The vast majority of structured settlements implemented in the United Kingdom have been RPI linked, thus ensuring that payments are protected against the erosive affects of inflation.

Structured Settlements and Mr Smith

17.112   We return to the case scenario. In order to prevent the case proceeding to trial the parties agree to jointly instruct a structured settlement intermediary.

17.113   The intermediary, aware of the conflicting aims of each party, will have to try and bridge the gap on the quantum of the case using the structured settlement. The following is the type of deal that could be put together:

Issue	Structured Solution	Benefit to claimant	Cost to the Defendant
1. Interim payment	Suggest £220,000 as a compromise figure of which the claimant uses £100,000 as a contingency fund, most of the balance having gone on the family home.	Allows for a sizeable fund for contingencies and the purchase of a suitable home.	£220,000
2. General damages			
3. Past losses			
4. Future loss of earnings	£7,000 per annum payable for 40 years. This sum will be payable for the term of 40 years, and will be paid on a level basis, free of any taxation.	Level of income to compensate for loss of earnings. The structured settlement will provide £7,000 free of any taxation, for the term of 40 years, the payments will remain level. Should anything happen to Mr Smith in the first 20 years, then payments will continue in any event for the balance of the 20 year minimum payment period	£112,000
5. Future costs of care and rehabilitation	£14,000 per annum, retail index linked, payable for life	Significant level of care costs ring-fenced and protected against the erosive effects of inflation. These structured settlement payments will also have the benefit of a 20-year minimum payment period.	£350,000

Issue	Structured Solution	Benefit to claimant	Cost to the Defendant
6. Future transport Costs	£10,000 every five years to provide a replacement vehicle. Fully RPI linked	Ensures that Mr Smith can replace his vehicle every five years. The first four payments to continue in any event.	£100,000
TOTAL COST			£782,000

Claimant's original valuation	£1,591,380
Defendant's original valuation	under £500,000

Outcome

17.114   While Northsouth Insurance have exceeded their initial evaluation of the case by over £250,000, the fact that the case has completed and the file can now be closed is a positive result. It was likely that once liability became a non-issue, unless they were willing to risk punitive costs and the associated risks with a full trial on quantum, their initial offer was inadequate.

17.115   From both parties' point of view a realistic compromise has been achieved. Significant trial costs will have been saved and this might have encouraged the Defendants to increase their offer to the extent that they did.

17.116   The settlement has been reached on a consensual basis. This approach is very much in the spirit of the Woolf reforms as more money goes to the claimant and less is spent on the litigation process. The claimant has not received an award of damages in the form of a large lump sum. He has received an award that goes some way to meeting his original claim. In terms of rehabilitation, the structured payments will aid Mr Smith returning to some form of atmosphere of normality. He requires annual payments to put him, as far as possible, back in the position he would have been in but for the accident.

17.117   Mr Smith will also have the stability of receiving a large proportion of his care regime each year free from the worries of inflation and secure in the knowledge that these payments will continue for his life. The structured settlement will also ensure that his other investments will not incur a massive tax liability over time, and with good advice he could further minimise his liability to tax.

17.118   One further point to highlight on the defendant's side is regarding the multiplier and the structured settlement. The lifetime retail price linked structured settlement has the equivalent return of a life multiplier of 25. While this does not 'beat' the claimant's multiplier of 24.66 and the defendant's of 20.10 (adopting a 3% discount rate), if one adopts a 2% discount rate then the multipliers would be 29.81 for the claimant and 23.45 for the defendant. With the current lobby for claimants pushing discount rates ever lower, the incidents of structured settlements 'beating' the multiplier gathers force and will become far more commonplace.

Structured Settlement Checklist

17.119   In order to ensure that the structured settlement is correctly implemented, and benefits from the tax-free status afforded to it, the following steps must be taken. The exact extent and requirement of each step will depend on the individual requirements of each case.

17.120   Required steps are as follows:

(a) detailed appraisal of the claimant's current and future needs;

(b) within the level of damages/reserve of the case, formulate the financial package best suited to meet those needs;

(c) broker the structured settlement annuity market with the use of all relevant medical information to identify the most appropriate and cost effective annuity and assurance products;

(d) meeting and/or liaising with the parties to assist in reaching agreement as to the form of the structure;

(e) drafting the appropriate orders and agreements to be used, taking into account the tax implications of such documents;

(f) preparation of forensic accountancy reports and other reports required as may be necessary to obtain the approval of the Inland Revenue, the Court of Protection, the courts, the Department of Health, HM Treasury and so on, and being available to deal with any matters which may arise, for example, court attendance to deal with questions raised by the judge;

(g) preparation of all the documentation required by the defendant for the purchase of the annuity package;

(h) monitoring, post-implementation, the actual working of the structure and ensuring that all payments flow to and from the correct parties and advising on annual changes.

17.121   When instructing an intermediary, it should be ensured that each of the above tasks is dealt with and that the letter of engagement clearly spells out the cost basis for dealing with the work. It should also be ensured that the defendant does not limit the costs of investigating the structure to the extent that it is so restrictive that it prevents an in-depth appraisal of the situation. The case of *Patel*[1] indicates that the claimant is entitled to recover 'reasonable costs' from the defendant in clinical negligence claims.

1   APIL Newsletter Vol 7, Issue 4.

CASE STUDIES

P v C – Structured Settlement January 1999

17.122   Mr P (now aged 32) sustained head injuries when he fell through a hole in a platform while at work. As a result of the accident, Mr P is now totally wheelchair dependent. He is also unable to manage his own affairs and so is under the protection of the Court of Protection. The accident occurred in 1992 and by 1997 it was clear from the size of the claim and the nature of Mr P's care requirements that a structured settlement would potentially be a viable option. It was the defendants who first considered the suitability of a structure in 1997.

17.123   Due to Mr P's recurring future care requirements, the following settlement package was initially proposed:

(1) To pay for adaptations to Mr P's home   £25,000
(2) Cost of providing residential care with   £30,000 per annum
    weekend relief
(3) Additional recurring costs such as holidays,   £20,000 every five years
    aids and appliances

17.124   It was proposed that items (2) and (3) be provided by two structured settlement annuities. The defendants were keen for this case to proceed on a pure 'bottom up' needs based approach. At no point did they want to make an alternative offer of a cash lump sum, which the claimant would then have invested on his behalf to produce income to provide for his care. Negotiations then slowed while the parties awaited the outcome of the *Wells v Wells* appeals.

17.125   Matters re-opened in November 1998. A revised, increased offer was put to Mr P. A report was prepared detailing the advantages to Mr P of receiving a proportion of his damages in inflation-proofed, lifetime, tax-free instalments. The Master of the Court of Protection approved the following settlement:

Interim payments already received   £459,176
To the Compensation Recovery unit   £25,424
Additional Payment   £100,000

17.126   The claimant was also provided a structured settlement on the following basis. An immediate annuity would provide £40,000 pa, payable free of any taxation, increasing each year in line with inflation as measured by the RPI. Payments guaranteed to continue for Mr P's life.

17.127   To produce the same level of income as provided by the structured settlement over a period of 50 years would have required an initial investment estimated at over £2,400,000, assuming that the claimant would take no investment risks, that is, reinvesting in a portfolio of gilts which produced a gross yield of 5% per annum. This would mean that on a 'conventional' basis, Mr P would have required nearly £3 million in his settlement. However, the size of his 'conventional' award is immaterial since he is receiving a significant proportion of his care costs each year, and this will continue for the rest of his life, no matter how long that will be.

M v P Health Authority

Structured Settlement December 1998
17.128   Child M (aged 11 at time of settlement) was injured at birth due to inappropriate standards of care and now suffers from cerebral palsy. Due to the level of damages claimed, it was apparent that a structured settlement would have obvious benefits.

17.129   Although child M is severely disabled physically, his mental capacity has not been affected. His award would therefore be under the supervision of the High Court until he attained the age of 18, at which point he would have access to a considerable fund of damages. The parties agreed to compromise the matter in the sum of £3,118,019, and adjourned to examine the merits of a structured settlement. Child M's care regime was in the region of £75,000 per annum. He also required a vehicle and other capital items every five years. Annuity quotations were obtained on the following bases:

(1) To provide £35,000 every five years would cost   £174,122
(2) To provide £54,528 per annum would cost   £1,500,000

17.130 The sums payable under the structured settlement are free of tax, will rise each year in line with the retail price index, and are fully guaranteed to continue for Child M's life.

17.131 Taking in to account interim payments, immediate capital requirements and the cost of the structured settlement package, Child M's residual fund to invest was just over £1.2 million.

17.132 Child M's solicitor and the structured settlement intermediary investigated the viability of setting up a trust until Child M attains age 18, at which stage he could either dissolve the trust, or continue the present regime.

17.133 The following settlement was achieved:

Interim payments	£250,000
To the Compensation Recovery Unit	£6,119
Past care to claimant's mother	£150,000
To be invested	£1,200,878

17.134 A structured settlement was established in line with the original investigation, consisting of an immediate annuity providing £54,528 per annum at a cost of £1.5 million, and a step annuity providing payments every five years of £35,000 costing £174,122.

17.135 One additional point to note is that the defendant Health Authority self-funded the structured settlement payments out of its own budget. Rather than pay out the full sum of £3,118,019 to be invested to provide income for the Child M, the defendant Health Authority retained £1,674,122 in house. This provided the defendant's with a significant cash flow saving (in present value terms), according to Treasury guidelines, of in the region of £75,000. It also assisted the defendant Health Authority in that they did not have the difficulty of raising the entire liability in one go.

S v T

17.136 Following a road traffic accident in March 1995, the claimant sustained a fracture to his spine, which together with several pre-existing conditions, meant that his health was deteriorating rapidly. He developed angina with the result that he suffers from chest pains and cannot walk more than 100 yards.

17.147 Alternatives of a lump sum of £80,000 or a series of regular annual payments were put to the claimant in settlement of the claim, but they were both rejected. The claimant's advisers stated that they were looking for at least £100,000 but that the claimant had expressed an interest in the idea of a lump sum followed by a series of payments into the future.

17.148   A revised proposal incorporating a lump sum of £50,000 plus a choice of four alternative structured settlement options was put forward.

17.149   The claimant finally settled for a cash lump sum of £50,000 plus a structured settlement providing for £11,642 every three years for four payments, the first three payments being guaranteed.

Cash lump sum	£50,000	
Plus	£11,642	after three years
	£11,642	after six years
	£11,642	after nine years
	£11,642	after twelve years
TOTAL	£96,568	

17.150   The amount needed to purchase the structured settlement providing £46,568 over 12 years was £30,000. Therefore, the overall cost of the settlement to the defendant was still £80,000.

17.151   The offer including a structured settlement was attractive to the claimant because he was concerned at dissipating the lump sum settlement. Payments under the structured settlement are tax-free in the future and are also 100% guaranteed by statute.

17.152   The insurer was happy because had the case not settled then it may have taken £90,000-£95,000 as a lump sum to settle the case.

17.153   This is the smallest amount used to fund a structured settlement in the UK. It reflects the trend of many insurers who now consider structured settlements on much smaller claims because of the benefits to claimants, while providing speedier and more cost effective settlement of claims.

17.154   The vast majority of personal injury claims are settled by agreeing a lump sum. In far too many instances a structured settlement is never even given consideration. Fortunately, this situation is changing as more and more claimants are requesting structured settlements and proactive insurers are offering settlements utilising a structured settlement.

E v T

17.155   Master E was involved in a road traffic accident on December 1990, at the age of eight. He was in a coma for around three months, as a result of which he is now severely brain damaged, and has a permanent injury to his left leg.

17.156   He was awarded nearly £1 million net of contributory negligence and CRU. Due to the reductions for contributory negligence, it was evident that it was too expensive to provide a structure to accommodate all E's future care needs.

17.157   It was evident that a certain level of risk and speculation was inevitable in order to secure E's needs for life. Accordingly, it was proposed that a large proportion of the award be placed on Special Account at the Court of Protection.

17.158   The claimant's family was advised that a small portion of the award be used to purchase a structured settlement annuity, in effect 'top slicing' the award to limit future income tax liability. The guaranteed regular income from the structure had the added advantage of allaying the family's fears about variations in returns from a conventional portfolio.

17.159   The following settlement was reached:

Interim payments	£30,000
House adaptations	£225,000
Contingency fund	£493,485
Cost of the structure	£250,000
Total	£998,485

17.160   Payments under the structure:

Type of annuity	Immediate
Initial net yield	3.6%
Initial tax free sum	£8,934
Equivalent gross yield after higher rate tax	6.0%
Minimum payment period	20 years

The International Dimension

17.161–17.164   With the advent of package holidays, cheap flights and the multinational nature of business today, it is hardly surprising to see cross-border litigation becoming more prevalent. Structured settlements have had to adapt to provide for this eventuality. Recent cases have seen structured settlements implemented for, among others; a US resident injured while visiting the UK, who subsequently returned home and required a structured settlement settled in accordance with UK law but written in US dollars; a UK resident injured while backpacking in Australia, who received his award via the Australian courts but his structure was from a UK life office. Cases are also being investigated in France, Spain, Germany, Holland and even Venezuela with payments in various currencies including Euros.

CONCLUSION

17.165   Eleven years on from the implementation of the first structured settlement, it can be said with confidence that structures are now firmly entrenched in personal injury and clinical negligence claims. The Woolf reforms, changes in discount rates for future losses and the reaction of claimants and their families to structures will mean that their use will continue to flourish in the future.

17.166   Practitioners who are involved in catastrophic cases, whether representing the claimant or the defendant, have a positive duty to consider and investigate structured settlements. The mutual benefits are clear. Guaranteed tax-free income for life for the claimant and the potential for saving time and costs for the defendant, can simply no longer be ignored. The competitive tendering of defendant work, the pressure on claimant-led firms to obtain a secure settlement for their client and the time constraints with costs sanctions contained within the

Woolf reforms means that cases need to be handled expeditiously. Structured settlements can play their part in solving the problems that face litigants involved in cases for damages from as low as £75,000.

17.167   Claimants are provided guarantees under structured settlements that no other investment vehicle can provide. It is this certainty and tax-free status that cannot be overlooked from a pure investment decision. It is for this reason that such cases should include a structured settlement as part of the claimant's investment portfolio. The structure can provide guaranteed income to act as the bedrock income to fund care, reduce the claimant's liability to high rate tax, allowing for the claimant to benefit from the peace of mind and ensure that in cases where the claimant has a long life expectation that a proportion of the damages will continue for as long as the claimant is alive. If a structured settlement is not implemented in cases of 'considerable' size, then the practitioner should ensure that the file contains full documentation showing that a structure has been investigated in full to prevent potential negligence claims at a later date.

17.168   To end this chapter, a quote from Cathy Kelly's father, Mr Adamson, who has given his views ten years after the implementation of the first structure for his daughter:

> 'I have never doubted for one minute that I was doing the right thing. I wanted the certainty of knowing that money would be available for the rest of Cathy's life. Looking back, the medical experts' views on her life expectation ranged from 5-10 years to 10-20 years. Physically, Cathy is in better shape now and if they came back today, they would say she could live another 20-30 years from now. They got it wrong.
>
> I would definitely recommend a structured settlement to anybody receiving a damages award. I have met other families who did not structure, and they regretted it. I have absolute peace of mind in knowing that, even if I am no longer here, there will still be money available for Cathy's needs for the rest of her life.'

Chapter 18

Nursing Care

James Rowley

THE FUNDAMENTAL PRINCIPLES
The Hierarchy of Decisions and the Basis of a Claim for Care

18.1   There are few decisions by way of principle directly on the point at House of Lords level.[1] Helpful dicta appear in *Wells* as to the evaluation of damages generally.

> 1   *Hunt v Severs* [1994] 2 AC 350 and *Wells v Wells* [1998] 3 WLR 329.

18.2   Earlier Court of Appeal decisions must be read in the light of the House of Lords decisions. Where they are inconsistent with those decisions they must be taken to have been overruled.

18.3   The historical evolution of claims for non-commercial care may be interesting but it should not cloud the current state of the law and practice. As the procedural framework has changed in recent months, so has the legal basis in recent years.

18.4   The fundamental basis of a claim for care should not be overlooked. It represents a mitigation of the claim for loss of amenity and sometimes pain and suffering. It should be viewed in the wider context of the principles of mitigation, in which past decisions by a claimant (and his agents), and genuinely held realistic intentions as to the future, are to be judged in the context of 'reasonableness' but viewed from the position of the individual claimant.

> 1   See the discussion in McGregor on Damages (16th edn, 1997) at 322 ff.

Decisions of the House of Lords

In the Context of Past Non-commercial Care
18.5   *Hunt v Severs:*[1]
> 'Reasonable value of/proper recompense for gratuitous services rendered' (363A/B-D) to be held on trust by the claimant for the provider, and hence a tortfeasor cannot recover damages if the care has been provided by him (363D).

> 1   [1994] 2 AC 350.

In the Context of Future Care

18.6 *Wells v Wells et al:*[1]

'Claimants are entitled to a reasonable standard of care to meet their requirements, but that is all' – Lord Lloyd at 345 E-F.

1 [1998] 3 WLR 329.

18.7 Dicta from *Wells* in a wider context:

'As nearly as possible, full compensation for the injury suffered' – Lord Lloyd at 332F.

'The sum should be calculated as accurately as possible, making just allowance, where this is appropriate, for contingencies' – Lord Lloyd at 332H – 333A.

'The calculation should make best use of such tools to assist that process as are available' – Lord Hope at 357E .

'There is no point in the courts making as accurate a prediction as they can of the [claimant's] future needs if the resulting sum is arbitrarily reduced for no better reason than that the prediction might be wrong. A prediction remains a prediction. Contingencies should be taken into account where they work in one direction, but not where they cancel out' – Lord Lloyd at 346 C-D.

'There is no room for a judicial scaling down' – Lord Lloyd at 333A.

'There is no room for any discount in the case of a whole life multiplier with an agreed expectation of life' – Lord Lloyd at 346C.

'The [Ogden] tables should now be regarded as the starting point, rather than a check. A judge should be slow to depart from the relevant actuarial multiplier on impressionistic grounds, or by reference to 'a spread of multipliers in comparable cases' especially when the multipliers were fixed before actuarial tables were widely used' – Lord Lloyd at 347 D-E.

'Since the effect of reducing the rate of discount will be to increase the multiplicand in every case, it is all the more important to keep firm control of the multiplicand' – Lord Lloyd at 345 E-F [in the context of reasonable as against extravagant care, and not an excuse to scale down or discount further from reasonable provision.]

Decisions of the Court of Appeal

18.8 *Donnelly v Joyce:*[1]

Established that the basis of a claim for care was the claimant's 'need for care', as against 'recompense to the providers themselves' – 462 B-C. Effectively overruled by the House of Lords in *Hunt v Severs*.

1 [1974] QB 454.

18.9 *Cunningham v Harrison:*[1]

In conflict with *Donnelly v Joyce* and foreshadowed *Hunt v Severs* in terms of the true basis of the claim – 952 A-B. It underlined what remains a fundamental point that damages will only be awarded for care that will actually be provided – 952 E and 954 G-955A.

1 [1973] QB 942.

18.10 The corollary in relation to past care is that the exercise is to award damages for what has actually been provided, whether commercial or non-commercial care. It is not to evaluate how the need should have been provided for, using an 'expert' standpoint. It is fundamentally a question of fact as to what really has been provided. Of course, when an expert makes an assessment of past care, given off and on over a 24-hour period, there will be elements of opinion as to how the actual provision translates into fair recompense on an hourly basis, but the starting point must be the actual care provided and not a theoretical one based on need.

18.11 *Housecroft v Burnett:*[1]

In so far as based on *Donnelly v Joyce*, in terms of the claimant's need for care, as against reasonable recompense to the carer for the non-commercial services provided, it has been overruled by *Hunt v Severs*.

1 [1986] 1 All ER 332.

18.12 The idea that damages for non-commercial care represent 'some monetary acknowledgement'– 343f – or 'a present or series of presents' – 343g – as against the 'reasonable value of the services' or 'proper recompense to the carer' is also inconsistent with *Hunt v Severs* and must be considered overruled.

18.13 The concept that the 'ceiling is the commercial rate' – 343e – in relation to non-commercial care may be regarded as of doubtful validity. It could easily be correct if the stress is placed entirely on one line of thought in *Hunt v Severs*, namely in the damages representing the reasonable value of the gratuitous services themselves.[1] In this way the sole consideration is the actual care provided as distinct from the circumstances of the provider.

1 [1994] 2 AC 350 at 363A.

18.14 Nevertheless, at least equally important a line of thought in *Hunt v Severs* brings the provider as well as the services into the equation:

'… to enable the voluntary carer to receive proper recompense for his or her services …' – 363 B-C and
'… the reasoning in *Donnelly v Joyce* diverts attention away from the award's central objective of compensating the voluntary carer.' – 363 D

18.15 It is not difficult to construct facts where the commercial ceiling would come into conflict with the basis of 'proper recompense to the carer' in this second consideration in *Hunt v Severs* and first principles in relation to mitigation of loss. It may be unreasonable for an airline pilot earning substantially more than a carer to give up work completely to provide non-commercial care. It is much less obviously so for him to take unpaid leave for a month when his severely injured child first comes out of hospital. One doubts that defendants would take a point against him that his loss of earnings during that month off should be capped at the commercial rate of a nurse. This is precisely because viewed in the round the care is reasonable. But the point in relation to the commercial ceiling is the same whether he takes one month or 10 years off. In the case of a mother earning slightly more than a full-time carer, far from being obviously unreasonable, it is surely reasonable for her to give up work to nurse her child. The question ought to be whether it is a reasonable mitigation, in all the circumstances, for the mother to nurse the child. If so, first principles would allow full recovery of the mother's lost wages in excess of the commercial rate as reasonable recompense to her.

18.16 For a similar approach on another head of loss which is fundamentally a mitigation of loss of amenity, as is care, see the case of *Roberts v Johnstone*.[1] In the context of the provision of accommodation, the Court of Appeal rejected the concept of 'betterment' in relation to the purchase of superior accommodation in favour of the question whether it was a reasonable mitigation. As it was a reasonable mitigation, the whole amount was allowed without any credit – 893 B-E.

1 [1989] QB 878.

18.17 Given that there is already the control mechanism of 'reasonable recompense', there is no need of a further control in the form of an arbitrary ceiling of the commercial rate. The commercial ceiling is a concept in conflict with the wider reasoning in *Hunt v Severs* and is therefore open to argument as impliedly overruled. The concept has also thrown the authorities at first instance into disarray – see paras 18.18 to 18.21.

Mills v British Rail Engineering Ltd[1]
18.18 In so far as the words 'modest and not extravagant' – Staughton LJ – Q138 – purport to qualify 'reasonable recompense' to reduce damages on account of non-commercial care, they are arguably inconsistent with earlier authorities and are certainly now inconsistent with *Hunt v Severs* and *Wells v Wells* – see paras 18.5 and 18.6.

1 [1992] PIQR Q130.

18.19 The concept that the care in a non-commercial context need be 'devoted' – Dillon LJ at Q137 – 'well beyond the ordinary call of duty for the special needs of the sufferer'-Dillon LJ at Q137 – or 'distinctly beyond that which is part of the ordinary regime of family life' – Staughton LJ at Q138, as if providing a threshold test to cut out the smaller claims, forms no part of the ratio in *Hunt v Severs*. It is contrary to a passage cited in *Hunt v Severs*[1] with apparent approval, from Lord Denning in *Cunningham v Harrison*:

'Even though she had not been doing paid work but only domestic duties in the house, nevertheless all extra attendance on him certainly calls for compensation.'

1 Lord Bridge [1994] 2 AC 350 at 360E.

18.20 *Mills* marks an attempt at judicial discounting or control of awards, prevalent in 1992. The above phrases appear to be essentially obiter and the case was really decided on the basis that the actual evidence of past care did not justify the figures awarded. While *Cunningham v Harrison* was mentioned in the judgment, the passage of Lord Denning (para 18.19) was not cited. *Mills* has rarely been followed even at first instance prior to *Hunt v Severs*. If the phrases were part of the ratio, *Mills* is inconsistent with *Hunt v Severs* and must considered as overruled.

18.21–18.29   A number of other authorities in the Court of Appeal deal with nursing care. However, they add nothing to the principles in *Hunt v Severs* and *Wells* as elaborated in connection with the previously leading Court of Appeal authorities considered above. Each case turns on its own facts in the authorities and in the actual preparation of a case to which this chapter now turns.

THE PRINCIPLES SUMMARISED AND CONVERTED INTO PRACTICAL ADVICE

Past Care

General Principles for Past Care
18.30   The first stage is to establish as a matter of fact what has been done

18.31   In relation to non-commercial care, the actual care requires to be valued by reference to proper recompense to the provider (see paras 18.36 to 18.50). Prima facie, this will be the reasonable value of the services subject to a 'non-commercial discount' unless there is something special about the provider. This gives the measure of loss subject to allegations of failure to mitigate (para 18.83).

18.32   In relation to commercial care, the cost requires to be proved and almost certainly by reference to invoices and receipts. This gives the measure of loss subject to allegations of failure to mitigate.

18.33   The final stage is to consider if there has been any element of failure to mitigate. It is not for the claimant to take this point, although a properly drawn claim will no doubt have considered it in the course of its formulation. It is for the defendant to plead it or take it clearly in a counter-schedule of loss.

- Has the actual care, whether commercial or non-commercial, gone beyond what was reasonably required from the standpoint of the individual claimant in all the circumstances of the case?
- Is the prima facie 'reasonable recompense' to the provider of non-commercial care (para 18.31) in all the circumstances unreasonable, in the sense that it exceeds the commercial ceiling, or in any other general sense on the facts of the case?
- Does the actual commercial cost paid go beyond what is reasonable for the actual commercial care provided? Are the hourly rates reasonable?

18.34   If consideration of the above questions in the round leads to the conclusion that there has been a failure to mitigate, adjust the figures to lead to a reasonable result.

18.35   It will be an unusual case where arguments of failing to mitigate a claim for past care are appropriate and even more succeed. It is usually the reverse in that the claimant will have struggled on with inadequate care.

Valuation of Reasonable/Proper Recompense for Non-Commercial Care

18.36 Appellate judgments give little guidance as to this important topic.

The Number of Hours

18.37 It is now universally accepted at first instance and in everyday negotiation that the assessment of reasonable recompense begins with the evaluation of the actual care in terms of hours spent or a fair reflection of hours spent in the case of long-term intermittent care or supervision. It stands to reason that unless there is attention to detail at this stage, so that the number of hours truly reflects the amount of work done, the end result will be unfair.

An Hourly Rate to Reflect the Work

18.38 A fair hourly rate is then taken by reference to the type of care and the circumstances, such as the place where it has been provided. Many different rates exist for different places and methods of provision and there is no uniformity of approach. The expert must chose a suitable rate closest to the care provided, set it out and be ready to justify it. Over long periods the rates change. It is no use providing rates for auxiliaries in a hospital setting where the care has been provided at home.[1]

> 1 See *Page v Sheerness Steel plc* [1996] PIQR Q26 at Q 39, Dyson J, and *Walsh v Allessio* (February 1996, unreported) Gage J.

Weekend, Anti-social Hours and Bank Holiday Rates

18.39 While the authorities and general practice attempt to find the rate closest to the type and place of the actual work, decisions at first instance generally refuse to use rates enhanced for weekends, anti-social hours and bank holidays.

18.40 In *Fairhurst v St Helens and Knowlsey Health Authority*,[1] HH Judge David Clark QC, sitting as a Deputy Judge of the High Court, rejected the weekend rates' argument without giving reasons, simply commenting at Q 4 that:

> 'Whereas commercial carers are necessarily paid more for weekend work, it does not follow that these enhanced rates should be taken when considering the basis of valuation of parental care.'

> 1 [1995] PIQR Q1.

18.41 The judge approached the matter as a jury point with a broad brush – Q 5.

18.42 The decision in *Fairhurst* may or may not have been correct on the facts, but an overall rationale to be applied to all cases is hard to divine in terms of reasonable recompense and it may well be that this weekend rates' 'rule' comes from a time before *Wells*, representing a tendency towards a judicial discount. From first principles, if the care really involves unremitting seven-day per week toil without a break, nursing a loved one in circumstances where the clinical detachment of the outsider who can go home to a different life is denied, one would expect some premium (or weekend rates). Nevertheless, the reader should be aware that the 'weekend rates' line has yet to make its mark post-*Wells* at first instance. However, as we shall see, various judges have found differing ways round the issue.

Non-commercial Discount
18.43 Once the number of hours has been applied to the hourly rate to give a 'gross' amount, consideration is then given to a discount on account of the 'non-commercial' element. This is generally done, looking at the individual circumstances of the case, by removing any element of agency commission (rare because the rate taken should not usually be an agency rate) and deducting a proportion on account of the tax and National Insurance contributions which would have been paid. Damages for personal injuries are not taxed and this deduction is perfectly logical, indeed required as a matter of principle. Another rationale put forward for some discount from the commercial rate is that the care is given within the home and some element of discount for travelling expenses and time travelling should be made. In fact, while there is justification as a matter of principle for a discount on this score, carers are generally paid expenses on account of travelling on top of the hourly rate, as anyone familiar with the formulation of claims for future commercial care will know.

Weekend Rates and Proper Recompense Revisited
18.44 Even setting aside the criticism regarding weekend rates, all is not quite so simple in practice. In some decisions, at first instance judges have refused to give a non-commercial discount at all on the ground that the care has been of an exceptional quality and amount. This is perfectly laudable on the facts of these cases and the Court of Appeal did not interfere when judges avoided the 'commercial ceiling' for one carer in *Housecroft* by categorising the care 'as equivalent to 1½ carers', provided the facts justified it.

> 1 See *Hogg v Doyle* – Kemp A2-006/1 – where Turner J had awarded 1½ times the net rate for a nurse; but also *Fitzgerald v Ford* [1996] PIQR Q72 where on the facts such an assessment was inappropriate.

18.45 The picture which emerges from the decisions at first instance, apart from being illogical, places claims in an artificial straitjacket, and is probably contrary to the wide statement of principle in *Hunt v Severs*. The problem lies not in the discounting exercise. It lies rather in the failure of the earlier exercise to assess a fair number of hours for the level of the care and/or to chose a rate that truly reflects reasonable recompense for the services rendered. If starting with too low a rate for the quality of care and one which does not reflect the unremitting work and anti-social hours in deserving cases, it is inevitable that there will be unease in the discounting exercise where the care has been extensive, without much outside help and of good quality. As with any other aspect of the assessment of damages, if there is unease at the final figure the answer is not to ignore principle and fudge the discount, but to revisit the earlier elements of the assessment.

18.46 Lord Clyde gave the following advice in *Wells v Wells*:[1]

> 'If at the conclusion of the exercise the judge is uneasy at the total result he should not seek to make any overall adjustment in either direction to the

total award to meet his unease; he should return to reconsider each element in the calculation and secure that there is no need for revision at that level.'

1 [1998] 3 WLR 329 at 361H – 362A.

18.47 In *Abdul-Hosn v Trustees of the Italian Hospital*,[1] Hirst J, as he then was, considered himself bound by the 'commercial ceiling' statement in *Housecroft v Burnett*. Of course, he decided the case in 1987, well before *Hunt v Severs* and before present practice became well founded. In failing to deduct on account of tax and NI from the agreed commercial rate for the care, he achieved the right result. However, it could have been better achieved had he simply gone behind that evidence, as he was entitled to do, to say that the 'agreed' commercial figure undervalued the care. That figure was based on the care of both parents being valued by reference to the commercial ceiling of one full-time carer. This was a manifestly incorrect basis, or at least manifestly so after *Hunt v Severs*.

1 Kemp A4-104.

18.48 In *Lamey v Wirral Health Authority*,[1] Morland J did not consider the 'commercial ceiling' point as a rule of law but rather as a guideline upper limit. In rejecting the submission of the defendants that a 25% deduction should be made from the commercial valuation, he again achieved the correct result but ignored the point of principle. It is clear from the judgment that he had unease at the way in which night care had been valued, although he agreed that the commercial rate for night care was inappropriate for parents at home. He bypassed the commercial ceiling argument on the basis that the quality of the care was so high that the commercial rate for 'routine care of the physically or mentally disabled by a carer with professional qualifications' was insufficient. The reasonable valuation was based on a quantitative and qualitative assessment with a broad brush after consideration of the evidence of the experts as to the 'commercial value'.

1 Kemp A4-120.

18.49 The approach of Turner J in the deserving case of *Hogg v Doyle*[1] accorded with principle at least in awarding 1½ times the net rates for a nurse. Whether enhanced weekend rates are used, or the ordinary rates or the overall hours simply increased as Turner J did, the exercise is to assess the proper recompense to the individual carer.

1 Kemp A2-006/1.

18.50–18.59 The moral of all this is that nursing experts should be alert in putting forward rates and hours that are truly appropriate, and if in doubt they should flag up the issue by providing alternative rates. It is submitted that the time has come to test the weekend and anti-social rates argument again at first instance in the light of *Hunt v Severs* and *Wells*. It is a mistake to think that the 'commercial ceiling' argument has any real place at this point. If truly suitable rates and hours are chosen there can be no conflict with the 'commercial ceiling'. Reasonable/ proper recompense for the services provided remains the measure without any unease in deserving cases. In those where the care is of a lesser calibre the lower rate is chosen, and/or with fewer hours, and a fair reflection of the care is awarded in damages.

FUTURE CARE

Assessment on the Basis of Fair Assumptions

Theoretical Framework

18.60 Future losses always involve elements of conjecture. The exercise is to assess damages on the basis of an assumption, or series of assumptions, which do justice between the competing contingencies.[1] There are two essential types of assumptions. In the first sense, used by Lord Hope in the above passage, the assumption balances competing contingencies so that, once the assumption is made, the calculation can proceed as if it is a certainty. This is the sort of assumption Lord Lloyd had in mind when he spoke of a prediction remaining a prediction and not to be arbitrarily discounted.[2] This type of assumption can be called a 'certain' assumption. However, not all assumptions are to be treated as if they are certain, in the sense that damages are assessed from that point without adjustment for chances. Suppose there is a medical dispute as to the size of a risk of late deterioration – one doctor putting the risk at 30% at or about age 50, and another at 20% at age 60. Based on that evidence the judge has to make an assumption even though it is impossible to make a prediction in the sense used by Lord Lloyd. Say, for example, the assumption is a 25% risk at 55, this type of assumption can be called a 'chance' assumption. Under the conventional approach to the assessment of damages, all contingencies, good and bad, have to be taken into account to arrive at a fair result. The 'chance' assumption in the above example is no less a prediction (except for 25% of the damages riding on the contingency) than a 'certain' assumption would be but for 100% of the damages.

1 See the speech of Lord Hope in *Wells v Wells* [1998] 3 WLR 329 and especially at 356F-357F.
2 *Wells v Wells* at 346 C-D.

Example Calculation

18.61 The assumptions in the short and medium term lead to a nursing package costing £50,000 p a for a man currently aged 40. The 'certain' assumption for life expectancy is to age 70. He might just manage all his life on essentially the same package, or one costing roughly the same. However, it is decided as a 'chance' assumption, that there is an 80% chance of requiring an extra £10,000 p a care because of the superimposed effects of ageing at age 60. In addition, there is a 25% chance, in the event of excessive weight-gain, of requiring two as against only one carer for transfers from the age of 65, requiring a further £15,000 p a. The calculation should make best use of the Ogden Tables, following the advice of the House of Lords in *Wells*. The method will be seen from the example, but different assumptions will require a little lateral thought and the use of different Ogden Tables.

'Certain' assumption for life (30 years: 40-70)
£50,000 p a   x 30 year arithmetical multiplier (Table 22 – 3%)
        x19.89

                                          £994,500

80% 'Chance' assumption of £10,000 at age 60
80% of £10,000 p a x [30 year – 20 year multiplier] (ditto)
      £ 8,000 x [19.89 – 15.10]
      £ 8,000 x 4.79

                                        £ 38,320

25% 'Chance' assumption of £15,000 at 65
25% of £15,000 p a x [30 year – 25 year multiplier] (ditto)
      £ 3,750 x [19.89 – 17.67]
      £ 3,750 x 2.22

                                        £ 8,325

                                    £1,041,145

18.62   The method is to subtract the multiplier appropriate to the period before the chance comes about from the multiplier over the whole period. There is no need to discount back to date of trial as the method leaves the already discounted final slice of the overall multiplier behind.

Defining the Medical Assumptions as a Framework for Future Care

The Question of Deterioration
18.63   The 'certain' assumptions in a case requiring nursing care usually revolve, by date of trial, around an assessment of the claimant's current condition. This is primarily a matter of fact to be gauged from the claimant's own evidence against the backdrop of the expert medical evidence. Having read the medical evidence the nursing expert can go ahead to assess the patient. However, in serious cases it will be comparatively rare for the disability to remain entirely static and the medical evidence should address the possible contingencies going to the claimant's condition. One of the main areas to consider is the long-term 'certain' and 'chance' assumptions on which the care package is to be founded. Might there be deterioration in the claimant's primary medical condition? What will be the likely superimposed effects of ageing on the already disabled patient? Will a previous care regime require stepping up as to hours or number of carers in attendance, for example in terms of transfers? What will be the position for the final year or so of life? Is there a chance of requiring nursing on a ventilator? Questions similar to these, based on the individual circumstances of the case, must be considered, as must the issue of provisional damages.

Life Expectancy
18.64   While addressing the contingencies, the medical evidence should address whether there are grounds to suppose that life expectancy is reduced below the average. If so, the medical evidence should state the fair 'certain' assumption on which life expectancy is to be considered. Again, this is not a statement on the balance of probabilities that the claimant will die at a certain age. It is an assumption based on mean life expectancy in all the circumstances, to be ascertained from the claimant's condition in the past and present, and bearing in

mind the claimant's likely provision for care and medical treatment in the future. Average life expectancy continues to lengthen, as seen from the Ogden Tables now including Tables for Projected Mortality. It would be surprising if the life expectancy of the disabled did not also lengthen, and perhaps disproportionately so, particularly when the best care and medical treatment will be provided, as in nearly all cases where damages are recovered. Caution should be exercised when using evidence of past mortality in cohorts who had little access to best treatment, either through lack of means or available technology. On the fixing of the medical assumption, and assuming there are no other contingencies to take into account, an arithmetical multiplier is used for future care.

Approaching the Nursing Assumptions

A Clinical Assessment as the Starting Point
18.65   Once the medical evidence is available to give the framework of assumptions, the nursing evidence must consider what are the fair assumptions in relation to a nursing package or series of packages. Where there are later 'chance' assumptions, different packages or, more often additional elements to a base package, have to be devised in case the chance comes about. Deciding what are the fair assumptions involves consideration of many issues. The starting point is the clinical or professional judgment of the nursing expert as to packages to mitigate the claimant's pain and suffering and loss of amenity. This is a judgment untrammelled at this stage by the litigation and without account of often woefully inadequate resources to care for those without entitlement to damages.

How Far to Mitigate the Suffering and Loss of Amenity?
18.66   How far should the attempt at such mitigation go? Here there is a tension in what the law aims to achieve ('full compensation' or the alleviation of the pain, suffering and loss of amenity in so far as it is possible) and the means ('reasonable' means) it is prepared to use. At first it may be thought that there are here mutually inconsistent concepts. While it must be acknowledged that the tension can never be removed, the concepts are not contradictory. A few examples might illustrate the point.

- Where it is relatively cheap to alleviate a facet of loss of amenity or an aspect of suffering completely, the law will not be satisfied with simply alleviating the loss of amenity to tolerable or 'reasonable' levels. 'Reasonable means' requires total alleviation in this case.
- Where it is simply not possible to achieve complete alleviation, the law will not countenance ever increasing expenditure for little incremental improvement. When reasonable means have been expended towards the overall goal, the law calls a halt.

18.67   Where is the line to be drawn and by what criteria?

18.68   As with many aspects of the law, it is a balancing exercise between the cost and likelihood of success of the provision against the levels of the claimant's suffering and loss of amenity, comparing him with and without the provision.

18.69   In this day and age, where the provision goes to an aspect of fundamental human dignity, the law is unlikely to be satisfied until all practicable measures have been taken. The same will be true where the provision goes to personal safety, when there is a more than minimal risk or involves substantial improvements in levels of suffering.

18.70 By way of contrast, if the provision relates to less fundamental aspects of life, reasonable measures will require a lesser provision.

A Practical Test: The Assumptions Must be Workable
18.71 All the time the exercise is carried out against the background of practicality in the sense that the law will not found a claim on the basis of an assumption which cannot or will not be put into effect.

18.72 This potential problem is not of the importance in practical terms that it used to be. The advent of the wider availability of skilled home-based nursing care and case managers, whose role it is to put into effect the care plan, makes this a much rarer situation. In *Cunningham v Harrison*[1] the commercial care plan was substantially discounted because it was unlikely to be capable of establishment on a continuous basis. This is unusual now in terms of being unable to find carers willing to undertake the management of even the most grievously injured or difficult patients. Nevertheless, especially in lower level claims, it is necessary to look at the true intentions of the claimant and the close family together with the long-term practicality of the proposed scheme. If the money will not be spent on care, it will not be awarded for care. If a proportion of the care will continue to be provided on a non-commercial footing, it will not be awarded on the false premise of a complete commercial package.

1 [1973] QB 942.

The Long-term Ability of Non-commercial Carers
18.73 The long-term ability of the carer to continue on a non-commercial footing must be considered. Age and infirmity are real considerations, as is the high divorce rate generally, when partners are contemplating long-term care. Where disability is imposed on a relationship, there is strong anecdotal evidence that separation is even more common. This is particularly so where brain injury is concerned and where children are present. These are important 'chance' assumptions which are often overlooked, but which should be built into the calculation where non-commercial care forms any substantial part of the package. Medical evidence as to the suitability of a carer to continue may often be appropriate, especially when the ability to transfer the patient is important.

Role of the Nursing Expert in Determining the True Intentions of the Patient
18.74 The role of the nursing expert is crucial in determining the true intentions of the people concerned. It is just as wrong to try to impose a totally commercial package when it will not be carried out, as it is to elicit, at an early interview, an intention on the part of a carer to carry on indefinitely on a non-commercial basis, and to proceed on that footing. Many spouses and especially mothers will evince an intention to carry on out of mixed and irrational motives, such as guilt and the fact that they have been forced by circumstance into the role of carer itself. Many see themselves as failures if they admit even the possibility that they cannot continue. Communication skills are essential.

18.75 If the initial intentions of the family members clash with the clinical judgment in terms of a refusal to accept help, it is as much a cause for serious concern as when the package is rejected insisting on a much higher level of provision. In either case, the duty of experts to the court is the same, whether on a jointly instructed basis or otherwise. It is to set out in straightforward and neutral terms their clinical judgment and the present intentions of those concerned. The overriding objective under the Civil Procedure Rules ('CPR') is to enable the court to deal with cases justly (Part 1.1(1)). The duty of experts is to help the court on matters within their expertise (Part 35.3 (1)). Therefore experts should give the court such help as they can to resolve the clash.

18.76 Resolution of a clash between clinical judgment and the initial intentions of family members might involve a practical compromise to achieve a scheme with long-term viability. Such a compromise is unlikely to be workable if arrived at without time for reflection. Where funds are available, it is best tested with an interim measure but remembering the stresses and strains imposed on those still in the throes of litigation, particularly if liability remains in dispute. Where appropriate, a split trial might be ordered to allow for a trial of the care package. It may be that the genuine long-term intentions do not crystallize until shortly before trial. Where they coincide with the clinical judgment after reflection and advice they are likely to be reliable.

Overview of the Role of Nursing Expert
18.77 The nursing evidence values the largest part of most serious claims, and awards of over £1m for future nursing care are now commonplace. It is a grave responsibility to report in such cases. It is also of the highest importance for expert and litigator to appreciate the intricacy of the exercise. Nursing reports are more effective when they take less space summarising the evidence of other experts, and concentrate on the task of identifying the aspects of suffering and loss of amenity which the nursing care is aimed at alleviating. Experts are to be encouraged to set out actual analysis to justify the proposed expense or saving by reference to the specific mitigation being attempted. The potential improvement or deterioration in quality of life or safety of the claimant could be set out, recognising the difference between fundamental and lesser aspects of the need for care. That is not to say that less essential aspects are not to be catered for, but simply that they require greater justification for the expenditure, in argument on the face of the report.

Chapter 19

Personal and Domestic Assistance; Occupational Therapy

Rosemary Statham DipCOT

INTRODUCTION

What is in a Name?

19.1   Uniquely to medico legal work, there have grown a number of anomalies in descriptions of the type of relevant expertise and services which do not necessarily relate to practice in the provision of services. These are listed below:

- People with disabilities are described as needing nursing care although it is only a small number who will need help of this sort.
- The word care is conveniently used as a generic term for provision of help but fails when it is not seen to encompass services which go beyond the provision of 'hands-on' personal care, such as enabling or loss of services and may or may not cover domestic help or gardening.
- Prescription and provision of equipment may be seen as the exclusive province of the occupational therapist, overriding or overlooking arrangements in practice of the team approach of physical, communication and occupational therapists and others.
- Other staff in addition to occupational therapists carry out assessments for provision of some basic equipment needs in the community through social services and much of the responsibility for physical therapy on a day-to-day basis is undertaken by families or care staff, albeit under the direction of qualified therapists.

19.2   The Civil Procedure Rules 1998 ('CPR') seem to suggest that focus should be on the subjects to be covered in reports rather than giving the report a sole name such as a nursing report, an occupational therapy report and so on.

19.3   The words nursing, care or occupational therapy expert and others are, therefore, avoided in this chapter in favour of the terms practitioner or quantum expert, although it should be recognised that the focus is on care, equipment provision and occupational therapy and not other provinces of the quantum expert, and is written by an occupational therapist.

Whom to Choose?

19.4   The choice of quantum expert is, of course, important and it is erroneous and an over-simplification to assume that a practitioner experienced in setting up packages of care for/with people with disabilities will automatically be proficient in assessment of functioning and associated needs for every medical condition.

19.5 Similarly, a lack of experience in provision of the services being recommended will limit the ability to quantify requirements however detailed the assessment of need and understanding of the condition.

Advance Planning

19.6 There has always been a need to co-ordinate how reports are produced, by whom, the subjects to be covered and the varying approaches according to the specific disciplines of the writers concerned but the CPR lay down that this will be planned in advance rather than evolved solely according to information being produced through quantum expert reports.

19.7 Gone are the days when the solicitor could send the quantum expert to the client to find out for themselves the subjects to be covered and to provide the solicitor's first introduction to any detail about their client, as some have done in the past. However, the CPR would also seem to encompass some of the good practice and aims which have been in existence for some time, albeit not universally.

19.8 Plans work well when the following needs are met:

- The solicitor has detailed knowledge of their client, the subjects they want covered in each of the reports and who will provide those reports.
- The quantum expert has the relevant knowledge of the client's condition and of the subjects to be reported on and has time to take on the work requested.
- The client has been told to expect contact from each of the quantum experts, the reason for the contact and that time will need to be set aside for the assessment.

19.9 However, the plan may require further refinement when:

- The quantum expert provides information discovered during assessment which requires the solicitor to reconsider the plan, the other experts to be instructed and the subjects to be covered.
- The client is required during the interview with the quantum expert to address long term plans, possibly hitherto unconsidered, and the views initially expressed to the solicitor and earlier visiting experts is changed.

PREPARATION

Framework

19.10 The following paragraphs aim to set a framework and provide background information whereby arrangements can run as smoothly as possible, that time is used as economically as possible and the end result is what the court requires.

19.11 In order to know whether instructions can be accepted, and whether the reporting practitioner has appropriate expertise, it is necessary for the following information to be provided on the client as a minimum requirement for consideration of the case and quotation of fees – name, age, home area, date of accident/negligence, details of injury, present condition, and time schedule for work to be completed.

19.12 Thereafter if instructions are to be given, the expert needs to know the following information.

The Client's Name and Address, Date of Birth, Telephone Number and/or Contact Details and Instructions on How and With Whom Contact Should be Made
19.13 It is important that it is established who should be seen for the purposes of the report as, for example, a client with memory problems from a brain injury may not be a sufficiently accurate historian on their own and a client with serious injuries may have been very ill in early stages and have no accurate knowledge of events. It is therefore necessary to ascertain the availability of others in the family or friends for interview in addition to the client.

19.14 While it is often unnecessary for details of the circumstances of an accident to be passed on beyond those immediately associated with understanding the injury, some details are pertinent in saving embarrassment when, for example, discussions about past and future transport needs make it obvious that the expert does not know that the car was 'written off' by the interviewee who was the one who drove their loved one into a tree. Such information goes beyond sensitivities, however, and the expert needs to be told if details for a valuation of extra services provided gratuitously are to be ignored for reasons of the case or there are other factors.[1]

1 *Hunt v Severs* [1994] 2 AC 350, [1994] 2 All ER 385.

19.15 The client should know that the contact is to be made and the reasons for the assessment visit and report. The solicitor who knows their client can help in this area by striking a balance regarding the importance of the interview. Without this the expert, hitherto a stranger, may inadvertently cause the client anxiety prior to their visit by the zeal expressed in the appointment letter, written to ensure that the client recognises the importance of giving time and preparing details for the examination. The client may respond with a 20-page list with resultant exhaustion, or the appointment letter is so low key and reassuring that the client forgets all about it and goes out.

Medical Condition, Date of Injury, Present Condition and Prognosis and Medical Opinion Being Relied On
19.16 The practitioner needs to know as much as possible as to how the medical position is to be presented in the claim. It is a waste of time and effort, and an unnecessary expense, for the practitioner to spend hours working out provision needed for a client through all stages of life into old age if a short life only is expected and, therefore, much of the report is to be ignored.

19.17 The medical view on any future changes in condition needs to be understood in terms of functional effect and likely timing for the practitioner then to apply their own knowledge of the impact of this on the help to be provided and the specific home and other circumstances of the client.

19.18 If medical advice proposes a home programme of rehabilitation it is necessary to know the details of this if the practitioner's report is to include details of the auxiliary staff needed to support the programme.

Subjects to be Covered in the Report and Other Experts Being Instructed
19.19 For reasons of economy and efficiency, and the avoidance of a variety of diverse costings on the same subject, it is important that the quantum expert understands the boundaries to their report expected by the solicitor and the CPR require that experts must now always quote the instructions they have been given within their report. The request to cover 'subjects within your expertise' may be convenient and technically correct but could result in straying into areas not required of an expert, particularly if the expert has had a long and varied career.

19.20 Should quantum experts liaise before completion of each of the reports where there are recognised possible areas of overlap? Examples would be gardening, home maintenance and decorating which could be included in a report dealing generally with paid help or which might be considered the province of a housing expert as part of extra costs generally involved in the client's need to move to a larger home. There is no point in one report claiming long-term extra costs of heating when another reports advocates extra expenditure to put in a heating system and double glazing to reduce heating costs, or laundry if clothing protection and continence is being allowed for in consideration of equipment.

Time Schedule for the Completion of a Report

Additional Relevant Information, Issues or Constraints and/or Special Features of the Claim
19.21 The practitioner dealing with additional help needs to know whether it is intended that previous working hours are to be excluded from the valuation of past care hours provided by the care giver in favour of a loss of earnings claim.

19.22 It is necessary to know if extra input from a specific care giver is to be excluded owing to the particular nature of the accident.[1]

1 *Hunt v Severs* [1994] 2 AC 350, [1994] 2 All ER 385.

19.23 Information already held by the solicitor, such as records of journeys to visit hospital, will need to tally with the number of visits being claimed in the valuation of extra input from the family.

19.24 Statements help as clients are sometimes reluctant to answer questions again which they think they have already covered in a statement with their solicitor. Provision of background information in advance, together with preparation by the practitioner, allows past issues to be checked with the client rather than through a more laborious means of discovery, thereby saving concentration which may be limited and saving time in favour of the assessment of current functioning and discussion of future plans.

19.25 Full medical records are not usually needed but a synopsis of dates of hospital admissions, home visits and discharge is helpful, particularly where the client/family has not kept a diary or dates have been forgotten by the family giving the history for the past care claim.

19.26–19.29 Other reports, such as those from therapists, the statement of special educational needs and notes from review meetings will be particularly important for some reports.

SEEING THE CLIENT – ASSESSMENT

19.30 Choose the method of interview. A long interview without breaks may be too demanding and is counterproductive for people with some injuries, for example, brain injury. Some details may best be provided by informants other than the client on their own although some clients will seek to be fully involved in all stages.

19.31 Skill is required of the assessor in order to make the interview as positive as possible, to avoid confirming any paranoid ideas or anger about the cause of the injury and to confine the interview to the purpose for which it is intended. However, it is also necessary to strike a balance between ensuring that the information required on the subjects to be covered is obtained and allowing the client freedom to air other thoughts which, hitherto unexpressed, may prove to be very relevant to the report/claim.

19.32 A direct assessment of abilities and difficulties is made usually at home but sometimes elsewhere.

19.33 Various assessment tools will be used and choice is made according to the type of injury sustained. Understanding physical functioning may be helped by standardised assessment procedures as may assessment of cognitive functioning, although care needs to be taken that the latter does not influence testing being carried out by the neuropsychologist.

19.34 Demonstration of daily living activities, as far as is practical within the home and neighbourhood, provides objective information about levels of functioning for comparison with the client's description of difficulties in other situations which do not lend themselves to direct testing.

19.35 Methods used by clients may need to be challenged as it may be that some lateral thinking as to how an activity is undertaken will result in a new approach and independent completion by the client, as opposed to the provision of additional help.

19.36 Verbal reporting by the client, family and significant others is essential for understanding of such matters as levels of pain during activities, fatigue, ability to prioritise and organise life.

Aspirations and Lifestyle
19.37 Details are taken of the client's lifestyle and aspirations before the injury for comparison with that found afterwards. It is not appropriate to make a claim for the loss of an ability to do a task or replacement of this by employed help if it was never to be done by the client in the first place or additional help had always been used.

19.38   The client's perspective is noted, along with that of their family and it is necessary to ascertain the client's intentions and plans for the future, their general attitude to the employment of help and the ongoing input, for example, from family and friends. Ideally, precise arrangements should be discussed. The independent assessor may be clear about the amount of employed help needed but this is worthless if the client and the family have no intention of using it.

19.39   It may be relatively easy to form an opinion on the amount of help that is needed, but less so as to how it is to be provided. It may be necessary to try and resolve difficult issues before the report can be written.

19.40   A florid and dysfunctional brain injured person's assertion that they need no help at all which, in itself, may be a product of their injury, will need to be challenged before they reduce their caring relative to complete breakdown.

19.41   Parents of a young child may be looking no further than next week when they are asked to give a considered view of their child's and their own aspirations decades ahead (and the very process of discussion at the time with the assessor and later between themselves may result in change to an outcome initially rejected).

19.42   The client or family may have an unrealistically strong view of the intrusion and loss of autonomy in the use of outside help or, conversely, have too high expectations of that which will be resolved by the provision of extra help.

19.43–19.49   The expert may need to weigh the issue that the client does not intend to use outside help with their own knowledge that, over time, they probably will have to, or though their knowledge of families who have completely changed their view and future plans when help has been introduced and previous fears proved unfounded.

WHAT CAN BE CLAIMED

19.50   The history given by the client and family of past care/services given should be subject to scrutiny and comparison with that which would have been provided in any event, that which can be combined with other tasks and that which would seem to have been reasonable in terms of the medical condition and the helpers available.

19.51   Not only should the issue for direct help and/or supervision for the client be addressed, but the services they previously provided which have been assumed by others since the injury should not be overlooked.

19.52   Care needs to be taken to avoid that which would constitute double recovery, such as the hours of the partner visiting the injured party in hospital counted in addition to the hours of childcare with which they would have otherwise been involved and which were covered by others in their absence.

19.53   It is necessary to look at the pattern of family input prior to discharge from hospital. In busy hospital wards it is not uncommon for family and friends to be involved in personal care and therapies with their loved ones, and some patients may prefer aspects of their intimate care to be undertaken by a relative rather than a nurse. In some circumstances the relative is given a specific role and may need to stay at the hospital to learn about care and therapies prior to the patient's discharge from hospital.

19.54 Choosing the rate of pay which best equates to the services given by the family/friends needs thought and questioning. Identifying the main area of the work, be this domestic, household management, direct care, enabling, nursing, therapy, behaviour modification or teaching, or a combination of these, is sometimes difficult and there may be no precise published rate of pay which exactly equates to the activity performed.

19.55 Privately employed domestic workers providing small packages of hours for which they need to travel may necessitate higher rates than the trained care worker providing a larger number of hours on a formal contract basis. The former rates may not, therefore, be appropriate for the family working at home, for which there is no travel, even if the input is more domestic than care.

19.56 Nursing care, in the strict sense of the word, or therapy rates can be argued against on the grounds that the family helper has not undergone years of formal training and as family helpers or care staff they would be working under the guidance of a trained therapist.

19.57 An alternative of attempting to apportion hours to various disciplines may add more time-consuming consideration and further complicated discussion of past care in terms of other factors set out below.

19.58 Factors affecting the valuation of past extra services will include time divisions according to marked changes in needs and provision at various times and complex discounting for help provided from elsewhere such as that from statutory services and respite care.

19.59 In the case of children, there is the need to consider the amount of help which would anyway have been needed had the child not been injured, which adds another time division.

19.60 The detail given may not be justified in outcome in terms of valuation of time/sums of money but this may not be apparent until the detailed evaluation is done.

19.61 It is recognised that the court may make a deduction for tax and national insurance contributions which would have been required to be paid by employed staff and for the commercial element, which does not apply for family and friends providing help out of affection. It may be most practical to take a broad brush approach and apply a percentage deduction, although there would seem to be anomalies which can occur, such as tax and National Insurance ('NI') deductions being made on amounts which are too small to fall into the tax and NI contribution brackets. Also a commercial element could be deducted from an already discounted sum, that is, when the full commercial rate has not been applied by the quantum expert in the first place.

19.62 Continuing and future extra help may be provided by the family/friends as in the past or may be supplemented or replaced by employed help.

19.63 The employed helper may be one of three main groups working in the home.

Domestic Worker/Housekeeper
19.64 Responsibilities include all household tasks of cleaning, cooking, laundry, ironing, shopping, errands and such like. Therefore, there is no direct input to client who does not necessarily need to be present.

Personal Assistant/Home Care Worker
19.65 Employed to help with dressing, toileting, bathing, mobility/transport, input to activities and interests, help with therapies, enabling and so on, there is direct input to/with client.

Nurse
19.66 Direct supervision, advice and input to administration of medication, treatment, skin care, nutritional status, bladder/bowel care, training and monitoring of care provided by family/other helpers, information on changing symptoms and support to patient and family again involves direct input to patient.

19.67 There can be some carryover between tasks in that a personal assistant may do some direct domestic tasks in association with, or during, duty periods of personal care. However, there is unlikely to be carryover in other areas in that the worker paid on a domestic rate would not be expected to undertake personal care, a care attendant/assistant would not expect to undertake those tasks which may be considered invasive and/or treatment requirements and a nurse would not be expected to do general domestic tasks.

19.68 Selecting the appropriate rate of pay requires careful consideration of the client's needs, factors which will affect job satisfaction or otherwise of the worker and the degree of autonomy and responsibility under which staff are required to work. Factors, such as local rates being paid with which the employer needs to compete for staff, are starting points, as are nationally agreed and published rates of pay which have the added advantage of vouching for medico legal purposes.

19.69 The means by which the client will find staff needs to be considered for costing implications. Some clients or their families will find recruitment easier than others and some will feel impotent and unable to proceed without additional help.

19.70 For some families, it is unacceptable that, in order to have the help they need to relieve the high pressure on their time, they should be required to find even more time to recruit and organise that help. In any event, the time-consuming process of drafting job descriptions, contracts and advertisements, responding to enquiries, sending out application forms, short-listing applicants, interviewing, dealing with PAYE and accounting, which tends to be proportionally more time consuming on a one-off basis than with specialists in the field, needs to be taken into account either in valuing family services or the appointment of recruitment specialists. In some cases, use of recruitment agencies may be the most reasonable way of getting help and in others it will be part of the remit of a case manager.

19.71   Testing the viability of the proposed scheme should be carried out.

19.72–19.79   Interim funding has the advantage of enabling arrangements for use of employed help to be set up and tested in advance of the final settlement of the claim, thereby putting into practice the starting point from which the quantum expert works in terms of hours and pay considered in the report to be required. By using this method it will be discovered whether it is possible to recruit/keep staff on the pay scale offered and whether the hours can be reduced or need to be extended in practice. Such matters as the client's reluctance or over-optimism about employed help can be tested and a future plan gauged with increased accuracy. However, it is important that the client understands that the assessed level of need by one expert does not automatically mean that it will be universally accepted or agreed to be paid for by the other side when final settlement is made and, in this context, the reluctance of some clients to commit interim funding until they know the final sum being awarded can be understood.

OCCUPATIONAL THERAPIST INPUT

19.80   The College of Occupational Therapists' definition of occupational therapy states that:

> 'Occupational Therapy is the treatment of people with physical and psychiatric illness or disability through specific selected occupation for the purpose of enabling individuals to reach their maximum level of function and independence in all aspects of life. The occupational therapist assesses the physical, psychological and social functions of the individual, identifies areas of dysfunction and involves the individual in a structured programme of activity to overcome disability. The activities selected will relate to the consumer's personal, social, cultural and economic needs and will reflect the environmental factors which govern his/her life.'

19.81   As can be seen, occupational therapists work within a wide field and it is, therefore, necessary to consider for medico legal reporting purposes that the request for a report from an occupational therapist will not in itself always result in the same subjects being covered each time by every occupational therapist. It is, therefore, most important that subjects sought to be covered are clearly identified at the outset.

19.82   Some 'care' reports have come to be called occupational therapy reports when they have involved assessment and reporting on the subject of additional help by a quantum expert who is an occupational therapist, in the same way as reports from a nurse came to be known as 'nursing reports'.

Clinically Based Occupational Therapists
19.83   These therapists are competent in devising hospital and community or home based programmes of therapeutic intervention, clinical assessment and treatment,

Community-based Occupational Therapists
19.84   In contrast, such therapists have their focus on the client at home and what is required in the way of changing methods to increase independence, house

adaptations, equipment provision and, when the former prove insufficient, help from other people. Community based occupational therapists may refer clients for assessment by the clinical occupational therapist according to the latter's area of expertise and assessment facilities.

19.85   Many occupational therapists will have both hospital and community experience.

Equipment and Transport

19.86   Assessment will include demonstration, wherever practical, in and around the home from which will be extrapolated other areas of difficulty in activities outside the home.

19.87   Recommendations for provision of equipment may be straightforward where the prescription is so precise as to warrant only one possibility, successful provision is already established and replacements of the same models only are needed and/or the client's condition is unlikely to change.

19.88   Other recommendations may be more problematical. The prescribing therapist may want to try out a number of options involving trials over a period of time, take advice from other therapists treating the patient and seek input from representatives of supply companies. However, this would be expensive in terms of time and therefore outside the remit of the expert witness. Some recommendations for the future cannot be tested, such as those associated with potential deterioration in condition with ageing.

19.89   Methods for reducing or overcoming difficulties are reviewed with the client and may include development of a different method to achieve the same end, alteration of the immediate environment (sometimes as simple as moving furniture or reorganising kitchen work areas) and lead on, if these are not sufficient, to equipment provision, house adaptations and/or provision of additional help.

19.90   The best the quantum expert can do, therefore, is express an opinion on the equipment which is representative of that needed and the point at which they would start in finding the most suitable piece of equipment. However, some requirements are so specialised and customising so precise (with marked variances in costs accordingly) that further assessments for individual provision need to be undertaken in order to reach any sort of costing consensus.

19.91   The need to make a discount for that which would have been needed in any event may require only minimal consideration for a wheelchair user who could walk before the injury, but other subjects, such as transport, are more complicated. There is the need to consider stages of a client's life and the practitioner may find himself in a position more accurately described as a second hand car sales expert than anything else.

19.92   The teenage motorcyclist rendered paraplegic will need to replace his motorbike with a car (a new and reliable one at that) probably at an age earlier than would otherwise have been necessary and at this point the extra cost is easily identifiable. The car which will be sold on, however, will be newer and therefore of greater value than would otherwise have been the case and in later life the need for a car may be no more than otherwise anticipated. The career path and earnings potential otherwise anticipated would also affect the client's ability to purchase a car or type of car and reference is needed to what is being claimed in loss of earnings.

19.93 Mobile and portable telephones and the basic provision of computers, which can be very important tools for people with disabilities, are increasingly viewed as tools which the general population uses in any event, although the need for additional phones when employing staff is still likely to be extra.

19.94 It is essential to keep up to date with the development of new equipment, technological changes, new suppliers, relevant research and assessment projects, hazard warnings, lifting and handling rules and requirements associated with provision such as servicing needs and safety issues, in addition to up-to-date costings. It is not sufficient, in practice, to rely on knowledge of a relatively small selection of a therapist's favoured items as there will be new models becoming available which may be as successful but less expensive. Some items may seem expensive in terms of initial purchase price but become more economical viewed over time if infrequent replacement is needed. Technological advances can increase the range of activities and degree of independence for the client and may have the result of reducing the amount and costs of help required.

19.95 The temptation to provide ballpark figures only (with inevitable wide ranges in actual costs) can be great when experience shows that negotiation of parts of the claim and the hard work in achieving precision and accuracy is compromised in negotiations for settlement of the claim. However, a broad brush approach to accurate figures has to be better than a broad brush approach applied twice and the practitioner is saved from criticism from the client about inaccuracies in reports when the client comes to buy the piece of equipment recommended.

19.96 Alternative sources of equipment and funding, such as statutory provision of wheelchairs, the wheelchair voucher scheme, the Motability scheme and social services need to be considered to determine if they are applicable to the specific client. However, some caution also needs to be applied because, for example, social services provision may look comprehensive on paper but in practice may have resource limitation resulting in long waiting lists on which some clients never reach the top. There is an increasing pressure for those who can contribute financially to do so and there is no guarantee that services provided free of charge at present will continue to be so in the future (for example, the old Home Help service used to be a free provision but is not now).

Accommodation

19.97 The specialist architect or surveyor reporting will need to know recommendations for housing features, structural alterations, some equipment provision and about employed help being proposed by other experts in order to complete their report and costings. Similarly, the occupational therapist will need to ensure that fitting costs of equipment being recommended are covered in the housing report if it is not to be included their own and that advice is sought where specialist assessment of technical feasibility and particular design is required.

19.98   Recommendations for adaptations to the existing home of the client are relatively straightforward in approach and in quantifying that which is extra. Moving a client to different accommodation is altogether more complicated in the assessment and quantification of the claim.

19.99   The occupational therapy practitioner needs to be involved in advising on suitability for purchase and adaptations which will be required, although care should also be taken to ensure that this remains strictly confined to the needs for reporting for the claim and not the provision of services which should come out of the client's damages claim under ongoing therapy provision. Again, it is relatively simple to consider the suitability of housing in physical terms, but whether the property meets other needs and all the needs is altogether more complex.

19.100   Expert advice aiming to achieve the most suitable and economical solution, and being mindful of the need to mitigate loss, may result in a client being sent to a home or place in which they do not wish to live, on the basis that this is best in terms of their functional abilities, maximising independence and/or maximising their housing claim.

19.101   There are a number of clients who live in splendid isolation in their large ranch style bungalows which, being so large, were advantageous as they needed little or no adaptation for a wheelchair user. These individuals are away from their friends, neighbours and the enjoyment of feeling part of a community.

Extra Costs

19.102   It is recognised that some people with some disabilities may incur extra costs at home and on holiday, although it is important to stress that not all will. Investigation needs to be made to ascertain whether and where there may be extra expenditure.

Heating
19.103   For reasons such as an inability to exercise to help keep warm, poor temperature control (when cooling aids may also be necessary at times), poor circulation and more time spent at home because of mobility problems and/or that the person is no longer out at work.

19.104   There are a variety of routes to follow in gauging the amounts which could be considered extra. Comparison of bills before and after the injury works well if the client still lives in the same house and has kept records. Applying a percentage to current bills is possible and easier in some cases than others but applying the old DHSS supplementary benefit, identifiable in the 1980s, and adding for inflation becomes increasingly inaccurate as time passes.

Telephone
19.105   For contact with services, medical appointments and needs, a family may be less able to go out to meet people and collect supplies and may need to have extra telephones.

Laundry
19.106   Extra changes of clothes and bedding due to drooling, spillages and incontinence, together with personal care routines, temperature control problems

and that dirt is easily transferred when using a wheelchair outdoors create extra laundry.

Holidays
19.107   There are additional costs in terms of larger accommodation, car hire and extra travel costs for a wheelchair user, as well as that helpers may need to be taken and will incur expenses for which the client needs to pay.

Household
19.108   Household costs such as extra for special diets, cleaning of carpets and replacement of decorations damaged through wheelchair use, cleaning of extra equipment, cost of staff refreshments during duty periods, staff expenses on outings with the client and extra toiletries.

Clothes
19.109   It is likely that additional expenditure will be incurred on clothes damaged through wheelchair use, special clothes for use with a wheelchair and alterations to assist un/dressing.

Travel Expenses
19.110   Walking distances or using public transport, which would have otherwise been used, are no longer alternatives. A second vehicle may need to be taken for some outings and holidays owing to the extra equipment and staff to be transported and upgrading to club class from economy air travel may be required because of mobility problems and/or the space required for a helper to attend to the client.

Insurance
19.111   Insurance would be required associated with employing staff, equipment and that more people may need to drive the client's vehicle.

FORMAT OF REPORTS

19.112   The report writer should strike a balance in the length of a report. While brevity may result in little more than a shopping list from which it is difficult to know why and for whom the list is needed, the longer the report the greater will be the expense of the writer's time, followed by that of the reader. Further, length often equates to prolixity, lack of clarity and difficulty in assimilation.

19.113   The report needs to stand according to the purpose for which it is intended and, therefore, there may be parts of the interview with the client which do not find their way into the written report as they are irrelevant. However, care also needs to be taken that there are no omissions which might be seen to counter the strength of the view being put forward by the writer. The purpose of a report is to identify a need, to justify the view of need and to cost it.

19.114   The CPR require that the experts address their report to the court and declare that their first duty in writing the report and giving evidence is to the court. Sources of information being relied on in reaching an opinion need to be identified and a declaration of truth made about the contents of the report.

Part 4
Finalising the Claim

Chapter 20

Preparing for Trial

Iain Goldrein QC
Margaret de Haas QC

INTRODUCTION

Cutting Back on the Paper Mountain

20.1   Hitherto it was regularly the practice to build up a file on quantum, however poor were the prospects on liability. The rationale was that the insurer would be more likely to buy off a claim if it were quantified. Hence the focus in the Civil Procedure Rules 1998 ('CPR') on the facility to try issues separately such as liability and quantum.

Quantum

20.2   The approach to quantum has tended to be haphazard, with the potential for file management to run without an agenda. Post 'Woolf', it is submitted that to approach quantum without an agenda is fiscally suicidal particularly in the context of capped/conditional fees. Furthermore, the calculation of the heads of damage must be carefuly scrutinised. As Lord Lloyd said in *Wells v Wells*.[1]

> 'In my view the Court of Appeal was right to scrutinise the individual items which went to make up the multiplicand. Since the effect of reducing the rate of discount will be to increase the multiplier in every case, it is all the more important to keep firm control of the multiplicand. [Plaintiffs] are entitled to a reasonable standard of care to meet their requirements, but that is all.'

1   [1998] 3 WLR 329 at 345 E-F.

Costs

20.3   Only that paper which is necessary should be created. If liability is in issue, no-win-no-fee predicates that costly paper is to be at the litigator's account if the action fails. If quantum is in issue and documents are created unnecessarily, then on detailed assessment it is open to argue that costs have been unreasonably incurred.

Reports

20.4   All reports should be in a font size of at least 14 with line spacing of at least 1½, with margins wide enough to annotate. Each page should carry the name of the expert making the report, his speciality, for whom he has prepared it, the date and page number. The report must be signed (with the expert's declaration).

Expert Evidence and the Devil's Advocate

20.5   As a general rule, experts should be retained only if they have experience of acting for both claimant and defendant. No report should be provided without the expert first considering robustly what the other side's argument will be. If the expert is of the view that such an argument will succeed, then the opinion should be given by reference to what can be established. If the expert anticipates arguments which he believes to be weak, he should recite the arguments and explain why they are misconceived.

LIABILITY

Preserving Evidence

20.6   If liability is in issue, the priority is to access and preserve the evidence. For example:

- (a) *road traffic accident*: visit the scene, photograph any skid marks and also the overall environment (including damage to vehicles if still possible), interview witnesses;
- (b) *clinical negligence:* secure the medical notes, ask the hospital trust to preserve any equipment which may be relevant, confirm that they will keep records on all staff (and where they may move to) who are directly or indirectly relevant.

Who Should Interview Witnesses?

20.7   The interview of a witness performs the following functions:

- (a) first, it is the evidence-in-chief of that witness. Thus, ensure that it is taken without leading questions;
- (b) second, the interviewing of witnesses is a risk management tool. It is the litigator's opportunity to assess the witness for himself.

What Should be in a Witness Statement?

20.8   Those facts relevant to the issues to be proved are those be included. The distillation of those issues is a matter of litigator judgment/analysis. Constantly, the focus of the litigator's mind should be on the question: 'What are the issues on which this case is going to turn?'

What is a Statement of Truth?

20.9   Assuming the statement of truth is the 'Uberimma fides' declaration at the end of a claimant's proposal form for conditional fee assurance the following points can be made:

- (a) the litigator who is seduced by a witness is fooled by his statement of truth;

(b) the credibility risk (a witness not being believed in court) can be reduced by inviting the defendant litigator to be present when the claimant witnesses are interviewed for the purposes of finalising their statements for exchange and the making of statements of truth?

The Inter-Action of Expert Evidence and Witness Evidence as to Fact

20.10–20.19 Experts provide opinions in the context of facts to be proved. As a general rule, it is for the litigator to establish the facts. Often, this is delegated. For example, how often is an accident investigator instructed to proof witnesses and photograph the scene of an accident? Such delegation almost of necessity divorces the litigator from the 'feel' of the case and equally delegates to the accident investigator the findings of fact. The litigator has reduced himself to a postal facility. Experts are not trained litigators. Their understanding of facts relevant to legal issues may not be correct. The following is the essential framework for the opinion of an expert:

(a) what are the issues on which you are invited to express an opinion?
(b) in relation to each issue, what is your opinion?
(c) what are the primary facts which you invite the judge to find to establish your opinion?
(d) do you draw any inferences from the primary facts and if so, what are they and on what basis do you draw them?
(e) what is the evidence admissible in law to support the primary facts?
(f) what are the grounds for the opinion that you have expressed as (b) above.

QUANTUM
Lead Medical Expert

20.20 The nature of the injury (for example, spinal) will predicate the speciality of the lead medical expert. His role is to advise on pain, suffering and loss of amenity; earning capacity; any need for care/attendance, housing, aids/equipment, sexual aids/assistance and so on.

The Check List For Pain, Suffering and Loss of Amenity

20.21 To assess the cost, the following list can be used:

(a) pain and suffering;
(b) awareness of accelerated death;
(c) distress and its effect on the family;
(d) sexual dysfunction;
(e) loss of joy in work;
(f) loss of holiday;
(g) more work for same pay;
(h) impairment of housekeeping ability;
(i) psychological problems including post-traumatic stress disorder.

Prognosis

20.22 Central to file management is prognosis. Prognosis sets the timetable for trial/settlement. The lead medical expert must be instructed when he anticipates being able with confidence (not certainty) to report on prognosis on the balance of probabilities. If he persistently says he cannot, then a question may arise as to the extent of his experience with people injured in this category.

Timetabling

20.23   Given the prognosis, it is then feasible to address the question of which expert is required to report on which issue and when. Reports are of no use if bespoken, only to be left in the file. They are a waste of money for they will have to be updated. A good example of the problem is nursing care reports and occupational therapy reports. It is no use commissioning these if there is a split trial and liability has yet to be proved unless their purpose is to found an interim payment application. Equally, if the prognosis is not yet clear, final settlement/trial may be some time (even years) away. If an interim payment is to be applied for, what will be required (say, in the nursing context) is a report focusing on the terms of that application. Far too much money can be spent on reports which do not focus on the right issue at the right time. This leads to a plethora of paper, time wasted in reading it and the cost of preparing it in the first place.

Money Claims

20.24   Issues which arise in money claims necessitate timetabling for the gathering of the primary evidence and the relevant reports:

(a) loss of earnings are net of tax and national insurance and include the value of lost fringe benefits. Check also promotion prospects and handicap in the labour market;

(b) cost of care and/or value of gratuitous nursing care (cross reference with expert evidence as to need, and lay evidence as to extent);

(c) aids/equipment (occupational therapy, computer/communication expertise);

(d) cost of mobility/extra transport;

(e) extra wear and tear on bedding, extra laundry, clothing;

(f) cost of additional domestic help;

(g) cost of purchasing/altering/adapting accommodation (including any removal costs, estate agents and conveyancing fees) also extra cost of running home (heating, rates, damage to decor, insurance);

(h) cost of travel of close friends and relatives to aid rehabilitation;

(i) medical costs/prescription;

(j) extra cost of holidays;

(k) cost of therapies (physio, occupational and speech – note: speech therapy can extend life expectation by training to swallow: similarly physiotherapy by reducing the risk of respiratory tract infection and so on);

(l) DIY/gardening;

(m) Court of Protection.

(n) Interest on past losses, but not on claims for 'handicap in the labour market.'

20.25   Note deductions:

(a) Compensation Recovery Unit ('CRU');
(b) cost of maintenance in a hospital, nursing home or other institution, to be set off against a claim for loss of earnings;
(c) *Avon County Council v Hooper*[1] (the re-imbursement situation).

1 [1997] I WLB 1605, CA.

Interim Payment

20.26   Given the prognosis and given this check list, the questions arise:

(a) does the claimant need money now?
(b) if so, for what?
(c) does the lead medical expert confirm the need?
(d) is other expertise required, precisely on what issue?

Explanation of 'Need'

20.27   A brain damaged victim will require a comprehensive regime of nursing care. Frequently parents provide this care prior to trial. There are two factors which warrant particular comment:

(a) the longer parental care lasts the more likely it is that a defendant will contend that the parents will *in fact* continue to look after the child;
(b) parental care can tend to endure by default when the litigator fails to address specifically the issue of nursing care early on in the context of an interim payment application. If there is a split trial, ask for a speedy hearing if the parents are struggling with care.

20.28   Given a need for, say, nursing provision the reports required are:

(a) the lead of medical expert to confirm need;
(b) a nursing expert, to advise on the regime of care which is necessary, and its costs;
(c) a housing expert, to advise on the accommodation required, given that regime of nursing care.

20.29–20.39   The figure should then be calculated and the interim payment application launched.

NURSING REPORT

Introduction

20.40   These are given a separate section because regularly they generate figures for compensation of over £1 million. It is a sobering thought to realise that were a commercial action being run for a figure of that magnitude, much forensic skill may be expected to be brought to bear with detailed arguments. To what extent should nursing reports contain material sufficient to justify claims at that level?

Past Care – Evidence

20.41   It is for the litigator to elicit from the family, the detailed extent of past nursing care/attendance. If possible this should be with reference to diarised daily notes. This evidence (with a declaration of truth) can then be supported by a nursing expert and the lead medical expert as care reasonably necessitated by the injury concerned.

Future Care

20.42–20.49   This should be addressed with great care and detail. To say that 24-hour care will be necessary, and little more, is grossly inadequate. There must be set out:

(a)   precisely the regime of care necessary;
(b)   why it is necessary;
(c)   what European Regulations would justify such regime;
(d)   to what extent the claimant is put at risk by less care and what could go wrong?
(e)   to what extent is the condition of the claimant preserved/advanced by the care advised?
(f)   explain how, with the regime of care so advised, parents can perform the role of parents rather than nursing carers;
(g)   to what extent life expectancy is secured by the degree of care advised;[1]
(h)   explain how an average day in the life of the claimant would unfold, given the regime of nursing care recommended as contrasted with, say, the proposed regime advanced by the defence;
(I)   what literature is there to support the claim?
(j)   are there any parallel cases of which transcripts may be available from the court shorthand writers.[2]

1   See Article 2, European Convention of Human Rights.
2   See Division X, Butterworths Personal Injury Litigation Service where several transcripts are reported.

OTHER REPORTS

Physiotherapy
20.50   These claims are rarely worth more than £50,000. The reports are often the largest in the bundle. All that is required:

(a)   the regime recommended;
(b)   the length of time over which the regime is to run;
(c)   the costs;
(d)   what advantages enure to the claimant if there is such physiotherapy (including, for example, life expectation in the context of chest physiotherapy);
(e)   what disadvantages would arise without that physiotherapy.

Occupational Therapy

20.51   The criterion is reasonable need, not to provide for the claimant as much as possible. If the latter is the criterion by which the recommendations are to be made, the whole report will be out of balance. What is required is:

> (a) the items reasonably necessary (the explanation as to why they are reasonably necessary to be expressed in simple focused sentences, not exceeding for each item a paragraph);
> (b) the costs;
> (c) a picture (if otherwise not clear) of the item recommended, to be included (through use of a computer) alongside the text where it is mentioned.

20.52 The lead medical experts should confirm the validity of the need in relation to each item, perhaps a schedule format.

CHECK LIST FOR TRIAL

Trial Bundle

Liability
20.53 It is suggested:

> (a) pleading file: white;
> (b) claimant's witness evidence as to fact: blue;
> (c) defendant's witness evidence as to fact: orange;
> (d) claimant's expert evidence: green;
> (e) defendant's expert evidence: yellow;
> (f) medical evidence: red;
> (g) literature: black.

Quantum
20.54 Suggestions here are:

> (a) claimant's evidence as to fact: white;
> (b) claimant's medical expert evidence: red;
> (c) defendant's medical expert evidence: blue;
> (d) claimant's occupational therapy, nursing and housing report: green;
> (e) defendant's occupational therapy, nursing and housing report: orange.

20.55 Aim to keep the entire trial bundle below 250 sides of A4. One way of achieving this is to have one set of facts incorporated by reference into each expert report after the experts have liaised. So much time is wasted on reading 'the facts' in a myriad of reports. Do the facts on current living conditions have to be recited at all if there is a contemporary video film showing the problems? The aim must be to keep paper to a minimum.

Compilation of Trial Bundle

20.56 Strong ring binder/files, indexed, paginated, reports separated by coloured index guide cards, no binder to be more than two-thirds full.

Schedule Of Loss

20.57 Separate file, each figure cross-referencing with the passage in respect of a report from which it flows.

Witnesses as to Fact

20.58   Details to check are as follows:

    (a) statements cover all issues of fact?
    (b) statement of truth?
    (c) up to date?
    (d) witness warned?
    (e) witness timetabled?

Expert Evidence

20.59   Again, details to check include:

    (a) report/reports up to date?
    (b) experts met without prejudice?
    (c) issues to find?
    (d) witness warned?
    (e) witness time-tabled?
    (f) has he seen/checked the skeleton argument?

Estimated Length of Hearing

20.60   Is the original estimate sound? Can the issues be narrowed? Check:

    (a) reasonableness and Part 44?
    (b) cost of issues – Part 36 offer on issues?
    (c) skeleton argument/opening?

Forensic Accountancy

20.61   Forensic expertise can assist particularly in relation to:

    (a) complex calculations involving tax in the context of past and future loss of earnings;
    (b) discounted actuarial schedules of cost of chattels;
    (c) calculation of pension loss.

20.62   Generally, however, these reports should do no more than calculate figures (cross-referencing with reports) from the data contained in the expert evidence. A criterion for using a forensic accountant should be whether it will be cheaper to sub-contract this, than to produce the equivalent product in the office?

Employment Consultant

20.63   Any projection should be founded, not on abstract statistics but firmly in reference to *this* claimant in *this* area, with his pre/post accident skills. It is misconceived to project a high earning capacity if school records and pre-accident proved earnings and IQ (as assessed with an educational psychologist) suggest otherwise. Litigation tips are:

    (a) caution before using such an expert;
    (b) if instructing try to provide:

(i)   a comprehensive profile of the family and the achievements of the individual members;

(ii)   all educational records;

(iii) the report of an educational psychologist;

(iv) plans which the family had for the claimant (particularly if a child) pre-accident, substantiated by firm evidence;

(v)   accurate employment, pay and tax records.

Electronic Aids/Communication

20.64 Litigation tips:

(a) it is misconceived to recommend items of such equipment if a psychologist explains that it is not practicable to use it;

(b) the lead medical expert should justify the need;

(c) the communication expert should advise what benefit there is to the claimant arising from having the equipment and/or the disadvantage there is to the claimant in not having it.

Housing

20.65 The information needed by the judge includes:

(a) the size of the house the claimant will need;

(b) what house he would otherwise have had and when he would have acquired it (this is an issue of fact, to be elicited by the litigator);

(c) how much extra the house required will be?

(d) what adaptations are required and why, and what will they cost?

(e) how much extra such a house will cost to run annually.

Conclusion

20.66 Keep paper to a minimum. What paper there is should set out the issues and opinion with simple clarity. 'Boiler plate' in reports should be avoided at all costs; that is, material which is produced from computer databases irrespective of the specific case on which expert opinion is sought. In relation to each head of claim the court should be entitled to a clear answer to the following simple question: What is the issue on which this head of claim turns and what precisely is the opinion of the expert on this issue?

Chapter 21

The Court of Protection

Denzil Lush

INTRODUCTION

21.1 The Court of Protection is an office of the Supreme Court. Its function is to protect and manage the property and financial affairs of persons who are incapable, by reason of mental disorder, of managing and administering their property and affairs themselves.[1] Such people are technically known as patients and their affairs are managed on a day-to-day basis by a receiver.

    1   Mental Health Act 1983, s 93(2).

21.2 Although the court has 'power over the purse', it has no 'power over the person' and cannot make medical treatment decisions on behalf of patients or personal decisions, such as where to live, with whom they may or may not have contact,[1] or whether they can marry.[2]

    1   *DR v DR* (1999) Times, 8 February.
    2   A guardian appointed under Part II of the Mental Health Act 1983 has the limited powers over a patient's person set out in s 8(1) of the Act. In recent years the declaratory jurisdiction of the High Court, both inherent and governed by Order 15 rule 16 of the Rules of the Supreme Court, has been invoked to assist in making various medical treatment and personal decisions.

Patients

21.3 The court has more than 22,000 patients[1] and they fall into four main groups:

- Elderly people suffering from the mental infirmities of old age, such as Alzheimer's disease or multi-infarct dementia. 70% of the court's patients are aged 70 or over.
- People with mainstream mental illnesses, such as schizophrenia and hypomania.
- People who are mentally handicapped or have learning difficulties.
- People who have suffered brain damage at birth or as a result of medical negligence, or who have acquired head injuries in an accident or assault, and have been awarded damages for personal injuries.

    1   The National Audit Office report on the Public Trust Office (HC 206 Session 1998-99), published on 12 February 1999, states at para 1.31 that the court currently oversees 22,000 receiverships; it handles 6,500 applications to have a receiver appointed; and 8,000 receiverships are in the process of being wound up.

History of the Court

21.4   The court's origins date back to the Middle Ages. During the reign of King Edward I (1272-1307) the Crown assumed responsibility for the management of the estates of persons lacking mental capacity to protect them from exploitation and abuse by their feudal superiors. This jurisdiction was later exercised by the Court of Wards (1540-1660) and thereafter by the Lord Chancellor personally. In 1842 the Lord Chancellor delegated many of his functions in this area to two Masters in Lunacy: the number of Masters was later reduced to one. In 1934 the Office of the Master in Lunacy was renamed the Management and Administration Department, and in 1947 it became the Court of Protection.[1]

1   Patients' Estates (Naming of Master's Office) Order 1947 (SR & O 1947/ 1235).

Powers of the Court

21.5   The court's current powers are contained in the:

- Mental Health Act 1983, Part VII (ss 93-113).
- Court of Protection Rules 1994.
- Enduring Powers of Attorney Act 1985.
- Court of Protection (Enduring Powers of Attorney) Rules 1994.

21.6   Section 95(1) of the Mental Health Act 1983 sets out the general powers of the court with respect to the property and affairs of a patient. It has an extremely wide discretion to do or secure the doing of all such things as appear necessary or expedient:

(a)   for the maintenance or other benefit of the patient;[1]

(b)   for the maintenance or other benefit of members of the patient's family;

(c)   for making provision for other persons or purposes for whom or which the patient might be expected to provide if he were not mentally disordered; or

(d)   otherwise for administering the patient's affairs.

1   In *Re W (EEM)* [1971] Ch 123 Ungoed-Thomas J held that the word 'benefit' is of wide significance comprehending whatever would be beneficial in any respect, material or otherwise.

21.7   The court must have regard first to the requirements of the patient, but may also take into account the interests of creditors and the desirability of making provision for obligations of the patient, notwithstanding that they may not be legally enforceable.[1] Section 96 of the Act sets out a lengthy list of specific powers conferred on the court, and s 99 empowers the court to appoint a receiver for a patient.

1   Mental Health Act 1983 s 95(2).

Personnel

21.8   The court's staff consists of the Master, a Court Manager, three Assistant Masters, two Nominated Officers, and the Registrar and his assistants. The Master must be a lawyer with at least a seven years' general qualification[1] and is of similar rank to a circuit judge and the senior masters of the divisional courts. The Master deals with all originating applications where the patient's net income exceeds a certain amount (currently £15,000 a year) and all subsequent applications and directions in such matters. In practice, all major personal injury and medical negligence awards are in the Master's list.

1   Supreme Court Act 1981, Sch 2, Pt II

Review and Appeal

21.9   Anyone who is aggrieved by a decision of the court which was not made at an attended hearing may apply to the court within eight days of the decision to have it reviewed by the court. On hearing the application the court may either confirm or revoke its previous decision, or make any other order or decision it thinks fit.[1] Anyone who is aggrieved by an order or decision made at a hearing or review may appeal to a nominated judge within fourteen days.[2] A 'nominated judge' for this purpose could be any High Court Judge assigned to the Chancery Division or Family Division.

1   Court of Protection Rules 1994 (SI 1994/3046) r 56.
2   Court of Protection Rules 1994 r 57.

Proposed Reforms

21.10–21.14   In its report, *Mental Incapacity*, published in March 1995, the Law Commission recommended that the present Court of Protection should be abolished and that, in its place, a new superior court of record – also to be called the Court of Protection – should be established. The jurisdiction of the new court will extend to personal and medical decision-making in addition to financial decision-making, and will be exercised by nominated district, circuit and High Court judges sitting at any place in England and Wales designated by the Lord Chancellor. The Law Commission's report also proposes abolishing receivership and authorising the court to appoint managers instead, who will have power to deal with a patient's capital as well as his income. The report was further considered in a consultation paper, *Who Decides?*, issued by the Lord Chancellor's Department in December 1997, followed by a policy statement, *Making Decisions*, published in October 1999. The government intends to implement the Law Commission's proposals when parliamentary time allows.

THE PUBLIC TRUST OFFICE

Relationship with the Court

21.15   Since January 1987 the Court of Protection and the Public Trust Office have shared the same building. The relationship between these two organisations can be summarised by saying that the court exercises judicial functions in relation to a patient's property and financial affairs, whereas the Public Trust Office carries out the orders of the court and exercises administrative functions.

1   Stewart House, 24 Kingsway, London WC2B 6JX.

Divisions

21.16   The Public Trust Office employs approximately 535 people, excluding casual staff and agency staff, and consists of four divisions:

- Receivership Division, where the Public Trustee acts as the receiver for a patient.
- Protection Division, which deals with external receivers such as members of the patient's family, solicitors and local authorities.
- Trust Division, where the Public Trustee has been appointed as an executor or trustee.
- Court Funds Office, which provides a banking and investment service for funds deposited in court.

Personnel

21.17   The day-to-day management of a patient's affairs is carried out within the Public Trust Office by caseworkers. These are civil servants of administrative officer, executive officer, higher executive officer or senior executive officer rank, and cases are allocated to, and certain decisions are made by, these different ranks according to their complexity. Most major personal injury and medical negligence cases are handled by HEOs.

21.18   The Protection Division, which looks after 90% of patients' estates, is divided into four branches, each of which has an SEO branch manager:

- Branch 1 deals with patients whose surnames range from A to COS, and all cases where an officer of a local authority is the receiver.
- Branch 2 deals with patients with surnames from COT to HUW.
- Branch 3 from HUX to REA.
- Branch 4 from REB to Z.

Complaints

21.19   If for any reason it is necessary to complain about the service provided by the Public Trust Office, the complaint should be addressed first to the caseworker; and then to the relevant divisional manager, the Principal of the Protection Division or, if the Public Trustee is the receiver, the Principal of the Receivership Division. If the response is unsatisfactory, then the complaint should be referred to the Director of Mental Health Services and thence to the Chief Executive. The Public Trust Office has produced a leaflet *How to Complain*, which is available free of charge.

Proposed Reforms

21.20–21.24   The Public Trust Office became an executive agency within the Lord Chancellor's Department on 1 July 1994. All executive agencies are subject to a thorough review, usually every five years. The Quinquennial Review of the Public Trust Office was carried out between May and October 1999 by Miss Ann Chant CB. Her report was published on 18 November 1999, and its principal recommendations are as follows:[1]

    (1)   The current Public Trust Office should cease to exist as a separate Executive Agency with effect from 1 April 2001, although the need for

its functions to be performed as the responsibility of Ministers still remains. Responsibility for the Court Funds Office should pass to the Court Service, and the Official Solicitor's Office should become responsible for Protection, Receivership and Trust work.

(2) Specialist client services should not be provided by Public Trust Office staff but by appropriate private, not-for-profit and public sector organisations under contract. Principal among these might be trust and receivership work done by solicitors; all fund management done by the private financial sector; visiting Court of Protection patients by charities, local authorities and the Benefits Agency; and collection of receivers' annual accounts by the Inland Revenue.

(3) The main role of Public Trust Office staff should be to regulate quality control, monitor and analyse the performance and delivery of services to their clients.

(4) The Public Trust Office building should eventually be sold by the Lord Chancellor's Department for commercial redevelopment.

1 The Lord Chancellor's Paper of 12 April 2000 makes changes and the future of the Public Trust Office has now committed the LCD to the earlier proposals for change that were being recommended.

DECIDING WHETHER SOMEONE IS A PATIENT

21.25 The statutory definition of a patient as stated by s 94(2) of the Mental Health Act 1983 is that:

The functions of the judge under this Part of this Act shall be exercisable where, after considering medical evidence, he is satisfied that a person is incapable, by reason of mental disorder, of managing and administering his property and affairs; and a person as to whom the judge is so satisfied is referred to in this Part of this Act as a patient.

Medical Evidence

21.26 The medical evidence to be considered by the court generally consists of a printed certificate (form CP3) which should be completed by a registered medical practitioner. There is no requirement that the certificate be completed by a psychiatrist or neurologist, and in practice it is usually completed by the patient's GP.

21.27 Occasionally there have been problems where the form CP3 has been completed by a clinical psychologist. It is acknowledged that clinical psychologists are experts in assessing an individual's cognitive skills, but regrettably, because of the wording of the statute, the court cannot accept a certificate completed by anyone other than a registered medical practitioner.[1]

1 'A medical certificate' means a certificate by a registered medical practitioner: Court of Protection Rules 1994 (SI 1994/3046) r 36(2).

21.28 Although the court will consider medical reports other than in form CP3, the prescribed certificate, which was prepared in consultation with the Royal College of Psychiatrists and the British Medical Association, contains some useful additional information which assists the court in making decisions on investment policy and on whether a patient's name should be placed on the Lord Chancellor's Visitors' list.[1]

1   For further information on the Lord Chancellor's Visitors, see Mental Health Act 1983, ss 102 and 103.

21.29   The British Medical Association makes a recommendation each year as to the fees medical practitioners may charge for the completion of certificates and other work done in connection with Court of Protection matters. The fees recommended with effect from 1 April 2000 are:

(a)   for completion of the medical certificate (form CP3) with an examination of the patient – £81;

(b)   for serving notice of an application for the appointment of a receiver (form CP7) – £40.50. If travelling is involved, the fee may be higher.

21.30   In order to be classified as a patient, a person must:

(a)   be suffering from mental disorder;

(b)   have property and financial affairs that need to be managed and administered; and

(c)   be incapable of managing and administering such property and affairs.

Minors

21.31   Claimants in personal injury and medical negligence actions who are minors present a particular difficulty in terms of jurisdiction. It is not always clear whether they incapable of managing their affairs by reason of mental disorder (even if they are mentally disordered) or whether their incapacity is the result of their age. There was a time when the Court of Protection was reluctant to assume jurisdiction in the case of children, but more recently, where the injury is such that it is unlikely that the claimant will be able to manage his or her own affairs at eighteen, the court will agree to become involved because it is in the claimant's best interests that a long-term, long-lasting regime of investment and management should be put in place at an early stage.[1]

1   See *Stringman v McArdle* [1994] 1 WLR 1653 CA.

Mental Disorder

21.32   Mental disorder is defined in s 1(2) of the Mental Health Act 1983:[1]

'"Mental disorder" means mental illness, arrested or incomplete development of mind, psychopathic disorder and any other disorder or disability of mind and 'mentally disordered' shall be construed accordingly.'

1   An acquired head injury after an accident or assault often falls within the definition and diagnostic guidelines of organic personality disorder: ICD10.F.07.0.

21.33   Section 1(3) of the Act, however, states that a person is not to be regarded as suffering from mental disorder by reason only of promiscuity or other immoral conduct, sexual deviancy or dependence on alcohol or drugs.

Incapacity to Manage

21.34   Although 'mental disorder' is defined by statute, unfortunately there is no reported decision in English law on the meaning of the expression 'incapable of managing his property and affairs'. In *Heywood & Massey*, the standard textbook on Court of Protection practice, the authors state (12th edition, page 17) that:

> 'The question of the degree of incapacity of managing and administering a patient's property and affairs must be related to all the circumstances including the state in which the patient lives and the complexity and importance of the property and affairs which he has to manage and administer.'

21.35 The authority for this statement is an unreported decision of Mr Justice Wilberforce (as he then was) on 23 March 1962 in *Re CAF*. It is doubly unfortunate that, not only was Lord Wilberforce's decision not reported, but also there is no surviving transcript of his judgment, because in Australia there has been a lively debate in the courts as to the meaning of this note in *Heywood & Massey*, and whether an individual's capacity to manage his affairs is subjective (following *Re CAF*) or objective.

21.36 In New South Wales, in the case of *PY v RJS* Mr Justice Powell tried to introduce a more objective test. He said:

> 'It is my view that a person is not shown to be incapable of managing his or her own affairs unless, at the least, it appears:
> (a) that he is incapable of dealing, in a reasonably competent fashion, with the ordinary routine affairs of man; and
> (b) that by reason of that lack of competence there is shown to be a real risk that either:
> (i) he may be disadvantaged in the conduct of such affairs; or
> (ii) that such moneys or property which he may possess may be dissipated or lost. It is not sufficient, in my view, merely to demonstrate that the person lacks the high level of ability needed to deal with complicated transactions or that he does not deal with even simple or routine transactions in the most efficient manner.'

1 [1982] 2 NSWLR 700, 702

21.37 However, in another Australian state, Victoria, in *Re MacGregor*,[1] Mr Justice Starke followed *Re CAF* and upheld the subjective test. He said:

> 'The Act itself appears to me to lay down the test. It speaks of 'managing his affairs', not the 'ordinary routine affairs of man'. The court under the Act is exercising its protective jurisdiction in respect of individuals, not a class of persons, albeit before the jurisdiction is exercised it must be shown that the person is an infirm persons for the purposes of the Act.'

1 [1985] VR 861.

21.38 Accordingly, in some personal injury cases, the claimant may be capable of handling relatively small sums of money, such as DSS benefits, but, as soon as a substantial damages award has been made, they lose the capacity to manage in view of the complexity and importance of the property and affairs that need to be managed.

21.39   In *White v Fell*[1] Mr Justice Boreham, as he then was, held that whether a person is capable of managing his property and affairs depends on whether or not he is capable of taking, considering and acting on appropriate advice.

1   (12 November 1987, unreported).

21.40–21.44   He held that to establish whether a claimant is capable of taking, considering and acting upon appropriate advice, one needs to ask the following questions:

- Does the claimant have the insight and understanding of the fact that he has a problem in respect of which he needs advice?
- Is the claimant capable of seeking an appropriate adviser and instructing him with sufficient clarity to enable him to understand the problem and to advise him appropriately?
- Does the claimant have sufficient mental capacity to understand and make decisions based on, or otherwise give effect to, such advice as he may receive?

WHEN TO APPLY TO THE COURT OF PROTECTION

21.45   In order to become a patient a person without capacity must have property and finances that need to be managed and administered. If he has no capital, and no income other than DSS benefits, the Secretary of State for Social Security will consider appointing an appointee to handle those benefits on his behalf.

21.46   In many personal injury and medical negligence claims there is no need to apply for the appointment of a receiver until an award, either interim or final, is imminent. If the claimant is mentally incapacitated, nobody has authority to deal with capital on his behalf until a receiver has been appointed. A next friend does not have that right, nor does the solicitor in the action.[1]

1   *Leather v Kirby* [1965] 1 WLR 1489; *M v Lester* [1966] 1 WLR 134.

WHO SHOULD BE THE RECEIVER?

21.47   Traditionally the court has tended to appoint a member of the patient's family as receiver, and more rarely a solicitor, accountant or the Director of Social Services for a local authority.[1] If no one else is able or willing to make the application, or if the court for any other reason thinks fit, the Public Trustee will be appointed.

1   The National Audit Office report *Public Trust Office: Protecting the Financial Welfare of People with Mental Incapacity*, published in February 1999, contains a pie graph on page 14 showing that 54% of receivers are relatives (21% being close relatives, such as a spouse, parent or child of the patient); 13% are solicitors; 12% are local authorities; and in 11% of cases the Public Trustee is the receiver.

21.48   However, the British Association of Brain Injury Case Managers ('BABICM') has recently questioned the court's policy of appointing family members in cases where the patient has an acquired brain injury It has recommended that, in all but exceptional cases, professionals rather than members of the family should be appointed as receivers for people with an acquired brain injury, and that the receiver, whoever is appointed, should have some basic training in the issues relevant to the long-term effects of brain injury. The following reasons have been given.

Amount of the Award
21.49   The amount of damages awarded nowadays can be very substantial, and in some cases comparable to a lottery jackpot. The families of the individuals concerned almost always have no experience of handling such large sums of money, and may be incapable of managing their own finances prudently, let alone those of a person under a disability.

Burden
21.50   The burden on families of people with an acquired brain injury increases, rather than decreases, over time. The administrative tasks of receivership often increase that burden and add to the stress levels already experienced by the family.

Dependency
21.51   There is a danger of mutual dependency in any family which has a disabled member. The involvement of a relative as receiver increases this risk, making it harder for the family to let go and allow the person with a head injury to begin to lead a life which is as independent as possible.

Inability to Refuse
21.52   Some people with a head injury have behavioural problems and can be intimidating and difficult to reason with. Family members often have problems in saying 'no' to demands, even though these may be clearly unreasonable and not in the best interests of the disabled person. Similarly, some families feel sorry for the disabled person and find it difficult to say 'no' because they do not wish to disappoint him.

Moral Conflict
21.53   People with a brain injury have the normal desires of other persons in their peer group. They may wish to spend some of their money on activities which could cause conflict with their parents or family: for example, pornography, prostitutes, alcohol, or illegal drugs. People who have not suffered a head injury may choose to indulge in these activities, and are able to do so not only without their parent's knowledge, but also without the need for family consent or financial support.

Financial Conflict
21.54   Families may be reluctant to spend money on appropriate items such as care, equipment, adaptations and case management, for fear of running out of money. Other families may regard a compensation award as a source of income or as a 'family fund' to use for the benefit of the whole of the family as they see fit. This often leads to the family providing substandard care against the advice of experienced professionals and against the interests of the injured person. The view of the fund as a family resource may also lead to the conservation of capital for the future beneficiaries of any will.

Personal Conflict
21.55   People with brain damage may be inhibited in expressing their own wishes and feelings, especially if they perceive these to conflict with those of

their family. It may be much easier for them to express their wishes to an independent receiver.

21.56   In any event, the court is reliant on the goodwill and professional judgment of solicitors or counsel in proposing a suitable candidate for appointment as a receiver in a particular case. The court itself has no knowledge of the applicant and, in most cases, will simply rubber-stamp the appointment unless objections are raised.

21.57   Usually the receiver and the next friend in the action leading to the award will be the same person, but in any case the next friend is likely to be authorised to continue the action on the claimant's behalf.

21.58–21.64   A receiver is entitled to recover his reasonable out-of-pocket expenses, such as postage, telephone calls and travelling expenses, but is granted remuneration only in exceptional circumstances, usually if he is a solicitor, accountant or other professional person.[1]

1   In *Re Rudy* (1995) 26 Alta LR (3d) 332, Nash J of the Surrogate Court of Alberta, Canada, held that a receiver is entitled to remuneration from the estate based on the quality of services rendered to the estate. The remuneration must be related to the work actually performed and the responsibility involved in the management of the estate. It is improper for a receiver to take remuneration without the prior approval of the court.

FIRST APPLICATION FOR THE APPOINTMENT OF A RECEIVER

21.65   The forms for applying for the appointment of a receiver can be obtained free of charge from the Customer Services Unit at the Public Trust Office.[1]

1   Stewart House, 24 Kingsway, London WC2B 6JX; telephone 020 7664 7300; fax 020 7774 7705; DX 37965 Kingsway; e-mail: enquiries@publictrust.gov.uk.

21.66   Before applying, the applicant must give notice of his intention to all the patient's relatives of a degree of relationship equal to, or nearer than, the applicant or the proposed receiver.[1] Where a solicitor is seeking to be appointed as receiver, it is sufficient to give notice of the proposed application to the patient's closest relatives, rather than the entire family.

1   Court of Protection Rules 1994 (SI 1994/3046) r 27.

21.67   The following documents should be completed and returned to the Public Trust Office:

(a)   two copies of the application (form CP1);
(b)   the Medical Certificate (form CP3);
(c)   the Certificate of Family and Property (form CP5);
(d)   a copy of the patient's will and other testamentary documents (if any);
(e)   a cheque for the commencement fee, currently £200 made payable to 'Public Trust Office'.

21.68   If immediate action is necessary, for example, the purchase of a property or access to the patient's account in order to pay care fees, an explanation why the matter is urgent should be given in both the form CP5 and a covering letter. The court will then issue an interim order, certificate or directions as appropriate.[1]

1   Court of Protection Rules 1994 r 44.

21.69   On receiving these documents the Public Trust Office will return one copy of form CP1 marked with the date and time when the court will consider the application. Unless the court directs otherwise, no attendance on that date will be necessary,[1] and the appointment of a receiver will be purely a paper transaction. An attended hearing will only be necessary if someone objects to the application.

1   Court of Protection Rules 1994 r 10.

21.70   The Public Trust Office also sends the applicant's solicitor a letter addressed to the patient, if aged 18 or over, telling him the date on which the application will be considered and explaining how representations and observations can be made (form CP6). Unless the court directs otherwise, this letter must be personally served on the patient,[1] and the person who serves it must complete a certificate of service (form CP7).[2] The letter must be delivered to the patient at least 10 clear days before the date when the application will be considered by the court.[3]

1   Court of Protection Rules 1994 r 26.
2   Court of Protection Rules 1994 r 28(1).
3   Court of Protection Rules 1994 r 48(1).

21.71   Although the court has power to dispense with serving notice on the patient, it is generally reluctant to do so because the patient may wish to object to the appointment of a particular person as receiver or may have useful information to contribute. The court is only likely to dispense with notification if it is satisfied, after considering medical evidence, that the patient is incapable of understanding the letter, or that such notification would be detrimental to his health.[1]

1   Court of Protection Rules 1994 r 26(2).

21.72   In most cases the Public Trust Office will take up a reference as to the suitability of the proposed receiver by sending a questionnaire (form CP8) to the referee named by the applicant in the Certificate of Family and Property.

21.73   Where an order is to be made appointing anyone other than the Public Trustee as receiver, the receiver may be required to give security for the due performance of his duties.[1] The amount covered by the security bond is usually based on 1½ times the patient's annual income. A small premium is payable, and this can be recovered from the patient's estate. The order will not be entered until evidence of the security given has been produced. The court's requirements will be explained in a letter to the applicant's solicitor.[2]

1   Court of Protection Rules 1994 r 58.
2   Court of Protection Rules 1994 r 59.

21.74–21.79   When everything is in order, the First General Order setting out the receiver's powers and duties will be issued. Any dealings with the patient's capital must be authorised in the First General Order or subsequent orders or directions.

THE RECEIVER'S DUTIES

Initial Duties

21.80 As soon as the receiver has been appointed he should:[1]

- Open a receivership bank account in his or her own name 'as receiver for [patient's name]'.
- Send an office copy of the order to each bank, building society or other financial institution having dealings with the patient's money and ask them to comply with the directions in the order.
- Pay any money received on the patient's behalf into the receivership bank account.
- Arrange for social security benefits and any occupational pensions or annuities or other income to be paid into the receivership bank account.
- Pay any outstanding bills referred to in the order of appointment.
- Arrange for the patient's valuables, such as jewellery and important documents, to be kept somewhere safe. The order of appointment will usually give directions in this respect.
- Inform the managers of the home or hospital where the patient lives that a receiver has been appointed for the patient, and liaise with them as to the patient's requirements.
- If the patient lives in his or her own home, contact all the authorities (gas, water, electricity, telephone, Council Tax) and inform them of the appointment.
- Arrange with the patient and his social worker, where appropriate, for the patient to have a weekly cash float for their day-to-day requirements.
- Keep records of all transactions: for example, receipts, vouchers and bank statements.

1 The Public Trust Office produces two brochures, *Duties of a Receiver* and *Handbook for Receivers*, which are available free of charge and are usually sent to receivers on their appointment.

Ongoing Duties

21.81–21.84 A receiver also incurs ongoing duties, for example:

- To spend as much as is required of the patient's income in maintaining the patient and providing him or her with clothing and extra comforts. If the patient's income is insufficient, prior authority must be obtained from the court or the Public Trust Office before resorting to the patient's capital.
- To notify the Public Trust Office of any change of address.
- To inform the Benefits Agency of any change in the patient's circumstances.
- To deal with the patient's tax affairs.
- To keep the patient's property secure and in a reasonable state of repair. Minor repairs up to a total cost of £500 a year can be carried out without reference to the Public Trust Office.
- To see that the patient's personal possessions are insured for their full replacement value.
- To complete and submit to the Public Trust Office an annual account or enquiry relating to the patient's financial affairs.
- Not to reveal to anyone else the contents of the patient's will during the patient's

lifetime without the prior and specific approval of the Court or the Public Trust Office.
- To notify the Public Trust Office if the patient dies. The powers of the receiver and the jurisdiction of the Court of Protection terminate on the patient's death.[1]

1 See generally Factsheet 4, *Death of a Patient*.

ACCOUNTS AND ENQUIRIES

21.85   A receiver is required to render an annual account of how he has dealt with the money received and spent on the patient's behalf.[1] A Receiver's Account (form CP28) is sent to the receiver about a week before the anniversary of the First General Order appointing him as receiver. The form should be completed and returned within one month together with:

- The bank statements relating to the receivership bank account.
- Dividend and interest counterfoils.
- Vouchers in support of miscellaneous receipts, such as tax repayments.
- Receipts for all payments, when specifically requested. This includes receipts for nursing home fees and sums spent on clothes and extra comforts.

[1]   Court of Protection Rules 1994 (SI 1994/3046) r 63.

21.86–21.88   In some cases a full account may not be necessary and the receiver will be asked to complete an annual enquiry (form CP27) instead. Both the annual account and annual enquiry forms require the receiver to forecast a budget for the coming year. Even though the figures are only estimates, the budget is a useful indication of whether there will be sufficient income to meet anticipated expenditure and whether recourse to the patient's capital will be necessary. A receiver may prepare and submit his own accounts or instruct a solicitor or accountant to prepare them for him. The Public Trust Office operates an Accounts Helpline[1] to assist in answering queries about completing the annual account or enquiry form.[2]

1   Telelphone 020 7664 7494.
2   Two factsheets are also available free of charge from the Public Trust Office's Customer Services Unit: Factsheet 1, *Accounts*; and Factsheet 2, *Annual Enquiry*.

COMPROMISE OF PROCEEDINGS

All Compromised Cases

21.89   Any proposed compromise of a personal injury or medical negligence action must be approved by the Court of Protection prior to approval by the Queen's Bench Division or District Registry.[1] This can usually be dealt with by correspondence, rather than by an attendance.

1   *Rhodes v Swithenbank* (1889) 22 ABD 577; *Re E (Mental Health Patient)* [1985] 1 All ER 609, 617.

21.90   Before it can approve the award, the court will need to see:

- The pleadings.
- Medical reports.

- Other experts' reports.
- The claimant's and defendant's schedules.
- Counsel's opinion on quantum.

Cases Involving a Structured Settlement

21.91   Before it can approve an award which includes a structured settlement, the court also needs to see the additional documents referred to in the practice note of 12 February 1992, namely:

- The forensic accountant's report setting out the advantages and disadvantages, if any, of structuring, bearing in mind the claimant's life expectancy and the anticipated costs of future care.
- The draft order and model agreement.
- If practicable, counsel's opinion on the structured settlement proposed.
- Sufficient material to satisfy the court that enough capital is available free of the structure to meet anticipated future needs. Particular reference to accommodation and transport needs will usually be helpful in this context.
- Sufficient material to satisfy the court that the structure is secure and backed by responsible insurers.
- Evidence of other assets available to the claimant beyond the award (unless this has already been provided in the certificate of family and property (form CP5) supporting the application for the appointment of a receiver.

  1   Practice Direction (Structured Settlements: Court's Approval) 1 All ER 862, sub nom Practice Note [1992] 1 WLR 328.

TRANSFER OF DAMAGES

Wording of the Order

21.92   The procedure for transferring damages from the Queen's Bench Division or District Registry to the Court of Protection is described in a practice note issued on 7 September 1990.[1]

  1   Practice Direction (Mental Health: Transfer of Damages) [1991] 1 All ER 436, sub nom Practice Note [1991] 1 WLR 2.

21.93   The transfer of funds will be facilitated if the judgment includes a provision to the following effect:

> 'that the defendant do within days pay the said sum of £ into court to be placed to and accumulated in a special account pending an application by the next friend to the Court of Protection for the appointment of a receiver for the [plaintiff] and that upon such an appointment being made the said sum of £ together with any interest thereon [subject to a first charge under the Legal Aid Act 1988] be transferred to the Court of Protection to the credit of the [plaintiff] to be dealt with as the Court of Protection in its discretion shall think fit.'

Legal Aid Reserve

21.94   If the claimant was legally aided in the action, the award will effectively be frozen because of the statutory charge unless and until a reserve for costs can be agreed with the Legal Aid Board. The claimant's solicitor should therefore take urgent steps to obtain and complete the appropriate form of undertaking, which is available from the area office, by inserting a figure which is sufficient to cover the full extent of their claim on the legal aid fund. This sum should take into account costs and disbursements already incurred or to be incurred, less any legal aid contribution which has been paid by the claimant and any inter partes costs which have been recovered from the defendant. The claimant's solicitor should return the signed undertaking to the legal aid area office (who will inform the Court Funds Office by letter of the amount to be retained to cover the statutory charge) and should obtain an order from the court making the award directing the Court Funds Office to release to the area office the amount from the award to cover the statutory charge. The balance will then be released to the Court of Protection once the Part II Order has been lodged.

Lodging the Part II Order

21.95   The claimant's solicitor should complete a payment schedule (Form 200). In the column headed 'Details of payments, transfers or other operation required', they should insert 'Transfer to Court of Protection credit', and in the second column they should give the full name and address of the patient. In the third column they should insert the figure which represents the award, less the figure to be reserved for costs. In the space below, they should insert in the first column 'Reserve for cost' and in the third column they should give details of that figure as shown in the undertaking to the legal aid area office mentioned above. The solicitor should then forward the Form 200 for authentication to the District Registry which made the award. If the award was made in London, and the patient is not also a minor, the Form 200 should be lodged in the Action Department of the Central Office at the Royal Courts of Justice. If the patient is also a minor, it should go to the Masters' Secretary's Office in the Royal Courts of Justice.

21.96–21.99   The court which made the award should be requested to forward the payment schedule (form 200) to the Court Funds Office.[1] As soon as it is received there, arrangements will be made to carry the bulk of the award over to the Court of Protection, leaving the amount reserved for costs in the Special Account at the Court Funds Office to gain interest until the legal aid area office confirms that it can be released to the Court of Protection or to itself, as the case may be.

   1   Queen's Bench Division, 22 Kingsway, London WC2B 6LE.

HANDING OVER TO THE COURT

The 'Handover' Meeting

21.100   As soon as the award has been received and carried over to the Court of Protection, it may be helpful to arrange a 'handover' meeting with the court. Such a meeting is by no means compulsory, but it can greatly assist the smooth running of the case in the future by allowing the patient and receiver to know what is expected of them and giving them the opportunity to find out what they can expect in return.

21.101   The meeting is usually held by the Master or the caseworker who deals with the matter on a day-to-day basis at the Public Trust Office and is attended by any one or more of the following people:

- The solicitor who has had conduct of the personal injury or medical negligence claim.
- The receiver.
- Members of the family or carers.
- The case manager.
- A representative from the Public Trust Office's Investments Branch or the panel brokers.
- Sometimes, the patient himself.

21.102   To facilitate the patient's attendance there is a ramp and doorway at the side of the building which can easily be manoeuvered by wheelchair and a lift to the Master's chambers on the first floor. These meetings are usually held at 2.30 p.m. but can be arranged at any time to suit the convenience of those attending, especially if they have a long journey. The meeting is very relaxed and informal and there is no need for anyone to be worried about it.

21.103   The purpose of the handover meeting is to reconsider the whole position and establish what the patient's capital and income needs are likely to be, how they can be met and what the investment policy should be. The assumptions on which the award was based at trial or settlement may not always be still applicable and sometimes it is not in the patient's interests to follow precisely the scheme that was envisaged in the claimant's schedule or the judge's decision, although obviously it is a useful guide.

21.104   If for any reason it is difficult to attend the court, perhaps because of distance or problems in getting someone to look after the patient for any length of time, the matters that would normally be discussed at the meeting can be dealt with by correspondence instead. These are discussed in para 21.105-21.121.

Capital Requirements

21.105   The first item to be considered is the patient's capital requirements, both immediate and in the foreseeable future. These are one-off items of expenditure, rather than ongoing payments which are more in the nature of income needs.

21.106   Capital expenditure includes, for example:

- The cost of purchasing suitable alternative accommodation, conversion and adaptations (see paras 21.120-21.126).
- Specialist equipment such as wheelchairs and hoists.
- Transport.
- Repayment of past expenses.
- Computer equipment.
- Holidays.

Income Requirements

21.107   The next point to consider is the patient's income requirements and to calculate how much is required each month from his contingency fund in addition to any social security benefits, structured settlement payments or other income he receives.

21.108 It is difficult to generalise on the amount that any patient will require each month. This is because each case differs from another. However, there are three fairly common scenarios where the patient is a child living at home with his parents. They are:

(a) where both parents are working, or are otherwise comparatively well-off;

(b) where one parent is working, but is earning only an average wage; and

(c) where neither parent is able to work because they both need to devote themselves full-time to the care of the patient and other children in the family.

21.109 In all of these cases there is probably professional, commercial care of one kind or another, and there will be additional costs to the family (for example: extra electricity costs, extra petrol, respite care, additional clothing costs, and so on) which are attributable solely to the injury and which should have been taken into account when making the award.

21.110 In the first case in para 21.108 the costs of professional care and the additional costs attributable solely to the injury may be the only costs the claimant is expected to provide from the award during his minority.

21.111 In case (b) the claimant may be expected not only to pay the costs of professional care and the additional costs attributable solely to the injury, but also to contribute towards expenditure on things like holidays, entertainment, respite care and so on, which would be for his benefit but which the parents could not wholly provide from just the one wage coming in.

21.112 In case (c) the claimant will, to all intents and purposes, be subsidising the living expenses for the whole of the family, which is not what the award was intended for but which may, nevertheless, be unavoidable. The financial consolation will be that his or her care will be less expensive than if it were provided professionally, but it can still be a great drain on the fund to have to support or partly support people other than the claimant. In appropriate cases the court will make an allowance from the patient's fund to a parent for the care he provides, but it will not be regarded as a salary or wage, and will not be paid under a contract of employment.[1] The allowance will vary from time to time, if the patient's needs so require.

1 In *Re B's Estate* (1999) Times, 26 January, Mr Justice Jonathan Parker held that where the Court of Protection made monetary contributions on a patient's behalf to the provision of accommodation and the running of a household, those payments could not properly be characterised as a contribution towards the 'reasonable needs' of the patient's mother for the purposes of the Inheritance (Provision for Family and Dependants) Act 1975, notwithstanding that the payments indirectly benefited the mother. Furthermore, it was impossible to infer that the patient, via the Court of Protection, assumed responsibility for the maintenance of her mother for the purposes of s 3(4) of the 1975 Act. Reversed by the Court of Appeal: [2000] 1 All ER 665.

Table1:

Expenditure	Monthly
Care: commercial	
Care: family	
Speech therapy	
Physiotherapy	
Hydrotherapy/swimming	
Food	
Gas	
Water	
Electricity	
Council Tax	
Telephone bills	
Mobile telephone	
TV licence	
Cable TV subscription	
Clothes	
Footwear	
Pet food/vet	
Car: petrol	
Car: servicing and maintenance	
Car: insurance	
Car: road tax	
Car: AA/RAC membership	
Spectacles/optician	
Dentist/Denplan	
Prescriptions	
Toiletries	
Hairdresser	
Cleaner/cleaning materials	
Dry cleaning/laundry	
Public transport	
Taxis	
Insurance: building	
Insurance: contents	
Insurance: medical	
Insurance: death of prime carer	
Domestic appliances	
Household decorating, repairs etc.	
Holidays	
Entertainment/social	
Birthday/Christmas presents	
Newspapers/magazines	
Case management	
Accountancy fees	
Income Tax	
Total	

Income	Monthly
Structured settlement Disability Living Allowance Severe Disablement Allowance	
Total	

Balance	Monthly
Expenditure Income	
Shortfall	

Monthly Budget

21.113   It is helpful if a budget can be drawn up by the receiver, with assistance from the solicitor where necessary, in advance of the handover meeting. The budget should set out the patient's monthly expenditure on care, outgoings in respect of accommodation, and his general living expenses. Some items of expenditure will be annual (in which case, divide the annual sum by 12 to arrive at a monthly figure): others will be weekly (in which case, use a calculator to multiply the weekly payments by 52 and then divide by 12 to reach the monthly figure).

21.114   When the patient's income requirements have been ascertained, the court will authorise monthly payments to cover the shortfall between expenditure and the income received from other sources such as a structured settlement or state benefits. The monthly payments are usually paid by standing order from the Court Funds Office to the receivership bank account.

21.115–21.119   The next task is to consider investment strategy (see para 21.130-21.142), and then to consider whether it would be appropriate for an adult patient to make a will or, if he lacks testamentary capacity, whether an application should be made to the court to authorise the execution of a statutory will on his behalf (see para 21.150-21.153). Finally, the receiver will be reminded to get in touch with the patient's local tax office and Benefits Agency to advise them of any change in circumstances arising from the award.

PURCHASING SUITABLE ACCOMMODATION

Negotiating the Price

21.120   When negotiating the purchase price of alternative accommodation, it is recommended that, wherever possible, the estate agents should not be told that a substantial damages award has been made or is in the pipeline. The agents are acting for the seller, and it has been noticed on many occasions that a patient has been required to pay the full asking price, sometimes more, even though the property may have been on the market for some time, and even though the evidence of value suggests that the property is worth less than the agreed price.

21.121   For similar reasons the court usually asks for three competitive estimates for the cost of altering or adapting the property to meet the patient's requirements. It does not automatically follow that the court will insist on the receiver accepting the cheapest quotation or tender. Other factors may be taken into account, such as when a builder can start, whether a particular builder has a good reputation, and what guarantees there are in respect of faulty workmanship.

The Court's Approval

21.122   Before it is able to approve a proposed purchase, the court requires sight of:

- A survey.
- Evidence of value, if not already contained in the survey.
- (If possible) a report from an architect specialising in building design for the disabled, or an occupational therapist's report, assessing the suitability of the external access, internal access and facilities within the property, and giving an estimate of the likely cost of adapting the building to meet the patient's requirements.
- (Where appropriate) planning permission for any proposed extension, ramps etc. It is recommended that contracts should not be exchanged until the requisite planning consents have been obtained.
- Evidence that there are, or will be, sufficient funds (say, from an interim payment) to cover the purchase price, the incidental costs of acquiring the property, and the cost of any alterations and adaptations.

21.123   The court will also need to be satisfied that the cost of the property and proposed adaptations is reasonable having regard to all the circumstances, and that it will not eat into capital that has been earmarked for the patient's care.

Order for Purchase Where the Patient is an Adult

21.124   Where the patient is aged 18 or over and is the only person contributing to the purchase price, an order for purchase will be issued authorising the receiver to sign the contract and transfer on the patient's behalf. The court issues a procedure note, PN 4, Procedure on Sale and Purchase of Property, which is available free of charge.

Procedure Where the Patient is a Minor

21.125   A minor cannot hold land. Accordingly, where the patient is under 18 the property must be transferred to at least two trustees to hold on his behalf. One of the trustees should be independent of the patient's family, preferably a solicitor. The trustees are required to execute a simple declaration of trust. For example:

THIS DECLARATION OF TRUST is made on (*date*) by (*full names of the patient's parents*) of (*address*) and (*full name of solicitor trustee*) of (*address*) ('the Trustees')

WHEREAS
1. The Trustees are the proprietors of the property known as (*address*) ('the property') title to which is registered at the Land Registry under title number (*number*)
2. The property was purchased entirely from [interim] damages awarded to (*full name of patient*) in respect of personal injuries

NOW THIS DEED WITNESSES that the Trustees HEREBY DECLARE that they hold the property on trust for (*full name of patient*) absolutely

SIGNED as a deed by (*all the trustees*)
in the presence of:

21.126–21.129   A restriction should be registered on the proprietorship register at the Land Registry. In some cases the court may require the trustees to give an undertaking in the following form, which can of course be included in the declaration of trust:[1]

WE (*full names and addresses of trustees*) HEREBY UNDERTAKE that during the incapacity of the above-named patient
a) we shall not exercise the statutory power of appointing new trustees without the prior consent of the Court of Protection
b) we shall not mortgage charge sell or otherwise dispose of the property without first obtaining the court's approval
c) in the event of sale we shall only deal with the patient's share of the proceeds of sale as the court directs

Signed ....
Dated ....

1   Master's Direction 1/93.

INVESTMENTS

Investment Policy

21.130   Although it seeks to attempt the impossible, the overall aim in damages cases is to ensure that, on the last day of the patient's life, the last pound of the patient's award is being spent. If the fund has been exhausted years before the patient's death, then everyone has been over-indulgent. Conversely, if a large capital sum is left on the patient's death, then everyone has been over-cautious or frugal and has not allowed the patient to enjoy the quality of life and care that the award was intended to provide.

21.131   An investment policy is set for each patient, usually when the First General Order is issued or at the handover meeting after the final award has been made. When selecting the appropriate investment policy the court first considers the patient's age and life expectancy. In the medical certificate (form CP3) the doctor is asked to express an opinion on whether the patient is expected to live for five years or more.

21.132 If the patient is unlikely to live for five years, a short-term ('ST') policy is set. This applies most frequently in the case of older patients and is usually designed to ensure that the funds are safe and available quickly. If the patient is expected to live for more than five years, a long-term ('LT') policy is set. There are eight separate investment codes within the LT specification depending on the amount of capital available and whether the requirement is for capital growth or high income. The investment codes which are generally selected for patients who have been awarded substantial damages for personal injury or medical negligence are LT7 and LT8. A factsheet is supplied by the Public Trust Office's Customer Services Unit free of charge.[1]

1   Factsheet 3: *Investments*, Public Trust Office 020-7664-7300.

Investing for Capital Growth

21.133 Investment code LT7 applies to funds over £150,000 where the requirement is solely for capital growth, or capital growth with some income, and some risk is acceptable.

21.134 The usual investment strategy is to set up a segregated portfolio to provide the required level of gross income with a cash balance held on Special Account and investments chosen from:

- Conventional and index-linked gilts, when anticipated returns exceed that on Special Account. The fixed interest portion of the fund may be reduced to 15% (or 10% for funds over £500,000, but for this to occur approximately half this liquidity should be retained on Special Account).
- Primarily individual UK ordinary shares and Common Investment Funds. There should be a minimum of 15 equity holdings for a portfolio valued at £150,000 (and usually at least 20 holdings for higher value funds) paying due regard to the FTSE100 market sector wightings. The foreign exposure will usually not exceed 20% of the equity exposure with no more than 5% in any one economic area, and should be achieved through commercial unit trusts and investment trusts. Direct foreign purchases can only be made with the court's approval. Exposure to *smaller companies* should also be achieved through commercial unit trusts and investment trusts.

Investing for High Income

21.135 Investment code LT8 applies where the fund exceeds £150,000 and the requirement is for growth of income and capital, or high income with resort to capital if income is insufficient to meet expenditure. Again, this code only applies if some risk is considered acceptable.

21.136 The usual investment strategy is to set up a segregated portfolio to provide, if possible, the required level of gross income with:

- 20-30% in Special Account or gilts, where the anticipated returns exceed that on Special Account. The balance on Special Account should be at least one year's estimated total expenditure.

- Primarily individual UK ordinary shares and Common Investment Funds. There should be a minimum of 15 equity holdings for a portfolio valued at £150,000 (and usually at least 20 holdings for higher value funds) paying due regard to the FTSE100 market sector wightings. The foreign exposure will usually not exceed 10% of the equity exposure with no more than 5% in any one economic area, and should be achieved through commercial unit trusts and investment trusts. Direct foreign purchases can only be made with the court's approval.

Funds in Court

21.137   The court will also decide whether a patient's investments are to be held 'in court' or 'out of court'. In practice, investments out of court are managed by stockbrokers other than the Public Trust Office's appointed panel brokers.

21.138   Where funds are held in court:

- The patient's assets are usually held in the name of the Accountant-General of the Supreme Court and are dealt with through the Court Funds Office.
- Ready cash is held on Special Account.
- Common Investment Funds are available.
- Only the appointed panel brokers are authorised to manage more substantial portfolios because of the administrative arrangements between the Court Funds Office and the Bank of England.
- The receiver does not receive company reports and accounts or have to deal with rights issues, bonus issues, takeover bids, mergers and so on.
- The Court Funds Office receives and accounts for dividend and interest payments, thereby relieving the receiver of administrative duties.
- The Court Funds Office makes regular (usually monthly) payments to the receivership bank account, or simply transfers dividends and interest when they are received.

Special Account

21.139   Special Account is a deposit account held in the name of the Accountant-General of the Supreme Court which pays a competitive rate of interest (currently 7% gross) without deduction of tax. No notice of withdrawal is required. Interest is credited half-yearly on the last Friday of May and November, though it accrues on a day-to-day basis.

Common Investment Funds

21.140   Common investment funds are similar to unit trusts and are managed by Flemings on behalf of the Accountant-General of the Supreme Court. Part I of the Administration of Justice Act 1965 authorised the creation of such funds for the investment of funds in court. There are now only two funds (a third, the Gross Income Fund, ceased to exist in 1999):

(a) Capital Fund, an equity fund aimed at capital growth; and
(b) High Yield Fund, which provides a greater income than the Capital Fund but still offers scope for capital growth.

The Panel Stockbrokers

21.141   The panel brokers are two firms of stockbrokers appointed by the Public Trust Office to manage patients' investments where there is no other suitable broker or financial adviser. The portfolios of patients with surnames from A to K are managed by Brewin Dolphin Bell Lawrie Ltd, and those from L to Z are managed by Capel Cure Sharp Ltd. The panel brokers do not charge a management fee for their services and are remunerated only by commission on any deals they transact with the approval of the Public Trust Office.

Funds Out of Court: Using Other Stockbrokers

21.142–21.149   There is a traditional predisposition towards the investment of a damages award with the Public Trust Office's appointed panel brokers. However, the court has a discretion in such matters and will consider allowing other stockbrokers to manage a patient's investments under what is known as a general powers authority if, having regard to all the circumstances, it is satisfied that the management of the fund out of court will be more beneficial to the patient than management in court.[1]

   1   *Morris v Zanki* (1997) 18 WAR 260; *Jones v Moylan* (1997) WAR 492 Supreme Court of Western Australia).

WILLS
If the Patient has Testamentary Capacity

21.150   If a patient is aged 18 or over and wishes to make a will, medical evidence should be obtained as to whether he has testamentary capacity. The criteria for capacity to make a will were set out in *Banks v Goodfellow*,[1] namely that a person must be able to:

(a) understand the nature of the act and its effects;
(b) understand the extent of the property of which he is disposing;
(c) comprehend and appreciate the claims to which he ought to give effect.

   1   (1870) LR 5 QB 549 p 566.

21.151   If a patient has testamentary capacity, the court will authorise his solicitor to take instructions for the preparation of a will. Procedure Note PN5 gives instructions on the procedure.

If the Patient Lacks Testamentary Capacity

21.152   If the patient lacks testamentary capacity, an application may be made to the court for an order authorising the execution of a 'statutory will' on the patient's behalf. The procedure is set out in Procedure Note PN9, and details of the principles to be considered by the court when making such a will are given in *Re D(J)*.[1]

   1   [1982] 1 Ch 237; [1982] 2 WLR 373; [1982] 2 All ER 37.

21.153–21.154   An application for a statutory will may be advisable to resolve some apparent injustice in the intestacy rules. Anyone who may be adversely affected by the proposed will is usually notified of the application and has the opportunity to make his representations.[1]

> 1 *Re B (Court of Protection)(Notice of Proceedings)* [1987] 1 WLR 552; [1987] 2 All ER 475; [1987] 2 FLR 155.

FEES
Recoverability from the Defendant

21.155 Court of Protection fees are payable to the Public Trust Office and are governed by Part XVIII of The Court of Protection Rules 1994. The current fees payable are specified in the Appendix to those Rules and are described in paras 21.156 and 21.159-21.162. These fees are recoverable from the defendant.[1] However, there is some uncertainty as to the effect which contributory negligence will have on the amount of fees recoverable.[2]

> 1 *Futej v Lewandowski* (1980) 124 Sol Jo 777, approved by the Court of Appeal in *Rialas v Mitchell* (1984) Times, 17 July.
> 2 *Ellis v Denton* Rougier J (30 June 1989, unreported), *Kemp & Kemp*, C2-002. Compare *Cassel v Riverside Health Authority* [1992] PIQR Q168.

Commencement Fee

21.156 A commencement fee of £200 is payable on the issue of any first application for the appointment of a receiver or any other originating process in respect of any patient (for example, a short order or a direction of the Public Trustee).[1]

> 1 Court of Protection Rules 1994 (SI 1994/3046) r 79, as amended by the Court of Protection (Amendment) Rules 1999 (SI 1999/2504).

Administration Fee[1]

21.157 An annual administration fee is payable in respect of the clear annual income at the disposal of the patient from the date of issue of the first application for the appointment of a receiver, or other originating process, until the termination of the proceedings.[2]

> 1 At the time of finalising this chapter, there is a draft Statutory Instrument due to be laid before Parliament in September 2000 that fundamentally changes the basis of the COP annual charges to a flat fee of £205 pa for cases where the Public Trustee is not the Receiver and £1,750 p a where the Public Trustee is the Receiver.
> 2 Court of Protection Rules 1994 r 80(1).

21.158 The Public Trustee will annually, or at any other convenient interval, issue a certificate stating the amount of the administration fee payable in respect of the patient, the period in respect of which it is payable and the name of the person by whom the payment is to be made.

Income Band	Exceeding	Not Exceeding	Fee
(i)	-	£2,000	£100
(ii)	£2,000	£5,000	£180
(iii)	£5,000	£10,000	£450
(iv)	£10,000	£15,000	£800
(v)	£15,000	£25,000	£1,200
(vi)	£25,000		£1,750

Transaction Fee

21.159   A transaction fee of £100 is payable on the making by the Court of any order authorising the execution of a statutory will on behalf of a patient.[1] Other transaction fees are set out in the Appendix to the Court of Protection Rules 1994.

1   Court of Protection Rules 1994 r 83(1) and Appendix para 5.

Fees Payable Where the Public Trustee is the Receiver

21.160   An *appointment fee* of £250 is payable on the appointment of the Public Trustee as receiver for a patient,[1] except where it appears that the patient's clear annual income is less than £1,000.

21.161   An annual fee is payable comparable to, but on a higher scale than, the annual administration fee payable where there is an external receiver.[1] The annual fee is payable on the passing of the account and is based on the clear annual income at the patient's disposal. Income which accrued and became payable more than six months prior to the date when the court's jurisdiction was first exercised in relation to the patient is disregarded. No annual fee is taken where the proceedings are terminated less than four weeks from the date of issue of the first application for the appointment of a receiver.

Income Band	Exceeding	Not Exceeding	Fee
(i)	-	£2,000	£200
(ii)	£2,000	£5,000	£600
(iii)	£5,000	£10,000	£1,500
(iv)	£10,000	£15,000	£3,000
(v)	£15,000	£25,000	£3,800
(vi)	£25,000		£4,600

1   Court of Protection Rules 1994 Appendix Table 2. Table 1 relates to the annual administration fee payable where there is an external receiver.

21.162   A winding up fee is payable on the death of a patient for whom the Public Trustee had been appointed receiver, amounting to £250 on the date of cessation of the receivership and £100 on each anniversary of such date until the matter is completed.

Treatment of Structured Settlements

21.163   Special provisions apply where any structured payment of damages or any payment which is intended as part of a series of payments arising from an annuity, insurance bond or similar arrangement is made for the benefit of a patient.[1] In such a case only 50% of the payment is treated as the patient's income for the purposes of calculating any fee payable which requires ascertainment of the clear annual income at the patient's disposal.

1   Court of Protection Rules 1994 r 85(1).

Remission, Postponement and Exemption

21.164–21.169　The Public Trustee may remit or postpone the whole or part of any fee where in his opinion hardship might otherwise be caused to the patient or his dependants, or where the circumstances are otherwise exceptional.[1] No review lies from the Public Trustee's decision in this respect.[2] He may also remit the payment of the whole or part of any fee where the cost of calculation and collection would be disproportionate to the amount involved.[3]

1　Court of Protection Rules 1994 r 86(1).
2　Court of Protection Rules 1994 r 56(2).
3　Court of Protection Rules 1994 r 86(2).

SOLICITORS' COSTS

Recoverability from the Defendant

21.170　In addition to Court of Protection fees (see paras 21.155-21.164), the claimant can recover from the defendant the cost of instructing a solicitor in relation to the application to the court for the appointment of a receiver and the costs of continued dealings with the court, if reasonably incurred.[1]

1　*Hodgson v Trapp* [1988] 1 FLR 69.

21.171　Legal aid is not available for proceedings in the Court of Protection. All costs incurred in relation to proceedings under the Court of Protection Rules 1994 are in the discretion of the court or the Public Trustee.[1] Generally, they are awarded out of the patient's estate,[2] although in disputed cases there may be circumstances where some other order will be made. There are three options: taxation, fixed costs or agreed costs.

1　Court of Protection Rules 1994 r 87(1).
2　*Re Cathcart* [1893] 1 Ch 466.

Detailed Assessment of Costs

21.172　Detailed assessment is the usual method of dealing with costs, which are normally awarded on an indemnity basis.[1] The Court of Protection (Amendment) Rules 1999 (SI 1999/2504) also came into force on 1 October 1999. They amend rule 89 of the Court of Protection Rules 1994 so as to apply, with certain modifications, the costs provisions in Parts 43, 44, 47 and 48 of the Civil Procedure Rules 1998 to Court of Protection proceedings.

1　The question of costs was considered in detail by Sir Robert Megarry V-C in *Re D(J)* [1982] Ch 237.

Fixed Costs

21.173　Fixed costs were introduced in 1983 and are reviewed annually by the Court of Protection and the Law Society. Solicitors are under no obligation to accept fixed costs and retain the option of having a bill of costs drawn-up and taxed, if they prefer.

21.174　There are five categories of fixed costs, and in addition to the following figures, VAT and disbursements are allowed:

- Category I covers work up to and including the date on which the First General Order is entered. The current (2000) level is £600.
- Category II applies to the preparation and lodgment of a receivership account. The level is currently £155, or, where the receivership account has been certified by a solicitor under the provisions of the Practice Directions dated 13 September 1984 and 5 March 1985, £170.[1]
- Category III covers general management work in the second and subsequent years. The current level is £475 where there is a lay receiver, and £530 where a solicitor is the receiver. Categories II and III may be claimed together.
- Category IV relates to applications under the Trustee Act 1925, s 36(9) for the appointment of a new trustee in place of the patient and for the purpose of making title to land. The current level is £290.
- Category V applies to conveyancing costs. Two elements are allowable: (a) a fixed sum of £110 in respect of correspondence with the court or Public Trust Office, and (b) a value element of 0.5% of the consideration up to £400,000 and 0.25% thereafter, with a minimum value element of £305.

1   See [1984] 3 All ER 320 and [1985] 1 All ER 884 respectively.

Agreed Costs

21.175–21.179   Agreed costs were introduced in 1990, and the level of agreed costs has been raised on several occasions since then. If a solicitor's bill for costs incurred in the Court of Protection does not exceed £1,000 excluding VAT and disbursements, the solicitor may submit the bill to the court and suggest a figure which he would accept by way of costs. The bill submitted should contain a narrative of the work done, the time spent and the level of fee-earner involved, together with receipts for any disbursements. If the amount sought is reasonable, it will be agreed by the court.

ALTERNATIVES TO RECEIVERSHIP

Criticism of Receivership

21.180   In its report, *The Incapacitated Principal*, which was published in July 1983 and led to the Enduring Powers of Attorney Act 1985, the Law Commission said:

> 'The underlying complaint is not that the Court of Protection is unapproachable or unnecessarily slow or inflexible. It is none of these things. Inevitably, however, it has procedures, and procedures always involve time and expense. For example, before making a receivership order the court always requires production of *medical evidence* because it has to be satisfied that the proposed patient is indeed a 'patient'. The originating application must usually be accompanied by a substantial (*certificate* of family and property) to enable the court to judge the suitability of the proposed receiver and (looking to the future) to assist the court to give directions on questions relating to the administration of the patient's estate. Furthermore, the receiver may as a condition of his appointment be required to provide *security*. He will also usually be required to render annual *accounts* to the court and ... have these passed. Finally, in order to finance the court's activities, *fees* are payable by the patient's estate. At the outset each originating application bears a commencement fee. Additionally, there are fairly substantial fees charged

annually on the patient's clear annual income as well as 'transaction fees' for some individual dealings with the patient's estate (including the making of a statutory will).'

1   Law Com No 122 (Cmnd 9877), at para 2.27.

21.181   These comments are as true today as they were in 1983. As a former Law Commissioner put it, 'the Court of Protection does things properly, but paternalistically and at a price'.[1] Anyone working in the mental health sector has to tread a line between autonomy on the one hand, and paternalism on the other. The court is no exception and is keen allow patients and receivers as much autonomy as it considers appropriate in the circumstances.

1   JT Farrand in *An Aging World: Dilemmas and Challenges for Law and Social Policy*, John Eekelaar and David Pearl (eds) (1989) Clarendon Press, Oxford, p 641.

21.182   There are two alternatives to receivership: a private trust and an enduring power of attorney.

Private Trusts

21.183   The High Court has no power to order the settlement of an award of damages which is the absolute property of a patient. The Court of Protection, however, does have the power to authorise the creation of a trust or settlement of a patient's assets,[1] and will consider the creation of a private trust if it is satisfied that, having regard to all the circumstances, a trust – including a special needs trust – will be more beneficial to the patient than a receivership.[2] An application for the creation of a private trust is formal, and the Official Solicitor will be asked to represent the patient for the purposes of that application. The court usually requires that the trust be revocable, and that there should always be at least one professional trustee who is independent of any family trustees.

1   Mental Health Act 1983 s 96(1)(d). Applications for a private trust are usually formal, and the Official Solicitor is often asked to represent the patient. The procedure for making an application is described in Procedure Note PN9.
2   See, generally, the Court of Protection's Practice Note of 15 November 1996 on the procedure for the settlement of personal injury awards to patients.

Enduring Powers of Attorney

21.184   An enduring power of attorney is a deed in which one person (the donor) gives another person (the attorney) authority to act on his behalf. It endures, or remains in force, after the donor has become mentally incapable of managing his property and affairs, provided it is registered with the Public Trust Office.[1]

1   Enduring Powers of Attorney Act 1985, ss 1 and 4. The mental capacity required to create an enduring power of attorney was described by Hoffmann J (as he then was) in *Re K, Re F* [1988] 1 All ER 358.

21.185   Enduring powers are ideally suited for older people who wish in advance to appoint someone to manage their affairs if they should become mentally incapacitated. Generally speaking, however, they are not suitable for the management of a substantial damages award because of the high incidence of abuse.[1] An attorney is not obliged to account to anyone, is unable to provide security in the event of default because no insurance company is prepared to cover such a risk, is not obliged to pursue any particular investment policy or even to take investment advice and has unlimited access to the donor's capital and income.[2]

1 See, generally, Denzil Lush, *Taking liberties: enduring powers of attorney and financial abuse,* Solicitors Journal, Vol 142 No 34, 11 September 1998, pp 808, 809.
2 The court can refuse to register an enduring power of attorney or can cancel the registration of a power if it is satisfied that, having regard to all the circumstances, the attorney is unsuitable to be the donor's attorney: Enduring Powers of Attorney Act 1985 ss 6(7) and 8(4)(g).

21.186 Nevertheless, in a few appropriate cases the court has authorised a patient to execute an enduring power of attorney and, once it has been registered with the Public Trust Office, has discharged the receiver.

Part 5
Appendices

Appendix 1

Selected List of Rehabilitation Units

BRAIN INJURY

Area Rehabilitation Service for Younger Disabled People, Stirling Royal Infirmary NHS Trust
Bill Anderson, Service Manager   01786 434096

Astley Ainslie Hospital Edinburgh
Mrs Yvonne Jones   0131 537 9039

Astley Ainslie Hospital - Driving Assessment Centre   0131 537 9192

Aylesbury Vale Community Healthcare NHS Trust, Physical Rehabilitation Service
Ms Veronica Wheeler, General Manager   01296 393319

Banstead Place Brain Injury Rehabilitation Centre, Surrey
Ms Judith Oliver, Manager   01737 356222

Bath Head Injury and Neuro-rehabilitation Unit + Bath Children's Head Injury Unit
Royal National Hospital for Rheumatic Diseases
Dr A L Clarke + Mrs S Phillips, Clinical Director   01225 473458

Brain Injury Rehabilitation Centre (BIRC), Rathbone Hospital, Liverpool
Dr Kieran O'Driscoll   0151 250 3062

Brain Injury Rehabilitation Trust (BIRT), Thomas Edward Milton House, Milton Keynes
Mr Bob Merriman, Services Manager   01908 504778
BIRT also have units in Leeds, Birmingham, and Liverpool

Burden Neurological Hospital, Bristol
Dr D Rogers + Dr J M Bird   0117 970 1212

Cambridge Rehabilitation Unit, Herts and Essex Hospital
Dr Whale, Consultant in Rehabilitation   01279 827235

Centre for Brain Injury Rehabilitation, Royal Victoria Hospital, Dundee
Mrs L Pape (Specialty Manager) + Mr Douglas Gentleman   01382 527806

Children's Trust at Tadworth, Tadworth Court, Surrey
Dr Stephane Duckett, Director of Rehabilitation Services   01737 357171

Christchurch Court, Northampton
Ms Jakki Turnbull + Ms Ann Goodman   01604 603533

David Lewis Centre for Epilepsy, Cheshire
Alison Sutherland, Services and Support Manager   01565 640003

Defence Medical Rehabilitation Centre, Headley Court
Officer Commanding Rehabilitation Division   01372 378271

Dorset Brain Injury Service, c/o Poole General Hospital
Dr J P S Burn, Consultant   01202 665511

Douglas Grant Rehabilitation Unit, Ayrshire Central Hospital
Dr P G Mattison, Consultant   01294 274191

Elm Park Brain Injury Services, Colchester
Unit Manager   01206 231055

Fife Rehabilitation Service, Sir George Sharp Unit, Cameron Hospital
Dr R L Sloan, Consultant in Rehabilitation Medicine   01592 712472 Ext 259

Floyd Unit for Neurological Rehabilitation, Birch Hill Hospital, Rochdale
Dr K Walton   01706 755815

Frenchay Centre for Brain Injury Rehabilitation, Frenchay Park Road, Bristol
BS16 1UU
Mr Marc Evans   0117 956 2697

Grafton Manor Brain Injury Rehabilitation Unit, Northants
Annie Gent, Director   01908 543131

Haywood Hospital Neurobehavioural Unit, Stoke-on-Trent
Dr Ken Barrett, Consultant Neuropsychiatrist   01782 425780

Head Injuries Trust for Scotland (HITS) - information service   0141 332 6104

Head Injury Rehabilitation Centre, Sheffield
Mrs Jane Collins, Centre Manager   0114 273 7451/2

Head Injury Therapy Unit, Frenchay Hospital, Bristol
Ms Christel Brugeman, Clinical Co-ordinator   01179 186522

Highbank Brain Injury Rehabilitation Unit, Bury
Mr Phillip Thomas, General Manager   01706 829540

Homerton Regional Neurologic Rehabilitation Unit, London
Dr R J Greenwood   020 8510 5555 ext 7970

Hume Neurological Rehabilitation Unit, Sunderland
Consultant   0191 565 6256 ext 43296

Hunters Moor Regional Neurorehabilitation Centre, Newcastle-upon-Tyne
Professor Michael Barnes, Professor of Neurological Rehabilitation
0191 219 5661

Links Rehabilitation Service, National Society for Epilepsy, Buckinghamshire
Dr Pam Thompson (Consultant) C Farley (Links Manager)   01494 601333

Lishman Brain Injury Unit, Maudsley Hospital, London
Dr Simon Fleminger, Consultant Neuropsychiatrist   020 7919 2092

Lynne House Rehabilitation Unit for Children and Adolescents, Bury
Mr Phillip Thomas   01706 829540

Murdostoun Brain Injury Rehabilitation Unit, Lanarkshire
Miss Ann Hunter, Unit Manager   01698 384055

National Centre for Brain Injury Rehabilitation (Kemsley Division),
St Andrew's Hospital, Northants
Mrs Doreen Maggs, Referral Co-ordinator   01604 29696

National Hospital for Neurology and Neurosurgery, London
Ms Ellis Maher, Director of Therapy & Rehabilitation
020 7837 3611 ext 3654

Oak Farm Physical Rehabilitation Unit, Norwich
Mr N C Williamson, Rehabilitation Manager   01603 868953

Oakwood Cheshire Services (Leonard Cheshire), Stockport
General Manager or Clinical Services Co-ordinator   0161 419 9139

Oliver Zangwill Centre for Neuropsychological Rehabilitation
Princess of Wales Hospital, Cambridgeshire
Jonathan Edwards, Clinical Director   01353 6552165

Papworth Trust, Cambridge
Ms Karen Speare, Business Manager, Rehab Programmes   01480 357276

Raigmore Hospital NHS Trust Rehabilitation Department, Inverness
Dr L Fisher   01463 704000 ext 4291

Rivermead Rehabilitation Centre, Oxford
Dr Derick T Wade, Consultant in Neurological Disability   01865 240321

Robert Fergusson Unit, Royal Edinburgh Hospital
Dr L Langwill, Clinical Manager   0131 537 6000

Royal Hospital for Neuro-disability, London
Dr Keith Andrews (Medical Director)   020 8780 4500

Royal Leamington Spa Rehabilitation Hospital
Mr D A H Badwin, Consultant in Rehabilitation Medicine
01926 317700 ext 7716

Southampton Rehabilitation Unit
Professor D L McLellan   01703 794580

Thames Brain Injury Unit, 80-82 Blackheath Hill, London SE10 8AB
Mr Sayed Bel Barco   020 8691 0102   or   020 8692 4007

Ticehurst House Hospital Brain Injury Services
Director of Head Injury Services   01580 200391

Unstead Park Rehabilitation Hospital,Surrey
Consultant   01483 892061

Wirral Neurorehabilitation Unit, Wirral Hospital Trust, Clatterbridge Hospital
Jo Goodfellow, Directorate Manager   0151 334 4000 ext 4321

Wolfson Neuro-rehabilitation Centre, Atkinson Morley's Hospital, London
Dr Richard Hardie, Clinical Director   020 8725 4765

SPINAL INJURY

Duke of Cornwall Spinal Treatment Centre, Salisbury
Mr Tony Tromans, Consultant   00722 336262

Hexham General Hospital, Northumbria
Mr R A Sutton, Consultant   01434 655655

Midland Spinal Injuries Unit, Oswestry
Mr W El Masry, Consultant   01691 655311

Musgrave Park Hospital, Belfast
Dr J McCann, Consultant   01232 669501 ext 3041

National Spinal Injuries Centre, Stoke Mandeville Hospital
Miss Catherine Dover, General Manager   01296 315820

Royal National Orthopaedic Hospital Spinal Injuries Unit, Stanmore
Head of Service Department   020 8954 2300 ext 592

Princess Royal Spinal Injuries Unit, Sheffield
Mr D G Thomas, Consultant   01142 715647

Queen Elizabeth National Spinal Injuries Unit, Glasgow
Mr Peter Edmond, Consultant   0141 201 2555

Southport Regional Spinal Injury Centre, Merseyside
Mr B M Soni, Consultant   01704 547471

Welsh Spinal and Rehabilitation Unit, Cardiff
Mrs D Martin   01222 566281

Yorkshire Spinal Injuries Centre, Pinderfields Hospital, Wakefield
Mr Y S Ahmed, Consultant   01924 201688 ext 2273

Appendix 2

The Ogden Tables

Government Actuary's Department Actuarial Tables
with explanatory notes for use in Personal Injury and Fatal Accident cases
(Third edition)

*Prepared by an Inter-disciplinary Working Party of Actuaries, Lawyers, Accountants
and other interested parties*

MEMBERS OF THE WORKING PARTY RESPONSIBLE FOR THE THIRD EDITION

Sir Michael Ogden QC	*Chairman*
Chris Daykin, CB, FIA	*The Government Actuary*
Ray Sams	*Lord Chancellor's Department*
Professor Burrows	*The Law Commission*
Harvey McGregor QC	*Invited by the Chairman*
John Crowley QC	*Invited by the Chairman*
Ashton West ACII, Chartered Insurer	*Association of British Insurers*
Alistair Kinley	*Association of British Insurers*
Dr Harry Reid, FIA	*Association of British Insurers*
Mrs Caroline Harmer, Barrister	*Association of Personal Injuries Lawyers*
Allan C Martin, FFA	*Faculty of Actuaries and Institute of Actuaries*
Mrs Ann Paton QC	*Faculty of Advocates*
Nicholas Mostyn QC	*Family Law Bar Association*
Tim Lawrence, FCA	*Family Law Bar Association*
Humphrey Morison, FCA	*Family Law Bar Association*
Tim Sexton, FIA	*Family Law Bar Association*
Martin Brufell, Solicitor	*Forum of Insurance Lawyers*
Graeme Garrett, Solicitor	*Law Society of Scotland*
Matthias Kelly, Barrister	*Personal Injuries Bar Association*
Andrew Dismore, MP	*Association of Personal Injury Lawyers*
Graham Codd	*Association of Personal Injury Lawyers*
John Horne, BCL, Barrister	*The General Council of the Bar*
	(Secretary to the Working Party)

Table of Contents

Explanatory Notes
Section A: General
Section B: Contingencies other than mortality
Section C: Summary

Appendix A
Rates of mortality expressed as percentages of 1911 rates

Appendix B
Selecting an appropriate real rate of return based on market considerations

Appendix C
Comments by the Association of British Insurers (ABI)

Tables 1 to 10 (ELT15)
Table 11   Multipliers for pecuniary loss for life (males)
Table 21   Multipliers for pecuniary loss for life (females)
Table 31   Multipliers for loss of earnings to pension age 65 (males)
Table 41   Multipliers for loss of earnings to pension age 65 (females)
Table 51   Multipliers for loss of earnings to pension age 60 (males)
Table 61   Multipliers for loss of earnings to pension age 60 (females)
Table 71   Multipliers for loss of pension commencing age 65 (males)
Table 81   Multipliers for loss of pension commencing age 65 (females)
Table 91   Multipliers for loss of pension commencing age 60 (males)
Table 10   Multipliers for loss of pension commencing age 60 (females)

Tables 11 to 20 (Prudent estimate of future mortality)
Table 11   Multipliers for pecuniary loss for life (males)
Table 12   Multipliers for pecuniary loss for life (females)
Table 13   Multipliers for loss of earnings to pension age 65 (males)
Table 14   Multipliers for loss of earnings to pension age 65 (females)
Table 15   Multipliers for loss of earnings to pension age 60 (males)
Table 16   Multipliers for loss of earnings to pension age 60 (females)
Table 17   Multipliers for loss of pension commencing age 65 (males)
Table 18   Multipliers for loss of pension commencing age 65 (females)
Table 19   Multipliers for loss of pension commencing age 60 (males)
Table 20   Multipliers for loss of pension commencing age 60 (females)

Tables 21 and 22 (Tables for term certain)
Table 21   Discounting factors for term certain
Table 22   Multipliers for pecuniary loss for term certain
Actuarial formulae and basis

Introduction to the Third Edition

A2.1   This new edition of the tables has been prompted by the publication of English Life Tables No 15. The increased longevity shown in ELT 15 has resulted in changes to the tables published in the second edition.

It will also be seen that opportunity has been taken to make other significant changes and improvements, including the provision of tables which make appropriate prudent allowance for future improvements in mortality. Where appropriate the tables have been extended to ages below 16 and above 70. Relevant tables have also been included for terms certain.

Once the Lord Chancellor has been able to consider the speeches in the House of Lords in *Wells v Wells* which is due to be heard in May, it is anticipated that Commencement Orders will be made bringing into force the Civil Evidence Act 1995 Section 10 and the Damages Act 1996 Section 1, which latter provision is likely to result in the Lord Chancellor fixing the rate of return. Consequently, this edition makes no reference in the main text to the choice of the rate of return, since the Court of Appeal in *Wells* decided that the appropriate rate is 4.5%. However, material relating thereto published in the Second Edition is to be found in Appendix B, so that it will be available if the House of Lords takes a view different from that taken by the Court of Appeal.

After the Lord Chancellor has fixed the rate of return, a fourth edition of the tables will almost certainly be necessary to take account of that and what is said in the House of Lords in *Wells*. Happily, since pursuant to the Civil Evidence Act, the Government Actuary will become responsible for the tables, a fourth edition will be his responsibility, thereby releasing me from the task of being Chairman of the working party, which I was asked to undertake 15 years ago.

SIR MICHAEL OGDEN QC
May 1998

Introduction to the Second Edition

A2.2 The principal reason for this edition is that it is now possible to give assistance about contingencies other than mortality. Tables A, A(60) and A(F)[1] together with explanatory notes, in which those tables are set out, show how these contingencies can be taken into account.

In addition, four further tables have been added so that figures for men and women whose retirement ages are 60 and 65 are now available.

The six original tables have been revised in the light of changes in life expectancy. All 10 tables are based on English Life Tables No 14. It is intended to revise the tables when new Life Tables are published.

In Scotland in *O'Brien's Curator Bonis v British Steel plc* 1991 SLT 477 the Inner House concluded that the tables can be used as a check on a multiplier arrived at by the conventional method. There has been no decision in the English Court of Appeal concerning use of the tables; however, they are now widely used by Judges at first instance. The Law Commission's Consultation Paper No 125 'Structured Settlements and Interim and Provisional Damages' states that, subject to the view of consultees, the Commission believes that the time has come to encourage the general use of the tables by legislation.

The Working Party is greatly indebted to Professor S Haberman and Mrs D S F Bloomfield who undertook much of the work which has enabled the Working Party to provide the new information contained in this edition.

SIR MICHAEL OGDEN
November 1993

1   In the Third Edition these tables have been relabelled as Tables A, B and C.

Introduction to the First Edition

A2.3   Proposals have been made from time to time that actuarial tables might be produced to assist in assessing damages in cases of personal injuries and fatal accidents, for example, by the Law Commission (Law Com No 56, 1973) and by the former Solicitor-General during the passage of the Administration of Justice Act 1982. Both branches of the legal profession in Great Britain have recently co-operated with the Faculty of Actuaries and the Institute of Actuaries to produce the following tables and notes. The tables have been prepared by the Government Actuary's Department and the explanatory notes by actuaries and lawyers nominated by all their professional bodies in Great Britain. I am particularly grateful to the actuaries for having nominated representatives of the highest calibre including a former President of the Institute and the Government Actuary.

The Lord Chancellor, Lord Hailsham of St Marylebone, was informed in advance of the proposal that the actuarial and legal professions should co-operate in the production of such tables and agreed that it would be helpful if this avenue of co-operation between the professions could be explored. Of course, it must be understood that the tables have not been prepared under his direction nor published with his authority.

The purpose of the tables is to help courts in determining on the appropriate figure for what lawyers describe as the 'multiplier'.

It must be emphasised that the tables do not take account of contingencies other than mortality. Consequently the court will need to adjust the multiplier contained in the tables to take account of other factors.

Notwithstanding the need to adjust the multipliers contained in the tables, the size of some of the figures in the tables will undoubtedly come as a surprise to lawyers. However, the members of the Working Party unanimously concluded that the reasoning which leads to such figures could not be faulted. As will be seen, the existence of a new type of Government stock played a significant part in our reasoning.

The Present Position

A2.4   The courts seek, by the award of a lump sum, to put the wage earner or, if he has been killed, his dependant into the same financial position as if the accident had not happened. It is up to the claimant to invest that lump sum as best he can to replace the income lost for which he is being compensated. The courts have decided that, in the majority of cases, inflation is to be disregarded when assessing damages, one reason being that inflation is best left to be dealt with by prudent investment policy (see *Lim v Camden Health Authority*, [1980] AC 174 and cases cited therein). The courts have taken the view that investment of the lump sum award in ordinary shares or a 'basket' of equities and gilts would enable the claimant to have an income derived from dividends and sales of shares which would broadly match the income he had lost; inflation would increase the dividends and market prices at which he would gradually be able to realise his holdings over the years to which the loss relates. Such presumed matching is of necessity imprecise and there is an unavoidable risk of injustice either to the claimant or the defendant.

Index-Linked Government Stock

A2.5 Currently, the courts are using multipliers which implicitly assume a discount rate of between 4% and 5% (*Lim v Camden*). This rate compares with the rate of about five per cent currently obtainable on a spread of ordinary shares if no allowance is made for the effects of future inflation or for the relative future prosperity or adversity of the companies which issued those shares. However, the issue of Index-Linked Government Stock since 1981 has now made it possible to match the receipts from the investment of a lump sum almost precisely to the income loss for which the claimant is being compensated. Such stocks are now an established part of the investment market. The nature of these stocks is such that the dividends rise in accordance with the rise in the Retail Price Index as does the payment on maturity.

A claimant who has purchased ordinary shares or a basket of gilts and equities will receive interest and prices on sale which reflect market forces. In particular, market forces reflect views about anticipated inflation and, in the case of ordinary shares, views of the future prosperity of the particular company relative to other companies. As a result, particularly in the case of ordinary shares, the market price can alter considerably and very rapidly.

A claimant who has bought Index-Linked Government Stock is in a very different position. The future payments under the stock reflect price inflation almost exactly and there is no question of the Government failing to make the stipulated payments. The market value of such stocks represents the value of the future stipulated payments of interest and capital (ignoring the effects of future inflation thereon) discounted at a rate usually lying in the bracket 2 ½% to 3½% per annum. It is within that bracket that the yield on index-linked stocks has generally lain since their introduction to the market. Therefore, it is possible to provide a claimant with such index-linked stocks on which the sums received as interest and payments received on maturity and sale would almost exactly replace the income lost by the claimant in respect of which he is being compensated over the period to which the loss relates.

It is because the effect of inflation, on capital and income alike, is taken into account in the case of Index-Linked Government Stocks that the yield on such stocks is lower and their capital value more stable than in the case of non-index-linked stocks. Whereas, in general, interest rates reflect expectations as to inflation based on past and existing inflation, and the fear of its continuance, the yield on index-linked stocks is simply a measure of the real return which the market expects on invested capital which is assumed to keep its value in real terms.

Obviously, if the courts cease using multipliers which assume a discount rate of between four% and five% and use multipliers based on the assumption that funds are to be invested in index-linked stocks discounted at a rate of between 2½% and 3½%, it is inevitable that the size of the multipliers will increase. The conversion of prospective income which has been lost to the claimant into a capital sum of equivalent value would accordingly be by means of a multiplier which embodies a discount rate in the range 2½% to 3½% and also allows for the effects of mortality. That is in the first instance; the Courts will need to make such adjustments as are necessary, for example to reflect the possibility that receipt of the lost income was not certain (as a result of ill health, redundancy, early retirement and so on), or that the income might have increased otherwise than as a result of inflation (because of promotion and so on), or that the claimant's chances of survival to draw the lost income are not properly represented by the mortality rates of which the multiplier takes account.

Our Reasoning

A2.6 The Working Party concluded that the following arguments could not be faulted. The courts seek to put the wage earner, or, if he has been killed, his dependant, into the same financial position as if the accident had not happened. Investment policy, however prudent, involves risks and it is not difficult to draw up a list of blue chip equities or reliable unit trusts which have performed poorly and, in some cases, disastrously. Index-Linked Government stocks eliminate the risk. Whereas, in the past, a claimant has had to speculate in the form of prudent investment by buying equities or a 'basket' of equities and gilts or a selection of unit trusts, he need speculate no longer if he buys Index-Linked Government Stock. If the loss is, say, £5,000 per annum, he can be awarded damages which, if invested in such stocks, will provide him with almost exactly that sum in real terms.

It may be said that, in practice, the claimant, having been awarded damages on the basis of assumed investment in Index-Linked Government Stocks, may invest in equities. However, the Working Party concluded that it is difficult to argue that any claimant should be obliged to speculate if he does not wish to do so, when there exists an investment which enables him to avoid doing so. In any event, a claimant has been able to do the equivalent in the past in that he may not buy a prudent basket of equities or other investments, damages having been awarded on that basis, but may invest the entire sum in a single venture, for example a small shop. Alternatively, a claimant may invest in a very speculative and imprudent investment or in something such as Krugerrands. For these reasons, the Working Party concluded that the fairest approach to the problem is to work on the basis of multipliers calculated on the basis of presumed investment in Index-Linked Government Stock.

Since reaching this conclusion, the Working Party has read with great interest the speech of Lord Diplock in *Wright v British Railways Board* 1983 (2 AER 698) on the subject of Index-Linked Government Stock.

The Tables[1]

A2.7 The tables take account of ordinary mortality risks. They are based on the assumption that a capital sum will be awarded and that this sum will be exhausted at the end of the period during which the loss will occur.

The tables contain multipliers to be applied to figures of income after deduction of tax. If tax will be payable on the income derived from investing the award, the multiplier which is otherwise appropriate will need adjusting as described in the explanatory notes.

The tables take no account of risks other than mortality. For example, permanent ill health leading to loss of employment, whether due to accident or illness, is something to which any apparently healthy person is to some extent at risk, but which is not reflected in the tables. Of course the tables do not take account of factors such as loss of employment due to redundancy, early retirement and so on.

It will be seen that the tables cover rates between 1½% and 5%. This has been done in case the Courts do not accept the Working Party's view that the fairest solution is to use tables based on Index-Linked Government Stocks.

I am grateful for the assistance given by members of the stock-broking firm of Grieveson, Grant & Co.

MICHAEL OGDEN

1   What is said under this heading must now be read subject to what is included in the later editions.

EXPLANATORY NOTES

Section A: General

Purpose of Tables

A2.8   1. The tables have been prepared by the Government Actuary's Department. They provide an aid for those assessing the lump sum appropriate as compensation for a continuing future pecuniary loss or consequential expense in personal injury and fatal accident cases.

Application of Tables

A2.9   2. The tables set out multipliers. These multipliers enable the user to assess the present capital value of future annual loss (net of tax) or annual expense calculated on the basis of various assumptions which are explained below. Accordingly, to find the present capital value of a given annual loss or expense, it is necessary to select the appropriate table, find the appropriate multiplier and then multiply the amount of the annual loss or expense by that figure.

3. Tables 1 to 20 deal with annual loss or annual expense extending over three different periods of time. In each case there are separate tables for men and women.

- – In Tables 1, 2, 11 and 12 the loss or expense is assumed to begin immediately and to continue for the whole of the rest of the claimant's life, allowing for the possibility of early death or prolonged life. ('The claimant' here includes the deceased in fatal accident cases.)
- – In Tables 3 to 6 and 13 to 16 the loss or expense is assumed to begin immediately but to continue only until the claimant's retirement or earlier

death. The age of retirement is assumed to be 65 in Tables 3 and 4 (and 13 and 14) and 60 in Tables 5 and 6 (and 15 and 16).

– In Tables 7 to 10 and 17 to 20 it is assumed that the annual loss or annual expense will not begin until the claimant reaches retirement but will then continue for the whole of the rest of his or her life.

4. In Tables 7 and 17 (males) and Tables 8 and 18 (females) the age of retirement is assumed to be 65. In Tables 9 and 19 (males) and Tables 10 and 20 (females) the age of retirement is assumed to be 60. The tables make due allowance for the chance that the claimant may not live to reach the age of retirement.

Mortality Assumptions for Tables 1 to 10

A2.10   5. As in previous editions of these tables, Tables 1 to 10 are based on the mortality rates experienced in England & Wales in a three-year period, in this case the years 1990 to 1992, and published by the Government Actuary's Department as English Life Tables No 15 (ELT 15). Given this assumption about mortality, the accuracy of these tables, which were prepared by the Government Actuary's Department, has been accepted by all the actuaries on the Working Party, which included actuaries nominated by the Institute and the Faculty of Actuaries, the Association of British Insurers ('ABI') and the Family Law Bar Association. Consequently, the Courts can have confidence in the mathematical accuracy of these tables. Members of the Working Party nominated by the ABI have reservations about the application of the Tables and other matters and these are set out in Appendix C.

6. On the basis of some reported cases, it appears that tables for pecuniary loss for life, for example, cost of care, may have been misunderstood. As stated hereafter in paragraph 21, the tables take account of the possibilities that the claimant will live for different periods, for example, die soon or live to be very old. The mortality assumptions relate to the general population of England and Wales. Unless there is clear evidence in an individual case to support the view that the individual is atypical and will enjoy longer or shorter than average life, no further increase or reduction is required for mortality alone.

Tables Adjusted to take Account of Projected Mortality (Tables 11 to 20)

A2.11   7. The actuaries on the Working Party consider that failure to have regard to reasonable projected improvements in mortality rates will result in claimants receiving awards of damages which are lower than they should be. At Appendix A is an extract from ELT 15 which shows graphs indicating rates of mortality expressed in percentages of 1911 rates on a logarithmic scale. They demonstrate in a stark fashion the improvement in longevity which has taken place since 1911. The sole exception is a small increase recently in the mortality of males in their late twenties and early thirties due to AIDS and increasing numbers of suicides, the same effect being present, but to a lesser degree, for females. Even if this slight worsening of mortality at these ages were to continue, the effect on the tables of multipliers would not be significant. (For comments by the ABI see Appendix C.)

8. The graphs, and the figures on which they are based, point to the conclusion that, on the balance of probabilities, the mortality rates which will actually be

experienced in future by those who are alive today will be lower than in ELT 15, and increasingly so the further into the future one goes. This, of course, would imply the need for higher multipliers. For the purposes of preparing the official national population projections, the Government Actuary makes a considered estimate of the extent of future improvements in mortality. Tables 11 to 20 show the multipliers which result from the application of these projected mortality rates. The actuaries on the Working Party (save for the dissenting views expressed at Appendix C) consider that these alternative tables may provide a more appropriate estimate of the value of future income streams than Tables 1 to 10, which are based on historic mortality and almost certainly underestimate future longevity of the population as a whole. The Working Party therefore recommends the Courts to use Tables 11 to 20 rather than Tables 1 to 10.

Use of Tables

A2.12   9. To find the appropriate figure for the present value of a particular loss or expense the user must first choose that table which relates to the period of loss or expense for which the individual claimant is to be compensated and to the sex of the claimant.

10. If for some reason the facts in a particular case do not correspond with the assumptions on which one of the tables is based, (if, for instance, it is known that the claimant will have a different retiring age from that assumed in the tables) then the tables can only be used by making an appropriate allowance for this difference; for this purpose the assistance of an actuary should be sought.

Rate of Return

A2.13   11. The basis of the multipliers set out in the tables is that the lump sum will be invested and yield income (but that over the period in question the claimant will gradually reduce the capital sum so that at the end of the period it is exhausted). Accordingly, an essential factor in arriving at the right figure is to choose the appropriate rate of return. The tables set out multipliers based on rates of return ranging from 1½% to 5%, as in previous editions.

12. Currently, the rate of return to be applied is 4.5% (*Wells v Wells* [1997] 1 WLR 652). (N.B. this differs from the figures stated in *Hodgson v Trapp* [1989] AC 807, namely 4% to 5%, which allowed a degree of flexibility according to the prevailing economic circumstances). After a Commencement Order has been made in respect of the Damages Act 1996 Section 1, the rate or rates of return are likely to be specified by the Lord Chancellor after receiving advice from the Government Actuary and the Treasury. Should it become necessary, further tables will be issued.

13. Previous editions of these tables explained how the current yields on index-linked government bonds could be used as an indicator of the appropriate real rate of return for valuing future income streams. Since such considerations could apply again following the commencement of Section 1 of the Damages Act 1996, it has been thought desirable to retain tables for a range of possible rates of return, notwithstanding the Appeal Court judgment in *Wells v Wells*. A description of how to use market rates of return on index-linked gilts to determine the appropriate rate of return is given in Appendix B. In cases outwith the scope of these tables, the advice of an actuary should be sought.

Tax

A2.14 14. In order to arrive at a true present capital value of the claimant's future loss or expense it is necessary to consider whether he or she will have to pay a significant amount of tax on the investment return arising from his compensation. If he or she will pay little or no tax, no adjustment of the rate of return will be required. If he or she will have to pay a significant percentage of that income in tax, then the rate of return chosen to determine the present capital value of the loss or expense should be reduced accordingly. Attention is drawn to the decision of the House of Lords in *Hodgson v Trapp* [1989] AC 807 concerning the treatment of the incidence of higher rate tax on the income arising from a compensatory fund.

15. In cases where the impact of personal Income Tax and Capital Gains Tax is likely to be significant, more accurate calculation of the value net of tax of payments to the individual may be desirable. Such calculations can be carried out by using software of the type referred to in paragraph 45 or the advice of an actuary should be sought.

Different Retirement Ages

A2.15 16. In paragraph 10 above, reference was made to the problem that will arise when the claimant's retiring age is different from that assumed in the tables. Such a problem may arise in valuing a loss or expense beginning immediately but ending at retirement; or in valuing a loss or expense which will not begin until the claimant reaches retirement but will then continue until death. In the former case, this is where the loss or expense to be valued covers the period up to retirement, the following procedure will be found to be satisfactory in most cases. Where the claimant's actual retiring age would have been earlier than that assumed in the tables, he or she is treated as correspondingly older than his or her true age. Thus a woman of 42 who would have retired at 55 is treated as though she were 47 and retiring at 60. The appropriate multiplier is then obtained from the table (Table 6 or 16). A further correction should then be made, because the claimant's chances of survival are greater at 42 than if she were in fact 47. There should therefore be added to the multiplier one quarter of 1% for each year (here 5 years) by which the claimant's personal retiring age is earlier than 60. In the case of a man the correction required is a ½% for each such year. This difference is because, on average, women live longer than men.

17. When the claimant would have expected to retire later than the age assumed in the table, the procedure is reversed. Thus a man of 42 who would have retired at 70 is treated as though he were 37 and retiring at 65. The appropriate multiplier is then obtained from the table (in this case Table 3 or 13) and the further correction required is made by reducing the multiplier by one half of 1% for each year by which the retiring age of the claimant exceeds the retiring age assumed in the table. In the case of a woman the reduction would, of course, be by one quarter% for each year.

18. When the loss or expense to be valued is that from the date of retirement to death, and the claimant's date of retirement differs from that assumed in the tables, a different approach is necessary. The first step is to assume that there is a present loss which will continue for the rest of the claimant's life and from Table 1 or 2 (or

11 or 12) establish the value of that loss or expense over the whole period from the date of assessment until the claimant's death. The second step is to establish the value of such loss or expense over the period from the date of assessment until the claimant's expected date of retirement following the procedure explained in paragraphs 16 and 17 above. The third step is to subtract the second figure from the first. The balance remaining represents the present value of the claimant's loss or expense between retirement and death.

Younger Ages

A2.16   19. Tables 1, 2, 11 and 12, which concern pecuniary loss for life, and Tables 7 to 10 and 17 to 20, which concern loss of pension from retirement age, have been extended down to age 0. In some circumstances the multiplier at age 0 is slightly lower than that at age 1; this arises because of the relatively high incidence of deaths immediately after birth.

20. Tables for multipliers for loss of earnings (Tables 3 to 6 and 13 to 16) have not been extended below age 16. In order to determine the multiplier for loss of earnings for someone who has not yet started work, it is first necessary to determine an assumed age at which the claimant would have commenced work and to find the appropriate multiplier for that age from Tables 3 to 6 or 13 to 16, according to the assumed retirement age. This multiplier should then be multiplied by the deferment factor from Table 21 which corresponds to the appropriate rate of return and the period from the date of the trial to the date on which it is assumed that the claimant would have started work. A similar approach can be used for determining a multiplier for pecuniary loss for life where the loss is assumed to commence a fixed period of years from the date of the trial. For simplicity the factors in Table 21 relate purely to the impact of the rate of return and ignore mortality. At ages below 30 this is a reasonable approximation (for example allowance for ELT 15 male mortality from age 5 to 25 would only reduce the multiplier by a further 1%) but at higher ages it would normally be appropriate to allow explicitly for mortality and the advice of an actuary should be sought.

Contingencies

A2.17   21. Tables 1 to 10 have been calculated to take into account the chances that the claimant will live for different periods, including the possibility that he or she will die young or live to be very old, based on current levels of population mortality. Tables 11 to 20 make reasonable provision for the levels of mortality which members of the population of England and Wales may expect to experience in future. The tables do not take account of the other risks and vicissitudes of life, such as the possibility that the claimant would for periods have ceased to earn due to ill-health or loss of employment. Nor do they take account of the fact that many people cease work for substantial periods to care for children or other dependants. Section B suggests ways in which allowance may be made to the multipliers for loss of earnings to allow for certain risks other than mortality.

Impaired Lives

A2.18   22. In some cases medical evidence may be available which asserts that a claimant's health impairments are equivalent to adding a certain number of years to the current age, or to treating the individual as having a specific age different from the actual age. In such cases, Tables 1, 2, 11 and 12 can be used with respect to the deemed higher age. For the other tables the adjustment is not so straightforward, as adjusting the age will also affect the period up to retirement age, but the procedures described in paragraphs 16 to 18 may be followed, or the advice of an actuary should be sought.

Fixed Periods

A2.19 23. In cases where pecuniary loss is to be valued for a fixed period, the multipliers in Table 22 may be used. These make no allowance for mortality or any other contingency but assume that regular frequent payments will continue throughout the period. These figures should in principle be adjusted to allow for less frequent periodicity of payment, especially if the payments in question are annually in advance or in arrears. An appropriate adjustment is to multiply by one plus half the rate of return for annual payments in advance (that is, by 1.02 for a rate of return of 4%) and to divide the term certain multiplier by one plus half the rate of return for annual payments in arrears.

Variable Loss or Expense

A2.20 24. The tables do not provide an immediate answer when the loss or expense to be valued is not assumed to be stable; where, for instance, the claimant's lost earnings were on a sliding scale or he was expected to achieve promotion. It may be possible to use the tables to deal with such situations by increasing the basic figure of annual loss or expense; or by choosing a lower rate of interest and so a higher multiplier than would otherwise have been chosen. More complicated cases may be suited to the use of the software referred to in paragraph 45.

25. If doubt exists that the tables are appropriate to a particular case which appears to present significant difficulties of substance it would be prudent to take actuarial advice.

SECTION B: CONTINGENCIES OTHER THAN MORTALITY

A2.21 26. As stated in paragraph 21, the tables for loss of earnings (Tables 3 to 6 and 13 to 16) take no account of risks other than mortality. This section shows how the multipliers in these tables may be reduced to take account of risks other than mortality. This is based on work commissioned by the Institute of Actuaries and carried out by Professor S Haberman and Mrs D S F Bloomfield. (*Work time lost to sickness, unemployment and stoppages: measurement and application* (1990), Journal of the Institute of Actuaries 117, 533-595). Although there was some debate within the actuarial profession about the details of this work, and in particular about the scope for developing it further, the findings were broadly accepted and were adopted by the Government Actuary and the other actuaries who were members of the Working Party when the Second Edition of the Tables was published.

27. Reported cases suggest that the Courts have hesitated to accept these findings, which were based on scientific research, and continue to make reductions of as much as 20%, which appears to have been a figure adopted before any work on the subject had been carried out. Since the risk of mortality has already been taken into account in the Tables, the principal contingencies in respect of which a further reduction is to be made are illness and

unemployment. Even with the effective disappearance of the 'job for life' there appears to be no scientific justification in the generality of cases for assuming significantly larger deductions than those given in this section. It should be noted that the authors of the 1990 paper (Professor Haberman and Mrs Bloomfield) wrote 'All the results discussed in this paper should be further qualified by the caveat that the underlying models ... assume that economic activity rates and labour force separation and accession rates do not vary in the future from the bases chosen. As mentioned already in the text, it is unlikely to be true that the future would be free from marked secular trends.' The paper relied on Labour Force Surveys for 1973, 1977, 1981 and 1985 and English Life Tables No. 14 (1980-82). However, although it is now somewhat out of date, it is the best study presently available. It is hoped to commission some further research into the impact of contingencies other than mortality.

28. Specific factors in individual cases may necessitate larger reductions. By contrast, there will also be cases where the standard multipliers should be increased, to take into account positive factors of lifestyle, employment prospects and life expectancy.

29. The extent to which the multiplier needs to be reduced will reflect individual circumstances such as occupation and geographical region. In the short term, levels of economic activity and unemployment, including time lost through industrial action, are relevant. Reductions may be expected to be smaller for clerical workers than for manual workers, for those living in the South rather than the North, and for those in 'secure' jobs and in occupations less affected by redundancy or industrial action.

30. The suggestions which follow are intended only to provide a 'ready reckoner' as opposed to precise figures.

The Basic Deduction for Contingencies other than Mortality

A2.22   31. Subject to the adjustments which may be made as described below, the multiplier which has been selected from the tables, that is, in respect of risks of mortality only, should be reduced by *multiplying* it by a figure selected from the table below, under the heading 'Medium'.

Table A
Loss of Earnings to Pension Age 65 (Males)

Age at date of trial	High	Medium	Low
20	0.99	0.98	0.97
25	0.99	0.98	0.96
30	0.99	0.97	0.95
35	0.98	0.96	0.93
40	0.98	0.96	0.92
45	0.97	0.95	0.90
50	0.96	0.93	0.87
55	0.95	0.90	0.82
60	0.95	0.90	0.81

Levels of Economic Activity and Employment

A2.23 32. The medium set of reductions is appropriate if it is anticipated that economic activity is likely to correspond to that in the 1970s and 1980s (ignoring periods of high and low unemployment). The high set is appropriate if higher economic activity and lower unemployment rates are anticipated. The low set is appropriate if lower economic activity and higher unemployment rates are anticipated.

33. Whereas it is possible to reach conclusions about these factors in the short term the Courts are not prepared to speculate about such matters beyond the short term (*Auty v National Coal Board* [1985] 1 WLR 784). Consequently the headings 'High' and 'Low' may only be of limited value.

Lower Pension Age (Males)

A2.24 34. The figures will be higher for a lower pension age. For example, if pension age is 60, the figures should be as shown in Table B.

Table B
Loss of Earnings to Pension Age 60 (Males)

Age at date of trial	High	Medium	Low
20	0.99	0.99	0.98
25	0.99	0.99	0.97
30	0.99	0.98	0.97
35	0.99	0.98	0.96
40	0.98	0.97	0.94
45	0.98	0.96	0.93
50	0.97	0.94	0.92
55	0.96	0.93	0.88

Female Lives

A2.25 35. As a rough guide, for female lives between ages 35 and 55 with a pension age of 60, the figures should be as shown in Table C.

Table C
Loss of Earnings to Pension Age 60 (Females)

Age at date of trial	High	Medium	Low
35	0.95	0.95	0.94
40	0.93	0.93	0.92
45	0.90	0.90	0.88
50	0.91	0.90	0.88
55	0.95	0.94	0.93

Variations by Occupation

A2.26 36. The risks of illness, injury and disability are less for persons in clerical or similar jobs, for example, civil sevants, the professions and financial services industries, and greater for those in manual jobs, for example, construction, mining, quarrying and ship-building. However, what matters is the precise nature of the work undertaken by the person in question; for example, a secretary in the Headquarters office of a large construction company is at no greater risk than a secretary in a solicitor's office.

37. In less risky occupations the figures in Tables A to C should be *increased* by a maximum of the order of 0.01 at age 25, 0.01 at age 40 and 0.03 at age 55.

38. In more risky occupations the figures in Tables A to C should be *reduced* by a maximum of the order of 0.01 at age 25, 0.02 at age 40 and 0.05 at age 55.

Variations by Geographical Region

A2.27 39. For persons resident in the South East, East Anglia, South West and East Midlands, the figures in Tables A to C should be *increased* by a maximum of the order of 0.01 at age 25, 0.01 at age 40 and 0.03 at age 55.

40. For persons resident in the North, North West, Wales and Scotland, the figures in Tables A to C should be *reduced* by a maximum of the order of 0.01 at age 25, 0.02 at age 40 and 0.05 at age 55.

SECTION C: SUMMARY

A2.28 41. To use the tables take the following steps:

(1) Choose the tables relating to the appropriate period of loss or expense.
(2) Choose the table, relating to that period, appropriate to the sex of the claimant.
(3) Choose the appropriate rate of return, before allowing for the effect of tax on the income to be obtained from the lump sum.
(4) If appropriate, allow for a reduction in the rate of return to reflect the effect of tax on the income from the lump sum.
(5) Find the figure under the column in the table chosen given against the age at trial (or, in a fatal accident case, at the death) of the claimant.
(6) Adjust the figure to take account of contingencies other than mortality, as specified in Section B above.
(7) Multiply the annual loss (net of tax) or expense by that figure.

42. In principle an allowance for an expected increase in the annual loss or expense (not due to inflation) can be made by choosing a lower rate of return or by increasing the figure of annual loss or expense. In cases where the claimant's expected age of retirement differs from that assumed in the tables the more complicated procedure explained in paragraph 16 to 18 should be followed.

43. An example is given below:

A2.29 The claimant is female, aged 35. She lives in London and is an established civil servant working in an office at a salary of £25,000 net of tax. As a result of her injuries, she has lost her job. The task of estimating her loss of earnings to retirement age of 60 is to be undertaken as follows:

(1) Tables 6 and 16 assume a retirement age of 60 for females. If the projected mortality tables are accepted, then Table 16 is relevant.
(2) The appropriate rate of return is decided to be 4.5% (based on *Wells v Wells* [1997] 1 WLR 652).
(3) Table 16 shows that, on the basis of a 4.5% rate of return, the multiplier for a female aged 35 is 14.94.
(4) It is now necessary to take account of risks other than mortality. Let us assume that economic activity for the next few years, for the purpose of this exercise, is regarded as being 'high'. Table C would require 14.94 to be multiplied by 0.95.
(5) Further adjustment is necessary because the claimant (a) is in a secure non-manual job, and (b) lives in the South East.

The adjustments should be made as follows:

Basic adjustment to allow for short-term high economic activity

(Table C)	
	0.95
Adjustment to allow for occupation, say	+0.01
	0.96
Adjustment for geographical region, say	+0.01
	0.97

The original multiplier taken from Table 16, namely 14.94, must therefore be multiplied by 0.97 resulting in a revised multiplier for use of 14.49.

The example takes no account of the incidence of tax on investment (see paragraph 14) above. It is assumed that this was taken into account when determining the 4½% rate of return.

Final Remarks

A2.30 44. These tables are designed to assist the Courts to arrive at suitable multipliers in a range of possible situations. However, they do not cover all possibilities and in more complex situations advice should be sought from a fellow of the Institute of Actuaries or a Fellow of the Faculty of Actuaries.

45. In the Family Division a software program (the Duxbury Method) is used for making similar calculations in complex cases. A similar facility would be useful for more complex personal injury and fatal accident cases and it is intended that such a programme will be made available shortly.

Christopher Daykin CB, MA, FIA	London
Government Actuary	May 1998

APPENDIX A

Rates of mortality expressed as percentages of 1911 rates (logarithmic scale)

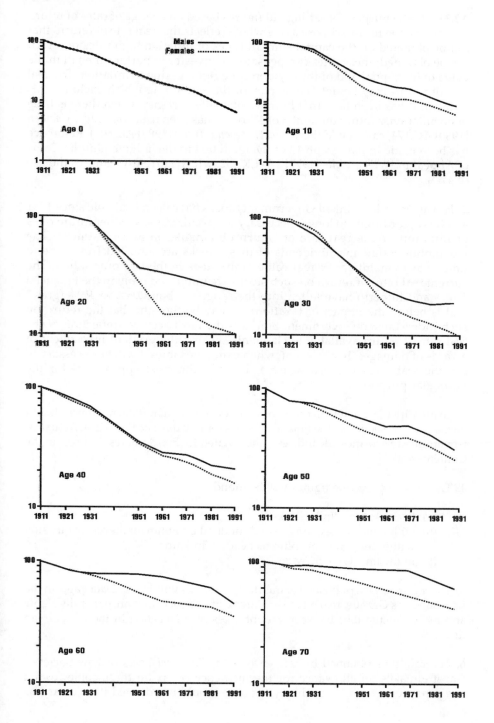

APPENDIX B

Selecting an appropriate real rate of return based on market considerations

A2.31   1. The purpose of setting out figures based on a range of rates of return is to enable the user to choose a rate which reflects the 'real rate of return' that can be obtained on the capital sum. In times of inflation high rates of return can be obtained; these rates compensate the investor in part for the fall in the value of his capital and of the dividends he receives due to inflation. The real rate of return may be defined as part of the actual rate which excludes this element. It has been held that in times of stable currency, when there is little or no inflation, a return on capital of 4% or 5% has been usual (see *Lim v Camden* [1980] AC 174, cases cited there and *Hodgson v Trapp* [1989] AC 807). Reference has been made in paragraph 12 of the main text to the judgment of the Court of Appeal in *Wells v Wells* [1997] 1 WLR 652, which currently requires the use of 4½%.

2. However, Index-Linked Government Stocks have been available since 1981 and it is accordingly no longer necessary to speculate about either future rates of inflation or the real rate of return obtainable on an investment. The redemption value and dividends of these stocks are adjusted from time to time so as to maintain the real value of the stock in the face of inflation. The current real rates of return on such stocks are published daily in the Financial Times and hitherto have fallen into the range of about 2½% to 4½% (gross, that is before the impact of taxation). It may be thought that the return on such Index-Linked Government Stocks is the most accurate reflection of the real rate of return available to claimants seeking the prudent investment of awards of damages. In any event, when using the tables it will be necessary to use the real rate of return which is deemed the most appropriate for the particular purpose.

3. To identify the real return on such stocks on a particular date, reference should be made to the section of the Financial Times for that day entitled 'FTSE Actuaries Government Securities UK Indices' (abbreviated to 'Fixed interest indices' in the Contents list).

4. The most appropriate figures will be found:

   (a) in the section 'Index-linked'
   (b) within the sub-section on yields under the column for the day in question within the group of columns headed 'Inflation 5%'
   (c) in the line 'Over 5 Years'.

5. This figure is also published at quarterly intervals within the 'Data Page' in the Law Society's Gazette; real returns on index-linked securities are generally stable and major fluctuations between the intervals of publication in the Gazette are unusual.

6. The rate thus obtained by reference to the *Financial Times* or Law Society's Gazette makes no allowance for the incidence of tax on the income from a compensation award. Accordingly, the rate should be adjusted if necessary, as

described in paragraphs 14 and 15 of Section A, in order to identify the correct column of the table to be used.

APPENDIX C

Comments by the Association of British Insurers (ABI)

Introduction

A2.32 1. The Association of British Insurers (ABI) represents companies transacting some 95% of insurance company business in the United Kingdom. The Forum of Insurance Lawyers (FOIL) fully supports the comments made in this appendix. Both ABI and FOIL are pleased to have participated for the first time in the Working Party which was responsible for the third edition of these tables and explanatory notes.

2. We believe that the central issue in the debate on the calculation of damages for future losses and expenses is ensuring that the claimant, the recipient of the compensation, is able to meet his or her future needs and requirements for as long as they arise. There may be a number of ways of calculating what the claimant needs for the future. Using multipliers is one. Purchasing an annuity may be another. There is perhaps a danger that the use of any scientific approach in this area may bring a spurious accuracy to a calculation which, almost by definition, will prove wrong in the future.

3. Our contention is that none of the methods above addresses this key question. All that any of the currently used methods do is to calculate a sum of money which is given to the claimant to do with as he or she wishes or sees fit. We nonetheless accept that a wider review of the means of addressing future financial provision for the victims of personal injury is outside the scope of this Working Party.

The Tables in the Third Edition

A2.33 4. What the tables do is to give a multiplier for a particular individual in his or her particular circumstances which is based on the general mortality of the population at large. Insurers have no objection to the actuarial principles underlying the tables, because the figures which they include are derived from objective actuarial science applied to real mortality data from current English Life Tables.

5. The figures in the tables have been produced by the Government Actuary. We have no reason to dispute the mathematical accuracy or the rigour of the calculations used to derive any of the figures in any of the tables. What may be open to discussion is the suitability of using data drawn from a population of millions as a tool to predict what may be appropriate for an individual claimant in his or her own particular environment.

6. The figures in Tables 1-10 could provide a useful starting point for assessment of an individual case, and will need adjustment to reflect accurately the individual circumstances of the person concerned. As the Chairman of this Working Party noted in the discussions prior to publication of this edition:

'People show a marked disinclination to die in strict accordance with their life expectancy.'

Projected Mortality Tables

A2.34   7. Paragraphs 7 and 8 of the explanatory notes state that Tables 11-20 are concerned with projected improvements in mortality rates. It is noted that the Government Actuary makes a considered estimate of the future improvements in mortality for national population projections. We accept that the evidence of the twentieth century demonstrates that the mortality of the population as a whole has been improving. We understand that these improvements could provide a basis for projections for the national population as a whole. Nevertheless, we are aware of a number of factors which tend to question the continuation of such improvements.

8. We note that there is no objective evidence to which we have access of how the mortality patters of a particular injury group are developing. We would strongly suggest that movements in the mortality of the group of victims of personal injury (of which an individual claimant in his or her particular circumstances is a member) may not be properly represented by the projected improvement in mortality of the whole of the population of the United Kingdom.

9. For example, whilst the development of improved methods of resuscitation and treatment may result in fewer fatalities, those who survive as a consequence of these procedures may bring with them a heavier pattern of mortality which is at variance with national experience.

10. In our view the use of Tables 11-20 is not supportable for two reasons. First, because of uncertainty about the future movements in national mortality and second because of uncertainty about the movement of the mortality of victims of personal injury relative to it.

11. Our conclusion on mortality is that whilst we accept with some reservations the updating of the tables of multipliers represented by Tables 1-10, we see no valid argument for further modifying the mortality basis to include speculative assessments of future changes. For these reasons, insurers are unable to recommend the use of Tables 11-20 to the courts.

Explanatory Notes – Section B: Contingencies Other Than Mortality

A2.35   12. Paragraphs 26-40 attempt to deal with the deductions to be made for contingencies other than mortality, especially the risk of unemployment. A 'ready reckoner' to assess the deduction to be made from the multiplier is proposed at paragraphs 31-40.

13. A different approach is generally adopted in the courts when assessing the deduction to be made for these contingencies. The practice is to consider all the evidence relating to how the individual is affected in his or her own particular circumstances, and then to decide on an appropriate adjustment which reflects these circumstances.

14. The paper from which Section B is derived is now over eight years old and was based on data which is at least thirteen years old. Some of the data analysed in the paper is now twenty-five years old. It is our considered view that the use of such limited and out of date information which does not accurately reflect economic conditions at the time of trial or settlement is wholly anomalous.

15. Paragraph 27 mentions that further research is being considered. ABI is keen to facilitate and contribute to such research and, at the time of writing, is in discussion with the Government Actuary's Department on this subject.

Rates of Return

A2.36 16. It is not for this Working Party to advocate the use of any particular rate of return. Under the Damages Act 1996, this is a matter for the Lord Chancellor (if he is so minded) who is likely to make his decision after the House of Lords has given its judgment in *Wells v Wells*. Until *Wells* is decided and until the Lord Chancellor has considered exercising his power under the Damages Act, we would therefore caution against adoption of the argument in support of Index-Linked Government Stock; proposed in the 'Introduction to the First Edition' which is found in this (third) edition at pages 12-14 and further discussed in paragraphs 2-5 of Appendix B at page 31.

17. FOIL suggests that in changing economic conditions there may be a case for including rates of return beyond the 1-5% range, which earlier editions of these tables adopted and which is used in the current edition.

Association of British Insurers
6 April 1998

Table 1: Multipliers for pecuniary loss for life (males)

Age at date of trial	Multiplier calculated with allowance for population mortality and rate of return of:								Age at date of trial
	1.5%	2.0%	2.5%	3.0%	3.5%	4.0%	4.5%	5.0%	
0	43.97	38.02	33.25	29.38	26.22	23.60	21.41	19.57	0
1	43.98	38.08	33.34	29.49	26.34	23.72	21.53	19.68	1
2	43.66	37.86	33.18	29.38	26.26	23.67	21.49	19.66	2
3	43.32	37.62	33.01	29.26	26.17	23.60	21.45	19.62	3
4	42.98	37.37	32.84	29.13	26.08	23.53	21.40	19.58	4
5	42.63	37.12	32.65	29.00	25.98	23.46	21.34	19.54	5
6	42.27	36.86	32.47	28.86	25.88	23.39	21.28	19.50	6
7	41.90	36.59	32.27	28.72	25.77	23.31	21.22	19.45	7
8	41.53	36.32	32.07	28.57	25.66	23.22	21.16	19.41	8
9	41.16	36.05	31.87	28.42	25.55	23.14	21.10	19.35	9
10	40.77	35.76	31.66	28.26	25.43	23.05	21.03	19.30	10
11	40.38	35.48	31.44	28.10	25.31	22.95	20.95	19.24	11
12	39.99	35.18	31.22	27.93	25.18	22.85	20.88	19.19	12
13	39.59	34.88	30.99	27.76	25.05	22.75	20.80	19.12	13
14	39.19	34.58	30.76	27.58	24.91	22.65	20.72	19.06	14
15	38.78	34.27	30.53	27.41	24.77	22.54	20.63	18.99	15
16	38.37	33.96	30.29	27.22	24.63	22.43	20.55	18.93	16
17	37.96	33.65	30.05	27.04	24.49	22.32	20.46	18.86	17
18	37.55	33.33	29.82	26.86	24.35	22.21	20.38	18.79	18
19	37.13	33.02	29.57	26.67	24.21	22.10	20.29	18.72	19
20	36.71	32.70	29.33	26.48	24.06	21.98	20.20	18.65	20
21	36.29	32.37	29.07	26.28	23.90	21.86	20.10	18.57	21
22	35.86	32.03	28.82	26.08	23.74	21.74	20.00	18.49	22
23	35.42	31.69	28.55	25.87	23.58	21.60	19.90	18.41	23
24	34.97	31.35	28.27	25.65	23.41	21.47	19.79	18.32	24
25	34.52	30.99	27.99	25.43	23.23	21.33	19.67	18.23	25
26	34.06	30.63	27.70	25.20	23.04	21.18	19.55	18.13	26
27	33.59	30.26	27.41	24.96	22.85	21.01	19.43	18.03	27
28	33.12	29.88	27.10	24.72	22.66	20.86	19.30	17.92	28
29	32.64	29.49	26.79	24.47	22.45	20.70	19.16	17.81	29
30	32.15	29.10	26.47	24.21	22.24	20.52	19.02	17.69	30
31	31.65	28.70	26.15	23.94	22.02	20.34	18.87	17.57	31
32	31.15	28.29	25.81	23.67	21.80	20.16	18.71	17.44	32
33	30.64	27.87	25.47	23.38	21.56	19.96	18.55	17.30	33
34	30.12	27.44	25.12	23.09	21.32	19.76	18.38	17.16	34
35	29.60	27.01	24.76	22.80	21.07	19.55	18.21	17.01	35

36	29.07	26.57	24.40	22.49	20.82	19.34	18.03	16.86	36
37	28.54	26.13	24.03	22.18	20.56	19.12	17.84	16.70	37
38	28.00	25.68	23.65	21.86	20.29	18.89	17.64	16.53	38
39	27.45	25.22	23.26	21.54	20.01	18.65	17.44	16.36	39
40	26.90	24.76	22.87	21.20	19.73	18.41	17.23	16.18	40
41	26.34	24.28	22.47	20.86	19.43	18.16	17.02	15.99	41
42	25.78	23.80	22.06	20.51	19.13	17.90	16.79	15.80	42
43	25.21	23.32	21.64	20.15	18.82	17.63	16.56	15.60	43
44	24.63	22.83	21.22	19.79	18.51	17.36	16.32	15.39	44
45	24.05	22.33	20.79	19.41	18.18	17.07	16.07	15.17	45
46	23.47	21.82	20.35	19.03	17.85	16.78	15.82	14.94	46
47	22.89	21.31	19.91	18.65	17.51	16.48	15.55	14.71	47
48	22.30	20.80	19.46	18.25	17.16	16.18	15.28	14.47	48
49	21.71	20.28	19.01	17.85	16.81	15.87	15.01	14.22	49
50	21.11	19.76	18.55	17.45	16.45	15.55	14.72	13.97	50
51	20.52	19.24	18.09	17.04	16.09	15.22	14.43	13.71	51
52	19.93	18.72	17.62	16.62	15.72	14.89	14.14	13.44	52
53	19.33	18.19	17.15	16.20	15.34	14.55	13.83	13.17	53
54	18.74	17.66	16.68	15.78	14.96	14.21	13.52	12.89	54
55	18.15	17.13	16.20	15.35	14.57	13.86	13.21	12.60	55
56	17.55	16.60	15.72	14.92	14.18	13.51	12.88	12.31	56
57	16.97	16.07	15.24	14.49	13.79	13.15	12.56	12.01	57
58	16.38	15.54	14.76	14.05	13.39	12.79	12.23	11.71	58
59	15.80	15.01	14.28	13.61	13.00	12.42	11.89	11.40	59
60	15.22	14.49	13.81	13.18	12.60	12.06	11.56	11.09	60
61	14.66	13.97	13.33	12.74	12.20	11.69	11.22	10.78	61
62	14.10	13.45	12.86	12.31	11.80	11.32	10.88	10.46	62
63	13.55	12.95	12.40	11.88	11.40	10.95	10.54	10.15	63
64	13.01	12.45	11.94	11.46	11.01	10.59	10.20	9.83	64
65	12.48	11.97	11.49	11.04	10.62	10.23	9.86	9.52	65
66	11.96	11.49	11.04	10.63	10.24	9.87	9.53	9.21	66
67	11.46	11.02	10.61	10.22	9.86	9.52	9.20	8.90	67
68	10.97	10.56	10.18	9.82	9.49	9.17	8.87	8.59	68
69	10.49	10.11	9.76	9.43	9.12	8.82	8.55	8.28	69
70	10.02	9.67	9.35	9.04	8.75	8.48	8.22	7.98	70
71	9.55	9.24	8.94	8.66	8.39	8.14	7.90	7.68	71
72	9.10	8.81	8.54	8.28	8.04	7.80	7.58	7.37	72
73	8.67	8.40	8.15	7.91	7.69	7.47	7.27	7.08	73
74	8.25	8.00	7.77	7.56	7.35	7.15	6.97	6.79	74
75	7.84	7.62	7.41	7.21	7.02	6.84	6.67	6.50	75

76	7.44	7.24	7.05	6.87	6.69	6.53	6.37	6.22	76
77	7.05	6.87	6.70	6.53	6.37	6.22	6.08	5.94	77
78	6.69	6.52	6.36	6.21	6.07	5.93	5.80	5.67	78
79	6.33	6.18	6.04	5.90	5.77	5.65	5.53	5.41	79
80	5.99	5.86	5.73	5.61	5.49	5.37	5.26	5.16	80
81	5.67	5.55	5.43	5.32	5.21	5.11	5.01	4.91	81
82	5.36	5.25	5.14	5.04	4.94	4.85	4.76	4.67	82
83	5.06	4.96	4.86	4.77	4.68	4.60	4.52	4.44	83
84	4.77	4.68	4.60	4.52	4.44	4.36	4.28	4.21	84
85	4.50	4.42	4.35	4.27	4.20	4.13	4.06	4.00	85
86	4.25	4.17	4.10	4.04	3.97	3.91	3.85	3.79	86
87	4.01	3.94	3.88	3.82	3.76	3.70	3.65	3.59	87
88	3.78	3.72	3.67	3.61	3.56	3.51	3.46	3.41	88
89	3.57	3.52	3.47	3.42	3.37	3.32	3.28	3.24	89
90	3.36	3.31	3.27	3.23	3.18	3.14	3.10	3.06	90
91	3.15	3.11	3.07	3.03	3.00	2.96	2.92	2.89	91
92	2.95	2.92	2.88	2.85	2.81	2.78	2.75	2.72	92
93	2.77	2.74	2.70	2.67	2.64	2.61	2.59	2.56	93
94	2.60	2.57	2.54	2.52	2.49	2.46	2.44	2.41	94
95	2.45	2.42	2.40	2.37	2.35	2.33	2.30	2.28	95
96	2.31	2.29	2.26	2.24	2.22	2.20	2.18	2.16	96
97	2.18	2.16	2.14	2.12	2.10	2.08	2.06	2.04	97
98	2.06	2.04	2.02	2.00	1.98	1.97	1.95	1.93	98
99	1.94	1.92	1.91	1.89	1.87	1.86	1.84	1.83	99
100	1.83	1.81	1.80	1.78	1.77	1.76	1.74	1.73	100

Table 2: Multipliers for pecuniary loss for life (females)

| Age at date of trial | Multiplier calculated with allowance for population mortality and rate of return of | | | | | | | | Age at date of trial |
	1.5%	2.0%	2.5%	3.0%	3.5%	4.0%	4.5%	5.0%	
0	45.85	39.35	34.21	30.08	26.73	23.99	21.70	19.79	0
1	45.82	39.38	34.27	30.16	26.83	24.08	21.80	19.88	1
2	45.53	39.18	34.14	30.07	26.76	24.04	21.77	19.86	2
3	45.21	38.97	33.99	29.97	26.69	23.99	21.73	19.84	3
4	44.90	38.75	33.83	29.86	26.61	23.93	21.69	19.81	4
5	44.57	38.52	33.67	29.75	26.53	23.87	21.65	19.78	5
6	44.24	38.28	33.51	29.63	26.45	23.81	21.61	19.75	6
7	43.90	38.05	33.34	29.51	26.36	23.75	21.56	19.71	7
8	43.56	37.80	33.16	29.38	26.27	23.68	21.51	19.68	8
9	43.21	37.55	32.98	29.25	26.17	23.61	21.46	19.64	9
10	42.86	37.30	32.80	29.12	26.08	23.54	21.41	19.60	10

11	42.50	37.04	32.61	28.98	25.97	23.47	21.35	19.56	11
12	42.13	36.78	32.42	28.84	25.87	23.39	21.29	19.51	12
13	41.76	36.51	32.22	28.69	25.76	23.31	21.23	19.46	13
14	41.39	36.23	32.02	28.54	25.65	23.22	21.17	19.42	14
15	41.01	35.95	31.81	28.39	25.54	23.14	21.10	19.37	15
16	40.63	35.67	31.60	28.23	25.42	23.05	21.03	19.31	16
17	40.24	35.38	31.39	28.07	25.30	22.95	20.96	19.26	17
18	39.85	35.09	31.17	27.91	25.17	22.86	20.86	19.20	18
19	39.45	34.80	30.95	27.74	25.04	22.76	20.82	19.15	19
20	39.05	34.49	30.72	27.57	24.91	22.66	20.74	19.08	20
21	38.64	34.18	30.48	27.39	24.77	22.55	20.65	19.02	21
22	38.22	33.87	30.24	27.20	24.63	22.44	20.57	18.95	22
23	37.80	33.55	30.00	27.01	24.48	22.33	20.48	18.88	23
24	37.37	33.22	29.74	26.82	24.33	22.21	20.38	18.81	24
25	36.94	32.88	29.49	26.61	24.17	22.09	20.29	18.73	25
26	36.50	32.54	29.22	26.41	24.01	21.96	20.18	18.65	26
27	36.05	32.20	28.95	26.19	23.84	21.82	20.08	18.56	27
28	35.59	31.84	28.67	25.97	23.67	21.68	19.97	18.47	28
29	35.13	31.48	28.39	25.75	23.49	21.54	19.85	18.38	29
30	34.67	31.11	28.09	25.52	23.30	21.39	19.73	18.28	30
31	34.20	30.74	27.80	25.28	23.11	21.23	19.60	18.18	31
32	33.72	30.36	27.49	25.03	22.91	21.07	19.47	18.07	32
33	33.23	29.97	27.18	24.78	22.71	20.91	19.34	17.96	33
34	32.74	29.58	26.86	24.53	22.50	20.74	19.20	17.84	34
35	32.25	29.18	26.54	24.26	22.28	20.56	19.05	17.72	35
36	31.75	28.77	26.21	23.99	22.06	20.38	18.90	17.59	36
37	31.24	28.36	25.87	23.71	21.83	20.19	18.74	17.46	37
38	30.73	27.94	25.53	23.43	21.60	19.99	18.58	17.32	38
39	30.21	27.51	25.18	23.14	21.36	19.79	18.41	17.18	39
40	29.68	27.08	24.82	22.84	21.11	19.58	18.23	17.03	40
41	29.15	26.64	24.45	22.54	20.85	19.37	18.05	16.88	41
42	28.61	26.19	24.08	22.22	20.59	19.14	17.86	16.72	42
43	28.07	25.74	23.70	21.91	20.32	18.92	17.67	16.55	43
44	27.53	25.28	23.31	21.58	20.04	18.68	17.46	16.38	44
45	26.98	24.82	22.92	21.25	19.76	18.44	17.25	16.20	45
46	26.42	24.35	22.52	20.91	19.47	18.19	17.04	16.01	46
47	25.86	23.88	22.12	20.56	19.17	17.93	16.82	15.82	47
48	25.30	23.40	21.71	20.21	18.87	17.67	16.59	15.62	48
49	24.73	22.91	21.29	19.85	18.56	17.40	16.36	15.41	49
50	24.16	22.42	20.87	19.48	18.24	17.12	16.11	15.20	50

51	23.59	21.92	20.44	19.11	17.91	16.84	15.86	14.98	51
52	23.01	21.42	20.00	18.73	17.58	16.55	15.61	14.76	52
53	22.43	20.92	19.56	18.34	17.24	16.25	15.35	14.52	53
54	21.84	20.41	19.12	17.95	16.90	15.94	15.07	14.28	54
55	21.26	19.89	18.66	17.55	16.54	15.63	14.80	14.03	55
56	20.67	19.38	18.21	17.15	16.19	15.31	14.51	13.78	56
57	20.08	18.86	17.75	16.74	15.82	14.98	14.22	13.52	57
58	19.49	18.33	17.28	16.33	15.45	14.65	13.92	13.25	58
59	18.91	17.81	16.82	15.91	15.08	15.32	13.62	12.98	59
60	18.32	17.29	16.35	15.49	14.70	13.98	13.31	12.70	60
61	17.74	16.77	15.88	15.07	14.32	13.63	13.00	12.42	61
62	17.16	16.25	15.41	14.64	13.94	13.29	12.69	12.13	62
63	16.58	15.73	14.94	14.22	13.55	12.93	12.36	11.84	63
64	16.01	15.21	14.47	13.79	13.16	12.58	12.04	11.54	64
65	15.45	14.70	14.00	13.37	12.77	12.11	11.71	11.24	65
66	14.89	14.19	13.54	12.94	12.38	11.87	11.38	10.94	66
67	14.33	13.68	13.07	12.51	11.99	11.50	11.05	10.63	67
68	13.77	13.17	12.61	12.08	11.59	11.14	10.71	10.32	68
69	13.23	12.66	12.14	11.65	11.20	10.77	10.37	10.00	69
70	12.68	12.16	11.68	11.23	10.80	10.40	10.03	9.68	70
71	12.14	11.66	11.21	10.79	10.40	10.03	9.68	9.36	71
72	11.61	11.17	10.75	10.36	10.00	9.65	9.33	9.03	72
73	11.09	10.68	10.30	9.94	9.60	9.28	8.98	8.70	73
74	10.58	10.21	9.86	9.53	9.21	8.92	8.64	8.38	74
75	10.08	9.74	9.42	9.11	8.83	8.56	8.30	8.06	75
76	9.58	9.27	8.98	8.70	8.44	8.19	7.95	7.73	76
77	9.09	8.81	8.54	8.29	8.05	7.82	7.60	7.40	77
78	8.62	8.36	8.12	7.89	7.67	7.46	7.26	7.07	78
79	8.16	7.93	7.71	7.50	7.30	7.11	6.93	6.75	79
80	7.72	7.51	7.31	7.12	6.94	6.76	6.60	6.44	80
81	7.29	7.10	6.92	6.75	6.58	6.43	6.28	6.13	81
82	6.88	6.70	6.54	6.39	6.24	6.10	5.96	5.83	82
83	6.47	6.32	6.18	6.04	5.90	5.77	5.65	5.53	83
84	6.09	5.95	5.82	5.69	5.57	5.46	5.35	5.24	84
85	5.71	5.59	5.48	5.36	5.26	5.15	5.05	4.96	85
86	5.36	5.25	5.15	5.05	4.95	4.86	4.77	4.68	86
87	5.04	4.94	4.85	4.76	4.67	4.59	4.51	4.43	87
88	4.72	4.64	4.56	4.48	4.40	4.32	4.25	4.18	88
89	4.42	4.34	4.27	4.20	4.13	4.06	4.00	3.94	89
90	4.14	4.07	4.00	3.94	3.88	3.82	3.76	3.71	90

91	3.87	3.81	3.75	3.70	3.64	3.59	3.54	3.49	91
92	3.63	3.57	3.52	3.47	3.42	3.37	3.33	3.28	92
93	3.40	3.35	3.31	3.26	3.22	3.18	3.13	3.09	93
94	3.19	3.15	3.11	3.07	3.03	2.99	2.95	2.92	94
95	2.99	2.95	2.92	2.88	2.85	2.81	2.78	2.75	95
96	2.82	2.78	2.75	2.72	2.69	2.66	2.63	2.60	96
97	2.66	2.63	2.60	2.57	2.54	2.52	2.49	2.47	97
98	2.50	2.49	2.45	2.43	2.40	2.38	2.35	2.33	98
99	2.35	2.32	2.30	2.28	2.26	2.23	2.21	2.19	99
100	2.20	2.18	2.16	2.14	2.12	2.10	2.08	2.06	100

Table 3: Multipliers for loss of earnings to pension age 65 (males)

Age at date of trial	Multiplier calculated with allowance for population mortality and rate of return of								Age at date of trial
	1.5%	2.0%	2.5%	3.0%	3.5%	4.0%	4.5%	5.0%	
16	33.54	30.32	27.54	25.14	23.05	21.23	19.63	18.23	16
17	33.05	29.93	27.23	24.89	22.86	21.07	19.51	18.12	17
18	32.56	29.54	26.92	24.65	22.66	21.91	19.38	18.02	18
19	32.07	29.15	26.61	24.39	22.45	20.75	19.24	17.91	19
20	31.57	28.75	26.28	24.13	22.24	20.57	19.10	17.80	20
21	31.07	28.34	25.95	23.86	22.02	20.39	18.96	17.68	21
22	30.55	27.92	25.61	23.58	21.79	20.21	18.80	17.55	22
23	30.03	27.49	25.26	23.29	21.56	20.01	18.64	17.42	23
24	29.50	27.05	24.90	23.00	21.31	19.81	18.48	17.28	24
25	28.96	26.61	24.53	22.69	21.06	19.60	18.30	17.14	25
26	28.41	26.15	24.15	22.38	20.80	19.39	18.12	16.98	26
27	27.85	25.69	23.77	22.05	20.53	19.16	17.93	16.82	27
28	27.29	25.22	23.77	21.72	20.24	18.92	17.73	16.65	28
29	26.71	24.73	22.96	21.38	19.95	18.67	17.52	16.48	29
30	26.13	24.24	22.54	21.02	19.65	18.42	17.30	16.29	30
31	25.54	23.73	22.11	20.66	19.34	18.15	17.07	16.10	31
32	25.94	23.22	21.68	20.28	19.02	17.87	16.84	15.89	32
33	24.33	22.70	21.23	19.89	18.69	17.59	16.59	15.68	33
34	23.71	22.17	20.77	19.50	18.34	17.29	16.33	15.45	34
35	23.08	21.62	20.29	19.09	17.98	16.98	16.06	15.22	35
36	22.45	21.07	19.81	18.67	17.62	16.66	15.78	14.97	36
37	21.81	20.51	19.32	18.24	17.24	16.33	15.49	14.71	37
38	21.16	19.94	18.82	17.79	16.85	15.98	15.18	14.44	38
39	20.50	19.35	18.30	17.34	16.45	15.63	14.87	14.16	39
40	19.83	18.76	17.78	16.87	16.03	15.26	14.54	13.87	40

41	19.15	18.16	17.24	16.39	15.60	14.87	14.19	13.56	41
42	18.47	17.55	16.69	15.90	15.16	14.48	13.84	13.24	42
43	17.78	16.92	16.13	15.39	14.71	14.06	13.47	12.91	43
44	17.07	16.29	15.56	14.87	14.24	13.64	13.08	12.56	44
45	16.36	15.64	14.97	14.34	13.75	13.20	12.68	12.19	45
46	15.64	14.99	14.37	13.79	13.25	12.74	12.26	11.81	46
47	14.92	14.32	13.76	13.22	12.74	12.27	11.83	11.41.	47
48	14.18	13.64	13.14	12.66	12.21	11.78	11.37	10.99	48
49	13.44	12.96	12.50	12.07	11.66	11.27	10.91	10.56	49
50	12.69	12.26	11.85	11.47	11.10	10.75	10.42	10.10	50
51	11.93	11.55	11.19	10.85	10.52	10.21	9.92	9.63	51
52	11.16	10.83	10.52	10.22	9.93	9.65	9.39	9.14	52
53	10.38	10.10	9.83	9.56	9.31	9.07	8.84	8.62	53
54	9.60	9.35	9.12	8.90	8.68	8.48	8.28	8.08	54
55	8.80	8.60	8.40	8.21	8.03	7.85	7.68	7.52	55
56	7.99	7.82	7.66	7.51	7.36	7.21	7.07	6.93	56
57	7.17	7.04	6.91	6.78	6.66	6.54	6.43	6.31	57
58	6.34	6.23	6.13	6.04	5.94	5.85	5.76	5.67	58
59	5.49	5.42	5.34	5.27	5.19	5.12	5.05	4.99	59
60	4.63	4.58	4.52	4.47	4.42	4.37	4.32	4.27	60
61	3.75	3.72	3.68	3.67	3.61	3.58	3.55	3.51	61
62	2.85	2.83	2.81	2.79	2.77	2.75	2.73	2.72	62
63	1.93	1.92	1.91	1.90	1.89	1.89	1.88	1.87	63
64	0.98	0.98	0.98	0.97	0.97	0.97	0.97	0.97	64

Table 4: Multipliers for loss of earnings to pension age 65 (females)

| Age at date of trial | Multiplier calculated with allowance for population mortality and rate of return of | | | | | | | | Age at date of trial |
	1.5%	2.0%	2.5%	3.0%	3.5%	4.0%	4.5%	5.0%	
16	34.08	30.78	27.93	25.47	23.34	21.47	19.84	18.41	16
17	33.59	30.39	27.62	25.23	23.14	21.32	19.72	18.31	17
18	33.10	30.00	27.31	24.98	22.94	21.16	19.59	18.21	18
19	32.60	29.60	26.99	24.72	22.73	20.99	19.46	18.10	19
20	32.09	29.19	26.66	24.45	22.52	20.82	19.31	17.98	20
21	31.57	28.77	26.32	24.18	22.30	20.64	19.17	17.86	21
22	31.05	28.34	25.98	23.90	22.07	20.45	19.01	17.74	22
23	30.52	27.91	25.62	23.61	21.83	20.25	18.85	17.61	23
24	29.98	27.47	25.26	23.31	21.58	20.05	18.69	17.47	24
25	29.43	27.02	24.89	23.00	21.33	19.84	18.51	17.32	25

26	28.87	26.56	24.51	22.69	21.07	19.62	18.33	17.17	26
27	28.31	26.09	24.11	22.36	20.79	19.39	18.14	17.01	27
28	27.74	25.61	23.71	22.02	20.51	19.16	17.94	16.84	28
29	27.16	25.12	23.30	21.68	20.22	18.91	17.73	16.66	29
30	26.57	24.62	22.88	21.32	19.92	18.65	17.51	16.48	30
31	25.97	24.12	22.45	20.96	19.61	18.39	17.29	16.29	31
32	25.36	23.60	22.01	20.58	19.28	18.11	17.05	16.08	32
33	24.75	23.07	21.56	20.19	18.95	17.83	16.80	15.87	33
34	24.13	22.54	21.10	19.79	18.61	17.53	16.55	15.65	34
35	23.50	21.99	20.63	19.39	18.26	17.22	16.28	15.42	35
36	22.86	21.44	20.14	18.97	17.89	16.90	16.00	15.17	36
37	22.21	20.87	19.65	18.53	17.51	16.57	15.71	14.92	37
38	21.55	20.30	19.15	18.09	17.12	16.23	15.41	14.65	38
39	20.89	19.71	18.63	17.63	16.72	15.87	15.09	14.37	39
40	20.22	19.11	18.10	17.17	16.30	15.50	14.77	14.08	40
41	19.53	18.51	17.56	16.68	15.87	15.12	14.42	13.78	41
42	18.84	17.89	17.01	16.19	15.43	14.72	14.07	13.46	42
43	18.14	17.26	16.44	15.68	14.97	14.31	13.70	13.12	43
44	17.43	16.62	15.86	15.16	14.50	13.89	13.31	12.77	44
45	16.71	15.97	15.27	14.62	14.01	13.44	12.91	12.41	45
46	15.98	15.31	14.67	14.07	13.51	12.99	12.49	12.02	46
47	15.25	14.63	14.05	13.51	12.99	12.51	12.05	11.62	47
48	14.50	13.95	13.42	12.93	12.46	12.02	11.60	11.21	48
49	13.75	13.25	12.78	12.33	11.91	11.51	11.13	10.77	49
50	12.98	12.54	12.12	11.72	11.34	10.98	10.64	10.31	50
51	12.20	11.81	11.44	11.09	10.75	10.43	10.12	9.83	51
52	11.42	11.08	10.75	10.44	10.15	9.86	9.59	9.33	52
53	10.62	10.33	10.05	9.78	9.52	9.27	9.03	8.81	53
54	9.81	9.56	9.32	9.09	8.87	8.66	8.45	8.25	54
55	8.99	8.79	8.58	8.39	8.20	8.02	7.85	7.68	55
56	8.16	7.99	7.83	7.66	7.51	7.36	7.21	7.07	56
57	7.32	7.18	7.05	6.92	6.79	6.67	6.55	6.44	57
58	6.46	6.36	6.25	6.15	6.05	5.96	5.86	5.77	58
59	5.59	5.51	5.44	5.36	5.29	5.21	5.14	5.07	59
60	4.71	4.65	4.60	4.54	4.49	4.44	4.39	4.34	60
61	3.81	3.77	3.73	3.70	3.66	3.63	3.60	3.56	61
62	2.89	2.87	2.85	2.83	2.81	2.79	2.77	2.75	62
63	1.95	1.94	1.93	1.93	1.91	1.90	1.89	1.88	63
64	0.99	0.98	0.98	0.98	0.98	0.97	0.97	0.97	64

Table 5: Multipliers for loss of earnings to pension age 60 (males)

Age at date of trial	Multiplier calculated with allowance for population mortality and rate of return of								Age at date of trial
	1.5%	2.0%	2.5%	3.0%	3.5%	4.0%	4.5%	5.0%	
16	31.43	28.64	26.20	24.07	22.20	20.55	19.09	17.79	16
17	30.91	28.22	25.86	23.79	21.97	20.36	18.93	17.66	17
18	30.39	27.79	25.51	23.51	21.74	20.17	18.78	17.54	18
19	29.86	27.36	25.16	23.22	21.50	19.98	18.62	17.40	19
20	29.33	26.92	24.80	22.92	21.26	19.77	18.45	17.26	20
21	28.78	26.47	24.43	22.61	21.00	19.56	18.27	17.12	21
22	28.23	26.01	24.05	22.30	20.74	19.34	18.09	16.96	22
23	27.67	25.55	23.66	21.97	20.46	19.11	17.90	16.80	23
24	27.11	25.07	23.26	21.64	20.18	18.87	17.69	16.63	24
25	26.53	24.59	22.85	21.29	19.89	18.62	17.48	16.45	25
26	25.94	24.09	22.43	20.93	19.58	18.37	17.26	16.26	26
27	25.34	23.58	21.99	20.56	19.27	18.10	17.03	16.07	27
28	24.74	23.06	21.55	20.18	18.94	17.82	16.79	15.86	28
29	24.12	22.53	21.09	19.79	18.60	17.52	16.54	15.64	29
30	23.50	21.99	20.63	19.39	18.25	17.22	16.28	15.41	30
31	22.87	21.44	20.15	18.97	17.89	16.91	16.00	15.17	31
32	22.22	20.88	19.66	18.54	17.52	16.58	15.72	14.92	32
33	21.57	20.31	19/16	18.10	17.13	16.24	15.42	14.66	33
34	20.91	19.73	18.64	17.65	16.73	15.88	15.10	14.38	34
35	20.24	19.13	18.12	17.18	16.32	15.52	14.78	14.09	35
36	19.55	18.53	17.58	16.70	15.89	15.14	14.44	13.79	36
37	18.87	17.91	17.03.	16.21	15.45	14.74	14.08	13.47	37
38	18.17	17.28	16.47	15.70	14.99	14.33	13.71	13.14	38
39	17.46	16.65	15.89	15.18	14.52	13.91	13.33	12.79	39
40	16.74	16.00	15.30	14.65	14.04	13.46	12.93	12.42	40
41	16.01	15.33	14.70	14.10	13.53	13.01	12.51	12.04	41
42	15.21	14.66	14.08	13.53	13.02	12.53	12.07	11.64	42
43	14.53	13.97	13.44	12.95	12.48	12.04	11.62	11.22	43
44	13.77	13.27	12.80	12.35	11.93	11.53	11.15	10.78	44
45	13.00	12.56	12.14	11.74	11.36	10.99	10.65	10.32	45
46	12.22	11.83	11.46	11.10	10.77	10.44	10.14	9.84	46
47	11.43	11.09	10.77	10.45	10.16	9.87	9.60	9.34	47
48	10.63	10.34	10.06	9.79	9.53	9.28	9.04	8.81	48
49	9.82	9.57	9.33	9.10	8.88	8.67	8.46	8.26	49
50	9.00	8.79	8.59	8.40	8.21	8.03	7.85	7.98	50

51	8.17	8.00	7.83	7.67	7.52	7.37	7.22	7.08	51
52	7.33	7.19	7.05	6.93	6.80	6.68	6.56	6.44	52
53	6.47	6.36	6.26	6.16	6.06	5.96	5.87	5.78	53
54	5.60	5.52	5.44	5.36	5.29	5.22	5.15	5.08	54
55	4.71	4.65	4.60	4.55	4.49	4.44	4.39	4.34	55
56	3.81	3.77	3.74	3.70	3.67	3.63	3.60	3.57	56
57	2.89	2.87	2.85	2.83	2.81	2.79	2.77	2.75	57
58	1.95	1.94	1.93	1.92	1.91	1.90	1.89	1.88	58
59	0.99	0.98	0.98	0.98	0.98	0.97	0.97	0.97	59

Table 6: Multipliers for loss of earnings to pension age 60 (females)

| Age at date of trial | Multiplier calculated with allowance for population mortality and rate of return of | | | | | | | | Age at date of trial |
	1.5%	2.0%	2.5%	3.0%	3.5%	4.0%	4.5%	5.0%	
16	31.81	28.97	26.50	24.33	22.42	20.74	19.26	17.94	16
17	31.29	28.55	26.15	24.05	22.19	20.56	19.11	17.82	17
18	30.76	28.12	25.80	23.76	21.96	20.37	18.95	17.69	18
19	30.23	27.68	25.44	23.47	21.72	20.17	18.79	17.55	19
20	29.68	27.23	25.07	23.16	21.47	19.96	18.62	17.41	20
21	29.13	26.78	24.70	22.85	21.21	19.75	18.44	17.26	21
22	28.57	26.31	24.31	22.53	20.94	19.52	18.25	17.11	22
23	28.00	25.84	23.91	22.20	20.66	19.29	18.06	16.94	23
24	27.42	25.35	23.51	21.86	20.38	19.05	17.85	16.77	24
25	26.83	24.86	23.09	21.50	20.08	18.80	17.64	16.59	25
26	26.24	24.35	22.66	21.14	19.77	18.53	17.42	16.40	26
27	25.63	23.84	22.22	20.77	19.45	18.26	17.18	16.20	27
28	25.02	23.31	21.77	20.38	19.12	17.98	16.94	15.99	28
29	24.40	22.78	21.31	19.99	18.78	17.69	16.69	15.77	29
30	23.77	22.23	20.84	19.58	18.43	17.38	16.42	15.55	30
31	23.12	21.68	20.36	19.16	18.07	17.06	16.15	15.30	31
32	22.47	21.11	19.87	18.73	17.69	16.73	15.86	15.05	32
33	21.82	20.53	19.36	18.29	17.30	16.39	15.56	14.79	33
34	21.15	19.95	18.84	17.83	16.90	16.04	15.24	14.51	34
35	20.47	19.35	18.32	17.36	16.48	15.67	14.92	14.22	35
36	19.78	18.74	17.77	16.88	16.05	15.29	14.58	13.92	36
37	19.09	18.12	17.22	16.38	15.61	14.89	14.22	13.60	37
38	18.38	17.48	16.65	15.87	15.15	14.48	13.85	13.27	38
39	17.67	16.84	16.07	15.35	14.68	14.05	13.47	12.92	39
40	16.94	16.18	15.47	14.81	14.19	13.61	13.06	12.55	40

41	16.21	15.51	14.86	14.26	13.68	13.15	12.64	12.17	41
42	15.46	14.83	14.24	13.69	13.16	12.67	12.20	11.76	42
43	14.70	14.14	13.60	13.10	12.62	12.17	11.75	11.34	43
44	13.94	13.43	12.95	12.49	12.06	11.66	11.27	10.90	44
45	13.16	12.71	12.28	11.87	11.49	11.12	10.77	10.44	45
46	12.37	11.98	11.60	11.24	10.89	10.56	10.25	9.95	46
47	11.58	11.23	10.90	10.58	10.28	9.99	9.71	9.45	47
48	10.77	10.47	10.18	9.91	9.64	9.39	9.15	8.91	48
49	9.95	9.69	9.45	9.21	8.99	8.77	8.56	8.36	49
50	9.11	8.90	8.69	8.50	8.31	8.12	7.94	7.77	50
51	8.27	8.09	7.92	7.76	7.60	7.45	7.30	7.16	51
52	7.41	7.27	7.14	7.00	6.88	6.75	6.63	6.51	52
53	6.54	6.43	6.33	6.22	6.12	6.03	5.93	5.84	53
54	5.65	5.57	5.49	5.42	5.34	5.27	5.20	5.13	54
55	4.75	4.70	4.64	4.59	4.53	4.48	4.43	4.38	55
56	3.84	3.80	3.77	3.73	3.69	3.66	3.63	3.59	56
57	2.91	2.89	2.86	2.84	2.82	2.80	2.78	2.77	57
58	1.96	1.95	1.94	1.93	1.92	1.91	1.90	1.89	58
59	0.99	0.99	0.98	0.98	0.98	0.98	0.97	0.97	59

Table 7: Multipliers for loss of pension commencing age 65 (males)

Age at date of trial	Multiplier calculated with allowance for population mortality and rate of return of								Age at date of trial
	1.5%	2.0%	2.5%	3.0%	3.5%	4.0%	4.5%	5.0%	
0	3.76	2.62	1.83	1.28	0.90	0.63	0.45	0.32	0
1	3.85	2.69	1.89	1.33	0.94	0.66	0.47	0.34	1
2	3.91	2.75	1.94	1.37	0.97	0.69	0.49	0.35	2
3	3.97	2.81	1.99	1.41	1.01	0.72	0.52	0.37	3
4	4.03	2.86	2.04	1.46	1.04	0.75	0.54	0.39	4
5	4.09	2.92	2.09	1.50	1.08	0.78	0.56	0.41	5
6	4.15	2.98	2.14	1.55	1.12	0.81	0.59	0.43	6
7	4.22	3.04	2.20	1.59	1.16	0.84	0.62	0.45	7
8	4.28	3.10	2.25	1.64	1.20	0.88	0.64	0.47	8
9	4.34	3.16	2.31	1.69	1.24	0.91	0.67	0.50	9
10	4.41	3.23	2.37	1.74	1.28	0.95	0.70	0.52	10
11	4.48	3.29	2.43	1.79	1.33	0.99	0.73	0.55	11
12	4.55	3.36	2.49	1.85	1.38	1.03	0.77	0.57	12
13	4.61	3.43	2.55	1.90	1.42	1.07	0.80	0.60	13
14	4.68	3.50	2.62	1.96	1.47	1.11	0.84	0.63	14
15	4.76	3.57	2.68	2.02	1.53	1.15	0.88	0.67	15

16	4.83	3.64	2.75	2.08	1.58	1.20	0.92	0.70	16
17	4.90	3.71	2.82	2.15	1.64	1.25	0.96	0.73	17
18	4.98	3.79	2.89	2.21	1.69	1.30	1.00	0.77	18
19	5.06	3.87	2.97	2.28	1.76	1.35	1.05	0.81	19
20	5.14	3.95	3.04	2.35	1.82	1.41	1.10	0.85	20
21	5.22	4.03	3.12	2.42	1.88	1.47	1.15	0.90	21
22	5.31	4.12	3.20	2.50	1.95	1.53	1.20	0.94	22
23	5.39	4.20	3.29	2.57	2.02	1.59	1.25	0.99	23
24	5.48	4.29	3.37	2.65	2.09	1.66	1.31	1.04	24
25	5.56	4.38	3.46	2.74	2.17	1.72	1.37	1.09	25
26	5.65	4.47	3.55	2.82	2.25	1.79	1.43	1.15	26
27	5.74	4.57	3.64	2.91	2.33	1.87	1.50	1.21	27
28	5.83	4.66	3.73	3.00	2.41	1.94	1.57	1.27	28
29	5.92	4.76	3.83	3.09	2.50	2.02	1.64	1.33	29
30	6.02	4.86	3.93	3.19	2.59	2.11	1.72	1.40	30
31	6.11	4.96	4.03	3.28	2.68	2.19	1.79	1.47	31
32	6.21	5.06	4.14	3.39	2.78	2.28	1.88	1.55	32
33	6.31	5.17	4.24	3.49	2.88	2.37	1.96	1.63	33
34	6.41	5.28	4.35	3.60	2.98	2.47	2.05	1.71	34
35	6.52	5.39	4.47	3.71	3.09	2.57	2.15	1.80	35
36	6.62	5.50	4.59	3.83	3.20	2.68	2.25	1.89	36
37	6.73	5.62	4.71	3.95	3.32	2.79	2.35	1.99	37
38	6.84	5.74	4.83	4.07	3.44	2.91	2.46	2.09	38
39	6.95	5.87	4.96	4.20	3.56	3.03	2.58	2.20	39
40	7.07	5.99	5.09	4.33	3.69	3.15	2.70	2.31	40
41	7.19	6.12	5.23	4.47	3.83	3.28	2.82	2.43	41
42	7.31	6.26	5.37	4.61	3.97	3.42	2.96	2.56	42
43	7.43	6.40	5.51	4.76	4.12	3.57	3.09	2.69	43
44	7.56	6.54	5.66	4.91	4.27	3.72	3.24	2.83	44
45	7.69	6.68	5.82	5.07	4.43	3.88	3.39	2.98	45
46	7.83	6.84	5.98	5.24	4.60	4.04	3.56	3.14	46
47	7.97	6.99	6.15	5.41	4.77	4.22	3.73	3.30	47
48	8.12	7.16	6.32	5.59	4.96	4.40	3.91	3.48	48
49	8.27	7.33	6.50	5.78	5.15	4.59	4.10	3.67	49
50	8.43	7.51	6.70	5.98	5.35	4.80	4.30	3.87	50
51	8.59	7.69	6.89	6.19	5.57	5.01	4.52	4.08	51
52	8.77	7.89	7.10	6.41	5.79	5.24	4.74	4.30	52
53	8.95	8.09	7.32	6.64	6.03	5.48	4.99	4.55	53
54	9.14	8.31	7.56	6.88	6.28	5.74	5.25	4.80	54
55	9.35	8.53	7.80	7.14	6.55	6.01	5.52	5.08	55

56	9.56	8.77	8.06	7.41	6.83	6.30	5.82	5.38	56
57	9.79	9.03	8.33	7.70	7.13	6.61	6.13	5.70	57
58	10.04	9.30	8.63	8.02	7.45	6.94	6.47	6.04	58
59	10.31	9.59	8.94	8.35	7.80	7.30	6.84	6.41	59
60	10.59	9.91	9.28	8.71	8.18	7.69	7.24	6.82	60
61	10.90	10.25	9.65	9.10	8.58	8.11	7.67	7.26	61
62	11.24	10.62	10.05	9.52	9.02	8.57	8.14	7.75	62
63	11.61	11.03	10.48	9.98	9.51	9.07	8.66	8.28	63
64	12.02	11.47	10.96	10.48	10.04	9.62	9.23	8.87	64
65	12.48	11.97	11.49	11.04	10.62	10.23	9.86	9.52	65

Table 8: Multipliers for loss of pension commencing age 65 (females)

Age at date of trial	Multiplier calculated with allowance for population mortality and rate of return of								Age at date of trial
	1.5%	2.0%	2.5%	3.0%	3.5%	4.0%	4.5%	5.0%	
0	5.11	3.53	2.45	1.70	1.19	0.83	0.58	0.41	0
1	5.22	3.63	2.53	1.77	1.24	0.87	0.61	0.43	1
2	5.30	3.70	2.59	1.82	1.28	0.91	0.64	0.46	2
3	5.38	3.78	2.66	1.88	1.33	0.94	0.67	0.48	3
4	5.47	3.85	2.72	1.93	1.37	0.98	0.70	0.50	4
5	5.55	3.93	2.79	1.99	1.42	1.02	0.73	0.53	5
6	5.63	4.01	2.86	2.05	1.47	1.06	0.77	0.55	6
7	5.72	4.09	2.94	2.11	1.52	1.10	0.80	0.58	7
8	5.80	4.17	3.01	2.18	1.58	1.15	0.84	0.61	8
9	5.89	4.26	3.09	2.24	1.63	1.19	0.87	0.64	9
10	5.98	4.34	3.16	2.31	1.69	1.24	0.91	0.67	10
11	6.07	4.43	3.24	2.38	1.75	1.29	0.96	0.71	11
12	6.16	4.52	3.32	2.45	1.81	1.34	1.00	0.74	12
13	6.26	4.61	3.41	2.52	1.88	1.40	1.04	0.78	13
14	6.35	4.70	3.49	2.60	1.94	1.45	1.09	0.82	14
15	6.45	4.80	3.58	2.68	2.01	1.51	1.14	0.86	15
16	6.55	4.90	3.67	2.76	2.08	1.57	1.19	0.90	16
17	6.65	5.00	3.76	2.84	2.15	1.64	1.25	0.95	17
18	6.75	5.10	3.86	2.93	2.23	1.70	1.30	1.00	18
19	6.85	5.20	3.96	3.02	2.31	1.77	1.36	1.05	19
20	6.96	5.31	4.06	3.11	2.39	1.84	1.42	1.10	20
21	7.06	5.41	4.16	3.20	2.48	1.92	1.49	1.16	21
22	7.17	5.52	4.27	3.30	2.56	1.99	1.55	1.21	22
23	7.28	5.64	4.37	3.40	2.65	2.07	1.62	1.28	23
24	7.39	5.75	4.48	3.51	2.75	2.16	1.70	1.34	24
25	7.51	5.87	4.60	3.61	2.84	2.24	1.78	1.41	25

26	7.62	5.99	4.71	3.72	2.94	2.34	1.86	1.48	26
27	7.74	6.11	4.83	3.83	3.05	2.43	1.94	1.55	27
28	7.86	6.23	4.96	3.95	3.16	2.53	2.03	1.63	28
29	7.98	6.36	5.08	4.07	3.27	2.63	2.12	1.71	29
30	8.10	6.49	5.21	4.19	3.38	2.74	2.22	1.80	30
31	8.23	6.62	5.34	4.32	3.50	2.85	2.32	1.89	31
32	8.35	6.76	5.48	4.45	3.63	2.96	2.42	1.99	32
33	8.48	6.90	5.62	4.59	3.76	3.08	2.53	2.09	33
34	8.62	7.04	5.76	4.73	3.89	3.21	2.65	2.19	34
35	8.75	7.18	5.91	4.88	4.03	3.34	2.77	2.30	35
36	8.89	7.33	6.06	5.03	4.17	3.47	2.90	2.42	36
37	9.03	7.49	6.22	5.18	4.32	3.61	3.03	2.54	37
38	9.17	7.64	6.38	5.34	4.48	3.76	3.17	2.67	38
39	9.32	7.80	6.55	5.51	4.64	3.92	3.31	2.81	39
40	9.47	7.97	6.72	5.68	4.81	4.08	3.47	2.95	40
41	9.62	8.13	6.89	5.85	4.98	4.24	3.63	3.10	41
42	9.77	8.31	7.07	6.03	5.16	4.42	3.79	3.26	42
43	9.93	8.48	7.26	6.22	5.35	4.60	3.97	3.43	43
44	10.10	8.66	7.45	6.42	5.54	4.79	4.15	3.60	44
45	10.26	8.85	7.65	6.62	5.75	4.99	4.35	3.79	45
46	10.44	9.04	7.85	6.83	5.96	5.20	4.55	3.99	46
47	10.61	9.24	8.07	7.05	6.18	5.42	4.76	4.20	47
48	10.80	9.45	8.29	7.28	6.41	5.65	4.99	4.41	48
49	10.99	9.66	8.51	7.52	6.65	5.89	5.23	4.65	49
50	11.18	9.88	8.75	7.76	6.90	6.14	5.48	4.89	50
51	11.38	10.11	9.00	8.02	7.16	6.41	5.74	5.15	51
52	11.59	10.34	9.25	8.29	7.44	6.68	6.02	5.43	52
53	11.81	10.59	9.52	8.57	7.72	6.98	6.31	5.72	53
54	12.03	10.84	9.79	8.86	8.03	7.28	6.62	6.03	54
55	12.26	11.11	10.08	9.16	8.34	7.61	6.95	6.36	55
56	12.51	11.38	10.38	9.48	8.68	7.95	7.30	6.71	56
57	12.76	11.67	10.70	9.82	9.03	8.31	7.67	7.08	57
58	13.03	11.98	11.03	10.17	9.40	8.70	8.06	7.48	58
59	13.31	12.30	11.38	10.55	9.79	9.10	8.48	7.90	59
60	13.61	12.64	11.75	10.95	10.21	9.54	8.92	8.36	60
61	13.93	13.00	12.15	11.37	10.66	10.00	9.40	8.85	61
62	14.27	13.38	12.57	11.82	11.13	10.50	9.92	9.38	62
63	14.64	13.79	13.01	12.30	11.64	11.03	10.47	9.95	63
64	15.03	14.23	13.49	12.81	12.18	11.60	11.07	10.57	64
65	15.45	14.70	14.00	13.37	12.77	12.22	11.71	11.24	65

Table 9: Multipliers for loss of pension commencing age 60 (males)

Age at date of trial	Multiplier calculated with allowance for population mortality and rate of return of								Age at date of trial
	1.5%	2.0%	2.5%	3.0%	3.5%	4.0%	4.5%	5.0%	
0	5.40	3.83	2.72	1.94	1.39	0.99	0.71	0.51	0
1	5.53	3.94	2.81	2.01	1.45	1.04	0.75	0.55	1
2	5.62	4.02	2.88	2.08	1.50	1.08	0.79	0.57	2
3	5.70	4.10	2.96	2.14	1.55	1.13	0.82	0.60	3
4	5.79	4.18	3.03	2.20	1.61	1.17	0.86	0.63	4
5	5.88	4.27	3.11	2.27	1.66	1.22	0.90	0.66	5
6	5.97	4.35	3.19	2.34	1.72	1.27	0.94	0.70	6
7	6.06	4.44	3.27	2.41	1.78	1.32	0.98	0.73	7
8	6.15	4.53	3.35	2.48	1.84	1.37	1.03	0.77	8
9	6.24	4.62	3.43	2.56	1.91	1.43	1.07	0.81	9
10	6.34	4.72	3.52	2.63	1.98	1.49	1.12	0.85	10
11	6.43	4.81	3.61	2.71	2.05	1.55	1.17	0.89	11
12	6.53	4.91	3.70	2.80	2.12	1.61	1.22	0.93	12
13	6.63	5.01	3.79	2.88	2.19	1.67	1.28	0.98	13
14	6.73	5.11	3.89	2.97	2.27	1.74	1.34	1.03	14
15	6.84	5.21	3.99	3.06	2.35	1.81	1.40	1.08	15
16	6.94	5.32	4.09	3.15	2.43	1.88	1.46	1.14	16
17	7.05	5.43	4.19	3.25	2.52	1.96	1.53	1.20	17
18	7.16	5.54	4.30	3.35	2.61	2.04	1.60	1.26	18
19	7.27	5.66	4.41	3.45	2.70	2.12	1.67	1.32	19
20	7.39	5.78	4.53	3.56	2.80	2.21	1.75	1.39	20
21	7.51	5.90	4.64	3.67	2.90	2.30	1.83	1.46	21
22	7.63	6.02	4.76	3.78	3.01	2.40	1.91	1.53	22
23	7.75	6.15	4.89	3.90	3.11	2.49	2.00	1.61	23
24	7.87	6.27	5.01	4.02	3.23	2.60	2.09	1.69	24
25	7.99	6.41	5.14	4.14	3.34	2.70	2.19	1.78	25
26	8.12	6.54	5.28	4.27	3.46	2.81	2.29	1.87	26
27	8.25	6.68	5.41	4.40	3.59	2.93	2.39	1.96	27
28	8.38	6.81	5.55	4.54	3.71	3.05	2.50	2.06	28
29	8.51	6.96	5.70	4.68	3.85	3.17	2.62	2.17	29
30	8.65	7.10	5.85	4.82	3.99	3.30	2.74	2.28	30
31	8.79	7.25	6.00	4.97	4.13	3.44	2.87	2.39	31
32	8.93	7.40	6.15	5.12	4.28	3.58	3.00	2.52	32
33	9.07	7.56	6.31	5.28	4.43	3.72	3.14	2.65	33
34	9.22·	7.72	6.48	5.45	4.59	3.88	3.28	2.78	34
35	9.36	7.88	6.65	5.62	4.76	4.04	3.43	2.92	35

36	9.52	8.05	6.82	5.79	4.93	4.20	3.59	3.07	36
37	9.67	8.22	7.00	5.97	5.11	4.38	3.76	3.23	37
38	9.83	8.39	7.18	6.16	5.29	4.56	3.93	3.40	38
39	9.99	8.57	7.37	6.36	5.49	4.75	4.11	3.57	39
40	10.16	8.76	7.57	6.56	5.69	4.94	4.31	3.76	40
41	10.33	8.95	7.77	6.76	5.90	5.15	4.51	3.95	41
42	10.50	9.15	7.98	6.98	6.12	5.37	4.72	4.16	42
43	10.68	9.35	8.20	7.20	6.34	5.59	4.94	4.37	43
44	10.87	9.56	8.42	7.44	6.58	5.83	5.17	4.60	44
45	11.05	9.77	8.65	7.68	6.83	6.08	5.42	4.84	45
46	11.25	9.99	8.89	7.93	7.08	6.34	5.68	5.10	46
47	11.45	10.22	9.14	8.19	7.35	6.61	5.95	5.37	47
48	11.66	10.46	9.40	8.47	7.64	6.90	6.24	5.66	48
49	11.88	10.71	9.67	8.75	7.93	7.20	6.55	5.96	49
50	12.11	10.97	9.96	9.05	8.24	7.52	6.87	6.29	50
51	12.35	11.24	10.25	9.37	8.57	7.86	7.21	6.63	51
52	12.60	11.53	10.56	9.70	8.92	8.21	7.58	7.00	52
53	12.86	11.83	10.89	10.05	9.28	8.59	7.96	7.39	53
54	13.14	12.14	11.24	10.42	9.67	8.99	8.38	7.81	54
55	13.43	12.47	11.60	10.81	10.08	9.42	8.82	8.26	55
56	13.75	12.82	11.99	11.22	10.52	9.88	9.29	8.74	56
57	14.08	13.20	12.40	11.66	10.98	10.36	9.79	9.26	57
58	14.43	13.60	12.83	12.13	11.48	10.89	10.33	9.82	58
59	14.81	14.03	13.30	12.63	12.02	11.45	10.92	10.43	59
60	15.22	14.49	13.81	13.18	12.60	12.06	11.56	11.09	60

Table 10: Multipliers for loss of pension commencing age 60 (females)

| Age at date of trial | Multiplier calculated with allowance for population mortality and rate of return of | | | | | | | | Age at date of trial |
	1.5%	2.0%	2.5%	3.0%	3.5%	4.0%	4.5%	5.0%	
0	6.88	4.83	3.41	2.41	1.71	1.22	0.87	0.62	0
1	7.03	4.96	3.52	2.50	1.78	1.28	0.92	0.66	1
2	7.14	5.06	3.61	2.58	1.85	1.33	0.96	0.69	2
3	7.25	5.17	3.70	2.65	1.91	1.38	1.00	0.73	3
4	7.36	5.27	3.79	2.73	1.98	1.44	1.05	0.76	4
5	7.47	5.38	3.89	2.82	2.05	1.49	1.09	0.80	5
6	7.58	5.49	3.98	2.90	2.12	1.55	1.14	0.84	6
7	7.70	5.60	4.08	2.99	2.20	1.62	1.19	0.88	7
8	7.81	5.71	4.19	3.08	2.27	1.68	1.25	0.93	8
9	7.93	5.82	4.29	3.17	2.35	1.75	1.30	0.98	9
10	8.05	5.94	4.40	3.27	2.43	1.82	1.36	1.02	10

11	8.17	6.06	4.51	3.37	2.52	1.89	1.42	1.08	11
12	8.30	6.18	4.62	3.47	2.61	1.97	1.49	1.13	12
13	8.42	6.31	4.74	3.57	2.70	2.05	1.56	1.19	13
14	8.55	6.44	4.86	3.68	2.80	2.13	1.63	1.25	14
15	8.68	6.57	4.98	3.79	2.89	2.22	1.70	1.31	15
16	8.81	6.70	5.11	3.91	3.00	2.30	1.78	1.37	16
17	8.95	6.83	5.24	4.02	3.10	2.40	1.86	1.44	17
18	9.08	6.97	5.37	4.15	3.21	2.49	1.94	1.52	18
19	9.22	7.11	5.50	4.27	3.32	2.59	2.03	1.59	19
20	9.36	7.26	5.64	4.40	3.44	2.70	2.12	1.67	20
21	9.51	7.41	5.79	4.53	3.56	2.81	2.22	1.76	21
22	9.65	7.56	5.93	4.67	3.69	2.92	2.32	1.84	22
23	9.80	7.71	6.08	4.81	3.82	3.04	2.42	1.94	23
24	9.95	7.87	6.24	4.96	3.95	3.16	2.53	2.04	24
25	10.10	8.03	6.40	5.11	4.09	3.29	2.65	2.14	25
26	10.26	8.19	6.56	5.27	4.24	3.42	2.77	2.25	26
27	10.41	8.36	6.72	5.43	4.39	3.56	2.89	2.36	27
28	10.57	8.53	6.90	5.59	4.54	3.70	3.03	2.48	28
29	10.74	8.70	7.07	5.76	4.71	3.85	3.16	2.60	29
30	10.90	8.88	7.25	5.94	4.87	4.01	3.31	2.73	30
31	11.07	9.06	7.43	6.12	5.04	4.17	3.46	2.87	31
32	11.24	9.25	7.62	6.30	5.22	4.34	3.61	3.02	32
33	11.42	9.44	7.82	6.50	5.41	4.52	3.78	3.17	33
34	11.60	9.63	8.02	6.69	5.60	4.70	3.95	3.33	34
35	11.78	9.83	8.22	6.90	5.80	4.89	4.13	3.50	35
36	11.96	10.03	8.44	7.11	6.01	5.09	4.32	3.67	36
37	12.15	10.24	8.65	7.33	6.22	5.30	4.52	3.86	37
38	12.34	10.45	8.88	7.56	6.45	5.51	4.72	4.06	38
39	12.54	10.67	9.11	7.79	6.68	5.74	4.94	4.26	39
40	12.74	10.90	9.34	8.03	6.92	5.97	5.17	4.48	40
41	12.94	11.13	9.59	8.28	7.17	6.22	5.41	4.71	41
42	13.15	11.36	9.84	8.54	7.43	6.48	5.66	4.95	42
43	13.37	11.60	10.10	8.81	7.70	6.74	5.92	5.21	43
44	13.59	11.85	10.36	9.08	7.98	7.02	6.19	5.48	44
45	13.81	12.11	10.64	9.37	8.27	7.32	6.48	5.76	45
46	14.05	12.37	10.93	9.67	8.58	7.62	6.79	6.06	46
47	14.28	12.65	11.22	9.98	8.89	7.94	7.11	6.37	47
48	14.53	12.93	11.53	10.30	9.23	8.28	7.44	6.71	48
49	14.78	13.22	11.84	10.64	9.57	8.63	7.80	7.06	49
50	15.05	13.52	12.17	10.98	9.93	9.00	8.17	7.43	50

51	15.32	13.83	12.51	11.35	10.31	9.39	8.56	7.82	51
52	15.60	14.15	12.87	11.73	10.71	9.79	8.98	8.24	52
53	15.89	14.49	13.24	12.12	11.12	10.22	9.41	8.69	53
54	16.19	14.83	13.62	12.53	11.56	10.67	9.88	9.16	54
55	16.50	15.20	14.02	12.97	12.01	11.15	10.37	9.66	55
56	16.83	15.57	14.44	13.42	12.49	11.65	10.88	10.19	56
57	17.17	15.97	14.88	13.89	13.00	12.18	11.43	10.75	57
58	17.54	16.39	15.34	14.40	13.53	12.74	12.02	11.36	58
59	17.92	16.83	15.83	14.93	14.10	13.34	12.64	12.00	59
60	18.32	17.29	16.35	15.49	14.70	13.98	13.31	12.70	60

Table 11: Multipliers for pecuniary loss for life (males)

Age at date of trial	Multiplier calculated with allowance for population mortality and rate of return of								Age at date of trial
	1.5%	2.0%	2.5%	3.0%	3.5%	4.0%	4.5%	5.0%	
0	45.80	39.31	34.17	30.05	26.70	23.96	21.68	19.77	0
1	45.73	39.31	34.20	30.10	26.77	24.04	21.76	19.85	1
2	45.43	39.09	34.06	30.00	26.70	23.99	21.73	19.83	2
3	45.11	38.87	33.90	29.89	26.62	23.93	21.69	19.80	3
4	44.78	38.64	33.74	29.78	26.54	23.87	21.64	19.76	4
5	44.45	38.41	33.57	29.66	26.46	23.81	21.60	19.73	5
6	44.11	38.17	33.40	29.54	26.37	23.74	21.55	19.69	6
7	43.76	37.92	33.22	29.41	26.27	23.67	21.50	19.65	7
8	43.41	37.67	33.04	29.28	26.18	23.60	21.44	19.61	8
9	43.05	37.41	32.86	29.14	26.08	23.53	21.38	19.57	9
10	42.69	37.15	32.67	29.00	25.97	23.45	21.33	19.53	10
11	42.32	36.88	32.47	28.85	25.86	23.37	21.26	19.48	11
12	41.94	36.61	32.27	28.70	25.75	23.28	21.20	19.43	12
13	41.57	36.33	32.06	28.55	25.64	23.20	21.13	19.38	13
14	41.18	36.05	31.85	28.40	25.52	23.11	21.06	19.32	14
15	40.79	35.76	31.64	28.24	25.40	23.01	20.99	19.27	15
16	40.40	35.47	31.42	28.07	25.27	22.92	20.92	19.21	16
17	40.01	35.18	31.20	27.91	25.15	22.82	20.84	19.15	17
18	39.62	34.89	30.98	27.74	25.02	22.72	20.77	19.09	18
19	39.22	34.59	30.76	27.57	24.90	22.63	20.70	19.04	19
20	38.83	34.30	30.54	27.40	24.77	22.53	20.62	18.98	20
21	38.42	33.99	30.31	27.23	24.63	22.43	20.54	18.91	21
22	38.02	33.68	30.08	27.05	24.49	22.32	20.46	18.85	22
23	37.60	33.37	29.83	26.87	24.35	33.21	20.37	18.78	23
24	37.18	33.04	29.59	26.67	24.20	22.09	20.28	18.71	24
25	36.75	32.71	29.33	26.48	24.05	21.97	20.18	18.63	25

26	36.31	32.38	29.07	26.27	23.89	21.85	20.08	18.55	26
27	35.87	32.04	28.80	26.06	23.72	21.72	19.98	18.47	27
28	35.42	31.69	28.53	25.85	23.55	21.58	19.87	18.38	28
29	34.97	31.33	28.25	25.63	23.38	21.44	19.76	18.29	29
30	34.50	30.96	27.96	25.40	23.19	21.29	19.64	18.20	30
31	34.02	30.59	27.66	25.16	23.00	21.14	19.51	18.10	31
32	33.54	30.20	27.36	24.91	22.81	20.98	19.38	17.99	32
33	33.05	29.81	27.04	24.66	22.60	20.81	19.25	17.88	33
34	32.56	29.42	26.72	24.40	22.39	20.64	19.11	17.76	34
35	32.05	29.01	26.39	24.13	22.17	20.46	18.96	17.64	35
36	31.54	28.59	26.05	23.85	21.94	20.27	18.80	17.51	36
37	31.01	28.16	25.70	23.57	21.70	20.07	18.64	17.37	37
38	30.48	27.73	25.34	23.27	21.46	19.87	18.47	17.23	38
39	29.94	27.29	24.98	22.97	21.21	19.66	18.29	17.08	39
40	29.40	26.84	24.61	22.66	20.95	19.44	18.11	16.92	40
41	28.85	26.38	24.23	22.34	20.68	19.22	17.92	16.76	41
42	28.29	25.92	23.84	22.02	20.41	18.98	17.72	16.59	42
43	27.73	25.44	23.44	21.68	20.13	18.74	17.52	16.42	43
44	27.15	24.96	23.04	21.34	19.83	18.49	17.30	16.23	44
45	26.57	24.47	22.62	20.98	19.53	18.23	17.08	16.04	45
46	25.98	23.96	22.19	20.61	19.21	17.96	16.84	15.84	46
47	25.37	23.45	21.75	20.23	18.89	17.68	16.60	15.62	47
48	24.76	22.93	21.30	19.85	18.55	17.39	16.34	15.40	48
49	24.14	22.39	20.84	19.45	18.20	17.08	16.08	15.16	49
50	23.52	21.86	20.37	19.04	17.85	16.78	15.80	14.93	50
51	22.90	21.32	19.90	18.63	17.49	16.46	15.53	14.68	51
52	22.28	20.78	19.43	18.22	17.12	16.14	15.24	14.43	52
53	21.65	20.23	18.95	17.79	16.75	15.80	14.95	14.16	53
54	21.02	19.67	18.46	17.36	16.37	15.46	14.64	13.89	54
55	20.38	19.11	17.96	16.92	15.98	15.12	14.33	13.62	55
56	19.75	18.55	17.47	16.48	15.58	14.77	14.02	13.33	56
57	19.12	17.99	16.97	16.04	15.19	14.41	13.70	13.04	57
58	18.50	17.44	16.47	15.59	14.78	14.05	13.37	12.74	58
59	17.87	16.87	15.97	15.14	14.38	13.68	13.03	12.44	59
60	17.24	16.31	15.46	14.68	13.96	13.30	12.69	12.13	60
61	16.61	15.74	14.94	14.21	13.54	12.92	12.34	11.81	61
62	15.98	15.17	14.43	13.74	13.11	12.52	11.98	11.48	62
63	15.35	14.60	13.90	13.26	12.67	12.12	11.62	11.14	63
64	14.72	14.02	13.38	12.78	12.23	11.72	11.24	10.80	64
65	14.09	13.45	12.85	12.30	11.78	11.31	10.86	10.45	65

Age									Age
66	13.46	12.87	12.32	11.81	11.33	10.89	10.48	10.09	66
67	12.85	12.30	11.80	11.32	10.88	10.47	10.09	9.73	67
68	12.24	11.74	11.28	10.84	10.44	10.06	9.70	9.36	68
69	11.64	11.19	10.76	10.36	9.99	9.64	9.31	9.00	69
70	11.06	10.65	10.26	9.89	9.55	9.23	8.92	8.64	70
71	10.51	10.13	9.77	9.44	9.12	8.83	8.55	8.29	71
72	9.97	9.63	9.30	9.00	8.71	8.44	8.18	7.94	72
73	9.45	9.14	8.84	8.56	8.30	8.05	7.82	7.59	73
74	8.95	8.67	8.40	8.15	7.91	7.68	7.46	7.26	74
75	8.46	8.21	7.97	7.74	7.52	7.31	7.11	6.93	75
76	8.00	7.77	7.55	7.34	7.14	6.95	6.77	6.60	76
77	7.56	7.35	7.15	6.96	6.78	6.61	6.45	6.29	77
78	7.14	6.95	6.77	6.60	6.43	6.28	6.13	5.99	78
79	6.73	6.56	6.40	6.25	6.10	5.96	5.82	5.70	79
80	6.35	6.20	6.06	5.92	5.78	5.65	5.53	5.41	80
81	6.00	5.86	5.73	5.60	5.48	5.36	5.25	5.14	81
82	5.66	5.54	5.42	5.30	5.19	5.09	4.99	4.89	82
83	5.35	5.24	5.13	5.03	4.93	4.83	4.74	4.65	83
84	5.07	4.97	4.87	4.78	4.69	4.60	4.52	4.43	84
85	4.81	4.72	4.63	4.54	4.46	4.38	4.30	4.23	85
86	4.56	4.48	4.40	4.32	4.24	4.17	4.10	4.04	86
87	4.32	4.24	4.17	4.10	4.03	3.96	3.90	3.84	87
88	4.07	4.01	3.94	3.88	3.82	3.76	3.70	3.64	88
89	3.84	3.78	3.72	3.66	3.61	3.56	3.50	3.45	89
90	3.62	3.56	3.51	3.46	3.41	3.36	3.32	3.27	90
91	3.40	3.35	3.31	3.26	3.22	3.17	3.13	3.09	91
92	3.19	3.14	3.10	3.06	3.02	2.99	2.95	2.91	92
93	2.99	2.96	2.92	2.88	2.85	2.81	2.78	2.75	93
94	2.82	2.78	2.75	2.72	2.69	2.66	2.63	2.60	94
95	2.65	2.62	2.59	2.56	2.53	2.50	2.48	2.45	95
96	2.48	2.45	2.43	2.40	2.38	2.35	2.33	2.31	96
97	2.32	2.29	2.27	2.25	2.23	2.21	2.19	2.16	97
98	2.15	2.13	2.11	2.10	2.08	2.06	2.04	2.02	98
99	1.99	1.98	1.96	1.94	1.93	1.91	1.90	1.88	99
100	1.83	1.82	1.81	1.79	1.78	1.76	1.75	1.74	100

Table 12: Multipliers for pecuniary loss for life (females)

Age at date of trial	Multiplier calculated with allowance for population mortality and rate of return of								Age at date of trial
	1.5%	2.0%	2.5%	3.0%	3.5%	4.0%	4.5%	5.0%	
0	47.34	40.38	34.93	30.59	27.10	24.25	21.90	19.94	0
1	47.25	40.36	34.95	30.64	27.16	24.31	21.97	20.01	1
2	46.97	40.18	34.82	30.55	27.10	24.28	21.94	19.99	2
3	46.67	39.97	34.69	30.46	27.04	24.23	21.91	19.97	3
4	46.37	39.77	34.54	30.36	26.97	24.18	21.88	19.94	4
5	46.06	39.55	34.40	30.26	26.89	24.13	21.84	19.92	5
6	45.74	39.34	34.24	30.15	26.82	24.08	21.80	19.89	6
7	45.42	39.11	34.09	30.04	26.74	24.02	21.76	19.86	7
8	45.09	38.88	33.93	29.93	26.66	23.97	21.72	19.83	8
9	44.76	38.65	33.76	29.81	26.58	23.91	21.68	19.80	9
10	44.42	38.41	33.59	29.69	26.49	23.84	21.63	19.76	10
11	44.08	38.17	33.42	29.56	26.40	23.78	21.58	19.72	11
12	43.73	37.92	33.24	29.44	26.31	23.71	21.53	19.69	12
13	43.38	37.67	33.06	29.30	26.21	23.64	21.48	19.65	13
14	43.02	37.41	32.87	29.17	26.11	23.56	21.42	19.60	14
15	42.65	37.15	32.68	29.03	26.01	23.48	21.36	19.56	15
16	42.29	36.88	32.49	28.89	25.90	23.41	21.30	19.52	16
17	41.91	36.61	32.29	28.74	25.79	23.32	21.24	19.47	17
18	41.54	36.34	32.09	28.59	25.68	23.24	21.18	19.42	18
19	41.15	36.05	31.88	28.43	25.56	23.15	21.11	19.37	19
20	40.77	35.77	31.67	28.28	25.44	23.06	21.04	19.32	20
21	40.37	35.48	31.45	28.11	25.32	22.97	20.97	19.26	21
22	39.97	35.18	31.23	27.94	25.19	22.87	20.90	19.20	22
23	39.57	34.88	31.00	27.77	25.06	22.77	20.82	19.14	23
24	39.16	34.57	30.77	27.59	24.93	22.67	20.74	19.08	24
25	38.74	34.25	30.53	27.41	24.79	22.56	20.65	19.01	25
26	38.32	33.93	30.28	27.11	24.64	22.44	20.56	18.94	26
27	37.89	33.61	30.03	27.03	24.49	22.33	20.47	18.87	27
28	37.46	33.27	29.78	26.83	24.34	22.21	20.38	18.79	28
29	37.01	32.93	29.51	26.63	24.18	22.08	20.28	18.71	29
30	36.57	32.59	29.24	26.42	24.01	21.95	20.17	18.63	30
31	36.11	32.23	28.97	26.20	23.84	21.81	20.06	18.54	31
32	35.65	31.87	28.68	25.98	23.66	21.67	19.95	18.45	32
33	35.18	31.50	28.39	25.75	23.48	21.52	19.83	18.35	33
34	34.70	31.13	28.10	25.51	23.29	21.37	19.71	18.25	34
35	34.22	30.74	27.79	25.26	23.09	21.21	19.58	18.15	35

36	33.73	30.35	27.48	25.01	22.89	21.05	19.44	18.04	36
37	33.23	29.96	27.16	24.75	22.68	20.88	19.30	17.92	37
38	32.72	29.55	26.83	24.49	22.46	20.70	19.16	17.80	38
39	32.21	29.14	26.50	24.22	22.24	20.51	19.00	17.67	39
40	31.69	28.72	26.16	23.94	22.01	20.33	18.85	17.54	40
41	31.17	28.29	25.81	23.65	21.77	20.13	18.68	17.41	41
42	30.64	27.86	25.45	23.36	21.53	19.93	18.51	17.26	42
43	30.10	27.42	25.09	23.06	21.28	19.72	18.34	17.12	43
44	29.56	26.97	24.71	22.75	21.02	19.50	18.16	16.96	44
45	29.00	26.51	24.33	22.43	20.75	19.28	17.97	16.80	45
46	28.44	26.04	23.94	22.10	20.48	19.04	17.77	16.63	46
47	27.88	25.57	23.55	21.77	20.20	18.80	17.56	16.46	47
48	27.30	25.09	23.14	21.42	19.90	18.55	17.35	16.27	48
49	26.72	24.60	22.73	21.07	19.60	18.30	17.13	16.08	49
50	26.14	24.10	22.30	20.71	19.30	18.03	16.90	15.88	50
51	25.54	23.60	21.87	20.34	18.98	17.76	16.66	15.68	51
52	24.95	23.09	21.44	19.97	18.65	17.48	16.42	15.47	52
53	24.36	22.58	21.00	19.59	18.33	17.20	16.17	15.25	53
54	23.78	22.09	20.58	19.22	18.01	16.92	15.93	15.04	54
55	23.21	21.59	20.15	18.85	17.69	16.64	15.68	14.82	55
56	22.63	21.10	19.72	18.47	17.36	16.35	15.43	14.60	56
57	22.05	20.59	19.27	18.09	17.02	16.05	15.16	14.36	57
58	21.46	20.07	18.82	17.69	16.66	15.74	14.89	14.12	58
59	20.85	19.54	18.35	17.27	16.30	15.41	14.60	13.86	59
60	20.22	18.98	17.86	16.84	15.91	15.07	14.29	13.58	60
61	19.57	18.40	17.35	16.38	15.50	14.70	13.97	13.29	61
62	18.90	17.81	16.81	15.91	15.08	14.32	13.62	12.98	62
63	18.21	17.19	16.26	15.41	14.63	13.92	13.26	12.65	63
64	17.52	16.57	15.70	14.90	14.17	13.50	12.88	12.31	64
65	16.81	15.94	15.13	14.39	13.70	13.07	12.49	11.95	65
66	16.11	15.30	14.55	13.86	13.23	12.64	12.09	11.59	66
67	15.42	14.67	13.98	13.34	12.75	12.20	11.69	11.22	67
68	14.75	14.05	13.42	12.82	12.27	11.76	11.29	10.85	68
69	14.08	13.45	12.86	12.31	11.80	11.33	10.89	10.47	69
70	13.44	12.85	12.31	11.81	11.34	10.90	10.49	10.11	70
71	12.8	12.28	11.79	11.32	10.89	10.48	10.10	9.74	71
72	12.2	11.74	11.28	10.85	10.45	10.08	9.72	9.39	72
73	11.7	11.21	10.79	10.40	10.03	9.68	9.35	9.05	73
74	11.1	10.69	10.31	9.94	9.60	9.28	8.98	8.70	74
75	10.6	10.18	9.83	9.50	9.19	8.89	8.61	8.35	75

76	10.0	9.68	9.36	9.06	8.77	8.50	8.25	8.00	76
77	9.5	9.19	8.90	8.62	8.36	8.11	7.88	7.66	77
78	9.0	8.70	8.44	8.19	7.95	7.73	7.51	7.31	78
79	8.5	8.22	7.99	7.76	7.55	7.34	7.15	6.96	79
80	8.0	7.76	7.55	7.34	7.15	6.96	6.79	6.62	80
81	7.5	7.32	7.12	6.94	6.76	6.60	6.44	6.28	81
82	7.1	6.89	6.72	6.55	6.39	6.24	6.10	5.96	82
83	6.7	6.49	6.33	6.19	6.04	5.91	5.78	5.65	83
84	6.3	6.12	5.98	5.85	5.72	5.59	5.47	5.36	84
85	5.9	5.78	5.65	5.53	5.42	5.30	5.20	5.09	85
86	5.6	5.46	5.35	5.24	5.13	5.03	4.93	4.84	86
87	5.3	5.16	5.06	4.96	4.86	4.77	4.68	4.60	87
88	5.0	4.88	4.79	4.70	4.61	4.53	4.45	4.37	88
89	4.7	4.62	4.53	4.45	4.37	4.30	4.22	4.15	89
90	4.5	4.37	4.30	4.22	4.15	4.08	4.02	3.95	90
91	4.2	4.13	4.07	4.00	3.93	3.87	3.81	3.75	91
92	4.0	3.90	3.84	3.78	3.72	3.67	3.61	3.56	92
93	3.7	3.68	3.62	3.57	3.52	3.47	3.42	3.37	93
94	3.5	3.46	3.41	3.36	3.32	3.27	3.23	3.18	94
95	3.3	3.25	3.21	3.16	3.12	3.08	3.04	3.00	95
96	3.1	3.05	3.01	2.97	2.93	2.90	2.86	2.83	96
97	2.9	2.87	2.83	2.80	2.77	2.73	2.70	2.67	97
98	2.7	2.70	2.67	2.64	2.61	2.58	2.55	2.53	98
99	2.6	2.53	2.51	2.48	2.45	2.43	2.40	2.38	99
100	2.4	2.37	2.34	2.32	2.29	2.27	2.25	2.23	100

Table 13: Multipliers for loss of earnings to pension age 65 (males)

| Age at date of trial | Multiplier calculated with allowance for population mortality and rate of return of | | | | | | | | Age at date of trial |
	1.5%	2.0%	2.5%	3.0%	3.5%	4.0%	4.5%	5.0%	
16	33.83	30.56	27.74	25.30	23.19	21.34	19.72	18.30	16
17	33.34	30.17	27.43	25.05	22.99	21.18	19.59	18.20	17
18	32.85	29.78	27.12	24.80	22.79	21.02	19.47	18.09	18
19	32.36	29.38	26.80	24.55	22.58	20.85	19.33	17.99	19
20	31.86	28.98	26.48	24.29	22.37	20.68	19.19	17.87	20
21	31.35	28.57	26.15	24.02	22.15	20.51	19.05	17.76	21
22	30.84	28.16	25.81	23.75	21.93	20.32	18.90	17.63	22
23	30.32	27.73	25.46	23.46	21.70	20.13	18.74	17.50	23
24	29.78	27.29	25.10	23.17	21.46	19.93	18.58	17.37	24
25	29.25	26.85	24.74	22.87	21.21	19.73	18.41	17.23	25

26	28.70	26.40	24.36	22.56	20.95	19.51	18.23	17.08	26
27	28.15	25.94	23.98	22.24	20.68	19.29	18.04	16.92	27
28	27.58	25.47	23.59	21.91	20.41	19.06	17.85	16.76	28
29	27.01	24.99	23.18	21.57	20.12	18.82	17.64	16.59	29
30	26.43	24.50	22.77	21.22	19.82	18.57	17.43	16.40	30
31	25.84	24.00	22.34	20.86	19.52	18.30	17.21	16.21	31
32	25.24	23.49	21.91	20.49	19.20	18.03	16.98	16.01	32
33	24.63	22.97	21.46	20.10	18.87	17.75	16.73	15.80	33
34	24.02	22.44	21.01	19.71	18.53	17.46	16.48	15.59	34
35	23.39	21.90	20.54	19.30	18.18	17.15	16.21	15.36	35
36	22.76	21.34	20.06	18.89	17.81	16.83	15.94	15.11	36
37	22.11	20.78	19.56	18.45	17.44	16.50	15.65	14.86	37
38	21.45	20.20	19.06	18.01	17.05	16.16	15.34	14.59	38
39	20.79	19.62	18.54	17.55	16.64	15.80	15.03	14.31	39
40	20.12	19.02	18.02	17.09	16.23	15.44	14..70	14.02	40
41	19.44	18.42	17.48	16.61	15.80	15.05	14.36	13.72	41
42	18.75	17.80	16.93	16.12	15.36	14.66	14.01	13.40	42
43	18.05	17.18	16.37	15.61	14.91	14.25	13.64	13.07	43
44	17.34	16.54	15.79	15.09	14.44	13.82	13.25	12.72	44
45	16.63	15.89	15.20	14.55	13.95	13.38	12.85	12.35	45
46	15.90	15.22	14.59	14.00	13.44	12.92	12.43	11.97	46
47	15.15	14.54	13.97	13.43	12.92	12.44	11.99	11.56	47
48	14.40	13.85	13.33	12.84	12.38	11.94	11.53	11.14	48
49	13.64	13.15	12.69	12.24	11.83	11.43	11.05	10.70	49
50	12.88	12.44	12.02	11.63	11.25	10.90	10.56	10.24	50
51	12.10	11.72	11.35	11.00	10.67	10.35	10.04	9.76	51
52	11.32	10.98	10.66	10.35	10.06	9.78	9.51	9.25	52
53	10.52	10.23	9.96	9.69	9.44	9.19	8.96	8.73	53
54	9.72	9.48	9.24	9.01	8.79	8.58	8.38	8.18	54
55	8.91	8.70	8.50	8.31	8.13	7.95	7.78	7.61	55
56	8.09	7.92	7.75	7.59	7.44	7.29	7.15	7.01	56
57	7.25	7.12	6.99	6.86	6.73	6.61	6.50	6.38	57
58	6.41	6.30	6.20	6.10	6.00	5.91	5.81	5.72	58
59	5.55	5.47	5.39	5.32	5.24	5.17	5.10	5.03	59
60	4.67	4.62	4.56	4.51	4.46	4.41	4.36	4.31	60
61	3.78	3.75	3.71	3.67	3.64	3.61	3.57	3.54	61
62	2.87	2.85	2.83	2.81	2.79	2.77	2.75	2.73	62
63	1.94	1.93	1.92	1.91	1.90	1.89	1.89	1.88	63
64	0.98	0.98	0.98	0.98	0.97	0.97	0.97	0.97	64

Table 14: Multipliers for loss of earnings to pension age 65 (females)

Age at date of trial	Multiplier calculated with allowance for population mortality and rate of return of								Age at date of trial
	1.5%	2.0%	2.5%	3.0%	3.5%	4.0%	4.5%	5.0%	
16	34.22	30.89	28.03	25.55	23.40	21.53	19.89	18.45	16
17	33.73	30.50	27.72	25.31	23.21	21.37	19.76	18.35	17
18	33.23	30.11	27.40	25.05	23.01	21.21	19.63	18.24	18
19	32.73	29.70	27.08	24.79	22.80	21.04	19.50	18.13	19
20	32.22	29.29	26.75	24.53	22.58	20.87	19.36	18.02	20
21	31.70	28.87	26.41	24.25	22.36	20.69	19.21	17.90	21
22	31.17	28.45	26.06	23.97	22.13	20.50	19.06	17.77	22
23	30.64	28.01	25.71	23.68	21.89	20.30	18.90	17.64	23
24	30.10	27.57	25.34	23.38	21.64	20.10	18.73	17.50	24
25	29.55	27.12	24.97	23.07	21.39	19.89	18.55	17.36	25
26	28.99	26.66	24.59	22.76	21.13	19.67	18.37	17.21	26
27	28.43	26.19	24.20	22.43	20.86	19.45	18.18	17.05	27
28	27.86	25.71	23.80	22.10	20.58	19.21	17.99	16.88	28
29	27.28	25.22	23.39	21.75	20.29	18.97	17.78	16.71	29
30	26.69	24.73	22.97	21.40	19.99	18.71	17.56	16.52	30
31	26.09	24.22	22.54	21.03	19.68	18.45	17.34	16.33	31
32	25.48	23.70	22.10	20.66	19.35	18.17	17.10	16.13	32
33	24.87	23.18	21.65	20.27	19.02	17.89	16.86	15.92	33
34	24.24	22.64	21.19	19.87	18.68	17.59	16.60	15.70	34
35	23.61	22.09	20.72	19.47	18.33	17.29	16.33	15.47	35
36	22.97	21.54	20.23	19.04	17.96	16.97	16.06	15.22	36
37	22.32	20.97	19.74	18.61	17.58	16.64	15.77	14.97	37
38	21.66	20.39	19.23	18.17	17.19	16.29	15.46	14.70	38
39	20.99	19.81	18.71	17.71	16.79	15.94	15.15	14.42	39
40	20.32	19.21	18.19	17.24	16.37	15.57	14.82	14.13	40
41	19.63	18.60	17.64	16.76	15.94	15.18	14.48	13.83	41
42	18.94	17.98	17.09	16.27	15.50	14.79	14.13	13.51	42
43	18.24	17.35	16.53	15.76	15.04	14.38	13.76	13.18	43
44	17.53	16.71	15.95	15.24	14.57	13.95	13.37	12.83	44
45	16.81	16.06	15.35	14.70	14.08	13.51	12.97	12.46	45
46	16.08	15.39	14.75	14.15	13.58	13.05	12.55	12.08	46
47	15.33	14.71	14.13	13.58	13.06	12.57	12.11	11.68	47
48	14.58	14.02	13.49	13.00	12.52	12.08	11.66	11.26	48
49	13.82	13.32	12.85	12.40	11.97	11.57	11.18	10.82	49
50	13.05	12.61	12.18	11.78	11.40	11.03	10.69	10.36	50

51	12.27	11.88	11.50	11.15	10.81	10.48	10.17	9.88	51
52	11.48	11.14	10.81	10.49	10.20	9.91	9.64	9.37	52
53	10.68	10.38	10.10	9.83	9.57	9.32	9.08	8.85	53
54	9.87	9.62	9.38	9.14	8.92	8.70	8.50	8.30	54
55	9.05	8.84	8.63	8.44	8.25	8.07	7.89	7.72	55
56	8.21	8.04	7.87	7.71	7.55	7.40	7.26	7.11	56
57	7.37	7.23	7.09	6.96	6.84	6.71	6.59	6.48	57
58	6.50	6.40	6.29	6.19	6.09	5.99	5.90	5.81	58
59	5.63	5.55	5.47	5.39	5.32	5.24	5.17	5.10	59
60	4.73	4.68	4.62	4.57	4.51	4.46	4.41	4.36	60
61	3.82	3.79	3.75	3.72	3.68	3.65	3.61	3.58	61
62	2.90	2.88	2.86	2.84	2.82	2.80	2.78	2.76	62
63	1.95	1.94	1.93	1.92	1.92	1.91	1.90	1.89	63
64	0.99	0.99	0.98	0.98	0.98	0.98	0.97	0.97	64

Table 15: Multipliers for loss of earnings to pension age 60 (males)

| Age at date of trial | Multiplier calculated with allowance for population mortality and rate of return of | | | | | | | | Age at date of trial |
	1.5%	2.0%	2.5%	3.0%	3.5%	4.0%	4.5%	5.0%	
16	31.58	28.77	26.31	24.16	22.28	20.61	19.14	17.84	16
17	31.06	28.34	25.97	23.88	22.05	20.42	18.99	17.71	17
18	30.53	27.91	25.62	23.60	21.81	20.23	18.83	17.58	18
19	30.00	27.48	25.26	23.30	21.57	20.04	18.67	17.45	19
20	29.47	27.04	24.90	23.01	21.33	19.83	18.50	17.31	20
21	28.92	26.59	24.53	22.70	21.07	19.62	18.32	17.16	21
22	28.37	26.13	24.15	22.38	20.81	19.40	18.14	17.01	22
23	27.81	25.67	23.76	22.06	20.54	19.17	17.95	16.85	23
24	27.24	25.19	23.36	21.72	20.25	18.94	17.75	16.68	24
25	26.66	24.70	22.95	21.38	19.96	18.69	17.54	16.50	25
26	26.08	24.21	22.53	21.02	19.66	18.43	17.32	16.31	26
27	25.48	23.70	22.10	20.65	19.35	18.17	17.09	16.12	27
28	24.88	23.19	21.66	20.28	19.02	17.89	16.86	15.92	28
29	24.27	22.66	21.21	19.89	18.69	17.60	16.61	15.70	29
30	23.64	22.12	20.74	19.49	18.34	17.30	16.35	15.48	30
31	23.01	21.57	20.26	19.07	17.98	16.99	16.08	15.24	31
32	22.37	21.01	19.78	18.65	17.61	16.66	15.79	14.99	32
33	21.72	20.44	19.28	18.21	17.23	16.32	15.49	14.73	33
34	21.06	19.86	18.77	17.76	16.83	15.97	15.18	14.46	34
35	20.38	19.27	18.24	17.29	16.42	15.61	14.86	14.17	35

36	19.70	18.66	17.70	16.81	15.99	15.23	14.52	13.86	36
37	19.01	18.04	17.15	16.32	15.55	14.83	14.17	13.55	37
38	18.30	17.41	16.58	15.81	15.09	14.42	13.80	13.21	38
39	17.59	16.77	16.00	15.29	14.62	14.00	13.41	12.87	39
40	16.87	16.12	15.41	14.75	14.13	13.55	13.01	12.50	40
41	16.14	15.45	14.81	14.20	13.63	13.10	12.59	12.12	41
42	15.40	14.77	14.19	13.63	13.11	12.62	12.16	11.72	42
43	14.65	14.08	13.55	13.05	12.58	12.13	11.70	11.30	43
44	13.89	13.38	12.90	12.45	12.02	11.62	11.23	10.86	44
45	13.11	12.66	12.24	11.83	11.45	11.08	10.73	10.40	45
46	12.33	11.93	11.55	11.19	10.85	10.53	10.22	9.92	46
47	11.53	11.18	10.85	10.54	10.24	9.95	9.67	9.41	47
48	10.72	10.42	10.13	9.86	9.60	9.35	9.11	8.88	48
49	9.90	9.64	9.40	9.17	8.94	8.73	8.52	8.32	49
50	9.07	8.85	8.65	8.45	8.26	8.08	7.90	7.73	50
51	8.22	8.05	7.88	7.72	7.56	7.41	7.26	7.12	51
52	7.37	7.23	7.10	6.97	6.84	6.72	6.60	6.48	52
53	6.50	6.40	6.29	6.19	6.09	5.99	5.90	5.81	53
54	5.62	5.54	5.47	5.39	5.32	5.24	5.17	5.10	54
55	4.73	4.67	4.62	4.57	4.51	4.46	4.41	4.36	55
56	3.82	3.79	3.75	3.71	3.68	3.65	3.61	3.58	56
57	2.90	2.88	2.85	2.83	2.81	2.79	2.78	2.76	57
58	1.95	1.94	1.93	1.92	1.92	1.91	1.90	1.89	58
59	0.99	0.99	0.98	0.98	0.98	0.98	0.97	0.97	59

Table 16: Multipliers for loss of earnings to pension age 60 (females)

Age at date of trial	Multiplier calculated with allowance for population mortality and rate of return of								Age at date of trial
	1.5%	2.0%	2.5%	3.0%	3.5%	4.0%	4.5%	5.0%	
16	31.88	29.03	26.55	24.37	22.46	20.77	19.28	17.96	16
17	31.36	28.61	26.20	24.09	22.23	20.59	19.13	17.84	17
18	30.83	28.17	25.85	23.80	21.99	20.40	18.98	17.71	18
19	30.29	27.73	25.49	23.50	21.75	20.19	18.81	17.57	19
20	29.74	27.28	25.11	23.20	21.50	19.99	18.64	17.43	20
21	29.18	26.82	24.73	22.88	21.24	19.77	18.46	17.28	21
22	28.62	26.35	24.35	22.56	20.97	19.55	18.27	17.12	22
23	28.05	25.88	23.95	22.23	20.69	19.31	18.07	16.96	23
24	27.47	25.39	23.54	21.88	20.40	19.07	17.87	16.79	24
25	26.88	24.90	23.12	21.53	20.10	18.82	17.66	16.61	25

26	26.28	24.39	22.69	21.17	19.80	18.56	17.43	16.42	26
27	25.68	23.88	22.26	20.80	19.48	18.28	17.20	16.22	27
28	25.06	23.35	21.81	20.41	19.15	18.00	16.96	16.01	28
29	24.44	22.82	21.35	20.02	18.81	17.71	16.71	15.79	29
30	23.81	22.27	20.88	19.61	18.46	17.41	16.44	15.56	30
31	23.17	21.72	20.40	19.19	18.09	17.09	16.17	15.32	31
32	22.52	21.15	19.90	18.76	17.72	16.76	15.88	15.07	32
33	21.86	20.57	19.40	18.32	17.33	16.42	15.58	14.81	33
34	21.19	19.98	18.88	17.86	16.93	16.06	15.27	14.53	34
35	20.51	19.38	18.35	17.39	16.51	15.69	14.94	14.24	35
36	19.82	18.77	17.80	16.91	16.08	15.31	14.60	13.94	36
37	19.12	18.15	17.25	16.41	15.64	14.91	14.24	13.62	37
38	18.42	17.52	16.68	15.90	15.18	14.50	13.87	13.28	38
39	17.70	16.87	16.10	15.38	14.70	14.07	13.48	12.93	39
40	16.97	16.21	15.50	14.84	14.21	13.63	13.08	12.57	40
41	16.24	15.54	14.89	14.28	13.71	13.17	12.66	12.18	41
42	15.49	14.86	14.27	13.71	13.18	12.69	12.22	11.78	42
43	14.73	14.17	13.63	13.12	12.64	12.19	11.77	11.36	43
44	13.97	13.46	12.98	12.52	12.09	11.68	11.29	10.92	44
45	13.19	12.74	12.31	11.90	11.51	11.14	10.79	10.46	45
46	12.40	12.00	11.62	11.26	10.91	10.59	10.27	9.97	46
47	11.60	11.25	10.92	10.60	10.30	10.01	9.73	9.46	47
48	10.79	10.49	10.20	9.93	9.66	9.41	9.16	8.93	48
49	9.97	9.71	9.46	9.23	9.00	8.78	8.57	8.37	49
50	9.13	8.92	8.71	8.51	8.32	8.14	7.96	7.79	50
51	8.28	8.11	7.94	7.77	7.62	7.46	7.31	7.17	51
52	7.42	7.28	7.15	7.01	6.89	6.76	6.64	6.52	52
53	6.55	6.44	6.34	6.23	6.13	6.03	5.94	5.85	53
54	5.66	5.58	5.50	5.43	5.35	5.28	5.21	5.13	54
55	4.76	4.71	4.65	4.59	4.54	4.49	4.44	4.39	55
56	3.84	3.81	3.77	3.74	3.70	3.67	3.63	3.60	56
57	2.91	2.89	2.87	2.85	2.83	2.81	2.79	2.77	57
58	1.96	1.95	1.94	1.93	1.92	1.91	1.90	1.90	58
59	0.99	0.99	0.98	0.98	0.98	0.98	0.98	0.97	59

Table 17: Multipliers for loss of pension commencing age 65 (males)

Age at date of trial	Multiplier calculated with allowance for population mortality and rate of return of								Age at date of trial
	1.5%	2.0%	2.5%	3.0%	3.5%	4.0%	4.5%	5.0%	
0	5.17	3.58	2.48	1.72	1.20	0.84	0.59	0.42	0
1	5.28	3.67	2.55	1.79	1.25	0.88	0.62	0.44	1
2	5.36	3.74	2.62	1.84	1.30	0.91	0.65	0.46	2
3	5.44	3.81	2.68	1.89	1.34	0.95	0.68	0.48	3
4	5.52	3.89	2.75	1.95	1.39	0.99	0.71	0.51	4
5	5.60	3.97	2.82	2.01	1.44	1.03	0.74	0.53	5
6	5.68	4.05	2.89	2.07	1.48	1.07	0.77	0.56	6
7	5.77	4.13	2.96	2.13	1.54	1.11	0.81	0.59	7
8	5.85	4.21	3.03	2.19	1.59	1.16	0.84	0.62	8
9	5.94	4.29	3.11	2.26	1.64	1.20	0.88	0.65	9
10	6.02	4.37	3.18	2.32	1.70	1.25	0.92	0.68	10
11	6.11	4.46	3.26	2.39	1.76	1.30	0.96	0.71	11
12	6.20	4.55	3.34	2.46	1.82	1.35	1.00	0.75	12
13	6.29	4.63	3.42	2.54	1.88	1.40	1.05	0.78	13
14	6.38	4.73	3.51	2.61	1.95	1.46	1.09	0.82	14
15	6.48	4.82	3.59	2.69	2.02	1.52	1.14	0.86	15
16	6.57	4.91	3.68	2.77	2.09	1.58	1.19	0.91	16
17	6.67	5.01	3.77	2.85	2.16	1.64	1.25	0.95	17
18	6.77	5.11	3.87	2.94	2.23	1.70	1.30	1.00	18
19	6.87	5.21	3.96	3.02	2.31	1.77	1.36	1.05	19
20	6.97	5.31	4.06	3.11	2.39	1.84	1.42	1.10	20
21	7.07	5.42	4.17	3.21	2.48	1.92	1.49	1.16	21
22	7.18	5.53	4.27	3.30	2.56	1.99	1.56	1.22	22
23	7.29	5.64	4.38	3.40	2.65	2.07	1.63	1.28	23
24	7.39	5.75	4.48	3.50	2.75	2.16	1.70	1.34	24
25	7.50	5.86	4.60	3.61	2.84	2.24	1.77	1.41	25
26	7.61	5.98	4.71	3.72	2.94	2.33	1.85	1.48	26
27	7.73	6.10	4.83	3.83	3.04	2.43	1.94	1.55	27
28	7.84	6.22	4.94	3.94	3.15	2.52	1.02	1.63	28
29	7.95	6.34	5.07	4.06	3.26	2.62	2.11	1.71	29
30	8.07	6.46	5.19	4.18	3.37	2.73	2.21	1.79	30
31	8.18	6.59	5.32	4.30	3.49	2.83	2.31	1.88	31
32	8.30	6.72	5.45	4.43	3.61	2.94	2.41	1.97	32
33	8.42	6.85	5.58	4.56	3.73	3.06	2.52	2.07	33
34	8.54	6.98	5.72	4.69	3.86	3.18	2.63	2.17	34
35	8.66	7.11	5.85	4.83	3.99	3.31	2.74	2.28	35

36	8.78	7.25	5.99	4.97	4.13	3.44	2.87	2.39	36
37	8.90	7.39	6.14	5.11	4.27	3.57	2.99	2.51	37
38	9.03	7.53	6.29	5.26	4.41	3.71	3.12	2.64	38
39	9.15	7.67	6.44	5.41	4.56	3.85	3.26	2.77	39
40	9.28	7.81	6.59	5.57	4.72	4.01	3.41	2.90	40
41	9.41	7.96	6.75	5.73	4.88	4.16	3.56	3.04	41
42	9.54	8.11	6.91	5.90	5.05	4.33	3.71	3.19	42
43	9.67	8.27	7.08	6.07	5.22	4.49	3.88	3.35	43
44	9.81	8.42	7.25	6.25	5.40	4.67	4.05	3.52	44
45	9.94	8.58	7.42	6.43	5.58	4.85	4.23	3.69	45
46	10.08	8.74	7.60	6.61	5.77	5.04	4.41	3.87	46
47	10.22	8.91	7.78	6.80	5.96	5.24	4.61	4.06	47
48	10.36	9.07	7.96	7.00	6.17	5.44	4.81	4.26	48
49	10.50	9.24	8.15	7.20	6.38	5.65	5.02	4.47	49
50	10.65	9.42	8.35	7.42	6.60	5.88	5.25	4.69	50
51	10.80	9.60	8.56	7.64	6.83	6.11	5.48	4.92	51
52	10.96	9.79	8.77	7.86	7.07	6.36	5.73	5.17	52
53	11.12	9.99	8.99	8.10	7.31	6.61	5.99	5.43	53
54	11.29	10.20	9.22	8.35	7.58	6.88	6.27	5.71	54
55	11.47	10.41	9.46	8.61	7.85	7.17	6.56	6.01	55
56	11.67	10.64	9.71	8.89	8.14	7.47	6.87	6.32	56
57	11.87	10.88	9.98	9.18	8.45	7.80	7.20	6.66	57
58	12.09	11.13	10.27	9.49	8.78	8.14	7.55	7.02	58
59	12.32	11.41	10.57	9.82	9.13	8.50	7.93	7.41	59
60	12.57	11.69	10.90	10.17	9.50	8.89	8.34	7.82	60
61	12.83	12.00	11.23	10.54	9.90	9.31	8.77	8.27	61
62	13.11	12.32	11.60	10.93	10.32	9.75	9.23	8.75	62
63	13.41	12.67	11.98	11.35	10.77	10.23	9.73	9.27	63
64	13.73	13.04	12.40	11.81	11.26	10.75	10.27	9.83	64
65	14.09	13.45	12.85	12.30	11.78	11.31	10.86	10.45	65

Table 18: Multipliers for loss of pension commencing age 65 (females)

| Age at date of trial | Multiplier calculated with allowance for population mortality and rate of return of | | | | | | | | Age at date of trial |
	1.5%	2.0%	2.5%	3.0%	3.5%	4.0%	4.5%	5.0%	
0	6.35	4.36	3.00	2.08	1.44	1.00	0.70	0.49	0
1	6.47	4.47	3.09	2.15	1.50	1.05	0.73	0.52	1
2	6.57	4.56	3.17	2.21	1.55	1.09	0.77	0.54	2
3	6.67	4.65	3.25	2.28	1.60	1.13	0.80	0.57	3
4	6.77	4.74	3.33	2.35	1.66	1.18	0.84	0.60	4
5	6.87	4.83	3.41	2.42	1.72	1.22	0.87	0.63	5

6	6.97	4.93	3.50	2.49	1.78	1.27	0.91	0.66	6
7	7.07	5.03	3.58	2.56	1.84	1.32	0.95	0.69	7
8	7.18	5.13	3.67	2.64	1.90	1.38	1.00	0.73	8
9	7.28	5.23	3.76	2.72	1.97	1.43	1.04	0.76	9
10	7.39	5.33	3.86	2.80	2.04	1.49	1.09	0.80	10
11	7.50	5.43	3.95	2.88	2.11	1.55	1.14	0.84	11
12	7.61	5.54	4.05	2.97	2.18	1.61	1.19	0.88	12
13	7.72	5.65	4.15	3.05	2.26	1.67	1.24	0.92	13
14	7.83	5.76	4.25	3.14	2.33	1.74	1.30	0.97	14
15	7.95	5.87	4.35	3.24	2.41	1.81	1.35	1.02	15
16	8.07	5.99	4.46	3.33	2.50	1.88	1.41	1.07	16
17	8.18	6.11	4.57	3.43	2.58	1.95	1.48	1.12	17
18	8.30	6.23	4.69	3.53	2.67	2.03	1.54	1.18	18
19	8.43	6.35	4.80	3.64	2.77	2.11	1.61	1.24	19
20	8.55	6.48	4.92	3.75	2.86	2.19	1.69	1.30	20
21	8.67	6.60	5.04	3.86	2.96	2.28	1.76	1.36	21
22	8.80	6.73	5.16	3.97	3.07	2.37	1.84	1.43	22
23	8.93	6.86	5.29	4.09	3.17	2.47	1.92	1.50	23
24	9.06	7.00	5.42	4.21	3.28	2.56	2.01	1.58	24
25	9.19	7.14	5.56	4.34	3.40	2.66	2.10	1.65	25
26	9.33	7.28	5.69	4.47	3.51	2.77	2.19	1.74	26
27	9.46	7.42	5.83	4.60	3.63	2.88	2.29	1.82	27
28	9.60	7.56	5.98	4.73	3.76	2.99	2.39	1.91	28
29	9.74	7.71	6.12	4.87	3.89	3.11	2.50	2.01	29
30	9.88	7.86	6.27	5.02	4.02	3.24	2.61	2.11	30
31	10.02	8.01	6.43	5.17	4.16	3.36	2.72	2.21	31
32	10.17	8.17	6.58	5.32	4.31	3.50	2.85	2.32	32
33	10.31	8.33	6.74	5.47	4.45	3.63	2.97	2.44	33
34	10.46	8.49	6.91	5.63	4.61	3.78	3.10	2.56	34
35	10.61	8.65	7.07	5.80	4.77	3.93	3.24	2.68	35
36	10.76	8.82	7.25	5.97	4.93	4.08	3.38	2.81	36
37	10.91	8.99	7.42	6.14	5.10	4.24	3.53	2.95	37
38	11.06	9.16	7.60	6.32	5.27	4.41	3.69	3.10	38
39	11.22	9.33	7.78	6.51	5.45	4.58	3.85	3.25	39
40	11.38	9.51	7.97	6.70	5.64	4.76	4.02	3.41	40
41	11.54	9.69	8.16	6.89	5.83	4.95	4.20	3.58	41
42	11.70	9.88	8.36	7.09	6.03	5.14	4.39	3.76	42
43	11.86	10.06	8.56	7.30	6.24	5.34	4.58	3.94	43
44	12.03	10.26	8.77	7.51	6.45	5.55	4.79	4.14	44
45	12.20	10.45	8.98	7.73	6.67	5.77	5.00	4.34	45

46	12.37	10.65	9.20	7.96	6.90	5.99	5.22	4.55	46
47	12.54	10.86	9.42	8.19	7.14	6.23	5.45	4.78	47
48	12.72	11.06	9.65	8.43	7.38	6.48	5.69	5.02	48
49	12.90	11.28	9.88	8.68	7.63	6.73	5.95	5.26	49
50	13.08	11.50	10.12	8.93	7.90	7.00	6.21	5.53	50
51	13.27	11.72	10.37	9.20	8.17	7.28	6.49	5.80	51
52	13.47	11.95	10.63	9.47	8.46	7.57	6.78	6.09	52
53	13.68	12.20	10.90	9.77	8.76	7.88	7.10	6.40	53
54	13.92	12.47	11.20	10.08	9.09	8.21	7.44	6.74	54
55	14.16	12.76	11.52	10.42	9.44	8.57	7.79	7.10	55
56	14.42	13.05	11.84	10.76	9.80	8.94	8.17	7.48	56
57	14.68	13.36	12.18	11.13	10.18	9.33	8.57	7.89	57
58	14.95	13.67	12.53	11.50	10.57	9.74	8.99	8.31	58
59	15.22	13.99	12.88	11.88	10.98	10.17	9.43	8.76	59
60	15.49	14.30	13.24	12.27	11.40	10.60	9.88	9.22	60
61	15.75	14.62	13.59	12.67	11.82	11.05	10.35	9.71	61
62	16.00	14.93	13.96	13.07	12.26	11.52	10.84	10.22	62
63	16.26	15.25	14.33	13.49	12.72	12.01	11.36	10.76	63
64	16.53	15.58	14.72	13.92	13.20	12.52	11.91	11.33	64
65	16.81	15.94	15.13	14.39	13.70	13.07	12.49	11.95	65

Table 19: Multipliers for loss of pension commencing age 60 (males)

| Age at date of trial | Multiplier calculated with allowance for population mortality and rate of return of | | | | | | | | Age at date of trial |
	1.5%	2.0%	2.5%	3.0%	3.5%	4.0%	4.5%	5.0%	
0	6.94	4.88	3.44	2.43	1.73	1.23	0.88	0.63	0
1	7.08	5.00	3.54	2.52	1.80	1.28	0.92	0.66	1
2	7.19	5.10	3.63	2.59	1.86	1.34	0.96	0.70	2
3	7.30	5.20	3.72	2.67	1.92	1.39	1.01	0.73	3
4	7.41	5.31	3.81	2.75	1.99	1.44	1.05	0.77	4
5	7.52	5.41	3.91	2.83	2.06	1.50	1.10	0.81	5
6	7.63	5.52	4.01	2.92	2.13	1.56	1.15	0.85	6
7	7.74	5.63	4.10	3.00	2.20	1.62	1.20	0.89	7
8	7.85	5.74	4.21	3.09	2.28	1.69	1.25	0.93	8
9	7.97	5.85	4.31	3.18	2.36	1.75	1.31	0.98	9
10	8.08	5.97	4.42	3.28	2.44	1.82	1.37	1.03	10
11	8.20	6.08	4.52	3.38	2.53	1.90	1.43	1.08	11
12	8.32	6.20	4.64	3.48	2.61	1.97	1.49	1.13	12
13	8.44	6.32	4.75	3.58	2.71	2.05	1.56	1.19	13
14	8.57	6.45	4.87	3.69	2.80	2.13	1.63	1.25	14
15	8.69	6.57	4.99	3.80	2.90	2.22	1.70	1.31	15

16	8.82	6.70	5.11	3.91	3.00	2.30	1.78	1.37	16
17	8.95	6.84	5.24	4.02	3.10	2.40	1.86	1.44	17
18	9.08	6.97	5.37	4.14	3.21	2.49	1.94	1.51	18
19	9.22	7.11	5.50	4.27	3.32	2.59	2.03	1.59	19
20	9.36	7.26	5.64	4.40	3.44	2.70	2.12	1.67	20
21	9.50	7.40	5.78	4.53	3.56	2.80	2.21	1.75	21
22	9.65	7.55	5.93	4.67	3.68	2.92	2.31	1.84	22
23	9.79	7.70	6.08	4.81	3.81	3.03	2.42	1.93	23
24	9.94	7.86	6.23	4.95	3.95	3.16	2.53	2.03	24
25	10.08	8.01	6.38	5.10	4.09	3.28	2.64	2.13	25
26	10.24	8.17	6.54	5.25	4.23	3.41	2.76	2.24	26
27	10.39	8.33	6.71	5.41	4.38	3.55	2.89	2.35	27
28	10.54	8.50	6.87	5.57	4.53	3.69	3.02	2.47	28
29	10.70	8.67	7.04	5.74	4.69	3.84	3.15	2.59	29
30	10.86	8.84	7.22	5.91	4.85	3.99	3.29	2.72	30
31	11.01	9.01	7.40	6.09	5.02	4.15	3.44	2.86	31
32	11.18	9.19	7.58	6.27	5.19	4.32	3.59	3.00	32
33	11.34	9.37	7.77	6.45	5.37	4.49	3.75	3.15	33
34	11.50	9.55	7.96	6.64	5.56	4.67	3.92	3.31	34
35	11.67	9.74	8.15	6.84	5.75	4.85	4.10	3.47	35
36	11.84	9.93	8.35	7.04	5.95	5.04	4.28	3.64	36
37	12.01	10.12	8.56	7.25	6.16	5.24	4.47	3.82	37
38	12.18	10.32	8.76	7.46	6.37	5.45	4.67	4.01	38
39	12.35	10.52	8.98	7.68	6.59	5.66	4.88	4.21	39
40	12.53	10.72	9.20	7.91	6.82	5.89	5.10	4.42	40
41	12.71	10.93	9.42	8.14	7.05	6.12	5.32	4.64	41
42	12.89	11.14	9.65	8.38	7.30	6.36	5.56	4.87	42
43	13.08	11.36	9.89	8.63	7.55	6.62	5.81	5.11	43
44	13.27	11.58	10.13	8.89	7.81	6.88	6.07	5.37	44
45	13.46	11.81	10.38	9.15	8.08	7.15	6.34	5.64	45
46	13.65	12.03	10.64	9.42	8.36	7.44	6.63	5.92	46
47	13.84	12.27	10.89	9.70	8.65	7.73	6.92	6.21	47
48	14.04	12.51	11.16	9.98	8.95	8.04	7.23	6.52	48
49	14.25	12.75	11.44	10.28	9.26	8.36	7.56	6.85	49
50	14.46	13.01	11.72	10.59	9.59	8.70	7.90	7.19	50
51	14.68	13.27	12.02	10.91	9.93	9.05	8.26	7.56	51
52	14.91	13.54	12.33	11.25	10.29	9.42	8.64	7.95	52
53	15.14	13.83	12.65	11.60	10.66	9.81	9.05	8.36	53
54	15.39	14.13	12.99	11.97	11.05	10.22	9.47	8.79	54
55	15.65	14.44	13.34	12.36	11.47	10.66	9.92	9.26	55

56	15.93	14.77	13.72	12.77	11.91	11.12	10.41	9.75	56
57	16.23	15.12	14.12	13.20	12.37	11.61	10.92	10.28	57
58	16.54	15.49	14.54	13.67	12.87	12.14	11.47	10.86	58
59	16.88	15.89	14.98	14.16	13.40	12.70	12.06	11.47	59
60	17.24	16.31	15.46	14.68	13.96	13.30	12.69	12.13	60

Table 20: Multipliers for loss of pension commencing age 60 (females)

| Age at date of trial | Multiplier calculated with allowance for population mortality and rate of return of | | | | | | | | Age at date of trial |
	1.5%	2.0%	2.5%	3.0%	3.5%	4.0%	4.5%	5.0%	
0	8.19	5.71	4.00	2.81	1.98	1.40	1.00	0.71	0
1	8.34	5.85	4.12	2.91	2.06	1.47	1.05	0.75	1
2	8.47	5.97	4.22	2.99	2.13	1.52	1.09	0.79	2
3	8.60	6.09	4.32	3.08	2.21	1.59	1.14	0.83	3
4	8.73	6.21	4.43	3.18	2.28	1.65	1.19	0.87	4
5	8.85	6.33	4.54	3.27	2.36	1.71	1.25	0.91	5
6	8.99	6.46	4.65	3.37	2.45	1.78	1.30	0.96	6
7	9.12	6.58	4.77	3.47	2.53	1.85	1.36	1.00	7
8	9.25	6.71	4.89	3.57	2.62	1.93	1.42	1.05	8
9	9.39	6.85	5.01	3.68	2.71	2.00	1.49	1.11	9
10	9.53	6.98	5.13	3.79	2.80	2.08	1.55	1.16	10
11	9.67	7.12	5.26	3.90	2.90	2.17	1.62	1.22	11
12	9.81	7.26	5.39	4.01	3.00	2.25	1.69	1.28	12
13	9.96	7.40	5.52	4.14	3.11	2.34	1.77	1.34	13
14	10.10	7.55	5.66	4.26	3.21	2.43	1.85	1.41	14
15	10.25	7.70	5.80	4.39	3.33	2.53	1.93	1.48	15
16	10.40	7.85	5.94	4.52	3.44	2.63	2.02	1.55	16
17	10.55	8.00	6.09	4.65	3.56	2.74	2.11	1.63	17
18	10.71	8.16	6.24	4.79	3.69	2.85	2.20	1.71	18
19	10.87	8.32	6.40	4.93	3.81	2.96	2.30	1.80	19
20	11.03	8.49	6.55	5.08	3.95	3.08	2.41	1.89	20
21	11.19	8.65	6.72	5.23	4.08	3.20	2.51	1.98	21
22	11.35	8.83	6.88	5.38	4.23	3.33	2.63	2.08	22
23	11.52	9.00	7.05	5.54	4.37	3.46	2.74	2.18	23
24	11.69	9.18	7.23	5.71	4.52	3.30	2.87	2.29	24
25	11.86	9.36	7.41	5.88	4.68	3.37	2.99	2.40	25
26	12.04	9.54	7.59	6.05	4.84	3.89	3.13	2.52	26
27	12.21	9.73	7.78	6.23	5.01	4.04	3.27	2.65	27
28	12.39	9.92	7.97	6.42	5.19	4.20	3.41	2.78	28
29	12.57	10.12	8.16	6.61	5.37	4.37	3.57	2.92	29
30	12.76	10.31	8.37	6.81	5.55	4.54	3.73	3.07	30

31	12.94	10.52	8.57	7.01	5.74	4.72	3.89	3.22	31
32	13.13	10.72	8.78	7.21	5.94	4.91	4.07	3.38	32
33	13.32	10.93	9.00	7.43	6.15	5.10	4.25	3.55	33
34	13.51	11.14	9.22	7.65	6.36	5.31	4.44	3.72	34
35	13.71	11.36	9.44	7.87	6.58	5.52	4.64	3.91	35
36	13.91	11.68	9.67	8.10	6.81	5.73	4.84	4.10	36
37	14.11	11.81	9.91	8.34	7.04	5.96	5.06	4.30	37
38	14.31	12.03	10.15	8.59	7.29	6.20	5.28	4.52	38
39	14.51	12.27	10.40	8.84	7.54	6.44	5.52	4.74	39
40	14.72	12.51	10.66	9.10	7.80	6.70	5.77	4.98	40
41	14.93	12.75	10.92	9.37	8.07	6.96	6.02	5.22	41
42	15.15	13.00	11.18	9.65	8.35	7.24	6.29	5.48	42
43	15.37	13.25	11.46	9.93	8.64	7.52	6.57	5.76	43
44	15.59	13.51	11.74	10.23	8.93	7.82	6.87	6.04	44
45	15.81	13.77	12.02	10.53	9.24	8.13	7.18	6.34	45
46	16.04	14.04	12.32	10.84	9.57	8.46	7.50	6.66	46
47	16.28	14.32	12.63	11.17	9.90	8.80	7.83	6.99	47
48	16.51	14.60	12.94	11.50	10.24	9.15	8.19	7.34	48
49	16.76	14.89	13.26	11.84	10.60	9.51	8.56	7.71	49
50	17.01	15.18	13.59	12.20	10.98	9.90	8.94	8.10	50
51	17.26	15.49	13.94	12.57	11.36	10.30	9.35	8.51	51
52	17.52	15.80	14.29	12.95	11.77	10.72	9.78	8.94	52
53	17.81	16.14	14.67	13.36	12.20	11.16	10.24	9.40	53
54	18.12	16.51	15.07	13.80	12.66	11.64	10.73	9.90	54
55	18.45	16.89	15.50	14.26	13.15	12.15	11.25	10.43	55
56	18.79	17.29	15.94	14.74	13.66	12.68	11.80	11.00	56
57	19.14	17.70	16.40	15.24	14.19	13.24	12.38	11.59	57
58	19.50	18.12	16.88	15.76	14.74	13.82	12.99	12.22	58
59	19.86	18.55	17.36	16.29	15.32	14.43	13.62	12.89	59
60	20.22	18.98	17.86	16.84	15.91	15.07	14.29	13.58	60

Table 21: Discounting factors for term certain

	Factor to discount value of multiplier for a period of deferment								
Term	1.5%	2.0%	2.5%	3.0%	3.5%	4.0%	4.5%	5.0%	Term
1	0.9852	0.9804	0.9756	0.9709	0.9662	0.9615	0.9569	0.9524	1
2	0.9707	0.9612	0.9518	0.9426	0.9335	0.9246	0.9157	0.9070	2
3	0.9563	0.9423	0.9286	0.9151	0.9019	0.8890	0.8763	0.8638	3
4	0.9422	0.9238	0.9060	0.8885	0.8714	0.8548	0.8386	0.8227	4
5	0.9283	0.9057	0.8839	0.8626	0.8420	0.8219	0.8025	0.7835	5

6	0.9145	0.8880	0.8623	0.8375	0.8135	0.7903	0.7679	0.7462	6
7	0.9010	0.8706	0.8413	0.8131	0.7860	0.7599	0.7348	0.7107	7
8	0.8877	0.8535	0.8207	0.7894	0.7594	0.7307	0.7032	0.6768	8
9	0.8746	0.8368	0.8007	0.7664	0.7337	0.7026	0.6729	0.6446	9
10	0.8617	0.8203	0.7812	0.7441	0.7089	0.6756	0.6439	0.6139	10
11	0.8489	0.8043	0.7621	0.7224	0.6849	0.6496	0.6162	0.5847	11
12	0.8364	0.7885	0.7436	0.7014	0.6618	0.6246	0.5897	0.5568	12
13	0.8240	0.7730	0.7254	0.6810	0.6394	0.6006	0.5643	0.5303	13
14	0.8118	0.7579	0.7077	0.6611	0.6178	0.5775	0.5400	0.5051	14
15	0.7999	0.7430	0.6905	0.6419	0.5969	0.5553	0.5167	0.4810	15
16	0.7880	0.7284	0.6736.	0.6232	0.5767	0.5339	0.4945	0.4581	16
17	0.7764	0.7142	0.6572	0.6050	0.5572	0.5134	0.4732	0.4363	17
18	0.7649	0.7002	0.6412	0.5874	0.5384	0.4936	0.4528	0.4155	18
19	0.7536	0.6864	0.6255	0.5703	0.5202	0.4746	0.4333	0.3957	19
20	0.7425	0.6730	0.6103	0.5537	0.5026	0.4564	0.4146	0.3769	20
21	0.7315	0.6598	0.5954	0.5375	0.4856	0.4388	0.3968	0.3589	21
22	0.7207	0.6468	0.5809	0.5219	0.4692	0.4220	0.3797	0.3418	22
23	0.7100	0.6342	0.5667	0.5067	0.4533	0.4057	0.3634	0.3256	23
24	0.6995	0.6217	0.5529	0.4919	0.4380	0.3901	0.3477	0.3101	24
25	0.6892	0.6095	0.5394	0.4776	0.4231	0.3751	0.3327	0.2953	25
26	0.6790	0.5976	0.5262	0.4637	0.4088	0.3607	0.3184	0.2812	26
27	0.6690	0.5859	0.5134	0.4502	0.3950	0.3468	0.3047	0.2678	27
28	0.6591	0.5744	0.5009	0.4371	0.3817	0.3335	0.2916	0.2551	28
29	0.6494	0.5631	0.4887	0.4243	0.3687	0.3207	0.2790	0.2429	29
30	0.6398	0.5521	0.4767	0.4120	0.3563	0.3083	0.2670	0.2314	30

Table 22: Multipliers for pecuniary loss for term certain

	Multiplier for regular frequent payments for a term certain at rate of return of								
Term	1.5%	2.0%	2.5%	3.0%	3.5%	4.0%	4.5%	5.0%	Term
1	0.99	0.99	0.99	0.99	0.98	0.98	0.98	0.98	1
2	1.97	1.96	1.95	1.94	1.93	1.92	1.91	1.91	2
3	2.93	2.91	2.89	2.87	2.85	2.83	2.81	2.79	3
4	3.88	3.85	3.81	3.77	3.74	3.70	3.67	3.63	4
5	4.82	4.76	4.70	4.65	4.59	4.54	4.49	4.44	5
6	5.74	5.66	5.58	5.50	5.42	5.35	5.27	5.20	6
7	6.65	6.54	6.43	6.32	6.22	6.12	6.02	5.93	7
8	7.54	7.40	7.26	7.12	6.99	6.87	6.74	6.62	8
9	8.42	8.24	8.07	7.90	7.74	7.58	7.43	7.28	9
10	9.29	9.07	8.86	8.66	8.46	8.27	8.09	7.91	10

11	10.15	9.88	9.63	9.39	9.16	8.93	8.72	8.51	11
12	10.99	10.68	10.39	10.10	9.83	9.57	9.32	9.08	12
13	11.82	11.46	11.12	10.79	10.48	10.18	9.90	9.63	13
14	12.64	12.23	11.84	11.46	11.11	10.77	10.45	10.14	14
15	13.44	12.98	12/54	12.12	11.72	11.34	10.98	10.64	15
16	14.24	13.71	13.22	12.75	12.30	11.88	11.48	11.11	16
17	15.02	14.43	13.88	13.36	12.87	12.41	11.97	11.55	17
18	15.79	15.14	14.53	13.96	13.42	12.91	12.43	11.98	18
19	16.55	15.83	15.17	14.54	13.95	13.39	12.87	12.38	19
20	17.30	16.51	15.78	15.10	14.46	13.86	13.30	12.77	20
21	18.03	17.18	16.39	15.65	14.95	14.31	13.70	13.14	21
22	18.76	17.83	16.97	16.17	15.43	14.74	14.09	13.49	22
23	19.48	18.47	17.55	16.69	15.89	15.15	14.46	13.82	23
24	20.18	19.10	18.11	17.19	16.34	15.55	14.82	14.14	24
25	20.87	19.72	18.65	17.67	16.77	15.93	15.16	14.44	25
26	21.56	20.32	19.19	18.14	17.18	16.30	15.48	14.73	26
27	22.23	20.91	19.71	18.60	17.59	16.65	15.80	15.01	27
28	22.90	21.49	20.21	19.04	17.97	16.99	16.09	15.27	28
29	23.55	22.06	20.71	19.47	18.35	17.32	16.38	15.52	29
30	24.20	22.62	21.19	19.89	18.71	17.64	16.65	15.75	30
31	24.83	23.17	21.66	20.30	19.06	17.94	16.91	15.98	31
32	25.46	23.70	22.12	20.69	19.40	18.23	17.16	16.19	32
33	26.07	24.23	22.57	21.08	19.73	18.51	17.40	16.40	33
34	26.68	24.74	23.01	21.45	20.04	18.78	17.63	16.59	34
35	27.28	25.25	23.43	21.81	20.35	19.04	17.85	16.78	35
36	27.87	25.74	23.85	22.16	20.64	19.28	18.06	16.96	36
37	28.45	26.23	24.26	22.50	20.93	19.52	18.26	17.13	37
38	29.02	26.70	24.65	22.83	21.20	19.75	18.45	17.29	38
39	29.58	27.17	25.04	23.15	21.47	19.97	18.64	17.44	39
40	30.14	27.63	25.42	23.46	21.73	20.19	18.81	17.58	40

ACTUARIAL FORMULAE AND BASIS

The functions tabulated are:

Tables 1, 2, 11 and 12	$\overline{a}_x$
Tables 3, 4, 13 and 14	$a_x : \overline{65 - x}$
Tables 5, 6, 15 and 16	$a_x : \overline{60 - x}$
Tables 7, 8, 17 and 18	$(65 - x) \mid {}^a 65$
Tables 9, 10, 19 and 20	$(60 - x) \mid {}^a 60$
Table 21:	$1 / (1 + i)^n$
Table 22:	$\overline{a}_{\overline{n}}$

Mortality: English Life Tables No. 15 (Tables 1 to 10)
Mortality assumptions for 1996-based official population projections for England and Wales (Tables 11 to 20)
Loadings: None
Rate of return: As stated in the Tables

Ogden Tables – Press Release*

The assumed rate of return on the investment of damages should be 2%, to reflect the recent low levels of return on index-linked government stocks.

The working party chaired by Sir Michael Ogden, QC, which produces the so-called Ogden actuarial tables for use in personal injury and fatal accident cases, pointed out that the actual rate of return on the index-linked stocks used to compile the tables had been consistently below 2.5% gross from the end of October 1998, and was 1.72% met in April.

In *Wells v Wells* (Times July 20, 1998; [1998] 3 WLR 329) the House of Lords had decided that the assumed rate of return should be 3%.

In cases awaiting trial claimants were arguing that a different rate should be applied, the working party said.

A minority of the working party would have preferred to recommend principles by which the rate should be fixed, rather than saying what the rate should be. The working party did not want to express a view about whether courts should depart from the House of Lords' 3% rate but intended its recommendation to provide assistance should the courts decide that a new rate should be set.

The working party would prefer the Lord Chancellor to use his power under section 1 of the Damages Act 1996 to set the return to be expected from the investment of a sum awarded as damages.

* As reported in the Times Law Reports on 3 May 1999.

Appendix 3

JSB Figures – Guidelines for the Assessment of General Damages in Personal Injury Cases

1. INJURIES INVOLVING PARALYSIS

(a) Quadriplegia £160,000 to £200,000
The level of the award within the bracket will be affected by the following considerations:

(i) the extent of any residual movement;
(ii) the presence and extent of pain;
(iii) depression;
(iv) age and life expectancy.

The top of the bracket will be appropriate only where there is significant effect on senses or ability to communicate.

(b) Paraplegia £110,000 to £140,000
The level of the award within the bracket will be affected by the following considerations:

(i) the presence and extent of pain;
(ii) the degree of independence;
(iii) depression;
(iv) age and life expectancy.

The presence of increasing paralysis or the degree of risk that this will occur, for example, from syringomyelia, might take the case above this bracket. The latter might be the subject of a provisional damages order.

2. HEAD INJURIES

(A) Brain Damage

(a) Very Severe Brain Damage £140,000 to £200,000
In cases at the top of this bracket the injured person will have a degree of insight. There

may be some ability to follow basic commands,
recovery of eye opening and return of
sleep and waking patterns and postural reflex
movement. There will be little, if any, evidence
of meaningful response to environment,
little or no language function, double incontinence
and the need for full-time nursing care.

The level of the award within the bracket will
be affected by:

    (i) the degree of insight;
    (ii) life expectancy;
    (iii) the extent of physical limitations.

The top of the bracket will be appropriate only
where there is significant effect on the senses.
Where there is a persistent vegetative state
and/or death occurs very soon after the injuries
were suffered and there has been no
awareness by the injured person of his or her
condition the award will be solely for loss of
amenity and will fall substantially below the
above bracket.

(b) Moderately Severe Brain Injury   £110,000 to £140,000
The injured person will be very seriously
disabled. There will be substantial dependence
on others and a need for constant care.
Disabilities may be physical, for example,
limb paralysis, or cognitive, with marked
impairment of intellect and personality. Cases
otherwise within (a) above may fall into this
bracket if life expectancy has been greatly
reduced.

The level of the award within the bracket will
be affected by the following considerations:

    (i)   the degree of insight;
    (ii)   life expectancy;
    (iii) the extent of physical limitations;
    (iv) the degree of dependence on others;
    (v)   ability to communicate;
    (vi) behavioural abnormality;
    (vii) epilepsy or a significant risk of epilepsy.

(c) Moderate Brain Damage
This category is distinguished from (b) by the fact
that the degree of dependence is markedly lower.

(i) Cases in which there is moderate to severe intellectual deficit, a personality change, an effect on sight, speech and senses with a significant risk of epilepsy. £75,000 to £110,000

(ii) Cases in which there is a moderate to modest intellectual deficit, the ability to work is greatly reduced if not removed and there is some risk of epilepsy. £45,000 to £75,000

(iii) Cases in which concentration and memory are affected, the ability to work is reduced, where there is a small risk of epilepsy and any dependence on others is very limited. £21,500 to £45,000

(d) Minor Brain Damage £7,750 to £21,500

In these cases the injured person will have made a good recovery and will be able to take part in normal social life and to return to work. There may not have been a restoration of all normal functions so there may still be persisting problems such as poor concentration and memory or disinhibition of mood, which may interfere with lifestyle, leisure activities and future work prospects. At the top of this bracket there may be a small risk of epilepsy.

The level of the award within the bracket will be affected by:

(i) the extent and severity of the initial injury;
(ii) the extent of any continuing, and possible permanent, disability;
(iii) the extent of any personality change.

(B) Minor Head Injury £1,000 to £6,250

In these cases brain damage, if any, will have been minimal.

The level of the award will be affected by the following considerations:

(i) the severity of the initial injury;
(ii) the period taken to recover from any severe symptoms;
(iii) the extent of continuing symptoms;
(iv) the presence or absence of headaches.

(C) Epilepsy

(a)Established Grand Mal   £50,000 to £75,000
(b)Established Petit Mal   £27,500 to £65,000
The level of the award within these brackets
will be affected by the following factors:

(i)   whether attacks are successfully controlled
      by medication and the extent to
      which the need for medication is likely
      to persist;
(ii) the extent to which the appreciation of
      life is blunted by such medication;
(iii) the effect on working and/or social life;
(iv) the existence of associated behavioural
      problems;
(v)   the prognosis.

(c)Other Epileptic Incidents   £5,250 to £13,000
Cases where there are one or two discrete
epileptic episodes but there is no risk of
recurrence beyond that applicable to the population
at large. The level of the award within
the bracket will be affected by the extent of
any consequences of the attacks on, for
example, education, sporting activities, working
and social life, and their duration.

4. INJURIES AFFECTING THE SENSES

(A) Injuries affecting Sight

(a) Total Blindness and Deafness   £200,000
Such cases must be considered as ranking with
the most devastating injuries.

(b) Total Blindness   £135,000
**(c) Loss of Sight in One Eye with Reduced
     Vision in the Remaining Eye**

(i) Where there is serious risk of further
     deterioration in the remaining eye,
     going beyond some risk of sympathetic
     ophthalmia.   £48,000 to £90,000

(ii) Where there is reduced vision in the
     remaining eye and/or additional problems
     such as double vision.   £32,000 to £53,000

(d) Total Loss of One Eye   £28,000 to £33,000
The level of the award within the bracket will
depend on age and cosmetic effect.

(e) Complete Loss of Sight in One Eye   £25,000 to £28,000
This award takes account of some risk of
sympathetic ophthalmia. The upper end of the
bracket is appropriate where there is scarring
in the region of the eye which is not sufficiently
serious to merit a separate award.

(f) Cases of serious but incomplete loss of vision
in one eye without significant risk of loss or
reduction of vision in the remaining eye, or
where there is constant double vision.   £12,000 to £20,000

(g) Minor but permanent impairment of vision in
one eye, including cases where there is some
double vision, which may not be constant.   £6,250 to £10,500

(h) Minor Eye Injuries   £2,000 to £4,250
In this bracket fall cases of minor injuries,
such as being struck in the eye, exposure to
fumes including smoke, or being splashed by
liquids, causing initial pain and some interference
with vision, but no lasting effects.

(i) Transient Eye Injuries   £1,000 to £2,000
In these cases the injured person will have
recovered completely within a few weeks.

(B) Deafness

The word 'deafness' is used to embrace total and
partial hearing loss. In assessing awards for hearing
loss regard must be had to the following:

    (i) whether the injury is one that has an
immediate effect, allowing no opportunity
to adapt, or whether it occurred
over a period of time, as in noise
exposure cases;
    (ii) whether the injury or disability is one
which the injured person suffered at an
early age so that it has had or will have
an effect on his or her speech, or is one
that is suffered in later life;
    (iii) whether the injury or disability affects
balance;
    (iv) in cases of noise-induced hearing loss
(NIHL) age is of particular relevance as
noted in paragraph (d) below.

(a) **Total Deafness and Loss of Speech**   £55,000 to £70,000
Such cases arise, for example, where deafness
has occurred at an early age (for example,

rubella infection) so as to prevent or seriously
to affect the development of normal speech.

(b) **Total Deafness** £45,000 to £55,000
The lower end of the bracket is appropriate for
cases where there is no speech deficit or
tinnitus. The higher end is appropriate for
cases involving both of these.

(c) **Total Loss of Hearing in One Ear** £16,000 to £23,000
Cases will tend towards the higher end of the
bracket where there are associated problems,
such as tinnitus, dizziness or headaches.

(d) **Partial Hearing Loss/Tinnitus**
This category covers the bulk of deafness
cases which usually result from exposure to
noise over a prolonged period. The disability
is not to be judged simply by the degree of
hearing loss; there is often a degree of tinnitus
present. Age is particularly relevant because
impairment of hearing affects most people in
the fullness of time and impacts both upon
causation and on valuation.

(i) Severe tinnitus/hearing loss. £15,000 to £23,000

(ii) Moderate tinnitus/hearing loss. £7,500 to £15,000

(iii) Mild tinnitus with some hearing loss. £6,250 to £7,500

(iv) Slight or occasional tinnitus with slight
hearing loss. £3,750 to £6,250

(C) Impairment of Taste and Smell

(a) **Total Loss of Taste and Smell** £20,000

(b) **Total Loss of Smell and Significant Loss of
Taste** £16,500 to £19,000

It must be remembered that in nearly all cases
of loss of smell there is some impairment of
taste. Such cases fall into the next bracket.

(c) **Loss of Smell** £12,500 to £16,500

(d) **Loss of Taste** £9,500 to £12,500

Appendix 4

The Criminal Injuries Compensation Scheme

Neil Sugarman

A4.1 The first ever scheme designed to compensate the victims of crimes of violence was announced in both Houses of Parliament on 24 June 1964 and in its original form came into force on 1 August 1964. The scheme was subsequently modified in a number of respects until its most radical revision by virtue of the Criminal Injuries Compensation Act 1995. The fundamental difference resulting from this legislation was to transform the previously discretionary scheme administered by the Criminal Injuries Compensation Board ('CICB') on common law principles to a statutory 'tariff base' system with limits on the compensation that could be awarded.

A4.2 The extent to which victims of violence should be compensated by the state inevitably raises issues of political ideology. One view is that the innocent victims of violent crime should be in no worse position than those people injured as result of the acts of negligence of others in circumstances where a tortfeasor has sufficient means to satisfy an award of compensation, in the majority of instances as a result of being fully and properly insured. The contrary view is that it is inappropriate for the public purse to bear responsibility for the criminal acts of individuals in circumstances where the state already has the burden of providing medical treatment under a National Health Service and financial assistance by way of the provision of benefits. The latter view would only appear to be tenable if full and adequate medical assistance, together with complete financial provision for loss of earnings and paid care, is genuinely achieved by the state, particularly in circumstances where overall public funding requirements already impose a heavy burden on the Treasury.

A4.3 What is beyond doubt is that the principle of compensating the victims of violence in Great Britain is now well established. The scheme pursuant to the Criminal Injuries Compensation Act 1995 and administered by the Criminal Injuries Compensation Authority ('CICA') is still somewhat in its infancy and its adequacy compared to its predecessor is gradually being tried and tested.

CRIMINAL INJURIES COMPENSATION BOARD AND CRIMINAL INJURIES COMPENSATION AUTHORITY

A4.4 It is evident that by virtue of the nature of injury sustained by the victims of violent crime, in particularly severe cases there will be a large number of claims still pending under the pre-1995 scheme. There are cases where the medical prognosis may still be uncertain or those involving young children that may still take some considerable time to resolve and on that basis it is important to establish under which scheme the matter is proceeding and to be aware of the crucial differences both of procedure and the nature of the awards that are available.

CICB

A4.5 The CICB had set itself a target to encourage the disposal of pending cases by April 2000 but many serious cases are likely to proceed beyond that date. Where a claim was lodged before 1 April 1996 it will be dealt with under the old scheme. Those applications received by the CICB on or after that date will be passed to the CICA to be dealt with. There are transitional provisions set out in the Criminal Injuries Compensation Scheme effected on 12 December 1995 by the Secretary of State in exercise of the powers conferred on him by ss 1-6 and 12 of the Criminal Injuries Compensation Act 1995.[1] The CICA has an internal mechanism to identify pending cases, some of which will only remain outstanding on the question of quantum. It is notable that under the old scheme there is a procedure for the listing of matters, particularly in the event of the non co-operation of the applicant where there appears to have been some delay on their part.[2] This should serve as a warning to Applicants and their representatives that they must ensure the efficient and speedy preparation and progress of claims to avoid them being forced through when inadequately prepared, and not really ready for conclusion.

1   Criminal Injuries Compensation Scheme paras 83-87.
2   Criminal Injuries Compensation Scheme 1990 para 6b.

Key Differences

A4.6 It is assumed that practitioners have a basic understanding of the content and the workings of the respective schemes. Nevertheless, it is evident that applications are often being made and indeed are being pursued by representatives who appear to have failed to grasp the essential differences between the two schemes and this can again cause delay, additional cost and can even lead to under-compensation.

Table 1: Major Differences Between CICB and CICA

Criminal Injuries Compensation Board pre 1 April 1996	Criminal Injuries Compensation Authority Post 1 April 1996
Discretionary scheme	Statutory scheme
Common law basis of assessment of award	Tariff based awards for injury
No 'cap' on damages	Limits on awards for loss of earnings, special expenses and cap on damages

Board membership available to practising barristers/advocates, solicitors or persons having held judicial office	Wider membership of Appeal panel
General time limit – three years from date of incident giving rise to injury	Two year time limit from date of incident
(See post for exceptions)	(See post for exceptions)

A4.7 In purely financial terms, it is important to recognise the impact of the restricted awards that can be made under the tariff-based scheme in relation to what are known as 'loss of earnings and special expenses'. Generally, claims for special damage and future loss form by far the most substantial part of awards made in claims for compensation for personal injury. Under the scheme applicable from 1 April 1996 an award can be made for loss of earnings or earning capacity provided that the applicant has been incapacitated for more than a full 28 weeks and no compensation is payable for the first 28 weeks. Similarly, the main eligibility rule for a claim for 'special expenses' is that those expenses must be as a direct result of an injury which caused the applicant to lose earnings or earning capacity or to be similarly incapacitated for longer than 28 weeks. If an applicant qualifies on these grounds then the award can actually cover those first 28 weeks, in addition to future losses. For those applicants not normally employed, the CICA will assess the extent of the incapacity from medical information. Nevertheless, it is to be noted that the total maximum amount payable in respect of the claim as a whole, including both the tariff amount, loss of earnings and/or special expenses, is £500,000.[1] Some degree of proportionality must always be kept in mind in the work that is done and the compilation of evidence in order to achieve that maximum award.

1   Criminal Injuries Compensation Scheme 1995 para 23.

Source of Funds

A4.8 Budget estimates for the scheme are prepared by the Home Office on an annual basis and controlled by the Treasury. Both the CICB and CICA publish annual reports, showing the amount of expenditure and can be held to budget. The annual report and accounts are open to debate in Parliament.

Organisation and Staffing

A4.9 As indicated, appointments to the CICB were made by the Secretary of State after consultation with the Lord Chancellor (and where appropriate the Lord Advocate). Those appointed were limited to barristers practising in England and Wales, advocates practising in Scotland, solicitors practising in England, Wales or Scotland or a person who had held judicial office in England, Wales or Scotland. The Chairman and other members would be appointed to serve for up to five years in the first instance and then appointments would be renewable for such periods as the Secretary of State felt appropriate. The Board or members of its staff would be entirely responsible for deciding what compensation should be paid in individual cases and would not be subject to appeal or ministerial review (nevertheless see judicial review para A4.58).

A4.10   In comparison, claims to the CICA are determined by claims officers who are civil servants and appeals against decisions taken on reviews under the scheme are determined by adjudicators, appointed as members of the Criminal Injuries Compensation Appeals Panel. They are appointed by the Secretary of State.[1]

> 1   Criminal Injuries Compensation Scheme 1995 para 2.

A4.11   Internally, staff are graded with financial limits on the amounts that they are authorised to pay. Administration officers undertake much of the preparatory work, such as obtaining medical reports and Department of Social Security ('DSS') reports but do not make decisions. Executive officers have power to make awards of up to £5,000.00. Beyond that, matters are referred to higher executive officers. There is a Senior Executive Officer who exercises a management role and finally, there are claims officers and legal advisors (formerly Board's advocates under the old scheme who are legally qualified). In comparison with the Board, the Criminal Injuries Compensation Appeals Panel is selected from a cross section of the community. There will be generally one legally qualified member appointed by the Secretary of State. It is their responsibility to make decisions about both eligibility and tariff.

Funding

A4.12   1999 saw radical changes to the civil litigation system and rules of civil procedure, the principal aim of which was undoubtedly to achieve cost effectiveness and 'proportionality'. Nowhere can the importance of this objective be more relevant than in the pursuance of claims for compensation for criminal injury. These requirements are given more focus by the abiding principle that exists under both schemes whereby the costs of representation are not recoverable.[1] There is no discretion.

> 1   Criminal Injuries Compensation Scheme 1990; Criminal Injuries Compensation Scheme 1995 para 74.

A4.13   So far as pure legal representation is concerned, applicants must therefore be advised that the costs in question will not be recoverable and must therefore be paid for privately or borne out of any compensation that is awarded. Legal aid, for so long as it has existed for pursuing any form of claim for compensation for injuries, has never been available for representation as such for claims under both schemes. The provision of some advice could be covered by the 'green form' scheme. It is therefore imperative that a legal representative of an applicant acting formally establishes a clear retainer in accordance with professional rules and guidance current at the time of the acceptance of instructions. In the event of dispute it would be open to an applicant to have a detailed assessment of the bill of costs of a solicitor on a private retainer basis. In addition, in cases of applicants under a disability (minors or patients) where there is the appointment of a Receiver through the Court of Protection the claim for costs must be submitted and assessed by the Supreme Court Taxing Office on behalf of the Court of Protection. This can be a lengthy process and care should be taken to ensure that the Court of Protection makes the appropriate orders to facilitate a detailed assessment to avoid long delays in the recovery of costs at the conclusion of a claim.

A4.14   Interestingly, while the concept of a conditional fee agreement[1] is not applicable to this type of claim, it is arguable, perhaps surprisingly, that the legal services in question, just as with applications to many of other forms of tribunal, fall within the definition of 'non contentious business'. The presentation of these claims are not regarded as an action, suit or other contentious proceedings. On that basis, it would strictly appear permissible to represent an applicant on a contingency fee basis. In recent times, professional rules and regulations governing the nature of the retainer between solicitor and client have been moving and developing rapidly. Contingency arrangements of a number of descriptions have become acceptable. The length of time before pure contingent litigation becomes commonplace remains to be seen but there does appear to be a rapid move in that direction.

   1   Courts and Legal Services Act 1990 s 58, as amended by Access to Justice Act 1999.

A4.15   Notwithstanding the purely professional requirements to be considered when entering an agreement on a contingency fee basis, careful thought should be given as to whether this type of funding is realistic or appropriate depending on the circumstances of each case. It can be anticipated that detailed assessment would still be a remedy available to a client in such a situation. Nevertheless, circumstances can be envisaged in which a contingency arrangement could represent a real way forward to overcome the uncertainty that might surround a claim for criminal injuries compensation, in particular as to eligibility under the scheme. A representative may have to invest many hours of skilled investigative work on what might be a speculative venture but at the same time, an applicant having suffered a severe injury may have no other conceivable means or method of funding an investigation of that potential claim. It is suggested that in particular where an applicant is under a disability (children and head injury type cases) it would be sensible to seek prior approval of such arrangements from the Court of Protection, who will be happy to consider proposals put forward.

A4.16   Of equal importance is the issue of disbursements. With claims under the scheme this will normally concern the expense of obtaining medical evidence to support an application although the need may also arise to submit other types of expert evidence as with any serious injury compensation claim. The CICB has a discretion to pay the expenses of the applicant and witnesses at a hearing. The CICA expressly states that it will not pay for medical examinations or reports, other than those specifically requested by the Authority in the course of its enquiries, and this would tend to imply that to have any possibility of recovering a disbursement there must be prior authorisation. The safest course in either case would be to indicate in advance the intention to obtain the particular form of evidence and when the matter falls for final consideration or should it proceed to a hearing all relevant fee vouchers should be scheduled and submitted in advance for consideration. In Board cases the advocates have the power to agree disbursements or can refer to a member if in doubt.

A4.17   The degree to which expert evidence is necessary or justifiable is a matter for careful judgment. It must be borne in mind that it is for an applicant to prove his case and the representative must be satisfied that sufficient evidence has been compiled by the Board or authority to do this. If there is doubt, then the applicant's representative should set about ensuring that the relevant evidence is compiled and submitted, while keeping an eye on the proportionate cost of obtaining that evidence. Special care and attention should be given in claims to the CICA in respect of the 'non medical issues' which arise in relation to claims for loss of earnings, special expenses and in fatal cases. Extremely useful and 'user-friendly' guides are provided to applicants and their representatives in respect of these aspects by the CICA.[1] Nevertheless, in cases of the utmost severity representatives should keep in mind that the maximum tariff level of compensation (level 25) is £250,000 and that the total maximum amount payable in respect of the same injury will not exceed £500,000.[2]

1   Issue Number One (4/96).
2   Criminal Injuries Compensation Scheme para 23.

A4.18   The cost of obtaining lengthy and indepth evidence from experts, such as forensic accountants or care and occupational therapy/assistance experts, can be extremely expensive. While representatives may not wish to dispense completely with expert evidence if it is required to establish a full entitlement to the part of an award that relates to financial aspects, it may be that the evidence does not need to be as 'indepth' as might be the case with other common law types of claim for compensation for injury. Similar considerations will apply to evidence that might be provided in respect of an applicant's accommodation requirements. The CICB and CICA are likely to discourage applicants or their representatives from the compilation of expensive evidence but equally caution ought to be exercised so as to guard against the possibility of the under-provision of necessary evidence resulting in an award being made that is too low.

Time Limits

A4.19   Under the 1990 scheme, applications had to be brought within three years of the incident giving rise to the injury, with the proviso that the requirement could be waived in exceptional cases. A decision by the chairman was final on this point. In comparison, under the 1995 scheme the application must be received by the CICA within two years of the date of the incident. A claims officer may waive the time limit if it is considered that it is reasonable and in the interests of justice to do so in the particular circumstances of the case.[1] It is anticipated that the authority may be more willing to be lenient in relation to time limits than its predecessor, although it is unlikely to wish to build up the hopes of an applicant only to refuse the application on other grounds. As guidance, similar criteria as to those that arise under the Limitation Acts are likely to be used. The rationale behind the time limit is the difficulty involved in investigating and substantiating claims which are made late because of the problems caused in obtaining both police and medical evidence once records are no longer available. Nevertheless, it is made clear that sympathetic consideration will be given to late applications by victims who have some form of impaired ability or who were under the age of 18 at the time of the incident, provided that the application is received within a reasonable time of the victim attaining 18 years.

1   Criminal Injuries Compensation Scheme 1995 para 17.

A4.20 For applicants who allege that they are the victims of child abuse, the CICA provides a separate leaflet 'Child Abuse and the Criminal Injuries Compensation Scheme'. Those applying on behalf of applicants under 18 must be adult, with parental responsibility and should submit a copy of the child's birth certificate together with the application form.

A4.21 It is very important for representatives to address the issue of time limits carefully and thoroughly at the outset of the claim. If it appears that the application is being made outside the normal time limits then every effort should be made to give a full and detailed explanation of the reasons, with supporting evidence, wherever it is available. This will inevitably save time and expense to both the CICA and the applicant or their representative.

A4.22 It is also notable that under both schemes there are provisions for the reopening or reconsideration of claims. Normally, the decision of the CICB is final but a decision can be reconsidered after a final award if it is accepted that there has been such a serious change in the medical condition of the applicant that it would be unjust if the original assessment stood.[1] Similarly, under the tariff-based scheme it is possible for a claims officer to reopen a case where there has been such a material change in the medical condition of the applicant that injustice would occur if the original assessment of compensation were allowed to stand, and also in circumstances where the applicant has subsequently died as a result of the injury.[2] This forms an interesting parallel with common law claims for provisional damages and it is suggested that those representing applicants should always keep this possibility in mind and indeed draw it to the attention of the applicant. In the case of those applicants that may not be capable of appreciating a deterioration in a medical condition themselves, care should be taken to draw these provisions to the attention of those with responsibility for the injured person.

1 Criminal Injuries Compensation Scheme 1990 para 13.
2 Criminal Injuries Compensation Scheme 1995 para 56.

The Application Form

A4.23 The importance of the full and careful completion of the application form cannot be over emphasised. The forms themselves and related guides are obtainable from the Criminal Injuries Compensation Authority.[1] There are separate application forms for 'personal injury' and 'fatal injury'. There is also a supplementary form where there is a claim for 'loss of earnings and special expenses'.

1 Criminal Injuries Compensation Authority, Tay House, 300 Bath Street, Glasgow G2 4JR. (Telephone: 0141 331 2726, fax: 0141 331 2287).

A4.24 Although on receipt of instructions it is incumbent on the representative to proceed promptly, there is a danger that inadequate completion of the application form will inevitably lead to delay and even rejection. Provided that there is no danger of falling outside the time limits, representatives should endeavour to complete all aspects of the application in a concise manner. The application form must be signed by the applicant or somebody regarded as a proper person on their behalf. The CICA can appoint a person regarded as suitable to act as an applicant's representative for the purposes of the scheme. If a child is in care the application should be made by the local authority if it has assumed parental responsibility in which case the application will have to be signed by a responsible officer on behalf of the local authority.

A4.25 Care should be taken to include the full name of the applicant. Failure to do so can often cause difficulty. For example, the CICA will wish to investigate whether the applicant has any convictions and incorrect identification of the applicant can result in inaccurate information being provided. Furthermore, it is important that the application form gives precise information about dates and locations. The CICA will have to liaise with the relevant police force and again if incorrect information is provided it will not tally with the information retained by the police authority resulting in delay, further investigation and increased costs.

A4.26 Representatives should be careful to provide a complete description of the injuries suffered by the applicant. This is important in relation to the tariff scheme whereby different bands of compensation are available and applicable for different types of injury suffered. There is a danger that if a representative fails to obtain full instructions as to the extent of all injuries, a potential band of the tariff may be lost. Furthermore, representatives should be sure to explore not merely physical injuries but any accompanying psychological or psychiatric problems and to deal thoroughly with this in the relevant section of the application form.

A4.27 It is often the case that severely injured victims will have visited more than one hospital. Full information must be given about all medical treatment that has been provided, whether by hospitals within the National Health Service, private hospitals or General Practitioners and it will further assist the smooth processing of the application if the sequence in which hospitals have been visited is specified. Again, failure to identify a relevant hospital may lead to a potential head of claim under the tariff being overlooked.

Claims Processing

A4.28 Within the CICA there is an initial action section which will deal with the acknowledgement of the application form. It will be logged onto a computer and proforma documents will be sent to the relevant police authority and hospitals. The file will be allocated to a case working section (there are seven such sections at the CICA's offices in Glasgow and three in London). The case working section will await responses from police and hospitals. In the absence of a response, computerised reminders are generated. As soon as it is felt that there is enough information for a decision to be made, the papers are referred to a claims officer. It is anticipated that the procedures will be quicker and more efficient than under the 1990 scheme. At this point, if there appear to be sufficient grounds for refusal the CICA will endeavour to do so as quickly as possible in order to avoid further unnecessary costs being incurred. It is suggested that it is open to the representatives of applicants to actively seek a decision on eligibility as a separate issue, so as to avoid unnecessary cost and expense. It is unlikely that such a decision will be made without a police report.

A4.29 In relation to medical evidence, three separate sheets are sent to the doctor or medical officer concerned, including details of the claim, a request for information and details of payment. Discretion as to the amount of information to be provided remains with the doctor or medical staff concerned. The CICA retains computerised database fields for identification of the type of injury and if any qualifying injuries have been overlooked there are remedies available at the point of a first offer being made, but it is obviously preferable if this can be avoided. It is rare for the CICA to request further information in comparison with the CICB whereby a Board member might have given an indication that additional evidence was required and further questions had to be put to the doctor concerned. Claims officers can ask for information but prefer to release a decision as soon as possible. Accordingly, unless the medical evidence provided by the doctor is ambiguous they will endeavour to reach a decision quickly as to the appropriate tariff band to be applied. On the notification of the making of an award, there is a time limit for a Review of 90 days. On receipt of a request for a Review the papers are passed to a Review section where they are dealt with by a different case worker who will ultimately pass the papers to a reviewing claims officer. It is open to an applicant at this point to submit further evidence and it is suggested that very careful consideration ought to be given to this possibility. Indeed, reasons and evidence to support the request for a Review should be submitted by the applicant.[1] It may be that in cases of severity, additional time is going to be needed to compile the relevant evidence and requests for more time will be considered sympathetically if submitted with a covering letter and an explanation of the reasons for the request being made.

1 Criminal Injuries Compensation Scheme 1995 para 59.

A4.30   In the event of dissatisfaction with the outcome of a Review, it is open to the applicant to appeal by way of written Notice of Appeal to the panel, again supported by reasons and additional material or evidence. The notice must be received by the panel within 30 days of the date of the Review decision, although again it is open to the panel to waive the time limit, provided that there are good reasons or that it is in the interests of justice to do so.

1 Criminal Injuries Compensation Scheme 1995 para 61/62.

A4.31   It is imperative that representatives should promptly notify the CICA of procedural matters, such as a change of address, and whenever additional information comes to light. Common sense needs to be exercised as to whether the applicant can assist in speeding up the claims process. A skilfull representative will anticipate problems and gaps in information and try to deal with them. It is open to a representative to write in to the CICA to see if they can assist. The provision of basic information such as hospital reference numbers and crime references can be extremely important, emphasising once again the need to provide accurate information from the outset of the claim and thereafter.

Informing and Co-operation with the Police and the CICA, Conduct and Good Character

A4.32   There are a number of key areas to be addressed to protect applicants against the risk of having an award refused or reduced. There may be a number of circumstances in which this can happen. As an example, in the year 1997/98 of 27,445 disallowed claims 2,661 were disallowed on a finding that the injury had not resulted from a crime of violence, 2,175 due to a failure to report without delay to the police, 4,812 as result of failure to co-operate with the police in bringing an assailant to justice, 3,134 resulting from the applicant's conduct before, during and after the incident, and 2,333 as a consequence of the applicant's criminal record.

Informing the Police

A4.33 It has never been necessary for an offender to be convicted before an award could be made and often offenders are never found. However, the Criminal Injuries Compensation schemes have always attached great importance to the need to inform the police or other relevant authorities promptly of the circumstances of the crime to facilitate the apprehension of offenders and as a safeguard to the public purse against fraudulent claims. Similarly, applicants are encouraged to co-operate fully with the police and authorities in bringing an offender to justice. Consequently, in circumstances where for some reason neither of these requirements have been complied with, it is imperative that applicants provide a comprehensive and cogent explanation of the reasons. If it is clear at the outset that a question is likely to arise about failure to report or co-operate, then representatives should anticipate and deal with this on making the application or so soon as possible thereafter. Similarly, if the CICA feels that an applicant is failing to co-operate by refusing to provide information or to give all reasonable assistance an award can be withheld or reduced. Representatives should be fully aware of this, particularly where there is a danger that their clients may, by virtue of their injuries, have difficulty in co-operating for physical or psychological reasons and should act in liaison with the CICA to ensure that there is no breakdown in the supply of information, or indeed in communication.

Conduct

A4.34 Bad conduct including provocative behaviour and offensive language can be taken into account in deciding whether an award should be reduced or withheld. Once again, it is sensible for representatives to anticipate such an issue arising and to address this at the earliest possible opportunity.

Criminal Convictions

A4.35 The CICA ignores convictions which are spent under the Rehabilitation of Offenders Act 1974, whereas the CICB had previously been entitled to take account of such convictions. Convictions are seen to be relevant to the applicant's character and can count against an award. The CICA adopts a system of penalty points outlined in its guide which will result in a percentage reduction from 0-100%. The CICA commissions an immediate search for police records and will obtain a list of convictions. In practical terms, the CICA sometimes has difficulty where the police can provide a report but are unable to provide an early list of convictions. This could result in a change of a decision if convictions only come to light at a later date. It is notable that a claims officer can take account of not only character, criminal convictions and unlawful conduct but of all other available information. This may leave the way open for wider and even moral issues to be taken into account. Representatives, out of caution, need to obtain full and thorough instructions from their clients dealing with all of these issues and to ensure that clients understand the relevance of the facts and the issues. In particular, when dealing with clients with head injury or psychological or psychiatric injury, representatives may wish to carry out thorough independent inquiries to satisfy themselves that these areas have been properly addressed. It is suggested that early investigation may well save a good deal of wasted time and effort and subsequent disappointment for applicants later on.

Compilation of Evidence

A4.36 Subject to the constraints of legal costs and expenses outlined in paras A4.12-A4.18), the compilation of evidence on behalf of a seriously injured claimant will follow a similar model to that required in other types of personal injury compensation claims. This is particularly so with regard to CICB cases, bearing in mind the common law method of assessment of compensation. In CICA cases efforts must be made to ensure that all aspects of injury, both physical and psychological, are examined. The evidence obtained by the CICA should be supplemented wherever necessary in order to result in the proper level of the tariff award being made, with the maximum target of level 25 at £250,000. Similarly, with regard to loss of earnings and special expenses the necessary evidence must be compiled in a cost-effective manner. The team approach necessary to achieve full and proper compensation is equally applicable in cases of this nature. Generally, the legal representatives (solicitor and counsel) are at the hub of the team, supported wherever possible by medical and other experts. The aim must be to ultimately present evidence in written form, generally by way of schedule of claim, supported by documentary evidence in the form of appendices. Presentation skills are as important in this type of claim as any other and the clear and lucid submission of evidence addressing all the issues will be appreciated by the Board or CICA giving time and costs saving.

A4.37 Under the tariff-based scheme, when addressing the issue of compensation for loss of earnings and special expenses, it should not be assumed that the claims put forward will be accepted. The CICA must be satisfied that the loss of earnings results directly from the criminal injury and will consider whether there are other influencing factors. For example, the CICA can look at health problems that arose before the injury, previous unconnected injuries, insecurity in the type of employment of the applicant, or in the case of those applicants who are self-employed, trading and cashflow problems unconnected with the injury. It is also necessary to show that the loss of earnings could not reasonably have been offset by an applicant who is able to find some form of alternative employment. Principles of mitigation do apply. Representatives should be able to anticipate and foresee these issues arising and to address them in the evidence submitted.

A4.38 Furthermore, financial benefits attributable to and received as a result of the injury are deductible, including any social security benefits, insurance payments and pensions which have become payable to the applicant during the period of loss and any other pension which has become payable to the applicant during the period of loss whether or not as a result of the injury.[1] If in the opinion of a claims officer an applicant might be eligible for benefits and payments, an award can be withheld until the applicant has taken reasonable steps to claim them.[2] Consequently, a thorough investigation of the availability to the applicant of state benefits and other pension payments should be undertaken by representatives, particularly in case the need arises to challenge any proposed deductions.

1   Criminal Injuries Compensation Scheme 1995 para 31 (D)(E).
2   Criminal Injuries Compensation Scheme 1995 para 46.

A4.39   With regard to special expenses, under the tariff-based scheme this will cover practical, medical and care costs provided that there has been incapacity for longer than 28 weeks as a direct result of the injury. Once more, medical issues need to be addressed to ensure that an applicant can satisfy the CICA that the injury is responsible. Again, there will be deductions for social security benefits. Awards can be made to cover damage to property or equipment belonging to an applicant which was relied on as a physical aid, and expenses such as NHS prescriptions, dental and optical charges and the costs of travel to and from hospital for treatment are covered. It is open to the CICA to consider the cost of private treatment provided that both the treatment itself and its cost is found to be reasonable in the circumstances of a particular case. The onus is on the applicant to show that private treatment is a reasonable option and the issue of whether or not it might be routinely available under the NHS or in a particular area should be addressed. As an example, some types of cosmetic surgery or special dental treatment can be considered and evidence may need to be adduced to address those needs.

A4.40   In relation to special equipment, this can include home adaptations and the cost of care at home or in a nursing home. Special equipment will include aids to mobility, both at home and outside, including specially adapted vehicles, wheelchairs, walking aids and kitchen implements designed to help those with a weakened grip. Receipts or estimates of costs must be provided.

A4.41   Adaptations to accommodation might include internal and external work with a view to improving mobility and access. Once more, plans and estimates should be submitted. Care costs are addressed on the basis of what is reasonably necessary in each individual case. The CICA will take account of services which might be provided free of charge from other sources such as the NHS or a local authority and will be need to be satisfied about the costs of a particular carer and the level of care if an applicant is being looked after at home by a relative or friend. It is therefore sensible to submit evidence to outline and support the existing or proposed care regime, preferably in the form of supporting statements.

A4.42   Should there be recurring annual or periodic special expenses then a multiplicand/multiplier approach is adopted.[1]

1   Criminal Injuries Compensation Scheme 1995 para 35.

Directions and Case Management

A4.43   From April 2000 the CICB scheme has been administered by its successor, the CICA and its officers (see para A4.5). It is anticipated that procedures under the Criminal Injuries Compensation Scheme will increasingly mirror the approach of the civil procedural rules with active case management. In particular, the CICB scheme now encourages directions hearings. Where an applicant has generated a care report there will almost certainly be a directions hearing so that the Board can review the evidence and progress of the claim and make decisions as to whether it wishes to compile its own evidence, in addition to providing a mechanism to ensure that cases move speedily.

Hearings

A4.44 Under the CICB scheme, an initial decision on an application may be made by a single member of the Board or any member of the Board's staff given authority to determine applications on behalf of the Board. If an award is made, the applicant will be given a breakdown of the assessment of compensation unless the Board considers this to be inappropriate and in the event of refusal or reduction, reasons for the decision will be given. It is open to the applicant to apply for an oral hearing if dissatisfied with the decision and this application must be made within three months of notification of the initial decision. The Board has a discretion to waive this time limit where an extension is requested with good reason within the three-month period or where it would otherwise be in the interests of justice to do so. However, it is open to a member of the Board or nominated member of the Board's staff to refer an application to a hearing where it is considered that it might not be possible for a just and proper decision to be made by an individual. It is suggested that in cases of severity or extreme difficulty it will always be appropriate for the matter to proceed to such a hearing and practitioners should try to give an early indication to the Board that this is felt appropriate, so as to try to ensure that the case is dealt with other than as a routine application.

A4.45 It will often be beneficial if supporting evidence and documents are lodged with the Board so that the members can consider them two weeks in advance of the hearing. To ensure this, it is generally useful for the Board Advocate to receive the documents 28 days before the hearing and although the Board will do so itself, it is most helpful if four bundles are prepared and lodged.

A4.46 For claims of the utmost severity it is preferable that there should be three members of the Board sitting but at least two members will sit. There are often late cancellations due to the commitments of Board members but the minimum number is two. The applicant and the Board Advocate will be entitled to call, examine and cross examine witnesses and relevant hearsay evidence can be taken into account. A decision is reached solely on the basis of the evidence given at the hearing and all such evidence will be made available to an applicant or their representative at the hearing, if not before. Hearings can be adjourned and it is possible that the assessment of compensation can be remitted to a single member for determination. In those circumstances, the applicant still has a right to a further hearing if not satisfied with the final assessment. This makes it imperative that any experts who are not going to attend the hearing should produce clear reports addressing all the issues and it is incumbent on representatives to be entirely satisfied that this has been done before the evidence is lodged. Failure to do so is likely to mean that a decision is reached on the basis of incomplete evidence or alternatively, that there has to be an adjournment occasioning further costs. It is open to a representative to liaise with the presenting officer or Board Advocate to discuss and decide on the format of the evidence to be presented. A dialogue of this nature can be extremely useful with a view to the saving of costs and time.

A4.47 It is open to the Board to use its experience to override medical and expert evidence provided that it complies with the principles of natural justice.[1] The venue of the hearing will generally be the hearing centre for the police force area in which the incident occurred but for issues related solely to assessment will be the hearing centre nearest to the home of the applicant. There are in the order of one dozen hearing centres around the country.

1   *R v CICB, ex p Catterall* (1997) PIQR 128.

A4.48 Similarly, appeals to the Criminal Injuries Compensation Appeals Panel will proceed after completion of the review procedure. A member of the staff of the Panel will refer the claim for an oral hearing and appeal against the decision taken on review to withhold an award, to make a reduced award or to seek repayment of an award provided that it meets the necessary criteria to go to a hearing.[1] The hearing will take place before at least two adjudicators. Alternatively, the hearing can be generated where a member of staff of the Panel has referred the matter to an adjudicator who, himself, will refer the claim to an oral hearing:

> (a) if he considers, on the evidence available, that a review decision to withhold an award on the ground that the injury was not serious enough to qualify, by virtue of a minimum tariff level was taken in circumstances where an award could have been made; or
>
> (b) in any other case where there is a dispute as to material facts or conclusions on which the review decision was based and where a different decision could have been reached.[2]

1   Criminal Injuries Compensation Scheme 1995 para 69.
2   Criminal Injuries Compensation Scheme 1995 para 70.

A4.49 In the second case, the adjudicator who has made the referral will not take part in the hearing. The procedure is a matter for the adjudicators themselves.[1]

1   Criminal Injuries Compensation Scheme 1995 para 72.

A4.50 An applicant will receive written notice of the hearing at least 21 days beforehand and similarly, evidence and documents provided by either the applicant or the CICA must be made available at the hearing, if not before. Clearly, in severe cases it is preferable for there to be a prior exchange. The procedure is informal with the adjudicators not being bound by the rules of evidence. It is open to the appellant, the claims officer and the adjudicators to call witnesses to give evidence and for there to be cross examination. Consequently, similar considerations with regard to the presentation of expert evidence apply. It is open to adjudicators to adjourn a hearing with the power for an interim payment to be made. In serious cases, representatives should be aware of this facility, as an interim award may be very important to a client to assist with care and financial loss and it may be some time before the appeal hearing can be re-instated.

A4.51 In reality, the format of hearings and appeals will vary greatly depending on the composition and preferences of the sitting members. There is strictly no need for any form of legal qualification in order to represent an applicant at a hearing, with applicants being entitled to bring a friend or legal advisor. It is a matter for individual practitioners as to whether they feel that they have relevant experience and expertise in presenting claims of this nature but it is suggested that careful thought should be given as to who is to undertake this responsibility. In particular, it will often be appropriate for counsel and leading counsel to appear. Nevertheless, if counsel is to be instructed, care should be taken at the outset to identify an advocate who has a full and proper understanding of the Criminal Injuries Compensation schemes.

A4.52   As with any other forum, representatives should take the time and trouble to ensure that the format of the hearing is explored, discussed and explained in 'client friendly' terminology with the applicant, and/or the relevant members of their family in the case of applicants who are unable to understand for themselves by reason of minority of infirmity. It will often be the case that the applicant or family members have to give evidence at a hearing and care should be taken to ensure that this possibility is discussed and that applicants are therefore not taken by surprise. Early preparation (rather than 10 minutes before the commencement of the hearing!) should be strongly encouraged.

A4.53   Out of caution, representatives should also make every effort to be sure that practical considerations have been addressed, such as checking that the building in which the hearing is to take place can accommodate disabled applicants, ensuring that all documents being relied on have been received, verifying that up-to-date financial information is available (benefits details, adoption allowances and so on) and if video evidence is to be relied on, that suitable facilities are available.

Awards and How they are Made

A4.54   Normally, a decision will be delivered and an award will be made on the day of the hearing. It is very rare for there to be any form of reserved decision, except in those circumstances where the quantification can be remitted to a single member under the 1990 scheme.

A4.55   At the conclusion of a hearing, it is important for representatives and applicants to remain and conclude any necessary documentation with the relevant officers. This might seem self-evident but failure to do so can result in a delay in the making of payments. The mechanics for payment are such that there will be a short delay until the Board officers are able to return to their office which may be the following week. A payment voucher will be produced after internal procedures have been undertaken and it is the aim that payment will normally be made within 28 days. The payment is generated internally by the Board or CICA. There are different types of form of acceptance for minors and in the case of fatal accidents claims.

A4.56   Compensation will normally be paid as a single lump sum, subject to any interim awards that have already been made. It has, however, been possible since 1996[1] for an award to be made consisting in whole or in part of an annuity or annuities ('structured settlements'). As in any other form of substantial personal injury compensation, depending on the individual circumstances of the applicant a structured settlement can be extremely attractive. Representatives should familiarise themselves with the benefits available under such an arrangement and carefully consider whether it will be beneficial to their client. They should generally be prepared to take the initiative in investigating this possibility. It may well be that the Board Advocate or claims officer will explore the question of a structured settlement with an applicant's advisors but primary responsibility for this consideration rests with the representative and it is strongly suggested that this should be done well in advance of the hearing. The Board or CICA cannot be expected to anticipate such a requirement. In the event that a representative fails to prepare for this option by taking the necessary advice and obtaining the appropriate quotations and projections, there can be lengthy delay after the hearing. It could take many months for a structure to be put in place and in order to obtain the tax advantages the award cannot be concluded, thus potentially causing a loss of substantial interest to the applicant. If it is decided to proceed with a Structured Settlement the Board Advocate or claims officer will make arrangements internally and will often be able to deal directly with the instructed financial advisors to ensure smooth administration which again can be important to ensure that arrangements are finalised during the currency of insurance and annuity quotations.

1   Criminal Injuries Compensation Act 1995 s 8 amending Income and Corporation Taxes Act 1988 s 329(b).

A4.57   In many cases of severity, the appointment of a Receiver through the Court of Protection will be required, generally in the same circumstances of those pertaining to any other form of award. The timing of an application will again mirror that of other personal injury litigation. The Court of Protection should certainly be involved if substantial interim awards are sought and made, for example to deal with accommodation and equipment requirements. Court of Protection costs are also a legitimate head of claim. It should be noted that if there has been an appointment at an early stage, care should be taken with the First General Order to ensure that power is granted to conduct the application for compensation and that it is relevant to the correct scheme pre- or post- 1 April 1996. It should also be noted that the court may appoint the official solicitor to be a guardian of the estate of a child where the CICB or CICA notifies it that it has made, or intends to make, an award to a child.[1]

1   Part 21(12) Civil Procedure Rules.

Judicial Review

A4.58   It is open to applicants who are dissatisfied with the procedures or decisions of the CICB, CICA or Criminal Injuries Compensation Appeals Panel to apply for Judicial Review in the High Court in England and Wales or the Court of Session in Scotland. It is necessary to apply for leave for Judicial Review.

A4.59   There are a variety of circumstances that might give rise to applications for Judicial Review in this way. Notably, evidential and procedural matters might be challenged. A refusal by the Board to award compensation in a case where the applicant failed to advise the police of the identity of his attacker out of fear resulted in a successful application. The Board's decision was quashed with directions for a rehearing on the basis that the failure by the Board to give reasons which 'precluded' compensation meant no reasons had in fact been given. It was found that the failure to give adequate reasons in a decision letter was perverse.[1] Similar considerations applied in a case in which the Board was found to have relied on conclusions which undermined the factual and expert evidence relied on, in turn, by the applicant and further on principles for calculating future losses which were erroneous in law. There had been no notification of either line of approach to the applicant's counsel nor had the Board sought assistance. It was held that the Board should have advised the applicant of its intention so to do and invited any appropriate submissions from counsel. Failure to do so was an irregularity.[2]

1   *R v CICB, ex p Powell* (1994) PIQR P77.
2   *R v CICB, ex p C (a minor)* (1977) PIQR P128.

A4.60   Although Judicial Review proceedings are not in the nature of an appeal as such, they can often represent the only real route to correct irregularities that might otherwise result in an injustice either in terms of qualification for an award or the amount of the award itself.

CONCLUSION

A4.61   The foregoing paragraphs are meant to be a simple and practical guide to practitioners with an emphasis on 'cost effective case management'. In terms of the technicalities of the Criminal Injuries Compensation Schemes themselves, there is absolutely no substitute for an indepth analysis of their narrative. The framework of both schemes is reasonably short and the accompanying guides are extremely helpful. A working knowledge of those schemes is therefore assumed.

A4.62   On the assumption that practitioners are skilled in the presentation of major personal injury compensation schemes, the aim of the foregoing paragraphs is to attempt to highlight some practical considerations to enable those representing the victims of violence to pursue claims with speed and efficiency and not to fall into traps that can result in delay and duplication. By exercising foresight and a thorough appreciation of these schemes, legal representatives and practitioners can properly fulfil the responsibility that they have undertaken on behalf of those who have been let down by one section of society, thus ensuring that another section of society helps to redress the balance.

Appendix 5

Rules and Practice Directions 29, 35 and 40

PART 29
THE MULTI-TRACK

CPR 29.1

29.1 Scope of this Part
This Part contains general provisions about management of cases allocated to the multi-track and applies only to cases allocated to that track.
(Part 27 sets out the procedure for claims allocated to the small claims track)
(Part 28 sets out the procedure for claims allocated to the fast track)

CPR 29.2

29.2 Case Management
(1) When it allocates a case to the multi-track, the court will–
   (a) give directions for the management of the case and set a timetable for the steps to be taken between the giving of directions and the trial; or
   (b) fix –
      (i) a case management conference; or
      (ii) a pre-trial review,
   or both, and give such other directions relating to the management of the case as it sees fit.
(2) The court will fix the trial date or the period in which the trial is to take place as soon as practicable.

(3) When the court fixes the trial date or the trial period under paragraph (2), it will –
    (a) give notice to the parties of the date or period; and
    (b) specify the date by which the parties must file a listing questionnaire.

CPR 29.3

29.3 Case Management Conference and Pre-trial Review
(1) The court may fix –
    (a) a case management conference; or
    (b) a pre-trial review, at any time after the claim has been allocated.
(2) If a party has a legal representative, a representative –
    (a) familiar with the case; and
    (b) with sufficient authority to deal with any issues that are likely to arise,
        must attend case management conferences and pre-trial reviews.
(Rule 3.1(2)(c) provides that the court may require a party to attend the court)

CPR 29.4

29.4 Steps Taken by the Parties
If –
    (a) the parties agree proposals for the management of the proceedings
        (including a proposed trial date or period in which the trial is to take
        place); and
    (b) the court considers that the proposals are suitable, it may approve them
        without a hearing and give directions in the terms proposed.

CPR 29.5

29.5 Variation of Case Management Timetable
(1) A party must apply to the court if he wishes to vary the date which the court
    has fixed for –
    (a) a case management conference;
    (b) a pre-trial review;
    (c) the return of a listing questionnaire under rule 29.6;
    (d) the trial; or
    (e) the trial period.
(2) Any date set by the court or these Rules for doing any act may not be varied
    by the parties if the variation would make it necessary to vary any of the
    dates mentioned in paragraph (1).
(Rule 2.11 allows the parties to vary a date by written agreement except where
the rules provide otherwise or the court orders otherwise)

CPR 29.6

29.6 Listing Questionnaire
(1) The court will send the parties a listing questionnaire for completion and
    return by the date specified in directions given under rule 29.2(3) unless it
    considers that the claim can be listed for trial without the need for a listing
    questionnaire.
(2) Each party must file the completed listing questionnaire by the date specified
    by the court.

(3) If –
- (a) a party fails to file the completed questionnaire by the date specified;
- (b) a party has failed to give all the information requested by the listing questionnaire; or
- (c) the court considers that a hearing is necessary to enable it to decide what directions to give in order to complete preparation of the case for trial, the court may fix a date for a listing hearing or give such other directions as it thinks appropriate.

CPR 29.7

29.7 Pre-trial Review
If, on receipt of the parties' listing questionnaires, the court decides –
- (a) to hold a pre-trial review; or
- (b) to cancel a pre-trial review which has already been fixed, it will serve notice of its decision at least 7 days before the date fixed for the hearing or, as the case may be, the cancelled hearing.

CPR 29.8

29.8 Setting a Trial Timetable and Fixing or Confirming the Trial Date or Week
As soon as practicable after –
- (a) each party has filed a completed listing questionnaire;
- (b) the court has held a listing hearing under rule 29.6 (3); or
- (c) the court has held a pre-trial review under rule 29.7,

the court will –
- (i) set a timetable for the trial unless a timetable has already been fixed, or the court considers that it would be inappropriate to do so;
- (ii) fix the date for the trial or the week within which the trial is to begin (or, if it has already done so, confirm that date); and
- (iii) notify the parties of the trial timetable (where one is fixed under this rule) and the date or trial period.

CPR 29.9

29.9 Conduct of Trial
Unless the trial judge otherwise directs, the trial will be conducted in accordance with any order previously made.

CPR PD 29 PRACTICE DIRECTION – THE MULTI-TRACK

This Practice Direction Supplements CPR Part 29

General
1.1 Attention is drawn in particular to the following Parts of the Civil Procedure Rules:

Part 1	The overriding objective
Part 3	The court's case management powers
Part 26	Case management preliminary stage
Part 31	Disclosure and inspection of documents

Parts 32 to 34   Evidence
Part 35   Experts and assessors and to the practice directions which relate
                     to those Parts.

1.2 Attention is also drawn to Part 49 of the Rules (Specialist Jurisdictions) and
to the practice directions which apply to those jurisdictions.

Case Management in the Royal Courts of Justice

2.1 This part of the practice direction applies to claims begun by claim form
issued in the Central Office or Chancery Chambers in the Royal Courts of
Justice.

2.2 A claim with an estimated value of less than £50,000 will generally, unless:
   (a) it is required by an enactment to be tried in the High Court,
   (b) it falls within a specialist list (as defined in CPR Part 49), or
   (c) it falls within one of the categories specified in 2.6 below or is otherwise
       within the criteria of article 7(5) of the High Court and County Courts
       Jurisdiction Order 1991, be transferred to a county court.

2.3 Paragraph 2.2 is without prejudice to the power of the court in accordance
with Part 30 to transfer to a county court a claim with an estimated value
that exceeds £50,000.

2.4 The decision to transfer may be made at any stage in the proceedings but
should, subject to paragraph 2.5, be made as soon as possible and in any
event not later than the date for the filing of listing questionnaires.

2.5 If an application is made under rule 3.4 (striking out) or under Part 24
(summary judgment) or under Part 25 (interim remedies), it will usually
be convenient for the application to be dealt with before a decision to
transfer is taken.

2.6 Each party should state in his allocation questionnaire whether he considers
the claim should be managed and tried at the Royal Courts of Justice and,
if so, why. Claims suitable for trial in the Royal Courts of Justice include:

(1) professional negligence claims,
(2) Fatal Accident Act claims,
(3) fraud or undue influence claims,
(4) defamation claims,
(5) claims for malicious prosecution or false imprisonment,
(6) claims against the police,
(7) contentious probate claims.

Such claims may fall within the criteria of article 7(5) of the High Court and County
Courts Jurisdiction Order 1991.

2.7 Attention is drawn to the practice direction on transfer (Part 30).

Case Management – General Provisions

3.1
(1) Case management of a claim which is proceeding at the Royal Courts of Justice will be undertaken there.
(2)
    (a) Case management of any other claim which has been allocated to the multi-track will normally be undertaken at a Civil Trial Centre.
    (b) The practice direction supplementing Part 26 provides for what will happen in the case of a claim which is issued in or transferred to a court which is not a Civil Trial Centre.

3.2 The hallmarks of the multi-track are:
(1) the ability of the court to deal with cases of widely differing values and complexity, and
(2) the flexibility given to the court in the way it will manage a case in a way appropriate to its particular needs.

3.3
(1) On allocating a claim to the multi-track the court may give directions without a hearing, including fixing a trial date or a period in which the trial will take place,
(2) Alternatively, whether or not it fixes a trial date or period, it may either—
    (a) give directions for certain steps to be taken and fix a date for a case management conference or a pre-trial review to take place after they have been taken, or
    (b) fix a date for a case management conference.
(3) Attention is drawn to rule 29.2(2) which requires the court to fix a trial date or period as soon as practicable.

3.4 The court may give or vary directions at any hearing which may take place on the application of a party or of its own initiative.

3.5 When any hearing has been fixed it is the duty of the parties to consider what directions the court should be asked to give and to make any application that may be appropriate to be dealt with then.

3.6 The court will hold a hearing to give directions whenever it appears necessary or desirable to do so, and where this happens because of the default of a party or his legal representative it will usually impose a sanction.

3.7 When the court fixes a hearing to give directions it will give the parties at least 3 days' notice of the hearing unless rule 29.7 applies (7 days notice to be given in the case of a pre-trial review).

3.8 Where a party needs to apply for a direction of a kind not included in the case management timetable which has been set (for example to amend his statement of case or for further information to be given by another party) he must do so as soon as possible so as to minimise the need to change that timetable.

3.9 Courts will make arrangements to ensure that applications and other hearings are listed promptly to avoid delay in the conduct of cases.

3.10

(1) Case management will generally be dealt with by:

    (a) a Master in cases proceeding in the Royal Courts of Justice,

    (b) a district judge in cases proceeding in a District Registry of the High Court, and

    (c) a district judge or a Circuit Judge in cases proceeding in a county court.

(2) A Master or a district judge may consult and seek the directions of a judge of a higher level about any aspect of case management.

(3) A member of the court staff who is dealing with the listing of a hearing may seek the directions of any judge about any aspect of that listing.

Directions on Allocation

4.1 Attention is drawn to the court's duties under rule 29.2.

4.2 The court will seek to tailor its directions to the needs of the case and the steps which the parties have already taken to prepare the case of which it is aware. In particular it will have regard to the extent to which any pre-action protocol has or (as the case may be) has not been complied with.

4.3 At this stage the court's first concern will be to ensure that the issues between the parties are identified and that the necessary evidence is prepared and disclosed.

4.4 The court may have regard to any document filed by a party with his allocation questionnaire containing further information, provided that the document states either that its contents has been agreed with every other party or that it has been served on every other party, and when it was served.

4.5 On the allocation of a claim to the multi-track the court will consider whether it is desirable or necessary to hold a case management conference straight away, or whether it is appropriate instead to give directions on its own initiative.

4.6 The parties and their advisers are encouraged to try to agree directions and to take advantage of rule 29.4 which provides that if:

(1) the parties agree proposals for the management of the proceedings (including a proposed trial date or period in which the trial is to take place), and

(2) the court considers that the proposals are suitable,

    it may approve them without a hearing and give directions in the terms proposed.

4.7

(1) To obtain the court's approval the agreed directions must

    (a) set out a timetable by reference to calendar dates for the taking of steps for the preparation of the case,

    (b) include a date or a period (the trial period) when it is proposed that the trial will take place,

    (c) include provision about disclosure of documents, and

    (d) include provision about both factual and expert evidence.

(2) The court will scrutinise the timetable carefully and in particular will be concerned to see that any proposed date or period for the trial and (if provided for) for a case management conference is no later than is reasonably necessary.

(3) The provision in (1)(c) above may
    (a) limit disclosure to standard disclosure or less than that, and/or
    (b) direct that disclosure will take place by the supply of copy documents
        without a list, but it must in that case say either that the parties must
        serve a disclosure statement with the copies or that they have agreed to
        disclose in that way without such a statement.
(4) The provision in (1)(d) about expert evidence may be to the effect that none is
    required.

4.8 Directions agreed by the parties should also where appropriate contain
    provisions about:
(1) the filing of any reply or amended statement of case that may be required,
(2) dates for the service of requests for further information under the practice
    direction supplementing Part 18 and of questions to experts under rule 35.6
    and by when they are to be dealt with,
(3) the disclosure of evidence,
(4) the use of a single joint expert, or in cases where it is not agreed, the exchange
    of expert evidence (including whether exchange is to be simultaneous or
    sequential) and without prejudice discussions between experts.

4.9 If the court does not approve the agreed directions filed by the parties but
    decides that it will give directions of its own initiative without fixing a case
    management conference, it will take them into account in deciding what
    directions to give.

4.10
    Where the court is to give directions on its own initiative without holding a
    case management conference and it is not aware of any steps taken by the
    parties other than the exchange of statements of case, its general approach
    will be:
(1) to give directions for the filing and service of any further information required
    to clarify either party's case,
(2) to direct standard disclosure between the parties,
(3) to direct the disclosure of witness statements by way of simultaneous
    exchange,
(4) to give directions for a single joint expert on any appropriate issue unless
    there is a good reason not to do so,
(5) unless paragraph 4.11 (below) applies, to direct disclosure of experts' reports
    by way of simultaneous exchange on those issues where a single joint expert
    is not directed,
(6) if experts' reports are not agreed, to direct a discussion between experts for
    the purpose set out in rule 35.12(1) and the preparation of a statement under
    rule 35.12(3),
(7) to list a case management conference to take place after the date for compliance
    with those directions, and
(8) to specify a trial period.

4.11
    If it appears that expert evidence will be required both on issues of liability
    and on the amount of damages, the court may direct that the exchange of
    those reports that relate to liability will be exchanged simultaneously but

that those relating to the amount of damages will be exchanged sequentially.

4.12

(1) If it appears to the court that it cannot properly give directions on its own initiative and no agreed directions have been filed which it can approve, the court will direct a case management conference to be listed.
(2) The conference will be listed as promptly as possible.

4.13

Where the court is proposing on its own initiative to make an order under rule 35.7 (which gives the court power to direct that evidence on a particular issue is to be given by a single expert) or under rule 35.15 (which gives the court power to appoint an assessor), the court must, unless the parties have consented in writing to the order, list a case management conference.

Case Management Conferences

5.1 The court will at any case management conference:
(1) review the steps which the parties have taken in the preparation of the case, and in particular their compliance with any directions that the court may have given,
(2) decide and give directions about the steps which are to be taken to secure the progress of the claim in accordance with the overriding objective, and
(3) ensure as far as it can that all agreements that can be reached between the parties about the matters in issue and the conduct of the claim are made and recorded.

5.2

(1) Rule 29.3(2) provides that where a party has a legal representative, a representative familiar with the case and with sufficient authority to deal with any issues that are likely to arise must attend case management conferences and pre-trial reviews.
(2) That person should be someone who is personally involved in the conduct of the case, and who has the authority and information to deal with any matter which may reasonably be expected to be dealt with at such a hearing, including the fixing of the timetable, the identification of issues and matters of evidence.
(3) Where the inadequacy of the person attending or of his instructions leads to the adjournment of a hearing, the court will expect to make a wasted costs order.

5.3 The topics the court will consider at a case management conference are likely to include:
(1) whether the claimant has made clear the claim he is bringing, in particular the amount he is claiming, so that the other party can understand the case he has to meet,
(2) whether any amendments are required to the claim, a statement of case or any other document,
(3) what disclosure of documents, if any, is necessary,
(4) what expert evidence is reasonably required in accordance with rule 35.1 and how and when that evidence should be obtained and disclosed,
(5) what factual evidence should be disclosed,

(6) what arrangements should be made about the giving of clarification or further information and the putting of questions to experts, and

(7) whether it will be just and will save costs to order a split trial or the trial of one or more preliminary issues.

5.4 In all cases the court will set a timetable for the steps it decides are necessary to be taken. These steps may include the holding of a case management conference or a pre-trial review, and the court will be alert to perform its duty to fix a trial date or period as soon as it can.

5.5

(1) The court will not at this stage give permission to use expert evidence unless it can identify each expert by name or field in its order and say whether his evidence is to be given orally or by the use of his report.

(2) A party who obtains expert evidence before obtaining a direction about it does so at his own risk as to costs. except where he obtained the evidence in compliance with a pre-action protocol.

5.6 To assist the court, the parties and their legal advisers should:

(1) ensure that all documents that the court is likely to ask to see (including witness statements and experts' reports) are brought to the hearing,

(2) consider whether the parties should attend,

(3) consider whether a case summary will be useful, and

(4) consider what orders each wishes to be made and give notice of them to the other parties.

5.7

(1) A case summary:

    (a) should be designed to assist the court to understand and deal with the questions before it,

    (b) should set out a brief chronology of the claim, the issues of fact which are agreed or in dispute and the evidence needed to decide them,

    (c) should not normally exceed 500 words in length, and

    (d) should be prepared by the claimant and agreed with the other parties if possible.

5.8

(1) Where a party wishes to obtain an order not routinely made at a case management conference and believes that his application will be opposed, he should issue and serve the application in time for it to be heard at the case management conference.

(2) If the time allowed for the case management conference is likely to be insufficient for the application to be heard he should inform the court at once so that a fresh date can be fixed.

(3) A costs sanction may be imposed on a party who fails to comply with sub-paragraph (1) or (2).

5.9 At a case management conference the court may also consider whether the case ought to be tried by a High Court judge or by a judge who specialises in that type of claim and how that question will be decided. In that case the claim may need to be transferred to another court.

Variation of Directions

6.1 This paragraph deals with the procedure to be adopted:
(1) where a party is dissatisfied with a direction given by the court,
(2) where the parties have agreed about changes they wish made to the directions given, or
(3) where a party wishes to apply to vary a direction.

6.2
(1) It is essential that any party who wishes to have a direction varied takes steps to do so as soon as possible.
(2) The court will assume for the purposes of any later application that a party who did not appeal, and who made no application to vary within 14 days of service of the order containing the directions, was content that they were correct in the circumstances then existing.

6.3
(1) Where a party is dissatisfied with a direction given or other order made by the court he may appeal or apply to the court for it to reconsider its decision.
(2) Unless paragraph 6.4 applies, a party should appeal if the direction was given or the order was made at a hearing at which he was present, or of which he had due notice.
(3) In any other case he should apply to the court to reconsider its decision.
(4) If an application is made for the court to reconsider its decision:
    (a) it will usually be heard by the judge who gave the directions or another judge of the same level,
    (b) the court will give all parties at least 3 days notice of the hearing, and
    (c) the court may confirm its directions or make a different order.

6.4 Where there has been a change in the circumstances since the order was made the court may set aside or vary a direction it has given. It may do so on application or on its own initiative.

6.5 Where the parties agree about changes they wish made to the directions given:
(1) If rule 2.11 (variation by agreement of a date set by the court for doing any act other than those stated in the note to that rule) or rule 31.5, 31.10(8) or 31.13 (agreements about disclosure) applies the parties need not file the written agreement.
(2)
    (a) In any other case the parties must apply for an order by consent.
    (b) The parties must file a draft of the order sought and an agreed statement of the reasons why the variation is sought.
    (c) The court may make an order in the agreed terms or in other terms without a hearing, but it may direct that a hearing is to be listed.

Failure to Comply with Case Management Directions

7.1 Where a party fails to comply with a direction given by the court any other party may apply for an order that he must do so or for a sanction to be imposed or both of these.

7.2 The party entitled to apply for such an order must do so without delay but should first warn the other party of his intention to do so.

7.3 The court may take any such delay into account when it decides whether to make an order imposing a sanction or to grant relief from a sanction imposed by the rules or any other practice direction.

7.4
(1) The court will not allow a failure to comply with directions to lead to the postponement of the trial unless the circumstances are exceptional.
(2) If it is practical to do so the court will exercise its powers in a manner that enables the case to come on for trial on the date or within the period previously set.
(3) In particular the court will assess what steps each party should take to prepare the case for trial, direct that those steps are taken in the shortest possible time and impose a sanction for non-compliance. Such a sanction may, for example, deprive a party of the right to raise or contest an issue or to rely on evidence to which the direction relates.
(4) Where it appears that one or more issues are or can be made ready for trial at the time fixed while others cannot, the court may direct that the trial will proceed on the issues which are then ready, and direct that no costs will be allowed for any later trial of the remaining issues or that those costs will be paid by the party in default.
(5) Where the court has no option but to postpone the trial it will do so for the shortest possible time and will give directions for the taking of the necessary steps in the meantime as rapidly as possible.
(6) Litigants and lawyers must be in no doubt that the court will regard the postponement of a trial as an order of last resort. Where it appears inevitable the court may exercise its power to require a party as well as his legal representative to attend court at the hearing where such an order is to be sought.
(7) The court will not postpone any other hearing without a very good reason, and for that purpose the failure of a party to comply on time with directions previously given will not be treated as a good reason.

Listing Questionnaires and Listing

8.1
(1) The listing questionnaire will be in Form N170.
(2) Unless it dispenses with listing questionnaires and orders an early trial on a fixed date, the court will specify the date for filing completed listing questionnaires when it fixes the trial date or trial period under rule 29.2(2).
(3) The date for filing the completed listing questionnaires will be not later than 8 weeks before the trial date or the start of the trial period.
(4) The court will serve the listing questionnaires on the parties at least 14 days before that date.
(5) Although the rules do not require the parties to exchange copies of the questionnaires before they are filed they are encouraged to do so to avoid the court being given conflicting or incomplete information.
(6) The file will be placed before a judge for his directions when all the questionnaires have been filed or when the time for filing them has expired.

8.2 The court's general approach will be as set out in the following paragraphs. The court may however decide to make other orders, and in particular the court will take into account the steps, if any, of which it is aware which the parties have taken to prepare the case for trial.

8.3
(1) Where no party files a listing questionnaire the court will normally make an order that if no listing questionnaire is filed by any party within 3 days from service of the order, the claim and any counterclaim will be struck out.
(2) Where a party files a listing questionnaire but another party (the defaulting party) does not do so, the court will fix a listing hearing. Whether or not the defaulting party attends the hearing, the court will normally fix or confirm the trial date and make other orders about the steps to be taken to prepare the case for trial.

8.4 Where the court decides to hold a listing hearing the court will fix a date which is as early as possible and the parties will be given at least 3 days notice of the date.

8.5 Where the court decides to hold a pre-trial review (whether or not this is in addition to a listing hearing) the court will give the parties at least 7 days notice of the date.

Directions the Court will give on Listing

9.1 Directions the court must give.
The court must fix the trial date or week, give a time estimate and fix the place.

9.2 Other directions
(1) The parties should seek to agree directions and may file an agreed order. The court may make an order in those terms or it may make a different order.
(2) Agreed directions should include provision about:
   (a) evidence especially expert evidence,
   (b) a trial timetable and time estimate,
   (c) the preparation of a trial bundle, and
   (d) any other matter needed to prepare the case for trial.
(3) The court will include such of these provisions as are appropriate in any order that it may make, whether or not the parties have filed agreed directions.
(4) Unless a direction doing so has been given before, a direction giving permission to use expert evidence will say whether it gives permission to use oral evidence or reports or both and will name the experts concerned.

9.3 The principles set out in paragraph 6 of this practice direction about variation of directions applies equally to directions given at this stage.

The Trial

10.1 The trial will normally take place at a Civil Trial Centre but it may be at another court if it is appropriate having regard to the needs of the parties and the availability of court resources.

10.2 The judge will generally have read the papers in the trial bundle and may dispense with an opening address.

10.3 The judge may confirm or vary any timetable given previously, or if none has been given set his own.

10.4 Attention is drawn to the provisions in Part 32 and the following parts of the Rules about evidence, and in particular:
(1) to rule 32.1 (court's power to control evidence and to restrict cross-examination), and
(2) to rule 32.5(2) statements and reports to stand as evidence in chief.

10.5 In an appropriate case the judge may summarily assess costs in accordance with rule 44.7. Attention is drawn to the practice directions about costs and the steps the parties are required to take.

10.6 Once the trial of a multi-track claim has begun, the judge will normally sit on consecutive court days until it has been concluded.

PART 35
EXPERTS AND ASSESSORS

Rule 35.1	Duty to restrict expert evidence	CPR 35.1
Rule 35.2	Interpretation	CPR 35.2
Rule 35.3	Experts – overriding duty to the court	CPR 35.3
Rule 35.4	Court's power to restrict expert evidence	CPR 35.4
Rule 35.5	General requirement for expert evidence to be given in written report	CPR 35.5
Rule 35.6	Written questions to experts	CPR 35.6
Rule 35.7	Court's power to direct that evidence is to be given by a single joint expert	CPR 35.7
Rule 35.8	Instructions to a single joint expert	CPR 35.8
Rule 35.9	Power of court to direct party to provide information	CPR 35.9
Rule 35.10	Contents of report	CPR 35.10
Rule 35.11	Use by one party of expert's report disclosed by another	CPR 35.11
Rule 35.12	Discussions between experts	CPR 35.12
Rule 35.13	Consequence of failure to disclose expert's report	CPR 35.13
Rule 35.14	Expert's right to ask to court for directions	CPR 35.14
Rule 35.15	Assessors	CPR 35.15
Practice Direction – 35 Experts and assessors		CPR PD 35

CPR 35.1

35.1 Duty to Restrict Expert Evidence
Expert evidence shall be restricted to that which is reasonably required to resolve the proceedings.

CPR 35.2

35.2 Interpretation
A reference to an 'expert' in this Part is a reference to an expert who has been instructed to give or prepare evidence for the purpose of court proceedings.

CPR 35.3

35.3 Experts – Overriding Duty to the Court
(1) It is the duty of an expert to help the court on the matters within his expertise.
(2) This duty overrides any obligation to the person from whom he has received instructions or by whom he is paid.

CPR 35.4

35.4 Court's Power to Restrict Expert Evidence
(1) No party may call an expert or put in evidence an expert's report without the court's permission.
(2) When a party applies for permission under this rule he must identify –
    (a) the field in which he wishes to rely on expert evidence; and
    (b) where practicable the expert in that field on whose evidence he wishes to rely.
(3) If permission is granted under this rule it shall be in relation only to the expert named or the field identified under paragraph (2).
(4) The court may limit the amount of the expert's fees and expenses that the party who wishes to rely on the expert may recover from any other party.

CPR 35.5

35.5 General Requirement for Expert Evidence to be Given in a Written Report
(1) Expert evidence is to be given in a written report unless the court directs otherwise.
(2) If a claim is on the fast track, the court will not direct an expert to attend a hearing unless it is necessary to do so in the interests of justice.

CPR 35.6

35.6 Written Questions to Experts
(1) A party may put to –
    (a) an expert instructed by another party; or
    (b) a single joint expert appointed under rule 35.7,
    written questions about his report.
(2) Written questions under paragraph (1) –
    (a) may be put once only;
    (b) must be put within 28 days of service of the expert's report; and
    (c) must be for the purpose only of clarification of the report;
    unless in any case,
        (i) the court gives permission; or
        (ii) the other party agrees.
(3) An expert's answers to questions put in accordance with paragraph (1) shall be treated as part of the expert's report.

(4) Where –
- (a) a party has put a written question to an expert instructed by another party in accordance with this rule; and
- (b) the expert does not answer that question,

the court may make one or both of the following orders in relation to the party who instructed the expert –
- (i) that the party may not rely on the evidence of that expert; or
- (ii) that the party may not recover the fees and expenses of that expert from any other party.

CPR 35.7

35.7 Court's Power to Direct that Evidence is to be Given by a Single Joint Expert
(1) Where two or more parties wish to submit expert evidence on a particular issue, the court may direct that the evidence on that issue is to given by one expert only.
(2) The parties wishing to submit the expert evidence are called 'the instructing parties'.
(3) Where the instructing parties cannot agree who should be the expert, the court may –
- (a) select the expert from a list prepared or identified by the instructing parties; or
- (b) direct that the expert be selected in such other manner as the court may direct.

CPR 35.8

35.8 Instructions to a Single Joint Expert
(1) Where the court gives a direction under rule 35.7 for a single joint expert to be used, each instructing party may give instructions to the expert.
(2) When an instructing party gives instructions to the expert he must, at the same time, send a copy of the instructions to the other instructing parties.
(3) The court may give directions about –
- (a) the payment of the expert's fees and expenses; and
- (b) any inspection, examination or experiments which the expert wishes to carry out.
(4) The court may, before an expert is instructed –
- (a) limit the amount that can be paid by way of fees and expenses to the expert; and
- (b) direct that the instructing parties pay that amount into court.
(5) Unless the court otherwise directs, the instructing parties are jointly and severally liable(GL) for the payment of the expert's fees and expenses.

CPR 35.9

35.9 Power of Court to Direct a Party to Provide Information
Where a party has access to information which is not reasonably available to the other party, the court may direct the party who has access to the information to –
- (a) prepare and file a document recording the information; and
- (b) serve a copy of that document on the other party.

CPR 35.10

35.10 Contents of Report
(1) An expert's report must comply with the requirements set out in the relevant practice direction.
(2) At the end of an expert's report there must be a statement that –
    (a) the expert understands his duty to the court; and
    (b) he has complied with that duty.
(3) The expert's report must state the substance of all material instructions, whether written or oral, on the basis of which the report was written.
(4) The instructions referred to in paragraph (3) shall not be privileged[GL] against disclosure but the court will not, in relation to those instructions –
    (a) order disclosure of any specific document; or
    (b) permit any questioning in court, other than by the party who instructed the expert,
unless it is satisfied that there are reasonable grounds to consider the statement of instructions given under paragraph (3) to be inaccurate or incomplete.

CPR 35.11

35.11 Use by One Party of Expert's Report Disclosed by Another
Where a party has disclosed an expert's report, any party may use that expert's report as evidence at the trial.

CPR 35.12

35.12 Discussions Between Experts
(1) The court may, at any stage, direct a discussion between experts for the purpose of requiring the experts to –
    (a) identify the issues in the proceedings; and
    (b) where possible, reach agreement on an issue.
(2) The court may specify the issues which the experts must discuss.
(3) The court may direct that following a discussion between the experts they must prepare a statement for the court showing –
    (a) those issues on which they agree; and
    (b) those issues on which they disagree and a summary of their reasons for disagreeing.
(4) The content of the discussion between the experts shall not be referred to at the trial unless the parties agree.
(5) Where experts reach agreement on an issue during their discussions, the agreement shall not bind the parties unless the parties expressly agree to be bound by the agreement.

CPR 35.13

35.13 Consequence of Failure to Disclose Expert's Report
A party who fails to disclose an expert's report may not use the report at the trial or call the expert to give evidence orally unless the court gives permission.

CPR 35.14

35.14 Expert's Right to Ask Court for Directions

(1) An expert may file a written request for directions to assist him in carrying out his function as an expert.
(2) An expert may request directions under paragraph (1) without giving notice to any party.
(3) The court, when it gives directions, may also direct that a party be served with –
 (a) a copy of the directions; and
 (b) a copy of the request for directions.

CPR 35.15

35.15 Assessors
(1) This rule applies where the court appoints one or more persons (an 'assessor') under section 70 of the Supreme Court Act 1981 or section 63 of the County Courts Act 1984.
(2) The assessor shall assist the court in dealing with a matter in which the assessor has skill and experience.
(3) An assessor shall take such part in the proceedings as the court may direct and in particular the court may –
 (a) direct the assessor to prepare a report for the court on any matter at issue in the proceedings; and
 (b) direct the assessor to attend the whole or any part of the trial to advise the court on any such matter.
(4) If the assessor prepares a report for the court before the trial has begun –
 (a) the court will send a copy to each of the parties; and
 (b) the parties may use it at trial.
(5) The remuneration to be paid to the assessor for his services shall be determined by the court and shall form part of the costs of the proceedings.
(6) The court may order any party to deposit in the court office a specified sum in respect of the assessor's fees and, where it does so, the assessor will not be asked to act until the sum has been deposited.
(7) Paragraphs (5) and (6) do not apply where the remuneration of the assessor is to be paid out of money provided by Parliament.

CPR PD 35 – PRACTICE DIRECTION – EXPERTS AND ASSESSORS

This Practice Direction Supplements CPR Part 35

Part 35 is intended to limit the use of oral expert evidence to that which is reasonably required. In addition, where possible, matters requiring expert evidence should be dealt with by a single expert. Permission of the court is always required either to call an expert or to put an expert's report in evidence.

Form and Content of Expert's Reports

1.1 An expert's report should be addressed to the court and not to the party from whom the expert has received his instructions.

1.2 An expert's report must:
(1) give details of the expert's qualifications,
(2) give details of any literature or other material which the expert has relied on

in making the report,

(3) say who carried out any test or experiment which the expert has used for the report and whether or not the test or experiment has been carried out under the expert's supervision,

(4) give the qualifications of the person who carried out any such test or experiment, and

(5) where there is a range of opinion on the matters dealt with in the report:
    (i) summarise the range of opinion, and
    (ii) give reasons for his own opinion,

(6) contain a summary of the conclusions reached,

(7) contain a statement that the expert understands his duty to the court and has complied with that duty (rule 35.10(2)), and

(8) contain a statement setting out the substance of all material instructions (whether written or oral). The statement should summarise the facts and instructions given to the expert which are material to the opinions expressed in the report or upon which those opinions are based (rule 35. 10(3)).

1.3 An expert's report must be verified by a statement of truth as well as containing the statements required in paragraph 1.2(7) and (8) above.

1.4 The form of the statement of truth is as follows:
'I believe that the facts I have stated in this report are true and that the opinions I have expressed are correct.'

1.5 Attention is drawn to rule 32.14 which sets out the consequences of verifying a document containing a false statement without an honest belief in its truth.

(For information about statements of truth see Part 22 and the practice direction which supplements it.)

1.6 In addition, an expert's report should comply with the requirements of any approved expert's protocol.

Information

2. Under Part 35.9 the court may direct a party with access to information which is not reasonably available to another party to serve on that other party a document which records the information. The document served must include sufficient details of all the facts, tests, experiments and assumptions which underlie any part of the information to enable the party on whom it is served to make, or to obtain, a proper interpretation of the information and its significance.

Instructions

3. The instructions referred to in paragraph 1.2(8) will not be protected by privilege (see rule 35.10(4)). But cross-examination of the expert on the contents of his instructions will not be allowed unless the court permits it (or unless the party who gave the instructions consents to it). Before it gives permission the court must be satisfied that there are reasonable

grounds to consider that the statement in the report of the substance of the instructions is inaccurate or incomplete. If the court is so satisfied, it will allow the cross-examination where it appears to be in the interests of justice to do so.

Questions to Report

4.1 Questions asked for the purpose of clarifying the expert's report (see rule 35.6) should be put, in writing, to the expert not later than 28 days after receipt of the expert's report (see paragraphs 1.2 to 1.5 above as to verification).

4.2 Where a party sends a written question or questions direct to an expert and the other party is represented by solicitors, a copy of the questions should, at the same time, be sent to those solicitors.

4.3 The party or parties instructing the expert must pay any fees charged by that expert for answering questions put under rule 35.6. This does not affect any decision of the court as to the party who is ultimately to bear the expert's costs.

Single Expert

5.   Where the court has directed that the evidence on a particular issue is to be given by one expert only (rule 35.7) but there are a number of disciplines relevant to that issue, a leading expert in the dominant discipline should be identified as the single expert. He should prepare the general part of the report and be responsible for annexing or incorporating the contents of any reports from experts in other disciplines.

Assessors

6.1 An assessor may be appointed to assist the court under rule 35.15. Not less than 21 days before making any such appointment, the court will notify each party in writing of the name of the proposed assessor, of the matter in respect of which the assistance of the assessor will be sought and of the qualifications of the assessor to give that assistance.

6.2 Where any person has been proposed for appointment as an assessor, objection to him, either personally or in respect of his qualification, may be taken by any party.

6.3 Any such objection must be made in writing and filed with the court within 7 days of receipt of the notification referred to in paragraph 6.1 and will be taken into account by the court in deciding whether or not to make the appointment (section 63(5) of the County Courts Act 1984).

6.4 Copies of any report prepared by the assessor will be sent to each of the parties but the assessor will not give oral evidence or be open to cross-examination or questioning.

CPR PD 40C – PRACTICE DIRECTION – STRUCTURED SETTLEMENTS

This Practice Direction Supplements CPR Part 40

Structured Settlements

1.1 A structured settlement is a means of paying a sum awarded to or accepted by a claimant by way of instalments for the remainder of the claimant's life. The payments are either funded by an annuity from an insurance company or, where the party paying is a government body, by payments direct from that body.

1.2 The agreed sum which purchases the annuity or provides for payments (including any sum to be retained as capital for contingencies) is based on the sum offered or awarded on a conventional basis, less an amount representing the tax benefits obtained by the structure.

1.3 This type of order may be used both on settlement of a claim and after trial where the judge has found in favour of the claimant. In the latter case the claimant or his legal representative should ask the judge:
(1) not to provide for entry of judgment,
(2) to state the total amount to which the judge has found the claimant to be entitled, and
(3) for an adjournment to enable advice to be sought as to the formulation of a structured settlement based on that amount.

1.4 Where a claim settles before trial, an application should be made in accordance with Part 23 for the consent order embodying the structured settlement to be made, and for the approval of the structured settlement where the claimant is a child or patient'.

1.5 If the claimant is not a child or patient, the consent order may be made without a hearing.

1.6 Where a hearing is required and as the annuity rate applicable to the structure may only remain available for a short time, the claimant's legal representative on issue of his application notice, should immediately seek an early date for the hearing.

1.7 At such a hearing the court will require the following documents and evidence to be filed not later than midday on the day before the hearing is to take place:
(1) Counsel's or the legal representative's opinion of the value of the claim on the basis of a conventional award (unless approval on that basis has already been given or the judge has stated the amount as in paragraph 1.3(2) above), For the definition of child or patient see Part 21,
(2) a report of forensic accountants setting out the effect of a structured settlement bearing in mind the claimant's life expectancy and the anticipated cost of future care,
(3) a draft of the proposed structure agreement,
(4) sufficient information to satisfy the court that –
    (a) enough of the agreed sum is retained as a contingency fund for anticipated future needs, and

(b) the structured settlement is secure and the annuities are payable by
    established insurers,

(5) details of any assets available to the claimant other than the agreed sum
    which is the subject of the application, and

(6) where the claimant is a patient, the approval or consent of the Court of
    Protection.

1.8 To obtain the approval of the Court of Protection the claimant's legal
    representative should lodge the documents and information set out in
    paragraph 1.7(1) to (5) above together with a copy of the claim form and
    any statements of case filed in the proceedings in the Enquiries and
    Acceptances Branch of the Public Trust Office, Stewart House, 24 Kingsway,
    London WC2B 6JH by midday on the fourth day before the hearing.

1.9 If an application for the appointment of a receiver by the Court of Protection
    has not already been made:

(1) two copies of the application seeking his appointment (form CP1),

(2) a certificate of family and property (form CP5), and

(3) a medical certificate (form CP3)
    should be lodged at the same time as the documents and information
    mentioned in paragraph 1.8 above. Forms CP1, 3 and 5 may be obtained
    from the address set out in paragraph 1.8.

1.10
    Wherever possible a draft order should also be filed at the same time as
    the documents in paragraph 1.7 above.

1.11
    Examples of structured settlement orders are set out in an Annex to this
    practice direction which may be adapted for use after trial or as the
    individual circumstances require. It should be noted that the reference in
    the second paragraph of the Part 2 – structured settlement order to the
    'defendant's Insurers' means the Life Insurer providing the annuity on
    behalf of the defendant.

1.12
    Where it is necessary to obtain immediate payment out of money in court
    on the order being made, the claimant's legal representatives should;

(1) contact the officer in charge of funds in court at the Court Funds Office at
    least 2 days before the hearing, and arrange for a cheque for the appropriate
    sum made payable to the insurers or government body to be ready for
    collection,

(2) notify the court office the day before the hearing so that the court is aware
    of the urgency, and

(3) bring to the hearing a completed Court Funds Office form 200 for
    authentication by the court upon the order being made.

ANNEX – PART 1 – STRUCTURED SETTLEMENT ORDER

(Order to settle for conventional sum and for an adjournment to seek advice on the formulation of a structured settlement).

Title of Claim

UPON HEARING (Counsel/solicitor) for the claimant and (Counsel/solicitor) for the defendant

AND UPON the defendant by (Counsel/solicitor) having undertaken to keep open an offer of £   in full and final settlement of the claim and the claimant having undertaken to limit the claim to £

AND UPON the claimant's solicitors undertaking to instruct appropriate advisers to advise upon a structured settlement and to use their best endeavours promptly to make proposals to the defendant's solicitors as to the most equitable formulation of a structured settlement and after to seek (further directions/approval) from the court if necessary

IT IS ORDERED that this claim is adjourned with permission to both parties to apply in respect of the further hearing relating to further directions providing for a structured settlement as undertaken by the claimant's solicitors and that these proceedings be reserved to the (trial judge) unless otherwise ordered

AND IT IS ORDERED that the costs of these proceedings together with the costs relating to any proposal for a structured settlement be (*as ordered*)

PART 2—STRUCTURED SETTLEMENT ORDER

(Order giving effect to and approval of a structured settlement)

Title of Claim

UPON HEARING Counsel/solicitors for the claimant and Counsel/solicitors for the defendant

AND the claimant and defendant having agreed to the terms set forth in the Schedule to this order in which the claimant accepts the sum of £   (*overall sum*) in satisfaction of the claim of which the sum of £   is to be used by the [defendant's insurers for the purchase of an annuity] [defendant for the provision of the appropriate payments]

AND UPON the Judge having approved the terms of the draft minute of order, the agreement and the schedule to this order

AND UPON the claimant and the insurer (*name*) undertaking to execute the agreement this day

BY CONSENT

IT IS ORDERED
(1) that of the sum of £00000000 (*total sum in* 0000000000 *court*) now in court standing to the credit of this claim the sum of £00000000 be paid out to (*insurers/payee*) on behalf of the defendant for the purchase of an annuity as specified in the payment schedule to this order
(2) (*other relevant orders*)
   (00) that all further proceedings in this claim be stayed except for the purpose of carrying the terms into effect
   (00) that the parties have permission to apply to carry the terms into effect –

SCHEDULE

(Attach draft agreement and set out any other terms of the settlement)

Appendix 6

Limitation

2001 R No. 847

IN THE HIGH COURT OF JUSTICE
QUEEN'S BENCH DIVISION
BARCHESTER DISTRICT REGISTRY

BETWEEN:

JOHN ROE Claimant
and
BARCHESTER HEALTH AUTHORITY Defendant

MODEL SKELETON ARGUMENT FOR CLAIMANT
LIMITATION ISSUE – DATE OF KNOWLEDGE
ATHETOID CEREBRAL PALSY

A6.1 Format for this Skeleton

The propositions of law and the framework of the argument are set out in the body of the Skeleton which is to be found in page 1-14 inclusive.

Scheduled off in pages A-P inclusive are the statutory provisions and those dicta from the cases which substantiate the propositions of law and arguments advanced.

The purpose of splitting this 'Skeleton' in that ways is to avoid cluttering the arguments which could have the effect of confusing rather than identifying issues.

A6.2 Factual Introduction

1. The claimant was the second of a twin birth, and was delivered 45 minutes after his brother.

2. The delay resulted in oxygen starvation to the brain with the consequence that the claimant suffers from 'athetoid cerebral palsy'; while his intellect is preserved, his musculature and its control are catastrophically damaged. He is wheelchair

bound and while able to articulate speech, his delivery is such that it is almost impossible to understand what he is saying without an interpreter.

3. His case is that by the age of 15 he actually knew that his brain had been damaged by oxygen starvation arising from a delay in delivery. His parents had told him so.

4. But he did not know that the delay in delivery was by reference to the act or omission alleged to constitute negligence, namely the omission on the part of the hospital to have an anaesthetist standing ready at the time of the delivery of the first twin, thus able immediately to intervene to facilitate speedy delivery of the second twin.

5. The fact that the absence of an anaesthetist until it was too late was the problem is averred by the claimant and acknowledged by the defendant's expert: see report of Dr Marie Antoinette, exhibit WJ 1 to the affidavit of defence witness William Jones.

6. The claimant will contend that he did not have actual knowledge until receipt of the expert obstetric evidence.

7. In the alternative, he will aver that it is proper for the court to disapply the time bar, given the balance of fairness and prejudice between the parties.

A6.3   Representation

1. Claimant:
   (a) Leading Counsel: F E Smith QC
   (b) Junior Counsel: Patrick Hastings

2. Defendant:
   (a) Leading Counsel: Marshall Hall QC
   (b) Junior Counsel: Thomas Erskine.

A6.4   Dramatis Personae – Witnesses

1. The following will give evidence from the witness box:
   (a) The claimant (who will speak through an interpreter, one of his carers). Speaking appears to cause him very considerable suffering. He instructs, however, that notwithstanding appearances, speaking does not cause him pain.
   (b) The claimant's parents: Mr and Mrs Roe.

2. The claimant will rely on the following expert evidence by reference to their reports:
   (a) Liability – obstetric:
      (i) Professor Kielands
      (ii) Professor Ventouse
   (b) Causation – neonatology: Professor Apgar.

A6.5   Chronology

- 26 March 1975: Birth
- 1990: Claimant aged 15 years. Told [along the lines of] 'your arrival was delayed

and you suffered from a lack of oxygen: see paragraph 7(a) of claimant's affidavit.

- August 1994: Claimant took up residence at Trafalger House in Waterloo, a home for the disabled. (Prior to this the claimant had been cared for in residential schools).
- Late 1999/early 2000: Claimant first began to question whether what had happened to him at birth could have been avoided.
- 3 April 2000: Claimant's father met with solicitor from Donoghue, Stevenson & Co – the claimant's present solicitor.
- 12 April 2000: Claimant confirmed his instructions to his solicitors (Coward Turner and Co) to proceed with his potential claim.
- 31 September 2000: Legal aid granted to claimant.
- 30 November 2000: Medical case notes disclosed by the Royal Bracton General Hospital.
- 28 March 2001: Report received from obstetric expert.
- 25 May 2001: Report received from neonatal expert.
- 5 October 2001: Writ issued.

A6.6　Statutory Provisions

The relevant provisions of the Limitation Act 1980 are:

    (a) s 11 (provisions as to the primary limitation period of three years);
    (b) s 14 (provisions as to actual and constructive knowledge); and
    (c) s 33 (the discretion to disapply the time bar).

These provisions are set out in Schedule to this Skeleton.

Reference will also be made to s 14A of the Act.

A6.7　The Legal Principles relating to 'Date of Knowledge' (actual and constructive) and 'Disapplying' the Time Bar

The following is a summary of the relevant principles:

A. *Actual Knowledge:*

    (a) The test is subjective, that is, the actual knowledge of this claimant.
    (b) The knowledge has to be of 'the act or omission alleged to constitute negligence', that is, it is not enough that the claimant knows that the damage was attributable to an act or omission of the defendant. The omission of which the claimant must have knowledge must be that which is casually relevant for the purposes of an allegation of negligence: *Hallam-Eames v Merrett Syndicates Ltd* [1995] 7 Med LR 122.
    (c) It 'is impossible to identify an omission except by reference to an act which could have been done ... the claimant's injury cannot be said to be attributable to any omission by the defendant unless the defendant could have acted to prevent it ...' see Evans LJ in *Forbes v Wandsworth Health Authority* [1997] QB 402 at 420G-H [1996] 3 WLR 1108 at 1123H-1124A.
    (d) The burden of proof is on the claimant.
    (e) Primary cases on the interpretation of s 14 are: *Spargo v North Essex District Health Authority* [1997] 8 Med LR 125 and *Kyriacou v Camden and Islington*

Health Authority [1997] unreported per Sedley J [Lexis Transcript] and *Smith v Leicestershire* [1998] Lloyd's Rep Med 77.

B. *Constructive Knowledge*

(a) Rationale for the 'constructive knowledge' provisions: Per Colman J in *Parry v Clwyd Health Authority* [1997] PIQR P4:

> '... The function of that sub-section is to prevent the [Plaintiff] from remaining inactive in circumstances where, although he does not have actual knowledge of the facts which show that his injury is, as a matter of a real, as distinct from a fanciful, possibility, capable of being attributable to the act or omission of the defendant, he might reasonably be expected to acquire such actual knowledge from ...'

(b) Objective Test: The rationale is explained by Evans LJ in *Forbes v Wandsworth Health Authority* per Evans LJ [1997] QB 402 at 420G-H, [1996] 3 WLR p 1108 at 1125G:

> 'Since there is a wide discretionary power to extend the period in circumstances which Parliament has defined in s 33, there is no clear requirement to construe the knowledge provisions in s 14 narrowly or in favour of individual [Plaintiffs]. I therefore consider that they should be interpreted neutrally so that in respect of constructive knowledge under s 14(3) an objective standard applies.'

(c) What is to be disregarded when applying the objective test? The claimant's individual characteristics which might distinguish him from the reasonable man are to be disregarded: *Smith v Leicestershire Health Authority* [1998] Lloyd's Rep Med 77 at 86 (a case of tetraplegia):

> '... the [Plaintiff's] individual characteristics which might distinguish her from the reasonable woman should be disregarded. Thus her fortitude, her lack of bitterness at becoming tetraplegic and the determination and devotion she has shown to making herself as independent and useful a member of her family and society as she can which have surpassed what might be expected, are to be put on the side.'

(d) What is to be taken into account when applying the objective test? The following characteristics can properly be taken into account vis-à-vis this claimant, John Roe:

> • He has been at all material times in a wheelchair.
> • He has been without means of his own.
> • He was, and is virtually unable to communicate. The grounds for that submission are the following dicta on page 88 (second column, third down) of *Smith*:

> 'In our judgment it would be quite unrealistic to expect a reasonable person in the [Plaintiff's] situation, that is to say in a wheelchair with no means of his own ...'

That submission is supported by the following dicta of Evans LJ in *Forbes v*

Wandsworth Health Authority at [1997] QB 402 at 423A-C, [1996] 3 WLR 1108 at 1126A-C:

'This leads to the disquiet expressed by Stuart-Smith and Roch LJJ as to the statement in the judgment of this court in *Nash v Eli Lilly & Co* [1993] 1 WLR 782, 799: "In considering whether or not the inquiry is or is not, reasonable, the situation, character and intelligence of the [Plaintiff] must be relevant."

As to the situation, there is no difficulty. The reasonable man must be placed in the situation that the [plaintiff] was. The references to character and intelligence, however, suggest that regard should be had to personal characteristics of the [plaintiff], and this I find difficult to square with the application of an objective and, therefore, equal standard.'

And also in *Forbes* Stuart-Smith LJ adopted the same approach [1997] QB 402 at 413E-F; [1996] 3 WLR 1108 at 117B-C:

'In my judgment, a reasonable man in the position of the deceased ...'

(e) Burden of proving the date when the claimant had constructive knowledge. On the defendant, see *Forbes* [1997] QB 402 at 419E, [1996] 3 WLR 1108 at page 1122F-G; per Evans LJ.

C. *The Discretion to Disapply the Time Bar – Legal Principles*

(a) The burden of proof: On the claimant.
(b) This issue is: Balancing the prejudice to each party and in all the circumstances, can the claimant prove that it is equitable to disapply the time bar?
(c) Criteria to assist the court in relation to that issue: Set out in ss 33(3)a-(3)(g). These statutory criteria are not exclusive. The court must have regard to all the circumstances of the case: *Taylor v Taylor* (1984) Times, 14 April, CA.
(d) Discretion – unfettered: The court has an unfettered discretion to disapply the three-year time bar: *Conry v Simpson* [1983] 3 All ER 369, *Nash v Eli Lilly and Co* [1993] 1 WLR 782 at (802F-G).

D. *Issues for Adjudication*

1. As to 'Knowledge'.

(a) Did the claimant's date of knowledge occur more or less than three years prior to the issue of the writ?
(b) What is the 'act or omission' alleged to constitute negligence; relevant case law is cited in Schedule 2.
(c) When was there 'actual knowledge' of that act or omission alleged to constitute negligence?
(d) With what constructive knowledge is the claimant fixed? Is the test that of the reasonable man, or the reasonable man who is suffering from catastrophic athetoid cerebral palsy?
(e) Is the 'knowledge' that of the parents, or that of the son? And is there in fact a difference in this case in the respective states of knowledge of the parents and the son? Relevant case law is cited in Schedule 4.

(2) As to 'discretion to disapply the time bar.' If (which is denied) knowledge was or ought to have been acquired more than three years before the date of the writ, the claimant will contend that the balance of equity/justice is in his favour, and that the court should exercise its powers under s 33 of the Limitation Act 1980 by ordering that the provisions of s 11 should not apply to this claim.

E. *Matters which are not in Issue*

The fact that the injury was 'significant' is not in issue. The claimant adopts the following dicta of Colman J in *Parry v Clwyd Health Authority* [1997] PIQR at 4:

> 'Of those matters which are material for the purposes of s 14 of the 1980 Act, there is no issue but that the [plaintiff] did have knowledge that her injury was significant and that, if anybody was responsible for it, it was the defendant.'

A6.8 Claimant's Legal Submissions on the Issue of 'Date of Knowledge'

A. *Actual Knowledge*

The claimant's primary submissions vis-à-vis date of 'actual' knowledge:

(a) The negligence in the instant case is an 'act of omission'.

(b) Where an 'omission' is relied on as the basis of the alleged negligence, the claimant must know the facts constituting the omission, that is to say the claimant must know what was not done which it is said ought to have been done: see Colman J in *Parry* at 4.

(c) Knowledge of an 'omission' is not sufficient, unless such 'omission' is the omission 'alleged to constitute negligence.'

(d) In the instant case, the 'omission alleged to constitute negligence' is the lost opportunity to deliver within 20 minutes of his older twin, because an anaesthetist was not present for the twin delivery; see dicta of Evans LJ in *Forbes* [ibid] [1997] QB at 420H-421A.

(e) The claimant only had actual knowledge of that act or omission when he received the obstetric report in or about early March 2000 (the affidavit of the claimant's solicitor, Coward Turner, deposes that a preliminary report was received from the obstetric expert on 27 February 2000). The Court of Appeal authority closest in relevance is, it is submitted, *Smith v Leicestershire Health Authority* [1998] Lloyd's Rep Med 77.

(f) In contrast with the instant case, in the case of *Forbes v Wandsworth* [1997] QB 402, [1996] 3 WLR 1108, the 'delay' in carrying out the second operation was the only allegation of negligence which could be made.

(g) Submission: The delay in delivery [of which the client did know, see his affidavit at para 7(a)] is not 'knowledge'. There had to have been knowledge that the relevant delay was over 20 minutes and was the result of an anaesthetist not being present for the twin delivery.

B. *Constructive Knowledge*

By reference to the dicta of Colman J at 14 in *Parry* the claimant did not have constructive knowledge prior to the period of three years culminating in the issue of the writ:

'... There is no evidence that ordinary woman of moderate intelligence and of no more than average understanding and sophistication, even if sufferers from cerebral palsy, could reasonably have been expected to infer from those facts known to the [plaintiff] that there was a real possibility that an act or omission of the defendants' medical staff had caused her injury.'

See for further argument, Schedule 3.

A6.9 Submissions on the Discretion to Disapply the Time Bar

The provisions of s 33 are set out in Schedule 5, together with dicta from the cases supporting the arguments set out below:

1. *The Length of and Reasons for the Delay*
The explanation is set out above. There is no suggestion that the claimant wilfully delayed: see *Common v Croft* [1980] LS Gaz Rep 358 which is authority for the proposition that delay in this context means 'unlawful, culpable delay and not that delay which was lawful and permitted by the Limitation Act and the Rules of the Supreme Court, per Stephenson LJ. Reference can also be made to *Thompson v Brown Construction (Ebbw Vale) Ltd* [1981] 1 WLR 744 at 751 HL, which is authority for the proposition that the delay is that delay arising after the primary limitation period has expired (which in the instant case would be after the 21st birthday in 1991).

2. *The Extent to Which the Evidence is Likely to be Less Cogent*
There is no real prejudice here: see the cases in Schedule 5. Further, had the claimant's brain damage been diffuse rather than just to the basal ganglia, he would have been able to bring proceedings at any time throughout his life, s 28 of the Limitation Act 1980.

3. *The Conduct of the Defendant*
Not an issue.

4. *The Duration of any Disability*
To his 21st birthday in 1996.

5. *The Extent to Which the Claimant Acted Promptly*
There is no suggestion of delay after the claimant had decided to have investigations made.

6. *The Steps to Take Advice*
There is no suggestion of dilatoriness.

7. *Other Matters*
(a) Other defendants? No – there is no other potential defendant.
(b) Size of claim: The impact of losing must be much greater vis-à-vis the defendant.
(c) Prospects of success: See dicta of Dillon LJ in *Dale v British Coal Corpn* [1993] 1 All ER 317. It is submitted that here the prospects of success are substantial. This is dealt with separately, immediately below.

A6.10   Prospects of Success

1. The Pleadings
(a) Paragraphs 3(b) and 3(c)(i) of the Amended Statement of Claim set out the essence of the claimant's case on negligence.
(b) Paragraph 3 of the defence sets out the following defence to this issue – namely the hospital did not have its own anaesthetic team in full attendance.

2. There is No Dispute About the Significance of the Absence of an Anaesthetist
The defence expert Dr Antoinette says (in page 2 of her report exhibited as WJ 1 to the affidavit of Mr William Jones):

> 'It is claimed that there was a failure to appreciate the need urgently to delivery the baby. In fact, such delay as there was would be accounted for by the need to summon the anaesthetist, because delivery was not possible without general anaesthetic.'

3. Evidence of the Claimant's Expert Evidence
The clear and unequivocal expert evidence of the claimant is that it was negligent for there not to be an anaesthetist in attendance. See Exhibit JR2 to the claimant's affidavit, namely a report from obstetrician Professor Kiellands, at 6:

> 'If Mrs Roe's recollection is correct and the delay was caused in part at least because an anaesthetist had to come from another hospital to administer a general anaesthetic for the delivery of the second baby, this was inexcusable ...
>
> ... In any event, the delivery of twins should not have been started without an anaesthetist being immediately at hand, still less an operative delivery ...'

And continuing at the bottom of page 8:

> 'The mechanism of the distress is not of importance. It should have been detected and the delivery expedited before damage was done. This would have been possible if an anaesthetist had been present and ready to administer a general anaesthetic as soon as the need became clear ...'

And continuing on page 9:

> 'An anaesthetist and a paediatrician should have been called before the delivery of John simply because this was a twin delivery but given the fact that there had been such a prolonged second stage, that an oxytocin infusion was necessary to enhance uterine activity after the delivery of twin 1 and that an operative delivery was to be undertaken, the need for the presence of these additional doctors was even greater. Knowing that there was no anaesthetist on the premises made it foolhardy in the extreme to proceed without have secured his attendance.'

4. Exhibit CT 2 to the Affidavit of Clifford Turner (Claimant Solicitor)
This is a supplemental report from the claimant's second obstetric expert, Professor Apgar. In para 4 he inter alia quotes from 'Practical Obstetric Problems' page 252.

'... An anaesthetist should always be present throughout the second and third stage of all variable twin deliveries, prepared to induce an anaesthetic at a moment's notice ...'

Professor Apgar continues in para 5:

'... There is a much higher possibility of operative intervention being required for twin 2.'

5. *The Significance of the Second Stage of Labour*

Full dilatation of the cervix marks the commencement of what is called 'the second stage of labour' and it is this stage which ushers in delivery. The defendant had ample time to call an anaesthetist: See exhibit JR 2 (see above). On page 4 Professor Kiellands records:

'The second stage of labour was allowed to go on for 4 hours and 30 minutes.'

In the same context, Professor Kiellands says at page 6 of his report:

'When there had been no progress for an hour, the midwife should have called for medical assistance and preparations made for delivery. This should have included the calling of an anaesthetist.'

FE Smith QC
Birkenhead Chambers
Atlantic Wharf
Liverpool

Patrick Hastings
Equity Court
Temple
London EC4

1998 R No. 847

IN THE HIGH COURT OF JUSTICE
QUEEN'S BENCH DIVISION
BARCHESTER DISTRICT REGISTRY

BETWEEN;

JOHN ROE Claimant

and

BARCHESTER HEALTH AUTHORITY Defendant

Claimant SKELETON ARGUMENT ON LIMITATION HEARING

Coward Turner and Co
Tower of London (River Entrance)
London EC2

SCHEDULE 1

A6.11   THE STATUTORY PROVISIONS

1. *Section 11(4)*

'... the period applicable is three years from:
(a) the date on which the cause of action accrued; or
(b) the date of knowledge (if later) of the person injured.'

2. *Section 14*

(1) In ss 11 and 12 of this Act references to a person's date of knowledge are references to the date on which he first had knowledge of the following facts:

(a) that the injury in question was significant;
(b) that the injury was attributable in whole or in part to the act or omission which is alleged to constitute negligence, nuisance or breach of duty;
(c) the identity of the defendant;
(d) if it is alleged that the act or omission was that of a person other than the defendant, the identity of that person and the additional fact supporting the bringing of an action against the defendant, and knowledge that any acts or omissions did or did not, as a matter of law, involve negligence, nuisance or breach of duty is irrelevant.

(2) For the purposes of this section an injury is significant if the person whose date of knowledge is in question would reasonably have considered it sufficiently serious to justify his instituting proceedings for damages against a defendant

who did not dispute liability and was able to satisfy a judgment.

(3) For the purposes of this section a person's knowledge includes knowledge which he might reasonably have been expected to acquire:

(a) from facts observable or ascertainable by him;
(b) from facts ascertainable by him with the help of medical or other appropriate expert advice which it is reasonable for him to seek; but a person shall not be fixed under this subsection with knowledge of a fact ascertainable only with the help of expert advice so long as he has taken all reasonable steps to obtain (and, where appropriate, to act on) that advice.'

SCHEDULE 2

A6.12   CASE LAW RELATING TO 'DATE OF KNOWLEDGE'

Citations from the Relevant Authorities

A. *Spargo v North Essex District Health Authority* [1997] 8 Med LR 125. This case is the 'locus classicus' on 'date of knowledge'. Per Brooke LJ at page 129, towards the bottom of column 2:

'This branch of the law is already so grossly overloaded with reported cases, a great many of which have been shown to us or cited by counsel, that I can see no reason to add to the overload by citation from other decisions. I have considered the judgments of this court in *Halford v Brooks* [1991] 1 WLR 443; Nash v Eli Lilley & Co [1993] 1 WLR 782; *Broadley v Guy Clapham* [1993] 4 All ER 439; *Dobbie v Medway Health Authority* [1994] 1 WLR 1234; *Smith v Lancashire Health Authority* [1995] PIQR 514; and *Forbes v Wandsworth Health Authority* [1996] 7 Med LR 175. From these decisions the following principles are drawn:

(1) The knowledge required to satisfy s 14(1)(b) is a broad knowledge of the essence of the causally relevant act or omission to which the injury is attributable.
(2) 'Attributable' in this context means 'capable of being attributed to', in the sense of being a real possibility.
(3) A [Plaintiff] has the requisite knowledge when she knows enough to make it reasonable for her to begin to investigate whether or not she has a case against the defendant. Another way of putting this is to say that she will have such knowledge if she so firmly believes that her condition is capable of being attributed to an act or omission which she can identify (in broad terms) that she goes to a solicitor to seek advice about making a claim for compensation.
(4) On the other hand, she will not have the requisite knowledge if she thinks she knows the acts or omissions she should investigate but in fact is barking up the wrong tree; or if her knowledge of what the defendant did or did not do is so vague or general that she cannot fairly be expected to know what she should investigate; or if her state of mind is such that she thinks her condition is capable of being attributed to the act or omission alleged to constitute negligence, but she is not sure about this, and would need

to check with an expert before she could be properly said to know that it was.'

B. *Forbes v Wandsworth Health Authority* [1997] QB 402 at 420F-421A; [1996] 7 Med LR 175 – dealing with 'knowledge' in the context of an 'omission' per Evans LJ:

'... in my judgment it is impossible to identify an omission except by reference to an act which could have been done. It would be wrong and contrary to section 14 to say "should have been done" or "ought to have been done", but the fact that nothing was done does not constitute an "omission" in my view, unless something could have been done, regardless of whether it ought to have been done or not. Certainly the [plaintiff's] injury cannot be said to be attributable to any omission by the defendant unless the defendant could have acted to prevent it.

'Of what fact therefore was the decreased ignorant until he received medical advice which led him to bringing these proceedings for negligence in 1992? I would say that he did not know until then, that there was, as is now alleged, a lost opportunity to prevent the injury which he later suffered. That is a question of medical science of which he was unaware. It is a different question depending on medical practice whether the operation should have been carried out sooner than it was. That is the question whether the omission was negligent, which is not relevant under section 14(1).'

Vis-à-vis the instant case, the submission evolves (transposing the dicta of Evans LJ in the last paragraph cited above).

'Of what fact, therefore, was Mr Roe ignorant until he received the medical advice which led to him bringing these proceedings for negligence in 1995. I would say that he did not know until then, that there was, as is now alleged, a lost opportunity to prevent the injury which he later suffered. That is a question of medical science of which he was unaware ...'

C. *Kyriacou v Camden and Islington Health Authority* 13 October 1997 – Lexis: Inguinal hernia repair – cut of the urinary bladder. This case demonstrates on its facts the degree of 'knowledge' that is required before there is 'knowledge of the act or omission alleged to constitute negligence' Per Sedley J in *Dobbie v Medway Health Authority* [1994] 4 All ER 450, the Master of the Rolls quoted with approval the words which Hoffman LJ had used in *Broadley* when he had rejected the submission that the claimant must know that the defendants' act or omission was capable of being attributed to some fault on his part and he had said:

'I think counsel was right when he said that the words "which is alleged to constitute negligence, nuisance of breach of duty" serve to identify the facts of which the [Plaintiff] must have knowledge without implying that he should know that they constitute a breach of a rule whether of law or some other code of behaviour. Section 14(1)(b) requires that one should look at the way the [Plaintiff] puts his case, distil what he is complaining about and ask whether he had, in broad terms, knowledge of the facts on which the complaint if made.'

But more recently, those earlier cases were considered in *Hallam-Eames v Merrett Syndicates Ltd* (1995) Times 25 January 1995. That, of course, was not a medical negligence case but a case involving constructive knowledge on the part of names at Lloyds. But in the course of giving judgment, Hoffman LJ considered the most recent decisions of the Court of Appeal on s 14(1)(b) of the Limitation Act and in particular the authorities of *Broadly* and *Dobbie* to which I have just referred. What he said in relation to those cases is this:

> 'If all that was necessary was that the [Plaintiff] should have known that the damage was attributable to an act or omission of the defendant that statute would have said so, instead it speaks of the damage being attributable to "the act or omission which is alleged to constitute negligence". In other words the act or omission of which the [Plaintiff] must have knowledge must be that which is causally relevant for the purposes of an allegation of negligence.'

> In considering these authorities it seemed to me to be significant that the act or omission to which the [Plaintiff's] significant injury is attributable has in all the cases been something other than simply the carrying out of an operation.

> On the facts of this case the connection between the pain being suffered in the groin and the puncturing of the bladder is not an attribution readily occurring to a layman. Indeed the defendants' experts deny that it is capable of such an attribution. In my judgment therefore, what the [Plaintiff] has to know before time begins to run against him is that the injury which he now suffers, namely the pain in the groin, the paraesthesia over the scar area and the limp are all attributable to the incision made in the bladder at the operation on 30 March 1992.'

Submission
Adopting this framework of words and adapting them to the instant case the argument runs:

> 'On the facts of this case the connection between the delay and oxygen starvation at birth because of there not being an anaesthetist present for the twin birth is not an attribution readily occurring to a layman ... In my judgment therefore, what the [Plaintiff] has to know before time begins to run against him is that the injury, which he now suffers, namely the brain damage, is attributable to an omission to have present an anaesthetist in time for the twin birth thereby to have enabled the [Plaintiff] to have been delivered within 20 minutes of his older twin.'

D. *Anderson v Associated Co-operative Creameries Ltd* (15 December 1997, unreported) CA. By reference to the actual facts of this case, it is instructive as to how much knowledge is required before the statutory threshold of 'date of knowledge' is reached.

> 'Mr Hare contends that the [Plaintiff] here had knowledge of the attributability of his back problem to the system of work about which he now complains at the very latest when he was told by the chiropractor early in 1993 that his back problem might have been caused by his work. That, he submits, indicated a "real possibility" that the condition was capable of being attributed to work. Indeed, his submissions go further still, because his first line of contention is that this [Plaintiff] ought really to be taken as having appreciated the link at the very moment when he suffered the first acute incident in May 1992, given his presently pleased

case that it was obvious that the system of work exposed him to the hazard of back injury. For my part, however, I reject both that more extreme submission and the narrower one dependent upon the later remark by the chiropractor.

'It seems to me strongly arguable indeed that it was not in fact until a medical report was prepared upon the [Plaintiff] on 1 February 1994 that he had the required knowledge. After all, it was not until then that medical evidence existed that: "It is possible that continuing lifting and turning with rotation of the lumbar spine could exacerbate this [degeneration in his intervertebral disc] but the disc itself would have to be abnormal prior to this to allow a prolapse to occur.

'Be that as it may, I cannot regard the chance remark made by a chiropractor, put in the loosest and most general terms, as sufficient to impute to the [Plaintiff] the requisite knowledge for s 14(1)(b) purposes. At the very least his state of mind seems to me to have been akin rather to that described in the concluding lines of Brooke LF's formulation in Spargo. Certainly I do not find the evidence in this case such as to compel a different factual conclusion from that reached by the judge below. He, after all, had the benefit of hearing oral evidence on the point.'

E. *O'Driscoll v Dudley Health Authority [1998] 30 April CA.*
This case is fundamentally different from the instant case. In this case, the claimant was born with cerebral palsy in 1970 and he was held to be statute barred after launching proceedings in May 1994. It is clearly distinguishable from the instant case, on its facts: see the head-note in the Lexis report which explains that the claimant know of the ability to make a claim at the age of 15 and deliberately did not:

'In about 1985 when the [Plaintiff] was 15 years old, the family read a newspaper and saw a television programme concerning the case of a brain damaged child whose family were claiming compensation from the Health Authority. The judge accepted that this programme led them to believe that the reason for Rosanna's condition might be some fault or failure in management at birth. There was a family discussion about a possible claim between the father, mother, Mrs O'Driscoll's mother and sister-in-law in which the [Plaintiff] was also involved. The decision was taken which (it was to transpire) determined the fate of the subsequent litigation. It was decided that when the [Plaintiff] became an adult at the age of 21 years they would write to the Health Authority making a claim. Thus the child, having become an adult, could bring this claim in her own right. Until then they would do nothing. The child was so informed and agreed. Thus the child, having become an adult, could bring this claim in her own right. The father said in evidence (and the judge accepted) that this decision was taken because he believed that she would become an adult on her 21st birthday, and accordingly no advice, either medical or legal during the six years that passed before Rosanna's 21st birthday, was sought.'

The position becomes clearer again when reference is made to the dicta of Slade LJ. He inter alia said at page 13 of the Lexis Transcript:

'The "act" or "omission" which is alleged to constitute negligence in the present case is the defendant's failure to deliver the [Plaintiff] by timeous Caesarean section as soon as a diagnosis of cord prolapse was made.

'The word "attributable" in section 14(1)(b) does not mean "caused by". It merely means "capable of being attributed": see *Dobbie v Medway Health Authority* [1994] 1 WLR 1234.

'The issue relating to actual knowledge in the present case thus resolves itself to the question: When did the [Plaintiff] first know that her brain damage was capable of being attributed to the defendant's failure to deliver her by timeous Caesarean section?'

Submission (1)

Adapting those dicta to the instant case, the issue as to 'actual knowledge' becomes:

'When did Mr Roe first know that his brain damage was capable of being attributed to the defendant's failure to have present in time for the twin delivery an anaesthetist thereby to enable him to be delivered within 20 minutes of his older twin?'

Submission (2)

Simon Brown LJ in *O'Driscoll* inter alia adapted the dicta of Brooke LJ in *Spargo* saying at page 15 of the Lexis transcript:

'Applying the second of the Spargo principles usefully drawn by Brooke LJ from earlier authorities – see *North Essex District Health Authority v Spargo* [1997] 8 Med LR – the question can be reformulated thus: When did the [Plaintiff] first know that there was a real possibility that her injury was a result of a failure to deliver her by Caesarean section.'

Adapting those dicta to the instant case:

'When did Mr Roe first know that there was a real possibility that his injury was a result of a failure to have the anaesthetist present for the twin birth thereby to enable him to be delivered within 20 minutes of his older twin?'

SCHEDULE 3

A6.13 SUBMISSIONS RELATING TO 'CONSTRUCTIVE KNOWLEDGE'

Submission

The 'constructive date of knowledge was within 3 years of issue of the writ'. That submission is advanced by adapting the material dicta of Roch in LJ in *Smith v Leicestershire Health Authority* [1998] Lloyd's Rep Med 77 to the instant case:

'... [page 86, towards top of second column] What was the [Plaintiff's] situation in 1969 when he suffered brain damage? He had just been born. He lived, when not in hospital, with his parents. He was told and accepted that the oxygen starvation which had rendered him brain damaged was the result of a delay in his being born. That is what his parents were told and what he and his parents believed. Until 1993 at no time did it ever occur to him that the treatment his mother had

had at the ... hospital had played any part in his becoming brain damaged or that the doctors at the hospital might have delivered the mother differently from the way they did in fact deliver her.

'... [page 86, second column] Would these things have occurred to a reasonable man in the [Plaintiff's] position? We do not believe that the defendants can establish or that the defendants did establish that these matters would have occurred to a reasonable person or that a reasonable person would have sought medical expert advice ...

'... [page 87, first column] What the [Plaintiff] has to know in cases of omission such as the present is, as Evans LJ pointed out in Forbes sup at page 420G, that there was a lost opportunity to prevent the injury, his brain damage. That knowledge could only be gained by the [Plaintiff] seeking expert medical advice ...

'If the decision in Forbes is being read as saying that every time a patient has an operation and, following the operation, is significantly disabled, the patient has some 12 to 18 months to decide consciously or unconsciously whether to investigate a possible claim against those who operated, then in our view the decision in Forbes is being misinterpreted and misapplied ...'

2. That submission is supported by the following dicta of Colman J in *Parry v Clywd Health Authority* [1997] PIQR at page 14:

'The burden of proof of constructive knowledge is on the defendant. There is no evidence that ordinary women of moderate intelligence and of no more than average understanding and sophistication, even if sufferers from cerebral palsy, could reasonably have been expected to infer from those facts known to the [Plaintiff] that there was a real possibility that an act or omission of the defendants' medical staff had caused her injury. As I have already found, the evident suggests that people would not generally have considered that those facts known to the [Plaintiff] pointed to that possibility. If average people would not have had that perception, it is impossible to see why they should reasonably be expected either to acquire additional information or to consult medical or other expert advice in order to acquire such information.

'On the whole of the evidence, it is not established that even those of average moderate intelligence and understanding, suffering from cerebral palsy, would, prior to the end of 1989, have connected their condition with mismanagement of delivery, even as a possibility worth investigating. The [Plaintiff] and her mother were not, in my judgment, excessively unquestioning or outside the range of moderate intelligence and medical understanding of the reasonable, average, relatively unsophisticated person. Their failure to appreciate the possible medical significance of the facts known to them was therefore not unreasonable. Nor, therefore, was the [Plaintiff's] failure to institute further investigations earlier than she did.'

SCHEDULE 4

A6.14 IS THE KNOWLEDGE OF THE PARENTS ATTRIBUTED TO THE SON?

A. Per Colman J in *Parry v Clywd Health Authority* [1997] PIQR at page 13:

> 'It was argued that before the time when the [Plaintiff] reached majority the court must have regard to the actual or constructive knowledge of the parent and not to that of the child. I reject that construction of sections 11 and 14. The words very clearly indicate that one looks exclusively to the knowledge of the [Plaintiff]. The fact that under section 28 a person's majority can be a starting point for the running of time under the 1980 Act shows that the policy of the Act is not to introduce the imputation of knowledge from parent to child.'

SCHEDULE 5

A6.15 THE DISCRETION TO DISAPPLY UNDER SECTION 33

Section 33(1) of the Limitation Act 1980:

> 'If it appears to the court that it would be equitable to allow an action to proceed having regard to the degree to which:
>
> (a) the provisions of ss 11 ... or 12 of this Act prejudice the claimant or any other person whom he represents; and
> (b) any decision of the court under this subsection would prejudice the defendant or any person whom he represents:
>
> the court may direct that those provisions shall not apply to the action, or shall not apply to any specified cause of action to which the action relates.'

Section 33(3) provides:

> 'In acting under this section the court shall have regard to all the circumstances of the case and in particular to:
>
> (a) the length of, and the reasons for, the delay on the part of the claimant;
> (b) the extent to which, having regard to the delay, the evidence adduced or likely to be adduced by the claimant or the defendant is or is likely to be less cogent than if the action had been brought within the time allowed by section 1 ...
> (c) the conduct of the defendant after the cause of action arose, including the extent (if any) to which he responded to requests reasonably made by the claimant for information or inspection for the purpose of ascertaining facts which were or might be relevant to the claimant's cause or action against the defendant;
> (d) the duration of any disability of the claimant arising after the date of the accrual of the cause of action;
> (e) the extent to which the claimant acted promptly and reasonably once he knew whether or not the act of omission of the omission of the

defendant, to which the injury was attributable, might be capable at that
time of giving rise to an action for damages;

(f) the steps, if any, taken by the claimant to obtain medical, legal or
other expert advice and the nature of any such advice he may have
received.'

The primary arguments:

1. The instant case would probably have turned (whenever litigated) on an
interpretation of the medical case notes, whenever brought. As Roch LJ said in
Smith v Leicestershire Health Authority [1998] Lloyd's Rep Med 77 at page 92:

> 'The remaining factor, and of greater weight than the last, in respect of
> which we think the judge erred was his rejection of Mr Stembridge's
> submission that this is a case which turned on documents and X-rays
> and that the defendant's evidential disadvantage was not great. In the
> light of the judge's observations when reaching his finding that the
> radiologist was negligent, we are quite unable to identify any evidence
> that the defendants could have adduced on that issue which might have
> assisted them. Indeed we were told during the appeal that there was no
> evidence as to the availability of the radiologist concerned although there
> was evidence as to the unavailability of some of the clinicians responsible
> for the treatment of the [Plaintiff] in 1954 and 1955. The defendant
> maintained a total silence as to the whereabouts and availability of the
> radiologist.'

2. The case could have been pursued up to 1991, the 21st birthday of the claimant
without the issue of 'limitation' being raised.

3. See also *Farthing v North East Essex Health Authority* [1998] Lloyd's Rep Med 37
at page 42 per Simon Brown LJ:

> '... the case must inevitably turn not upon the recollection of witnesses
> like these doctors as to precisely what they did or observed when
> variously they saw the [Plaintiff] (and, in the case of Dr Yashlaha and
> Mr Hunt, operated upon her) but rather upon what is stated in the
> contemporaneous material in the way of hospital records, notes and
> correspondence. I have already read extracts from the letters written
> by Dr Yashlaha and Mr Hunt after they had played their respective
> parts in this story. Their findings recorded there seem to me the all-
> important parts of the contemporary evidence. The experts will then given
> [sic] their opinion as to whether the negligence is properly to be inferred
> from it.'

Index